Frontiers of
Development Economics

Frontiers of Development Economics

THE FUTURE IN PERSPECTIVE

Gerald M. Meier
Joseph E. Stiglitz
editors

A COPUBLICATION OF THE WORLD BANK AND OXFORD UNIVERSITY PRESS

Oxford University Press

OXFORD NEW YORK ATHENS AUCKLAND BANGKOK BOGOTA BUENOS AIRES
CALCUTTA CAPE TOWN CHENNAI DAR ES SALAAM DELHI FLORENCE HONG KONG
ISTANBUL KARACHI KUALA LUMPUR MADRID MELBOURNE MEXICO CITY
MUMBAI NAIROBI PARIS SÃO PAULO SINGAPORE TAIPEI TOKYO TORONTO WARSAW

and associated companies in

BERLIN IBADAN

© 2001 The International Bank for Reconstruction
and Development / The World Bank
1818 H Street, N.W., Washington, D.C. 20433, USA

Published by Oxford University Press, Inc.
198 Madison Avenue, New York, N.Y. 10016

Oxford is a registered trademark of Oxford University Press.

Manufactured in the United States of America
First printing December 2000

1 2 3 4 5 03 02 01 00

The findings, interpretations, and conclusions expressed in this study are entirely those of the authors and should not be attributed in any manner to the World Bank, to its affiliated organizations, or to members of its Board of Executive Directors or the countries they represent. The boundaries, colors, denominations, and other information shown on any map in this volume do not imply on the part of the World Bank Group any judgment on the legal status of any territory or the endorsement or acceptance of such boundaries.

Library of Congress Cataloging-in-Publication Data

Frontiers of development economics : the future in perspective / edited by Gerald M. Meier, Joseph E. Stiglitz.
    p. cm.
    Revised papers and commentary from the symposium, "The Future of Development Economics," held in Dubrovnik in May 1999 and sponsored by the University of Zagreb and the World Bank.
    Includes bibliographical references and index.
    ISBN 0-19-521592-3
    1. Development economics. I. Meier, Gerald M. II. Stiglitz, Joseph E.

HD75 .F77 2000
338.9—dc21
                                                 00-020985

Contents

Appendixes

Foreword

THIS VOLUME IS A VALUABLE contribution to our understanding of the evolution of development thought and its relation to development policy. Over the past 50 years, two generations of development economists have sought to analyze the process of development and to formulate policies that might reduce international poverty. Building on their assessment of what we do—and do not—know about development, the contributors to this volume emphasize issues that will challenge the next generation of development academics and practitioners alike.

Development economics is about the big issues: how economies and societies grow and change. They are the issues that were at the heart of the work of classical economists— in particular, Smith, Ricardo, and Marx. The "pioneers" of development economics, writing soon after World War II, were firmly aware of these intellectual connections and roots. They initially recognized the heritage of classical growth economics. The pioneers were also directly concerned with the role of changing behavior and institutions in the process of development, issues that those working in development economics have been emphasizing strongly in recent years. It is therefore now of great value for a new generation of development economists to interact with the earlier generations. They have much to learn, not only in terms of ideas and concepts but also in terms of wise judgment on what is important. Of special relevance for future examination are the unsettled issues highlighted in this volume.

Development economists have, throughout the last 50 years, been strongly involved with issues of policy. This involvement implies that the role of the state must be at center stage. On this subject there has been a fundamental change in development thinking. In the early years, following World War II, there was, broadly speaking, a mistrust of markets, including world markets, influenced in large part by the experience of the Great Depression. There was also confidence in the ability of government to take an effective and productive role in directing investment. The experience of the 1950s and 1960s did not support this confidence, and the 1970s and 1980s saw strong moves to liberalize and privatize.

By the end of the 1990s, we had seen many countries embark on market reform. Again, we have learned from experience. We see that market reforms can be, and on the whole have been, an engine of growth. But we have also seen that if they are not supported by sound institutions and good governance, they can stall or fail. Hence, the focus now is on the relations between institutions and markets.

The centrality of policy to development economics also requires specificity on goals. Here the subject has broadened its perspectives. While income distribution was an issue from the early days following World War II, it began to be emphasized more strongly in the 1960s. And in 1974, Robert McNamara, then president of the World Bank, in his Annual Meeting speech in Nairobi, made overcoming poverty a key goal for the Bank. The understanding of well-being, and thus poverty, has gone beyond income, and now most of those working in the subject would place strong emphasis on improving health and education as part of the development goals and as instrumental in generating growth of income. More broadly still, development is increasingly seen as expanding freedom of choice and action.

This broader perspective on the goals of development and the return to the interests of some of the pioneers makes this millennial publication particularly timely and significant. The broadening of the agenda, together with the emphasis on institutions, also reminds us that development economists need to be aware of contributions from the other social sciences: they have much to learn from economic historians, political scientists, and anthropologists, for example. The potential fruitfulness of some of these new interactions is well illustrated in this volume.

The contributors and commentators in the volume provide many insights and examine some new questions that make the subject both more interesting and more difficult. We have, it is true, learned much in the last half century about the effectiveness of different kinds of policy interventions and structures. Indeed, one of the more beneficial advances is that the subject has become much more focused on evidence, in part in response to, and in part due to, the greater availability of data. The challenge now is to apply what we know with judgment and wisdom while taking on the very serious research challenges ahead of us. In this task, the World Bank has a responsibility to work closely with researchers throughout the developing and industrial world.

NICHOLAS STERN
Chief Economist and Senior Vice President
  for Development Economics
World Bank

Preface

IT IS NOW TIMELY AND CHALLENGING to contemplate the future of development economics in light of the past half-century's experience of development thought and practice. This volume does so as an outgrowth of an intergenerational symposium on "The Future of Development Economics," held in Dubrovnik in May 1999 under the sponsorship of the University of Zagreb and the World Bank. The Bank had previously organized a series of retrospective lectures by the first generation of development economists (approximately 1950–75). These were published in *Pioneers in Development* (1984) and *Pioneers in Development—Second Series* (1987).

At Dubrovnik, representatives of the first and the second (approximately 1975 to the present) generations of development economists presented papers that have been revised for this volume. Most of the contributors are now instructing the next generation of development economists. Viewing the past as prologue—and as a sequel to the previous two volumes by the Pioneers—they now look toward the unsettled issues that will confront the next generation. About 15 discussants comment on the main papers. Two appendixes offer reflections on the future by several Nobel laureates and first-generation pioneers.

The editors greatly appreciate the efforts of the large number of contributors. All who attended the Dubrovnik symposium are also grateful for the splendid hospitality provided by Professor Soumitra Sharma and the Faculty of Economics of the University of Zagreb. The World Bank furnished logistical support for the meeting, but the views of the contributors are their own and should not be attributed to the World Bank.

The editors have benefited greatly from the assistance of David Ellerman, Noemi Giszpenc, and Paola Scalabrin at the World Bank and Kenneth MacLeod at Oxford University Press. Yuri Woo at Stanford University was especially helpful in maintaining overall control of the manuscript and in bringing uniformity to a variety of bibliographical styles. Her patience and proficiency in dealing with all the details, from the first e-mail to the last footnote, were unsurpassed. Without her keen attention to the needs of so many authors and the editors, the manuscript would not have reached its present form.

GERALD M. MEIER
Stanford University

JOSEPH E. STIGLITZ
Stanford University

Introduction:
Ideas for Development

Gerald M. Meier

OVER THE PAST HALF-CENTURY, we have witnessed an unprecedented effort by the international community to accelerate the development of poor countries. This effort has been based on an evolution in thinking about economic development—its nature, its causes, and the choice of policies for improving the rate and quality of the development process. Although the development record exhibits many successes, there are also failures and disappointed expectations. And while the first two generations of development economists brought about much progress in the evolution of the subject, many unsettled questions and central issues remain to be resolved by the next generation. Accordingly, the contributors to this volume consider the future of development economics from the perspective of the development record and development thought.

Ideas as Framework and as Productive Factors

Underlying all the papers collected here is the recognition that ideas are fundamental to the future progress of development. No formula exists for development. Aid alone cannot yield development. As a former chief economist of the World Bank observed,

> [M]ore than ever before, the central priority for the World Bank . . . is to create and help implement improved strategies for economic development. These strategies must rely, to a greater extent than before, on the transfer and transformation of knowledge, so as to compensate for the expected paucity of development assistance. . . . To put it bluntly, since there will not be much development money over the next decade, there had better be a lot of good ideas. (Summers 1991: 2)

Working from the recognition that the knowledge gap between rich and poor countries is as significant as the savings gap or the foreign exchange gap, the World Bank's *World Development Report 1998/99* was devoted to the theme of "knowledge for development." As Joseph Stiglitz, the chief economist of the Bank at the time of the Dubrovnik conference, observed,

> Today the World Bank has shifted much of its emphasis to the intangibles of knowledge, institutions, and culture in an attempt to forge a more comprehensive New Development Framework for our work. We want, for instance, to be a Knowledge Bank, not just a bank for infrastructure finance. We now see economic development as less like the construction business and more like education in the broad and comprehensive sense that covers knowledge, institutions, and culture. (Stiglitz 1999a)

In a similar vein, the growth economist Paul Romer asserts that

> Ideas should be our central concern. . . [I]deas are extremely important economic goods, far more important than the objects emphasized in most economic models. In a world with physical limits, it is discoveries of big ideas, together with the discovery of millions of little ideas, that make persistent economic growth possible. Ideas are the instructions that let us combine limited physical resources in arrangements that are ever more valuable. (Romer 1993b: 64)

Although the World Bank has been an intellectual actor (Stern 1997), ideas for development have come more naturally from university economists and research institutes. This volume considers the future of development economics from the perspective of the advances in development thought made by both World Bank and academic economists. The evolution has been along several dimensions of analysis and policy implications. In successive order, the focus has been as shown in Figure 1.

As Irma Adelman observes in this volume, there have been "twists and turns" in the evolution of development thinking. Nonetheless, the subject matter of development economics has evolved with increasing analytical rigor, and policy implications have become more definitive. Yusuf and Stiglitz, in their chapter, can point to seven major issues as settled and as representing "normal science" and "common wisdom."

The ultimate objective is for appropriate ideas on development to be absorbed and implemented in developing countries. These ideas include both concepts of development policy, in a macro sense, and ideas about technical progress, in a micro or enterprise sense.

The "new growth theory" emphasizes the role of ideas in promoting growth through the aggregation of advances at the micro level. Within a developing country, the implementation of ideas is essential for rais-

Figure 1. The Evolution of Development Thought

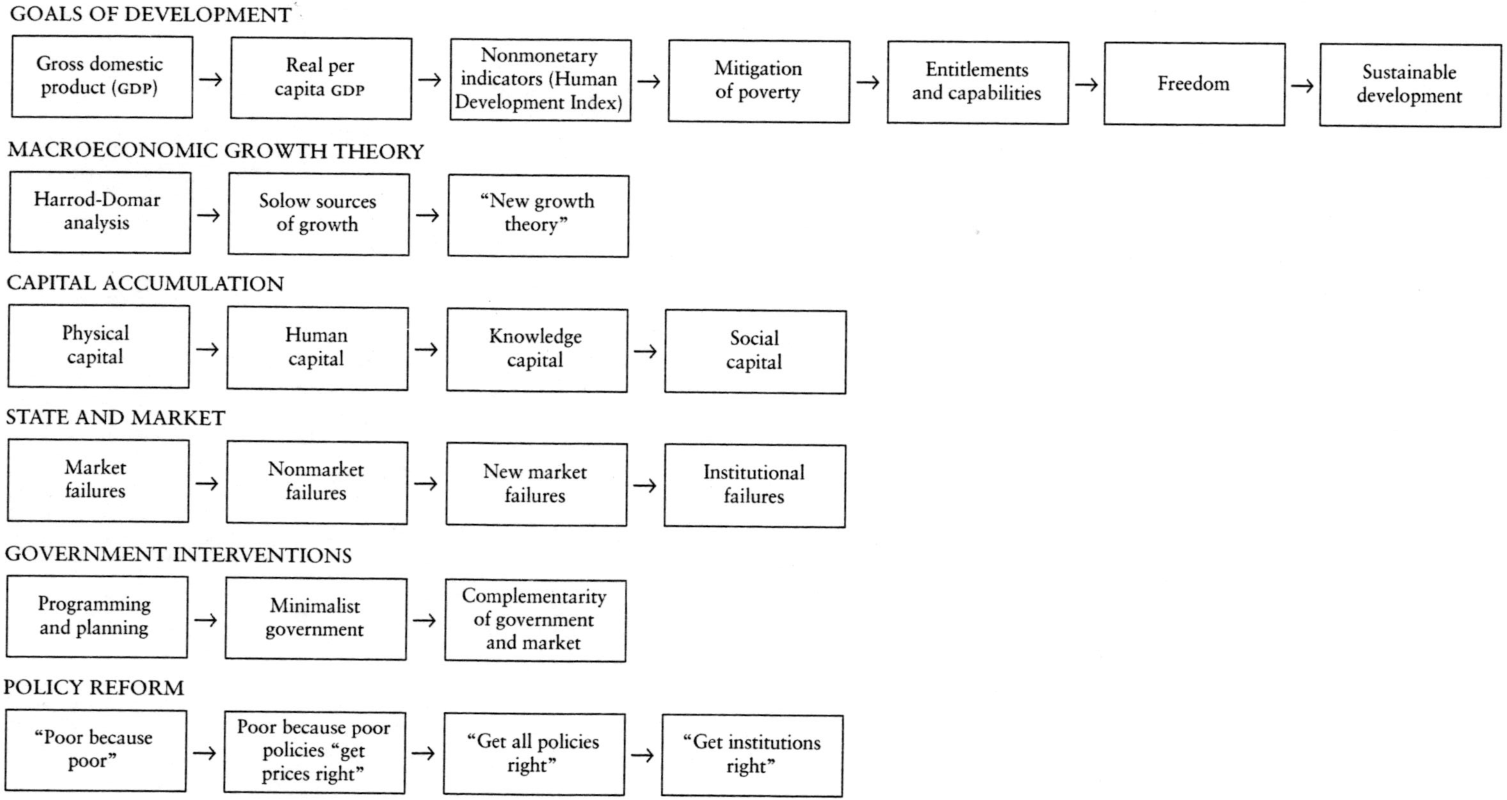

GOALS OF DEVELOPMENT

| Gross domestic product (GDP) | → | Real per capita GDP | → | Nonmonetary indicators (Human Development Index) | → | Mitigation of poverty | → | Entitlements and capabilities | → | Freedom | → | Sustainable development |

MACROECONOMIC GROWTH THEORY

| Harrod-Domar analysis | → | Solow sources of growth | → | "New growth theory" |

CAPITAL ACCUMULATION

| Physical capital | → | Human capital | → | Knowledge capital | → | Social capital |

STATE AND MARKET

| Market failures | → | Nonmarket failures | → | New market failures | → | Institutional failures |

GOVERNMENT INTERVENTIONS

| Programming and planning | → | Minimalist government | → | Complementarity of government and market |

POLICY REFORM

| "Poor because poor" | → | Poor because poor policies "get prices right" | → | "Get all policies right" | → | "Get institutions right" |

ing total factor productivity. (See the chapters by Meier and by Crafts, in this volume.)

Schumpeter's emphasis on innovations is highly relevant for development. He distinguishes between "inventions"—that is, ideas or concepts—and "innovations" (Schumpeter 1939). For development to occur, ideas have to produce "new combinations of productive means"—that is, innovations. These include the introduction of a new good or a new quality of a good, the introduction of a new method of production, the opening of a new market, the introduction of a new source of supply, or the carrying out of new organization of an industry (Schumpeter 1949). Such innovations can offset diminishing returns.

The Schumpeterian type of competition, based on innovations, depends on entrepreneurial performance. To accelerate development, the supply of entrepreneurship has to be increased. This depends on ideas being accepted as individual knowledge and implemented through human capabilities. Entrepreneurial ability is thus a form of human capital.[1]

Beyond contributing to technical change and raising the growth rate, the absorption of ideas may also facilitate the structural transformation of the economy, allow better control of demographic changes, and improve the distribution of income. In an even deeper sense, scientific ideas and rationality can change a society's values and can give support to modernization.

The backwardness of individuals as economic agents is an unfortunate cause and result of poverty. Schooling and training are commonly advocated as means of raising creative capacity and inspiring achievement. Beyond this, a facilitating environment can be promoted through the establishment and protection (but not overprotection) of intellectual property rights, through use of regulatory and tax measures to reward enterprises that innovate, and through intensified competition among decentralized enterprises.[2]

There is certainly an important role for the production of ideas, knowledge, and information by the developing country itself. But in the earlier phases of the development process, reliance may have to be placed on the transmission of ideas via international trade, foreign direct investment, and technology transfer. Perhaps of even greater value than the importation of material goods is the fundamental "educative effect" of trade (Myint 1971). A deficiency of knowledge is a more pervasive handicap to development than is the scarcity of any other factor. Knowledge, however, is a global public good (Stiglitz 1999b), and contact with more advanced economies provides an expeditious way of overcoming this deficiency.[3] The importation of technical know-how and skills is an indispensable source of technical progress, and the importation of ideas in general is a potent stimulus to development—vital not only for economic change but also for political and sociocultural advances that may be necessary preconditions of economic progress. By providing the opportunity to learn from the achievements and failures of the more advanced economies, and by facilitating selective borrowing and adaptation, foreign trade can help considerably in accelerating a country's development.

In the mid-19th century, J. S. Mill observed, "It is hardly possible to overrate the value in the present low state of human improvement, of placing human beings in contact with persons dissimilar to themselves, and with modes of thought and action unlike those with which they are familiar . . . Such communication has always been and is peculiarly in the present age, one of the primary sources of progress."[4] In the 21st century, the pattern and pace of change still differ among countries, thereby allowing trade in ideas to yield dynamic gains from trade. Indeed, Romer (1993a: 543) can assert, "Nations are poor because their citizens do not have access to the ideas that are used in industrial nations to generate economic value."[5]

Although the creation of ideas is a necessary condition for development, it is not a sufficient condition. The absorptive capacity of the developing country is crucial. If development economists and visiting missions are not listened to, their ideas will come to naught. The same is true if ideas on policy reform require political conditions for their implementation and these conditions do not exist, or if the absorptive capacity depends on institutional change that is not forthcoming. In the organization of government and the design of information and an incentives system, the preconditions must be in place for the acceptance and implementation of ideas. The chapter by Grindle in this volume throws additional light on the problem.

The rejection of bad ideas is as important as the acceptance of good ideas. In the 1960s a too-ready importation of the Harrod-Domar analysis overemphasized physical capital accumulation and misinterpreted an idea that was meant in a special way for industrial, not developing, countries. The acceptance of ideas about import-substitution industrialization also turned out to have adverse consequences. So too, at the micro level there have been mistaken ideas. Foreign direct investment may bring benefits, but it may also be overly capital intensive when there is surplus labor, or multinationals may present costs to the host country that mount over time and alter the cost-benefit ratio unfavorably.

The absorption of wrong ideas may make it necessary to reverse or end policies—a difficult task. In general, ideas that become embedded in human capital as knowledge need to be "appropriate knowledge," analogous to appropriate technology. Indeed, inappropriate human capital may be more of a handicap than inappropriate physical capital because human capital cannot be scrapped. A bad practice is not conveniently ended, and a bad idea may drive out a good idea.

Whether ideas are imported from abroad or produced within the developing countries, they should avoid the biases of ideology. Ideological beliefs have only too easily permeated development thought. With postwar decolonization, development economics was initially often viewed as the economics of resentment or discontent. Center and periphery were emotive—not logical—categories. As a policy-oriented and problem-solving subject, development economics was also susceptible to the ideologies of both the left and the right. Disciplined thinking on the proper balance between state and market has only too often been neglected (see Stiglitz 1999a).

If ideas are to be more influential, they will have to evolve from rigorous analysis and empirical testing. To this end, multiple sources of analytical arguments and empirical evidence should be promoted in both industrial and developing countries. As in the past, so too in the future will ideas for development be improved by learning from experience and subjecting ideas to open debate. The emotive and ideological may then be reduced in favor of disciplined analysis that will strengthen development economics.

Contents of This Volume

With the above premises in mind, we turn to the next chapters, which look to future ideas for development. In so doing, we may heed Samuelson's observation (1996: 27): "It is a mistake in science to think that any generation arrives at the banquet table late, after the feast has been consumed. Science's work is never done. Science is a movable feast. One solved problem fans out into many new open questions that beg in turn for solutions." Not only will new issues confront the next generation of development economists: more elegant analytical techniques should allow them to refine and extend some of the insights of earlier generations.

In the next chapter, "The Old Generation of Development Economists and the New," Gerald M. Meier summarizes the past and future of development economics from the viewpoint of the "older generation." To put the future of development economics in perspective, Meier reviews the development ideas of the first (approximately 1950–75) and second (approximately 1975–present) generations of development economists. Against this background, he then considers the unsettled questions and unfinished tasks for the next generation. These involve the recognition of an expanded meaning of "economic development"; more attention to the residual (total factor productivity) in the production-function approach to the sources of growth; refinement and extension of new growth theories in relation to the economics of ideas and knowledge; interpretation of the "right institutions"; determination of the sources and consequences of social capital; undertaking of multidisciplinary analysis; recognition of historical lessons; examination of the opportunities and problems being created by globalization; and attention to new perspectives on the interdependence of the state and the market in the development process.

Meier distinguishes between ordinary neoclassical economic analysis of development and a more comprehensive approach that looks to the operation of large, innovative changes and to political-economy issues in development policymaking. All these issues are subsumed in the general question of whether development economics is to be regarded simply as applied economics or whether there is a need for a special development theory to supplement general economic theory.

In "On the Goals of Development," Kaushik Basu maintains that new goals for development—beyond simply increasing the rate of economic growth—are implied by the movement toward "human development" or "comprehensive development." But can these larger social and political goals be given more precise meaning, let alone be subjected to measurement and some operational metric for purposes of evaluation? This question receives prime attention. To the extent that income growth is relevant, Basu suggests that the focus should be on how the poorest people are faring and on the growth rate of the per capita income of the poorest quintile of the population. Of special interest is the relatively ignored subject of the strategic interaction between the goals of different countries and the issue of "conditional morality" that they present. Such an analysis is relevant for the design of coordinated actions by nations to achieve developmental objectives.

Irma Adelman, in "Fallacies in Development Theory and Their Implications for Policy," identifies three major misconceptions: (a) underdevelopment has but a single cause (whether it be low physical capital, missing entrepreneurship, incorrect relative prices, barriers to international trade, hyperactive government, inadequate human capital, or ineffective government); (b) a single criterion suffices to evaluate development performance; and (c) development is a log-linear process. Adelman maintains that development should be analyzed as a highly multifaceted, nonlinear, path-dependent, dynamic process involving systematically shifting interaction patterns that require changes in policies and institutions over time.

Three chapters look at how some of the development strategies proposed in the World Bank's *World Development Reports* of the early 1990s have fared. In "Revisiting the Challenge of Development," Vinod Thomas argues that development outcomes in the past decade confirm the essential contribution of market-friendly actions but also highlight missing or underemphasized ingredients. Foremost among the latter are the distribution of human development, the protection of the environment, globalization and financial regulation, and the quality of governance. Giving top priority to these issues would mean integrating the quality dimension into development approaches instead of striving to maximize short-term growth. It would also replace one-track efforts to hasten the pace of market liberalization and would expand the attention given to consensus building in civil society, along with the concern for policy changes.

In "The Evolution of Thinking about Poverty: Exploring the Interactions," Ravi Kanbur and Lyn Squire describe the progressive broadening of the definition and measurement of poverty, from command over market-purchased goods (income) to other dimensions of living standards such as longevity, literacy, and health and, most recently, to concern about risk and vulnerability, and about powerlessness and lack of voice. Kanbur and Squire argue that although there are some correlations among these different dimensions, the broadening of the definition significantly changes our thinking about how to reduce poverty. The broader concept expands the set of relevant policies, but it also emphasizes that poverty-reducing strategies must recognize interactions among policies: the impact of appropriately designed combinations will be greater than the sum of the individual parts. The authors maintain that additional research is required to increase our understanding of those interactions; that in-depth country case studies are needed to explore the best policy combinations for countries with different problems and different capacities; and that institutional innovations designed to overcome information failures and knowledge gaps need to be carefully evaluated.

Shahid Yusuf and Joseph E. Stiglitz, in "Development Issues: Settled and Open," consider which issues in development economics appear settled and which require future attention. Settled issues have to do with the following questions: What are the sources of growth? Does macroeconomic stability matter, and how can it be sustained? Should developing countries liberalize trade? How crucial are property rights? Is poverty reduction a function of growth and asset accumulation, or are poverty safety nets required? Can developing countries defer or downplay environmental problems? How closely should the state manage and regulate development?

Current trends reveal a range of issues that are likely to call for future analysis and action. These trends relate to globalization, localization, environmental degradation, demographic change, food and water security, and urbanization. The issues can be grouped under two headings: (a) multilevel governance and regulation issues (participatory politics, organizational capability, decentralization, inequality, and urban governance) and (b) issues related to managing human capital and natural resources (cross-border migration, aging and capital supplies, management of the global commons, and food and water security). Convergence of both income levels and human development levels could be accelerated by responding to these issues. Fresh thinking on governance, institutions, regulatory policies, and measures for managing resources will lead to the highest payoff.

Institutions and incentive structures are also central in Pranab Bardhan's discussion of "Distributive Conflicts, Collective Action, and Institutional Economics." Drawing the connections between the new institutional economics and development economics, Bardhan gives particular attention to some issues that have been neglected in the theoretical institutional economics literature, in particular, (a) the persistence of dysfunctional institutions in poor countries, (b) institutional impediments as outcomes of distributive conflicts, (c) the collective action problems these conflicts exacerbate, and (d) a more complex and nuanced role of the state, to deal with the need for coordination. The analysis focuses on the effects of distributive conflicts among different social groups and asymmetries in their bargaining power. In this light, Bardhan explains institutional failures and draws attention to the inevitable collective action problems at both state and local levels.

In "Historical Perspectives on Development," Nicholas Crafts asks whether development economics has much to gain from resuming a closer relationship with economic history. To answer this question, Crafts appraises the legacy of the two older generations of economic historians: the postwar pioneers who linked economic history and development economics, and the more recent practitioners of the new economic history of the later 1960s and 1970s. Moving beyond growth regressions, the analysis is focusing less on production and more on living standards—an area, Crafts suggests, in which development economists and economic historians can interact fruitfully.

Central to both long-run economic history and development are endogenous institutional and technological changes. Crafts emphasizes the importance of solving agency and appropriation problems in creating an environment conducive to innovation and productivity improvement. Looking to future collaboration between historians and development economists, he advises against forcing patterns of economic growth and development into the framework of the augmented-Solow neoclassical growth model. Crafts emphasizes institutions but recognizes that different countries can be expected to diverge in their institutional arrangements. He notes the changing relationship between growth in real wages and in gross domestic product (GDP) per capita and improvement of living standards. The next generation of development economists, Crafts observes, should be able to gain more insights from economic history than did the second generation.

Although progress has been made in understanding the intersection of policies and politics, Merilee S. Grindle ("In Quest of the Political: The Political Economy of Development Policymaking") asserts that there is still much to explain about development policymaking from a political-economy perspective. Grindle explicates two divergent traditions of political economy, based on economics and on sociological theory, that offer different interpretations of decisionmaking and the process of policy reform. Neither of these contending paradigms, Grindle argues, is adequate for understanding four real-world puzzles: Why and when are politicians interested in supporting policy change? How do political institutions affect the choices made by politicians? How are new institutions created or transformed? What are the consequences of new rules of the game for economic and political interaction?

Grindle asserts that political-economy analyses should be able to model reality by reflecting the dynamics of policy interactions in the design and implementation of development policy and in the creation or transformation of institutions. Political-economy analysis can then provide helpful ideas about what might be done to improve practice, not only for macroeconomic management but also as regards a number of new issues related to institutional change, social policies, and decentralized and participatory forms of governance. The author emphasizes that if development economists are to understand political decision-making, inquiry into political processes is especially needed. In addition, leadership, ideas, and improved institutions are important determinants of successful policy outcomes that are not yet sufficiently explained in political-economy theory.

Throughout this volume, there are two pivotal questions: What are the forces that can explain the divergence in incomes across countries? What interventions are most likely to promote development? In the final chapter, "Modern Economic Theory and Development," Karla Hoff and Joseph E. Stiglitz focus directly on these questions. Their answers reflect recent advances in the economics of imperfect information and the economics of coordination failures. Instead of assuming that information costs are negligible and the capacity to contract is limitless, Hoff and Stiglitz make explicit assumptions about individual-specific information constraints and the set of feasible transactions. Ultimately, development economists have to endogenize the institutions that affect information and enforcement costs. This means that institutions, history, and distributional considerations do matter and that the analyst must go beyond the usual fundamentals of resources, technology, and preferences. Neither government-induced distortions nor low capital accumulation have proved adequate for explaining underdevelopment. Rather than concentrate on differences between industrial and developing countries in levels of physical capital, human capital, or government-induced distortions, Hoff and Stiglitz emphasize that the two groups are on different production functions and are organized in different ways.

In contrast to earlier models in development economics, the authors provide many examples of models with multiple equilibria that can explain why poor countries may be caught in a low-level equilibrium trap from which they cannot be freed by market forces. They present three complementary hypotheses relating to gaps in knowledge, institutions that may be dysfunctional, and an ecological perspective on social, economic, and political institutions. They formulate a number of models with "development traps" that arise from coordination failures as a result of interaction effects among agents that are not fully mediated through prices. The models indicate multiple Pareto-ranked equilibria.

Of special interest from the standpoint of the chapter's emphasis on modern theory is the demonstration that the modeling of coordination failures may provide insights into economic policies for resolving them. From this new perspective, more appropriate policies can be recommended that will coordinate good equilibria, affect information, or change incentives and organizational structures.

The volume closes with two sections that present reflections on the future of development economics by Nobel laureates and some original "Pioneers."

Notes

1. The central role of entrepreneurship has long been emphasized in development literature. See Leibenstein (1968).

2. For a discussion of the wide variety of approaches to encouraging the production and use of ideas, see Romer (1993b).

3. To the extent that an idea is nonrivalrous but excludable, it is an impure public good.

4. Mill (1848): vol. 2, book 3, ch. 17, sect. 5.

5. For an analysis of ideas as nonrival goods that give rise to increasing returns and nonconvexities, see Romer (1993a) and the discussion of new growth theory in the chapters by Meier and by Adelman in this volume. For the links between trade, innovation, and growth, see Grossman and Helpman (1991).

References

Grossman, Gene, and Elhanan Helpman. 1991. *Innovation and Growth in the Global Economy.* Cambridge, Mass.: MIT Press.

Leibenstein, Harvey. 1968. "Entrepreneurship and Development." *American Economic Review* 58 (2, May): 72–75.

Mill, J. S. 1848. *Principles of Political Economy,* vol. 2, book 3, ch. 17, sect. 5. London.

Myint, Hla. 1971. *Economic Theory and Underdeveloped Countries.* New York: Oxford University Press.

Romer, Paul M. 1993a. "Idea Gaps and Object Gaps in Economic Development." *Journal of Monetary Economics* 32 (December): 543–73.

———. 1993b. "Two Strategies for Economic Development: Using Ideas and Producing Ideas." In *Proceedings of the World Bank Annual Conference on Development Economics 1992,* 63–91. Washington, D.C.: World Bank.

Samuelson, Paul A. 1996. "The Age of Bhagwati et al." In Robert C. Feenstra, Gene M. Grossman, and Douglas A. Irwin, eds., *The Political Economy of Trade Policy.* Cambridge, Mass.: MIT Press.

Schumpeter, Joseph A. 1939. *Business Cycles.* New York: McGraw-Hill.

———. 1949. *The Theory of Economic Development.* Cambridge, Mass.: Harvard University Press.

Stern, Nicholas. 1997. "The World Bank as an Intellectual Actor." In Davesh Kapur, John P. Lewis, and Richard Webb, eds., *The World Bank: Its First Half Century,* vol. 2, ch. 12. Washington, D.C.: Brookings Institution.

Stiglitz, Joseph E. 1999a. "Knowledge for Development: Economic Science, Economic Policy, and Economic Advice." In Boris Plesovic and Joseph E. Stiglitz, eds., *Annual World Bank Conference on Development Economics 1998.* Washington, D.C.: World Bank.

———. 1999b. "Knowledge as a Global Public Good." In Inge Kaul, Isabelle Grunberg, and Marc A. Stern, eds., *Global Public Goods: International Cooperation in the 21st Century,* 308–25. New York: Oxford University Press.

———. 1999c. "Public Policy for a Knowledge Economy." Remarks at the Department for Trade and Industry and Center for Economic Policy Research, London, January 27. At <http://www.worldbank.org/html/extdr/extme/jssp012799a.htm>.

Summers, Lawrence. 1991. "Research Challenges for Development Economists." *Finance and Development* 28 (3, September): 2–5.

World Bank. 1999. *World Development Report 1998/99: Knowledge for Development.* New York: Oxford University Press.

The Old Generation of Development Economists and the New

Gerald M. Meier

NEAR THE END OF THE 19TH CENTURY, in a retrospective review of economic theory entitled "The Old Generation of Economists and the New," Alfred Marshall wrote of "the relation to which the older generation of economists, which is coming near the close of its activity, stands to the work which appears to lie before the coming generation" (Marshall 1897: 115). Now, at the end of the 20th century, we may attempt a similar exercise for development economists.

This chapter does so by appraising the progress in the evolution of ideas made by the first two generations of development economists over the past 50 years. The next two sections are devoted to the first generation (roughly 1950–75) and the second generation (roughly 1975–present). The final section outlines the unsettled questions and unfinished tasks that the next generation will face. The intention is not to present yet another survey of the literature but rather to offer a subjective summary appraisal of the past and future of the subject from the viewpoint of the "older generations."[1]

The First Generation

After World War II the subject of development was thrust upon economists as newly independent governments in emerging countries sought advice for the acceleration of their development. Political independence could be obtained from Whitehall, but for economic independence the new governments of Asia and Africa turned to economists in the United Kingdom and America. As a discipline, however, development economics had to be rediscovered or newly founded.[2]

At the outset in the 1950s, development economists were more confident than now. They formulated grand models of development strategy that involved structural transformation and a correlative role for extensive government involvement in development programming or planning.[3] The models were visionary, looking to the requirements for an increase in per capita real income. Because population—the denominator—was increasing, the emphasis had to be on a rapid rate of growth of the numerator, gross domestic product (GDP). Capital accumulation, as the necessary requirement, was the central focus of the models. The Harrod-Domar equation, although originally formulated for conditions of full growth in an industrial economy, was applied to estimate capital requirements in developing countries.[4]

Growth accounting also emphasized the contribution of capital. The simple Solow (1957) decomposition of growth into factor contributions and a residual was based on a differentiation of a production function, $Y = F(K, L, t)$, where Y is output, K is capital, L is labor, and t is time, to form

$$\frac{\dot{Y}}{Y} = \left(\frac{F_K K}{Y} \right) \frac{\dot{K}}{K} + \left(\frac{F_L L}{Y} \right) \frac{\dot{L}}{L} + \frac{F_t}{Y}.$$

(Subscripts denote partial derivatives.)

The contribution of capital accumulation to growth is measured by $(\dot{K}/K)$ multiplied by the share of capital in national income (Stern 1991). The residual—growth in total factor productivity (TFP)—was left to be explained exogenously by technical progress.

Other early models of development strategy also featured capital accumulation: Rostow's "stages of growth," Nurkse's "balanced growth," Rosenstein-Rodan's external economies and "big push," Lewis's unlimited supply of labor and dual-sector model, the Prebisch-Myrdal-Singer hypotheses about terms of trade and import substitution, Leibenstein's "critical minimum effort" thesis, and Chenery's "two-gap model."[5]

The models and hypotheses had policy implications that involved strong state action. To many of the early development economists, a less-developed economy was characterized by pervasive market failures. To correct or avoid market failure, they advocated central coordination of the allocation of resources. The newly expanding subject of welfare economics also provided considerable rationale for government action to correct market failures. Furthermore, the structuralist school criticized the market price system by emphasizing rigidities, lags, shortages and surpluses, low elasticities of supply and demand, structural inflation, and export pessimism.[6]

Believing that a developing country did not have a reliable market price system, that the supply of entrepreneurship was limited, and that large structural changes—not merely marginal adjustments—were needed, the first generation of development advisers turned to the state as the major agent of change. The government of a developmental state was to promote capital accumulation, utilize reserves of surplus labor, undertake policies of deliberate industrialization, relax the foreign exchange constraint through import substitution, and coordinate the allocation of resources through programming and planning.

A growing number of visiting missions and foreign advisers cooperated with local planning agencies and industrial development corporations in producing the analyses and policy recommendations underlying national development plans. To provide tests for the consistency, balance, and feasibility of plans, they utilized modern techniques of economic analysis, especially input-output analysis, dynamic programming, and simulation of growth models.

The advocacy of inward-looking policies derived from a belief that export earnings were inelastic. This gave support to the two-gap model of savings-and-investment and the balance of trade (Bruno and Chenery 1962). According to this model, extra savings cannot be converted into imports of capital goods and is therefore frustrated, but foreign aid can allow investment to expand by relaxing the constraint in foreign exchange. There was also belief in structural inflation, in which the marginal propensity to import exceeds the marginal propensity to export, and in the need for balanced growth (Lewis, in Meier and Seers 1984).

At the same time as pessimistic conclusions were reached about developing countries' capacity to export primary products and to pursue export-led development, optimistic conclusions were expressed about capacity to accelerate development through the extension of the public sector and through wide-ranging governmental policies. This combination of external pessimism and internal optimism dominated the thinking of the first generation.

With these macro-strategies it was believed that government could accomplish a structural transformation in the developing economy. Government would give reality to the slogans of the first generation by breaking Nurkse's "vicious circle of poverty" via Rosenstein-Rodan's "big push" and through "balanced growth" that would establish complementarity in demand, achieve Leibenstein's "critical minimum effort," break out of the "low-level equilibrium trap," and fulfill the conditions of Rostow's "takeoff."[7]

Both the models and the policy advocacy of the first generation were subsequently criticized.[8] The models lacked sufficient empirical content. Moreover, as Krugman observes, the development theorists of the 1950s were

at first unable, and later unwilling, to codify [their insights] in clear, internally consistent models. At the same time the expected standard of rigor in economic thinking was steadily rising. The result was that development economics as a distinctive field was crowded out of the mainstream of economics. Indeed, the ideas of "high development theory" (of the 1950s) came to seem not so much wrong as incomprehensible. (Krugman 1993: 29)

Furthermore, in the 1960s the initial concentration on physical capital accumulation was giving way to the concept of investment in human capital and its implications for development. It was increasingly recognized that development depended on productive human agents who, through their acquisition of knowledge, better health and nutrition, and increase in skills, could raise total factor productivity.

Above all, criticisms of the early models were reinforced by experience with the adverse effects of government intervention. Economists became increasingly disenchanted with development programming or planning. Despite the optimism of the earlier generation and the deliberate efforts of governments to accelerate development, it became only too painfully evident in many countries that mass poverty still existed, that more people were unemployed or underemployed, that the numbers in "absolute poverty" were increasing, and that the distribution of income and assets was becoming more unequal.

To explain these disappointments, many blamed the policy-induced distortions and the nonmarket failures resulting from public policies. Particular criticisms were levied at the neglect of agriculture, the inefficiency of state-owned enterprises, the adverse effects of import-substitution industrialization, and balance of payments deficits.

In 1952 W. Arthur Lewis could say:

Planning in backward countries imposes much bigger tasks on governments than does planning in advanced countries. The government has too many things which can in advanced countries be left to entrepreneurs. It has to create industrial centers, to put through an agricultural revolution, to control the foreign exchanges more strictly, and in addition to make up a great leeway of public services and/or ordinary economic legislation. And all this has to be done through a civil service that is usually much inferior to that of an advanced country. Why then do backward countries take more readily to planning? Because their need is also so obviously much greater. And it is also this that enables them to carry it through in spite of error and incompetence. For, if the people are on their side, nationalistic, conscious of their backwardness, and anxious to progress, they willingly bear great hardships and tolerate many mistakes, and they throw themselves with enthusiasm into the job of regenerating their country. Popular enthusiasm is both the lubricating oil of planning, and the petrol of economic development—a dynamic force that almost makes all things possible. (Lewis 1952: 128)

By the late 1960s and early 1970s, however, deficiencies in industrial programming and comprehensive planning had become acute. Former supporters of development planning began to lament the "crisis in planning" (Streeten and Lipton 1969; Faber and Seers 1972). Critics now pointed to the causes of government failure: deficiencies in the plans, inadequate information and resources, unanticipated dislocations of domestic economic activity, institutional weaknesses, and failings on the part of the administrative civil service (Killick 1976: 164; Chakravarty 1991).

Although the rationale for government interventions had been to remedy market failure, the perverse result was only too often government failure. This was increasingly evident in the adverse effects of price distortions—distortions that were especially prevalent in wage rates, interest rates, and foreign exchange rates. The policy challenge now became to "get prices right." As Timmer (1973) expressed it, "getting prices right" does not guarantee economic development, but "getting prices wrong" frequently is the end of development. The logic of choice was again reasserting itself in economic analysis. The second generation of development economists was to give support to a "resurgence of neoclassical economics" (Little 1982: chs. 9–10).

The Second Generation

If the first generation of development economists was visionary and dedicated to grand theories and general strategies, the second generation was almost moralistic, dedicated to a somber realism grounded on fundamental principles of neoclassical economics. Harberger could say to the governments of developing countries, "Economics is good for you"—and by economics, he meant neoclassical analysis as the basis for policymaking (Harberger 1993).

Governments were admonished not only to remove price distortions but also to "get all policies right." Not differences in initial conditions but differences in policies were now thought to explain the disparate performances of developing countries. A country was not poor because of the vicious circle of poverty but because of poor policies. Markets, prices, and incentives should be of central concern in policymaking.

It had become evident that economic rationality characterizes agents in developing countries as well as in the more developed countries. Claiming that the usual postulates of rationality and the principles of maximization or minimization have general applicability, some economists emphasized the universality of neoclassical economics and dismissed the claim of the first generation that development economics was a special subdiscipline in its own right. Krueger, for example, maintained:

Once it is recognized that individuals respond to incentives, and that "market failure" is the result of inappropriate incentives rather than of nonresponsiveness, the separateness of development economics as a field largely disappears. Instead, it becomes an applied field, in which the tools and insights of labor economics, agricultural economics, international economics, public finance and other fields are addressed to the special questions and policy issues that arise in the context of development. (Krueger 1986: 62 f)[9]

In accordance with neoclassical economic theory, the second generation moved from highly aggregative models to disaggregated microstudies in which the units of analysis were production units and households. For offering policy advice, "grand theories" came to be viewed as less useful than highly specific applications. Microstudies, rather than the broader visionary models of the earlier period, could provide more direct policy implications for specific policies such as a change in tariffs or agricultural subsidies (Arrow 1988). There was a marked change from a focus on the process of development to an emphasis on particular features of underdevelopment. Quantitative analytical tools were used more extensively, especially for empirical analysis of microphenomena that were country specific, sector specific, or project specific. The greater availability of microdata sets allowed the modeling of household behavior and of human capital investments in education and health.

Studies concluded that how capital is allocated is more important than the level of capital accumulation. Growth could be slow despite high rates of saving, as in India; high rates of saving were seen to be neither necessary nor sufficient for success. Recognizing the importance of the allocation of capital, analysts gave more attention to refinements in the techniques of cost-benefit analysis and shadow pricing that lay behind project appraisal.

In earlier concepts of the aggregate production function, the residual was thought of as a coefficient of technical advance. The second generation, however, looked at the growth process in a more microeconomic fashion. The residual was recognized to be "a composite of the effects of many different forces: (i) improvements in the quality of labor through education, experience and on-the-job training; (ii) reallocation of resources from low-productivity to higher-productivity uses, either through normal market forces, or through the reduction of barriers or distortions; (iii) exploitation of economies of scale; (iv) improved ways of combining resources to produce goods and services, not just at the level of new machines or processes, but also by relatively mundane adjustments at the level of the factory or the farm" (Harberger 1983: 864 ff).

Numerous studies criticized price distortions, high effective rates of protection, and rent-seeking. Not adverse external conditions but inappropriate domestic policies explained why some countries were not taking advantage of their external economic opportunities. In contrast, the East Asian newly industrializing economies were viewed as the success stories of development.[10] The correct policies were to move from inward-looking strategies toward liberalization of the foreign trade regime and export promotion; to submit to stabilization programs; to privatize state-owned enterprises; and to follow the dictates of the market price system. Through its guidance toward the correct policies, neoclassical economics was believed to be the safeguard against policy-induced distortions and nonmarket failures.

Human Capital and the Power of Innovation

With the questioning of how strategic the role of physical capital is, more weight has been given to human capital—to creating agents who can become more productive through their acquisition of knowledge, better health and nutrition, and increased skills. The focus was on knowledge as a source of increasing returns. Near the end of the 19th century, Marshall (1890) had stated that "although nature is subject to diminishing returns, man is subject to increasing returns . . . Knowledge is the most powerful engine of production; it enables us to subdue nature and satisfy our wants." A little later, J. M. Clark observed that "knowledge is the only instrument of production that is not subject to diminishing returns" (1923: 120). Now, at the beginning of the 21st century, this view is reiterated in the new or newly rediscovered growth theory that treats knowledge as a nonrival good and emphasizes aggregate nonconvexities associated with investment in "knowledge" capital (Romer 1986). The theory explains technical progress as being determined by the "accumulation of knowledge by forward-looking, profit-maximizing agents" (Romer 1986: 1003). It thus supplements Solow's model, which emphasized capital accumulation. Although the "new growth theory" is not literally new, it does emphasize "newness" in production functions and in the goods produced (Romer 1994a, 1994b). The introduction of new goods is important to development and raises the problem of fulfilling total conditions (the introduction of an industry) rather than neoclassical marginal conditions (the production of additional units).[11]

By emphasizing knowledge and ideas, the new endogenous growth theory of the 1980s and 1990s brought about a marked change in the analysis of aggregate production functions (Romer 1986, 1989, 1990; Lucas 1988). Instead of the early Solow version of diminishing marginal returns to physical capital and to labor separately and constant returns to both inputs jointly, with technological progress as a residual, the new growth theory examines production functions that show increasing returns because of an expanding stock of human capital and as a result of specialization and investment in "knowledge" capital.[12] Technological progress and human capital formation are endogenized within general equilibrium models of growth. New knowledge is generated by investment in the research sector, and the technological progress residual is accounted for by endogenous human capital formation and the increases in the public stock of knowledge. With imperfect competition, the prospect of monopoly profits induces innovation. Knowledge or information, once obtained, can be used repeatedly at no additional cost. The new production processes and products then create spillover benefits to other firms. "[T]he creation of new knowledge by one firm is assumed to have a positive external effect on the production possibilities of other firms . . . [so that] production of consumption goods as a function of the stock of knowledge exhibits increasing returns; more precisely, knowledge may have an increasing marginal product" (Romer 1986: 1003). This allows aggregate investment in the public stock of knowledge to exhibit increasing returns to scale, to persist indefinitely, and to sustain long-run growth in per capita income.

For developing countries, the new growth theory implies a greater emphasis on human capital (including learning), even more than on physical capital, and recognition of the benefits from the international exchange of ideas that accompanies an open economy integrated into the world economy. The new growth theory is also relevant for the question of convergence.[13] Convergence occurs as the "technology gap" between countries is overcome and poor countries catch up with rich ones by growing faster. Free mobility of capital among countries will speed this convergence as the rate of diffusion of knowledge increases.

"Learning by doing" (Arrow 1962) and "learning by watching" (King and Robson 1989) are also knowledge-producing activities and sources of scale economies. Unlike growth theory that relies on discrete innovations, however, the "learning by doing" model emphasizes the increase in productivity from the important process of "continuous improvement" (Solow 1997: 40 f, 66 f).

The New Political Economy and the State

The second generation, which was able to reflect on two or three decades of development experience, recognized the increasing heterogeneity of developing countries and gave more attention to an explanation of differential rates of country performance. Cross-country econometric studies of the determinants of economic growth multiplied. A comparative approach was adopted in an attempt to understand why certain policies were effective in a given country while others were not, and why the same type of policy was effective in one country but not in another.

The inquiry into the causes of differential development performance led to more attention to the politics of policymaking. Elements of a "new political economy"—a positive theory of politics—were formulated. In this view, the analytical concepts and principles for interpreting why governments do what they do are analogous to those of neoclassical economic analysis. Postulates of rationality, the concept of self-interest or self-goal choice, and the techniques of marginal analysis and equilibrium outcomes have been applied to political markets and political objective functions. Whereas the first generation followed the usual approach of normative economic analysis, which assumed that the government is composed of Platonic guardians and that the state acts benevolently in seeking the public interest, proponents of the new political economy now focus on other types of states—the leviathan state, the bureaucratic state, or the factional state. To the first generation the government was an exogenous force, but the new political economy attempts to endogenize the decisions of politicians, bureaucrats, and administrators. It seeks to open windows in the black box of the "state" by using various strands of thought: public choice, collective choice, transaction costs, property rights, rent-seeking, and directly unproductive profit-seeking activities.

Whether a leviathan, bureaucratic, or factional model of the state is used, the thrust of the new political economy is that an underdeveloped economy has commonly given rise to an overextended state and to a negative or exploitative state. This implication appears in writings on price distortions (rent-seeking and directly unproductive profit-seeking activities), state-owned enterprises (patronage and bureaucracy), financial repression (politicized credit allocation and cheap credit to supporters), agricultural markets (pro-urban bias), inflation (populism), and tariffs and quotas (lobbying).

New Market Failures

A major modification of neoclassical analysis occurred in the 1980s and 1990s, when "new market failures" were analyzed. The recognition of the existence of imperfect and costly information, incomplete markets, and transaction costs and of the absence of futures markets extended the range of market failures beyond the earlier attention to public goods and externalities that required only selective government intervention (Stiglitz 1989b). Risk and information imperfections in the economy became highly relevant for development analysis. Correction of the new market failures provided a basis for a potential role for more pervasive government intervention. Nonetheless, in the 1990s more emphasis was actually given to government failures than to market failures, and concern about policy reform dominated (Krueger 1990). The recognition of risk and information imperfections did, however, improve analysis of two sectors that had been relatively neglected by the first generation: agriculture and finance.

Countering the first generation's emphasis on industrialization, the second generation evaluated policies that would promote rural development. The effects of government intervention in agricultural pricing became a major concern. Numerous studies presented evidence that misguided agricultural pricing policies were having an adverse effect on the gap between urban and rural incomes, the incentives to produce food and export crops, the ability of governments to establish food reserves, and employment opportunities in farming, processing, and rural industries. The theory of rural organization was advanced through the use of information, risk, and contract analyses (Binswanger and Rosenzweig 1981; Braverman and Guasch 1986; Stiglitz 1986). The microeconomics of the rural sector examined the organization and linkages of labor, land, and credit markets. The recognition of information constraints and transaction costs helped explain how rural institutions are a response to missing markets and also clarified the situations in which the potential benefits of government intervention are greatest.[14] Decisionmaking by members of rural households was studied from the perspective of the maximization behavior of a "household-firm" (Singh, Squire, and Strauss 1986).

Financial institutions and financial markets had been neglected by the first generation. A too facile approach had been taken, in the spirit of Joan Robinson's comment that "where enterprise leads, finance follows." Experience with financial bottlenecks and financial repression, however, led the second generation to become more concerned with the design of financial systems that would allow the banking system and money and capital markets to perform their proper functions of efficient investment allocation and financial intermediation between savers and investors. "New market failures" also gave due weight to transaction costs, adverse selection, and moral hazard in an analysis of capital market imperfections and the requirements for more effective financial policies (Stiglitz 1989a).

First-Generation Ideas Revisited

The second generation's recognition of new market failures has also renewed interest in the first generation's models that were concerned with issues of investment allocation and coordination activities. So, too, have elements of the new growth theory (knowledge, externalities, dynamic increasing returns), the new institutional economics (information, contracts, response to missing markets), and the new international economics (imperfect competition, strategic trade theory). This new or extended neoclassical analysis provides a basis for increasing returns and coordination of externalities resulting from capital accumulation. There is, accordingly, a return to the first generation's emphasis on the importance of increasing returns and pecuniary external economies arising from the effects of market size.

As Krugman now concludes, "intellectual credibility" can be restored to a useful set of core ideas from the early analysis of the 1950s.

> What was ironic was that a competitive neoclassical orthodoxy settled in on the development front just as the orthodoxy was breaking up in other fields. We can now see that whatever bad policies may have been implemented in the name of high development theory, the theory itself makes quite a lot of sense. Indeed, in some ways it was a remarkable anticipation of ideas that would come to analytical fruition thirty years later in the field, for example, of international trade and economic growth. (Krugman 1993: 29)

Bardhan (1993: 139) notes that "as economic theory has turned more toward the study of information-based market failures, coordination failures, multiple roles of prices and the general idea of the potential complexity of market interactions, it has inevitably turned to questions that have long exercised development economists."

Although a more meaningful case can now be made for a "big push" or for "balanced growth" (Murphy, Shleifer, and Vishny 1989), the experience with government failure has remained dominant in weighing against government intervention. The common consensus in the 1990s was for the promotion of policy reform. The state was believed to be overextended. A market price system was needed to get prices right. And to get policies right, there was a need for stabilization, liberalization, deregulation, and privatization. Supporting these policies were the International Monetary Fund's (IMF's) conditionality for loans and the World Bank's structural adjustment lending.

It is now, finally, recognized that to get prices right and to get policies right, it is also necessary to "get institutions right." As North (1997) observes, we now know a good deal about what makes for successful development, but we still know very little about how to get there—and especially how to establish the institutional and organizational structure that will support the desired rate and composition of economic change.

Tasks for the New Generation

Although, at the end of the 20th century, the second generation of development economists leaves the subject in a far more advanced state than at midcentury, there is clearly much unfinished business and many unsettled questions to be considered by the new generation. It would be presumptuous and unrealistic to dictate a future research agenda, but we may suggest some central topics that deserve consideration.

Beyond Income Growth: Patterns of Growth and Income Distribution

The new generation must still begin with an understanding of the meaning of "economic development." To the old generation, the objective of development was an increase in per capita real income (or in a purchasing power parity index of per capita income), to be attained by growth of GDP. But it was increasingly realized that "development" meant growth plus change and that change implied other objectives beyond simple GDP growth. Emphasis on "quality growth," or a desired pattern of growth, incorporates broader criteria of development such as poverty reduction, distributional equity, environmental protection, or Sen's emphasis on "entitlements" and enhancement of "human capabilities" (Sen 1983) and, more recently, development as freedom (Sen 1999). In this broader view "the growth of real income and output has to be put in its place as ultimately an instrumental concern—deeply conditional on its causal role in enhancing more intrinsically valued objects" (Sen 1994: 367). Successful development policies need to determine not only how more rapid growth of real income can be generated but also how real income can be used to achieve the other values incorporated in "development."

Not only the rate of growth but also the pattern of growth is relevant, especially for better understanding of the role of income distribution in the process of development. The persistence of poverty—even with creditable rates of growth—is the shame of inadequate development policy. The World Bank estimates (World Bank 2000: 25) that approximately 1.5 billion people in the developing world are consuming less than US$1 a day (at 1985 prices). If poverty is to be reduced, future analysis will have to give more attention to how the pattern of growth determines who are the beneficiaries of growth. Patterns of growth will have to be designed that avoid urban bias, displacement of unskilled labor, alteration of relative prices to the disadvantage of the poor, gender gaps, deterioration of child welfare, and the erosion of traditional entitlements that have served as safety nets. Moreover, insofar as experience indicates that economic growth does not always lead to widespread improvement in standards of health and education, special policies that differ from those for simply increasing income will have to be devised to improve the health and educational attainment of the poor (Squire 1993: 379).

Employment Creation

When forces in certain types of growth regimes can plunge some groups into poverty, it becomes all the more essential to devise government policies that are adequate to lift them out of poverty. A central problem of development will remain surplus labor. The need to create jobs will be especially pressing, given that the world's labor force will increase by 40 percent over the next two decades, with 95 percent of the increase in developing countries, where less than 15 percent of the world's capital investment will occur (Summers 1991: 5). To reduce poverty by increasing productivity and earnings, governments will have to devise appropriate policies in four crucial sectors of the economy: the rural sector, the urban informal sector, the export sector, and the social sector.

Understanding the Sources of Growth

In the future, the criteria of development that should guide policy may acquire even wider meaning, incorporating for the purpose of better governance such political objectives as the attainment of civil liberties, popular participation, and democracy. Although specific strategies will be necessary to achieve the nonmonetary objectives, growth and change will continue to be central to any explanation of the determinants of development.

Advancement in determining the sources of growth has been notable. Because of the importance of total factor productivity, however, future research will have to increase our understanding of the "unexplained residual factor" in aggregate production functions. Abramovitz (1956) originally called the residual "some sort of measure of ignorance," but he advised that it was also "some sort of indication of where we need to concentrate our attention." This is still true. Now, as Stern observes, "We seem to have too many theories claiming 'property rights' in the unexplained 'residual,' and have no reassurance that any of them, separately or together, really capture what is going on. Just as worrying is that they omit many issues which are probably crucial to growth in the medium run, including economic organization and the social and physical infrastructure" (Stern 1991: 131).

In the future search for the sources of growth, more attention should also be directed to the joint and interdependent action of the causes of growth (Abramovitz 1993: 237 f). There needs to be analysis of the dependence of both tangible and human capital accumulation on the pace and character of technological progress, as well as in the other direction—on how capital accumulation influences technological progress. How do capital accumulation and the advance of knowledge, arising in part from independent or poorly understood sources of growth, work together to produce joint effects (Abramovitz 1993: 236 f)? More generally, growth accounting still has to establish the interactions in the residual among technological progress, economies of scale and scope, tangible capital accumulation, human capital, knowledge capital, and institutional change.

Beyond disaggregating the residual into recognizable elements and coming to understand the joint and interdependent action of the main sources of growth, the ultimate task is to determine how these elements are to yield to policies. Many policies that economists have considered bear on the supply of inputs, but it will be a more difficult challenge to devise and implement policies to promote the income-raising forces constituting the residual.

To explain the residual, or total factor productivity, in growth accounting, refinement and extension of the new growth theories will be a major task for the next generation of development economists. To proceed *from* capital accumulation *to* technological progress, as in the new growth theories, is only part of the story. In the first place, as Abramovitz observes, "there is still far too much that is poorly understood about the influence of relative factor costs, about the evolution of science and technology, and about the political and economic institutions and modes of organization on which the discovery or acquisition of new knowledge depends. We cannot reduce the actual advance of technology, its direction as well as its pace, to a stable function of the supply of savings and costs of finance alone" (Abramovitz 1993: 237). Second, as urged above, there must also be the reverse concern, about the effect of technical progress on the rate of capital accumulation.

The economics of ideas and knowledge require extension. Central policy questions remain to be answered by endogenous innovation models. If deliberate technical progress is to be achieved, what is the institutional design that will motivate behavior for the creation of knowledge? Can governments encourage the production and use of new knowledge? What is the search mechanism for the discovery of the most productivity-enhancing ideas? Can the sectors or locations be identified in which spillover effects may be large? Given the forces of globalization, what are the extensions of endogenous growth theory to international trade, international capital flows, and the international diffusion of ideas? The developing economies, given their increasing openness, will be most affected by the international aspects of the new growth theory. What are the best institutional arrangements for gaining access to the knowledge that already exists in the world? More extensive analysis will have to be given to the nonconvexities involved in the process of diffusion and adoption of new goods and techniques in a developing economy.[15] All of this will have to be integrated with theories of imperfect competition.

The Influence of Institutions

To understand the heterogeneous experience of countries in achieving "development" in the broad sense, it will be necessary to appreciate more fully the role of organizations and institutions. It is common to say that institutions matter, and, as advice for overcoming dualism and establishing a robust market price system, it is now common to say "get institutions right." But what is the meaning of "right"? And how are the right institutions to be established? The model of the competitive ideal world is essentially institutionless and provides little guidance for the actual establishment of efficient markets. These are important questions for the new generation's research agenda.

Some preliminary insights have been offered by Douglass North (1994, 1997), who emphasizes that the incentive structure of society—which is fundamental for the process of change—is a function of the institutional structure of that society.[16] Institutions are "the rules of the game in society or . . . the humanly devised constraints that shape human interaction" (North 1990: 3)—not only formal rules (constitutions, laws, and regulations) but also informal constraints (norms of behavior, conventions, and self-imposed codes of conduct). It is the admixture of rules, norms, and enforcement characteristics that determines economic performance.

Oliver Williamson (1995) also interprets the new institutional economics from the perspective of the institutional environment—the macroanalytics of the political and legal rules of the game—and from the microanalytical perspective of the firm and market modes of contract and organization. Starting from the objective of economizing transaction costs, firms and markets establish institutions for governance of contracts, investment, and private ordering. There are alternative modes of organization: markets, hybrids, hierarchies, and public bureaus. Each mode establishes different incentives and controls that lead to different degrees of cooperation or competition, credible investment conditions, and credible contracting.[17]

Neoclassical institutional economists have tended to focus on institutions that improve allocative efficiency and have considered relative price changes to be the main motive force for institutional change (Bardhan 1989: 1391–93). Institutional change, however, also involves a redistributive change. This raises issues of collective action, bargaining power, state capacity (Evans 1992), and political processes that neoclassical institutional economics has ignored.

The future concern with incomplete or missing institutions may also lead to revision and extension of the first generation's dual-sector model. Early on, Myint (1985) suggested that dualism is preeminently a phenomenon of an underdeveloped organizational framework, characterized by the incomplete development not only of the market network but also of the government's administrative and fiscal system. In contrast to the first generation's reliance on the limited analysis of a two-sector model, the concept of "organizational dualism" moves the policy implications away from "getting prices right" to an examination of what constitutes the development of appropriate institutions.

So too does the new approach to institutional development in terms of game theory, especially evolutionary and repeated games. As analyzed by Aoki and others in the field of comparative institutional analysis, an institution is an equilibrium outcome of a game. Rather than being determined by the polity or by culture, an institution originates as an endogenously created solution of a game in the economic, social, or political exchange domain. This type of new analysis of comparative institutional issues calls for application of game theory, contract theory, and information economics in comparative and historical contexts (see Aoki forthcoming).

A type of "constitutional economics" will be required to determine what reforms of the political-institutional parameters will provide appropriate incentives and rules of behavior for persons entering into exchange relationships. In a developing economy it is especially important that institutions both facilitate and adapt to change (Stern and Stiglitz 1997: 273). To do this, and to realize its potential for development, a country must be capable of "much social invention—changes in arrangements by which people are induced to cooperate and participate in economic activity" (Kuznets 1966: 5). Or, there must be a sufficiently high level of "social capability" (Ohkawa and Kohama 1989: 207–16).

Catching Up: The Role of Technology and Social Capability

A prominent interpretation of "catch-up" and "convergence" emphasizes the forces of "technological congruence" and "social capability" between the productivity leader and the followers. Abramovitz and David (1996) analyze how these forces relate to a country's growth potential and its actual ability "to make the technological and organizational leaps" that the convergence hypothesis envisages. The constraints on the potentials of countries are divided into two categories. First are limitations of "technological congruence"—limitations that arise because the frontiers of technology do not advance evenly in all dimensions among nations, that is, with the same proportional impact on the productivities of labor, capital, and natural resource endowments, on the demands for the different factors of production, and on the effectiveness of different scales of output. The lagging countries have difficulty in adopting and adapting the current technological practices of the leader. The second class of constraints relates to "social capability": levels of education and technical competence; commercial, industrial, and financial institutions; and political and sociocultural characteristics that influence risk-taking, incentives, and rewards for economic activity.

Abramovitz and David summarize their general proposition as follows:

[C]ountries' *effective* potentials for rapid productivity growth by catch-up are not determined solely by the gaps in levels of technology, capital intensity, and efficient allocation that separate them from the productivity leaders. They are restricted also by their access to primary materials and more generally because their market scales, relative factor supplies, and income-constrained patterns of demand make their technical capabilities and their product structures incongruent in some degree with those that characterize countries that operate at or near the technological frontiers. And they are limited, finally, by those institutional characteristics that restrict their abilities to finance, organize, and operate the kinds of enterprises that are required to exploit the technologies on the frontiers of science and engineering. Taken together, the foregoing elements determine a country's effective potential for productivity growth. (Abramovitz and David 1996: 34)

Whether it is labeled "social capability," "social infrastructure," or "social capital," these empty boxes need to be filled with more substantial analysis of institutional arrangements.[18]

Defining Social Capital

Following the successive emphasis on tangible capital, human capital, and knowledge capital, some economists would now add "social capital" to the sources of growth. Collier (1998) characterizes "social capital" as the internal social and cultural coherence of society, the norms and values that govern interactions among people, and the institutions in which they are embedded. Social capital has an economic payoff when it is a social interaction that yield externalities and facilitates collective action for mutual benefit outside the market. Trust, reciprocity, interpersonal networks, cooperation, and coordination can be viewed as "civil social capital" that conditions the interaction of agents and yields externalities.[19]

"Government social capital" can incorporate the benefits of law, order, property rights, education, health, and "good government." To the extent that social capital reduces transaction costs and information costs and makes physical capital and human capital more productive, it could be interpreted as a source of total factor productivity (the Solow residual).

But does it have the attributes of "capital" (Solow 1995, 1999)? Is it empirically an important contribution to the residual in the decomposition of the aggregate production function? Are there operational guidelines for the accumulation of social capital? How can there be investment in social capital? Who should provide the social capital?

There is no gainsaying that economic behavior is socially conditioned. But, aside from the technical language, is the appeal to "social capital" anything more than an appeal to consider culture and institutions?

And while we may not expect studies to quantify the residual of "social capital" in a Solow-growth model, we can still explore behavioral patterns qualitatively.[20] More specific and more disciplined analysis can be devoted to issues of transparency in decisionmaking, an efficient administrative system, effective accounting, a reliable legal system, avoidance of corruption, improvements in corporate governance, social cohesion, and state capability and credibility. Some of this deeper analysis may come through establishing stronger linkages between development economics, the new institutional economics, and the new economic sociology.[21] Especially relevant will be attempts to undertake more empirical research on problems of risk and uncertainty, the reduction of information and transaction costs, and the yield of externalities in social interactions.

The emphasis on social capital—or culture, institutions, and behavioral patterns—should move the explanation of the process of change into a multidisciplinary endeavor. As North (1990, 1997) contends, cultural beliefs are a basic determinant of institutional structure. Not economics, but psychology, sociology, political science, anthropology, law, and history must then provide the answers regarding the origins of cultural beliefs and how they lead to institutional change and the formation of social capital over time. Interdisciplinary research is needed to understand the obstacles to change in the form of values and institutions. Only a beginning has been made in this area.

Indeed, the more general implications of culture remain underresearched. A strong statement of why this has happened is given by Landes:

> If we learn anything from the history of economic development, it is that culture makes all the difference. (Here Max Weber was right on.) Witness the enterprise of expatriate minorities—the Chinese in East and Southeast Asia, Indians in East Africa, Lebanese in West Africa, Jews and Calvinists throughout much of Europe, and on and on. Yet culture, in the sense of the inner values and attitudes that guide a population, frightens scholars. It has a sulfuric odor of race and inheritance, an air of immutability. In thoughtful moments, economists and social scientists recognize that this is not true, and indeed salute examples of cultural change for the better while deploring changes for the worse. But applauding or deploring implies the passivity of the viewer—an inability to use knowledge to shape people and things. The technicians would rather do: change interest and exchange rates, free up trade, alter political institutions, manage. Besides, criticisms of culture cut close to the ego, injure identity and self-esteem. Coming from outsiders, such animadversions, however tactful and indirect, stink of condescension. Benevolent improvers have learned to steer clear. (Landes 1998: 516–17)

An earlier statement by Ruttan recognizes the difficulty of a rigorous multidisciplinary analysis of culture, but his plea remains timely for the next generation:

> The first postwar generation of development economists gave prominence, at least at the rhetorical level, to the role of cultural endowments in constraining or facilitating economic growth. They accepted the body of scholarship in history, philosophy, anthropology, sociology and political science that insisted that cultural endowments exerted major impact on behavior and hence on the response in traditional societies to the opportunities associated with the modernization of community life and the possibilities of national economic development. Professional opinion has, however, not dealt kindly with the reputations of those development economists who have made serious attempts to incorporate cultural variables into development theory or into the analysis of the development process. But in spite of the failure of research on the economic implications of cultural endowments to find a secure place in economic development literature or thought, the conviction that "culture matters" remains pervasive in the underworld of development thought and practice. The fact that the scholars and practitioners of development are forced to deal with cultural endowments at an intuitive level rather than in analytical terms should be regarded as a deficiency in professional capacity rather than as evidence that culture does not matter. In my judgment, it is time for a new generation of development economists to again take stock of the advances in the related social sciences and attempt to assess what they can contribute to our understanding of the development process and to institutional design. (Ruttan 1989: 1385)

Attention to culture is related to institutional development and, in turn, to effective governance and its consequences for economic growth. What are the conditions for creating strong, responsive, effective representative institutions? As Putnam (1992) asks, can civics—social trust, cooperation, civic agreement—predict economics? Although Putnam's research has focused on North-South disparities in Italy, the analysis may also be relevant for the global North and South.

Exploration of the foregoing issues—and others such as those involving gender or the environment—would all benefit from multidisciplinary attention. It is important to correct economists' assumptions about institutions, values, and motivations that have been generally derived only from Western societies. The social infrastructure that underlies the process of development merits deeper analysis. So too does the contribution of sociocultural development and political development to economic development. Insofar as the elucidation of institutional change, culture, and social capital must go beyond the perfect competition and rational-choice framework of neoclassical analysis, development theory will not be locationless but will have to be more country specific and time specific.

The Evolution of Financial Institutions

As for economic institutions, it will be especially important to achieve a better understanding of the evolution of financial institutions in the process of a country's development. Regarding banks and other credit institutions, Stiglitz has said:

> There seems an almost universal underappreciation of the importance of the role played by these institutions in our society . . . Recent work on the economics of information has led us to understand better that what used to be thought of as "capital market imperfections" are simply the reflections of the informational imperfections which are endemic—and which it is the social function of these institutions to address. However, the [developing countries] should be wary in concluding from these theoretical assertions that the government can do the job better. While the market allocations may well not be (constrained) Pareto efficient, there is little evidence that governments can—without considerable thought about the design of appropriate institutions—improve upon the allocations, and there is considerable evidence that it can do worse. What is more, the discretionary power resulting from charging below-market rates of interest gives those in the government assigned the task of allocating credit enormous power, which can be and has been used either for the personal interests of these individuals or for the interests of the party in power. (Stiglitz 1989a: 61)

If institutional change is of prime importance in development, the new generation might also gain significant insights from more attention to the history of the evolution of markets and economic institutions as integral components of the development process. With Jeffrey Williamson we may lament that:

> Caught up in the urgency of contemporary crises, development economists today seem to be less interested in the big questions informed by economic history than was an older generation who eagerly read Kuznets when he began publishing his articles in *Economic Development and Cultural Change* in the 1950s. Indeed there seems to be a growing gap between contemporary development economics and economic history. What a great irony this is

since we know far more about past industrial revolutions than we did three decades ago. To put it quite bluntly, economic history is far better equipped to educate contemporary debate in the less developed world than it was back in the 1950s and 1960s. (Williamson 1991: 2–3)

The new generation might undertake, on the basis of a merging of endogenous growth theory and economic history, a more serious exploration of the effects of institutions and policies on economic development.[22]

The Implications of Globalization

As globalization deepens, new problems of undertaking national development in the context of an integrated world economy will become more prevalent. Even more than for the previous generations, open-economy models will be the rule. And whereas previous international policy issues revolved around trade policy, the next generation will have to devote more attention to determining the effects of international capital movements, migration, and technology transfer.

The previous provocations of dependency thinking and a New International Economic Order are passé. But there will be more controversy over whether globalization benefits the poor countries and whether it creates benefits for poor people within countries. The next generation will have to sort out the positive and negative impulses resulting from globalization.

Furthermore, because markets, technology, and corporations are global in scope, while the jurisdiction of the nation-state is only local, there will be a need for new actions by the World Bank, the IMF, and the World Trade Organization. As the main constituents of the international public sector, they will have to devise new programs to ensure that the benefits of global integration are more equally shared, that competitive policymaking is avoided, and that problems of incomplete risk markets are mitigated as international integration becomes ever more complex.

Complementarity of State and Market

If the future of development economics is to be dominated by any one theme, it will be, as in the past, that of the respective roles of the state and the market in reducing poverty. But there will be new perspectives on the role of the state. The issue will not be market failure or government failure, as viewed from the neoclassical perspective. Instead, future analysis will have to recognize the new market failures, undertake cost-benefit analysis of government policies, and determine how state action can support the institution and deepening of markets.

The future is likely to witness a reaction to the minimalist state that was advocated by the second generation. True, the state should not be overextended. And it is true that government cannot do better than the private sector in the direct production of consumer and producer goods or in inducing innovation and change. But government will still have extensive functions in dealing with the new market failures (imperfect information, imperfect and incomplete markets, dynamic externalities, increasing returns to scale, multiple equilibria, and path dependence), providing public goods, satisfying merit wants such as education and health, reducing poverty and improving income distribution, providing physical infrastructure and social infrastructure, and protecting the natural environment.

The objective will be to have government do what government does best. The challenge will be to obtain the benefits of government action at the least cost.

Although past generations have regarded the government and the market as alternative resource allocation mechanisms, it will be more useful to treat the government as an integral element of the economic system, functioning sometimes as a substitute for and at other times as a complement to other institutional elements. The complementary relationship of state and market will have to be emphasized in policymaking. This will require more extensive analysis of what Aoki has termed a "market-enhancing" view that examines the role of government policy in facilitating or complementing private sector coordination.

> Government should be regarded as an endogenous player interacting with the economic system as a coherent cluster of institutions rather than a neutral, omnipotent agent exogenously attached to the economic system with the mission of resolving its coordination failures . . . In this view, government policy is not aimed directly at introducing a substitute mechanism for resolving market failures, but rather at increasing the capabilities of private sector institutions to do so. (Aoki, Kim, and Okuno-Fujiwara 1997: 2)

Market-enhancing can take many forms—from indirect rule-making that affects incentives, to direct government interventions that structure markets. As an example of indirect rule-making, Aoki and others have applied the market-enhancing criterion to the deepening of financial markets (Hellmann, Murdock, and Stiglitz 1996). The government can support the banking system through deposit rate controls and restrictions on entry—that is, through the exercise of financial restraint—thereby avoiding excessive competition and creating rents that would increase the franchise value for banks and would induce banks to refrain from moral hazard and carry out more effective monitoring of loans and risks. The general principle is that government action can facilitate private sector coordination and provide the necessary incentives to the private sector by creating "contingent rents"—returns in excess of the competitive market, provided certain conditions are fulfilled (as for patents or export subsidies based on targets).

In the future, the theory and practice of development policymaking should give much more consideration to this type of interdependence between state and market in a variety of policy situations. As Stern (1997: 168 f) observes, this approach will make the tasks facing governments more subtle and more difficult. A blending of public policies with the market will involve much deeper conceptual issues than those that faced the managers of command economies. In many ways it will be more difficult to be a policymaker, policy adviser, or policy administrator.

Policymaking and Economic Advice

Although the new generation may focus on these policy issues, their efforts will be of little avail if governments do not heed their normative conclusions. Why do governments not listen to development economists? And how can economists' policy advice be better implemented? These questions will be a major preoccupation of the next generation.

To answer them, the new (neoclassical) political economy provides a beginning in helping economists understand the policymaking process, endogenize government, and identify the conditions that may be conducive to policy reform.[23] But the new generation will have to go beyond a neoclassical type of analysis of political preference functions, political resources, and political constraints as applied to political markets.[24] A deeper theory of politically constrained welfare analysis is necessary to support future empirical work.

Although the new political economy can provide some insights into what contributes to government failure, it is overgeneralizing to maintain that all policymaking can be explained in terms of rational-choice self-interest models (Green and Shapiro 1994; Friedman 1995). Other social-psychological elements enter into decisionmaking, especially when "bounded rationality" prevails (Simon 1957: 241–60). Indeed, no single universal characterization of political behavior is possible. Instead of a unitary state, there is, in reality, an aggregation of preferences. Moreover, at times altruism or some sense of the social good may be more operative than self-interest, and at times economic rationality can take precedence over political rationality. Nor should insights from the old political economy be ignored: historical tradition, social structure, ideologies, and institutions can all influence policy decisions at the expense of rational-choice models.[25]

The new political economy is most robust when illuminating instances of government failure ex post. But beyond its positive analysis, can the new political economy also have predictive and normative value in promoting policy reform? Its attention to policy reform ex ante has been negligible. The reason for the relative neglect of advocacy of political change for purposes of economic reform is that the new political

economy implies a minimal state. As Grindle observes, the new political economy "is weakened as an approach to understanding
policymaking in developing countries and as a policy analytic tool by
the assumption that politics is a negative factor in attempting to get
policies right" (Grindle 1991: 44). Politics, however, should not be
viewed as "a spanner in the economic works, but as the central means
through which societies seek to resolve conflict over issues of distribution and values. In such a perspective, politically rational behavior would
not be viewed as a constraint on the achievement of collectively beneficial public policy" (Grindle 1991: 45).

Crucial for policy reform is an understanding of the reasons for the
successes of government policy. The new political economy ignores what
Grindle calls the "critical moments"—the turning points when policy
changes occur; for example, from import-substituting policies to export promotion, from inflationary policies to successful stabilization,
from financial repression to financial liberalization. Given the heterogeneous experience with development policymaking, it will be vital to
know what has caused the positive "turning points" in policy reform in
various countries. What forces induce political innovations? Policy reform requires political entrepreneurship, but a theory of political entrepreneurship is yet to come.[26] For this, we must look beyond economists
to historians, social psychologists, and political scientists.[27] Simplified
public choice theory as in the new political economy is insufficient,
especially for the governments of developing countries. The analysis of
development policy will have to identify the functional relationships
between economic and noneconomic factors, and their quantitative significance, in order to determine how to operate on incentives, attitudes,
organizational structure, social relations, or any of the many other factors that connect noneconomic and economic change. Clearly, the future success of economic policies in achieving structural transformation
will depend on a better understanding of how to achieve social and
political transformations.

In the past, the critical moments and turning points have normally
involved what Hirschman calls "pressing" problems, as distinguished
from autonomously "chosen" ones (Hirschman 1963). Pressing problems are those "that are forced on the policymakers through pressure
from injured or interested outside parties." Chosen problems are those
that decisionmakers "have picked out of thin air" as a result of their
own perceptions and preferences. Pressing problems are generally those
in which a perception of crisis is apparent. Policy reform involving large,
innovative changes tends to be induced by pressing problems. But we
must now ask: do economists exercise sufficient influence over these
large, innovative changes?

Economists are most knowledgeable about situations susceptible to
"ordinary" economic analysis. Such situations occur in a policy space

characterized by incremental policy changes involving chosen problems. They are subject to more technical analysis and hence a "low" degree of politics (that is, politics as usual). The economist assumes that the government is interested in some form of welfare maximizing. The policy situations involve an instrumental type of rationality (technical policy instruments as the means of achieving policy objectives). The perspective is from a society-centered type of policy, with the government as a clearinghouse or broker among interest groups.[28] Institutions are taken as given or are ignored. These conditions prevail in the upper-left-hand quadrant in Figure 1, which is representative of ordinary neoclassical economic analysis with a high understanding by economists of the policymaking process.

Figure 1. Contrasting Analysis in Different Policy Situations

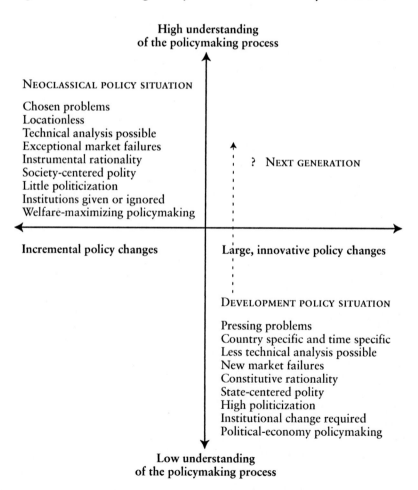

High understanding
of the policymaking process

NEOCLASSICAL POLICY SITUATION

Chosen problems
Locationless
Technical analysis possible
Exceptional market failures
Instrumental rationality
Society-centered polity
Little politicization
Institutions given or ignored
Welfare-maximizing policymaking

? NEXT GENERATION

Incremental policy changes

Large, innovative policy changes

DEVELOPMENT POLICY SITUATION

Pressing problems
Country specific and time specific
Less technical analysis possible
New market failures
Constitutive rationality
State-centered polity
High politicization
Institutional change required
Political-economy policymaking

Low understanding
of the policymaking process

In contrast, when economists have to deal with situations involving large, innovative policy changes associated with structural transformation, they are called on to advise developing countries in a political-economy context in which the economist has less understanding of the policymaking process. In this policy space (see the lower-right-hand quadrant in Figure 1), the problems are pressing problems. They are not amenable to as much technical analysis but, rather, are highly politicized and entail political and social change. The political process of economic policymaking matters. The rationality involved is of a constitutive type: that is, decisions have to be made about how decisions are to be made. A constitution is needed, and an institutional context for decisionmaking has to be established. The policymaking process is more state-centered. The nature and formation of social capital are highly relevant for facilitating dynamic choices. And institutional arrangements need to be changed.

If the new generation of development economists is to become more influential in advising on how to correct nonmarket failures and overcome resistance to policy reform, they will have to give more attention to the policy situations represented by the lower-right-hand quadrant in Figure 1. Their task will be to make policy changes transparent by identifying the distribution of not only the economic but also the political costs and benefits of policy changes and by identifying the gainers and losers. To promote policy reform, they will also have to examine feasible ways of compensating the losers, discover the possibilities for building supportive coalitions, and consider the scope for alternative institutional and administrative arrangements. It will be especially important to insulate policymakers from rent seekers and interest groups so that the government can give more attention to the efficiency of the economy and less to distribution for favor-seeking groups.

The new generation needs more insights from both the old and new political economy in order to better understand the causes of differential development performance and how to institute policy reform. Going beyond the limitations of formal rational-choice models, a richer analysis might be achieved by incorporating some concepts of the old political economy such as nationalism, power, ideology, class, and the relationship between the state and society. Future research may provide a synthesis of the old and new political economy that will point up the possibilities for designing policy changes on the basis of more political variables and a more favorable view of the political process.

So, too, will additional research be required if we are to understand the nature of institutional change and its effect on development performance. A beginning has been made in giving more attention to the functions of markets, property rights, formation of contracts, information problems, organizational change, and incentives. Beyond this, for a deeper understanding of the residual, economists will have to model how the formation of social capital and institutional arrangements make the complexity of dynamic policy choices more manageable in both the private and public sectors. The more manageable is the economy in terms of incentives and capabilities, the more productive it is. With this more comprehensive view of the policymaking process in practice, economists might be in a better position to advise on remedies not only for market failure but also for nonmarket failure and might better understand how to overcome resistance to policy advice.

Although data on aspects of underdevelopment have become more extensive, the very accumulation of ever more information challenges the next generation to formulate a relevant theoretical framework to bring some logical order to the data. Most important, a conjuncture with policymaking has to be established.

It is to be hoped that future research may allow the next generation to deal more effectively with the pressing problems of developing economies that are less tractable to technical analysis and more politicized, involve issues of constitutive rationality, and require social capital and institutional change. As analysts of development policymaking, the coming generation may then move from the lower-right-hand quadrant of Figure 1 to the upper-right-hand quadrant (dashed arrow). In so doing, the development textbook of the future will refine the standard neoclassical text. A distinct subdiscipline of "development economics" will not be simply equivalent to the application of universal economic principles.

In asserting the decline of development economics, Hirschman (1981) pointed to the dominance of "monoeconomics." Kreps (1997: 65–66) also characterized economics since World War II as having "a single methodological tongue" of mathematical modeling and a "sparse set of canonical hypotheses" that became the maintained hypotheses in almost all branches of the subject.[29] But as long as the developing countries have characteristics that distinguish them from industrial countries, a subdiscipline of development economics will be relevant. And even though there is a set of basic economic principles, their particular application to any one country will depend on the economic structure, institutions, political regime, administrative capacity, culture, and history of the particular country.

As Bliss states,

[G]eneral economic principles are precisely too general to give us insights into applications for less developed economies. Alone, the parts of economic theory and method they apply more or less universally tell us less than we need in particular application. To give them life they have to be enlarged and translated. When this is done a specialty is created. Development economics consists in part of the refinement of general economics to deal with questions that arise in the context of development, and partly of certain special ideas that have proved useful in studying developing countries. (Bliss 1989: 1188)

Notes

1. For comprehensive surveys of the literature, see the *Handbook of Development Economics* (Chenery and Srinavasan 1988, 1989; Behrman and Srinavasan 1995). See also Waelbroeck (1998).

A number of retrospective studies of the course of development economics were published in the 1980s; see Hirschman (1981); Livingstone (1981); Sen (1983); Bhagwati (1984); Lewis (1984); Arndt (1987); Stern (1989).

2. Although classical economists were concerned with economic growth and the "progressive state," interest ended with the marginalist revolution of the 1870s. At the start of modern development economics, W. Arthur Lewis could introduce his *Theory of Economic Growth* (1955) by saying, "A book of this kind seemed to be necessary because the theory of economic growth once more engages world-wide interests and because no comprehensive treatise on the subject has been published for about a century. The last great book covering this wide range was John Stuart Mill's *Principles of Political Economy* published in 1848."

Lewis began lecturing on development economics at the University of Manchester in 1950; the first seminar on development at the University of Oxford was offered by Hla Myint in 1950; the subject was introduced at Harvard and Yale in 1952–53. During the 1950s the number of journals devoted to economic development grew; as reported in the *Index of Economic Articles,* the number of development articles tripled in the decade 1950–54 to 1960–64.

3. Although we focus here on the general nature of the analysis, there were, of course, individual dissenters. See, for instance, Bauer (1957) and Myint (1967), discussed below.

4. The Harrod-Domar condition for the necessary growth rate of the capital stock is $\dot{K}/K = s/v$, where $\dot{K}$ is growth in capital, K is capital, s is the average saving rate, and v is K/Y, the capital-output ratio (Harrod 1948; Domar 1947).

5. See Meier and Seers (1984); Meier (1987). In these volumes, leading members of the first generation of development economists adopt a retrospective view and reflect on why they said what they did in their early work. The first volume contains essays by Lord Bauer, Colin Clark, Albert O. Hirschman, Sir Arthur Lewis, Gunnar Myrdal, Raúl Prebisch, Paul N. Rosenstein-Rodan, Walt W. Rostow, Sir Hans W. Singer, and Jan Tinbergen. Authors in the second volume are Celso Furtado, Gottfried Haberler, Arnold C. Harberger, Hla Myint, and Theodore W. Schultz.

6. The first generation had also been influenced by its experience with the Soviet way of industrialization, the practice of national economic management during the Great Depression, wartime mobilization of resources, and government-to-government assistance under the postwar Marshall Plan for the recovery of Western Europe.

7. See Meier and Baldwin (1957), chs. 1, 14, and 15.

8. Even earlier, Peter Bauer (1957:14–28) criticized "price-less" economics, and Hla Myint (1967: 119–21) criticized the lack of policy realism in the theoretical models.

9. It is striking that almost four decades after the first World Bank mission, this view was still similar to that expressed by Lauchlin Currie:

> When, in 1949, I was asked to organize and direct the first study mission of the World Bank, there were no precedents for a mission of this sort and indeed nothing called development economics. I just assumed that it was a case of applying various branches of economics to the problems of a specific country, and accordingly I recruited a group of specialists in public finance, foreign exchange, transport, agriculture, and so on. I did, however, include some engineers and public health technicians. What emerged was a series of recommendations in a variety of fields. I was at pains to entitle it "the basis of a program" rather than a socioeconomic plan. (Currie 1981: 54–58)

10. The generational contrast between the Economic Commission for Latin America (Prebisch 1950) and the World Bank (1993a) is vividly marked.

11. For the concept of "total conditions," see Hicks (1939: ch. 6).

12. For a comprehensive survey of endogenous growth theory and knowledge-based growth, see Aghion and Howitt (1998).

13. For an instructive empirical study, see Barro (1991).

14. For a review of the organization of rural institutions, see Hoff, Braverman, and Stiglitz (1993).

15. For a test of the impact of openness on the transmission of technical knowledge, see Coe and Helpman (1995); Coe, Helpman, and Hoffmaister (1997). A synthesis of new growth theory and trade theory has been offered by Grossman and Helpman (1991).

16. See also the chapters by North and Toye in Harriss, Hunter, and Lewis (1995). An early incisive statement on institutions (although not directed to developing countries) was given by Matthews (1986).

17. For a discussion of the possible convergence of the "new institutional economics" and the "old" institutional economics, see Hodgson (1998).

18. On social capability, see Adelman and Morris (1968); Temple and Johnson (1998). On social infrastructure see Stern (1991: 128 f). By "social infrastructure" is meant "the way in which business is done, rather than human capital. A system in which individuals behave dishonestly or where bureaucracy is obstructive, or where property rights are unclear may lead to a very wasteful allocation of resources in insuring against dishonesty, circumventing bureaucracy or enforcing property rights. The costs involved and the distortion of incentives may constitute serious impediments to growth" (Stern 1991: 128). On social capital, see Coleman (1988a, 1988b: esp. 392–99); Putnam (1993); Fukuyama (1997); Collier (1998); Dasgupta and Serageldin (1999). Collier characterizes "social capital" as the internal social and cultural

coherence of society, the norms and values that govern interactions among people, and the institutions in which they are embedded. Hall and Jones (1999) view institutions and government policies of "openness" as "social infrastructure." Their empirical study documents that differences in capital accumulation, productivity, and levels of output per worker are fundamentally related to their definition of "social infrastructure." For the promising emergence of a new field, comparative institutional analysis, see Aoki (1996); Grief (1998). Analysis of the political economy of institutions might also be extended by game theory and mechanism design, as indicated in Miller (1997).

19. Of trust, Arrow observes,

> Trust and similar values, loyalty or truth-telling, are examples of what the economist would call "externalities." They are goods, they are commodities; they have real, practical, economic value; they increase the efficiency of the system, enable you to produce more goods or more of whatever values you hold in high esteem. But they are not commodities for which trade on the open market is technically possible or even meaningful.
>
> It follows from these remarks that, from the point of view of efficiency as well as from the point of view of distributive justice, something more than the market is called for. Other modes of governing the allocation of resources occur. . . .
>
> Societies in their evolution have developed implicit agreements to certain kinds of regard for others, agreements which are essential to the survival of the society or at least contribute greatly to the efficiency of its working. It has been observed, for example, that among the properties of many societies whose economic development is backward is a lack of mutual trust. . . . And it is clear that this lack of social consciousness is in fact a distinct economic loss in a very concrete sense as well, of course, as a loss in the possible well-running of a political system. (Arrow 1974: 23, 26)

20. Although social capital is difficult to measure precisely, some empirical studies of the security of property rights, the enforceability of contracts, and the effectiveness of public bureaucracies do indicate that the quality of these indicators helps to explain differences in the rate of economic growth. See, for instance, Knack (1996); Clague and others (1997). For an empirical study of the relationship between interpersonal trust, norms of civic cooperation, and economic performance, see Knack and Keefer (1997).

21. For some initial suggestions, see Woolcock (1998).

22. For an illuminating discussion of this fruitful two-way relation, see Crafts (1997).

23. If the new political economy's positive theory of government endogenizes policymaking, can there be any degree of freedom for normative economics? For possible ways of resolving this "determinacy paradox" and defining the way welfare-theoretic economic policy analysis might be conducted, see the

symposium papers by Basu (1997), Dixit (1997), and O'Flaherty and Bhagwati (1997).

For formal political-economic models of behavioral rules for policymakers derived by solving optimization problems with well-defined objective functions, see Sturzenegger and Tommasi (1998).

24. For a discussion of game theory as an analytical methodology that can be applied to political competition as well as market competition, see Myerson (1997).

25. The political process in the making of economic policy is also emphasized by Dixit (1996).

26. See, however, the beginnings of some illuminating political-economic modeling of policy reform: Ranis and Mahmood (1992); Krueger (1993); Rodrik (1993); John Williamson (1994); Tommasi and Velasco (1996).

27. As Lipton (1970: 11) stated long ago, "explicit interdisciplinary studies are urgently needed for policy. Yet the talk/action ratio has surely been higher in interdisciplinary studies than in any other area of research."

28. For a more extensive discussion of the distinction between society-centered and state-centered policymaking, see Grindle and Thomas (1991).

29. Kreps recognizes, however, that after narrowing the issues addressed, in recent years "the field seems to be returning to something like the breadth of the discipline before World War II" (Kreps 1997: 66).

References

Abramovitz, Moses. 1956. "Resource and Output Trends in the United States since 1870." *American Economic Review* 46 (2, May): 5–23.

———. 1993. "The Search for the Sources of Growth: Areas of Ignorance, Old and New." *Journal of Economic History* 53 (2, June): 217–43.

Abramovitz, Moses, and Paul A. David. 1996. "Convergence and Deferred Catch-up: Productivity Leadership and the Waning of American Exceptionalism." In R. Landau, T. Taylor, and G. Wright, eds., *The Mosaic of Economic Growth*. Stanford, Calif.: Stanford University Press.

Adelman, Irma, and Cynthia Taft Morris. 1968. "Performance Criteria for Evaluating Economic Development: An Operational Approach." *Quarterly Journal of Economics* 82 (2, May): 260–80.

Aghion, Philippe, and Peter Howitt. 1998. *Endogenous Growth Theory.* Cambridge, Mass.: MIT Press.

Aoki, Masahiko. 1996. "Towards a Comparative Institutional Analysis: Motivations and Some Tentative Theorizing." *Japanese Economic Review* 47 (1, March): 1–19.

———. Forthcoming. *Towards a Comparative Institutional Analysis.* Cambridge, Mass.: MIT Press.

Aoki, Masahiko, Hyung-Ki Kim, and Masahiro Okuno-Fujiwara, eds. 1997. *The Role of Government in East Asian Development.* Oxford, U.K.: Clarendon Press.

Arndt, H. W. 1987. *Economic Development: The History of an Idea*. Chicago, Ill.: University of Chicago Press.

Arrow, Kenneth J. 1962. "The Economic Implications of Learning by Doing." *Review of Economic Studies* 29 (3): 155–73.

———. 1974. *The Limits of Organization*. New York: W. W. Norton.

———. 1988. "General Economic Theory and the Emergence of Theories of Economic Development." In Kenneth J. Arrow, ed., *The Balance between Industry and Agriculture in Economic Development*, vol. 1: 22–32. New York: St. Martin's Press.

Bardhan, Pranab. 1989. "The New Institutional Economics and Development Theory: A Brief Critical Assessment." *World Development* 17 (9, September): 1389–95.

———. 1993. "Economics of Development and the Development of Economics." *Journal of Economic Perspectives* 7 (2, spring): 129–42.

Barro, Robert J. 1991. "Economic Growth in a Cross Section of Countries." *Quarterly Journal of Economics* 106 (2, May): 407–43.

Basu, Kaushik. 1997. "On Misunderstanding Government: An Analysis of the Art of Policy Advice." *Economics and Politics* 9 (3, November): 231–50.

Bauer, P. T. 1957. *Economic Analysis and Policy in Underdeveloped Countries*. Durham, N.C.: Duke University Press.

Behrman, Jere, and T. N. Srinivasan, eds. 1995. *Handbook of Development Economics*, vols. 3A and 3B. Amsterdam: Elsevier.

Bhagwati, Jagdish. 1984. "Development Economics: What Have We Learned?" *Asian Development Review* 2 (1): 23–38.

Binswanger, Hans P., and Mark R. Rosenzweig. 1981. *Contractual Arrangements, Employment and Wages in Rural Labor Markets: A Critical Review*. New York: Agricultural Development Council.

Bliss, Christopher. 1989. "Trade and Development." In Hollis Chenery and T. N. Srinivasan, eds., *Handbook of Development Economics*, vol. 2. Amsterdam: North-Holland.

Braverman, Avishay, and J. Luis Guasch. 1986. "Rural Credit Markets and Institutions in Developing Countries." *World Development* 14 (10/11): 1253–62.

Bruno, Michael, and Hollis B. Chenery. 1962. "Development Alternatives in an Open Economy." *Economic Journal* 72 (285): 79–103.

Chakravarty, S. 1991. "Development Planning: A Reappraisal." *Cambridge Journal of Economics* 15 (March): 5–20.

Chenery, Hollis, and T. N. Srinivasan, eds. 1988. *Handbook of Development Economics*, vol. 1. Amsterdam: North-Holland.

———. 1989. *Handbook of Development Economics*, vol. 2. Amsterdam: North-Holland.

Clague, Christopher, Philip Keefer, Stephen Knack, and Mancur Olson. 1997. "Institutions and Economic Performance: Property Rights and Contract Enforcement." In Christopher Clague, ed., *Institutions and Economic Development*, ch. 4. Baltimore, Md.: Johns Hopkins University Press.

Clark, J. M. 1923. *Studies in the Economics of Overhead Costs.* Chicago, Ill.: University of Chicago Press.

Coe, David T., and Elhanan Helpman. 1995. "International R&D Spillovers." *European Economic Review* 39 (5, May): 859–87.

Coe, David T., Elhanan Helpman, and Alexander W. Hoffmaister. 1997. "North-South R&D Spillovers." *Economic Journal* 107 (440, January): 134–49.

Coleman, James S. 1988a. "Social Capital in the Creation of Human Capital." *American Journal of Sociology* 94 (supplement): S95–S120.

———. 1988b. "The Creation and Destruction of Social Capital: Implications for the Law." *Notre Dame Journal of Law, Ethics and Public Policy* 3 (spring): 375–404.

Collier, Paul. 1998. "Social Capital and Poverty." World Bank Social Capital Initiative Working Paper 4. Washington, D.C.

Crafts, N. F. R. 1997. "Endogenous Growth: Lessons for and from Economic History." In David M. Kreps and Kenneth F. Wallis, eds., *Advances in Economics and Econometrics: Theory and Applications,* vol. 2, ch. 2. Cambridge, U.K.: Cambridge University Press.

Currie, Lauchlin. 1967. *Obstacles to Development.* East Lansing: Michigan State University Press.

———. 1981. *The Role of Economic Advisers in Developing Countries.* Westport, Conn.: Greenwood Press.

Dasgupta, Partha, and Ismail Serageldin, eds. 1999. *Social Capital: A Multi-faceted Perspective.* Washington, D.C.: World Bank.

Dixit, Avinash. 1996. *The Making of Economic Policy: A Transaction-Cost Politics Perspective.* Cambridge, Mass.: MIT Press.

———. 1997. "Economists as Advisers to Politicians and to Society." *Economics and Politics* 9 (3, November): 225–30.

Domar, Evsey. 1947. "Expansion and Employment." *American Economic Review* 37 (1, March): 34–55.

Evans, Peter. 1992. "The State as Problem and Solution: Predation, Embedded Autonomy, and Structural Change." In Stephen Haggard and Robert R. Kaufman, eds., *The Politics of Economic Adjustment,* ch. 3. Princeton, N.J.: Princeton University Press

Faber, M. L. O., and Dudley Seers, eds. 1972. *The Crisis in Planning.* London: Chatto and Windus.

Friedman, J., ed. 1995. "Special Issue: Rational Choice Theory and Politics." *Critical Review* 9 (1–2, winter–spring).

Fukuyama, Francis. 1997. *The End of Order.* London: Social Market Foundation.

Green, D. P., and I. Shapiro. 1994. *Pathologies of Rational Choice Theory.* New Haven: Conn.: Yale University Press.

Greif, Avner. 1998. "Historical and Comparative Institutional Analysis." *American Economic Review* 88 (2, May): 80–84.

Grindle, Merilee S. 1991. "The New Political Economy: Positive Economics and Negative Politics." In Gerald M. Meier, ed., *Politics and Policy Making in Developing Countries: Perspectives on the New Political Economy.* San Francisco, Calif.: ICS Press.

Grindle, Merilee S., and John W. Thomas. 1991. *Public Choices and Policy Change: The Political Economy of Reform in Developing Countries.* Baltimore, Md.: Johns Hopkins University Press.

Grossman, Gene M., and Elhanan Helpman. 1991. *Innovation and Growth in the Global Economy.* Cambridge, Mass.: MIT Press.

Hall, Robert, and Charles Jones. 1999. "Why Do Some Countries Produce So Much More Output per Worker Than Others?" *Quarterly Journal of Economics* (February): 83–116.

Harberger, Arnold C. 1983. "The Cost-Benefit Approach to Development Economics." *World Development* 11 (10, October): 863–73.

———. 1993. "Secrets of Success: A Handful of Heroes." *American Economic Review* 83 (2, May): 343–50.

Harriss, John, Janet Hunter, and Colin M. Lewis, eds. 1995. *The New Institutional Economics and Third World Development.* London: Routledge.

Harrod, Roy. 1948. *Towards a Dynamic Economics.* London: Macmillan.

Hellmann, Thomas, Kevin C. Murdock, and Joseph Stiglitz. 1996. "Financial Restraint: Towards a New Paradigm." Working paper prepared for the World Bank Economic Development Institute workshop, "Role of Government in Economic Development: Analysis of East Asian Experiences," Kyoto, Japan, September 16–17.

Hicks, John. 1939. *Value and Capital.* Oxford, U.K.: Clarendon Press.

———. 1969. *A Theory of Economic History.* London: Oxford University Press.

Hirschman, Albert O. 1963. *Journeys toward Progress.* New York: Twentieth Century Fund.

———. 1981. "The Rise and Decline of Development Economics." In *Essays in Trespassing,* 1–24. Cambridge, U.K.: Cambridge University Press.

Hodgson, Geoffrey M. 1998. "The Approach of Institutional Economics." *Journal of Economic Literature* 36 (1, March): 166–92.

Hoff, Karla, Avishay Braverman, and Joseph E. Stiglitz, eds. 1993. *The Economics of Rural Organization: Theory, Practice, and Policy.* New York: Oxford University Press.

Killick, Tony. 1976. "The Possibilities of Development Planning." *Oxford Economic Papers* 28 (2, July): 161–84.

King, Mervyn A., and Mark Robson. 1989. "Endogenous Growth and the Role of History." NBER Working Paper 3151. National Bureau of Economic Research, Cambridge, Mass.

Knack, Stephen. 1996. "Institutions and the Convergence Hypothesis: The Cross-National Evidence." *Public Choice* 87 (June): 207–28.

Knack, Stephen, and Philip Keefer. 1997. "Does Social Capital Have an Economic Payoff? A Cross Country Investigation." *Quarterly Journal of Economics* 112 (4, November): 1251–88.

Kreps, David M. 1997. "Economics—The Current Position." *Daedalus* 126 (1, winter): 59–85.

Krueger, Anne O. 1986. "Aid in the Development Process." *World Bank Research Observer* 1 (1): 57–78.

————. 1990. "Government Failures in Development." *Journal of Economic Perspectives* 4 (3, summer): 9–23.

————. 1993. *Political Economy of Policy Reform in Developing Countries.* Cambridge, Mass.: MIT Press.

Krugman, Paul. 1993. "Towards a Counter-Counterrevolution in Development Theory." *Proceedings of the World Bank Annual Conference on Development Economics 1992.* Washington, D.C.: World Bank

Kuznets, Simon. 1966. *Modern Economic Growth: Rate, Structure, and Spread.* New Haven, Conn.: Yale University Press.

Landes, David S. 1998. *The Wealth and Poverty of Nations: Why Some Are So Rich and Some So Poor.* New York: W. W. Norton.

Lewis, W. Arthur. 1952. *The Principles of Economic Planning.* London: Allen and Unwin.

————. 1955. *The Theory of Economic Growth.* London: Allen and Unwin.

————. 1984. "The State of Development Theory." *American Economic Review* 74 (1, March): 1–10.

Lipton, Michael. 1970. "Interdisciplinary Studies in Less Developed Countries." *Journal of Development Studies* 7 (1, October): 5–18.

Little, Ian M. D. 1982. *Economic Development.* New York: Basic Books.

Livingstone, Ian. 1981. "The Development of Development Economics." *Overseas Development Institute Review* 1 (2): 1–19.

Lucas, Robert E. 1988. "On the Mechanics of Economic Development." *Journal of Monetary Economics* 22 (1, July): 3–42.

Marshall, Alfred. 1890. *The Principles of Economics.* London: Macmillan.

————. 1897. "The Old Generation of Economists and the New." *Quarterly Journal of Economics* 11 (2, January): 115–35.

Matthews, R. C. O. 1986. "The Economics of Institutions and the Sources of Growth." *Economic Journal* 96 (384, December): 903–18.

Meier, Gerald M., ed. 1987. *Pioneers in Development, Second Series.* New York: Oxford University Press.

Meier, Gerald M., and Robert E. Baldwin. 1957. *Economic Development: Theory, History, Policy.* New York: Wiley.

Meier, Gerald M., and Dudley Seers, eds. 1984. *Pioneers in Development.* New York: Oxford University Press.

Miller, Gary J. 1997. "The Impact of Economics on Contemporary Political Science." *Journal of Economic Literature* 35 (3, September): 1173–1204.

Murphy, Kevin M., Andrei Shleifer, and Robert W. Vishny. 1989. "Industrialization and the Big Push." *Journal of Political Economy* 97 (5, October): 1003–26.

Myerson, Roger B. 1997. "Economic Analysis of Political Institutions: An Introduction." In David M. Kreps and Kenneth F. Wallis, eds., *Advances in Economics and Econometrics: Theory and Applications. Seventh World Congress,* vol. 1, ch. 3. Cambridge, U.K.: Cambridge University Press.

Myint, Hla. 1967. "Economic Theory and Development Policy." Inaugural lecture, London School of Economics and Political Science, December 1, 1966. *Economica* (May): 117–30.

————. 1985. "Organizational Dualism and Economic Development." *Asian Development Review* 3 (1): 25–42.

North, Douglass C. 1990. *Institutions, Institutional Change, and Economic Performance.* Cambridge, U.K.: Cambridge University Press.

————. 1994. "Economic Performance through Time." *American Economic Review* 84 (3, June): 359–68.

————. 1997. *The Contribution of the New Institutional Economics to an Understanding of the Transition Problem.* WIDER Annual Lectures 1. Helsinki: United Nations University, World Institute for Development Economics Research.

O'Flaherty, Brendan, and Jagdish Bhagwati. 1997. "Will Free Trade with Political Science Put Normative Economists out of Work?" *Economics and Politics* 9 (3, November): 207–19.

Ohkawa, Kazushi, and Hirohisa Kohama. 1989. *Lectures on Developing Economies.* Tokyo: University of Tokyo Press.

Ohkawa, Kazushi, and Henry Rosovsky. 1972. *Japanese Economic Growth.* Stanford, Calif.: Stanford University Press.

Prebisch, Raúl. 1950. *The Economic Development of Latin America and Its Principal Problems.* New York: United Nations, Economic Commission for Latin America.

Putnam, Robert. 1992. "Democracy, Development, and the Civic Community: Evidence from the Italian Experiment." In Ismail Serageldin and June Taboroff, eds., *Culture and Development in Africa,* 33–74. Washington, D.C.: World Bank.

————. 1993. *Making Democracy Work: Civic Traditions in Modern Italy.* Princeton, N.J.: Princeton University Press.

Ranis, Gustav, and Syed Akhtar Mahmood. 1992. *The Political Economy of Development Policy Change.* Oxford, U.K.: Basil Blackwell.

Rodrik, Dani. 1993. "The Positive Economics of Policy Reform." *American Economic Review* 83 (2, May): 356–61.

Romer, Paul M. 1986. "Increasing Returns and Long-Run Growth." *Journal of Political Economy* 94 (5, October): 1002–37.

————. 1989. "Capital Accumulation in the Theory of Long-Run Growth." In R. J. Barro, ed., *Modern Business Cycle Theory,* ch. 2. Oxford, U.K.: Basil Blackwell.

————. 1990. "Endogenous Technical Change." *Journal of Political Economy* 98: 71–102.

————. 1994a. "New Goods, Old Theory, and the Welfare Costs of Trade Restrictions." *Journal of Development Economics* 43 (1, February): 5–38.

————. 1994b. "The Origins of Endogenous Growth." *Journal of Economic Perspectives* 8 (1, winter): 3–22.

Ruttan, V. W. 1989. "Institutional Innovation and Agricultural Development." *World Development* 17 (9): 1375–87.

Sen, Amartya. 1983. "Development: Which Way Now?" *Economic Journal* 93 (December): 745–62.

————. 1994. "Growth Economics: What and Why?" In Luigi L. Pasinetti and Robert M. Solow, eds., *Economic Growth and the Structure of Long-Term Development*. London: Macmillan.

————. 1999. *Development as Freedom*. New York: Knopf.

Simon, H. 1957. "A Behavioral Model of Rational Choice." In *Models of Man: Social and Rational; Mathematical Essays on Rational Human Behavior in a Social Setting*. New York: Wiley.

Singh, Inderjit, Lyn Squire, and John Strauss. 1986. "A Survey of Agricultural Household Models." *World Bank Economic Review* 1 (1, September): 149–54.

Solow, Robert M. 1957. "Technical Change and the Aggregate Production Function." *Review of Economics and Statistics* 39: 312–20.

————. 1995. "But Verify." Review of *Trust: The Social Virtues and the Creation of Prosperity*, by Francis Fukuyama. *The New Republic* 213 (11, September 11): 36–39.

————. 1997. *Learning from "Learning by Doing": Lessons for Economic Growth*. Stanford, Calif.: Stanford University Press.

————. 1999. "Notes on Social Capital and Economic Performance." In Partha Dasgupta and Ismail Seragelin, eds., *Social Capital: A Multifaceted Perspective*. Washington, D.C.: World Bank.

Squire, Lyn. 1993. "Fighting Poverty." *American Economic Review* 83 (2, May): 377–82.

Stern, Nicholas. 1989. "The Economics of Development: A Survey." *Economic Journal* 99 (397, September): 597–685.

————. 1991. "The Determinants of Growth." *Economic Journal* 101 (January): 122–33.

————. 1997. "Macroeconomic Policy and the Role of the State in a Changing World." In Edmond Malinvaud and Amartya K. Sen, eds., *Development Strategy and Management of Market Economy*, ch. 5. Oxford, U.K.: Clarendon Press.

Stern, Nicholas, and Joseph E. Stiglitz. 1997. "A Framework for a Development Strategy in a Market Economy." In Edmond Malinvaud and Amartya K. Sen, eds., *Development Strategy and Management of Market Economy*, ch. 8. Oxford, U.K.: Clarendon Press.

Stiglitz, Joseph E. 1986. "The New Development Economics." *World Development* 14 (2): 258–61.

————. 1989a. "Financial Markets and Development." *Oxford Review of Economic Policy* 5 (4): 55–66.

————. 1989b. "Markets, Market Failures, and Development." *American Economic Review* 79 (2, May): 197–203.

Streeten, Paul, and Michael Lipton, eds. 1969. *The Crisis of Indian Planning*. London: Oxford University Press.

Sturzenegger, F., and Mariano Tommasi, eds. 1998. *The Political Economy of Reform*. Cambridge, Mass.: MIT Press.

Summers, Lawrence. 1991. "Research Challenges for Development Economists." *Finance and Development* 28 (3, September): 2–5.

Temple, Jonathan, and Paul A. Johnson. 1998. "Social Capability and Economic Growth." *Quarterly Journal of Economics* 113 (3, August): 965–90.

Timmer, C. Peter. 1973. "Choice of Techniques in Rice Milling in Java." *Bulletin of Indonesian Economic Studies* 9 (2, July): 57–76.

Tommasi, Mariano, and Andres Velasco. 1996. "Where Are We in the Political Economy of Reform?" *Journal of Policy Reform* 1: 187–238.

Waelbroeck, Jean. 1998. "Half a Century of Development Economics: A Review Based on the *Handbook of Development Economics*." World Bank Policy Research Working Paper 1925. Research Advisory Group, World Bank, Washington, D.C.

Williamson, Jeffrey G. 1991. *Inequality, Poverty and History.* Cambridge, Mass.: Basil Blackwell.

Williamson, John, ed. 1994. *The Political Economy of Policy Reform.* Washington, D.C.: Institute for International Economics.

Williamson, Oliver E. 1995. "The Institutions and Governance of Economic Development and Reform." In *Proceedings of the World Bank Annual Conference on Development Economics 1994.* Washington, D.C.: World Bank.

———. 1998. "The Institutions of Governance." *American Economic Review* 88 (2, May): 75–79.

Woolcock, Michael. 1998. "Social Capital and Economic Development: Toward a Theoretical Synthesis and Policy Framework." *Theory and Society* 27: 151–208.

World Bank. 1993a. *The East Asian Miracle: Economic Growth and Public Policy.* New York: Oxford University Press.

———. 1993b. *Implementing the World Bank's Strategy to Reduce Poverty: Progress and Challenges.* Washington, D.C.

———. 2000. *World Development Report 1999/2000: Entering the 21st Century.* New York: Oxford University Press.

Comment

Philippe Aghion

GERALD MEIER'S CHAPTER PROVIDES an illuminating account of how the dominant thinking on development economics has evolved over the past 50 years: first, the "centralized" view that the state should step in directly to correct market failures and substitute for missing market institutions; second, the "neoclassical" view that development economics should essentially consist in applying standard economic analysis to the particular context of developing economies; and, more recently, what one might call a "transaction cost" approach that examines the sources of market imperfections in developing countries in more detail and tries to draw some of the implications of such imperfections for government policy and assess their effects on incentives and market performance. The chapter also puts the whole field of development economics in perspective by setting up intellectual challenges and offering a number of thought-provoking ideas for further thinking by "new generations" on development theory and policy. My discussion will focus entirely on that part of Meier's chapter. The suggestions made there are so relevant that a number of them have, in fact, already been taken up during the past 10 years of research on growth and development. Here, I just want to mention briefly some recent trends in growth theory, in development economics, and in the new field of transition economics.

New Growth Theories

The first generation of endogenous growth models (the "AK" approach—see Frankel 1962; Romer 1986) emphasizes externalities in capital accumulation as a major source of sustained productivity growth and uses this approach to discuss the effects of taxation, savings, education, and trade policies on long-run growth (see Rebelo 1991; Barro and Sala-i-Martin 1995). A second wave of endogenous growth models (the "neo-Schumpeterian" approach), which appeared in the early

1990s, with parallel work by Romer (1990) and by Aghion and Howitt (1992), takes a closer look at the economic sources of technological progress by focusing explicitly on innovations as a distinct economic activity with distinct economic causes and effects. This new approach has opened the door to a deeper understanding of how structural features of an economy such as the organization of firms, the degree of market competition in various sectors, the physical and legal infrastructure, the development of financial institutions, the distribution of income and wealth, the design of political institutions, and the endowment and accumulation of physical capital can affect long-run growth through their effects on economic agents' incentives and opportunities to engage in knowledge-producing (or innovative) activities.[1]

This more micro-founded approach has also changed the way of doing empirical work on growth. Departing somewhat from the aggregate cross-country regressions wave of the early 1990s, while at the same time taking due account of the pioneering work of Zvi Griliches and his prestigious "productivity" group, more recent contributions have explored in greater detail the sources of, and evolutions in, research productivity and productivity growth. For example, Caballero and Jaffe (1993) have developed a new methodology, using U.S. data on patents and patent citations, for measuring the extent of creative destruction, knowledge obsolescence, and knowledge spillovers in the growth process. More recently, Blundell, Griffith, and Van Reenen (1995) and Nickell (1996) have used U.K. firm-level panel data to show that both the arrival rate of innovations and the rate of productivity growth are positively correlated with various measures of product-market competition. Nickell, Nicolitsas, and Dryden (1997) have shown that the positive effects of competition on productivity growth tend to be reduced in firms with a dominant shareholder (and therefore less subject to agency problems). Similar work is being conducted on assessing the effects of financial depth and the organization of financial systems on the rate and nature of innovations.[2] And researchers working on trade and growth are trying to get a better grasp on the real sources of the positive correlation between openness and growth. Is it the result of a scale effect (larger markets encourage innovative activities by increasing the rents to innovation), or a consequence of the positive effects of trade on knowledge spillovers and knowledge diffusion (see Coe and Helpman 1995), or, instead, a result of the positive correlation between trade liberalization and product market competition?

Because of its explicit emphasis on the structural aspects of the innovation process, the neo-Schumpeterian approach has made it possible to bridge the gap between theorists and historians of growth and development. For example, the opposition between innovative forces and the vested interests of those working with the old technologies introduced during the Industrial Revolution may account for the industrial slowdown that occurred in Great Britain toward the end of the 19th century, as argued by Mokyr (1990). Also, recent theoretical work on innovation and growth has fostered synergies between theorists and historians interested in the phenomenon of general purpose technologies (GPT); in particular, they are analyzing several channels through which the introduction of a new GPT can temporarily contribute to a measured productivity slowdown even though it will eventually put the economy on a higher-growth path. Many people have come to the conclusion that the evolution in productivity growth, price of equipment, and wage inequality experienced by the world economy since the mid-1970s is related to the information revolution.

New Trends in Development Economics

Following the seminal work of Stiglitz (starting with Stiglitz and Weiss 1981) on adverse selection as a source of credit market imperfections and credit rationing, there has been a new wave of theoretical models—all based on a detailed formalization of the incentive problem underlying the imperfection of the capital market—that have analyzed the relationships between income and wealth inequality, the occupational division of society, and the resulting growth and development patterns.[3] More recently, increasing effort has been devoted to analyzing the effects of various kinds of institutional arrangement for insuring individuals in developing countries against different types of risks and facilitating their access to credit and investment. Examples include recent theoretical work on land reform and on microcredit.[4] This microfounded approach to economic development, which parallels the recent evolution in growth economics described above, has generated a new wave of microeconometric studies, starting with the work of Townsend (1994) on local insurance institutions in India and continuing with work by Banerjee, Mookherjee, and Ray (1998) and Banerjee and Duflo (1999) on contracts and incentives in selected Indian industries.

Transition Economics

Despite its newness as a separate field of research in economics, the "economics of transition"—the primary purpose of which is to analyze the transition of postsocialist economies in Central and Eastern Europe and the former Soviet Union from central planning to a market system—has taught us much about some of the questions that Gerald Meier raises in the last part of his chapter. Indeed, the postsocialist transition is the first institutional experiment ever conducted simultaneously on such a large scale and across so many countries that differ in history, starting point in the transition, openness to Western markets, knowledge or memory about market systems, and so on. After 10 years of transition, economists have learned much and are still discovering much about the institutional determinants of macroeconomic growth and stability, not only in Central and Eastern Europe but also in Western economies. For example, we have learned that privatization does not lead to more productive and allocative efficiency unless accompanied by suitable reforms of the overall institutional environment. The existence of effective product markets and political competition, enforceable laws, and adequate regulations for the financial system proved to make a great difference between successful countries such as Poland and far less successful countries such as Russia. Recent studies have also mentioned lack of "social capital"—of individuals' propensity to cooperate instead of pursuing rent-seeking objectives—as a potential source of failure in some transition countries. An interesting research question, recently taken up by Hellman and Schankerman (1999), is to what extent social capital (or, instead, corruption) in transition economies is being affected by the design and implementation of structural reforms such as privatization.[5] More generally, we still have much to learn about the interplay between formal contracting (that is, contracting that explicitly allocates decision rights or ownership rights) and informal, or "relational," contracting, which refers to sustainable trust and the absence of cheating between the contracting parties (see Baker, Gibbons, and Murphy 1997; Halonen 1997; Aghion, Dewatripont, and Rey 1999).

I hope that my remarks have convinced the reader that the avenues suggested by Gerald Meier for future research on growth and development economics are indeed the right way to go and that they feature prominently in more recent work in the field. I would like to conclude by mentioning an important question raised by Meier that, to my knowledge, has received very little attention so far: how to "measure" economic development as a whole once it is understood that growth is only one aspect of the development of societies and that there are other equally important dimensions such as political democracy and human rights, health, education, the environment, and equal access to opportunities. Although most of these other aspects interact with growth, the measurement question remains a considerable challenge for Meier's "new generation."

Notes

1. See Aghion and Howitt (1998) for more detailed analyses and discussions on each of these aspects.

2. The reference is to King and Levine (1993) and to more recent work on finance and growth in transition economies as reflected, for example, in EBRD (1998).

3. Here we should mention Banerjee and Newman (1993, 1994) and Galor and Zeira (1993). See also Aghion and Bolton (1997); Piketty (1997).

4. On land reform, see Mookherjee (1997); on microcredit, see Banerjee, Besley, and Guinnane (1994); Armendáriz de Aghion (1999); Ghatak (forthcoming); Armendáriz de Aghion and Gollier (forthcoming).

5. Whereas in Central Europe privatizations have gone along with improvements, both in the protection of minority shareholders' rights and in tax enforcement and other aspects of "social conduct," the opposite appears to be true in Russia, where insider privatizations have considerably increased the concentration of wealth, creating strong vested interests opposed to tax reform and enforcement of minority rights.

References

Aghion, Philippe, and Patrick Bolton. 1997. "A Theory of Trickle-Down Growth and Development." *Review of Economic Studies* 64 (2, April): 151–72.

Aghion, Philippe, and Peter Howitt. 1992. "A Model of Growth through Creative Destruction." *Econometrica* 60: 323–51.

_____. 1998. *Endogenous Growth Theory*. Cambridge, Mass.: MIT Press.

Aghion, Philippe, M. Dewatripont, and P. Rey. 1999. "Partial Contracting, Control Allocation, and Cooperation." Working Paper. University College London.

Armendáriz de Aghion, Beatriz. 1999. "On the Design of a Credit Agreement with Peer Monitoring." *Journal of Development Economics* 60 (1, October): 79–104.

Armendáriz de Aghion, Beatriz, and Christian Gollier. Forthcoming. "Peer Group Formation in an Adverse Selection Model." *Economic Journal*.

Baker, G., R. Gibbons, and K. Murphy. 1997. "Relational Contracts and the Theory of the Firm." Massachusetts Institute of Technology, Cambridge, Mass. Processed.

Banerjee, Abhijit V., and E. Duflo. 1999. "Reputation Effects and the Limits of Contracting: A Study of the Indian Software Industry." Massachusetts Institute of Technology, Cambridge, Mass. Processed. Forthcoming in *Quarterly Journal of Economics*, and available at http://web.mit.edu/eduflo/www/sofpap102-1.pdf.

Banerjee, Abhijit V., and Andrew F. Newman. 1993. "Occupational Choice and the Process of Development." *Journal of Political Economy* 101 (2, April): 274–98.

_____. 1994. "Poverty, Incentives, and Development." *American Economic Review* 84 (2): 211–15.

Banerjee, Abhijit V., Timothy Besley, and Timothy W. Guinnane. 1994. "Thy Neighbor's Keeper: The Design of a Credit Cooperative with Theory and Test." *Quarterly Journal of Economics* 109 (2, May): 491–515.

Banerjee, Abhijit V., and Dilip Mookherjee, Kaivan Munshi, and Debraj Ray. 1998. "Inequality, Control Rights and Rent Seeking: Sugar Cooperatives in Maharastra." Forthcoming in *Journal of Political Economy*.

Barro, Robert J., and Xavier Sala-i-Martin. 1995. *Economic Growth.* Cambridge, Mass.: MIT Press.

Blundell, Richard, Rachel Griffith, and John Van Reenen. 1995. "Dynamic Count Data Models of Technological Innovation." *Economic Journal* 105 (429): 333–44.

Caballero, R. J., and A. B. Jaffe. 1993. "How High Are the Giant's Shoulders: An Empirical Assessment of Knowledge Spillovers and Creative Destruction in a Model of Economic Growth." *NBER Macroeconomics Annual,* 15–74. Cambridge, Mass.: MIT Press.

Coe, David T., and Elhanan Helpman. 1995. "International R&D Spillovers." *European Economic Review* 39 (5, May): 859–87.

EBRD (European Bank for Reconstruction and Development). 1998. *Transition Report.* London.

Frankel, M. 1962. "The Production Function in Allocation and Growth: A Synthesis." *American Economic Review* 52: 995–1022.

Galor, Oded and Joseph Zeira. 1993. "Income Distribution and Macroeconomics." *Review of Economic Studies* 60 (1): 35–52.

Ghatak, Maitreesh. Forthcoming. "Joint Liability Credit Contracts and the Peer Selection Effect." *Economic Journal.*

Halonen, Maija. 1997. " A Theory of Joint Ownership." University of Bristol, Bristol, U.K. Processed.

Hellman, J., and M. Schankerman. 1999. "Government in Transition." European Bank for Reconstruction and Development, London. Processed.

King, Robert G., and Ross Levine. 1993. "Finance and Growth: Schumpeter Might Be Right." *Quarterly Journal of Economics* 108 (3): 717–37.

Laffont, J.-J., and T. T. N'Guessan. Forthcoming. "Group Lending with Adverse Selection." *European Economic Review.*

Mokyr, Joel. 1990. *The Lever of Riches.* New York: Oxford University Press.

Mookherjee, Dilip. 1997. "Informational Rents and Property Rights in Land." In *Property relations, incentives and welfare: Proceedings of a conference held in Barcelona, Spain, by the International Economic Association.* John E. Roemer, ed. New York: St. Martin's Press.

Nickell, S. J. 1996. "Competition and Corporate Performance." *Journal of Political Economy* 104 (4): 724–46.

Nickell, S. J., D. Nicolitsas, and N. Dryden. 1997. "What Makes Firms Perform Well?" *European Economic Review* 41 (3–5): 783–96.

Piketty, T. 1997. "The Dynamics of the Wealth Distribution and the Interest Rate with Credit Rationing." *Review of Economic Studies* 64 (2, April): 173–89.

Rebelo, S. 1991. "Long-Run Policy Analysis and Long-Run Growth." *Journal of Political Economy* 99: 500–521.

Romer, Paul M. 1986. "Increasing Returns and Long Run Growth." *Journal of Political Economy* 94 (5, October): 1002–37.

———. 1990. "Endogenous Technical Change." *Journal of Political Economy* 98 (5, part 2): 71–102.

Stiglitz, Joseph E. 1990. "Peer Monitoring and Credit Markets." *World Bank Economic Review* 4 (3): 351–66.

Stiglitz, Joseph E., and Andrew Weiss. 1981. "Credit Rationing in Markets with Imperfect Information." *American Economic Review* 71 (3): 393–410.

Townsend, Robert M. 1994. "Risk and Insurance in Village India. *Econometrica* 62 (3): 539–61.

Comment

Hla Myint

PROFESSOR MEIER'S PAPER suggests two central questions:

1. What is the future of development economics as a separate branch of economics in the aftermath of the "neoclassical consensus" that maintains a general economic theory is applicable to both industrial and developing countries?

2. Is development economics to be regarded simply as "applied economics," or is there a need for a special "development theory"?

This second question is something of a red herring, inasmuch as all development economists are "applied economists" seeking to apply economic theory to the facts and problems of developing countries. The real issue is whether development economists can do their job better by acquiring more empirical knowledge about these countries or whether they would become better *applied* economists if assisted by a special economic theory that supplements general economic theory, so as to get a better grip on the different economic settings of developing countries.

As an individual, the development economist may choose to become more empirically oriented or more theoretically oriented, according to his or her own interests and aptitude. But looking at the subject as a whole, the balance of advantage at present seems to have shifted in favor of a theoretical approach. In the 1950s the older development economists theorized about developing countries on the basis of very scanty facts. Now the situation is reversed, for there has been a vast outpouring of statistical and empirical information, not only from international organizations like the World Bank but also from individual researchers, covering various aspects of the economic life of the developing countries. The problem now is how to pull together this vast array of ad hoc descriptive and applied studies into an orderly framework and to convert the empirical information into useful hypotheses to be incorporated into standard theoretical analysis. I therefore agree with Bliss about the need for special "development theory."

But it is one thing to search for a more usable type of development theory and another to expect that it will lead to the "high understanding of the policymaking process" demanded by Meier's Figure 1. For instance, my own search for a development theory at the middle level of abstraction between high theory and down-to-earth applied economics will fall far short of these requirements. My approach may be regarded as a species of the "endogenous neoclassical growth theory" seeking the "residual factors" of growth in the changes in the domestic institutional framework of a developing country. It may have some uses, but like most types of neoclassical approach, it is embedded in the tradition of looking for "incremental policy changes" and is not likely to yield "large, innovative policy changes."

I now go on to make some brief comments on the detailed items listed in Figure 1. As far as I understand Hirschman's idea of the "pressing problems," they seem to arise from a familiar situation of macroeconomic disequilibrium with high inflation and balance of payments crisis. I admit that such macroeconomic crises are very painful and difficult to solve. But I see no special need to urge the economists to deal with this type of problem since, in any actual situation, most economists in the country suffering from a crisis will be automatically drawn into "crisis management." The danger in such a situation is that the economic advisers may be tempted (or politically pressured) into resorting to short-term panaceas—for example, foreign borrowing instead of devaluation and budget cuts—that would add to the longer-run difficulties. Thus while the "pressing problems" may be a necessary condition, they do not provide a sufficient condition for policy reforms for longer-run development. This will largely depend on the nature of the government in the country suffering the crisis. A semidemocratic government subject to "factional" pressures and vested interests may be driven into short-term panaceas, while a strong military government may "tough it out" and resist a great deal of pressure without any policy reforms.

I agree with Meier that the "nitty-gritty" part of policy changes may not require elaborate technical analysis precisely because economists wish to avoid being drawn into politics. In any case, a politician would regard himself a better judge of "the political costs and benefits" than any economist, whether a visiting foreign expert or the native economist. The visiting foreign economist cannot be expected to know much about a country's political situation, and it is extremely perilous for a native economic adviser to "politicize" his economic advice. If he swims with the political tide, he merely becomes a "spin doctor" for the ruling government and loses his professional integrity; if he swims against the tide, he may lose his job, or worse.

On the subject of "government failures," I subscribe to the "new political economy" concept of the "predatory state." I believe that most governments, whether democratic or military, would do almost anything to stay in power. Thus, political interference with the underdeveloped administrative system will tend to undermine the "functional efficiency" of that system, and I fear that "politicization" of economic policy would only make things worse. I admit, however, that it is not easy to reform the inefficient and corrupt administrative system of a developing country, even without the politicians throwing a spanner into the works. It used to be thought that the limited administrative capacity of a newly independent country could be increased by training, education, and experience. But university expansion in these countries has merely increased graduate unemployment, and the new political economy of the "bureaucratic-maximizing" state warns us about the difficulties of reforming enriched administrative practices designed to make the government "the employer of last resort."

Having seen the failure of the 1950s type of "big push" approach, I put my trust more in the "incremental" economic gains that, compounded over a few decades, have resulted in higher rates of economic growth than were ever thought possible in the 1950s.

On the Goals of Development

Kaushik Basu

THE DEVELOPMENT DEBATE appears to be, at last, coasting toward a consensus: developing nations must not focus their energies on the growth rates of their GDP, NNP, GNP, and the like but should instead try to achieve "human development" or "comprehensive development." A remarkable feature of these new goals is that everyone seems to be supporting them, although few know what the terms mean. This is in some sense understandable. First, the terms "human" and "comprehensive" are so enticing that no one can proclaim being against them without sounding absurd and boorish. And given that the aim of these new objectives is to go beyond narrow economic objectives to larger social and political goals, some vagueness in the target is inevitable. Attempts to give these goals sharper focus, as in the United Nations Development Programme's (UNDP's) construction of the Human Development Index, have inevitably been criticized for arbitrariness. Even on this, however, one may argue that it is better to be somewhat arbitrary but have your broad objective right than to have a sharply defined but morally indefensible objective.

In this chapter, I join the debate somewhat idiosyncratically. After a discussion of the concept of development as it has evolved over time, I propose and evaluate some particular goals that countries should adopt. I then suggest some perspectives on measuring and evaluating the progress of nations, without claiming that these measures should be the end-all of what nations strive to achieve; rather, they should be part of the larger goal of human development. Next, I discuss a relatively ignored subject: the interdependence of the goals of different nations. Even if all nations were to agree on the ultimate aims, there is enough interdependence in the global economy for the journey toward these goals to be marred by skirmishes, as each nation wants others to make certain moves first before it does so (if at all).

The strategic interaction between the goals of different nations has received little attention, the presumption being that strategic problems

arise when agents act selfishly and vanish when we put on our normative hats and try to advance general human well-being. But this
presumption is wrong. Some of the most serious problems of development—for instance, those related to labor standards and the environment—have remained unresolved because of strategic problems of
morality. The final sections of this chapter discuss the problem of the
interdependence of nations' goals and supply an illustrative example
on international labor standards.

The Idea of Development

By leafing through *Forbes* magazine and some recent *World Development Reports,* it is easy to compile the following facts. The total income, in 1998, of Hollywood's richest 50 individuals exceeds the total
income of Burundi's entire population of 7 million. If Bill Gates decided
to encash and consume the *increase* in the value of his total assets that
occurred over the past year, he would be able to consume more than the
total annual consumption of the 60 million people of Ethiopia. These
numbers reflect both the phenomenal scope for wealth and economic
well-being that the modern world makes possible and also how easy it
is for this enormous potential to bypass large masses of humanity. That
even today, in this unbelievably rich world, large numbers of children
have to work 12 to 14 hours a day to enable their families to barely
survive; that in many countries more than 100 babies die in the first
year of their lives for each 1,000 live births; and that in many countries
more than half the population does not have access to electricity or safe
drinking water—all this shows a massive failure not in our scientific
achievements (because technically we can provide for all) but in our
social and political institutions. Have we had our goals right? Have we
striven too hard for narrow economic amassment without paying adequate attention to basic human well-being and equity?

For long stretches of history, a nation's achievement was measured
by its territorial control, and progress was equated with sending out
armies and armadas. Although there was always trade, which could
create value simply by altering the ownership of goods and services, a
large part of the global game was viewed as a zero-sum competition.
As a consequence, development, which connotes advance and progress,
was not an important part of the human agenda. The aim of a state or
a kingdom was to have peace and general prosperity; expansion meant
encroachment into what belonged to others. One can see this in one of
the earliest books on economics, *The Arthashastra,* written by Kautilya
around 300 B.C. Despite its attempt to be a comprehensive treatise on
statecraft and the economic management of a nation (*arthashastra* literally means "the doctrine of wealth"), its obsession is with order and

static efficiency and on how the king should have a well-defined set of laws and punish anybody who disrupts the functioning of society. There are long tracts on the management of state finances, on how profligacy must be avoided, on fiscal discipline, and on effective tax collection. The concern about budgetary discipline is so great that in times of financial shortage the *Arthashastra* (272) permits the king to exploit the gullibility of the masses and raise funds by "building overnight, as if it happened by a miracle, a temple or a sanctuary and promoting the holding of fairs and festivals in honour of the miraculous deity" and (273) to use "secret agents to frighten people into making offerings to drive away an evil spirit." Despite such attention to detail and its range of concerns, which trespasses the boundaries of economics, politics, and sociology (not to mention morality), what is surprising about this classic work, viewed at the beginning of the 21st century, is how little it dwells on *progress* or growth of aggregate material well-being. This was, in general, true of the early view of the good life.

With the growth in trade and breakthroughs in science and technology, of which in theory there need be no end, this has changed. Our goals have moved away from purely tangible wealth such as land and gold and also away from static well-being. One can have a large income despite having little control over not just land but anything tangible. By sending one's capital to distant lands, one can partake in the success of faraway places without the aid of soldiers and guns. The discovery of a new technology in one laboratory in one city can spread to faraway lands. In principle, prosperity can extend to all, and greater income over time can accrue to all.

Yet that has not happened. China's per capita income grew at the astonishing rate of 6.7 percent a year for 30 years beginning in 1965; during the same period Sierra Leone's per capita income fell 1.4 percent a year. Chile's per capita income grew at the more sober rate of 1.6 percent a year over the same 30 years, while Ghana's declined at an annual rate of 0.9 percent. Negative average growth rates over the past 30 years were also observed in Bolivia, El Salvador, Madagascar, Senegal, and several other nations.[1] These anomalies raise a host of new questions concerning development and distribution. What policies should developing countries follow? What policies should global organizations such as the World Bank and the World Trade Organization follow or advocate?

With the rise in the popularity of measuring and monitoring national incomes (clearly a phenomenon of this century), progress and development also came to be measured in terms of gross national product (GNP) or the per capita income of a nation. This intellectual tradition, with its limited objective, helped nations focus their energies narrowly and must have played a role in the rapid growth of national incomes that this century has witnessed. But it also brought in its wake dissension and disappointments. To maximize income growth, environmental considerations were left to languish on the sidelines; the standard of living was often allowed to slide; large inequalities between classes, regions, and genders were ignored; and poverty was tolerated more than it should have been in the rush to generate maximum growth.

Fortunately, that has been changing. A large number of economists have argued the need for moving beyond this narrow goal.[2] This is precisely the line along which Stiglitz (1998a: 31), for instance, has contested the "Washington consensus." "The Washington consensus advocated use of a small set of instruments . . . to achieve a relatively narrow goal (economic growth). The post–Washington consensus recognizes both that a broader set of instruments are necessary and our goals are also much broader." Stiglitz goes on to emphasize, rightly, the need to focus attention on improvements in income distribution, environment, health, and education.

In a series of influential publications, Sen (1983, 1985, 1999) has contributed to the broadening of the goals of development. He has argued the need to move away from the commodity fetishism of the earlier approaches and toward the evaluation of development and progress in terms of functioning and capability. A functioning is what a person manages to do or be. A good can enable a functioning but is distinct from it. For example, a bicycle is a good, whereas being able to transport oneself rapidly to work is a functioning. Several persons, each owning a bicycle, may be able to achieve different kinds of functioning depending on their other attributes—how well fed they are, their morbidity statistics, and so on. As Sen has pointed out, this approach has its roots in an intellectual heritage that goes back to Adam Smith and Karl Marx (see the discussion in Basu and Lopez-Calva 1999), but it was lost in the increasing fervor of measuring the progress of nations by their incomes that we have seen in this century.

This broader approach to the concept of well-being and progress has generated two kinds of literature: one that formalizes this still somewhat nebulous idea (see, for instance, Atkinson 1995; Herrero 1996; Romer 1999; Suzumura 1999), and one that tries to put it into operation. Dasgupta and Weale (1992), Brandolini and D'Alessio (1998), and the UNDP's *Human Development Reports* are examples of the latter. Since I am concerned here with some of the more practical and policy-oriented issues of development goals, and the modifications I suggest are based on the latter approach, the next section begins with a statement of the method used by the UNDP.

Quintile Income and Quintile Growth

The UNDP, beginning with its *Human Development Report 1990,* has argued strongly for an indicator of a nation's progress that is a weighted average of the nation's literacy and educational achievement, the citizen's life expectancy, and the nation's per capita income. Recently, the World Bank has argued for widening our goals beyond the traditional macro-economic objectives, such as national income, fiscal health, and stability in the balance of payments, to encompass "societal development," including basic human rights, access to a just legal system, literacy, and good health (see Stiglitz 1998a; Wolfensohn 1999). Streeten (1994) has tried to bring order into these expanding objectives by classifying them into two categories, resource development and humanitarian progress, and by giving six reasons why we should be interested in human development. These reasons are, briefly, as follows:

- Human development is desirable as an end in itself.
- It can promote higher productivity and so enhance human command over goods and services.
- It reduces human reproduction, an outcome that is generally considered desirable.
- It is good for the environment.
- It can contribute to a healthy civil society and democracy.
- It can promote political stability.

Most of these objectives are related to the objective of equity and poverty reduction—of including people in the development process rather than excluding or abandoning them. Streeten points out that the poor are not just victims of environmental degradation but often its cause and shows how human development promotes a healthy civil society by improving the lot of the poorest people and making them feel included.

This suggests a natural correction for the way we evaluate different economies. Essentially, it says that in evaluating an economy's state or progress, we must focus primarily on how the poorest people are faring. A first cut at doing this—and the criterion that I want to advocate in this section—is to look at the economic condition of the poorest 20 percent of the population. In other words, instead of bothering about the per capita income of the nation as a whole, we should be concerned about the per capita income of the bottom quintile. Instead of equating a country's progress with the growth rate of per capita income in general, we should look at the growth rate of the per capita income of the poorest 20 percent of the population.

In recommending the use of these measures and commending them as goals of development, I am not taking issue with the advocacy of noneconomic goals, which has gathered strength in recent years with the publication of the UNDP's annual *Human Development Reports* and the World Bank's new interest in "comprehensive development." My suggestion is not meant to deny the larger aims of trying to achieve political stability, environmental goodness, and a higher general quality of human life. In understanding this recommendation, two factors have to be kept in mind. First, to the extent that we do look at income and income growth, I am suggesting that we should focus on the per capita income of the poorest 20 percent of the population ("quintile income") and the growth rate of the per capita income of that poorest 20 percent ("quintile growth rate"). Second, these quintile objectives are likely to correlate better with other noneconomic indicators, such as environmental conditions and social stability, for the reasons Streeten has suggested.[3] (See also Aturupane, Glewwe, and Isenman 1994.)[4] Thus, even when we decide to play the dismal scientist and focus on income, if the focus is on *quintile* income, we will automatically capture some of the social indicators emphasized in broader notions of human development.

Before proceeding further, it is useful to specify some definitions formally. Let us define the *income profile* of a country with n persons as a vector, $x = (x_1, x_2, \ldots x_n)$, of nonnegative numbers such that x_i denotes the income of person i. Without loss of generality, it will be assumed that if x is an income profile, then $x_1 \leq x_2 \leq \ldots \leq x_n$. This simply entails renaming the citizens so that the poorest person is named person 1, the second poorest person is named person 2, and so on, with ties being broken arbitrarily. Since populations can vary, we will, for explicitness, use $n(x)$ to denote the number of elements in x. Now, let $t(x)$ be the largest integer r such that $r/n(x) \leq 1/5$.

Given a country with an income profile x, the *quintile income* of the country is denoted by $q(x)$, which is defined as follows:

$$q(x) = [x_1 + \ldots + x_{t(x)}]/t(x).$$

Suppose a country's income profile changes from x^t in period t to x^{t+1} in period $t + 1$. Then the *quintile growth rate* (call it g) of this country between years t and $t + 1$ is defined as:

$$g = 100[q(x^{t+1}) - q(x^t)]/q(x^t).$$

Balancing Equality and Growth

This criterion for assessing the *economic* performance of an economy stems from a combination of normative and pragmatic considerations. Suppose one looks at the gross inequalities of income that prevail in the world, as suggested by the few striking examples cited at the start of the preceding section. A question that the lay person often asks, even though it may not arise in discussions among professional economists, is whether there is a case for limiting the incomes of the richest people. It seems to me that the answer should depend crucially on what such a policy would do to the poorest people. It is indeed a shame that Bill Gates earns so much more than the average person in Burundi and, for that matter, in the United States. But if trying to curb Bill Gates's income would cause poor people to be worse off, there would be no case for such a curb. Not only in distributional questions such as this but in deciding on any economic policy, it seems morally appealing to check what the policy change will do to the poorest people.[5] This is the normative consideration.

One may legitimately ask whether it is reasonable to hold up the progress of the better-off segment of a society's population for the sake of the bottom quintile, which may contain a disproportionate amount of dysfunctional individuals. There are several possible responses. First, thanks to a variety of market failures, a society's bottom quintile is likely to contain not just dysfunctional individuals but also many talented people whose talents are not realized or nurtured because of limited access to education and credit. Second, even for the dysfunctional people, there is a moral case for directly supporting them by taxing the rich. Of course, if the tax becomes too large and therefore inefficient, the society in question will do badly in the long run, and so, by the criterion of the long-run interest of the bottom quintile itself, such a policy will turn out to be undesirable. This criterion is thus attractive because it sets limits to how much the government should try to redistribute wealth and income to the poor through a self-referential calculation that looks at the long-run interests of the poor.

Although Rawls (1971), in his abstract models, could focus attention on *the* worst-off person, in reality we seldom know who the worst off is. Indeed, thanks to earnings from the informal sector, income data for the poorest persons are very difficult to collect. However, most nations do provide information on the income or expenditure share that goes to the poorest 20 percent of the population. So the suggestion that we concentrate on the poorest 20 percent is the pragmatic part of the recommendation.

An advantage of designing policy by focusing attention on the poorest 20 percent is that one cannot totally ignore the effect on people outside this group. If others fare too badly, they will become part of the poorest 20 percent and so will automatically come into focus. For this same reason, raising the quintile growth rate can never mean totally ignoring the overall growth rate of the country. For certain periods of time, a positive quintile growth rate can occur together with a negative per capita income growth rate. But if that happens for too long, there will be perfect equality of income in the country, and at that point the per capita growth rate will coincide with the quintile growth rate. For this reason, the criterion suggested here is distinct from that of mere poverty reduction. The objective of reducing poverty satisfies the property of satiation. That is, it is a self-liquidating objective: once poverty is removed, there is nothing more to strive for. The aim of improving the lot of the poorest 20 percent can never be satiated. It gives us a moving target.

The relation between this criterion and inequality reduction is more complicated. If a society is locked in a zero-sum game, to improve the condition of the bottom quintile of society is also to reduce inequality (for reasonable definitions of inequality), since in a zero-sum society one has to take from Peter to give to Paul. As discussed above, however, allowing some people to become richer may be essential to enable the bottom quintile of society to do better. In such situations my criterion will tend to exacerbate inequality. One may, of course, bring in a special consciousness of inequality by requiring that inequality reduction be a lexicographically secondary objective. That is, if there are two policies that leave the quintile income the same but one of them lowers inequality, we should choose the latter. In general, the principle worth upholding is that equality is a desirable objective as long as it does not occur at the expense of the poorest people. If some aggregate welfare has to be sacrificed for greater equality, that is worthwhile, but if poverty has to be increased in order to have greater equality, the greater equality is not worth it.

Measuring welfare in terms of the welfare of the bottom quintile of society also has the advantage of satisfying the criterion of anonymity and the weak Pareto principle. In other words, if two societies were such that one could be made to look just like the other through a permutation of the individuals, then under my criterion the two societies would be judged equally good. If everybody's income rises in a society, this will be considered a better society according to this criterion of evaluation.

There are, however, some desirable axioms that the quintile measure does not satisfy. One is what I will call the *weak transfer axiom*. This says that when a fixed sum of money is transferred from a rich person to a poorer person who also happens to be in the bottom quintile of society, such that the income ranking of people remains unchanged, the new income profile thus created should be considered socially superior to the old one. It is easy to see that when money is transferred from a person above the bottom 20 percent to someone in the bottom quintile, the quintile income will rise. When the transfer takes place from a person in the bottom quintile to someone poorer, the quintile income remains unchanged. Hence, the quintile income as a measure of welfare violates the weak transfer axiom.

This weakness may be rectified by using an index that I shall call the *rank-weighted quintile income*. This is essentially an ordinal index that penalizes a country if, within the poorest 20 percent, income is distributed in favor of the relatively rich. Let x be an income profile. Then the rank-weighted quintile income (RQI) is denoted by $\hat{q}(x)$ and is defined as follows:

$$\hat{q}(x) = \sum_{i=1}^{t(x)} [t(x) + 1 - i] \, x_i \, / \sum_{i=1}^{t(x)} [t(x) + 1 - i]$$

where $\hat{q}(x)$ is the weighted average of the incomes of the poorest 20 percent and the weight for the poorest ith person's income is given by $t(x) + 1 - i$. Hence, the poorest person gets the highest weight, $t(x)$, and the richest person in the bottom quintile is assigned the lowest weight, 1.

By rearranging terms, the above equation can be rewritten as:

$$\hat{q}(x) = 2q(x) - \frac{2 \sum ix_i}{t(x)[1 + t(x)]} .$$

One can proceed in this vein and create variants that are more complex. These more nuanced measures may be pursued in the future to yield more sophisticated measurements of welfare based on the general idea that the welfare of a society ought to be equated with the welfare of the poorest people. To spend more time on these variants here would distract us from our present objective. I will therefore focus on quintile income and quintile growth.

A Practical Illustration: Country Rankings

Some changes in welfare criteria may be important notionally but make very little actual difference when put into practice. This possibility prompts me to ask, if international organizations displaying comparative income and growth information, as in the World Bank's *World Development Reports,* instead gave data on quintile income and quintile growth, would this result in important changes in rankings? If not, the whole exercise outlined here would be academic and of little consequence from the practitioner's point of view. It is, however, easy to see that the changes in rankings could be quite sharp.

Table 1 shows the relative performance of a group of nations using the criteria of income and quintile income. The 40 countries selected include the world's 10 richest and 10 poorest nations. A handicap in doing the calculation was that for most nations, the share of income going to the bottom 20 percent is not available on an annual basis. I therefore use the latest available data on income shares.

Subject to this caveat, it is interesting to see how large a difference the shift from per capita income to quintile income makes. Switzerland, which was the richest nation in per capita income, drops below Norway and Denmark. The United States, which was the 4th richest country, drops to 10th place. Among poor nations, Sierra Leone's per capita income of US$160 dollars is already low, but its quintile income is a shocking US$9. The South Asian countries are very poor, but they do relatively better viewed through the lens of quintile income.

Table 1. Per Capita Income and Quintile Income,
40 Countries, 1997

Country	Percentage share of income of poorest 20 percent (various years)[a]		GNP per capita, 1997 (U.S. dollars)	Per capita income of poorest 20 percent or quintile income 1997 (U.S. dollars)
Ethiopia	7.1	(1995)	110	39
Sierra Leone	1.1	(1989)	160	9
Niger	2.6	(1995)	200	26
Rwanda	9.7	(1983–85)	210	102
Tanzania	6.8	(1993)	210	71
Nepal	7.6	(1995–96)	220	84
Guinea-Bissau	2.1	(1991)	230	24
Burkina Faso	5.5	(1994)	250	69
Madagascar	5.1	(1993)	250	69
Mali	4.6	(1994)	260	60
Vietnam	7.8	(1993)	310	121
Bangladesh	9.4	(1992)	360	169
India	9.2	(1994)	370	170
Pakistan	9.4	(1996)	500	235
China	5.5	(1995)	860	237
Ukraine	4.3	(1995)	1,040	224
Indonesia	8.0	(1996)	1,110	444
Egypt, Arab Rep.	8.7	(1991)	1,200	522
Romania	8.9	(1994)	1,410	627
Russian Federation	4.2	(1996)	2,680	563
Thailand	5.6	(1992)	2,740	767
South Africa	2.9	(1993–94)	3,210	465
Venezuela	4.3	(1995)	3,480	748
Poland	9.3	(1992)	3,590	1,669
Mexico	3.6	(1995)	3,700	666
Hungary	9.7	(1993)	4,510	2,187
Malaysia	4.6	(1989)	4,530	1,042
Brazil	2.5	(1995)	4,790	599
Chile	3.5	(1994)	4,820	844
Israel	6.9	(1992)	16,180	5,582
Netherlands	8.0	(1991)	25,830	10,332
Sweden	9.6	(1992)	26,210	12,581
France	7.2	(1989)	26,300	9,468
Belgium	9.5	(1992)	26,730	12,697
Austria	10.4	(1987)	27,920	14,518
Germany	9.0	(1989)	28,280	12,726
United States	4.8	(1994)	29,080	6,979
Denmark	9.6	(1992)	34,890	16,747
Norway	10.0	(1991)	36,100	18,050
Switzerland	7.4	(1982)	43,060	15,932

a. Figures in parentheses are the years for which the share data were obtained.
Source: World Bank (1998).

Recapturing Past Insights

It is one thing to present data and information on the bottom quintile of societies (as urged in this section) and another actually to design policy and set development goals. When we move to designing policy, there are two issues that I want to address: the tradeoff between economic well-being and other indicators of welfare, and conflicts between global goals and the goals of nations. The latter takes us into new analytical territory concerning strategic issues in policymaking and conditional morality. I will first briefly take up the matter of tradeoffs between different goals.

Given the recent effort to make economists, international bureaucrats, and policymakers aware that "there are things in life that matter, apart from income and wealth," one might be led to think that the focus on income had always been the principal focus of nations. But, as mentioned above, that is not so. Classical writers had considered the significance of a good quality of life, and their definitions typically went beyond material plentitude. Adam Smith, in a letter to Lord Carlisle written on November 8, 1779, wrote about how Ireland could make greater progress: "It wants order, police and a regular administration of justice both to protect and to restrain the inferior ranks of people, articles more essential to the progress of industry than both coal and wood put together" (Smith 1987: 243). In discussing the alienation of labor, Karl Marx (1844) stressed how a life in which only one's material wants are met is animalistic—freedom to choose being an essential constituent of good human life. These traditions, via modern formalizations, have influenced the construction of the Human Development Index.

The Relevance of Indexes for Policymakers

Before proceeding further, one question worth asking is this: even though the need to broaden our goals of development, as suggested in the *Human Development Reports,* has great normative appeal, is there a case for constructing a single index from a composite of varied indexes? While it is true that such an index can have (and indeed has had) the desirable effect of mobilizing popular opinion, its conceptual underpinnings are questionable. Ray (1998) has rightly questioned the method of aggregating diverse indicators of the quality of life, as is done in the *Human Development Reports.*

Another problem with the use of such aggregate measures has not always been noted. Let us suppose that we take all the variables that are worthwhile and construct a strictly concave welfare function in which these variables enter as arguments. For simplicity, we often use a linear aggregator, such as the Human Development Index, but clearly, as we have too much of one variable, we would expect the weight on that variable to decrease. Hence, the strict concavity is natural. What I am arguing is that if we use such an aggregate notion of welfare and do cost-benefit analysis to determine which projects are desirable, we are likely to run into important flaws in our decisionmaking.

Note that in standard treatments of cost-benefit analysis or project evaluation, the content of the project is considered unimportant. Whether it be a school or a dam, the same method of analysis is supposed to apply. This would be fine if all projects were fully specified, alternative courses of action open to a nation. But in reality, projects do not come in that form. Separate projects come up one at a time, and each is typically evaluated separately. And therein lies the problem of evaluating all projects against one aggregate measure of welfare.

Suppose that welfare depends on only two variables, income and literacy, and that the welfare function is strictly convex. Hence, the indifference curves (or, more precisely, the superior sets) in the income-literacy space are strictly concave. Suppose there are two projects: a school and a dam. The former generates two units of literacy and causes a drop of one unit of income, whereas the latter causes a rise of two units of income and a drop of one unit of literacy. It is entirely possible that if each project is evaluated individually (as is usually done in reality) by the yardstick of this all-embracing welfare function, each will be rejected, although the combination of the two projects is clearly desirable.

What this suggests is that either projects have to be bunched together and evaluated all at once, or we must evaluate different projects against different yardsticks. Since it is virtually impossible to conceive of all projects at once, we are forced to rely on the latter course. In other words, we must evaluate a school for what it does for schooling and literacy. If it contributes greatly to literacy without "too much" damage to other things, it must be considered desirable. Similarly, a dam may have to be evaluated in terms of what it does mainly for income. This is not a well-defined rule for project analysis (since the worth of a project depends on what other projects are *likely* to come up in the future, and there may be no hard information on that at the moment), but it is close to what policy planners, through their intuition, tend to do. I argue that the policy planners may in this case be right.

To reject the use of an aggregated index is, however, no reason to reject the importance of the components of an index. One way of capturing this importance is to look at a *vector* of a nation's achievements, leaving the exact tradeoffs one considers reasonable to be determined at the time of specific decisions and perhaps varied depending on the context. This section has argued that an important component of this vector should be quintile income. International organizations such at the World Bank and the UNDP should make data on quintile income widely available.

In addition, one can take the spirit of this proposal further and focus on the performance of the bottom 20 percent in various dimensions of well-being, such as life expectancy and sundry health indicators. Concerning literacy, one has to be more innovative because whenever a country has a literacy rate of less than 80 percent, the least literate quintile will be completely illiterate, and there will be little to distinguish among most developing nations on this score.

In a recent paper, James Foster and I argue that there are two kinds of illiterate persons: an "isolated illiterate," who lives in a household consisting of all illiterates, and a "proximate illiterate," who lives in a household that has at least one literate person (Basu and Foster 1998). We argue that a proximate illiterate's access to a literate person can relieve the darkness of illiteracy nonnegligibly.[6] Thus, a nation in which the literacy rate is 50 percent, with half the members of each household being literate, is much better off than one in which 50 percent of the people are literate and 50 percent are isolated illiterates (that is, all those who are illiterate live in households with no literate members). An implication is that if we were to start bottom up, as the quintile approach would require us to do, in devising literacy programs, we would first start with the isolated illiterates.

One reason why individual nations do not give adequate attention to quintile incomes, the environment, education, and minimal labor standards is that in the rough and tumble of international competition, they find little room for such soft targets. Just as, according to one theory, firms that do not maximize profit risk getting wiped out by the process of evolution, nations fear that to keep afloat in the global economy, they must try to achieve higher growth. Thus, a part of the problem is not so much to persuade leaders that quintile income matters, the environment matters, and so on (since not many national leaders will disagree *in principle*) but, rather, to create global institutions that make it possible for countries to pursue these goals. This requires us to understand why, even when each country wants to pursue a certain goal, in the strategic environment of the global economy countries may fail to do so. That is the subject matter of the next section.

Conditional Morality

Economists usually give advice on and write about the goals of development without specifying who the recipient of the advice is. This may be satisfactory for some very broad kinds of advice, but not for all. It seems eminently reasonable to give different advice to different agents, even when these pieces of advice are mutually inconsistent.

Consider the following example. Suppose you are a "good adviser" in the sense that you give advice in the best interests of the particular advisee, without allowing it to be distorted by your self-interest. If you are a doctor and a patient comes to you complaining of an ailment, "good advice" consists of recommending a medicine that, to the best of your knowledge, will cure the ailment, disregarding, for instance, the fact that the patient happens to be your tenant who is refusing to quit your apartment![7]

Now suppose that there are n nations in the world and that each of them seeks your advice individually. It is not unreasonable for you to advise each nation to aim for the highest possible growth rate of per capita income. If you know that each nation's aim is to achieve overall economic prosperity or to be the most powerful country in the world, then such advice is quite reasonable. Now assume that a truly international organization, one that represents global interests or the interests of all nations—in brief, an international organization of a kind that does not exist in today's world—seeks your advice on what each of the nations should do. It is entirely reasonable for you to advise it that the aim should be for countries not to grow too fast, since that may cause a deterioration in the global environment and create political and social tensions, and since you know that if every country tries to be the most powerful nation in the world, that can only make the world a worse place.[8] In other words, it may be reasonable for you to advise each nation to do what you would not advise all nations to do.

To see this even more transparently, consider two nations playing at prisoners' dilemma. Let the player choosing between rows be country 1 and the player choosing between columns be country 2.

Game 1

	C	D
C	5, 5	0, 6
D	6, 0	2, 2

Assume that the players know that they have to choose between C and D but do not know the payoffs. Country 1 contacts an expert (by definition, someone who does know the payoffs) for advice on what it should do. Clearly (since a good adviser gives the advice that is in the advisee's best interests), the correct advice is for the country to play D. This is the advice that the expert would give if he were called upon by each nation individually. If his advice were followed, the global economy would reach the outcome (D, D) in which both would be worse off than if they had chosen C. Now suppose the World Bank, trying to devise an outcome that serves the interests of the global economy, asks the expert what both countries should do. It is quite reasonable to respond by saying that both nations should choose C. Hence, the outcome, if the advice were followed, would be (C, C).

At one level, the three pieces of advice given—to 1 and 2, "choose D," and to the global organization, "choose (C, C)"—are contradictory, but this is exactly what a good adviser should do. Moreover, strictly speaking, there is no contradiction, since the advice given is a function not only of the question asked but also of who asked the question.

One can add flesh to this story by thinking of different accounts of what C and D represent. In one story, D could represent "go nuclear" and C, "shun nuclear." In that case the game describes the realistic possibility that each country stands to gain by having nuclear weapons but that both are better off if neither has nuclear weapons. In another story, D could be the strategy of rapid growth and C the strategy of moderate growth. Suppose that fast growth causes the environment to deteriorate but that a part of this environmental cost is borne by the other nation. It is now very possible to think of a case in which no matter what the other country does, it is better for each country to choose D, but the outcome if both choose D is worse than if both choose C, since the total environmental degradation causes an overall deterioration in living conditions.

In both these stories, knowing that you are advising both countries, you may be tempted to be moral and advise each nation to choose C and so create a better world. If, however, you want to carry out your job as adviser honestly and each nation has asked you, "Keeping only my interest in mind, tell me whether I should do C or D?" the correct answer is "D." Of course, in reality, you may decide to go beyond what you are asked and tell both nations that there is much to be gained by sitting down at a roundtable and trying to play cooperatively. But such options are not always available, and so there is an unavoidable moral conundrum here for the adviser.

In prisoners' dilemma–type games, the prospect of getting nations to cooperate seems hopeless at first sight. But the situation is not as bad as it seems because most nations, like most individuals, do adhere to some basic norms and morality. Now, conditional behavior is typically taken to be the domain of self-interested decisionmaking: "It is in my interest to confess if the other agent confesses." However, in reality, we often express even our morals in this form: "I believe in paying taxes because it is every citizen's duty to do so; however, I believe that this ceases to be a duty on my part, and indeed I would not pay taxes, if others did not." Similarly, nations may be willing to control environmental pollution as long as other nations also do so. This, of course, gives rise to a free-rider problem, but it is very different from the usual free-rider problem with self-interested agents because here even the cooperative outcome is not one that is in each agent's self-interest. I may be better off not paying taxes even if everybody does. A small nation may not benefit by controlling pollution even if other nations do.

Much of our morality, especially morality that translates into action, is conditional. "I will behave like a good utilitarian as long as others do, or I would be happy to play like a Rawlsian, but only as long as I know that others are not violating the Rawlsian norm for selfish gain." Such conditional morality stems from two urges, as basic to human nature as the propensity to maximize utility (and perhaps even more so): the urge to adhere to *some* morality, and the urge not to be a sucker. Unfortunately, the strategic aspects of moral behavior have not been discussed much in the literature—certainly not as much as the strategic problems of selfish behavior.[9]

Let us, for purposes of illustration, assume that the moral system that people adhere to is utilitarianism but that they do so conditionally. To keep the analysis tractable, let us assume that the conditionality works in the following way: agents take the view that they will behave according to utilitarian norms if and only if others behave like utilitarians;[10] if others do not do so, they will revert to selfish utility maximization. It is interesting to check what happens in Game 1 when it is played by two conditional utilitarians.[11] Place yourself in the shoes of agent 1. If the other person chooses D, clearly violating utilitarianism, you will behave selfishly and choose D. If the other person chooses C, behaving as a utilitarian, you will be a utilitarian and will choose C, since (C, C) generates a total utility of 10, while (C, D) gives a total of 6 utils.[12]

Let me now define a pair of strategies (or an *n*-tuple of strategies, in an *n*-player game) to be a *behavioral Nash equilibrium* if, given the other player's strategy, each player chooses not to alter his or her strategy. It follows that this game (with the conditional morality and consequent behavior that we have defined) has two behavioral Nash equilibria: (C, C) and (D, D), although (D, D) is the unique (conventional) Nash equilibrium. Given that human beings, across cultures and nations, do frequently subscribe to conditional morality, what the example illustrates is that an outcome that conventional game theory would not declare sustainable as an equilibrium may actually turn out to be an equilibrium.

I see illustrations of this abstract idea quite regularly in the town of Ithaca, New York. On Forest Home Drive there is a bridge so narrow that cars can travel on it in only one direction at any given time. The convention that has been established is that a convoy of three or four cars travels in one direction and the next car then stops and allows a convoy of three or four cars to come from the other side. There is no one to police the norm, but it seems to work well, with an occasional breakdown at the start of the academic year—no doubt because new students and faculty are unaware of the norm.

The fourth or fifth car that stops to allow cars to start up from the other side clearly makes a small sacrifice in self-interest in the larger interest of society. So what we have in Ithaca is a behavioral Nash equilibrium that leaves the whole society better off. What sustains this outcome is conditional morality; it seems unlikely that a driver would voluntarily stop to let oncoming cars pass if he believed that no one else in town adhered to this rule. In other words, what one is exercising is the norm that one will make small sacrifices for society as long as others are also willing to make such sacrifices.

I have not seen an equilibrium like this work in many other places, and I used to wonder whether it showed some innate differences in preferences or social norms between the citizens of Ithaca and those elsewhere. But I now believe that it is much more likely that people are at an innate level similar (at least more similar than their behavior, taken at face value, would lead us to believe) and that all human beings adhere to conditional morality. Once they do so, games like the bridge-crossing one and the prisoners' dilemma described above acquire multiple equilibria, and it becomes possible to think of different communities being caught in different equilibria even though the game being played and the preferences and values of the people may be identical.

International relations are riddled with conditional morality. Nations are often willing to make small sacrifices for the larger global good, but they do not want to do this alone. This is reason for hope because certain desirable outcomes that do not occur may nevertheless be potential equilibria, by this argument. Consider, for instance, the goal of limiting environmental pollution. Because of externalities, it is not always in a nation's self-interest to curtail pollution adequately (Repetto 1995). Similarly, any country trying to raise its labor standards risks losing capital to some other country with laxer standards. For these reasons, nations left to themselves are more likely to strive for faster growth to the neglect of these other objectives. This makes it difficult for countries to strive to improve the lot of their poorest people or to raise living standards generally. Yet, as the above argument clarifies, there is scope for coordinated behavior—in fact, even behavior that does not constitute an equilibrium in a conventional sense but that is a *behavioral* equilibrium and would lead to the global optimum.[13]

An Example: International Labor Standards

This section presents a small model on the pursuit of international labor standards to illustrate the problem of interdependence of moral goals. The subject is of some importance in its own right in this age of globalization and multinational action. I begin with a brief statement of the issues involved.

International labor standards (ILSs) are meant to be policy measures aimed at helping poor nations achieve certain minimal living standards. What is remarkable about these measures is that the most consistent opposition to them has come from the alleged beneficiaries. The fear of the poor nations is that labor standards are a Trojan horse which conceals the true agenda of industrial nations—protectionism. The fear is partly justified: the demand for labor standards, as it stands today, comes overwhelmingly from protectionist lobbies in industrial countries. Developing countries fear that once an international organization is empowered to enforce standards, it will use this power in the interest of the richer and more powerful nations. Indeed, we know that at the level of the nation, a government empowered to tax people often intervenes in practice in favor of the rich while using the rhetoric of helping the poor. Subtle systems of taxation and subsidy are often used to redistribute in favor of those who need the redistribution the least (see Stiglitz 1989: 46–48 for a discussion). This is a general problem, and there is no reason to expect that it will not make its appearance at the level of multinational organizations.

I have argued elsewhere that although labor standards as they are currently conceived ought to be rejected, there is nevertheless scope for a minimal and differently conceived set of international labor standards. But the construction of this argument requires us to recognize the strategic problems that arise *among* the developing nations.

As a general principle, hardly anyone can oppose the goal of international labor standards. Workers are among the poorest people in most developing economies, and a policy to raise their standard of living can be justified as a step to raise the quintile income of a nation. One important component of ILSs is the goal of putting an end to child labor. Given that it is the poorest households that send their children out to work, if the conditions of these households can be improved so that they do not have to do so, this can again be justified as a step toward raising the quintile income. The reason why poor countries have nevertheless resisted ILSs is that setting standards has been posed in most industrial nations as a tussle between developing and industrial countries, and the latter group has tried to use it as an instrument of protection (Bhagwati 1995; Srinivasan 1996).

I will illustrate my argument with the case of international child labor standards. A myth that has fueled support for protectionism among the uninitiated of the North is that the low labor standards in developing countries rob adults in industrial countries of their jobs. What is overlooked is that the products that are manufactured in the worst conditions in developing countries, often using child labor, are not those that involve any serious competition between industrial and developing countries.

A nice natural experiment actually occurred in the carpet industry. Hand-knotted carpets are a classic example of labor-intensive production. For historical reasons, Iran was the largest exporter of hand-knotted carpets to the United States. Then, in the late 1980s, the United States placed an embargo on imports from Iran. Did that boost production in industrial countries? The answer, not surprisingly, is no. China, India, Nepal, and other poor countries stepped in. India, which used to be a small exporter of carpets, suddenly became a big player. In 1996 the United States, which does not make any hand-knotted carpets, imported US$316 million worth of this product. The five biggest suppliers were India (45 percent), China (25 percent), Pakistan (16 percent), Turkey (6.5 percent), and Nepal (2.9 percent). The competition is clearly much more acute among developing countries than between developing and industrial countries.[14]

A natural consequence of this, often overlooked by the countries of the North, is that labor standards are of great concern *within* the developing countries. This concern is combined with a fear that any action on this front by any one country will cause a shift in production to some other developing country.[15] In today's world of mobile capital, each of these countries is aware of how easily capital can leave its territory and go elsewhere if its cost of labor goes up. If coordinated action is possible regarding certain kinds of labor standards (not necessarily the ones that industrial nations are campaigning for), this may be to the benefit of all nations. It is conceivable that if this happens, then—and this is my central argument here—even if there is scope for free-riding, each nation will be willing to forgo it as long as other nations do the same, in a manner reminiscent of traffic on the bridge on Forest Home Drive in Ithaca.

To illustrate this formally in a very simple model, assume that the developing world consists of T nations and N households. Each household has one adult and m children. Each adult produces 1 unit of labor, and each child produces γ (< 1) unit of labor.

Let each household's utility function be represented by:

$$(1) \qquad u = u(c, e), u_c \geq 0, u_e \leq 0$$

where c (≥ 0) denotes total consumption in the household and e is the amount of work done by each child. We assume that $e \in [0, 1]$ and, for algebraic simplicity, that all children work the same amount and that adults always work; that is, adults' labor supply is perfectly inelastic. It is easy to think of the utility function as having the property that if the wage drops too low—in particular, below ω—households will choose $e = 1$. This turns out to be a critical assumption in modeling child labor (Basu and Van 1998; Basu 1999).

Suppose that there are n firms operating in the developing world and that there is perfect capital mobility, so that firms will go wherever the most profit is to be made. Each firm's demand for labor is a function of the wage rate. Using w to denote the wage (for each unit of labor) and d for the demand for labor from each firm, we have:

(2) $$d = d(w), \, d'(w) < 0$$

First, consider a free-market equilibrium, that is, an equilibrium in which there is no law against the use of child labor. Let us suppose that the free-market equilibrium occurs at a wage below ω. Hence, the *free-market equilibrium* wage, w^*, is given by:

(3) $$nd(w^*) = N + \gamma mN.$$

Note that since w^* is less than ω, all children supply their labor. Hence, the total supply of labor is the total amount of adult labor (N) plus the total amount of child labor in the developing world (γmN). An equilibrium wage is one at which total labor supply equals total labor demand.

Next, consider the case in which ILSs are imposed, so that no child is allowed to supply labor. Let us call the equilibrium that prevails an *ILS equilibrium*. Clearly, in an ILS equilibrium, the wage, w^I, is given by:

(4) $$nd(w^I) = N.$$

Finally, consider the case in which only one country bans child labor, so that the labor standards are imposed only within the nation's boundary. Call this an *NLS equilibrium*. Evidently, in an NLS equilibrium, the wage, w^N, is given by:

(5) $$nd(w^N) = N + \gamma m(T - 1)N/T.$$

Note that (4) and (5) may be alternatively written as:

(4') $$nd(w^I) = [N + \gamma mN] - \gamma mN$$

and

(5') $$nd(w^N) = [N + \gamma mN] - \gamma mN/T.$$

It follows from (3), (4'), and (5') that

(6) $$nd(w^*) > nd(w^N) > nd(w^I).$$

Hence:

(7) $$w^* < w^N < w^I.$$

Let the utility levels of worker households in the three equilibria be denoted as follows. Let u^* and u^I be utilities in the free-market equilibrium and the ILS equilibrium. In an NLS equilibrium, let u^N and u^{-N} be the utilities of households in, respectively, nations that adopt the standard and nations that do not. There is much that one can do with this model, but for our present purpose it is enough to take note of two results that are easy to prove.

Result 1. Workers in a nation that imposes labor standards alone are worse off than workers in a world in which all countries impose labor standards; that is, $u^I > u^N$.

Result 2. If all developing countries impose labor standards, it is possible that all workers in these countries will be better off. But this is not necessarily so; it is possible that

(8) $$u^I > u^*$$

but it is also possible that

(9) $$u^I < u^*.$$

Now think of the developing world as consisting of only two nations ($T = 2$). Suppose that each nation has the policy option of banning child labor (strategy B) or not banning child labor (strategy N) and that each nation's own interest is to promote the welfare of its workers. Then, plainly, these two nations will be locked in the following game, in which nation 1 chooses between rows and nation 2 chooses between columns:

Game 2

	B	N
B	U^I, u^I	u^N, u^{-N}
N	U^{-N}, u^N	u^*, u^*

If (9) were true—which, by Result 2, we know is possible—ILSs would not be worthwhile from the point of view of the developing world, and so they should not be considered, assuming that the aim of ILSs is to help poor workers in poor countries and not to support small, special-interest groups. Since (9) and Result 1 imply $u^* > u^N$, (N, N) is a Nash equilibrium. It is easy to check that (B, B) is not a Nash equilibrium.

If, however, (8) happens to hold, it is in both nations' interest to reach the outcome (B, B). Given the parameters of this model, (B, B) may or may not be a Nash equilibrium, but (B, B) will be a behavioral Nash equilibrium whenever it is a Nash equilibrium, and it may be a behavioral Nash equilibrium even when it is not Nash. It is easy to check that a Nash equilibrium is always a behavioral Nash equilibrium (see note 11); hence, if (B, B) is a Nash equilibrium, it is also a behavioral Nash equilibrium. Next, consider the case in which (B, B) is not a Nash equilibrium but $u^{-N} + u^N < 2u^I$ and $u^N < u^*$. It is easy to check, using the above model, that these inequalities are feasible. Since (B, B) is not a Nash equilibrium, it must be that $u^{-N} > u^I$. Hence if a player plays B, it will be taken to be a utilitarian act by the other player, and so the other player will be willing to play B.

Once again we have reached the kind of impasse that we discussed in the preceding section: no nation will individually adopt labor standards, yet all nations as a whole may be interested in such a goal.

The contentious manner in which the debate on international labor standards has been conducted illustrates many of the issues discussed in this chapter. If only national income or even per capita income is at issue, there may not be any reason to be especially concerned about labor standards. As soon, however, as we begin to show special solicitude for the standard of living of the poorest people in a society, there arises reason to be concerned about labor standards. The debate on labor standards has been so contentious that one may be led to wonder whether all nations share this concern. The above discussion suggests that even if they did share these goals, this may not be manifested in their behavior because of conditional morality, leading to a refusal to partake in the program unless each country perceives that others are doing their share.

Conclusion

This discussion began by recounting the evolution of the goals of development and the management of the national economy. I argued that the recent and growing emphasis on goals that go beyond income and economic growth to broader objectives—a better quality of life, increased education, and a more equitable distribution of goods and services—actually represents a revival of objectives that were emphasized by classical writers but had fallen into disrepute during this century. This broadening of objectives, it was argued, is desirable, but it would be helpful to have some meaningful summary measures that capture some of these multiple objectives. I proposed that in evaluating an economy's performance we should pay much greater attention to the per capita income of the poorest 20 percent of the population and the growth rate of the per capita income of these poorest people. I did not suggest that we ignore all other indicators of the quality of life but, rather, that we use these measures in place of per capita income and the overall growth rate of an economy. The quintile income was shown to have many attractive properties, among them the fact that it probably correlates more strongly with other indicators of well-being, such as greater life expectancy and higher literacy, than does per capita income.

I raised the question of why many national goals, even when they are generally recognized as important, get ignored in practice. I argued that even in our normative pursuits, there are strategic considerations that come into play because most agents have an innate sense of conditional morality. To recognize this is important because it can enable the design of coordinated action on the part of nations for achieving developmental objectives that go beyond national income and income growth. The problem of conditional morality was illustrated with a simple example concerning international labor standards, where desirable actions are often thwarted for reasons of strategic disadvantage. It was argued that recognizing this problem can lead to a conception of minimal international labor standards that are different from those currently being demanded by many industrial nations and that, if pursued, could make a significant contribution to improving the quality of life in developing countries.

Notes

1. The statistics cited in this paragraph are from World Bank (1998).

2. For a lucid and comprehensive account of the changing objectives of development over the past 50 years, see Thorbecke (1999).

3. For certain kinds of social problems, such as crime, the crucial variable may be the *gap* between the per capita incomes of the richest and the poorest people in a society.

4. A similar exercise that broadens the idea of human well-being to take account more explicitly of political and civil liberties was undertaken by Dasgupta and Weale (1992).

5. Answering an interviewer's question about what is a "successful" economy, Amartya Sen (*Chicago Tribune*, March 28, 1999) pointed out, "This concerns how the worst-off members of society share in that society. Neglect of people at the bottom of the ladder would indicate a failed economy."

6. An empirical study by Basu, Narayan, and Ravallion (1999) based on individual income and literacy data from Bangladesh confirms the enormous externalities of having a literate person at home. Illiterate people in households with literate members seem to earn systematically more than isolated illiterate persons. Gibson (forthcoming) finds confirmation of this result in his study of nutrition in Papua New Guinea.

7. This somewhat chilling illustration of the problem of conflict between the interests of the adviser and advisee involves the *self*-interest of the adviser. But the same problem can arise even when the adviser distorts his advice because of some *moral* interest of his that happens to conflict with the interest of the advisee. These problems are addressed at length in Basu (1997) and O'Flaherty and Bhagwati (1997). In the present exercise I stay away totally from the problem of conflict of interest between the adviser and the advisee, whether it be self-centered or moral. My focus here is on the conflict of interest between various advisees and the dilemma that this creates for the adviser who happens to be advising several advisees.

8. I have often wondered about the merit of those popular books that tell people how to become leaders. For a single individual, the advice of such a book can indeed be valuable, but if everybody follows the advice in such a book, the world can only be a worse place.

9. An exception is Hardin (1988, ch. 2), although the particular problem that I am about to discuss is not a matter that he dwells on.

10. In a more sophisticated approach, we may want to add the proviso "as long as the personal loss from behaving like a utilitarian is not too large."

11. Singh (1995) has presented a related analysis in which one player plays entirely to maximize aggregate utility.

12. I have not defined precisely what "being a utilitarian" means, and indeed this is open to different interpretations. I shall here define a person choosing a certain action as being a utilitarian if that action cannot be justified in terms of his self-interest, no matter what the other person chooses, and it can be explained in utilitarian terms for some choice of action by the other person. By varying what we take to be evidence of utilitarian behavior, alternative definitions of equilibrium play are easy to create.

13. Frank (1999) makes a similar point at the level of individuals. Conspicuous consumption and materialist zeal in modern industrial societies reach the point at which the people who practice them are worse off in terms of their own preferences. Yet, short of some policy aimed at coordinated behavior, or taxes that create the right incentives, society cannot break out of this equilibrium once it is trapped in it.

14. All statistics quoted in this paragraph are from U.S. Department of Labor (1997).

15. This point has been made by several commentators, for instance, Grimsrud and Stokke (1997) and Harvey, Collingsworth, and Athreya (1998).

References

Atkinson, Anthony. 1995. "Capabilities, Exclusion and the Supply of Goods." In Kaushik Basu, Prasanta Pattanaik, and Kotaro Suzumura, eds., *Choice, Welfare and Development*. Oxford, U.K.: Oxford University Press.

Aturupane, Harsha, Paul Glewwe, and Paul Isenman. 1994. "Poverty, Human Development and Growth: An Emerging Consensus?" *American Economic Review* 84 (May): 244–49.

Basu, Kaushik. 1997. "On Misunderstanding Government: An Analysis of the Art of Policy Advice." *Economics and Politics* 9 (3, November): 231–50.

———. 1999. "Child Labor: Cause, Consequence and Cure, with Remarks on International Labor Standards." *Journal of Economic Literature* 37: 1083–1119.

Basu, Kaushik, and James Foster. 1998. "On Measuring Literacy." *Economic Journal* 108: 1733–49.

Basu, Kaushik, and Luis-Felipe Lopez-Calva. 1999. "Functionings and Capabilities." In Kenneth Arrow, Amartya Sen, and Kotaro Suzumura, eds., *Handbook of Social Choice and Welfare*. Amsterdam: North-Holland.

Basu, Kaushik, and Pham Hoang Van. 1998. "The Economics of Child Labor." *American Economic Review* 88 (3, June): 412–27.

Basu, Kaushik, Ambar Narayan, and Martin Ravallion. 1999. "Is Knowledge Shared within Households?" Policy Research Working Paper 2261. Office of the Chief Economist, Development Economics, and Poverty and Human Resources, Development Resource Group, World Bank, Washington, D.C.

Bhagwati, Jagdish. 1995. "Trade Liberalization and 'Fair Trade' Demands: Addressing the Environment and Labor Standards Issues." *World Economy* 18: 745–59.

Brandolini, Andrea, and G. D'Alessio. 1998. "Measuring Well-Being in the Functioning Space." Banca d'Italia. Processed.

Dasgupta, Partha, and Martin Weale. 1992. "On Measuring the Quality of Life." *World Development* 20 (1, January): 119–31.

Frank, Robert H. 1999. *Luxury Fever: Why Money Fails to Satisfy in an Era of Success.* New York: Free Press.

Gibson, J. Forthcoming. "Literacy and Intrahousehold Externalities." *World Development.*

Grimsrud, Bjørne, and Liv Jorunn Stokke. 1997. *Child Labour in Africa: Poverty or Institutional Failures?* Fafo Report 223. Oslo: Fafo Institute for Applied Social Science.

Hardin, Russell. 1988. *Morality within the Limits of Reason.* Chicago, Ill.: University of Chicago Press.

Harvey, Pharis J., Terry Collingsworth, and Bama Athreya. 1998. "Developing Effective Mechanisms for Implementing Labor Rights in the Global Economy." International Labor Rights Fund, Washington, D.C. Available at <http://www.laborights.org/ilrf.html>.

Herrero, Carmen. 1996. "Capabilities and Utilities." *Economic Design* 2: 69–88.

Kautilya. 1992. *The Arthashastra.* Edited by L. N. Rangarajan. New Delhi: Penguin.

Marx, Karl, 1844. *The Economic and Philosophic Manuscripts*, trans. London: Lawrence and Wishart.

O'Flaherty, Brendan, and Jagdish Bhagwati. 1997. "Will Free Trade with Political Science Put Normative Economists out of Work?" *Economics and Politics* 9 (3, November): 207–19.

Rawls, John. 1971. *A Theory of Justice.* Oxford, U.K.: Oxford University Press.

Ray, Debraj. 1998. *Development Economics.* Princeton, N.J.: Princeton University Press.

Repetto, Robert. 1995. "Trade and Sustainable Development." In M. G. Quibria, ed., *Critical Issues in Asian Development.* Hong Kong: Oxford University Press.

Romer, John. 1999. "What We Owe Our Children, They Their Children, and . . ." University of California at Davis. Processed.

Sen, Amartya. 1983. "Development: Which Way Now?" *Economic Journal* 93 (December): 745–62.

———. 1985. *Commodities and Capabilities.* Amsterdam: North-Holland.

———. 1999. *Development as Freedom.* New York: Knopf.

Singh, Nirvikar. 1995. "Unilateral Altruism May Be Beneficial: A Game-Theoretic Illustration." *Economics Letters* 47 (March): 275–81.

Smith, Adam. 1987. *The Correspondence of Adam Smith*. Edited by Ernest Mossner and Ian Ross. Indianapolis, Ind.: Liberty Fund.

Srinivasan, T. N. 1996. "International Trade and Labor Standards from an Economic Perspective." In P. van Dyck and G. Faber, eds., *Challenges to the New World Trade Organization*. Boston, Mass.: Kluwer Law International.

Stiglitz, Joseph. 1989. *The Economic Role of the State*. Oxford, U.K.: Basil Blackwell.

———. 1998a. "More Instruments and Broader Goals: Moving Towards the Post–Washington Consensus." WIDER Annual Lecture, Helsinki, January 7. Available at <http://www.worldbank.org/html/extdr/extme/js-010798/wider.htm>.

———. 1998b. "Towards a New Paradigm for Development: Strategies, Policies and Processes." Prebisch Lecture at the United Nations Conference on Trade and Development, Geneva, October 19. Available at <http://www.worldbank.org/html/extdr/extme/jssp101998.htm>.

Streeten, Paul. 1994. "Human Development: Means and Ends." *American Economic Review* 84 (May): 232–37.

Suzumura, Kotaro. 1999. "Consequences, Opportunities and Procedures." *Social Choice and Welfare* 16: 17–40.

Thorbecke, Erik. 1999. "The Evolution of the Development Doctrine and the Role of Foreign Aid, 1950–2000." Cornell University, Ithaca, N.Y. Processed.

UNDP (United Nations Development Programme). 1990. *Human Development Report 1990*. New York: Oxford University Press.

U.S. Department of Labor. 1997. *By the Sweat and Toil of Children*. Vol. 4: *Consumer Labels and Child Labor*. Washington, D.C.: Bureau of International Labor Affairs.

Wolfensohn, James. 1999. "A Proposal for a Comprehensive Development Framework." Washington, D.C.: World Bank. Processed.

World Bank. 1998. *World Development Indicators 1998*. Washington, D.C.

Comment

Paul P. Streeten

I AM IN GREAT SYMPATHY with the spirit of Kaushik Basu's chapter. In particular, I agree that poverty is not a technical or economic but a social and political problem. And I also agree with the emphasis on the poorest people in any given community. The measure proposed by Basu is appealing in its Rawlsian origins. To focus primarily on how the poorest people are faring is also reminiscent of the earlier basic-needs approach to poverty reduction, if basic needs are interpreted dynamically. I also welcome the introduction of moral considerations into the analysis of international relations.

Basu begins his essay by saying that "no one can proclaim being against [the term 'human development'] without sounding absurd and boorish." But I would suggest that one could be against the expression "human development" because it can be regarded as redundant: with whom else is development concerned but human beings? Surely not with stones or animals (Swift 1998). There are, however, certain questions that a measure which looks at the poorest 20 percent of the population raises.

First, the poorest 20 percent includes many lame ducks: the disabled, the physically and mentally ill, the handicapped, the old, the unemployable. The charismatic Indian planner Pitambar Pant advocated in the 1960s a minimum-needs strategy that wrote off completely the poorest 20 percent as beyond help. Without going as far as that, special measures are needed to help these people, and commonly recommended policies such as employment creation or access to credit may be of little use.

Second, much depends on how long the poor are in the quintile. Compare two societies with the same income distribution by quintile. They enjoy very different levels of welfare if, in one, the poor move rapidly up the income scale while some new entrants start poor, whereas in the other the poor and their children are condemned to languish permanently in poverty. Or compare two societies: in one, incomes are determined each year by a series of lotteries, voluntarily entered into by people who love gambling and who become rich and poor in quick succession, while in the other the same unequal income distribution that would result from such a lottery is permanent. Or consider a society in which there is no inheritance and everybody saves exactly the same amount each year between the ages of 21 and 65. At any given moment, the index of inequality would be quite high, yet, looking at the lifetime earnings of any given person, this would be a highly egalitarian society. Stephen Jenkins of Essex University reports evidence of considerable income mobility in Great Britain, where only 7 percent of the population remains in the bottom 20 percent of incomes for four consecutive years (*Economist* 1997: 60).

Third, inequality generally, even among comparatively well-off people and not just in the poorest quintile, can impede economic performance in several ways.

• Inequality is associated with political instability, violence, and crime, which are both undesirable in themselves and discourage investment and economic growth.

• It reduces the ability of social groups to arrive at mutually acceptable compromises.

• It discourages the evolution of efficiency-enhancing norms such as trust and the predisposition to commitment.

• It limits the effectiveness of incentive devices such as changes in prices or fines that may have unintended regressive or adverse effects. A small increase in diphtheria immunization fees, for example, might be imposed to increase revenues so that the immunization program can extend its coverage into new areas. But in the face of serious inequality, even that small rise in fees might prevent the poor from getting the shots. Usage might decline sufficiently to cause a drop in revenues, and outbreaks of diphtheria might actually increase.

There is another argument against concentrating only on the poverty of the bottom quintile. Recent research has shown that relative deprivation can cause absolute deprivation even among the well off. Richard Wilkinson (1996) of Sussex University found that inequality itself, irrespective of the absolute level of material standards, has adverse effects on the health of the relatively disadvantaged. Perceptions of inequality translate into psychological feelings of insecurity, lower self-esteem, envy, and unhappiness that, directly or through their effects on life-styles, cause illness (Cassidy 1999: 90).

Michael Marmot, a British epidemiologist, in a recent study suggested that relative deprivation can affect people's health, even among the rich. Between 1985 and 1988 Marmot and his colleagues studied the health records of 10,000 British civil servants age 35–55, all of whom were quite well paid. They found that the rate at which both women and men experienced life-threatening illnesses was inversely related to their employment grades. Workers who successfully climbed up in the hierarchy were much healthier than those stuck at the bottom (Marmot and others 1999).

There is some evidence that life expectancy is reduced by income inequality. Americans, who have greater income inequality, do not live as long as the Japanese, Germans, or Swiss, who enjoy less inequality. Of course, other factors besides income inequality play a role, such as more highway deaths and AIDS. But Christopher Jencks, a professor of sociology at the Kennedy School of Government at Harvard University who is conducting a study on the effects of inequality, has said, "The data seem to say that if you are of average income, living among people of average income, you are less likely to have a heart attack than if you live more stressfully in a community where there is you in the middle, and a bunch of rich people and a bunch of poor people. That seems hard to believe, but it is the direction in which the evidence seems to point" (Uchitelle 1998). "Income inequality and wage stagnation exacerbate each other; the inequality would not be such a problem if incomes were going up for everyone," says Frank Levy, a labor economist at the Massachusetts Institute of Technology who deals with this problem in an updated version of his 1988 book *Dollars and Dreams* (Levy 1998).

Basu writes, "Once poverty is removed, there is nothing more to strive for." This is not so. Poverty lines are dynamically defined and rise with rising average incomes. Poverty is at a different level in the United States than in Bangladesh, and it is different today from what it was 50 years ago or will be 20 years hence. Poverty, like basic needs, is a dynamic concept. Karl Marx wrote about the man who lived in a small cottage and was perfectly happy until a neighbor came along who constructed a palace.[1] Then the cottager began to feel deprived. Relative deprivation is deprivation that results from comparing our level of living with that of a reference group with higher incomes (Sen 1984: ch. 14).

It is, however, important to note that not all poverty resulting from rising average incomes is relative; *absolute* poverty can also result from higher average incomes. Sen analyzes this by saying that poverty can be an absolute notion in the space of capabilities, although relative in that of commodities or characteristics. A number of different factors can account for this: changes in the availability of goods and services, which may cease to be available or may rise in price more than money incomes; changes in conventions and laws; and deeper psychological causes, such as shame at not being able to afford what has become socially necessary.

If the benefits from a primary education depend on watching certain television programs at home, those who cannot afford a television set are absolutely worse off when the average family in the society acquires a set. The television set does not reflect a new need that arises as

incomes rise; rather, satisfaction of the same need (to be educated) requires a higher income. The poor in California are absolutely deprived
if they do not own a car, for public transport has deteriorated because
most people own cars. The wide availability of refrigerators and freez-
ers affects the structure of retailing and impoverishes those without
these durable consumer goods. Or, turning to low-income countries, as
some groups get richer, land is diverted from producing grain to producing fodder crops or meat and dairy products, so that grain becomes
more expensive, possibly increasing poverty among the poor. In these
cases the structure of supply is altered unfavorably for the poor. Or, if
an essential good is in inelastic supply, the growth of income of a particular group may raise its price so much that the poor are worse off.

In a rich society, poor people may be forced to buy overspecified
products to meet essential needs: food that is processed, packaged, ad-
vertised, and correspondingly more expensive; drip-dry shirts, even
though the poor may have preferred cheaper, no longer available shirts
that they ironed themselves. It is as if one had to buy a Dior dress to
keep warm. When buses offer less frequent service at higher fares, the
poor have the choice between waiting longer, and paying more for the
buses, or spending their scarce resources on a car. The disappearance of
low-cost items as incomes rise is well reflected in Marie Antoinette's
admonition to the poor, when bread was short, "Let them eat cake!"

Then there are changes in conventional standards and legal restrictions that accompany greater prosperity and that may be unfavorable
to the poor. If you are a rural dweller, you can pitch a tent that provides
shelter from the elements, but if you live in New York City, you must
not put up a tent on Madison Avenue. In the bush you can wear only a
loincloth, but if you work in London you have to wear a shirt, suit, tie,
and shoes and perhaps carry a neatly rolled umbrella. Higher minimum
standards of housing are imposed on you by the higher incomes of the
city dwellers, or by restrictions on what structures you can put up.

Adam Smith wrote in 1776 that customary standards also determine what is a necessity. To have no shoes in England was to be deprived of a necessity, although this was not so for women in Scotland
or for either men or women in France. But the shame that the shoeless
feel when appearing in public in a society in which wearing shoes is
part of social custom is not relative; they are not more ashamed than
others. It is an absolute deprivation. Bathrooms and telephones were
once luxuries, but most Americans now consider them necessities. Peter Townsend reports that in the 1980s in London it might be impossible to avoid shame if one could not give one's children treats.[2] These
feelings might in turn derive from a sense of lack of participation in
community life (social exclusion) or a lack of self-respect.

The view that shame in the face of others' possession of more goods
is an absolute form of poverty leads, however, to somewhat odd con-

clusions. As Robert H. Frank (1989: 666) has noted, "we may be prepared to believe, on the one hand, that the millionaire bond trader Sherman McCoy and his wife in Tom Wolfe's novel *Bonfire of the Vanities* really do *require* a chauffeur and limousine in order to transport themselves without shame to a dinner party just a few blocks from their apartment. On the other hand, few of us would feel comfortable calling them *impoverished* if they were suddenly deprived of their car and driver."

This view of shame also leads to odd remedies that may lie more in the realm of psychology than of economics. One cure is to educate people not to be ashamed when they do not have shoes (or linen shirts, another of Adam Smith's examples) but proudly to display their different life-style, in the manner of the members of the German *Wandervögel* before World War I, or the hippies more recently. Or it may become possible to reduce such forms of absolute poverty by taking the shoes or the linen shirts away from the better off or by imposing a heavy tax on shoes and linen shirts.

Since absolute poverty is partly a function of average living standards, it is clear that "absolute" does not mean fixed in time. The absolute level of poverty can rise as incomes increase. The capability of appearing in public without shame, of participating in the life of the community, or of maintaining self-respect will vary with the conventions, regulations, and material comforts of a society.

Basu's universal concern with the bottom quintile can also be questioned. In Sweden or Norway or the Netherlands, one should perhaps worry only about the bottom 5 percent, whereas in Bangladesh or India the bottom 40 or 50 percent should be a matter of concern.

Finally, Basu is entirely silent on income distribution among nations.

In the interesting section on "Conditional Morality," Basu inserts an element of morality into an analysis normally dominated by the assumption of undiluted self-interest. I welcome this unfashionable departure. The ranking of preferences with respect to, say, countries' decisions to ban child labor may be as follows:

1. My country does not ban, while others do (free-rider, defection of one).

2. My country bans together with others (cooperation; Basu's conditional morality).

3. No country bans (prisoners'-dilemma outcome).

4. My country bans while no other country does (on selfish motivation: sucker; on altruistic motivation: action according to the categorical imperative).

Behavior by each according to 1, or the fear of 4, leads, on conventional assumptions, to outcome 3. Although 2 is preferred to 3, we end up with the less preferred situation 3 unless rewards and penalties, autonomous cooperative motivations, or behavior according to Basu's conditional morality leads to 2. But countries do not behave like individuals. If hypocrisy is the compliment that vice pays to virtue, the evocation of national self-interest by politicians is the compliment virtue pays to vice. Citizens are often more moral, even in international relations, than their politicians. The situation is aggravated because the more countries there are, and the less trust exists, the more likely is a prisoners'-dilemma outcome.

In his discussion of labor standards, Basu does not mention that formal sector workers are not among the poorest in developing countries. In fact, they constitute a labor aristocracy to be counted among the top 20 percent of the population. They are certainly not to be found among the bottom quintile. Minimum wages, the right to collective bargaining, and so on are often achieved at the cost of higher unemployment and impoverishment of the workers outside the organized industrial sector. This does not, of course, apply to the banning of child labor, on which Basu has written illuminatingly.

Notes

1. Marx, "Wage Labour and Capital," in Marx and Engels (1958): 930–94.
2. Reported by Geoffrey Hawthorn in "Introduction," Sen (1987): xi.

References

Cassidy, John. 1999. "No Satisfaction. The Trials of the Shopping Nation." *New Yorker* (January 25): 90.

Economist. 1997. "Tony Blair's Big Idea" (December 8).

Frank, Robert H. 1989. Review of Amartya Sen, *The Standard of Living. Journal of Economic Literature* 27 (2, June): 666.

Levy, Frank. 1998. *The New Dollars and Dreams: American Incomes and Economic Change*. New York: Russell Sage.

Marmot, Michael G. 2000. "Multilevel Approaches to Understanding Social Determinants." In Lisa F. Berkman and Ichiro Kawachi, eds., *Social Epidemiology*. New York: Oxford University Press.

Marmot, Michael G., George Davey Smith, Stephen Stansfeld, Chandra Patel, Fiona North, J. Head, Ian White, Eric Brunner, and Amanda Feeny. 1999. "Health Inequalities among British Civil Servants: The Whitehall II Study." *Lancet* (June 8): 1387–95.

Marx, Karl, and Frederick Engels. 1958. *Selected Works*, vol. 1. Moscow: Foreign Languages Publishing House.

Sen, Amartya K. 1984. "Poor, Relatively Speaking." In Amartya Sen, ed., *Resources, Values and Development*, ch. 14. Oxford, U.K.: Basil Blackwell.

————. 1987. *The Standard of Living.* Edited by Geoffrey Hawthorn. Cambridge, U.K.: Cambridge University Press.

Smith, Adam. 1910. *An Inquiry into the Nature and Causes of the Wealth of Nations.* 2 vol. Everyman's Library. London: J. M. Dent. First published 1776.

Swift, Adam. 1998. Review of Paul Barker, ed., *Living as Equals. Times Literary Supplement* (April 17).

Uchitelle, Louis. 1998. "Even the Rich Can Suffer from Income Inequality." Economic View. *New York Times* (November 15), Money and Business section: 4.

Wilkinson, Richard G. 1996. *Unhealthy Societies: The Afflictions of Inequality.* London: Routledge.

Comment

Michael Lipton

BASU'S CHAPTER MAKES constructive proposals for achieving four shifts in focus:

- In growth, from the average income of a country to that of its poorest quintile
- In human development, from aggregated to disaggregated indices
- In advice, toward implicit joint maximization, using conditional morality
- In international issues, toward avoiding "bad" prisoners'-dilemma equilibria.

These shifts of focus go to the heart of why development economics matters. The emphasis is not mainly on the standard subject matter of economics—how to increase resources and incomes and how to improve the conversion efficiency of resources into incomes—but on how to improve the efficiency of societies' conversion of resources *and* incomes into well-being.[1]

The power of analytical economics rests in part on its combination of two strands: techno-economics, in the spirit of Cournot and Ricardo, and applied moral philosophy, in the spirit of Adam Smith. Recently, the balance has shifted dangerously away from the latter, leaving the former in danger of self-obsessed cleverness, isolated from humane or historical roots. Basu's chapter, without sacrificing rigor, helps show how to redress the balance. The following nitpicks and fine-tunings notwithstanding, I warmly agree with its approach and emphases.

Quintile Income

Country A will exceed Country B (or time t will exceed time $t - 10$ in the same country) in average income of the poorest quintile (APQ) to the extent that country A or time t has higher income: (a) at the line separating the poorest quintile from the rest (due to a higher mean or to less low-end inequality) or (b) for the average person below the initial line. The APQ in relation to mean income corresponds, as a measure of relative poverty, to the absolute poverty measure alpha-one (incidence × mean proportionate shortfall below the poverty line). The *rank-weighted* APQ, in relation to national mean income, would (with one plausible choice of weights) correspond to alpha-two; that is, it would give better marks to countries to the extent that they concentrated growth, within the lowest quintile, on the poorest. The APQ alone, even if rank-weighted, is a mixture of absolute and relative poverty. International differences in APQ level and growth—used, as in Basu's chapter, in comparison with average income growth—do measure a country's progress in reducing *relative* poverty, and they are consistent with standard measures of progress in reducing *absolute* poverty. But absolute poverty reduction is an important (and sometimes competing) policy goal. So, the APQ measure should play second fiddle to measures of the incidence and intensity of absolute poverty.

It is a good fiddle, but it needs tuning. I strongly agree with Basu that "the World Bank and the [United Nations Development Programme] should make data on quintile income widely available." But what data?

Basu's Table 1 and the discussion use current exchange rates. Purchasing power parity (PPP) data for average income are available, and should be used, for international comparisons. This might avoid the result that in 1997 the poorest quintile in Sierra Leone somehow lived on less than 2.5 U.S. cents per person per day and was 4.3 times poorer than the poorest quintile in Ethiopia. It is desirable, too, to develop PPP indicators for different income groups within countries; otherwise, in countries where food staples are relatively cheap or are becoming relatively cheaper, the APQ will appear to be lower (or improving more slowly) than is really the case, and it will appear to be larger (or rising faster) where food staples are relatively expensive or becoming more so.

The survey data in Table 1 sometimes report consumption instead of income (reducing *measured* inequality), or households instead of persons, usually with the same effect.[2] Correction factors (see, for example, Deininger and Squire 1996) should be used in comparing APQ levels or growth across countries.

Although more than 95 percent of the world population lives in countries with acceptable nationwide household surveys of income and expenditure, most countries, as Basu rightly observes, carry out such surveys infrequently. Before the early 1980s national income distributions changed only slowly, with no global pattern (Deininger and Squire 1996); hence, if the share of the poorest quintile was estimated by multiplying recent gross domestic product (GDP) or growth data by older survey data for that quintile's share, no great error or bias was likely. That is no longer the case because since the mid-1980s (where comparable surveys over time exist), income inequality has sharply risen in the transition economies, in East Asia, and to some extent in Latin America and Africa (Cornia 1999; Kanbur and Lustig 2000). Hence, in comparisons based on Table 1, income growth for the poorest quintile in these regions will be significantly overestimated—and increases in inequality will be overestimated—when, as often happens, old survey data for distribution are applied to recent (say, 1997) data for mean gross national product (GNP). Any allowance for this must be rough-and-ready, but it is necessary in APQ comparisons for recent decades.

Human Development: From the Human Development Index to "Another Day, Another Dollar"

Basu rightly stresses that human development is too important to be measured by one reductive indicator. It is bad enough that economists add up planes, trains, and violin concertos into GDP. However, unlike the Human Development Index (HDI), GDP is an aggregation for which there are (a) good reasons, (b) testable, micro-founded theories of the causes of change and of the tradeoffs, positive or negative, between such change and other desiderata, and (c) accessible measures of how components should be weighted (that is, by relative prices). Although extreme assumptions are required if such prices are to measure marginal cost of production and marginal utility to each consumer, ideal weights are at least conceivable.[3] Inclusions in, exclusions from, and weightings of elements within the HDI are all necessarily arbitrary. Moreover, any index of human development, gender equality, or human poverty loses information. We want to know where and when (for example) literacy indicators are higher, or health indicators lower, than would be predicted from mean income. The comparative behavior over space and time of an amalgam of indicators of health, schooling, and income—with the amalgam arbitrary, the social measures often unreliable, and, in recent versions, the income indicator arbitrarily truncated—tells us less than nothing.[4] Basu knocks another nail into the coffin: not only is the HDI obviously damned if it is not strictly convex in each component, but it is also damned if it is convex because then it is useless for benefit-cost analysis, for the subtle reason Basu adduces.[5]

Those who developed the HDI and its successors did well to build an alternative ladder that GDP-index-fixated politicians might climb to see the problems of health, literacy, gender, and poverty reduction. These indicators performed an important service, but they are deeply flawed. The ladder is rotten; throw it away.

Can one nevertheless find a single indicator of the socioeconomic good that is less incomplete than income or consumption and less arbitrary than the HDI? Amartya Sen has suggested that among countries with similar initial mortality, the rate of mortality decline is an overall guide to at least a large part of welfare improvement. Life is a precondition for welfare and utility, as well as for capabilities and functionings. Are amendments needed to life expectancy at birth as our overall indicator?

- Life in illness and pain can be a burden. For expectation of healthy life, we need an indicator such as "expected disability-adjusted life years" (EDALYs).
- Even healthy life may be converted into small welfare and few functionings by poverty. EDALYs should therefore be multiplied by average (not discounted) lifetime yearly consumption.[6] By using *expected* values for a newborn, calculated from current EDALYs and mean consumption by age groups, we should be able to derive a measure of expected disability-adjusted lifetime income per person, by a method similar to that used in estimating total fertility rate per woman.
- Perhaps better, one could estimate (EDALY × mean expected lifetime consumption per year) for the *median* adult-equivalent. This would avoid assigning greater weight to consumption and length of life for those fortunate enough to enjoy a lot of either and, in particular, would shift the focus of our measurement of well-being from such people toward the typical person, giving equal weight to each person who becomes poorer and each person who becomes richer instead of to each daily dollar.

This approach (clearly in need of refinement!) could combine consumption measures and EDALYs in a single measure. Unlike the HDI, it would exclude benefits from education or literacy. To justify including such benefits, one needs a defensible rule for evaluating them vis-à-vis consumption or EDALYs. If we use the market price of education or literacy, or its cost of production, we accept that willingness and ability to pay for these goods *should* determine their value relative to other commodities, even where information and market power, as well as the distribution of market demand, affect relative prices. To reject the market price, however, is to say that Nanny knows best or else that a just "political price" for (some products of) education can be established through open, democratic means.[7] A possible partial way out may be to use the relative market price of education or literacy as estimated in a more egalitarian society with similar mean income.

If a literacy component can be worked into a defensible replacement of the HDI, I am uncertain whether (as Basu proposes) isolated illiteracy should be considered worse than other forms, thus encouraging governments to devise literacy programs that start with the isolated illiterates. Basu's points are valid, but even if it were feasible, say, to deny an illiterate extra tuition because she had a literate spouse or parent, it might be wrong. First, over a lifetime, children gain much more from being made literate than do adults, yet adults are likelier to be isolated illiterates. Second, in much of rural Asia many adult women are illiterates, married to literate men; both facts reduce women's bargaining power within marriage. One would not want a welfare indicator to signal to a government that literacy for such women (or for the girls who might grow up to be such women) matters less because they are not "isolated." Third, since rapid "growth through trade" usually requires a literate work force (Wood 1994), the aging of the work force in many developing countries, combined with inadequate school education, suggests the need for increased spending on efficient adult education, irrespective of "isolation" or otherwise.[8]

Conditional Morality and Joint Maximization

Please forgive an apparent digression; the following discussion *is* relevant to the crucial development issues raised by Basu.

At Sussex University there is a T-junction of the main exit road with a feeder road that carries about one third of the heavy traffic leaving the university around 5 p.m. The "convention that has been established" is that after two or three cars crawl down the main exit road past the T-junction, the next car gives up its right-of-way to the next waiting car from the feeder road. Although this is apparently similar to the "behavioral Nash equilibrium" that Basu describes at Cornell, the differences underline the distinction between long-run-selfish reciprocal altruism and community morality.

As Basu describes the Cornell case, the two access roads to the one-way bridge are of equal rank. Unless a norm were established, chaos would delay all. At Sussex the cars on the main exit road have the right-of-way, and if they enforced it, the feeder-road cars would have to wait for a long time. As the two groups are mostly the same cars each day (from the same subject groups), drivers on the main exit road would lose nothing.

Basu's case can be explained as the result of a prisoners'-dilemma game with an open-ended number of repeats, similar in key respects to open-ended games that tend in practice to lead to tit-for-tat equilibrium (Axelrod 1984).[9] In prisoners'-dilemma one-shot games, noncooperative solutions dominate. This also applies (as a result of backward induction from the last play) to prisoners'-dilemma games with a known, finite number of repeats; stable cooperative outcomes, even if better for everyone ex post, have to be explained by either ignorance or some form of conditional morality. In infinitely repeated prisoners'-dilemma games, however, there is no barrier to cooperative outcomes, and one would expect them to "evolve." Open-ended prisoners'-dilemma games are in this respect like infinite games; even the selfish cannot identify the "last time" they will wish to leave by car and insist on the right-of-way, setting up the backward induction process that dooms cooperation. The Sussex case cannot be explained as an open-ended game, since the sacrificers (the cars on the main exit road) and the gainers (the feeder-road cars) are (pretty well) exclusive and stable sets. "Community morality" rather than reciprocal altruism is at work.

Another aspect of the Sussex case partly confirms this. When the traffic from the main exit road (joined by the feeder-road cars) reaches the main nonuniversity road, there is another T-junction. Almost nobody on the big public road ever stops for the university traffic. It is not rare for the drive from the university car park onto the main road to take 20 minutes at peak hours. But almost none of this is due to failures of interuniversity community morality; almost all is the result of the absence of a community morality embracing road users outside as well as inside the university.

As Basu says, "international relations"—and, one might add, the management of common property—"are riddled with conditional morality." The distinction between norms with and without community morality is similarly crucial. That is why, for example, it is easy to persuade the small growers of a crop such as tea, in a country where market share far exceeds the absolute value of the global price-elasticity of demand (E), to accept government taxes or restrictions on output volume if their neighbors face the same rules, since all producers in that country gain. It is much harder to persuade many small countries (with market shares well below E) to accept a global arrangement to this effect, especially if they also have comparative advantage in the crop, and it is almost impossible to persuade processing and retailing organizations in consumer countries not to "bribe" small producer countries to defect from such an agreement—even though, if all do defect (and especially if the large producer country "punishes" the small by unloading supplies), world prices and hence total producer income will fall.

The category analysis of international labor standards (ILS) equilibria is illuminating. Poor countries resist ILSs not only because they fear the abuse of the standards as "an instrument of protection" by rich ones but also because, as Basu points out earlier in his chapter, "nations are often willing to make small sacrifices for the larger global good, but they do not want to do this alone." Each developing country fears that if it accepts ILSs, it will lose out to others that do not accept them or that pretend to do so and then fail to enforce the rules.

This interacts with Basu's point that industrial countries, even if seeking to placate producer interests, have no reason to protect most products made with child labor because these products are competitive only among developing countries. This may be true only because "the international community," even among developing countries, has no enforceable consensus on child labor. The U.S. embargo on carpets from

Iran, as Basu points out, transferred production not to industrial countries but to other developing countries—but perhaps only because the latter used much child labor to cut production costs. Would industrial countries not have gained market share (at the cost of their own consumers) if developing countries had agreed on, and enforced, restrictions on the use of child labor?

It is in the common long-run interest of *each* developing country (as well as humane and right) that *all* developing countries, at the least, enforce regulations that prevent employment of children under age 10, require education for children under age 15, and protect child health, especially eyesight. But it is unhappily plausible that if all developing countries agreed to enforce such rules (a) some would fail or defect, raising their "carpet income" and short-run GDP at the cost of non-defectors, or (b) some production would be captured by capital-intensive competitors in industrial countries; the less (a) happened, the more (b) would happen. Assuming that individual poor-country losers can be compensated—a strong assumption—each developing country's long-run gain in child happiness and schooling, and perhaps in GDP, matters more. But how do we get there from here? Not by reciprocal altruism alone; community morality is needed too.

Notes

1. This question is probably more important, and almost certainly more tractable, than that of whether well-being means something like "utility" or something like "functionings" or "capabilities." Conversion efficiency also embraces issues—neglected by economists because they are wrongly believed to be simply resolved by revealed preference—of how *given* material intakes of food, housing, and so on can be transformed by individuals and families into more well-being.

2. It also greatly distorts *membership* of the lowest quintile (for example, by excluding many poor but very large households).

3. Actual market price weights derive from revealed preferences and production costs (a) conditioned by imperfect information and uncertainty, (b) transformed into weights in a way biased by distribution of income-based market demand, and (c) distorted, as are the weights, by market power. Estimating ideal shadow-price weights corrected for (b) and (c) is conceivable; less conceivable is further correction of such weights for (a), because of Arrow's impossibility theorem.

4. A country's HDI value (and thus all countries' ranks) can be no more reliable than its weakest HDI component.

5. However, because the weights of HDI components are inherently arbitrary, it would be baroque to worry much about convexity—that is, about an arbitrary inverse relationship of arbitrary weights to the size of the weighted components!

6. Consumption during each year of life, for the *individual* with expected-value EDALY, should be estimated in relation to "requirements" in that year (as in calculating *population* mean consumption per adult-equivalent). Convexity might be accommodated, but inevitably in an arbitrary way—for example, by using the logarithm of consumption.

7. This is not absurd. Working on the dual problem (in output space) and for health rather than education, Oregon state in the United States claims to be able to determine, by nested open meetings, which costs to support under budget constraints.

8. In South Asia at least 30 percent of the work force *in 2020* has already (in 2000) lived past standard secondary school age without acquiring functional literacy.

9. It is not clear whether the Axelrod condition that all agree somehow to punish deliberate defectors and also those who do not do so applies at Cornell.

References

Axelrod, Robert M. 1984. *The Evolution of Cooperation.* New York: Basic Books.

Cornia, Giovanni Andrea. 1999. "Liberalization, Globalization and Income Distribution." UNU/WIDER Working Paper Series 157. Helsinki: United Nations University, World Institute for Development Economics Research.

Deininger, Klaus, and Lyn Squire. 1996. "A New Data Set Measuring Income Inequality." *World Bank Economic Review* 10 (3): 565–91.

Kanbur, Ravi, and Nora Lustig. 2000. "Why Is Inequality Back on the Agenda?" In Boris Plesovic and Joseph E. Stiglitz, eds., *Annual World Bank Conference on Development Economics 1999.* Washington, D.C.: World Bank.

Wood, Adam. 1994. *North-South Trade, Employment and Inequality: Changing Fortunes in a Skill-Driven World.* IDS Development Studies Series. Oxford, U.K.: Clarendon Press.

Fallacies in Development Theory and Their Implications for Policy

Irma Adelman

NO AREA OF ECONOMICS HAS EXPERIENCED as many abrupt changes in its leading paradigm since World War II as has economic development. The twists and turns in development economics have had profound implications for development policy. Specifically, the dominant development model has determined policy prescriptions concerning the desirable role of government in the economy, the degree of government intervention, the form and direction of intervention, and the nature of government-market interactions.

Changes in both theory and policy prescriptions arise mainly from the following sources:

Learning. As our empirical and theoretical knowledge base is enlarged, new theoretical propositions, or new evidence of either resounding real-world successes or conspicuous real-world failures, become apparent. These feed into new theoretical or empirical paradigms.

Changes in ideology. As different power elites ascend and wane, their ideologies ascend and wane with them. New ideologies provide new prisms through which to view both old theories and old policy prescriptions. When the old ideas are inconsistent with new fundamental values, they are reformulated so as to achieve congruence.

Changes in the international environment. Significant technological innovations such as the Industrial Revolution and the communications revolution, and major global institutional transformations such as the post–Bretton Woods architecture of the global financial system, can have major implications for both theory and policy. They can raise new issues, open new opportunities, or close old avenues.

Changes in domestic institutions, constraints, and aspirations. The dynamic of development itself fundamentally restructures institutions, relaxes some constraints while tightening others, and brings new aspirations to the fore.

Finally, the *culture of the discipline,* which acts to structure the art of discourse and the manner of argumentation, determines how these four sources of change are incorporated into theories and models.

Here, I shall be concerned primarily with the impact that the culture of economics as a science has had on development economics. I shall argue that the discipline of economics has enshrined the "keep it simple, stupid" (KISS) principle as an overarching tenet, imbibed in graduate school, that can be violated only at the violator's peril. This principle demands simple explanations and universally valid propositions. It has led to three major fallacies, with significant deleterious consequences for both theory and policy: single-cause theories of underdevelopment; a single-figure-of-merit criterion for development; and the portrayal of development as a log-linear process. Each is taken up below. In this discussion, I am not arguing for complexity for its own sake but, rather, for theories rich enough to portray the changing reality that is relevant for correct policy prescriptions.

Three Fallacies

Fallacy 1: Underdevelopment has but a single cause.
The fundamental reason for the many sudden changes in the dominant paradigm in development economics has been the (inherently misguided) search for a single-cause, and hence a single-remedy, theory of development. The specific form of argumentation has been structured by the KISS principle and has remained fundamentally the same: underdevelopment is due to constraint X; loosen X, and development will be the inevitable result. The identification of the missing factor X has varied significantly over time, responding to empirical-historical learning from prior failures and successes, as well as to the other sources of paradigm change enumerated above. The universal remedy for underdevelopment, thought to be both necessary and sufficient for inducing self-sustained economic development, has varied over time, and so have recommendations for the optimal forms of state-market interactions and primary policy levers.

Alas, the search for a single open-sesame factor has been fundamentally misguided because it is based on a simplistic view of the mechanism of development and of the system in which it takes place. Unfortunately for the X-theory, as will be shown below, history demonstrates that the process of economic development is highly nonlinear and multifaceted. Nevertheless, like chemists' futile search for the philosopher's stone, the naive search for the X-factor has guided theoretical and empirical research in economic development during the past half-century. As a discipline, we seem unable to admit that the X-factor does not exist; that development policy requires a more complex understanding of social systems, combining economic, social, cultural, and political institutions and their changing interactions over time; that interventions may have to be multipronged; that what is good for one phase of the development process may be bad for the next phase; that there are certain irreversibilities in the development process that create path dependence; and, as a result of all this, that policy prescriptions for a given country at a given time must be anchored in an understanding of its situation at that point in time and of how it got there, not only recently but on a historical time scale.[1] Thus, although there are certain regularities and preferred time sequences in the development process, universal institutional and policy prescriptions are likely to be incorrect.

I now proceed to an identification of the sequence of Xs. The portrait of changes in leading development paradigms will be somewhat overdrawn. Like leading countries in the world economy, older paradigms, even after they are dethroned, continue to persist in a subsidiary position for some time before disappearing from the realm of discussion. This is nowhere clearer than in the successive editions of Gerald Meier's *Leading Issues in Development Economics,* the content of which varies drastically from edition to edition. But what is not overdrawn is the monocausal nature of explanations of underdevelopment and deficiencies in development performance.

I do not contend that any of the theories presented below is completely wrong, in the sense of having no applicability to any country, at any time. On the contrary, each is applicable to some countries, or to some groups of countries, at particular junctures in their evolution. What I do deny is that any of these theories offers the necessary and sufficient conditions for underdevelopment; that relaxing any particular X will automatically lead to development rather than to the emergence of a sequence of other binding constraints; and that there is a unique binding constraint X that applies to all countries at all points on their trajectory.

I am not saying, either, that all development economists have been guilty of monocausalism—just that the reigning paradigms have. Classical economists, comparative economic historians, dependency theorists, and modernization theorists offer important exceptions to the monocausal view of development. However, in the spirit of the KISS principle, the work of all these authors was largely ignored by the mainstream. Thus, the classical economists, from Adam Smith through Marx and Schumpeter, had a multidimensional view of the grand dynamics governing the economic fate of nations. Indeed, the general analytical framework I used in my first book to present their theories as special cases (Adelman 1958) was based on an expanded production function the arguments of which consisted of vectors describing not only the physical resources used in production but also the technical knowledge applied in various sectors and the different social and institutional structures within which the economy operates. Economic historians such as Kuznets (1966), North (1973, 1990), Abramovitz (1986), and Landes (1969, 1998) all had a multidimensional view of the sources of economic progress, which included institutions, culture, and technology. So did Polanyi (1944), Myrdal (1968), and the dependency theorists such as Baran (1957), Furtado (1963), and their followers. They all viewed economic retardation as being due not to resource constraints but rather to inimical domestic political structures, adverse international institutions, and path dependence. Finally, modernization theorists such as Lerner (1958), Hoselitz (1960), Black (1966), Inkeles and Smith (1966), and Adelman and Morris (1967) all adopted a multi-indicator theory of development that included transformations of production structures, as well as social, cultural, and political modernization.

I now turn to a brief sketch of the sequence of mainstream theoretical paradigms and their implications for the role of government.

X equals physical capital (1940–70).

The experiential roots of economic development can be found in the reconstruction of Western Europe after the end of World War II. There, the Marshall Plan, which financed the reconstruction of infrastructure and physical capital destroyed by the war, led to very quick economic recovery. By analogy, it was optimistically assumed that a similar injection of finance into now-independent former colonies would lead to their rapid economic development. The proposition that a deficiency in capital is the fundamental cause of underdevelopment was the basic principle underlying the Bretton Woods institutions—the International Bank for Reconstruction and Development (IBRD, now part of the World Bank) and the International Monetary Fund (IMF)—as well as bilateral foreign assistance programs. The charters of the international financial institutions reflected this philosophy, as did their activities. Both multilateral and bilateral aid programs concentrated on supplementing, on concessionary terms, the meager domestic savings available for domestic investment. The aid financed, almost exclusively, externality-generating large infrastructural projects in transport and energy and took the form of project, rather than program, assistance. Partial equilibrium–based project analysis was the main tool used to evaluate whether a proposed project should be financed. The macroeconomic implications of foreign assistance were almost totally ignored, as were the social and economic institutional requirements for project implementation.

The intellectual roots of economic development can be found in the writings of the pre-Marshallian classical economists, from Adam Smith on, and of their immediate post–World War II followers—the classical development theorists Rosenstein-Rodan (1943), Prebisch (1950), Nurkse (1953), Lewis (1954), Leibenstein (1957), and Hirschman (1958).

These theorists viewed economic development as a growth process that required the systematic reallocation of factors of production from a low-productivity, mostly primary-producing sector using traditional technology and with decreasing returns, to a high-productivity, modern, mostly industrial sector with increasing returns. But, unlike the later neoclassical development economists, who assumed that there were few technological and institutional impediments to the necessary reallocation of resources, classical development economists assumed that the resource reallocation process was hampered by rigidities that were both technological and institutional in nature. Investment lumpiness, inadequate infrastructure, imperfect foresight, and missing markets impeded smooth transfers of resources among sectors in response to individual profit maximization, and recognition of these constraints formed the bases for classical, structural approaches to economic development.

Much of the economic debate of the period centered on how to raise the national rate of saving above the threshold level of 15 percent (see, for example, Rostow 1960). All development economists saw foreign capital inflows as one answer to developing countries' low capacity to save. They therefore favored negative balances of trade, with the gap between imports and exports used to finance the difference between the levels of domestic savings and domestic investment. Most classical development economists favored a slightly inflationary framework to mobilize the necessary finance. Most regarded development-oriented governments as having a major role in the direct provision of finance, the subsidization of investment, and the direct undertaking of investment in infrastructural and "basic" industrial projects. These governmental activities were necessary to generate external economies and stimulate increased reallocation of private resources from agriculture to industry. The development economists of this era understood that both direct government investment and the provision of subsidized capital implied deficits in the government budget and would lead to some degree of inflation—hopefully not too high, and eventually diminishing as the production that had been financed in an inflationary manner came on line. Some development economists contended that a "big push" of simultaneously undertaken investments would maximize the external economies created by investment and would generate self-sustained, induced growth more quickly. Others contended that "balanced growth" would reduce the bottlenecks and import needs of the investment programs and thereby raise the marginal efficiency of investment.

Classical development theorists recognized that long-run economic growth is a highly nonlinear process characterized by the existence of multiple stable equilibria, one of which is a low-income-level trap (see, for example, Leibenstein 1957). They saw developing countries caught in that trap, which occurs at low levels of productive and infrastructural physical capital and is maintained by low levels of accumulation and by Malthusian population growth. Industrial production, the classical development theorists argued, is subject to technical indivisibilities that give rise to technological and pecuniary externalities. However, coordination failures lead to the realization of rates of return on investments based on (other things being equal) individual profit maximization that are systematically lower than those that could be realized through coordinated, simultaneous investment programs. Uncoordinated investments would not permit the realization of inherent increasing returns to scale and—in combination with low incomes, which restrict levels of savings and aggregate demand, and with Malthusian population growth—would ensnare an economy starting at low levels of income and capital in a low-income-level trap. Hence the need for government action to propel the economy from the uncoordinated, low-income, no-long-run-growth static equilibrium to the coordinated, high-income, dynamic-equilibrium, golden-growth path. In his seminal paper "Problems of Industrialization of Eastern and South-Eastern Europe," Rosenstein-Rodan (1943) posited the need for a government-financed series of interdependent investments to take advantage of external economies and economies of scale and propel developing countries from a low-level equilibrium trap, with no growth in per capita income, to a high-level equilibrium path characterized by self-sustained growth. Purely market forces, he argued, could not induce development.

Classical development economists were not unaware of the potential of international trade for stimulating economic growth (see, for example, Nurkse 1959). If trade were enough to induce the resource reallocation process, permit the capture of scale economies, and launch countries into a self-sustaining development process, there would, of course, be no need for direct government finance or direct government investment in infrastructure and industry. Free trade would induce domestic entrepreneurs to make the appropriate investments without special government intervention. The classical development economists, however, believed that international trade would not, in and of itself, suffice to induce development. Their first counterargument against the "trade will do the job" view was based on pessimism about elasticity and terms of trade (Prebisch 1950). Another reason for their skepticism about the development-inducing potential of free trade was that before World War II the growth process stimulated by the European Industrial Revolution in overseas territories was purely cyclical and was not accompanied by favorable structural change except when the overseas territories had sufficient political autonomy to impose import barriers.

In addition, the proponents of the "trade is not enough" view argued, even if one were to concede that trade could expand sufficiently to provide the necessary growth stimulus, trade by itself would not suffice to promote development because (a) nonprice barriers militate against the smooth transfer of resources among sectors in response to individual profit maximization; (b) in the absence of government action, the divergence between rates of return on uncoordinated and coordinated investments entangles the economy in the low-income trap; (c) the necessity of learning by doing implies the need for some initial infant-industry protection; and (d) nontradables, in the form of physical and social infrastructure, are required to enable competitive domestic industry to emerge. Both physical infrastructure, in the form of transport and energy, and social infrastructure, in the form of the requisite property rights, market institutions, social and political structures, and economic and political cultures, are lumpy and are hence subject to increasing returns to scale. Neither form of infrastructure will emerge spontaneously in response to uncoordinated market incentives.[2] In the view of the classical development economists, the conjunction of these factors meant that government action was needed to initiate the process of economic development. In the absence of appropriate government intervention, the Heckscher-Ohlin factor-price equalization theorem would not prevent the emergence of a low-income equilibrium trap.

X equals entrepreneurship (1958–65).

Around the mid-1960s development economists and development policymakers realized that there were serious absorptive capacity constraints on foreign assistance: beyond a certain point, the injection of additional capital became subject to sharply diminishing returns. As a result, foreign aid and government-sponsored investment projects were failing to induce sufficiently rapid growth of privately owned and privately managed industry. This failure was attributed to missing entrepreneurship. There were simply not enough potential industrialists willing and able to undertake industrial projects, especially when commercial, import-license-related, and "nonproductive" real estate investments provided such high rates of return in the inflationary and protected trade environments generated by government-sponsored accelerated development. A Schumpeterian school of economic development that studied the social origins of entrepreneurship emerged, and a sociocultural school of economic development (Hagen 1962; McClelland 1961) sought to analyze the sociocultural and psychological barriers to entrepreneurial attitudes and the differences in the prevalence of entrepreneurial attitudes among different cultures.

The classical development theorists provided several policy responses to the "deficiency in entrepreneurship" diagnosis. Most argued that in the absence of private entrepreneurship, governments would have to perform the entrepreneurial job while at the same time fostering the development of a cadre of private entrepreneurs willing and able to take over. Governments could encourage the development of this group by artificially increasing the rates of return on private investment through direct government subsidies, by engaging in joint government-private ventures, and by subsidizing management training programs. Other economists (primarily Hirschman) argued that what was needed was to economize on the need for private entrepreneurial talents by making the activities in which private investment would yield high returns more obvious, through unbalanced growth.

The realization that industrial entrepreneurship was scarce did not challenge the need for a continued substantial role of government in development. On the contrary, it reinforced it. By recognizing that a critical complementary factor in the government's efforts to promote development was missing, it emphasized that government policy would have to pay attention to structuring its own activities so as to increase the supply of entrepreneurship.

In the foreign aid area, the "missing entrepreneurship" school led to the establishment of the International Finance Corporation (IFC) within the World Bank Group to finance private entrepreneurial activity in developing countries. Aid programs began to funnel resources into training projects for the education of a cadre of potential entrepreneurs and policymakers in developing countries. The World Bank created its Economic Development Institute (EDI, now the World Bank Institute) to teach economics and management.

X equals incorrect relative prices (1970–80).

In the early 1970s several missions of the International Labour Organization analyzed the employment situation in developing countries (Emmerij 1986). The reports concluded that despite high rates of economic growth and industrialization, overt unemployment and underemployment were very high, of the order of 20 percent of the urban labor force. Moreover, unemployment had increased with the process of industrialization. The high rates of unemployment in turn induced an unequalizing process of economic growth: the owners of capital (the rich) and the owners of skills complementary to government-sponsored, capital-intensive development (the professional and bureaucratic middle class) were growing richer, but the owners of unskilled labor were not benefiting proportionately. Skilled and semiskilled workers who had been absorbed into modern industry had joined the middle class, while unemployed and underemployed workers in low-productivity sectors (agriculture and unskilled services) and in low-productivity enterprises (small-scale firms using traditional technology) were increasingly falling behind.

Several reasons were offered for this development failure. Some argued that the major culprit was technology that was inappropriate because it was too capital-intensive (Streeten 1986). Others contended that the main fault lay in the rapid rate of rural-urban migration (Harris and Todaro 1970), and still others saw the deficiency as arising from the relative bias toward inherently capital-intensive, large-scale formal industry and the corresponding neglect of more labor-intensive, small-scale, informal sector employment.

Essentially, all these explanations rested on the contention that the process of government-sponsored accelerated development had given rise to incorrect relative factor prices that did not reflect fundamental relative economic scarcities. Government subsidization of capital had led to capital being underpriced relative to its true scarcity and to labor being overpriced in relation both to capital and to the true abundance of labor. This had led to the adoption of inappropriate technology, induced not only by these incorrect relative factor prices but also by the direct transplantation of modern technology from industrial countries where capital-labor ratios were much lower than in developing countries. The migration explanation rested in part on the fact that unskilled wages in the urban-industrial sector were between twice and three times as high as rural per capita incomes. Even with 20 percent urban unemployment, the expected urban wage far exceeded actual rural per capita income, and therefore rural-urban migration would continue, swelling the ranks of the urban unemployed and underemployed. Rapid rural-urban migration was also the consequence of a process of industrialization that was forcibly transferring resources from agriculture to industry by lowering the agricultural terms of trade through foreign assistance–financed imports of grains, thereby keeping rural incomes low. The bias of development policy toward the urban and industrial sectors meant that large-scale industrial enterprises were subsidized, while the price of capital remained high for small-scale and informal sector activities. The unfavored sectors therefore had to pay low wages and could not expand their levels of employment enough to absorb the entire pool of the unemployed. Whatever the reasons for the relatively high capital-intensity of development, the remedy was to "get prices right" by reducing direct and indirect subsidies to industrialization. Raising interest rates on loans to large-scale industry and reducing tariff protection for capital-intensive, import-substituting industries were the policy remedies for overt urban unemployment.

Those who directly focused on the income distribution problem concluded that what was fundamentally wrong was not that relative factor prices were incorrect but that the labor-intensity of growth was too low (Adelman and Robinson 1978). They contended that the most effective way to remedy this major deficiency was to change relative prices indirectly, by choosing more labor-intensive sectors for government promotion and government-promoted exports. The result would be a growth pattern that would combine higher growth rates of per capita income with higher labor-output ratios and with the expansion of high-productivity unskilled and semiskilled employment. The end result would be a combination of accelerated growth and a nondeteriorating distribution of income. Streeten and Stewart (1976) argued that multipronged, simultaneous reforms of institutions, markets, and technology were required to rectify the unemployment and income distribution problems; single interventions might only make matters worse.

Although the classical development economists realized it only imperfectly at the time, the debate marked the beginning of the ascendancy of the neoclassical school of economic development. Rather than championing different forms of government intervention, the "getting prices right" school opened the door to the argument that government intervention should be curtailed, since it had obviously been counterproductive. The income distribution school continued to argue for a direct government role in the economy, but it called for a change in focus away from capital-intensive basic industries and toward labor-intensive consumer goods industries suitable for both domestic production and exports. The day was carried, however, by the "getting prices right" school.

X equals international trade (1980–).
Although the international trade explanation is a continuation of the "getting-prices-right" line of thought, its arguments against government intervention in the economic arena are sufficiently different to be a special paradigm. The proponents of this school argued that the government-promoted, protection- and subsidy-ridden industrialization process of past decades had led to inefficient growth by generating distortions in industry that kept industry inefficient and noncompetitive. The government-sponsored industrialization process was too costly and too far removed from the basic comparative advantage of the countries involved. Rather than urge governments to adopt different policies, the best remedy would be to look for a deus ex machina different from government to stimulate development, and this was found in international trade.

Neoclassical trade theorists (Krueger 1979, 1983; Bhagwati 1985) came to dominate the field of economic development. International trade, they emphasized, could provide a substitute for low domestic aggregate demand. The main thing governments needed to do to position an economy on an autonomous, sustained-growth path was to remove barriers to international trade in commodities.[3] According to this "trade is enough" school of thought, export-led rapid economic growth would be the inevitable result. Comparative advantage, combined with the Heckscher-Ohlin theorem, would then do the rest. Governments should also remove price distortions in domestic factor and commodity markets ("get prices right") to induce suitable movement of factors among sectors, encourage the adoption of appropriate technology, and increase capital accumulation. Thus, domestic and international liberalization programs would suffice to bring about sustained economic growth and structural change.

To the extent that deficient aggregate demand leads to a low-level equilibrium trap, international trade can indeed provide a substitute for deficient domestic demand. However, the moment one acknowledges that nontradable intermediate inputs, such as transport and power, are needed for efficient domestic production in modern manufacturing, international trade is seen to be inadequate. It cannot provide a perfect substitute for a government-promoted investment program in domestic infrastructure and interrelated industrial investments. A "big push" is still needed to lift the economy out of the low-level equilibrium trap.

Classical development economists argued that in an open economy, development would proceed faster and more efficiently. But for them and their followers, openness did not mean free trade. They favored mercantilist trade policies, and they believed that initial import substitution to protect infant industries, combined with selective export promotion, was needed to initiate development.

X equals hyperactive government (1980–96).

The "evil government" view represents the culmination of the neoclassical counterrevolution in economic development that was initiated by the "getting prices right" and "trade is enough" schools. Not coincidentally, it began life in the Reagan-Thatcher era of neoliberalism. According to this view, government is not the solution to underdevelopment; it is the problem (Krueger 1974). Government interventions are not needed, as trade liberalization can induce development, yield economies of scale, and make industries internationally more competitive. Greater domestic marketization of goods and services, including public goods, would make development more cost-effective and efficient. Governments are bloated; they are corrupt; they accept bribes for economic privileges generated by government interventions in the market; and they operate by distorting market incentives in mostly unproductive, foolish, and wasteful ways. Moreover, their discretionary interventions into markets, through regulation, tariffs, subsidies, and quotas, give rise to rent-seeking activities by private entrepreneurs that absorb large fractions of gross national product (GNP) and lead to significant economic inefficiencies. Reducing the role of government in the economy would therefore lead to more rapid and more efficient development. The best action a government can undertake to promote development is to minimize its own economic role.

The policy prescriptions call for liberalizing domestic and international markets for both factors and products and promoting the spread of markets and the rule of market incentives to improve the efficiency of the economy. Such actions by governments are taken as an indication of economic virtue, worthy of financial support by international agencies. A corollary is that starving the public sector of resources is a worthwhile undertaking, in and of itself.

The "evil government" period was one of a general slowdown in the world economy. It was marked by recessions in Japan, Europe, and the United States; a shift from growth-promoting to inflation-fighting policies in industrial countries; a slowing of the growth of world trade and an increase in trade restrictions in industrial countries; a rise in world interest rates and an effective devaluation of currencies against the dollar; the second oil shock; and a severe debt crisis in developing countries. A decade of drastic economic decline in developing countries ensued. During the 1980s average rates of economic growth either fell or were stagnant, balance of payments constraints became increasingly binding, and priorities shifted from economic development toward achieving external balance, mainly through restrictive macroeconomic policies. Most developing countries experienced rampant inflation, capital flight, low investment rates, large declines in living standards, increases in inequality, and substantial increases in urban and rural poverty. The average developing country transferred more than its entire growth of gross domestic product (GDP) abroad annually for debt service, but developing-country debt continued to increase, as two thirds of the countries failed to achieve a current balance surplus sufficient to service their debts.

The debt crisis was brought to a head by the inability of Mexico, Brazil, and Turkey to meet their debt-service obligations, whereupon commercial banks in industrial countries became unwilling to extend further loans to *any* developing countries. Developing countries became completely dependent on the Washington-based international institutions, the IMF and the World Bank, for economic survival, and these institutions used the opportunity to press their "evil government" philosophy on developing countries through loan conditionality. "Marketize, liberalize, and tighten your belt" policies—the "Washington consensus"—dominated development policy during this period. As a result, many of the economic and political institutions that form the core for capitalist development were created in a significant number of developing countries.

It is curious how completely neoclassical development theory came to dominate the policy agenda during this period, considering its numerous theoretical deficiencies:

• Neoclassical development economics ignored the fact that Marshallian neoclassical economics was never intended to be a growth theory, only a theory of static resource allocation. It must be supplemented by a theory of accumulation and growth to be a complete development theory. Markets may be efficient for static resource allocation but at the same time be inefficient vehicles for accumulation and growth; indeed, this is what classical development theorists would contend.

• Neoclassical development theory ignored the fact that the postulates of neoclassical economics, which are needed to ensure the efficiency of neoclassical market equilibria, are not applicable to developing countries. Developing countries are hardly characterized by smoothly mobile factors, complete and well-functioning markets, comprehensive information, and perfect foresight. The institutional bases for a neoclassical economy are missing in most developing countries and cannot be created overnight. But the absence of any of these characteristics implies that market equilibrium cannot be proved to be Pareto optimal and hence even statically efficient.

• Market equilibria depend on the initial distribution of wealth. If that distribution is not optimal, the Pareto optimality of a neoclassical economy will not maximize even static social welfare.

• The advocates of neoclassical development ignored the theory of the second best. Since it is impossible to remove all regulatory constraints on markets, it is quite possible that even when all neoclassical postulates hold, adding additional constraints on markets will improve, rather than reduce, market efficiency.

• Finally, all the objections to the "trade is enough" theory also apply to the "evil government" theory of development.

X equals human capital (1988–).

A different, more recent underdevelopment theory, associated with the Chicago school (Romer 1986; Lucas 1988), identifies low human capital endowments as the primary obstacle to the realization of the economies of scale inherent in the industrialization of developing countries. The productivities of raw labor and capital are assumed to be magnified by a factor, $A(k)^a$, that reflects the levels of human capital and knowledge, k. Various potential dynamic growth paths are open to countries. At one extreme, identified with low levels of human capital and knowledge, economic growth is characterized by low degrees of economies of scale, and the corresponding growth path is a low-factor-productivity, low-growth one that tends to a stationary state characterized by low per capita income levels. At the other extreme, identified with high levels of human capital and knowledge, economic growth is subject to increasing returns to scale, and the corresponding growth path is a high-factor-productivity, high-growth one that tends to a stationary state characterized by high levels of per capita income. According to this view, all that governments need to do to propel developing countries from a low-growth trajectory to a high-growth one is to invest in human capital and knowledge.

The "human capital is enough" development theory is open to objections that are analogous to those raised against the "trade is enough" development theory:

• Nonprice barriers militate against the smooth transfer of resources among sectors that is necessary in order to take advantage of potential scale economies.

• Missing markets, especially for capital, are likely to impede private individuals from undertaking the investments necessary to take advantage of potential scale economies.

• Appropriate trade policy is required to bring about the realization of the potential economies of scale inherent in industrialization. The necessity of learning by doing implies the need for some initial infant-industry protection, while the low aggregate demand induced by low income levels implies the need for export-led growth.

• Physical and institutional infrastructures are required to enable competitive domestic industry to emerge. Modernizing governments must provide both forms of infrastructure if the economies of scale posited by the Chicago production function are to materialize.

X equals ineffective government (1997–).

Several forces coalesced to lead to a reevaluation of the optimal role of government in economic development. First, economists came to realize that although most developing countries recorded poor growth performance during the 1980s, East Asian and some South Asian countries, in which governments continued to play an active role, had done remarkably well. Despite an unfavorable international environment, these countries were able to maintain and in some cases even improve on their previous development momentum. Rather than adopt deflationary government expenditure and macroeconomic policies and restrictive import and wage practices, the successful Asian countries exported their way out of the crisis. Their governments shifted from import-substitution to export-promotion regimes, devalued their currencies to promote expenditure switching among imports and domestic goods, undertook a set of market-friendly institutional and policy reforms, continued to invest in infrastructure and human capital, and engaged in the direct and indirect promotion of selected industries (World Bank 1993a; Stiglitz 1996).

Second, there was a backlash in the industrial countries against the neoliberal philosophy of the 1980s, which had led to slow growth and high unemployment, and toward a more activist government stance. Democrats replaced Republicans in the United States, Labor governments replaced conservative governments in most European countries, and the international influence of Japan, whose government had always played an active economic role, increased.

Third, the mixed success of developing countries' market reforms during the 1980s (Nogués and Gulati 1994) led international institutions to understand that it takes capable, committed governments to promote and manage successful reform (World Bank 1997). Without capable governments, even market-oriented reform efforts will flounder and be derailed or captured by special-interest groups of actual or potential losers from reform. A "revisionist" school of economic development, dubbed the "post–Washington consensus," appears to be in the making. This school advocates a dynamically changing mix of state-market interactions in which developmental governments play a significant role in investment and its finance, human capital formation, acquisition of technology, institution building, and the promotion of policy and institutional reforms. Development economics is returning full circle to the view of the classical development economists that the government has a critical role in economic development.

Fallacy 2: A single criterion suffices for evaluating development performance.

I will not dwell extensively on this fallacy, since it is well appreciated in the literature. The deficiencies of per capita GNP as a performance criterion have been extensively analyzed by, for example, Sen (1988). In brief, GNP only indicates national *potential* for improving the welfare of the majority of the population—not the extent to which the society delivers on this potential. To achieve a minimal appreciation of actual, rather than only potential, national development performance, what is required is a more multidimensional criterion such as the Human Development Index (UNDP various years) that takes account of dimensions of human welfare other than income, supplemented by a distribution-sensitive measure of aggregate income. I would prefer that a battery of disaggregated performance indicators, such as that originally proposed by Adelman and Morris (1967) or currently advocated by Wolfensohn (1998) and Stiglitz (1998), be used as indexes of the current state of national welfare and its likely future evolution. A more multidimensional statistical base for monitoring development would have enabled much earlier identification of the deficiencies of growth-oriented development policies during the 1950s and 1960s, as well as an earlier appreciation of the immense human costs of structural adjustment policies in Latin America during the 1980s. Improved development strategies and better responses to macroeconomic and financial crises could then have evolved earlier, and much human suffering could have been avoided.

Fallacy 3: Development is a log-linear process.

Following Solow (1957), a single production function is assumed to characterize all countries. This unique production function is presumed to be a function of supplies of inputs, capital, labor, and natural resources. Country deviations from this production function are taken to represent productivity differences, the source of which is left undefined. Accordingly, the rate of growth of total output becomes a function of the rate of change of the physical inputs, and the rate of growth of per capita output (identically equal to per capita income) becomes a function of the rate of change of the capital-labor ratio, the rate of change of the per capita endowment of natural resources (usually assumed to be zero), and the rate of change of the residual. Recently, cross-country empirical studies of the rate of growth of per capita GNP "explain" the rate of growth of the residual by assuming that it is a function of the X-factor of the day—the economy's openness (Krueger 1979; Bhagwati 1985; Balassa 1989); the degree of development of capitalist institutions (World Bank 1993a; De Melo, Denizer, and Gelb 1996); the availability of human capital (Lucas 1988 and his followers); the degree of democracy (Barro 1996 and his followers); the degree of corruption (Mauro 1995); or the degree of development of political institutions (Campos and Nugent 1999).

The unique production function approach leads to several erroneous implications. It suggests that (a) initial conditions do not matter; (b) levels do not matter; (c) there is no path dependence; and hence (d) universal policy prescriptions apply to all countries at all times, regardless of their current state of socioinstitutional and economic development, political structure, and policy objectives. Both the World Bank and the IMF fell prey to this postulate of universality and used a cookie-cutter approach in their policy prescriptions. They dismissed as special pleading developing-country governments' attempts to argue that particularly necessary conditions for the effectiveness of some policy prescriptions did not apply to their countries.

Unfortunately, both econometric analyses and historical case studies provide ample evidence that the log-linear, single-path, single-factor view of economic development is both erroneous and ahistorical. The following propositions (presented with supporting evidence for each) invalidate the view of development as a linear process.

Proposition 1: The development process is highly nonlinear.

1. In their original cross-country studies of development, Chenery (1960) and Chenery and Syrquin (1975) found the best fit to be nonlinear in logs. Chenery related intercountry differences in GNP to both the logs of the levels of per capita GNP and population and the logs of their squares.

2. As elaborated in the next section, interaction patterns among economic, social, and political institutions vary by level of socioeconomic development. The models of change thus differ in a systematic fashion as countries achieve higher levels of economic development.

3. More tellingly, not only do models of socioeconomic and political development alter as countries evolve, but even the same institutions and sectoral policies are transformed in predictable ways as development proceeds (Morris and Adelman 1988; Adelman and Morris 1989). The roles of government, agriculture, international trade, and politics alter as economies advance.

Initially, governments' primary roles consisted of social development, creation of political and economic institutions, and construction of infrastructure. The governments of the European latecomers in the 19th century first introduced the institutional changes required to strengthen responsiveness to market incentives during the early phases of the Industrial Revolution. They unified their countries and markets (Italy and Germany), eliminated legal barriers to trade and factor mobility (Russia's emancipation of the serfs), created credit institutions and promoted joint-stock companies (Germany), and facilitated transactions (Italy and Spain).

Once the institutional and physical frameworks for development were established, the primary function of government consisted of fostering industrialization while raising the productivity of agriculture. During both the 19th and the 20th centuries, an activist government that promoted the acquisition of dynamically changing comparative advantage was needed to attain the successive stages of industrialization. At this point the government used finance and subsidies to promote technologically sophisticated, interdependent, externality-inducing investments and also undertook such investments itself. It introduced the policy regimes needed to increase the profitability of private investment, through protection and subsidies, and it substituted for inadequate or missing markets, factors, finance, technology, and skills. Climbing the ladder of comparative advantage became the main thrust of government economic policy. This required changing international trade and commercial policies, as well as reorienting government finance, government investment, and government incentives. In each phase of industrialization, infant-industry protection had to be accorded to key sectors. Once the industries had become established, the goals of industrial policy with respect to that sector had to turn toward creating an export-competitive industry; at that point, infant-industry protection had to be gradually withdrawn and replaced by pressures and incentives to export. The government also had to maintain a certain degree of macroeconomic stability; to selectively promote not only foreign but also domestic competition; to help upgrade human resources and skills; and to foster social development.

Similarly, agriculture's main function had to alter with development. As we learned from Lewis, initially the primary job of the agricultural sector is to supply resources for industrialization—to release labor, accumulate and transfer capital, and earn foreign exchange. Large estates, worked with semiattached labor, and low agricultural terms of trade were best suited for this phase. Later, to enable industrialization to spread beyond a small enclave, agriculture must be capable of providing abundant food to the growing urban sector and supplying markets for urban manufactures. In this phase, the institutional structure of agriculture, terms of trade policies, and investments in agricultural infrastructure must be changed to yield incentives for improvements in the productivity of food agriculture. To enlarge the size of the domestic market for home-produced manufactures, the agricultural surplus must now become sufficiently widely distributed to enable generalized growth of farm income. Owner-operated farms that are large and productive enough to generate a marketable surplus are best suited to this stage. Thus, both historically and in our contemporary studies, we find that at low levels of development large estates are associated with more rapid growth and industrialization, while at later stages owner-cultivated farms are related to faster development.

The story with respect to international trade is similar. Not only should the main functions of government and the nature of agricultural institutions shift as development proceeds, but trade policies in support of industrialization must change as well. First, trade must open up possibilities for structural change in the economy's production patterns. To this end, it must generate sufficient domestic incentives to induce investment in initially inefficient infant industries. At the same time, trade must enable the economy to earn foreign exchange and buy the machinery and raw materials required for industrialization. In that phase, import substitution, promoted by modest subsidies, tariffs, and quotas, is the trade policy of choice. Next, trade and government investment policies must be structured so as to foster the continual acquisition of comparative advantage in higher-value-added, technologically more sophisticated industries. Exchange rate policy becomes critical in this phase. Trade policy should become selective. A gradual withdrawal of protection from adolescent industries, unification and reduction of tariff rates, and abolition of quotas on the older infants to force an increase in their competitiveness should be combined with selective, temporary protection of new infant industries. It is only when the economy has acquired the full panoply of industries characteristic of industrial economies that it should shift to completely free trade in order to induce increased competitiveness of domestic industry. Trade must now be allowed to act as a source of competition and a promoter of economies of scale by exposing domestic industry to foreign competition and by enlarging the markets for domestic industry.

These lessons concerning dynamically changing trade policy requirements are apparent both from the Industrial Revolution and from the policies adopted by the currently most successful industrialists, those in East Asia. All of the late industrialists of the 19th century practiced import substitution before shifting to export promotion. Even the earliest industrializers, which had no international competition at the time, used mercantilist policies during the period preceding the Industrial Revolution. By the same token, both the Republic of Korea and Taiwan (China), the most rapidly industrializing economies in the world, practiced import substitution for a short initial period. They then shifted to export orientation, rather than to free trade, and combined selective protection in successively higher industries with selective liberalization in earlier industrial specialties.

Finally, political transformations were required to enable successful development. At first, as we learn from 19th century overseas territories, the establishment of political stability and political support for the promulgation of laws furthering market development were sufficient to promote rapid expansion of primary exports. Dependent politics were sufficient for this stage. But unless the political institutions were later adapted so as to provide support for the economic needs of rising domestic commercial and industrial classes (as happened in Australia, Canada, and New Zealand), the translation of the initial impetus from exports into long-term economic development became blocked, as in Argentina and Brazil. At that point, a certain degree of domestic political autonomy became necessary.

Proposition 2: Development paths are not unique.

Point A. The present developed countries have followed alternative paths to development. We can distinguish at least three major distinct paths pursued by well-defined groups of countries during the Industrial Revolution (Morris and Adelman 1988).

1. *The largely autonomous industrialization of the first comers to the Industrial Revolution* (Great Britain and the United States). There was virtually no direct government investment in productive enterprises and very little direct financing of investment in industry and agriculture in these countries. Private enterprise financed a substantial amount of investment in infrastructure, facilitated by large government subsidies to private investment. For example, in the United States private investment in canals and railroads was subsidized through land grants to private entrepreneurs along rights-of-way.

However, even in those two countries governments had a pivotal function in promoting the Industrial Revolution. By 1870 in the United States and by 1850 in Great Britain, all premodern constraints on markets had been removed, major legal barriers to national mobility of labor (such as slavery in the United States) had been eliminated, and land transactions had been commercialized. The governments had created limited liability companies and had eliminated barriers to direct foreign investment. Prior to the Industrial Revolution, the British government had defended British entrepreneurs against outside competition through significant tariff protection and discriminatory shipping rules. Subsequently, British industrialization and competitiveness were promoted by a shift to free trade that allowed cheap raw material and food imports to come in from the Commonwealth countries. Moreover, throughout the 19th century the British government opened up its overseas territories to British industry by imposing free trade on its colonies and by investing in inland transport in the colonies (for example, railroads in India). It also provided externalities for private British ventures overseas by paying an important portion of the security and

administrative costs of the colonies and by developing capital markets
that enabled the export of enormous amounts of capital.

2. *The government-led industrialization process of the latecomers to
the Industrial Revolution* such as France, Germany, Italy, Japan, Russia, and Spain. For the 19th century latecomers, in contrast to the partially autonomous path of the first industrializers, government promotion
of industrialization was substantial and was positively, although not
perfectly, correlated with the magnitude of the development gap between Great Britain and the country in question. The government was
especially active in industrializing countries that were moderately backward but had administratively capable governments.

The governments of the latecomers responded to the military, political, and economic challenges posed by the British Industrial Revolution
by using a large variety of instruments to promote industrialization:
general and targeted subsidies, tariffs, incentives, monopoly grants,
quantitative restrictions, licensing, tax privileges, and even forced allocation of labor (Landes 1998: 235). Challenged by British industrialization, governments enlarged the sizes of their domestic markets by
providing support for the economic integration of urban-rural trade
networks, despite initial lack of effective political integration and significant economic dualism (between northern and southern Germany,
for instance); by investing in inland transport; by abolishing customs
duties and tolls to stimulate the evolution of national markets; by uni-
fying their countries politically; by strengthening their grip on overseas
colonies; and by engaging in territory-expanding wars. They also added
government demand for manufactures (for example, military uniforms
in Russia) to inadequate private demand. Governments substituted for
missing domestic factors through measures designed to enlarge the supply of skilled labor and finance. To increase the supply of skilled labor,
they invested in education, imported skilled technicians (especially in
Russia), and, where necessary, removed restrictions on labor mobility
(abolishing slavery and serfdom) and passed immigration laws favoring the influx of unskilled labor. If the country was too poor to support
the banks required to finance industry, the state promoted the establishment of financial intermediaries, invested in industrial enterprises
directly, or participated in industrial investment together with private
entrepreneurs. Thus, the governments of the follower countries engaged
in manifold entrepreneurial activities to catch up with Great Britain, in
an effort to reduce its military, economic, and political power.

3. *The government-assisted, open-economy, balanced-development
process of the small countries with high social capital* (Belgium, Denmark, the Netherlands, Sweden, and Switzerland). The role of the government in economic activity was less marked in this group than in the
latecomers to industrialization but more significant than in the early
industrializers. Governments were critical in the early development of

democracy and market institutions; in the provision of finance for interregional transport, agricultural infrastructure, and human resources; and in avoiding robber-baron capitalism by establishing a relatively extensive regulatory framework for private enterprise. But government provision of finance to the private sector and direct management of transport systems were less important than in the latecomers. The small size of these countries led to heavy export dependence and to emphasis on productivity improvements, in both agriculture and industry, as the countries shifted from extensive agriculture to intensive production of high-value crops. In addition, paucity of natural resources led to specialization in human resource–intensive industrialization. The results were not only economic growth and development but also widely shared improvements in living standards.

Point B. The end-points of development have differed among countries of the Organisation for Economic Co-operation and Development (OECD). Not only did the historical trajectories of the OECD countries differ during the 19th century, but they also exhibit distinct styles of mature capitalism today. Canada, France, Germany, Japan, the Scandinavian countries, the United Kingdom, and the United States all have mature capitalist systems, but their specific forms of capitalism are dissimilar (Maddison 1982, 1991; Artis and Lee 1994). Each pattern of capitalism is characterized by a special style of interaction between the government and the business sector; by a particular extent of government ownership of productive enterprises and infrastructure; by a specific relation of government to labor unions; by different methods of government regulation, control, and monitoring of the financial system; by the distinct structures of their financial systems, business organizations, and labor unions; and by disparate degrees of political decentralization. The relations between labor unions and business and labor unions and the polity have also differed. Finally, while they are all democracies, the particular forms of democracy (parliamentary or presidential), the relative importance of pressure groups (business, labor, farmers, and bureaucracies), and the role of political parties in forming policy have varied among them. The dissimilarities in capitalist styles are due both to the different development paths the countries have pursued and to differences in their initial cultures and values. The diversity in end-points, therefore, not only reinforces nonuniqueness but also indicates path dependence. Both the distinct paths of development and the distinct end-points of development have led to different national outcomes of inequality, welfare states, and evolutions over time in OECD countries.

Point C. The present developing countries have also been following alternative paths to development.

1. The pioneering studies of industrialization undertaken by Chenery (1960) and Chenery and Syrquin (1975) found systematic differences in the industrialization paths pursued by developing countries. Using country deviations from the average process, they distinguished four different country strategies: primary-oriented development, import substitution, balanced growth, and a strategy of industrialization. The contemporary variety in developing-country strategies is not unlike that evident during the 19th century, when both current OECD members and their overseas territories are included.

2. The role of the government in economic development shows significant contrasts among countries. In some East Asian countries the government has successfully played an entrepreneurial role, in much the same manner as in the latecomers to the Industrial Revolution (Amsden 1989; Wade 1990). The governments in East Asia shaped their financial, investment, trade, and commercial policies so as to promote their countries' climb up the ladder of comparative advantage. They restructured institutions to conform to their policy aims, changing old institutions or introducing new ones whenever they embarked on new policy initiatives. They exhibited high degrees of government commitment to development and enjoyed high degrees of autonomy from pressures by business or workers. Although at the beginning of each policy phase their initiatives were market-incentive distorting, the extent of market distortions was limited by tying subsidies to firms' export performance. As industries attained certain levels of proficiency, the government shifted to market-conforming policies and liberalized trade to spur competitiveness. By contrast, Latin American governments enjoyed less autonomy, exercised less direction, and had less commitment to the economic development of their countries (McGuire 1997). Their main struggle was over social reform rather than economic development. The governments, which started as captives of landed feudal elites and the foreign interests to which they were allied (Furtado 1963), tailored institutions, especially land tenure, to favor the interests of these elites. To benefit these interests when urban middle-class interests became important, they embarked on import-substitution policies and stayed with them until the 1980s.

3. Not only government roles but also patterns of accumulation differ among developing countries. While all developing countries have stressed accumulation as essential for development, countries have differed sharply in the extent to which they emphasized accumulation of human, as distinct from physical, capital. Some countries, primarily in East Asia, stressed the accumulation of human capital before embarking on serious industrialization, with favorable effects on income distribution, growth, industrialization, and productivity. Others, especially in Africa, imported the necessary human resources for industrialization and developed indigenous skills only subsequently. That accumulation

strategy resulted in a narrowly based, dualistic development path; little, low-productivity industrialization; natural resource–based exports; cyclically varying growth that responded to changes in world demand for raw material inputs; and shallow social change. Still other developing countries, mainly in Latin America, embarked on the accumulation of physical capital at an early stage in their development, widening inequality and developing an insufficient domestic market for the output of manufactures. They pursued low-productivity industrialization by engaging in import-substitution industrialization, starting with consumer goods and subsequently expanding to encompass industrial inputs. Thus, the different accumulation patterns pursued by developing countries in the 1950s and 1960s led to their subsequent achievement of comparative advantage in either labor-intensive or capital-intensive exports (Balassa 1979), with different consequences for inequality, industrial structure, domestic price levels, competitiveness, and optimal commercial policy. The dependence of current comparative advantage on prior accumulation patterns not only belies the "unique path" hypothesis but also indicates path dependence.

4. The sequence of industrialization and trade policies diverged among countries. Some developing countries, primarily in Latin America, pushed into the second phase of import substitution, in capital- and skill-intensive producer goods, after completing the first phase of concentration on labor-intensive consumer goods. Although they succeeded in promoting significant structural change in their economies, it was at the cost of slow growth, loss of competitiveness, and worsening income distribution (Krueger 1983). Other developing countries, mainly in East Asia, shifted immediately to export-led growth in labor-intensive consumer goods after a short period of import substitution (Kuo, Ranis, and Fei 1981; Wade 1990). These countries experienced egalitarian growth, increased competitiveness, and rapid economic growth.

5. Patterns of adjustment to the debt crisis of the 1980s have varied significantly among countries (Balassa 1989). Some developing countries, mostly in Latin America and Africa, adopted restrictive import regimes and deflationary macroeconomic policies. They also restrained wages, reduced subsidies, and liberalized their domestic markets to reduce their current account deficits, lower inflation, and increase competitiveness. Countries that followed this path experienced a lost development decade of substantial increases in poverty and inequality and low growth from which they began to emerge only in the 1990s. By contrast, a few countries, mostly in East Asia but also in Latin America (Brazil and Chile), coped with the adjustment problem by exporting their way out of the crisis. They shifted from import substitution to export promotion, devalued their currencies to promote expenditure switching among imports and domestic goods, and raised interest rates to increase net capital inflows. After a short period of

curtailed growth rates, these countries rebounded remarkably quickly and successfully grew their way out of the crisis.

6. Interaction patterns among economic, social, and political institutions, which are important for economic growth, have differed systematically at different levels of socioeconomic development. This is apparent from the statistical analysis of sources of intercountry differences in growth rates of per capita GNP between 1950 and 1965 by Adelman and Morris (1967). In developing countries at the lowest levels of socioeconomic development (Sub-Saharan Africa and a few very low income countries in Latin America and Asia), the primary explanatory variables for differences in economic growth were country differences in the degree of social development. Next, at a development level characteristic of the more developed but still transitional countries, the significant interactions were between economic growth, on the one hand, and, on the other hand, investment in infrastructure and the degree of development of economic institutions, particularly financial systems. Finally, in the most socioeconomically developed countries in the developing group, which had overcome the primary social development barriers, the significant interactions explaining cross-country differences in rates of economic growth were between growth rates, on the one hand, and, on the other, the effectiveness of economic institutions and a cluster of variables indicating the extent of national mobilization for economic development. This cluster combined the extent of leadership commitment to development, the investment rate, the rate of industrialization, and the degree of technological modernization in agriculture and industry.

7. Since 1980 the development paths of developing countries have differed systematically, not only according to their initial conditions but also given the same level of socioeconomic development (Adelman 1999). Thus, during 1980–94 some Sub-Saharan countries shifted to a broadly based rural development approach, while others continued their earlier trade-led, limited-industrialization pattern of narrowly based economic growth. Some countries at an intermediate social development level have continued their previous dualistic, export-oriented growth, while others have concentrated on developing the institutional bases for subsequent broadly based development without, however, achieving much growth during this period of structural change.

Proposition 3: Initial conditions shape subsequent development.

1. Abramovitz (1986) found that initial levels of social capability explained cross-country differences in the trajectories pursued by different European industrialists during the 19th century. His findings were confirmed for current developing countries by Temple and Johnson (1998). Using the Adelman-Morris index of socioeconomic development in 1960 as an indicator of initial levels of social capability, they

found that rates of growth in per capita income and in total factor productivity are strongly related to the extent of a country's initial level of social capability. They therefore reject the Solow model, in which technology is the same across countries, in favor of a model in which technology differs and preexisting social factors play a role in the speed of catching up.

2. Both economic history and contemporary development suggest that institutional readiness for capitalist economic growth is key to economic development, providing the conditions that enable technical progress and export expansion to induce widespread economic growth (Adelman and Morris 1967; North 1973, 1990). European countries that had achieved widespread economic growth by the end of the 19th century started with institutions better equipped for technological change than either the European latecomers or the developing countries of the 1950s (Kuznets 1968; Morris and Adelman 1988). They already had large preindustrial sectors well endowed with trained labor and entrepreneurs; governments that protected private property, enforced private contracts, and acted to free domestic commodity and labor markets; and leaderships responsive to capitalist interests that adopted trade, transport, and education policies which fostered technological progress in either industry (the early industrialists) or agriculture (the balanced-growth countries).

Similarly, those developing countries in the 1950s that were institutionally more advanced were the ones that benefited most from the growth impetus imparted by import demand from the OECD countries during the golden era of economic development. Their average rate of economic growth was 50 percent higher than that of the average nonoil country at the next-highest, intermediate level of socioinstitutional development (Adelman and Morris 1967). Furthermore, by 1973 the overwhelming majority of countries that were institutionally more developed in 1950 had become either newly industrialized countries (NICs) or industrial countries, while none of the countries at lower levels of socioinstitutional development had become NICs. Finally, upgrading financial and tax institutions was an important element in explaining intercountry differences in rates of economic growth at all levels of economic development in contemporary developing countries.

3. The extent of initial natural resource abundance mattered to development potential. During the 19th century some overseas territories with abundant land that had been settled by Europeans subsequently became developed. By contrast, all the land-scarce, densely populated former overseas European colonies are still underdeveloped today (for example, Egypt, India, and Myanmar).

4. The initial degree of government political autonomy and the initial distribution of assets determine whose interests the political system represents and hence the institutions and policies the state adopts (Morris

and Adelman 1988). The severely economically dependent colonies, which had no autonomy in setting their trade, immigration, and investment policies during the 19th century, were not able to pursue domestic development, as distinct from export-oriented, enclave, cyclical growth. It was not until they were decolonized that they could pursue development, and they are still struggling to develop today. By contrast, some of the less severely dependent Commonwealth countries (such as Australia and Canada) could set their economic policies to benefit their own industrialization and became OECD countries after World War II.

In the same vein, during the 19th century developing countries that were given sufficient political autonomy by their colonial rulers were able to translate growth impulses from export expansion into widespread economic development and to set their own economic policies so as to benefit domestic industrialization. Countries that were politically and economically so dependent on the center that they had no control over domestic economic policies (India and Myanmar) achieved only dualistic, enclave, sporadic growth (Morris and Adelman 1988: ch. 6).

Proposition 4: The development trajectory of countries is not only nonunique but also malleable.
1. Development is responsive to policy. (This would hardly be worth saying were it not for the contention of the rational-expectations school.) In both industrial and developing countries, economic outcomes have been influenced by the goals of economic policy. When, in the 1950–73 period, the OECD countries focused on economic growth, they got it. Similarly, after 1973, when they focused on economic stabilization, deliberately sacrificing economic growth and employment, they got that too (Maddison 1991). When, in the 1970s, developing countries chose not to curtail their development momentum but rather to pursue debt-led growth, they succeeded in raising their growth rates well beyond those of industrial countries. (This is not to say that it was a wise choice—only that it worked for a time.) When they had to shift to belt-tightening policies and make debt repayment their main objective, they succeeded in forcibly reducing their domestic standards of living and curtailing their growth rates. (This is also not to say that it was the best adjustment strategy—only that those governments that chose to pursue it had an effect on economic outcomes.)
2. As discussed to some extent in the previous section, our historical study has indicated that institutions and policies that were good for initiating economic growth were generally not appropriate for its continuation. For example, in the land-abundant non-European countries (Morris and Adelman 1988), foreign-dominated political institutions were a powerful force for the market-oriented institutional change that initiated strong expansion of primary exports. The institutions that were good for export growth, however, brought about neither systematic

agricultural improvement nor consistently rising standards of living. Yet successful development ultimately required that domestic economic institutions be transformed so that widely shared growth could ensue and a domestic market for manufactures could emerge.

3. Countries that got stuck in a given phase of their institutional structure or their policy orientation could not develop beyond a certain point. In backward European countries, governments and international resource flows could initially substitute for the missing institutional requirements for economic growth (Gershenkron 1962). At first, government demand for domestic manufacturing could successfully substitute for deficient home markets; government finance and foreign capital inflows could substitute for inadequate private domestic savings and underdeveloped financial institutions; and imports of skilled workers and technology could substitute for meager domestic human resources. But after a certain point, these substitutions became inadequate. To generate development, economic institutions and policies had to change so as to enable domestic, private provision of capital and skills and a broadly based expansion of domestic markets. For example, countries that were unable to selectively shift out of the import-substitution phase of their industrialization continued to have high-cost industry and captive bureaucracies. Similarly, nations that were unable to transform their agricultural institutions from forms suitable for extensive plantation agriculture have been unable to progress beyond relatively slow-growing industrialization and inequitable economic growth.

Governments must therefore retain a certain degree of autonomy from domestic and international pressures to enable them to switch from policies and institutions appropriate to earlier phases of their economic development that have outlived their primary usefulness. Whether governments do or do not have this capability depends on whose interests the political system represents; how entrenched, selfish and short-sighted the perspectives of these interests are; and what institutions exist for participation by the civil society in policy formulation. An illustration of this point is offered by the divergence in trajectories between two countries that had very similar initial conditions toward the third quarter of the 19th century: Argentina, whose polity represented the feudal landed elites, and Australia, where urban workers had captured the polity. Another example is the contrast today between countries that could not switch out of import substitution, except under external pressure, such as Colombia and Mexico, and countries that were capable of switching into early export orientation, such as Brazil, Korea, and Taiwan (China). Finally, the contrast between how Indonesia and Korea handled their recent financial crises illustrates the critical importance of governments' having enough political autonomy to undertake substantial institutional restructuring. Indonesia, mired in crony capitalism, has been unable to restructure its commercial and industrial organization toward greater competitiveness and fairness, whereas Korea, where the government has sufficient autonomy and credibility, is successfully mounting a forceful program of dismantling and rationalizing the chaebols.

Conclusion

Economic development is a highly multifaceted, nonlinear, path-dependent, dynamic process that involves systematically shifting interaction patterns among different aspects of development and therefore requires predictable changes in policies and institutions over time. By insisting on simplistic theories and on simple growth models that misspecify the process of economic development, development economists and aid agencies deliver to developing-country governments policy prescriptions that are mostly flawed and that, for most countries, are likely to be either completely or partially incorrect. The World Bank and the IMF must learn to accept that development is a complex, nonunique, nonlinear process that depends on countries' initial conditions and on their economic, institutional, sociocultural, and political histories. International aid institutions must start delivering a more state-specific, differentiated message to their clients, difficult as it might be. The cookie-cutter approach to policy is likely to be incorrect or irrelevant at least as often as it is right.

Notes

1. David Landes (1998) makes a convincing case that the current travails of the transition to market economy in Russia have their roots in the social structure prevailing in Russia under the tsars. The division of society into oppressed serfs, on the one hand, and profligate and incompetent noblemen, on the other, imprinted cultural attitudes that are inimical to interactions between labor, management, and government based on honesty, public-spiritedness, and hard work.

2. Bhagwati (1996) demonstrates that with increasing returns in a nontradable intermediate-goods sector, opening up the economy to international trade will not be enough to induce entrepreneurs to invest in the modern sector and so obviate the need for the "big push."

3. The models of Basu (1997) and Murphy, Shleifer, and Vishny (1989), which produce low-level equilibrium traps in a closed economy, lose the trap in an open economy, although Murphy and others claim that their model does not. By contrast, in Bhagwati (1996) the low-level equilibrium trap persists when the economy is opened up, and the need for a big push remains.

References

Abramovitz, Moses. 1986. "Catching Up, Forging Ahead, and Falling Behind." *Journal of Economic History* 46 (2, June): 385–406.

Adelman, Irma. 1958. *Theories of Economic Growth and Development.* Stanford, Calif.: Stanford University Press.

———. 1999. "Society, Politics and Economic Development, Thirty Years After." In John Adams and Francesco Pigliaru, eds., *Economic Growth and Change.* Aldwich, U.K.: Edward Elgar.

Adelman, Irma, and Cynthia Taft Morris. 1967. *Society, Politics and Economic Development: A Quantitative Approach.* Baltimore, Md.: Johns Hopkins University Press.

———. 1989. "Nineteenth-Century Development Experience and Lessons for Today." *World Development* 17 (9): 1417–32.

Adelman, Irma, and Sherman Robinson. 1978. *Income Distribution Policy in Developing Countries: A Case Study of Korea.* Stanford, Calif.: Stanford University Press.

Amsden, Alice H. 1989. *Asia's Next Giant.* New York: Oxford University Press.

Artis, M. J., and N. Lee. 1994. *The Economies of the European Union.* Oxford, U.K.: Oxford University Press.

Balassa, Bela. 1979. "A Stages Approach to Comparative Advantage." In I. Adelman, ed., *Proceedings of the Fifth World Congress of the International Economic Association,* 121–56. London: Macmillan.

———. 1989. "Exports, Policy Choices and Economic Growth in Developing Countries after the 1973 Oil Shock." In Bela Balassa, ed., *Comparative Advantage, Trade Policy and Economic Development,* 323–37. London: Harvester Wheatsheaf.

Baran, Paul A. 1957. *The Political Economy of Growth.* New York: Modern Reader Paperbacks.

Barro, Robert J. 1996. "Democracy and Economic Growth." *Journal of Economic Growth* 1: 1–27.

Basu, Kaushik. 1997. *Analytical Development Economics: The Less Developed Economy Revisited.* Cambridge, Mass.: MIT Press.

Bhagwati, Jagdish. 1985. *Essays on Development Economics,* vol. 1. Cambridge, Mass.: MIT Press.

———. 1999. "The 'Miracle' that Did Happen: Understanding East Asia in Comparative Perspective." *Taiwan's Development Experience: Lessons on Roles of Government and Market.* Erik Thorbecke and Henry Wan, Jr., eds. Boston: Kluwer Academic Publishers.

Black, Cyril E. 1966. *The Dynamics of Modernization: A Study of Comparative History.* New York: Harper and Row.

Campos, Nauro, and Jeffrey Nugent. 1999. "Development Performance and the Institutions of Governance: Evidence from East Asia and Latin America." *World Development* 27 (3, March): 439–52.

Chenery, Hollis. 1960. "Patterns of Industrial Growth." *American Economic Review* 50 (4, September): 624–54.

Chenery, Hollis, and Moises Syrquin. 1975. *Patterns of Development, 1950–1970.* London: Oxford University Press.

De Melo, Martha, Cevdet Denizer, and Alan Gelb. 1996. "Patterns of Transition from Plan to Market." *World Bank Economic Review* 10 (3, September): 397–424.

Emmerij, Louis. 1986. "Alternative Development Strategies Based on the Experience of the World Development Program." In Irma Adelman and Edward J. Taylor, eds., *The Design of Development Strategies*. Rohtak, India: Jan Tinbergen Institute of Development Planning.

Furtado, Celso. 1963. *The Economic Growth of Brazil.* Berkeley: University of California Press.

Gershenkron, Alexander. 1962. *Economic Backwardness in Historical Perspective.* Cambridge, Mass.: Belknap Press of Harvard University Press.

Hagen, Everett E. 1962. *On the Theory of Social Change.* Homewood, Ill.: Dorsey Press.

Harris, John R., and Michael P. Todaro. 1970. "Migration, Unemployment and Development: A Two-Sector Analysis." *American Economic Review* 60 (1, March): 126–42.

Hirschman, Albert. 1958. *The Strategy of Economic Development.* New Haven, Conn.: Yale University Press.

Hoselitz, Bernard. 1960. *Sociological Aspects of Economic Development.* Glencoe, Ill.: Free Press.

Inkeles, Alex, and David Horton Smith. 1966. *Becoming Modern.* London: Heinemann.

Krueger, Anne O. 1974. "The Political Economy of the Rent-Seeking Society." *American Economic Review* 64 (3, June): 291–303.

———. 1979. *The Developmental Role of the Foreign Sector and Aid.* Cambridge, Mass.: Harvard University Press.

———. 1983. *Trade and Employment in Developing Countries: Synthesis and Conclusions.* Chicago, Ill.: University of Chicago Press.

Kuo, Shirley, Gustav Ranis, and J. H. Fei. 1981. *The Taiwan Success Story.* Boulder, Colo.: Westview Press.

Kuznets, Simon. 1966. *Modern Economic Growth: Rate, Structure, and Spread.* New Haven, Conn.: Yale University Press.

———. 1968. *Toward a Theory of Economic Growth: With Reflections on the Economic Growth of Modern Nations.* New York: Norton.

Landes, David S. 1969. *The Unbound Prometheus.* Cambridge, U.K.: Cambridge University Press.

———. 1998. *The Wealth and Poverty of Nations: Why Some Are So Rich and Some So Poor.* New York: W. W. Norton.

Leibenstein, Harvey. 1957. *Economic Backwardness and Economic Growth.* New York: Wiley.

Lerner, Daniel. 1958. *The Passing of Traditional Society.* Glencoe, Ill.: Free Press.

Lewis, W. Arthur. 1954. "Economic Development with Unlimited Supplies of Labor." *Manchester School of Economic and Social Studies* 22: 139–91.

Lucas, Robert E. 1988. "On the Mechanics of Economic Development." *Journal of Monetary Economics* 22 (1, July): 3–42.

Maddison, Angus. 1982. *Phases of Capitalist Development.* Oxford, U.K.: Oxford University Press.

———. 1991. *Dynamic Forces in Capitalist Development.* Oxford, U.K.: Oxford University Press.

Mauro, Paulo. 1995. "Corruption and Growth." *Quarterly Journal of Economics* 110 (3, August): 681–712.

McClelland, David C. 1961. *The Achieving Society.* New York: Free Press.

McGuire, James W. 1997. *Rethinking Development in East Asia and Latin America.* Los Angeles, Calif.: Pacific Council on International Policy.

Meier, Gerald M. Various editions, 1964–2000. *Leading Issues in Development Economics.* New York: Oxford University Press.

Morris, Cynthia Taft, and Irma Adelman. 1988. *Comparative Patterns of Economic Development: 1850–1914.* Baltimore, Md.: Johns Hopkins University Press.

Murphy, Kevin M., Andrei Shleifer, and Robert W. Vishny. 1989. "Industrialization and the Big Push." *Journal of Political Economy* 97 (5, October): 1003–26.

Myrdal, Gunnar. 1968. *The Asian Drama.* Hammondsworth, U.K.: Penguin Books.

Nogués, Julio, and Sunil Gulati. 1994. "Economic Policies and Performance under Alternative Trade Regimes: Latin America during the 1980s." *World Economy* 17 (July): 467–96.

North, Douglass C. 1973. *The Rise of the Western World.* Cambridge, U.K.: Cambridge University Press.

———. 1990. *Institutions, Institutional Change and Economic Performance.* Cambridge, U.K.: Cambridge University Press.

Nurkse, Ragnar. 1952. "Some Aspects of Capital Accumulation in Underdeveloped Countries." Cairo. No publisher listed.

———. 1953. *Problems of Capital Formation in Underdeveloped Countries and Patterns of Trade and Development.* New York: Oxford University Press.

Polanyi, Karl. 1944. *The Great Transformation.* Boston, Mass.: Beacon Press.

Prebisch, Raúl. 1950. *The Economic Development of Latin America and Its Principal Problems.* New York: United Nations, Economic Commission for Latin America.

Romer, Paul M. 1986. "Increasing Returns and Long-Run Growth." *Journal of Political Economy* 94 (5, October): 1002–37.

Rosenstein-Rodan, Paul N. 1943. "Problems of Industrialization of Eastern and South-Eastern Europe." *Economic Journal* 53: 202–11.

Rostow, Walt W. 1960. *The Stages of Economic Growth: A Non-Communist Manifesto.* Cambridge, U.K.: Cambridge University Press.

Sen, Amartya. 1988. "The Concept of Development." In Hollis Chenery and
    T. N. Srinivasan, eds., *Handbook of Development Economics*. Amsterdam:
    North-Holland.

Solow, Robert M. 1957. "Technical Change and the Aggregate Production
    Function." *Review of Economics and Statistics* 39: 312–20.

Stiglitz, Joseph E. 1996. "Some Lessons from the East Asian Miracle." *World
    Bank Research Observer* 11 (2, August): 151–77.

———. 1998. "More Instruments and Broader Goals: Moving towards the
    Post–Washington Consensus." WIDER Annual Lecture, Helsinki, January 7.
    Available at <http://www.worldbank.org/html/extdr/extme/js-010798/
    wider.htm>.

Stiglitz, Joseph E., and others. 1989. *The Economic Role of the State,* edited
    by Arnold Heertje. London: Basil Blackwell.

Streeten, Paul P. 1986. "Basic Needs: The Lessons." In Irma Adelman and
    Edward J. Taylor, eds., *The Design of Development Strategies*. Rohtak, In-
    dia: Jan Tinbergen Institute of Development Planning.

Streeten, Paul P., and Frances Stewart. 1976. "New Strategies for Develop-
    ment: Poverty, Income Distribution and Growth." *Oxford Economic Pa-
    pers* 28: 113–28.

Temple, Jonathan, and Paul A. Johnson. 1998. "Social Capability and Eco-
    nomic Development." *Quarterly Journal of Economics* 113 (3, August):
    965–90.

UNDP (United Nations Development Programme). Various years. *Human De-
    velopment Report*. New York: Oxford University Press.

Wade, Robert. 1990. *Governing the Market: Economic Theory and the Role
    of Government in the East Asian Industrialization*. Princeton, N.J.: Princeton
    University Press.

Wolfensohn, James D. 1998. "The Other Crisis." Address to the Annual Meet-
    ings of the World Bank and the International Monetary Fund, Washington,
    D.C., October 6.

World Bank. 1993a. *The East Asian Miracle: Economic Growth and Public
    Policy.* New York: Oxford University Press.

———. 1997. *World Development Report 1997: The State in a Changing
    World*. New York: Oxford University Press.

Comment

David Vines

OVER THE 50-PLUS YEARS SINCE the end of World War II, there have been many shifts in view about how development might best be promoted. "No area of economics," says Irma Adelman, "has experienced as many abrupt changes in its leading paradigm."

Adelman charts these changes in a masterful way. She then makes two strong claims about them. The first of these is historical: that in these 50 years development economics has produced a mere passing parade of inadequate and oversimplified "single-cause" theories of economic development. The second claim is theoretical: this sorry state of affairs is the fault of the "culture of economics." "The discipline of economics has enshrined the 'keep it simple, stupid' (KISS) principle as an overarching tenet . . . that can be violated only at the violator's peril. This principle demands simple explanations and universally valid propositions." Adherence to this principle by economists has been the cause of the "twists and turns" from one view to another, and the cause of the inadequacy of what has appeared at every turn.

By presenting these stark views, Adelman does us all a great service. They are naturally views that are depressing to Adelman herself. In a spirit of some disappointment, she concludes that development economics has not yet evolved a body of development theory that is "rich enough to portray the changing reality that is relevant for correct policy prescriptions." This is a sad conclusion from one whose *Society, Politics and Economic Development: A Quantitative Approach* (Adelman and Morris 1967) did so much to add to our knowledge of development and was so ahead of its time.[1] The second half of her chapter is directed at what she sees as correcting the balance: showing—partly drawing on her own work—something of the complexity and subtlety that a good development theory needs to include.

Are things really this bad? In response, I also want to make two large claims, in a spirit of much greater optimism.

My first, historical, claim is that there have been only three grand phases, and two big turns, in the passing parade of development theory. And, I will argue, we have learned much from both shifts. We now know incredibly much more about development than our forebears did. And what we now know does not have the form of a single-cause theory.

My second, theoretical, claim is that—although I agree that economic theory has been driven by the KISS principle, and although I also agree that its effects have at times been malign—I think that adherence to this principle is necessary, can be benign, and is now in fact operating in a benign manner.

These are claims that I think Adelman would actually agree with. They suggest that development theory has moved, and is now moving further, in the direction that she would like. In fact, her chapter helps to chart a way forward.

An Alternative History of Development Economics

I do not think it is true that development economics has had more abrupt changes in its leading paradigm than other branches of economics. In my own major field, macroeconomics, there have been just three major paradigms, and thus two major paradigm shifts, in the past 50 years. These paradigms can be described, at one level, as the fiscalist demand-management views of the 1950s and 1960s, the monetarism of the 1970s and 80s, and now the central bank inflation-targeting of the 1990s. But at a deeper level, these were periods in which the dominant paradigms were the interventionism of the 1950s and 1960s, the laissez-faire of the 1970s and 1980s, and the emphasis on institutional design that characterizes the best work of the 1990s.

It is my contention that exactly these same three phases—no less and no more—can be found in development theory. In Phase 1 (in the 1950s and 1960s) there was a focus on and belief in the effectiveness of government intervention; in Phase 2 (in the 1970s and 1980s) there was a growing belief in the power of free markets; and in Phase 3 (in the 1990s and to the present) there has been a growing emphasis on the importance of institutional design.

Phase 1 was dominated by the ideas of what Krugman (1999) has called "high development theory." Loosely, this consisted of the view that development is a virtuous circle driven by external economies— that modernization breeds modernization. Some countries, according to this view, remained underdeveloped because they failed to get this virtuous circle going, and thus they were stuck in a low-level trap, as a result of a coordination failure. Consequently there was a powerful case for government activism as a way of breaking out of this trap.[2]

There were disputes, now famous, over the nature of the policies that might be required to break out of a low-level trap. Rosenstein-Rodan and others (for example, Nurkse 1952) advocated a broadly based investment program. Hirschman (1958) disagreed, arguing that a policy of promoting a few key sectors with strong linkages, then moving on to other sectors to correct the disequilibrium generated by these investments, and so on, was the right approach. But almost all argued that some government intervention might well be essential to break out of the trap. "Most classical development economists . . . regarded development-oriented governments as having a major role in the direct provision of finance, the subsidization of investment, and the direct undertaking of investment in infrastructural and 'basic' industrial projects" (Adelman, p. 107).

It is worth noting that there is a significant ambiguity in Adelman's description of development theory during what I have called Phase 1. She gives a long and careful account of the views of contemporary development economists on the interventions that might be required to solve the coordination problem. But she does this in the course of describing another view, which she claims was the prevalent one during Phase 1: that the accumulation of physical capital is *the* single necessary and sufficient condition for development. Her own discussion suggests, therefore, that many people at the time did not hold the kind of single-cause theory that she decries. Instead, they appear to have held the kinds of rich and complex views that she admires. Capital accumulation appears, on inspection, to be the proximate cause of development in this richer set of views; the interventions required to induce it seem to be the ultimate cause of development. In my view, the central search at the time was for a key set of interventions that, if taken together, would be both necessary and sufficient to bring about capital accumulation, which would, in turn, be necessary and sufficient for the sought-for development. [3]

In *Phase 2*, in the 1970s and 1980s, a reaction set in against interventionist policies. One reason had to do with questions about the analytical basis of these interventionist policies—a concern that worried many in the economics profession as early as the 1960s. (I return to this point in the next section.) More important, the period saw a pronounced series of macroeconomic shocks: the first energy crisis and the subsequent global recession; the second rise in oil prices, which flowed from the time of the Iranian revolution; the resulting global recession, which spawned the Latin American debt crisis; and the subsequent period of very low commodity prices in the mid-1980s. Such instability was a natural counterpart to and indeed a consequence of the end of the Bretton Woods regime, which was followed by a 15-year period of deep incoherence in the global macroeconomic policy framework. The effect of this incoherence on developing countries was to require large changes in macroeconomic policy and also substantial changes in microeconomic policy, as macroadjustments necessitated the removal of distortions and rigid policy frameworks—in particular, overvalued exchange rates and the dismantling of parastatal enterprises. Primary attention in developing countries turned to the removal of microeconomic and macroeconomic rigidities. The 1980s became the "adjustment decade." Finally, and perhaps most important, all this happened at a time when the ideology of the age was moving toward freer markets.[4] In the 1980s Ronald Reagan, Margaret Thatcher, and Helmut Kohl were elected leaders of the three most intellectually influential countries in the world.[5] The

Out of this changed intellectual climate grew the "Washington consensus."[6] Its advice for developing countries was, promote sound money and free trade, free up domestic markets, and encourage policymakers to go home early and stop interfering. A central part of this consensus was the view that openness and liberalization would lead to growth.[7] The intellectual implications of the Washington consensus were profound. Adelman discusses them at length in pages 113–15 of her chapter.

Phase 3, which we are now in, involves a reaction against this neoliberal agenda. The argument is that it is not just getting prices right, and the openness which comes from getting external prices right, that matter. Institutions also matter for growth. The manner in which this argument is made relies on variants of endogenous growth theory.

One way of constructing the argument is to note that the provision of basic services—health and education—is vitally important for growth. A second view is that the solution of coordination failures, through government subsidies and other kinds of more direct interventions, were crucial to the Asian miracle (Rodrik 1996; Stiglitz 1996). Finally, the efficacy of what happens when market liberalization is pursued without adequate attention to institutional structures has been seriously questioned as a result of the Asian financial crisis and the brutal experiences with liberalization in the transition economies (Stiglitz 2000). The less than satisfactory experiences with liberalization in generating growth in Latin America and Africa, and the growing concern about the increasing inequality and increasing volatility stemming from changes in technology and trade, also form part of the basis for much of the reassessment that is taking place.

Other types of evidence provide broader grounds for this kind of argument. One version has been put forward by Rodrik (1999), who argues that, in a volatile world, success in maintaining growth goes to those who are able to adjust. What, then, explains which countries have the capacity for adjustment? Rodrik links this capacity to a country's capacity to handle distributional changes. His empirical work on this issue directly challenges the Sachs and Warner (1995) correlation between openness and growth (see Rodrik 1998, 1999: ch. 4). He reconstructs the Sachs and Warner data and suggests that their openness measure picks up macroeconomic stability or even (what was more relevant for his argument) proxies for mechanisms for the management of distributional difficulties thrown up by the need for adjustment.

Thus, the professional and analytical literature has been evolving in interesting ways over the past decade. Looking back, it is now possible to see how contingent was the steady progress made by the countries that liberalized in the 1960s, 1970s, and 1980s. The construction, with government assistance, of industrial institutions that facilitated growth, the management of external volatility, and the containment of internal distributional conflict—all of these things were at the core of the successes of the period.[8] This understanding points to the crucial role of institutional frameworks in managing the growth process.

How have we come to these new Phase 3 beliefs? Not, clearly, through some linear process of intellectual development. Instead, there have been the two great turns that I have identified. These swerves, I have argued, owe much to what happened in industrial countries and perhaps too little to what actually happened on the ground in developing countries. Theoretical phases in mainstream economics in the West spilled over and influenced what was written about development theory, as my remarks about the parallel between development economics and macroeconomics were designed to emphasize. Also, what happened in development theory had a great deal to do with the climate of ideology in the West. As a result, theoretical developments and the ideological climate in industrial countries strongly influenced the policy advice that was given in developing countries. This point is brought out very clearly in the history of the World Bank (Kapur, Lewis, and Webb 1997; Kanbur and Vines forthcoming).

The new beliefs of Phase 3 point in important directions. They suggest that institutions can have many different forms and can manage the growth process in many different ways (Rodrik 1999). A natural corollary is an acceptance of a pluralism of views. Such a position is a complete change from the "getting-prices-right-is-everything" view of the neoliberal school that held sway at the time of the Washington consensus. It is also very much in line with the argument in the second half of Adelman's chapter.

KISS and Tell:
The Role of Theory in Development Economics

What should be the role of theory in the construction of development theory during Phase 3—the phase through which we are living?

Adelman's Apparent View: "Tell"

One reading of Adelman's chapter is that economists are too influenced by the KISS principle to provide the right theory for us. That reading suggests that neoclassical economists have little to tell us because the postulates of neoclassical economics "are not applicable to developing countries . . . The institutional bases for a neoclassical economy are missing . . . [and as a result] market equilibrium cannot be proved to be . . . efficient. . . . If [distribution of wealth] is not optimal [even efficient market outcomes] will not maximize . . . social welfare." In addition advice based on "neoclassical development [economics] ignore[s] the . . . second best" (p. 115).

What is the alternative to this? Adelman clearly thinks that economic development is a rich and complex process that is happening in a world very different from the kind of world described by "the postulates of neoclassical economists." Because of this, an important part of development theory may be summed up as "telling it the way it is." The second half of Adelman's chapter can be read as an indication that this is her preferred way of doing development theory: analytical, but nonformal, historical analysis that pays careful attention to institutional details.

Such an approach would cohere well with what she has done, to great effect, in her empirical work. First you do your historical analysis. Then you work with large panel data sets, as used in, for example, *Society, Politics and Economic Development.* You use these to look for empirical regularities that support the broad claims that your historical research throws up. Two examples of such regularities, taken almost at random from the last part of Adelman's chapter, are her claims about how the role of government in promoting agriculture needs to change as development proceeds and about the changing needs of trade policy as industrialization progresses. You study the extent to which such regularities are general. If they are general, then you have a theory. The formal mathematical models of modern economics seem unimportant for this process, especially if they bring along as baggage many of the silly assumptions identified above.

In my view this is a mistaken attitude to take toward economic theory. If this is indeed Adelman's view—a question I take up below—then I would disagree with her.

My View: "KISS and Tell"

In my view, the problem with economists in Phase 2 of development theory was not their use of the KISS principle. It was that economists at the time thought that the KISS principle implied the Washington consensus. "Just liberalize, and go home" was their advice to policymakers—

simple advice. And this was what their simple models, with all those silly assumptions, told them to say.

But the best neoclassical economists do not do theory like that any more, thanks to the industrial organization revolution of the 1980s, and thanks to the economics of regulation that it spawned. Market failure is the object of study of this new economics; intervention may be necessary for efficiency, and institutional rules are required. Second-best solutions are its stock in trade. Adelman's "neoclassical economist" is history.

The modern neoclassical economist is very interested in the kind of stories that Adelman tells in the second half of her chapter: they provide issues to work on. But, nevertheless, that economist will also want to follow the KISS principle. He or she will want to build a simple formal model. Why? To find exactly what intervention is necessary and sufficient to solve the market failure that the historical account has identified.

Consider the question that concerned economists in Phase 1 of development economics, discussed above—a question that is still relevant for some countries and in some circumstances (even now, when we are doing Phase 3 development theory). When will government intervention be necessary to solve the coordination problem of industrialization? Will it always be necessary? Will it always be sufficient? Will it never be sufficient?

"In most versions of this theory," writes Krugman (1999), the development trap comes from

> . . . an interaction between economies of scale at the level of the individual producer and the size of the market. Crucial to this interaction [is] some form of economic dualism, in which "traditional" production paid lower wages and/or participated in the market less than the modern sector. The story [goes] something like this: modern methods of production are potentially more productive than traditional ones, but their productivity edge is large enough to compensate for the necessity of paying higher wages only if the market is large enough. But the size of the market depends on the extent to which modern techniques are adopted, because workers in the modern sector earn higher wages and/or participate in the market economy more than traditional workers. So if modernization can be gotten started on a sufficiently large scale, it will be self-sustaining, but it is possible for an economy to get caught in a trap in which the process never gets going.

Any one with a smattering of game theory will know that what is being discussed is the question: "under what exact circumstances will there be multiple Nash equilibria in the modernization game?" or, in other words, "in what exact circumstances is there a coordination problem that requires intervention to solve?"

I defy my readers to answer this question unless they have worked their way through the Murphy, Shleifer, and Vishny (1989) paper, or at least the Krugman (1999) sketch-cartoon version of it. They certainly could not do so unless they have done what Adelman criticizes and have produced a single-cause theory of development. Indeed, it is relevant to remark that Adelman herself discusses the need for such intervention at some length in the first half of her chapter, and yet it is impossible to determine the answer to this question from her account.

Here is an account of how one can answer this question that draws on Krugman (1999) and shows exactly what the role of KISS theory can be in answering it. The precise answer to the question depends partly on whether it would be worthwhile for an individual producer to modernize if no other producer did. This, in turn, depends on whether the effect on costs of the higher wages in the modern sector dominates the effect on the costs of the high-fixed-cost/low-marginal-cost modern method of production at the *low* level of sales that would prevail if no other producer modernized. The answer also depends on whether it would be worthwhile for an individual producer to modernize if all the others had already done so. This, by comparison with the previous test, depends on whether the effect on costs of the higher wages in the modern sector dominates the effect on costs of the high-fixed-cost/low-marginal-cost modern method of production at the *high* level of output that prevails when all other producers have modernized.

This account enables one to see that an industrial policy that gave insurance to individual investors that other investors will also be investing would lead investors collectively to carry out investments which would justify each of them having done so ex post. But it also shows the circumstances in which such an approach to industrial policy would not be sufficient. It may be that the market is too small, so that a coordinated investment plan would not generate extra income for a market to satisfy the critical minimum push. The discussion also shows the circumstances in which such a coordinated plan would be unnecessary. Perhaps it would be possible to give a modest investment subsidy that was nevertheless large enough to make a single investment become profitable. This would solve the coordination problem through a simple marginal intervention. Once modernization had been achieved, with many firms paying higher wages, the subsidy could be withdrawn. Or it might be that modernization is possible without any intervention at all because the market is large enough to support modernizing producers even if other producers have not modernized.

Here is Krugman (1999) on why this kind of precisely focused discussion is helpful:

I can report from observation that until Murphy et al. published their formalization of Rosenstein-Rodan its conclusions were not obvious to many people, even those who have specialized in development. Economists tended to regard the Big Push story as essentially nonsensical—if modern technology is better, then rational firms would simply adopt it! (They missed the interaction between economies of scale and market size). Non-economists tended to think that Big Push stories necessarily involved some rich interdisciplinary stew of effects, missing the simple core. In other words, economists were locked in their traditional models, non-economists were lost in the fog that results when you have no explicit models at all.

Consider a second, more modern version of a related problem, of crucial importance to government policy in modern, Phase 3, development economics. Is there a need for concerted government intervention to solve an investment coordination problem in an outward-looking industrialization program? Here the size of the market is enormous: the world. So, coordination of investment cannot be necessary to create demand. This has long been a criticism of big push theory.[9] But intervention may still be necessary to solve problems on the supply side. Rodrik (1996) discusses the case in which successful outward-looking industrialization requires a critical intermediate input (which we could think of, if we like, as something like a skilled labor force). He examines what will happen if this input is available only if enough investors invest at the same time, because of the extra externality resulting from the training of any one worker. Under what circumstances will intervention in the provision of basic infrastructure (in this case education) be necessary? Under what circumstances will it be sufficient? Can this best be achieved by coordinated public provision or by a subsidy to producers? These are questions that simple theory can illuminate. Indeed Bhagwati (1996) has written a paper on exactly this topic, which Adelman admiringly quotes.

The purpose of theoretical papers in such circumstances is to show whether a particular intervention proposed to deal with the problem identified is necessary, or sufficient, to do so. One should tell a story so as to identify the market failures and then build a simple model to see whether the proposed solutions are necessary, or sufficient, to solve the problem. That is the role for KISS theory. It is not dispensable.

Adelman's Real View? "Do Not Just KISS"

I do not think that Adelman would actually disagree with any of this. In her chapter and in her other published work she shows great respect for the use of theory to work out the answer to focused questions, just as in the example I have described. I take her to be arguing that answers to the questions posed in these simple models are not enough. One sets out simple models to get at the underlying structure of issues. But—she is saying forcefully—one should not make policy on the basis of the simple insights obtained from these simple models. Models tell you what to think about, but they do not provide the answers to actual policy questions. As a result, the objects of Adelman's criticism are not so much the economic theorists who want to "keep it simple, stupid." Rather, she is opposed to those who would try to apply results obtained from simple models to actual policy without giving sufficient thought to their applicability.

We can all imagine the enthusiasm of the young electronics graduate, fresh from college, armed with the simple clarity of the Maxwell equations, turning up at a Boeing factory to make airplanes. He would quickly be told, "Get real, Sonny—get some experience." That is the admonition that comes from Adelman's chapter: "Get some good formal theory, sure. But get some wisdom too. Especially if you are a policy adviser flying in from the Bank or the Fund."

Notes

I am grateful to Ravi Kanbur for helpful discussions. In what follows I partly draw on Kanbur and Vines (forthcoming). Paul David commented on an earlier draft and saved me from serious error. Although this piece is now perhaps more as he would have wished, he still cannot be held responsible for it.

1. I remember vividly my excitement on reading this book as an undergraduate.

2. Krugman (1999): 1. This paragraph is taken, with adaptation, from Krugman's paper.

3. On one reading of Adelman's paper, the people who held these wider views during the time that I have labeled Phase 1 were "classical development theorists." They were not guilty of the single-cause view that she criticises; such views were held only by the "neoclassical development theorists." But, on this reading, for the argument of this section of the paper to succeed, she would have to establish that these "good guys" were somehow denied proper influence as a result of the undue influence of the "bad" single-cause people. This she does not do.

4. Thus, for example, macroeconomics underwent a similar paradigm shift, as has already been noted.

5. Of course this was not unconnected with the fact that the instabilities of the 1970s, in the face of which policy changes were clearly needed, were connected in the public mind, largely successfully, with the interventionism of the earlier era.

6. John Williamson has recently revisited the strange history of this term, which he invented in Williamson (1990). As he notes, "I find that the term has

been invested with a meaning that is significantly different from that which I had intended and is now used as a synonym for what is often called 'neo-liberalism' in Latin America, or what George Soros (1998) has called 'market fundamentalism'" (Williamson 2000: 251–52).

7. Balassa (1989) is an example of the literature of the 1980s. More recent support for this view is presented in Dollar (1992) and Edwards (1993). A recent restatement of the basic argument is to be found in Krueger (1998). Rodrik (1999) reviews and then criticizes the empirical literature claiming to support the connection between trade liberalization and growth.

8. Even though the growth of world trade was far from steady in the 1970s and early 1980s, developing countries that liberalized were not then exposed to the volatility of capital flows to which such countries are now exposed.

9. I am grateful to Katie Low for making this clear to me.

References

Adelman, Irma, and Cynthia Taft Morris. 1967. *Society, Politics and Economic Development: A Quantitative Approach.* Baltimore, Md.: Johns Hopkins University Press.

Balassa, Bela. 1989. "Exports, Policy Choices and Economic Growth in Developing Countries after the 1973 Oil Shock." In Bela Balassa, ed., *Comparative Advantage, Trade Policy and Economic Development,* 323–37. London: Harvester Wheatsheaf.

Bhagwati, Jagdish. 1999. "The 'Miracle' that Did Happen: Understanding East Asia in Comparative Perspective." *Taiwan's Development Experience: Lessons on Roles of Government and Market.* Erik Thorbecke and Henry Wan, Jr., eds. Boston: Kluwer Academic Publishers.

Dollar, David. 1992. "Outward-Oriented Developing Countries Really Do Grow More Rapidly: Evidence from 95 LDCs, 1976–85." *Economic Development and Cultural Change* 40 (April): 523–44.

Edwards, Sebastian. 1993. "Trade Orientation, Distortions, and Growth in Developing Countries." *Journal of Economic Literature* 31 (3, September): 1358–93.

Hirschman, Albert. 1958. *The Strategy of Economic Development.* New Haven, Conn.: Yale University Press.

Kapur, Devesh, John P. Lewis, and Richard Webb. 1997. *The World Bank: Its First Half Century.* Vol. 1: *History.* Washington, D.C.: Brookings Institution.

Kanbur, Ravi, and David Vines. Forthcoming. "The World Bank and Poverty Reduction: Past, Present, and Future." In Christopher L. Gilbert and David Vines, eds., *The World Bank: Structure and Policies,* ch. 5. New York: Cambridge University Press.

Krueger, Anne O. 1998. "Why Trade Liberalization Is Good for Growth." *Economic Journal* 108 (September): 1513–22.

Krugman, Paul. 1999. "The Fall and Rise of Development Economics." Available at <http:/web.mit.edu/krugman/www/dishpan.html>.

Murphy, Kevin M., Andrei Shleifer, and Robert W. Vishny. 1989. "Industrialization and the Big Push." *Journal of Political Economy* 97 (5, October): 1003–26.

Nurkse, Ragnar. 1952. "Some Aspects of Capital Accumulation in Underdeveloped Countries." Cairo. No publisher listed.

Rodrik, Dani. 1996. "Coordination Failures and Government Policy: A Model with Applications to East Asia and Eastern Europe." *Journal of International Economics* 40 (1–2, February): 1–22.

———. 1998. "TFPG Controversies, Institutions, and Economic Performance in East Asia." In Yujiro Hayami and Masahiko Aoki, eds., *The Institutional Foundations of Economic Development in East Asia*. London: Macmillan.

———. 1999. *The New Global Economy and Developing Countries: Making Openness Work*. Policy Essay 24. Washington, D.C.: Overseas Development Council.

Sachs, Jeffrey D., and Andrew M. Warner. 1995. "Economic Reform and the Process of Global Economic Integration." *Brookings Papers on Economic Activity* 1: 1–95.

Soros, George. 1998. *The Crisis of Global Capitalism: Open Society Endangered*. London: Little Brown.

Stiglitz, Joseph E. 1996. "Some Lessons of the East Asian Miracle." *World Bank Research Observer* 11 (2, August): 151–77.

———. 2000. "Whither Reform? Ten Years of the Transition." In Boris Pleskovic and Joseph E. Stiglitz, eds., *Annual World Bank Conference on Development Economics 1999*. Washington, D.C.: World Bank.

Williamson, John. 1990. "What Washington Means by Policy Reform." In John Williamson, ed., *Latin American Adjustment: How Much Has Happened?* Washington, D.C.: Institute for International Economics.

———. 2000. "What Should the World Bank Think about the Washington Consensus?" *World Bank,* Research Observer 15 (2, August): 251–64. Processed.

Comment

Sir Hans Singer

IRMA ADELMAN'S CHAPTER IS expectedly brilliant and thought provoking. Few will disagree with her conclusion that economic development is a highly multifaceted dynamic process in which many factors interact in a complicated way and that simple single-factor explanations claiming universal validity must be suspect. Similarly, this commentator would also agree with her closing admonition—addressed to the World Bank and the International Monetary Fund (IMF) but presumably valid for all donors, as well as analysts—to be more "state specific" and "differentiated" in giving advice to policymakers in the multitude of developing countries with their different histories, institutions, policies, and objectives. As far as the Bank and the IMF are concerned, I would add that her chapter also provides a case for a broader framework in structural adjustment discussions than the present narrow one, with Bank and IMF staff on one side of the table and ministry of finance and central bank representatives on the other.

But I have some doubts about the summary treatment of the various single-factor paradigms. Many of the single-factor fallacies that she presents—physical capital, entrepreneurship, relative prices, international trade, human capital, and hyperactive or ineffective government— were not put forward as sufficient explanations of development but rather as previous neglected factors that were important in combination with other factors. This is, in fact, apparent from Irma Adelman's own exposition and discussions of the various "X-factors" when, repeatedly, other factors enter the discussion. Some of these factors are themselves complex and multifaceted. The concept of human capital, for example, which she associates with the Chicago school (Lucas and Romer), but which some of us also associate with the United Nations Development Programme's *Human Development Reports,* is clearly multifaceted: low human capital can be the result of low income, poor education, poor health, poor training, lack of employment opportunities, and so on. The policy prescriptions for creating and upgrading

human capital must be correspondingly "state specific and differentiated" and dependent on history and institutions. *Pace* the "KISS" label,
there is nothing "simple" about this.

Another reservation concerns the clear distinction made throughout
the chapter between import substitution and export promotion. In practice, the distinction is quite complicated. Has Adelman herself become
a victim here of the KISS principle? A devaluation, of course, promotes
simultaneously import substitution and exports. The Republic of Korea has over long periods taken care to avoid currency overvaluation,
has often simultaneously promoted exports in one sector and import
substitution in another, and has promoted home production of inputs
needed for its export industries so as to increase the (initially often very
low) net value added of its exports. Should this import substitution for
inputs needed by exports be classified as import substitution or export
promotion? It seems to be a case of the glass of water being half-full or
half-empty. Such complications must throw doubt on any clear distinction, quite apart from the distinction made throughout the chapter between import substitution by newcomers trying to catch up when it is
appropriate (and indeed inevitable) and by mature economies, for which
it is more likely to be inappropriate as a guiding policy.

As for path dependency and the distinction between low-level equilibrium (the poverty trap) and paths leading to dynamic self-sustaining
development, the chapter is particularly impressive. I would perhaps
add an acknowledgement of Keynes, whose demonstration of the possibility of unemployment equilibrium was a clear forerunner of the
poverty trap. In fact, his advocacy of duo-economics (different policies
for conditions of unemployment and full employment) encouraged the
birth of development economics (different policies for rich and poor
countries). But one must agree with Adelman that the "duo" idea can
be misleading if it suggests a single "good" policy for all rich countries
and another single "good" policy for poor countries. "Solo versus or-
chestral" would be a better metaphor than "single versus duo."

There are other details one could debate—for example, that food
aid is an instrument for "keeping rural incomes low"; the Green Revolution in the Punjab happened at a time of massive U.S. food aid under
Public Law 480. But although it is the commentator's job to question
and raise doubts, in the face of such an original and significant contribution it would be wrong to conclude on a note of perhaps marginal
doubt rather than enthusiastic acclaim. In particular, Adelman shows
convincingly that history is not, as Henry Ford said, "bunk" but is with
us today and shapes the future.

Revisiting the Challenge
of Development

Vinod Thomas

THE DECADE OF THE 1990S was a dizzying period in development. One group of developing countries in East Asia experienced the fastest growth rates and then the sharpest declines. Free-market policies received both their strongest endorsement ever and a harsh indictment. The decade recapitulated many of the experiences of the past 50 years of development, yielding lessons of successful development approaches and cautionary tales to guide actions into the next century.

Assessing Progress

At the beginning of the decade *World Development Report 1990: Poverty* (World Bank 1990) recommended a twofold strategy for reducing poverty: broadly based growth combined with improved access to social services. *World Development Report 1992: Development and the Environment* (World Bank 1992) advocated another twofold strategy for sustainable development—reinforcing the positive links between development and protection of the environment, and breaking the negative links between economic growth and the environment.

Looking at 40 years of development experience, *World Development Report 1991: The Challenge of Development* (World Bank 1991) summed up the actions that differentiated high performers (measured by growth and social progress) from poor performers and that contributed to the success of East Asia, the setbacks in Sub-Saharan Africa, and the modest gains elsewhere in the developing world. On the basis of that record, it articulated an emerging consensus on a market-friendly approach to development, calling for a reappraisal of the roles of the state and the market. The state, said the report, has a crucial role in supporting, but not necessarily carrying out, key functions in which the private sector typically underinvests—provision of basic education, poverty reduction, environmental protection, establishment of a legal framework, and strengthening of the financial system. The report identified common behaviors engaged in by successful performers:

- Investing in people, through education and health care
- Improving market functioning, competition, and the climate for enterprise
- Opening economies to international trade and investment
- Getting macroeconomic policy right
- Blending government actions and market liberalization for maximum effect.

Development Outcomes

Development has to do with people's well-being, quality of life, and natural environment. It needs to be inclusive, mindful of future generations and the earth they will inherit. Development strategy has to engage people if it is to succeed over time. Measures of development must therefore include more than economic growth rates. The quality, dispersion, composition, and sustainability of that growth are just as important.[1]

Growth of gross domestic product (GDP) per capita has often been used as a proxy for social advance and sustainable progress in living standards, in part because social progress is associated with GDP growth and in part for expediency (GDP growth rates are relatively easy to quantify).[2] Today we know that reliance on GDP as the sole measure of welfare is limiting and misleading. Additional, multidimensional measures are needed, including indexes of human development and of natural resources and environmental sustainability.[3]

People value at least three dimensions of life over future as well as current time periods. They gain direct satisfaction from education and other stocks of human resources such as life expectancy or literacy (labeled H below), from stocks of natural resources such as clean air and clean water (N), and from flows of consumption goods such as food and shelter (C). They also care about the welfare of future generations and their enjoyment of all these aspects of life (at some discount rate). A society will try to get the most out of these dimensions, subject to the total resource constraint. The three dimensions, H, N, and C, are interrelated simultaneously. Together, increases in these dimensions signify development.

Each of these dimensions, as related to welfare, might be set out in reduced form as follows:

$$\dot{H} = \dot{h}(H_0, P_H; \dot{N}, \dot{C})$$
$$\dot{N} = \dot{n}(N_0, P_N; \dot{H}, \dot{C})$$
$$\dot{C} = \dot{c}(C_0, P_M, P_O, P_F, G; \dot{H}, \dot{N})$$

$\dot{H}$, $\dot{N}$, and $\dot{C}$ denote changes in human development, natural capital, and physical consumption (or gross national product, GNP). The dot indicates the percentage change in the variable; the subscript 0 indicates the initial level. P denotes policy variables such as macroeconomic policy (P_M), trade openness (P_O), financial depth (P_F), social spending (P_H), and environmental action (P_N). G denotes governance.

Ideally, we would start to assess development outcomes using measures of human and environmental progress and only then turn to intermediate indicators such as GNP or GDP growth. But because we lack the high-quality data needed to construct robust indicators of human and environmental progress, we still have to rely heavily on GNP and GDP. In this study we look at two sets of indicators relating to human development and environmental sustainability, along with GDP growth. Future work should move the discussion toward more direct consideration of other dimensions, including cultural well-being.

Looking at the three sets of indicators together is reassuring in some ways: it suggests that GDP growth is positively linked with indicators of human development and social progress. However, the correlations are often not statistically significant (see Table 1). The weak correlation between GDP growth and social progress may be partly attributable to the problems of measuring the quality and distribution of education and health status, but it reinforces the argument for including social indicators directly in measures of development.

Also supporting a broadening of the measurement of development is the finding that GDP growth is negatively linked with indicators of environmental sustainability (changes in carbon dioxide emissions and in forest cover). This finding is robust and is supported by data on other environmental indexes, such as particulate and sulfur dioxide emissions. Preliminary econometric analysis confirms the associations noted here.

The gains in human development over the past four decades have been enormous in some areas, such as infant mortality and adult literacy. The record in poverty reduction is spottier (Figure 1). Even worse is the record in environmental sustainability, as measured by trends in deforestation and emissions of carbon dioxide (Figure 2).

The developing world has seen steady progress in GDP growth in the three decades since 1965, and the average income gap between developing and high-income countries has been modestly reduced. Within the developing world, however, there have been marked differences, from the spectacular successes in East Asia to gloomier outcomes elsewhere (Figure 3). How growth rates are compared affects the outcomes. When growth rates are weighted by income levels, the decade of the 1980s is a lost decade for much of the world. The picture is more positive when growth rates are weighted by population because the losses among middle-income countries, especially in Latin America, weigh less and the gains in the larger low-income countries, China and India,

Table 1. Relations among Three Measures of Development, 1980–96

| | Human development | | | | Income growth (growth of GDP) | Environmental sustainability | | |
	Decrease in poverty	Increase in literacy	Decrease in infant mortality	Decrease in gender gap		Decrease in carbon dioxide emissions	Increase in forest cover	Decrease in water pollution
Human development								
Decrease in poverty	1	-0.24 0.25 25	0.36 0.07 25	-0.50 0.14 10	0.37 0.07 26	-0.46 0.02 27	-0.06 0.78 27	-0.33 0.27 13
Increase in literacy		1	0.02 0.84 66	0.02 0.92 30	0.24 0.04 76	0.02 0.87 90	-0.23 0.03 90	-0.15 0.32 44
Decrease in infant mortality			1	-0.12 0.59 21	0.07 0.58 63	-0.23 0.06 68	-0.25 0.04 69	-0.14 0.40 37
Decrease in gender gap				1	-0.02 0.90 29	0.18 0.32 31	0.00 0.99 28	-0.11 0.71 15

	Growth of GDP	Decrease in carbon dioxide emissions	Increase in forest cover	Decrease in water pollution
Income growth				
Growth of GDP	1	**-0.64**	-0.09	0.18
		0.00	0.45	0.25
		81	82	42
Environmental sustainability				
Decrease in carbon dioxide emissions		1	**0.22**	0.03
			0.04	0.82
			87	47
Increase in forest cover			1	-0.03
				0.82
				52
Decrease in water pollution				1

Note: The three values in each cell are the correlation coefficient, the significance level, and the number of countries. Entries in bold are significant at 10 percent or better.

Source: World Bank, *World Development Indicators 1998;* author's computations.

Figure 1. Poverty Gap Index, by Region, 1987, 1990, and 1993

Percentage of poverty line

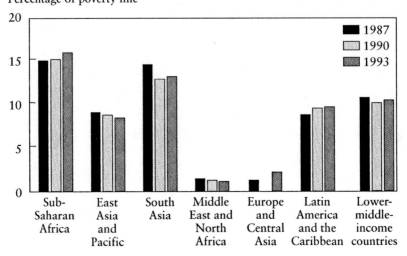

Source: Ravallion and Chen (1997).

Figure 2. Carbon Dioxide Emissions Per Capita, by Region, 1980 and 1995

Metric tons per capita

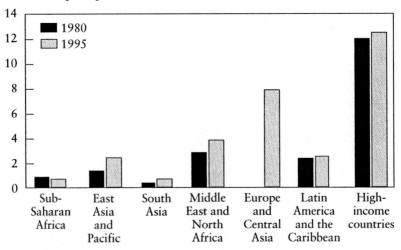

Source: World Bank data.

Figure 3. Growth of Average Income, Selected Countries, 1980–96

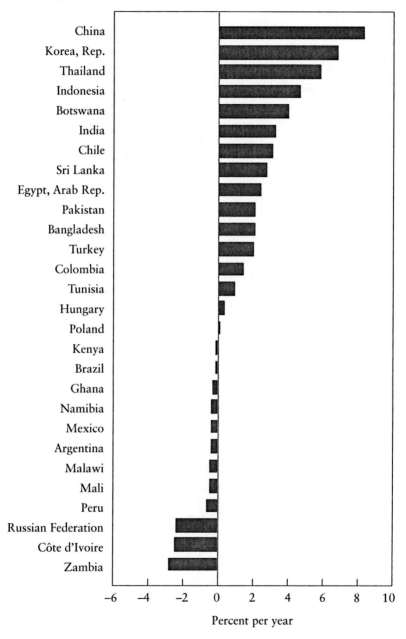

Note: Income is GDP per capita in purchasing power parity (PPP) terms, constant 1987 international dollars.

Source: World Bank data.

Table 2. Development Outcomes, by Growth Class

		Unweighted means		
Indicator	Period	High growth	Moderate or improved growth	Low growth
Number of countries		6	29	52
Poverty (percentage of	1990s	19.3	35.8	35.1
population living on	1980s	23.2	38.1	31.8
less than US$1 a day)				
Infant mortality (per	1990s	41.2	74.7	94.3
thousand live births)	1980s	62.5	83.9	124.9
Illiteracy (percent)	1990s	17.9	28.0	31.8
	1980s	24.8	33.2	42.5
Life expectancy (years)	1990s	67.9	62.2	59.4
	1980s	63.7	59.0	57.4
Income inequality	1990s	39.2	42.8	41.8
(Gini coefficient)	1980s	38.3	43.8	41.3
GDP growth (percent	1990s	7.5	4.8	0.7
per year)	1980s	7.1	2.0	2.4
Capital stock growth	1990s	9.4	2.4	2.0
(percent per year)	1980s	8.4	3.0	3.9
Growth of total factor pro-	1990s	2.9	1.6	−1.2
ductivity (percent per year)	1980s	1.9	−1.4	−0.7
Inflation, as measured by	1990s	7.8	40.8	174.6
consumer price index	1980s	7.1	173.6	43.9
(percent per year)				
Carbon dioxide emissions	1990s	3.1	1.9	2.0
(tons carbon per capita)	1980s	1.8	1.9	1.7
Deforestation (percent per year)	1990–95	1.1	1.2	0.9
Water pollution (kg of organic	1990s	0.16	0.18	0.20
water pollutants per worker				
per day)	1980s	0.17	0.22	0.22

Note: See text for details regarding country classification. Some variables are missing for some of the countries. In particular, poverty data are available for only a small number of countries.
Source: Various sources; author's computations.

weigh more. In the 1990s the growth rates of rich and poor countries converged, as growth rates improved in the middle-income countries of Latin America.

The same results can be seen in a different way by classifying developing countries in three groups: countries with high growth (more than 5 percent a year) in both the 1980s and the 1990s; those with moderate growth (between 4 and 5 percent in both decades) or improved growth (at least 2 percentage points a year higher in the 1990s than in the 1980s); and those with low or declining growth (see Table 2). Human development indicators improved generally, with the best performance among countries with better growth performance. Indicators of environmental sustainability show a mixed picture: the faster-growing groups have higher levels of carbon dioxide emissions per capita and higher deforestation rates but slightly lower levels of water pollution.

Market-Friendly Policies and Institutions

The policy measures needed to create a market-friendly approach to development were long resisted by a number of developing countries, and some policies remain politically contentious. Many developing countries, however, made efforts to follow them in the 1990s.

Investing in People. No country has achieved sustained development without investing substantially and efficiently in education and health. Developing countries have been spending increasing shares of public resources on social services (Figures 4 and 5), even protecting social service spending during periods of stabilization and fiscal austerity. Private spending on social services has been important in some regions, especially in East Asia, where the private share of total spending rose with economic growth. Public spending is more important in low-income Sub-Saharan Africa and South Asia. But whether public spending pro-

Figure 4. Expenditures on Education, by Region, Selected Years, 1980–94

Percentage of GNP

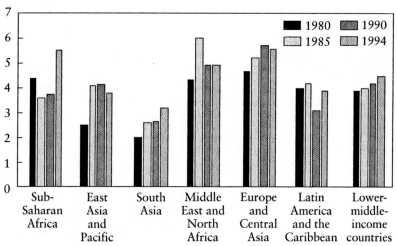

Note: Data are medians.
Source: World Bank, *World Development Indicators* (various years).

Figure 5. Expenditures on Health, by Region, 1990–95

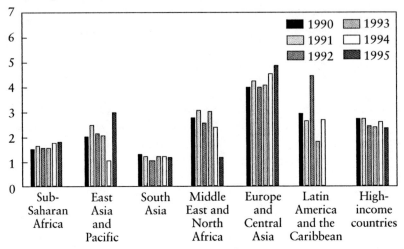

Percentage of GNP

Note: Data are medians.
Source: World Bank, *World Development Indicators* (various years).

duces good outcomes depends on its distribution and quality and on the incentives for increased private spending.

Openness and Competition. By any measure (price differences, volumes of trade and capital flows, or control regime), developing countries were more open in the 1990s. The ratio of trade to GDP rose in all developing regions, while average tariffs on manufactures fell following the Uruguay Round of trade negotiations (Figure 6). Openness to capital flows also increased in the 1990s—dramatically so in some regions. An index of financial controls shows a sharp decline in the 1990s, following a sharp increase in the previous decade.

Liberalization of domestic markets has also taken hold, as governments have become more willing to rely on markets and more aware of the need to attend to incentives for private initiatives. Governments are privatizing state-owned industries (Figure 7), putting public services to tender, deregulating utilities, and lifting other restraints on marketing and distribution. Many African countries that are exporters of primary commodities are liberalizing control boards and other institutional arrangements, permitting greater pass-through of international commodity prices to producers (Akiyama 1995).

Figure 6. Average Tariffs on Manufactures, by Region of Origin, before and after the Uruguay Round

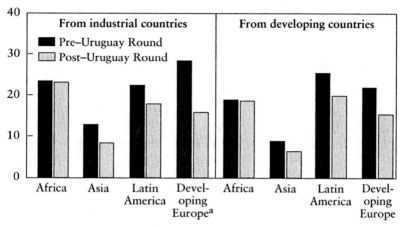

a. Low- and middle-income countries in Europe and central Asia.
Source: Development Economics Prospects Group, World Bank.

Figure 7. Privatization Trends, by Country Group, 1990–97

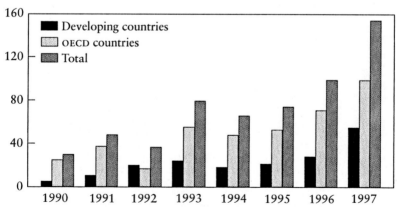

Source: OECD (various issues).

Macroeconomic Stability. Policies of openness and competition are closely related to macroeconomic stability. An indicator that captures their interaction is the parallel market premium for foreign exchange, which showed a sharp decline in the 1990s, even disappearing in most countries (Figure 8). Government deficits also declined steeply in most regions, with the exception of Europe and Central Asia, after sharp increases in the 1980s (Figure 9). Partly as a result, inflation declined in most developing countries.

Environmental Policies. An area of relative policy neglect is environmental management. There are no standard measures for evaluating the sustainability of a country's environmental policies. New indicators such as genuine saving, which measures the rate of saving after accounting for investments in human capital, depreciation of produced assets, and depletion and degradation of the environment, are still used only rarely and are available for only a handful of countries (World Bank 1999: 110). For this discussion, we seek to obtain a rough sense of countries' environmental commitment as evidenced by such actions as completion of a national environmental profile and formulation of

Figure 8. Parallel Market Premium, by Region, Selected Years, 1966–96

Percent

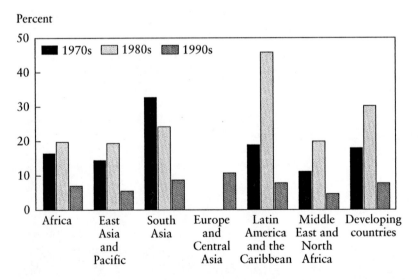

Note: The quantity plotted is (parallel market rate/official rate – 1) as a percentage for a unit of foreign currency in local currency units. Data are not available for all regions.

Source: Easterly and Yu (2000); World Bank, *World Development Indicators 2000.*

Figure 9. Overall Government Budget Balance, 1970–95

Percentage of GDP

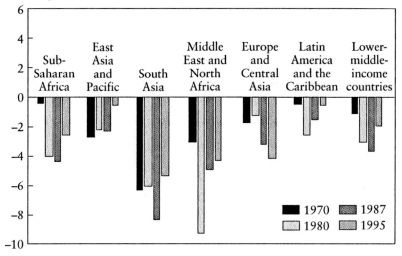

Note: Data are medians.
Source: World Bank, *World Development Indicators* (1997, 1998, 1999).

conservation and biodiversity strategies. Countries' commitment to issues of international environmental concern is gauged by participation in global efforts and the signing of treaties. These measures appear to be only weakly related to environmental outcomes. We need better ways of capturing the connections between countries' policies and environmentally sustainable development.

Missing Ingredients. We have seen that the developing world continued to make measurable progress in the 1990s, reducing trade and investment barriers, dismantling domestic price controls in agriculture and industry, reducing fiscal deficits, and investing in education and health (Table 3). Both the experience of the 1990s and the longer-term record show that these actions are associated with rapid economic growth. They also confirm the positive link between economic growth and poverty reduction. Application of these policies that boost economic growth is thus validated as a key element in the fight against poverty.

But the record also suggests that the positive actions, by government and others, which affect the quality and sustainability of growth have lagged seriously behind the liberalization measures. The imbalance can be linked not only to emphasis and capacity in country policymaking but also to the focus and advice of external agencies.

Table 3. Policy Performance, by Growth Class

| | | Unweighted means | | |
Indicator	Period (except as specified)	High growth	Moderate or improved growth	Low growth
Number of countries		6	29	52
Budget surplus (percentage of GDP)	1990s	−0.5	−1.2	−3.6
	1980s	−3.5	−4.7	−4.2
Effective tariff rate (percent)	1990s	24.8	30.0	18.5
	1980s	31.2	31.7	22.8
Trade as a share of GDP (percent)	1990s	26.2	22.9	19.2
	1980s	22.5	38.1	23.6
Capital account openness (index)	1996	2.5	3.0	2.9
	1988	2.0	1.9	1.6
Financial repression (index)	1996	3.8	3.0	3.8
	1973	5.4	6.8	5.8
M_2 as a share of GDP (percent)	1990s	60.2	34.7	27.9
	1980s	43.2	35.9	27.2
Bureaucratic efficiency (index)		1.6	1.3	1.5
Education spending (percentage of GDP)	1990s	3.5	3.8	4.2
	1980s	3.5	3.9	4.0
Health spending (percentage of GDP)	1990s	1.3	2.4	2.5
	1980s	1.4	2.7	2.4
Access to sanitation (percentage of population)	1990s	69.6	56.7	56.2
	1980s	54.3	50.2	44.7
Access to safe water (percentage of population)	1990s	80.7	64.7	60.1
	1980s	64.2	53.2	53.9
Environmental action (0–1 index)	International	1.00	0.96	0.88
	Domestic	0.83	0.81	0.76

Note: See text for details regarding country classification. Some variables are missing for some of the countries. In particular, the following variables are available for only a small number of countries: effective tariff rate, financial repression, and bureaucratic efficiency index.

Source: Various sources; author's computations.

These missing ingredients for development are the subject of the rest of this chapter.

In many parts of the world, social upheaval, civil strife, political unrest, and wars continued to derail progress in the 1990s. Although these events are not discussed here, their effects on development outcomes are all too apparent. Nearly two dozen countries, with half a billion people, were not even included in the analysis because of their highly unstable sociopolitical conditions. About one fifth of the developing world's population is living in conflict or postconflict conditions. Afghanistan, Iran, Iraq, Nigeria, Sierra Leone, Sudan, and Yugoslavia are just a few of the countries whose fortunes in the past two decades have been dominated more by sociopolitical crises than by economic policies.

Global and cross-border issues—capital flows, population pressures, labor migration, and environmental crises—continued to affect domestic outcomes. The number of people in the world will rise from 6 billion today to nearly 8 billion in 2025, even using a scenario with a low population growth rate of 1.5 percent. Despite progress in slowing population growth, many countries face large increases in population that undermine efforts to achieve sustainable development. Global warming, environmental degradation, and loss of biodiversity continue to worsen as a growing population strains limited global resources. These global pressures, while important for understanding country outcomes, are not assessed in this paper.

Underemphasized Lessons

What do the development outcomes for the countries examined tell us? Perhaps most important, the quality and sustainability of growth have been inadequate for making a fundamental difference in poverty reduction. In addition, rapid growth has frequently been associated with environmental degradation.

The achievement of growth that has a sustained impact on poverty and that is environmentally sustainable requires more than the standard set of policy prescriptions. It also requires the integration of positive actions into the foundations of market-friendly policies, not by governments alone but by other stakeholders as well. We can now see that over the past two decades a large number of countries followed a market-friendly approach in part, relying on a fairly standard set of policies that prominently featured trade liberalization and domestic deregulation. Another important set of actions was relatively neglected, and these now need attention to achieve the kinds of development outcome that really improve people's lives. Four areas seem especially critical and require action.

Investing in people. Access to social services is not adequate. The quality of education and its distribution (for example, access for girls and for the poor) need attention as population growth puts pressure on limited services. Supportive labor market policies and social protection are also needed. Governments have a crucial role in ensuring the quality and equitable distribution of social services (although not necessarily in providing them) and in promoting better utilization of the human capital of the poor through attention to the distribution of land and other assets essential for realizing the full benefits of better education and health.

Environmental management. Environmental degradation has worsened as a consequence of continuing poverty, increasing population pressure, and economic growth without regard for environmental consequences. The costs of environmental pollution and overexploitation of resources are enormous, and the losses are in some cases irretrievable. Few countries have actually taken explicit steps to confront the underlying causes of environmental and resource degradation, which include market failure, lack of information, and incentive problems of agents. Growth does not have to come at the expense of the environment. Better policies and a stronger combination of incentives, investments, and institutions can make environmentally sustainable growth a reality.

Managing financial risks. Global financial integration has undeniable benefits, but it has also made developing countries more vulnerable to sudden swings in investor sentiment, to capital flight, and to risks to the real sector. Internationally agreed standards and codes of good practice must be put in place to afford fiscal transparency, banking regulation, and corporate governance. Market-based instruments for managing risks are also important. Countries need to be cautious when opening up their capital accounts; they should guard against special incentives for short-term flows and should ensure that policy options, including reserve requirements and taxation of short-term flows, have been considered.

Securing good governance. Corruption is more than a matter of fairness or morality; it entails heavy social costs. Bad economic policies, weak legal frameworks, too many or the wrong kinds of regulations, too much regulatory discretion, and lack of professionalism all feed corruption. Civil liberties and the kind of political system matter enormously for governance and development. "Liberties appear to be strongly and positively associated with measures of welfare improvements," concluded *World Development Report 1991* (World Bank 1991: 50). Active civil societies, strong public oversight, and swift correction of policy distortions are crucial.

Investing in People

Over the past two decades, developing countries have increased the share of public resources spent on health and education services. Comparisons across countries, however, reveal little relationship between public spending on education or health and outcomes in these sectors, once country income levels are taken into account. In part, these findings reflect the limitations of cross-country averages. More important, they highlight two other related factors: outcomes depend in part on the quality of services and on the composition and allocation of spending (see Filmer, Hammer, and Pritchett 1998).

The quality of social services varies widely. In education such differences show up in a broad range of variables, from repetition and dropout rates to student scores on internationally comparable tests. For example, primary and secondary repeat rates are much lower in East Asia than in other developing countries at similar income levels. In the Republic of Korea dropout and repetition rates are extremely low, in part because of an automatic promotion system at all levels, while elimination of entrance examinations for middle school and high school ensures near-universal access (Thomas and Wang 1997a).

The distribution of services also varies greatly. For example, unequal distribution of education tends to have a negative impact on per capita income in most countries, after controlling for labor and physical capital (López, Thomas, and Wang 1998). A more equitable distribution contributes to higher income levels, with strong feedback effects on education demand and supply, the quality of education, and the outcome.

Improvement of distribution may even need to take precedence over quality improvements, at least until coverage is universal. López, Thomas, and Wang estimated Gini coefficients of educational attainment for 20 countries and found significant differences between rich and poor in the distribution of education.[4] Korea achieved the fastest expansion in education coverage and the most rapid reduction in its education Gini coefficient. (A lower coefficient indicates greater equality.) Education Gini coefficients for India and Pakistan are relatively high and have increased since 1980. India had an income Gini coefficient in 1992 similar to Korea's in 1988, implying that India's education distribution is much more skewed than its income distribution. The reverse has been true for Korea since the late 1980s.[5] China's income Gini coefficient was low in 1981 but rose in 1995, while its education Gini fell during the same period (Figure 10).

Although it might seem that the expansion of education would be uneven as a country reduces illiteracy from 60 to 20 percent or less, so that the education Gini would worsen before improving (similar to the Kuznets curve for income), country experience suggests the opposite. Argentina and Chile, for example, have had low education Gini coefficients throughout the period from the 1970s to the 1990s. Korea and many other countries have achieved substantial declines in the education Gini without any increases at the beginning. Only a few countries, including Algeria, India, Pakistan, and Tunisia, have seen a significant worsening of the education Gini. Thus, a worsening education distribution may not be an inevitable stage of the development process.

Figure 10. Gini Coefficients of Education, Selected Countries, 1970–95

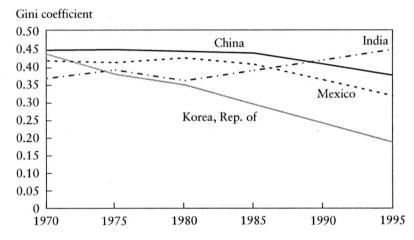

Note: A lower education Gini indicates greater equality.
Source: López, Thomas, and Wang (1998).

In addition to the links between the quality and distribution of social services and their impact, there is another link between economic policies and impact, especially for education. In a sample of 60 developing countries during 1965–87 (later updated to 1994), economic growth rates were especially high in countries with high levels of both education and macroeconomic stability and openness (World Bank 1991). The impact of trade openness on long-term growth thus depends on how well people are able to absorb and use the information and technology made available through trade and foreign investment. Similarly, Thomas and Wang (1997a) analyzed a sample of 1,265 World Bank projects and found that the rate of return was 3 percentage points higher in countries with both a more educated labor force and a more open economy than in countries that had only one or the other (Figure 11).[6] In a sample of 12 countries López, Thomas, and Wang (1998) found that a more educated labor force is associated with accelerated growth under conditions of market reform and an outward-oriented economic structure but that education has no significant impact on growth in the absence of these factors.

Managing the Environment

Many countries have taken a "grow first, clean up later" approach, arguing that they can ill afford to divert resources for environmental

Figure 11. Education, Openness, and Economic Rates
of Return of 1,265 World Bank Projects

Economic rate of return (percent)

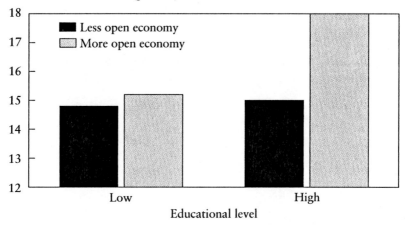

Low   High

Educational level

Note: Economic rates of return are from the evaluation database of the World
Bank's Operations Evaluation Department. Education is measured by the average level
of schooling of the labor force and openness by the logarithm of the foreign exchange
parallel-market premium.
    Source: Thomas and Wang (1997a).

protection. Now, evidence is flooding in from all parts of the world
showing that the rapid growth rates of the 1990s led to unprecedented
deforestation and environmental degradation and are not sustainable.
"Grow first, clean up later" is proving a costly strategy, socially and
ecologically, and a threat to the sustainability of growth itself. And
some environmental losses (in biodiversity and in human health, for
example) are irreversible, so that "clean up later" is foreclosed as an
option.

Environmental degradation can occur in both fast- and slow-growing economies (Table 4). East Asia's environmental record stands in
sharp contrast to its record of economic growth and poverty reduction.
In the past quarter-century incomes in East Asia grew 5 percent a year.
Poverty fell sharply—as much as 50 to 70 percent in Indonesia, Malaysia, and Thailand (Johansen 1993)—but environmental degradation
(pollution, congestion, deforestation, and loss of biodiversity) surpassed
that in all other regions in the world. About 20 percent of vegetated
land in East Asia suffers from soil degradation as a result of waterlog-
ging, erosion, and overgrazing. Biodiversity in 50 to 75 percent of coast-
lines and protected marine areas is classified as highly threatened. In

Table 4. Trade, Growth, Poverty, and the Environment
(percent, unless otherwise indicated)

Economy	Trade (annual growth of volume of merchandise exports), 1980–94	Growth (annual growth of GNP per capita), 1970–95	Poverty (population living on less than US$1 a day, PPP), various years[a]	Environment Annual deforest-ation (percentage change), 1981–90	Environment Total increase in carbon dioxide emissions, 1980–92
East Asia					
China	12.2	6.9	29.4 (1993)	0.7	79.2
Hong Kong	15.4	5.7	< 1	–0.5	81.3
Indonesia	9.9	4.7	14.5 (1993)	1.1	94.7
Korea, Rep. of	11.9	10.0	< 1	0.1	130.2
Malaysia	13.3	4.0	5.6 (1989)	2.1	150.0
Philippines	5.0	0.6	27.5 (1988)	3.4	35.1
Singapore	13.3	5.7	< 1	2.3	66.7
Thailand	16.4	5.2	< 1	3.5	180.0
Average	12.2	5.4	n.a.	1.6	85.6
Latin America					
Argentina	1.9	–0.4	—	0.1	9.3
Bolivia	–0.3	–0.7	7.1 (1990)	1.2	40.0
Brazil	6.2	—	28.7 (1989)	0.6	17.9
Chile	7.3	1.8	15.0 (1992)	–0.1	29.6
Costa Rica	6.6	0.7	18.9 (1989)	3.0	100.0
Mexico	13.0	0.9	14.9 (1992)	1.3	28.1
Peru	2.4	–1.1	49.4 (1994)	0.4	–8.3
Uruguay	0.9	0.2	—	–0.6	–16.7
Venezuela	1.1	–1.1	11.8 (1991)	1.2	28.9
Average	4.0	–0.1	n.a.	0.5	21.2

— Not available.

n.a. Not applicable.

a. PPP, purchasing power parity. The international poverty line is from World Bank, *World Development Indicators 1997*. Individual studies may give different estimates for the same country.

Sources: World Bank (1997a); Thomas and Wang (1997b).

countries that started liberalizing and growing rapidly in the 1980s, such as China, Malaysia, and Thailand, carbon dioxide emissions tripled.

But it is not only fast-growing countries that have experienced extensive environmental losses. Central America—where growth has been slow and poverty levels have remained stubbornly high—has also experienced extensive deforestation, soil degradation, overfishing, and coastal water pollution.[7]

Although rapid growth cannot itself be blamed for environmental degradation, it is not an automatic ally of the environment (Thomas and Belt 1997). Faster rates of growth tend to have a negative effect on the environment because of such accompanying factors as industrial expansion, urbanization, and increased exploitation of renewable and nonrenewable resources. At the same time, however, growth creates conditions for environmental improvement by raising the demand for better environmental quality and by making available the resources to supply it. Thus, the net effect could go either way.[8]

Experience argues against the "grow first, clean up later" approach. The health costs of delayed pollution control can exceed the costs of prevention. For example, the costs of cleanup and of compensation to the victims of itai-itai disease and yokkaichi asthma in Minamata, Japan, as a result of industrial mercury poisoning since the 1950s have ranged from 1.4 to 102 times the cost of up-front prevention (Kato 1996). Some damage, such as loss of terrestrial and aquatic biodiversity through habitat destruction, cannot ever be undone; in some areas, for example, pollution and destructive fishing techniques have damaged coral reefs, destroying or threatening to destroy animal and plant life that depends on complex coral reef ecosystems.

It is the poor and disadvantaged who bear the brunt of environmental pollution and resource degradation, whereas the rich are often responsible for the misuse. Deforestation is related to unsustainable timber extraction by large commercial logging companies, but it is poor indigenous communities whose sources of fuelwood, fodder, medicinal plants, and other forest products disappear. When water quality is degraded by industrial toxic effluents and pollution, the poor suffer most because they often lack access to municipal water supplies or do not have the resources to invest in water filters and other purification systems. Both indoor and outdoor air pollution also disproportionately hurt the poor, who cannot afford to switch to cleaner fuels or to purchase air filters and who tend to live closer to roads, where pollution levels are highest (UNDP, *Human Development Report 1998*).

Experience also points up a hopeful lesson: there are opportunities to promote a better environment that have not yet been fully exploited. Scarce resources can be put to multiple and sustainable high-return uses. In Latin America forests can be protected for their higher social value instead of being converted to ranches that generate negative social returns (Kishor and Constantino 1994). Management of tropical forests for such multiple uses as timber, nontimber goods, water and soil conservation, biological diversity, and other environmental services can yield high social returns while generating steady revenues.

The impacts of environmental degradation are not confined within political boundaries, as is becoming increasingly obvious in the cases of acid rain, global climate change, and such transboundary issues as polluted rivers. Although individual neglect of the environment may be tolerated by the ecosystem, persistent collective neglect can threaten global ecosystems and humanity itself—a powerful argument for promoting environmentally sustainable growth.

One key to reversing environmental degradation is to tax the activities that cause it. It is possible to use taxation to promote both environmental management and growth. Taxing the use of coal as fuel, for example, could make solar energy more economically competitive, reduce emissions, and increase revenues. The revenues can be used to scale down other distortionary taxes in the economy that are slowing growth. Similarly, taxing auto emissions makes cleaner forms of transport more attractive (Brown and Flavin 1999).

A switch from income to consumption taxes can have beneficial impacts on the environment and on growth. The production and consumption of luxury goods often make heavy demands on environmental resources. Consumption taxes would help to protect the environment by curbing the consumption of these goods. Steeply progressive consumption taxes would also promote equity and, by encouraging savings, would promote overall economic growth (Frank 1998).

Rapidly growing economies that ignored the environment have learned these lessons the hard way, and some are now being forced to take costly corrective actions. In the United States it will take hundreds of millions of dollars to remedy the damage done to the Everglades by shortsighted irrigation projects to aid sugarcane cultivation.[9] Economies embarking on a path of sustainable development still have time to incorporate environmental policies directly into their economic planning strategies.

Consider the alternative growth paths illustrated in Figure 12. An economy that values the environment will seek to balance accelerated growth with environmental quality by moving along *AD*. If the economy adopts a "grow now, clean up later" approach, it will go from *A* to *C*, with considerable environmental deterioration (China, Indonesia, and Thailand are examples). Or—a worse option—it may follow policies that yield slow growth and considerable environmental damage, moving from *A* to *B* (as has been the case in several countries in Central America and in Africa).

The economies represented by points *B* and *C* will incur serious losses related to ecosystem damage, including disease and death, degradation of forests and water bodies, and air pollution. Figure 12 suggests that economies at *C* can afford to improve their environmental management and move toward *D*, while those at *A* or *B* should strive to both raise the growth rate and improve the environment.[10] The costs of cleanup are likely to be much higher than the costs of prevention, and many losses are irreversible.

Figure 12. Alternative Growth Paths and Environmental Quality

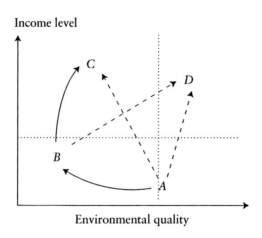

Managing Financial Risks

The expansion of international financial markets in the 1990s has been phenomenal: the value of financial transactions is more than five times that of world trade in goods and services. This increase in capital mobility in relation to world GDP means that disruptions in the financial system have far-reaching implications for development. Financial globalization in the 1990s has been characterized by vulnerability to liquidity and currency crises, as illustrated by the events in Mexico in 1994–95, Asia (Indonesia, Rep. of Korea, Malaysia, the Philippines, and Thailand) in 1997, and Brazil and Russia in 1998. This volatility has produced large welfare losses that have especially hurt the poor. Managing risks and balancing the benefits and costs of globalization are crucial concerns everywhere.

Risk Management. Fluctuations in investor confidence and capital flows present challenges that require a combination of market and official solutions to provide risk management. Countries continue to promote policies that encourage access to international capital markets. To inspire the necessary market confidence, the right mix of regulation, oversight, transparency, and market discipline is required, at both the international and the country levels.

Many developing countries have been liberalizing their financial markets and relaxing their restrictions on capital transactions. These are the correct policies, but in the absence of adequate institutional and regulatory frameworks (both national and international) for money, foreign exchange, and capital markets, problems have emerged. As countries liberalized, they gained access to a broader menu of foreign financing, with strong new incentives for recourse to foreign finance. For example, longer-maturity foreign capital was especially attractive for funding infrastructure projects, particularly in countries with exchange rates pegged to the U.S. dollar.

With increased capital mobility came increased vulnerability to sudden changes in investor sentiment, along with associated fluctuations in the supply and price of foreign capital. There was also a shift from official to private sources of capital, and from government to private entities as the main recipients of foreign capital. Suddenly, developing countries found themselves with new credit relationships and a variety of sources of international private finance, with the private sector a key recipient of foreign capital.

Neither the maturity structure nor the foreign exchange risk associated with foreign capital was properly taken into account, however. As the recent crises exposed the increased vulnerability of financial markets, many developing countries began to question the benefits of closer integration with global capital markets. Some, such as Malaysia, are reverting to capital controls or, like India, are slowing their move toward capital account convertibility to insulate their economies from external financial shocks. The critical question is, what is the best way forward?

Experience over the past two decades confirms that macroeconomic stability is vital. We have seen, however, that it cannot guarantee sustainable growth in today's globalized financial environment. Low inflation and conservative balance of payments policies remain necessary for growth, but they will not ensure sustained development in the absence of adequate institutional infrastructure, well-functioning financial markets, and good governance structures. The answer is not to roll back liberalization; rather, it is to put in place complementary regulatory and institutional mechanisms at the national and international levels.

A common thread runs through most of the analysis of financial cycles: systemic weaknesses in the domestic financial sectors of developing countries and in the international finance system. Lack of transparency and unavailability of data tend to mask the true state of financial markets, obscuring market failure in the face of increased global capital mobility. At the international level, globalization of capital calls for an institutional framework that can ensure transparency of accounts, security of property rights, enforcement of contracts, and mechanisms for managing risk. At the national level, poor control of risks, lax enforcement, weak prudential rules, inadequate supervision, and government-directed lending practices lead to a lower quality of investments and require attention. Also needed is a coherent perspective on external liabilities: on their maturities, the types of borrowers, and the various forms of explicit and implicit guarantees assumed by the government.

Balancing Gains and Risks. The world is still coming to grips with globalization. One view attaches considerable importance to increased globalization in the belief that crises can be overcome through better regulatory and institutional frameworks and, if necessary, through assistance from international financial organizations. Another perspective sees the costs and risks of closer financial integration as being too high, in relation to the potential benefits, and supports tighter controls on cross-border financial movements. An emerging consensus takes the middle ground, favoring the simultaneous opening up of financial markets and the establishment of an appropriate regulatory framework, avoidance of giving special incentives, and, possibly, some restrictions on short-term capital flows.

Financial liberalization offers clear economic gains, but it carries risks as well. Among 24 countries that experienced financial crises, Williamson and Mahar (1998) found that 13 had liberalized their capital accounts within five years of the crisis. The study concluded that the risks can be much reduced by giving proper attention to regulation and supervision; by maintaining a ceiling on the deposit interest rate, at least until the liberalized system is well established; and by delaying and perhaps limiting capital account convertibility.

Policy instruments that are increasingly being considered include incentive-based regulations such as risk-related capital adequacy requirements, higher liquidity requirements, and entry taxes on short-term capital inflows or reserve requirements. More fundamentally, motivating the private sector to invest in better quality and in long-term efforts could make a big difference. It will be necessary to find more effective ways of responding to crises. A key move is to shore up the confidence of creditors and investors and their willingness to supply capital to a borrower or to roll over existing claims. The international policy response to the recent crisis points in the right direction: prompt extension of large stand-by loans and of direct loans to refinance maturing foreign exchange obligations and restore confidence.

Proposals to underwrite Asia's economic recovery have included government guarantees of private sector liabilities that could mean an unbalanced sharing of risk, with the public sector assuming the full burden of failed projects and nonperforming loans. Guarantees impose a contingent liability on the government, with implications for future taxes and the credibility of the guarantor in international markets. Official assistance through multilateral institutions can make a positive difference in this context.

Financial market liberalization has yielded enormous benefits through economic growth but has also brought about greater volatility and welfare losses, especially for the poor. Moving forward will require actions at the national and international levels. It will take stronger regulatory mechanisms, better supervisory standards, greater transparency of financial transactions, better risk-control mechanisms for preventing liquidity crises, and better risk-sharing mechanisms between creditors and borrowers in dealing with existing debt overhangs.

Combating Corruption

Although the government's role in development has been studied intently, good governance has only recently been emphasized as a key development issue. The social costs of lack of good governance have been noted (see Table 5), and the pervasive impact of corruption on development is increasingly being recognized.

Corruption reduces domestic and foreign investments, lowers tax revenues, and, by skewing the composition of public expenditure away from social services that are important to the poor, worsens income distribution and diverts resources from poverty reduction. Misgovernance and corruption have increased the fragility of financial sectors. All these factors have been linked to the crises in Asian countries and elsewhere in the 1990s.

Evidence from a large cross-section of countries shows that corruption has a significant negative impact on domestic investment, making a large effect on economic growth likely as well. Tanzi and Davoodi (1997) found that corruption increases the size of public investment because of the opportunities for manipulation by corrupt officials. Corruption may also reduce tax revenue because it compromises the government's ability to collect taxes and tariffs, although the net effect depends on how the nominal tax rate and other regulatory burdens were chosen by corruption-prone officials (Kaufmann and Wei 1998).

Table 5. Liberties and Development, 1973–87

Indicator	1	2	3	4	5
1 Growth in GDP	2.00	0.30	0.23	0.39	0.19*
2 Decline in infant mortality		1.00	0.41	0.71	0.59
3 Change in female education			1.00	0.48	0.28
4 Level of female education				1.00	0.63
5 Political and civil liberties					1.00

Note: Numbers are period averages for 68 countries. All correlation coefficients except the one marked with an asterisk (*) are statistically significant at (at least) 10 percent.

Source: World Bank (1991).

Where corruption prevails, the poor face higher taxes and receive lower levels of social services; infrastructure investments are biased against projects that aid the poor; and the ability to escape poverty using small-scale entrepreneurial means is impaired (Wei 1997). Gray and Kaufmann (1998) find, for example, that corrupt regimes often budget defense contracts at the expense of rural health clinics, a policy bias that worsens income distribution and diverts resources from the countryside to the cities.

Contributing Factors. Political rights (democratic elections, a legislature, and opposition parties) and civil liberties (free and independent media, freedom of assembly, and freedom of speech) are negatively correlated with corruption, with the correlations somewhat stronger for civil liberties (Kaufmann and Sachs 1998). Similarly, there is a significant negative association between the rule of law (protection of property rights, an independent judiciary, and judicial resolution of conflict) and corruption, but no claims are made about the direction of causality.

Policy distortions and controls, state ownership, excessive regulation of business, arbitrary application of regulations, heavy trade restrictions, and protectionist and anticompetition measures are associated with a higher incidence of corruption. So is monopolization within economies.

Civil service professionalism, as manifested in training, hiring, and promotion systems, is negatively associated with corruption. The evidence on civil service pay is more ambiguous; the less robust relationship suggests that salary alone is not the answer in the fight against corruption. Salary corrections need to be combined with meritocractic recruitment and promotion and the creation of a professional cadre of civil servants.

Income per capita and education, holding other factors constant, are negatively correlated with corruption. There are exceptions, however. It may be that general development variables are merely proxies for more specific determinants of corruption, such as the rule of law, the quality of public sector institutions, the administration of the tax regime, or the amount of regulation. Focusing on more specific determinants helps us understand why corruption may be uncommon in some emerging economies despite relatively low levels of income per capita. These findings suggest that there may not be an inevitable link between corruption and lower income levels.

New studies are beginning to explore regional and country-specific variations in the determinants of corruption. For example, evidence suggests that administrative bribery is more prevalent than other forms of corruption in formerly socialist economies, a consequence of their often bloated bureaucracies. In Latin America there has been considerable economic and regulatory reform but less reform of the judiciary and other institutions that affect the rule of law.

Responses to Corruption. What kind of anticorruption program is likely to have the greatest impact? We know the elements of such a program: an independent judiciary, rule of law, good institutional and public sector management, strong political and civil liberties, oversight and involvement by civil society, deregulation, tax and budgetary reform, and financial and procurement reforms. We are less certain about how to put them together to achieve the greatest impact.

Increasingly, the evidence suggests that civil liberties, participation, and institutional capacity are important for protection against corruption and for the achievement of broadly based development. Analysis of more than 1,500 World Bank–financed projects shows a consistent, statistically significant, and empirically large effect of civil liberties on the economic rate of return to projects. Thus, for example, an improvement from worst (7) to best (1) on the Freedom House index of civil liberties would raise the economic rate of return (ERR) by 7.5 percentage points. On the Humana index of civil liberties, an improvement from the worst rating (13) to one of the best (91, Costa Rica) would boost the ERR by 22.5 percentage points.[11]

The strong empirical relationship between the performance of economic and social projects and civil liberties is striking. Combining these results with those noted earlier on the negative link between corruption and civil liberties provides a strong argument at the micro level for a more comprehensive, integrated approach to development that considers institutions and their effects on corruption, as well as economic policies.

Conclusion

We have focused on four broad policy and institutional concerns: the distribution of human development, environmental sustainability, financial risk management, and governance. What they have in common is their effect on the quality and sustainability of development, as measured by all three forms of wealth—human, natural, and physical. These issues also put the spotlight on distribution, which encourages attention to poverty as well as environmental sustainability.

Two broad categories of development strategies were recommended at the beginning of the 1990s. Some actions, such as trade and price liberalization and improved fiscal management, were strongly urged and were generally implemented, although with large variations. Other actions were either not recommended strongly enough or were opposed by special interests. Among these neglected areas were construction of an effective regulatory framework, improvement of the quality and distribution of education and other assets, and attention to environmental protection, governance, civil liberties, and institutional reform.

The evidence brought together here offers little support for the inevitability or the wisdom of sequencing economic growth (as a Kuznets curve might imply) before attending to greater equality of human development, environmental sustainability, and regulatory or anticorruption measures. Sequencing—whether it be "liberalize first, regulate later," "privatize first, ensure competition later," "grow first, clean up later," or "grow first, seek liberties later"—is far too costly. Regulatory actions, environmental management, and anticorruption measures must go hand in hand with liberalization in order to manage financial risks, ensure predictability, and sustain results.

These dimensions need to be an integral part of the package of liberalization policies, not an additional burden tacked on to an already challenging list of tasks. The additional actions are not necessarily to be taken by governments, which already have an overloaded agenda; they require actions by other stakeholders as well. That implies a change in emphasis in the following directions:

• Actions promoting equality of opportunity along with growth, instead of one-sided efforts to maximize short-term growth rates. The implication is not necessarily that long-term growth should be slowed but, rather, that attention has to be given to equality, quality, and sustainability, as well as to growth-oriented actions.

• A focus on building regulatory frameworks for competition and efficiency, along with liberalization and privatization, in place of one-track efforts to maximize the pace of market liberalization. Legal, judicial, and anticorruption reforms deserve greater attention. Again, the idea is not necessarily to slow liberalization but to speed regulatory actions in tandem with liberalization.

• Efforts to nurture civil liberties, participatory processes, and capacity building to complement policy changes rather than try to get only the government side of policies right. The goal is not to move the focus away from government policies and improvement of government capacity but to expand the scope of attention to include consensus building in civil society along with concern for policy change.

Notes

This paper draws on a report written with Mansoor Dailami, Ashok Dhareshwar, Daniel Kaufmann, Nalin Kishor, and Yan Wang. The author thanks Cary Anne Cadman, Xibo Fan, Deon Filmer, Stanley Fischer, Jeffrey Hammer, Ramon López, Lant Pritchett, Martin Ravallion, and Thomas Sterner for their inputs.

1. Many earlier studies had addressed the issue of multidimensional development objectives, for example, Sengupta and Fox (1969); Hicks and Streeten (1979); Hughes-Hallet (1989). Some studies conducted multivariate analysis of a large number of economic, social, and political variables, for example, Adelman and Morris (1967); UNRISD (1970); Baster (1972); Morris (1979).

2. See, for example, studies on growth theories, such as Barro (1990); World Bank (1991); Easterly and others (1992); Mankiw, Romer, and Weil (1992); Young (1992); Fischer (1993); King and Rebelo (1998); Easterly (1999).

3. Many economists have constructed indexes of quality of life or human development, for example, Goodman and Markowitz (1952); Drewnowski and Scott (1966); McGranahan and others (1972); Smith (1973); Fine and Fine (1974); Ram (1982); Diewert (1986); Dasgupta (1990); Slottje (1991). The most widely used is the UNDP's Human Development Index, which started in the 1980s (see UNDP various years).

4. Gini coefficients for education are calculated in two steps. First, Lorenz curves similar to those for income are drawn, with the percentage of the population age 15 and older on the horizontal axis and the percentage of cumulative education on the vertical axis. The Gini coefficient for education is then calculated as the ratio of the area between the diagonal and the Lorenz curve divided by the total area of the half-square in which the curve lies. Education was measured by the proportions of population with no schooling and with primary, secondary, and tertiary education, respectively (López, Thomas, and Wang 1998).

5. Income Gini coefficients are available only for selected years.

	1975	1983	1990	1992
India	41.8	32.9	32	33.6

	1970	1988
Korea, Rep. of	33.3	33.6

The income Gini for India was calculated on the basis of data in the *World Development Reports*, various years, 1979–97. Korea's income Gini is from Ahuja and others (1997): 27.

6. The cross-country project-level data set includes variables on education, per capita income, openness, government expenditure, and project performance. The project data cover 3,590 lending projects in 109 countries evaluated by the World Bank's Operations Evaluation Department (OED) in 1974–94 and include the OED rating of overall performance (satisfactory or not satisfactory) and economic rates of return (Thomas and Wang 1997b).

7. Central American economies have grown slowly for a variety of economic and sociopolitical reasons. Most Central American economies have been dominated by traditional exports, which have faced declining terms of trade, and they have highly unequal income distribution and inadequate educational investment, exacerbated by political instability.

8. Where the data support an environmental Kuznets curve (an inverted-U-shaped curve between per capita levels of income and environmental degrada-

tion), it is important to establish the underlying reasons—the policy and legislative frameworks, the institutional capacity, and the available technological
options. Isolating the relative importance of these factors will yield important
insights into approaches to environmental management. (For a recent analysis
of water pollution, see Hemamala, Mani, and Wheeler 1998.)

9. The widespread practice of illegal dumping of toxic wastes by industrial
firms in the United States and the establishment of Superfund for their cleanup
is another telling illustration of the high and inequitable costs of adopting a
"grow now, clean up later" approach. (For a poignant account of the effects of
these toxins on human health in the vicinity of Boston, Mass., see Harr 1995.)

10. East Asia provides an interesting case. The recent economic crisis has
taken countries such as Thailand and Indonesia from *C* to *B*. Hence they have
the tough task of implementing policies that clean up the environment and
raise economic growth at the same time.

11. Freedom House reports are available at <http://www.freedomhouse.org/
ratings>.

References

Adelman, Irma, and Cynthia Taft Morris. 1967. *Society, Politics and Eco-
    nomic Development: A Quantitative Approach.* Baltimore, Md.: Johns
    Hopkins University Press.

Ahuja, Vinod, and others. 1997. *Everyone's Miracle? Revisiting Poverty and
    Inequality in East Asia.* Directions in Development series. Washington, D.C.:
    World Bank,

Akiyama, Takamasa. 1995. "Has Africa Turned the Corner?" International
    Economics Commodities and Policy Unit, World Bank, Washington, D.C.
    Processed.

Barro, Robert. 1990. *Macroeconomic Policy.* Cambridge, Mass.: Harvard
    University Press.

Baster, Nancy. 1972. "Development Indicators: An Introduction." *Journal of
    Development Studies* 8 (3, April): 1–20.

Brown, Lester R., and Christopher Flavin. 1999. "It's Getting Late to Switch
    to a Viable World Economy." *International Herald Tribune,* 19 January.

Dasgupta, Partha. 1990. "Well-Being in Poor Countries." *Economic and Po-
    litical Weekly* (India) 25 (August 4): 1713–20.

Diewert, W. E. 1986. "Index Numbers." University of British Columbia,
    Vancouver. Processed.

Drewnowski, Jan F., and Wolf Scott. 1966. "The Level of Living Index."
    UNRISD Report 4. United Nations Research Institute for Social Develop-
    ment, Geneva.

Easterly, William. 1999. "Life during Growth: International Evidence on Quality
    of Life and Per Capita Income." Policy Research Working Paper 2110. De-
    velopment Research Group, World Bank, Washington, D.C.

Easterly, William and Hairong Yu (2000). Global Development Network Growth Database. Available at http://www.gdnet.org/data.htm.

Easterly, William, Robert King, Ross Levine, and Sergio Rebelo. 1992. *How Do National Policies Affect Long-Run Growth? A Research Agenda*. World Bank Discussion Paper 164. Washington, D.C.

Filmer, Deon, Jeffrey Hammer, and Lant Pritchett. 1998. "Health Policy in Poor Countries: Weak Links in the Chain." Policy Research Working Paper 1874. Poverty and Human Resources, Development Research Group, World Bank, Washington, D.C.

Fine, Ben J., and Kit Fine. 1974a. "Social Choice and Individual Rankings: I." *Review of Economic Studies* 44 (July): 303–22.

———. 1974b. "Social Choice and Individual Rankings: II." *Review of Economic Studies* 44 (October): 459–75.

Fischer, Stanley. 1993. "The Role of Macroeconomic Factors in Growth." *Journal of Monetary Economics* 32 (3, December): 485–512.

Frank, Robert H. 1998. *Luxury Fever: Why Money Fails to Satisfy in an Era of Excess*. New York: Free Press.

Goodman, L. A., and H. Markowitz. 1952. "Social Welfare Functions Based on Individual Rankings." *American Journal of Sociology* 58.

Gray, Cheryl W., and Daniel Kaufmann. 1998. "Corruption and Development." *Finance and Development* 35 (1): 7–10.

Harr, Jonathan. 1995. *A Civil Action*. New York: Vintage Books.

Hemamala, Hettige, Muthukumara Mani, and David Wheeler. 1998. "Industrial Pollution in Economic Development (Kuznets Revisited)." Policy Research Working Paper 1876. Development Research Group, World Bank, Washington, D.C.

Hicks, Norman, and Paul Streeten. 1979. "Indicators of Development: The Search for a Basic Needs Yardstick." *World Development* 7 (6, June): 567–80.

Hughes-Hallet, A. J. 1989. "Econometrics and the Theory of Economic Policy: The Tinbergen-Theil Contributions 40 Years On." *Oxford Economic Papers* 41 (January): 189–214.

Johansen, Frida. 1993. *Poverty Reduction in East Asia: The Silent Revolution*. World Bank Discussion Paper 203. Washington, D.C.

Kato, Kazu. 1996. "Grow Now, Clean up Later? The Case of Japan." In Ismail Serageldin and Alfredo Sfeir-Younis, eds., *Effective Financing of Environmentally Sustainable Development: Proceedings of the Third Annual World Bank Conference on Environmentally Sustainable Development*. Environmentally Sustainable Development Proceedings Series 10. Washington, D.C.: World Bank.

Kaufmann, Daniel, and Jeffrey Sachs. 1998. "Determinants of Corruption." Harvard University. Processed.

Kaufmann, Daniel, and Shan-Jin Wei. 1998. "Does 'Grease Money' Speed up the Wheels of Commerce?" Paper presented at the meeting of the American Economic Association, Chicago, Ill.

King, Robert, and Sergio Rebelo. 1998. "Public Policy and Economic Growth: Developing Neoclassical Implications." *Journal of Political Economy* (5, part 2): S126–S144.

Kishor, Nalin M., and Luis Constantino. 1994. "Sustainable Forestry: Can It Compete?" *Finance and Development* 31 (December): 36–39.

López, Ramón, Vinod Thomas, and Yan Wang. 1998. "Addressing the Education Puzzle: The Distribution of Education and Economic Reform." Policy Research Working Paper 2031. Economic Development Institute, World Bank, Washington, D.C.

Mankiw, N. Gregory, David Romer, and David N. Weil. 1992. "A Contribution to the Empirics of Economic Growth." *Quarterly Journal of Economics* 105 (2, May): 407–37.

McGranahan, D. V., and others. 1972. *Contents and Measurement of Socio-Economic Development*. New York: Praeger.

Morris, M. D. 1979. *Measuring the Condition of the World's Poor: The Physical Quality of Life Index*. New York: Pergamon Press.

OECD (Organisation for Economic Co-operation and Development). Various issues. *Trends in International Finance*. Paris.

Ram, Rati. 1982. "Composite Indices of Physical Quality of Life, Basic Needs Fulfillment, and Income: A 'Principal Component' Representation." *Journal of Development Economics* 11 (October): 227–47.

Ravallion, Martin, and Shaohua Chen. 1997. "What Can New Survey Data Tell Us about Recent Changes in Distribution and Poverty?" *World Bank Economic Review* 11 (2, May): 357–82.

Sengupta, Jati K., and Karl A. Fox. 1969. *Economic Analysis and Operations Research: Optimization Techniques in Quantitative Economic Models*. Amsterdam: North-Holland.

Slottje, Daniel J. 1991. "Measuring the Quality of Life across Countries." *Review of Economics and Statistics* 73 (November): 684–93.

Smith, J. H. 1973. "Aggregation of Preferences with Variable Electorate." *Econometrica* 41 (November): 1027–41.

Tanzi, Vito, and Hamid Davoodi. 1997. "Corruption, Public Investment, and Growth." IMF Working Paper WP/97/139. International Monetary Fund, Washington, D.C.

Thomas, Vinod, and Tamara Belt. 1997. "Growth and Environment: Allies or Foes?" *Finance and Development* 34 (June): 22–24.

Thomas, Vinod, and Yan Wang. 1997a. "Education, Trade and Investment Returns." Working Paper. Economic Development Institute, World Bank. Washington, D.C.

———. 1997b. "Missing Lessons of East Asia: Openness, Education, and the Environment." Paper presented at the Annual Bank Conference on Development in Latin America and the Caribbean, June 29–July 1, Montevideo.

UNDP (United Nations Development Programme). Various years. *Human Development Report*. New York: Oxford University Press.

UNRISD (United Nations Research Institute for Social Development). 1970. "Studies in the Methodology of Social Planning." Geneva.

Wei, Shang-Jin. 1997. "How Taxing Is Corruption on International Investors?" NBER Working Paper 6030. National Bureau of Economic Research, Cambridge, Mass.

Williamson, John, and Molly Mahar. 1998. "A Survey of Financial Liberalization." *Essays in International Finance* 211. Princeton, N.J.: International Finance Section, Department of Economics, Princeton University.

World Bank. 1990. *World Development Report 1990: Poverty.* New York: Oxford University Press.

———. 1991. *World Development Report 1991: The Challenge of Development.* New York: Oxford University Press.

———. 1992. *World Development Report 1992: Development and the Environment.* New York: Oxford University Press.

———. 1995. *World Development Report 1995: Workers in an Integrating World.* New York: Oxford University Press.

———. 1997a. *Can the Environment Wait? Priorities for East Asia.* Washington, D.C.

———. 1997b. *World Development Report 1997: The State in a Changing World.* New York: Oxford University Press.

———. 1999. *World Development Report 1998/99: Knowledge for Development.* New York: Oxford University Press.

———. 2000. *World Development Report 1999/2000. Entering the 21st Century.* New York: Oxford University Press.

———. Various years. *World Development Indicators.* Washington, D.C.

Young, Alwyn. 1992. "Tale of Two Cities: Factor Accumulation and Technical Change in Hong Kong and Singapore." In Olivier J. Blanchard and Stanley Fischer, eds., *NBER Macroeconomics Annual,* 13–54. Cambridge, Mass.: MIT Press.

The Evolution of
Thinking about Poverty:
Exploring the Interactions

Ravi Kanbur and Lyn Squire

ERADICATING, OR AT LEAST REDUCING, poverty lies at the heart of development economics. Although development seeks to benefit all members of society, the poor demand our special attention. Any reasonable definition of poverty implies that significant numbers of people are living in intolerable circumstances in which starvation is a constant threat, sickness is a familiar companion, and oppression is a fact of life. In Alfred Marshall's words, "The study of the causes of poverty is the study of the causes of degradation of a large part of mankind" (Marshall 1925). Improving the lives of the poor must be at the top of our agenda.

What does development economics have to say about reducing poverty? And how has our thinking evolved over the past quarter-century? This paper explores these issues through the evidence and analysis available in the literature in general and through the World Bank's *World Development Reports* on poverty (World Bank 1980, 1990, 2000).[1] These reports, drawing on evidence from around the world, summarize contemporary thinking on the subject and are therefore useful instruments for assessing progress in our understanding of the problem and our ability to solve it.

The breadth of the topic requires some selectivity. We focus on two questions: How should poverty be defined and measured? What policies and strategies reduce poverty, so defined? The questions are, of course, related—the definition of poverty drives the choice of policies. To organize the discussion, we take advantage of the broadening of the definition of poverty over the past quarter-century and the concomitant expansion of the relevant set of policies.

The definition of poverty, beginning with a focus on command over market-purchased goods (income), has expanded to embrace other dimensions of living standards such as longevity, literacy, and health. As we have learned more about and from the poor, the concept has developed further to reflect a concern with vulnerability and risk, and with powerlessness and lack of voice. Our review of the evolution of thinking about poverty leads us to two general conclusions.

First, broadening the definition of poverty does not change significantly who is counted as poor—at least not as far as aggregate measures are concerned. This is a simplification, and we can find evidence to the contrary in the literature, but it does reflect the fact that the many aspects of poverty—income, health, political rights, and so on—are often closely correlated. Although aggregate measures may not be greatly affected, the broader definitions do allow a better characterization of poverty and of the terrible hardships burdening the poor, and they therefore increase our understanding of poverty and the poor. This deeper understanding will often be critical to the design and implementation of specific programs and projects to help people escape poverty.

Second, broadening the definition changes significantly our thinking about strategies for reducing poverty. In part, this is obvious. As more aspects of poverty are recognized, so more policies become relevant to fighting poverty. Moving beyond income to include health, for example, introduces a new set of policy instruments. But there is another more subtle and more important consequence. The various aspects of poverty interact in such a way that policies do more than simply add up. For example, improved health increases income-earning potential, increased education leads to better health outcomes, provision of safety nets allows the poor to take advantage of high-return, high-risk opportunities, and so on. Poverty-reducing strategies must recognize these interactions among policies. The links among the various dimensions of poverty is a theme that runs throughout this review.

These two issues—definition and strategy—are explored in more depth in this chapter as we trace the historical evolution of poverty through its various manifestations. The next section looks at the definition of poverty as it emerged from Rowntree's pioneering efforts at the beginning of the 20th century. His focus on income (or expenditure) led naturally to a strategy based on growth in national income—which, however, would help the poor only if they shared in that growth. The key interaction, then, was the link between growth in national income and changes in inequality, and the fear was that progress on one front (growth) would lead to setbacks on the other (inequality), with uncertain implications for the poor.

We then explore the incorporation in the 1980s of other dimensions of poverty—longevity, literacy, and health. This broadening brought new policies into play. It also revealed two new interactions. One was within the new set of policies: healthier children perform better at school, better-educated mothers have healthier families, and so on. The other was between progress in human development and increases in national income. From one perspective, better health and education can be viewed as an investment in human capital that, like investment in physical capital, should yield a return in the form of increased income. From another perspective, better health and education can be seen as improvements in the quality of life in their own right—and, indeed, growth in national income has value only to the extent that it leads to longer lives, better health, and greater literacy. Either way, there is an interaction between the two sets of outcomes.

We then incorporate findings from analyses of panel data and from a range of participatory techniques that have recently come to the fore and that seek to elicit views about poverty from the poor themselves. This further broadening has led to today's concern with risk, vulnerability, powerlessness, and lack of voice. Here, too, important interactions emerge. Reducing exposure to risk offers an immediate benefit to the otherwise vulnerable, but it also provides a platform for escaping long-run poverty: lower exposure to risk frees the poor to engage in riskier, but more profitable, production and investment strategies, including investment in their children's education. Similarly, giving the poor voice reduces their sense of isolation—an immediate benefit— but, in addition, once poor people have a greater say in the selection and design of programs to assist them, they are more committed to implementation. In direct opposition to the isolation the poor often endure, successful implementation of income-earning projects, health programs, and safety nets calls for inclusion and active participation in a wide range of circumstances.

In the final section we sum up the central proposition of this review. As the definition of poverty has expanded and as new dimensions have been introduced, the degree of interaction among the elements has also increased; each element contributes to well-being in the broad sense but also contributes to the achievement of other elements. With this perspective as background, we offer some views on the most important outstanding issues in need of further research.

Measuring Poverty: Income and Consumption

According to *Merriam-Webster's Collegiate Dictionary,* poverty is "the state of one who lacks a usual or socially acceptable amount of money or material possessions." This definition contains two important ideas. First, the definition of poverty will be different at different times and in different societies: what is "socially acceptable" may differ in, say, India and the United States. Second, the focus is on the ability to purchase goods and services (thus, on money) or on their ownership (material possessions). As we shall see, many attempts to measure poverty incorporate these two ideas.

Benjamin Seebohm Rowntree, an early measurer of poverty, arrived at a "socially acceptable" amount of money by estimating the budget required "to obtain the minimum necessaries for the maintenance of merely physical efficiency" (Rowntree 1910: 86) in the specific circumstances of the city of York, England, at the beginning of the 20th century. Taking the nutritional content of various foods and their local prices as a basis, Rowntree concluded that 15 shillings would provide the minimum budget for food for a family of six for one week. Adding an allowance for shelter, clothing, fuel, and sundries, he arrived at a poverty line of 26 shillings for a family of six that implied a poverty rate of almost 10 percent in York.

The same approach has been used for other countries and other times. The resulting poverty line is sensitive to local circumstances. Thus, the Indian and U.S. poverty lines are based more or less on this approach, yet when both are expressed in 1985 purchasing power parity (PPP) dollars, the U.S. poverty line is 10 to 20 times as high as India's, depending on household size. This difference reflects the tendency for poverty lines to change over time within countries as average incomes rise and views about the "minimum necessaries" evolve. A study of poverty lines—budgets for "minimum subsistence"—used in the United States in the period 1905 to 1960 found that they rose 0.75 percent in real terms for each 1.0 percent increase in the real disposable income per capita of the general population (cited in Fisher 1996). Minimum subsistence budgets before World War I were, in constant dollars, between 43 and 54 percent of the absolute poverty threshold established by Mollie Orshansky, an economist with the U.S. Social Security Administration, for 1963; by 1923, a "minimum subsistence level" was 53 to 68 percent of the 1963 line. An "emergency" budget during the depression year 1935 was 65 percent of Orshansky's threshold, and a low-income line for 1957 was 88 percent.

That popular conceptions of the amount needed to "get along" rise with increases in overall incomes is neatly captured in an observation from 1938: "A standard budget worked out in the [1890s], for example, would have no place for electric appliances, automobiles, spinach, radios, and many other things which found a place on the 1938 comfort model. The budget of 1950 will undoubtedly make the present one look as antiquated as the hobble skirt" (cited in Fisher 1996).

As technology progresses and the general standard of living rises, three effects have an impact on poverty:

• New consumption items, initially viewed as luxuries, come to be seen as conveniences and then as necessities.
• Changes in the way society is organized may make it more expensive for the poor to accomplish a given goal—as, for example, when

widespread automobile ownership leads to a deterioration in public transport.

• General upgrading of social standards can make things more expensive for the poor; for example, housing codes requiring that all houses have indoor plumbing add to the cost of housing.

Once a poverty line has been established, it can be applied to data on incomes or on expenditure. Most analysts favor expenditure. In many cases it is far easier to measure, and it also has a conceptual advantage. If incomes vary over time in fairly predictable ways (as they are likely to do in, say, a rural economy), households can to some extent smooth their living standards despite income variability. Anand and Harris (1994) address the choice of a welfare indicator using data from Sri Lanka. They conjecture, and find, that income is a noisy indicator of "permanent" income, while household total expenditure per capita is less noisy and is thus preferred. (They go on to argue that household food expenditure is an even better indicator of permanent income.)

Within this broad approach, many attempts have been made to improve estimates of poverty lines and overcome a host of conceptual and empirical difficulties.[2] The value of this effort depends on the use to be made of poverty lines and hence the required level of precision. We discuss and judge some of these efforts from the perspective of two possible uses of poverty lines: as a means of measuring poverty worldwide and of monitoring changes over time, and as a means of designing specific actions oriented toward the poor.

A commonly used poverty line for monitoring progress in reducing poverty worldwide is the dollar-a-day measure introduced in *World Development Report 1990*. Based on the poverty lines actually used in several low-income countries, this poverty line is expressed in 1985 PPP dollars and refers to household expenditure per person.[3] It has well-known deficiencies: for example, it does not allow for cost of living differentials within countries (Ravallion and van de Walle 1991); it does not distinguish between transient and chronic poverty (World Bank 1990); it values only goods and services delivered through the market (van de Walle and Nead 1995); it does not consider intrahousehold allocation of expenditure (Haddad and Kanbur 1990); and it deals in only a rudimentary fashion with differences in household size and composition (Lanjouw and Ravallion 1995). Techniques exist for handling most of these concerns, but only at a cost and only given appropriate data. The relevant questions, therefore, are, when is it reasonable to ignore these complications, and when are they critical?

The broad elements of the answer are clear. As far as overall monitoring is concerned, the important issue is the extent to which the quantitative significance of the deficiencies changes over time or differs across countries. Although it is important to keep these factors in mind, their significance must be judged against our ability to measure poverty with any precision even in the best of circumstances. Measurement errors arising from different survey techniques, samples, timing, and so on make it doubtful that efforts to deal with some of the deficiencies noted above will greatly improve our ability to monitor progress in reducing poverty, broadly defined. Or, to put the same point differently, current methods, crude as they are, may well be adequate. Gauging the robustness of results through careful use of sensitivity analysis can provide some reassurance. Because the deprivation of someone living just above the poverty line is almost as severe as that of a person just below it, it makes sense to use more than one poverty line.[4]

It is reassuring that the use of more than one line generally gives the same overall picture regarding the worldwide distribution of poverty and how it is changing over time. Table 1 illustrates this point for two poverty lines, one identifying the poor and the other the extreme poor as defined in *World Development Report 1990*. Whichever poverty line one uses, the incidence of poverty in developing countries is highest in South Asia and Sub-Saharan Africa and lowest in the Middle East and North Africa and in East Asia. Similarly, whichever poverty line one uses, between 1985 and 1990 the incidence of poverty fell in South Asia but increased in Latin America and Sub-Saharan Africa. The survey data underlying these numbers cover 80 percent of the population in developing countries. Extrapolating to the total population under the higher of the two poverty lines—the widely used dollar-a-day poverty line for one individual at 1985 U.S. prices—about 1.3 billion people in the developing world, or a third of the world's population, were living in poverty in 1990.

The importance of precise measures of poverty increases when we turn to the design of specific poverty-reducing actions because equal

Table 1. Incidence of Poverty, Using Two Poverty Lines, 1985 and 1990

(poverty lines in 1985 PPP dollars per person per month)

Developing region	*Percentage of population under poverty line US$21.00*		*Percentage of population under poverty line US$30.42*	
	1985	*1990*	*1985*	*1990*
South Asia	36.76	33.31	60.84	58.60
Sub-Saharan Africa	31.65	33.44	51.40	52.89
Latin America and the Caribbean	13.23	17.21	23.07	27.77
East Asia	4.89	4.86	15.72	14.71
Middle East and North Africa	1.33	0.54	4.49	2.52
Total	18.25	17.79	33.88	33.52

Source: Chen, Datt, and Ravallion (1994).

treatment of equals is a fundamental principle of public policy. Take the issue of rural-urban differentials in the cost of living. People migrating from rural to urban areas in a developing country may find themselves facing an entirely new set of prices, especially for housing and food staples. For example, according to Ravallion and van de Walle (1991) average dwelling rents in 1981 were six times higher in urban Java than in rural Java. Incorporating such huge differences into location-specific poverty lines can, of course, change the focus of poverty-oriented actions from rural to urban areas. But the quality of the dwelling stock is often better on average in urban areas, and once allowance is made for this, Ravallion and van de Walle conclude, the differential is much smaller—about 10 percent between urban and rural Java. Thus, adjusting for cost of living differences may be important to ensure equal treatment of urban and rural dwellers, but the adjustment will usually be much less than that suggested by a simple comparison of prices.

Similarly, failure to allow for differential access to goods and services that are not purchased in the market can lead to misleading assessments of poverty. Two households that are equally poor according to the dollar-a-day definition could have quite different levels of well-being depending on their access to free or heavily subsidized goods and services or to public goods. For example, in Indonesia in 1987 the subsidy received by the poorest decile of the urban population through their use of hospitals and primary health centers was twice that received by the poorest decile of the rural population (van de Walle 1994). Similarly, if poor people are depleting common resources, the conventional estimates will overlook increases in pauperization. Jodha (1995) notes that between 1950 and the early 1980s common areas declined by 31 to 55 percent in study villages in dry regions of India. The premature harvesting of trees to make up for reduced availability of plant material once derived from the commons narrows the options for succeeding generations—a process that is not reflected in the national accounts.

Assume that we have accounted for cost of living differentials and similar problems such as differences in household size and composition and that we have identified two equally poor households during the survey period.[5] If one household is experiencing a temporary fall into poverty while the other is chronically poor, the appropriate policy responses toward the two households should probably be quite different. Alleviating chronic poverty demands increases in the physical and human capital of the poor or in the returns to their labor, while insurance and income-stabilization schemes are more appropriate for transient poverty. That said, instruments and objectives cannot be so easily segregated. The existence of an effective safety net or access to credit as a way of smoothing income fluctuations also has potentially important implications for the ability of the chronically poor to escape poverty, as we shall see.

Available panel data suggest that movement into and out of poverty is large. For example, data from a survey of six Indian villages by the International Crops Research Institute for Semi-Arid Tropics (ICRISAT) between 1975 and 1983 showed that 50 percent of the population was poor in a typical year but that only 19 percent was poor in every year (World Bank 1990). Thus, a substantial core of chronically poor coexists with considerable movement into and out of poverty. Jalan and Ravallion (1998), using panel data for rural China for six years, 1985 to 1990, found that transient poverty, defined as poverty that can be attributed to intertemporal variability in consumption, accounted for 37 percent of total poverty for households that were below the poverty line, on average. The extent of transient poverty was negligible for households with mean consumption more than 50 percent above the poverty line. The authors also found that in the poorer provinces about half of mean poverty is attributable to variability in consumption, while in a relatively well-off province with higher average consumption the proportion was much higher, 84 percent of mean poverty.

The distinction between transient and chronic poverty has emerged as an important issue in the context of the East Asian crisis. In Indonesia, the hardest-hit country, poverty is traditionally concentrated in rural areas. Rural poverty has been declining, but in 1997 it was still 12.4 percent, compared with 9.2 percent in the urban sector. As a result, 70 percent of Indonesia's poor were in rural areas in 1997 (Poppele, Sumarto, and Pritchett 1999). The immediate impact of the crisis, however, fell on the financial and corporate sectors and can therefore be expected to generate additional poverty in urban areas. Evidence in support of this view is beginning to appear. A survey of 2,000 households suggests that incomes in urban areas have fallen by one third, whereas in rural areas the decline has been less than 15 percent (Poppele, Sumarto, and Pritchett 1999). Allocation of income support schemes, such as public works programs, according to the precrisis distribution of poverty would have missed many of the newly poor in urban areas.

Imagine that we have constructed poverty lines that truly treat equal households equally. Does this necessarily imply the equal treatment of equal individuals? The answer depends on how households allocate income or food to individual household members. To test the quantitative importance of moving from household-based measures to individual-based ones, Haddad and Kanbur (1990) used data on calorie intake by individuals based on 24-hour recall by the mother in a sample of rural households in the southern Philippines. They found that ignoring within-household inequality understates total inequality; for example, the Gini index increases by about 35 percent when the base moves from households to individuals. Rankings across groups producing different crops or having different tenurial status were not affected by the change in base.

The way in which households allocate income among members can have a significant effect on policy formation and implementation. In the unitary model (Singh, Squire, and Strauss 1986), which assumes a single utility function that governs the household as a whole, policymakers can shift household allocation only by shifting relative prices. Other models move away from the notion of income pooling and a common utility function and assume that household members engage in a bargaining process or else behave independently (Manser and Brown 1980; McElroy and Horney 1981; Alderman and others 1995; Haddad, Hoddinott, and Alderman 1997). In these models the impact that public transfers have on welfare may be affected by the identity of the recipient. In support of this interpretation, Thomas (1990) shows that in Brazilian households the impact of nonlabor income accruing to women on per capita calorie and protein intake, fertility, child survival, and weight-for-height for children less than eight years old is different from what would have been the outcome had the income accrued to men. For example, unearned income accruing to the mother raises the probability of child survival by 20 times that of a similar increase in the unearned income of the father.

Similarly, if information is not pooled, it matters to whom policy initiatives are directed. Faulty policy assumptions may result in the nonadoption of, say, new technology or the adoption of projects that make a group worse off. For example, in the Dominican Republic a reforestation initiative assumed that men and women used wood for the same purposes and consequently discussed the project only with men until midway through the project. When women were finally consulted, it turned out that their needs for fuelwood were not met by the project—and it was too late for those needs to be addressed (Fortmann and Rocheleau 1989).[6]

The many difficulties of measuring poverty along conventional lines notwithstanding, considerable progress has been made in the past 25 years thanks to the expanding availability of household surveys. Between the World Bank's first progress report on poverty in 1993 and its second one in 1996, the number of low-income and middle-income countries with household data on income or expenditure more than doubled, from 31 to 71 (World Bank 1996). The availability of household surveys in one form or another has improved our knowledge of poverty substantially and has clarified the links between growth in national income and changes in inequality—the issue to which we now turn.

Growth, Inequality, and Poverty

Those who viewed poverty as a lack of income or commodities naturally turned their attention to ways of increasing per capita income—through economic growth—as a potential strategy for reducing poverty.

The question was whether income expansion accrued as much to the poor as to the rest of society or whether it left the poor behind. In 1955 Simon Kuznets called attention to the relation between economic growth and income inequality, describing it as "central to much of economic analysis and thinking" (Kuznets 1955). He examined the question with, by his own account, about 5 percent empirical information and 95 percent speculation, and he suggested explanations for—and theoretical arguments against—his scant data.[7] What is now known as the Kuznets curve, or the inverted U, comes from a hypothetical numerical exercise. The idea is that economies which are primarily agricultural start out with an initially equitable distribution and a low average income. As an economy develops, portions of the population migrate to other sectors with greater inequality but higher averages. Initially, this causes inequality to worsen, but with continued progress, more of the rural sector moves out of agriculture, and inequality eventually decreases. This picture was largely based on Lewis's dual-economy theory (Lewis 1954). In his numerical example Kuznets observed that the share of the lowest portion of the population fell in all cases (although no such pattern was found in his data).

Kuznets based his speculation on longitudinal data from the development of industrial countries, but many subsequent estimations used cross-country data to explore the hypothesis.[8] These studies found a pattern of significant increases in inequality as income levels rose, with ambiguous effects for poverty reduction, ranging from absolute impoverishment to slower than average gains. Later studies criticized the cross-country exercises for ignoring country-specific effects and measurement differences and looked at newly available country time-series data.[9] The Kuznets curve faded from view, leaving the conclusion that inequality and income are not systematically related according to some immutable law of development.[10] Thus, one study of 49 countries found no statistical relationship between inequality and income in 40 cases (more than 80 percent of the sample). Four of the remaining nine cases exhibited a U-shaped relationship rather than the inverted U hypothesized by Kuznets; the Kuznets curve appeared in only 5 out of 49 countries (Deininger and Squire 1998: 279). Nor does there seem to be a simple relationship between inequality and growth. Chen and Ravallion (1997) found that inequality was not correlated with growth of mean consumption in 43 spells (a spell being a period for which two household surveys are available for a country).

In place of the Kuznets curve, the recent literature points to a different empirical regularity. As more time-series data become available, it appears that aggregate inequality as measured by, say, the Gini index does not typically change dramatically from year to year. In fact, one study of panel data for 49 countries found that 91.8 percent of the variance in inequality was due to cross-country variance and that only

0.85 percent was attributable to variance over time (Li, Squire, and Zou 1998: 4) The same study showed that few countries exhibited statistically significant trends over time. Thirty-two out of 49 countries revealed no trend, while 10 showed an increasing trend toward inequality and 7 a decreasing one (Li, Squire, and Zou 1998: 32–33). This is not to say that inequality does not change. Obviously, it does, and in some cases—China, Eastern Europe, and the United Kingdom—quite rapidly. Nevertheless, for many countries over long periods of time, inequality has been surprisingly persistent, and where inequality has changed rapidly, it has increased. We do not have solid evidence of rapid reductions in inequality. For the seven countries in which inequality decreased in the Li, Squire, and Zou sample, the average rate of decrease was 0.3 Gini points a year. This implies that it would take about 60 years for a country with Latin American levels of inequality to move to the average of all developing countries. That said, even small changes in aggregate inequality can have a significant impact on poverty.

It is difficult to establish a simple formula relating changes in aggregate measures of inequality such as the Gini index to changes in poverty. The Gini index can increase or decrease, leaving poverty unchanged, if the distribution above the poverty line changes, and poverty can increase or decrease without any change in the Gini index if there are appropriate offsetting changes in distribution among the nonpoor. To explore the impact of inequality on the poor, we need to specify the change in distribution more precisely.

One specification that has received some attention (see Kakwani 1980; Lipton and Ravallion 1995) assumes that the Lorenz curve, which plots inequality, shifts by a constant proportion of the difference between the actual share of total income accruing to each income group and equal shares. This leads to analytically tractable elasticities of the poverty gap with respect to the Gini index.[11] Using the dollar-a-day poverty line, the elasticity can be as high as 8.2 (Brazil), 12.6 (Chile), and even 21.1 (Thailand). For countries with lower incomes and hence more poverty, however, the elasticities are much lower: 0.82 (India), 0.76 (Uganda), and 0.40 (Zambia). Nevertheless, we can see in the experience of two countries the significance of sustained falls in inequality over time. Between the early 1960s and the early 1990s Thailand's Gini index rose by 0.31 points a year while Norway's fell by a similar amount, 0.34 points a year. In Thailand the incomes of the poorest quintile grew at half the rate of mean per capita income; in Norway they grew almost 80 percent faster than the mean.[12]

Moreover, although there is no evidence of any systematic link between inequality and the level of income or between inequality and the rate of growth (see the evidence cited above), there may be a reverse relationship, from initial inequality in income or assets to growth. Clarke (1996), in one of the most careful econometric studies in the literature, found a strong negative and statistically significant effect of initial inequality in income on future growth. He concluded that a reduction in inequality from one standard deviation above the mean to one standard deviation below would increase the long-run growth rate by 1.3 percentage points a year. Subsequent research using higher-quality data has, however, found a positive impact of initial inequality on growth (Forbes 1998; Li and Zou 1998).

Although the evidence on initial income inequality is mixed, several authors have noted a strong relationship between growth and the initial distribution of various types of assets. Birdsall and Londoño (1997) found that the initial distribution of human capital affects future growth, while Deininger and Squire (1998) concluded that initial unequal distribution of land reduces future growth. A weakness in these aggregate growth regressions is the possibility of an aggregation bias. Ravallion (1998) found this bias to be quite large, and a consistent micromodel of consumption growth at the farm-household level indicated a far more harmful effect of asset inequality on consumption growth. These conclusions point to the possibility of identifying redistributive policies that increase growth and could therefore yield a double benefit for the poor.

From Mechanical Relationships to Policy

The search for a mechanical link between inequality and income is not likely to be fruitful, because of the large number and variety of experiences, nor does such an approach lead to policy insights (Kanbur 1998). Both growth and inequality are outcomes of economic policies, as well as of institutional capacity, and are subject to external trends and shocks. Moreover, there is now a substantial empirical literature on the range of factors that influence growth (Easterly and others 1993; Barro and Sala-i-Martin 1995) and a smaller one on the factors influencing inequality (Bourguignon and Morrison 1990; Li, Squire, and Zou 1998). It is odd, however, that analysts have typically looked for mechanical links, largely ignoring the role of policy, when investigating growth and inequality jointly, and when they have investigated the role of policy, they have usually looked at growth and inequality separately. Yet the key piece of information from the policymaker's standpoint is how policies influence both growth and inequality.

Policies to help the poor should examine how to increase growth and improve equality at the same time, or at least how to use propoor measures to mitigate inequality-generating growth. Lundberg and Squire (1999) demonstrated the importance of examining the impact of policy on both growth and inequality. They estimated separate "standard" growth and inequality equations based on the existing literature and found that one common variable—education—was significant in both equations. Education involves a tradeoff: it reduces growth but improves equality. This is immediate confirmation that the separate treatment of growth and inequality could be misleading from a policy perspective.

The estimation of separate standard models indicates that three variables—openness, civil liberties, and land distribution—are exclusively significant either for growth or for equality. This suggests that the policymaker has ample room to choose a package of policies that benefits both growth and equality. The three variables, however, have been treated as mutually exclusive by assumption. Lundberg and Squire reran the standard regressions but included all variables in both equations. In the joint model, land distribution and civil liberties are confirmed as mutually exclusive variables, but openness now signifies a tradeoff; it increases growth but worsens equality. Lundberg and Squire concluded that, at least for these simple models, the independent analysis of growth and inequality produces potentially misleading, or at least incomplete, results for the policymaker. Their results also suggest, however, that, even when growth and inequality are analyzed jointly, there are still likely to be mutually exclusive variables, implying a degree of flexibility for the policymaker.

Lundberg and Squire also examined the joint determination of growth and inequality in more realistic specifications. Openness, financial depth, and land redistribution emerge as policies that consistently spur growth across different specifications. The authors also found that with the significant exception of openness to trade, these policies benefit equality, although the results do not hold for all specifications, and their quantitative impact is small. Indeed, a general result emerging from this analysis is that growth is much more sensitive than equality to policy interventions. For example, the elasticity of growth with respect to the index of openness is minus 0.33; with respect to inequality, it is 0.01. In no case does a variable have a relatively larger influence on inequality than on growth. This is consistent with historical experience: growth rates are much more volatile than inequality.[13]

These results illustrate the importance of treating growth and inequality together. A strong growth performance with even a relatively modest reduction in inequality will have a tremendous impact on the incomes of the poor. Historical evidence supports this view. Data from the early 1960s to the early 1990s show that both Indonesia and Taiwan (China) experienced rapid growth and at least no deterioration in inequality. (Inequality fell in both countries, but the trend was not statistically significant.) During this period the incomes of the poorest quintile in Indonesia increased at a rate of 4.8 percent a year; in Taiwan the poorest quintile did even better, with an annual rate of growth of 5.8 percent.[14]

Understanding the policies and development strategies of these countries should provide valuable guidance for other countries. *World De-*

velopment Report 1990 enumerated as factors in the successes a stable macroeconomic environment (to encourage private investment), relatively undistorted sectoral terms of trade (to avoid bias against agriculture), relatively undistorted factor markets (to avoid capital-intensive production), and public provision of infrastructure, especially to rural areas (to avoid urban bias). Another feature underlying the successes in reducing poverty was emphasis on human development. The successful countries invested heavily in the education and health of their populations as contributing factors in growth and as benefits in their own right. We look at this additional dimension of poverty in more detail in the following section.

Human Development

A recent survey (Lipton and Ravallion 1995: 2573–74) concludes that "the generally preferred indicator of household living standards is a suitably comprehensive measure of current consumption, given by a price-weighted aggregate over all marketed commodities consumed by the household from all sources (purchases, gifts, and own production)." This carefully worded statement well summarizes the conventional view on measuring poverty. In principle, it captures the value of publicly provided goods and services that are often supplied free of charge or are highly subsidized, as long as there is a relevant market price. In practice, however, basic education and health services, which are almost always free or subsidized, may not have a readily comparable market price. The definition also fails to capture such public goods as spraying swamps to eliminate malaria that may influence health outcomes. Because the level and quality of basic education and health services, including public goods, vary significantly across countries, most analysts recommend the inclusion of social indicators in arriving at an overall assessment of living standards. For example, *World Development Report 1990* "supplements a consumption-based poverty measure with others, such as nutrition, life expectancy, under 5 mortality, and school enrollment rates" (World Bank 1990: 26).

The key word in that quotation is "supplements": the social indicators provide information not captured in conventional measures of poverty. Command over market-purchased commodities is important, but so is access to public goods. An alternative approach treats income (or expenditure) as an input to other, more fundamental goals. For example, the focus of *World Development Report 1980* "is on *absolute poverty*—a condition of life so characterized by malnutrition, illiteracy, and disease as to be beneath any reasonable definition of human decency" (World Bank 1980: 32). This represents a marked difference from conventional definitions in that it does not mention income or expenditure but focuses on well-being as revealed by nutritional status, educational attainment, and health status. To be sure, income may be important to the improvement of social indicators, but there is no universal or guaranteed transformation of income into these outcomes, and, in this perspective, it is the results that count.

This view has received intellectual support from Sen's definition of poverty in terms of "capabilities" (Sen 1981, 1984). Capability, in Sen's terminology, means the substantive freedoms people enjoy that permit them to lead the kind of life they have reason to value, such as social functioning, better basic education and health care, and longevity (Sen 1999). The arguments in favor of the capability approach are as follows:

- Poverty can be characterized by capability deprivation, since capabilities are intrinsically important, whereas low income is only instrumentally significant.
- Low income is not the only influence on capability deprivation.
- The impact of income on capabilities varies among communities, families, and individuals.

There is also a connection leading from capability improvement to greater earning power and not only the other way around. This points to the importance of the citizenry's being well prepared to take advantage of economic opportunities.

The United Nations Development Programme (UNDP) has played a leading role in defining poverty in terms of human development and has introduced several measures, including the Human Development Index and the Human Poverty Index (HPI). The HPI is of particular relevance to this discussion. It concentrates on three aspects of human deprivation: longevity, literacy, and living standard. Longevity is measured by the percentage of people who die before age 40, literacy by the percentage of adults who are literate, and living standard by a combination of the percentage of the population with access to health services, the percentage of the population with access to safe water, and the percentage of malnourished children under age 5.

Although information on each of these aspects is valuable, aggregation into a single index raises a host of serious issues. Apart from the loss of policy-relevant information, aggregation requires the arbitrary selection of weights—a feature that has met with considerable criticism in the literature.[15]

Unlike the conventional poverty measures discussed above, the HPI at best ranks countries. Because national HPIs, like gross domestic product (GDP) per capita, are national means, they tell us nothing about the poor. Although governments are presumably interested in the life expectancy of all their citizens, just as they are presumably interested in the incomes of all members of the population, a special focus on poverty requires that we look at those who can expect to live the fewest number of years. National averages do not allow ranking of households within countries and therefore cannot be used to distinguish the poor from the nonpoor. This, of course, reflects the lack of household surveys that would allow the computation of the relevant distributions. For some measures of human development, however, household-level data are beginning to become available, and where they are, households that are poor according to an expenditure-based measure invariably score badly on other indicators of well-being. Tables 2 and 3 illustrate this point.

Table 2 shows that the poorest households by income level in five Latin American countries attain fewer years of education than richer households. In the poorest households the number of years of education for 25-year-olds ranges from about one half to one fifth that attained by their counterparts in the wealthiest households. In each country the number of years of education increases steadily as one moves up the income scale.

Table 3 reveals an almost exactly comparable picture of sickness and wealth in developing countries. The very poor are generally much sicker than the rest of the population. For the sample of Asian and African countries shown in Table 3, the proportion of children born in the past five years but no longer living is between three and six times larger for the poorest decile than for the richest decile. In two of the countries, Tanzania and Uganda, almost half the children born in the poorest decile in the past five years have died. As with education, the table reveals a steady improvement as wealth increases.

It should not be concluded from this evidence that the identification of the poor according to different dimensions of poverty will lead to exactly the same results every time. A study using data collected in 1985 in Côte d'Ivoire showed relatively modest correlations between different measures of poverty. Less than half of the 30 percent of the population who were identified as poor by a measure based on consumption per capita adjusted for family composition were so identified when the criterion was the average educational level of adults (Glewwe

Table 2. Average Years of Education for 25-Year-Olds, by Income Decile, Five Latin American Countries

Country	1 (lowest)	2	3	4	5	6	7	8	9	10 (highest)
Chile	6.24	6.88	7.09	7.40	7.69	8.16	8.47	9.80	10.88	12.83
Brazil	1.98	2.49	2.97	3.41	3.66	4.40	4.49	5.98	7.43	10.53
Mexico	2.14	2.95	3.78	4.15	4.78	5.66	6.06	7.24	8.89	12.13
Peru	3.87	4.17	4.95	5.69	6.60	7.05	7.66	8.28	9.04	10.80
Venezuela	4.66	4.94	5.27	5.72	6.23	6.68	7.20	7.78	8.58	10.81

Note: Data are from recent household surveys.
Source: IADB (1998).

Table 3. Proportion of Children Born in the Past Five Years
Who Are No Longer Living, by Income Decile,
Selected Countries

Country	1 (lowest)	2	3	4	5	6	7	8	9	10 (highest)
Bangladesh	0.19	0.13	0.10	0.09	0.08	0.10	0.07	0.09	0.09	0.06
Indonesia	0.25	0.14	0.08	0.06	0.06	0.05	0.05	0.05	0.04	0.04
Madagascar	0.25	0.14	0.13	0.10	0.10	0.10	0.10	0.09	0.08	0.08
Pakistan	0.18	0.10	0.10	0.09	0.09	0.07	0.08	0.07	0.07	0.06
Tanzania	0.49	0.18	0.13	0.14	0.11	0.10	0.08	0.07	0.07	0.09
Uganda	0.48	0.19	0.16	0.14	0.13	0.09	0.12	0.09	0.09	0.07

Source: Bonilla-Chacin and Hammer (1999), from Demographic and Health Surveys (DHS) conducted by the MACRO Corporation for the U.S. Agency for International Development (USAID).

and van der Gaag 1990). A similar conclusion emerges from a study of six developing countries: "Individuals with lower incomes on average also have lower welfare in other dimensions . . . However, it is also noticeable that the correlations are rather modest—income usually explains very little of the variation in non-money metric welfare indicators" (Appleton and Song 1999: 25). The Appleton and Song study, however, makes no allowance for family composition in arriving at its measure of per capita consumption. Thus, while there is clearly an overlap—those who lack income are less well educated and suffer more sickness—the correspondence is less than complete and can in some cases be quite small.

We saw earlier that the poor, on balance, gain from broadly based growth (they certainly have little to gain from contraction or stagnation). From this perspective, a poverty-reducing strategy that does not give a central role to equity-improving growth is unlikely to be successful. How should the strategy change if the definition of poverty is expanded to incorporate human development as measured by, say, life expectancy or literacy? This extension captures important dimensions of poverty that are otherwise missed by conventional income or expenditure measures, especially as used in applied work. It reminds us that there are additional policy instruments that need to be kept in mind. Moreover, there are important interactions at play, both among various elements of human development and between those elements and growth.

The Seamless Web

A society faced with the task of providing social services to the poor may well wonder where to begin. The lives of the poor are ringed with a tangle of vicious circles, with the virtuous circles seemingly just out of reach. These interactions have been recognized for some time. *World Development Report 1980,* for example, stressed that the "different elements of human development are key determinants of each other" (World Bank 1980: 68) and spoke of the "seamless web of interrelations" (69). Efforts to improve on past performance in delivering social services are better informed than ever about these interactions.

For example, many studies have shown that mothers' education has a strong positive effect on their children's health. We now know that this occurs because education enables the mother to obtain and process information. Thus, a study using 1986 data from northeastern Brazil showed that parents who regularly made use of the mass media had healthier children, as measured by height-for-age. Once variables for use of the media are included, the mother's years of schooling no longer had an independent effect. One interpretation of this result is that education is necessary so that mothers can process information but that access to relevant material through the mass media is needed if education is to have an effect on child health (Thomas, Strauss, and Henriques 1991). A study using data for Morocco from 1990–91 provides support for this interpretation. It found that a mother's basic health knowledge had a direct effect on child health and that education and access to media were the vehicles for acquiring that knowledge (Glewwe 1997).

Many studies show that better health improves school attendance and performance. Often, however, these studies use cross-sectional data and rely on recall. To overcome this problem, a recent study used longitudinal data to investigate the effect of child health and nutrition on school enrollments in rural Pakistan. These data allow the authors to relax the assumption that child health and nutrition are predetermined rather than determined by household choices. Their preferred point-estimates indicate that the child health and nutrition factor is three times more important for enrollment than conventional approaches would suggest (Alderman and others 1997) and that the effects are larger for girls than for boys. Although the study had to do with the health-education link, its methodological point increases our confidence in the results of previous work that indicates a positive effect on performance as well.

Human Development and Growth

In addition to the interrelations among various aspects of human development, there are important linkages between human development and income-earning capacity; income is a major determinant and outcome of human development. The specific way in which the poor participate in growth tends to be through increased or more productive use of their most abundant asset, labor. But some of the intrinsic characteristics of poverty—lack of education, poor nutrition, and poor health—also have functional effects on poor people's capacity to work. Some of the links that enhance or impair the capabilities of the poor may give an idea of the multifarious interactions between human development and growth. For example, a well-nourished person can work more hours, thereby earning more, consuming more, and saving more and so ensuring future nourishment and work capacity. Similarly, a person with primary education can take a higher-paying job, allowing her children to attend school. We briefly illustrate from the extensive empirical literature on these links.

Drawing on data from a survey of 1,725 households in Conakry, Guinea, in 1990, Glick and Sahn (1997) examined the impact of education on labor earnings by sector of employment. Two results are noteworthy. First, education raises the earnings of men and women in the three sectors examined—self-employment, private wage employment, and public wage employment. Thus, even in a very low-income urban area such as Conakry, the benefits of schooling are clearly visible. Second, even in the informal sector (which overlaps with the small enterprises of the self-employed and which is expected to be an important source of job growth in Africa), earnings increase with level of education. For example, completed primary schooling raises the hourly enterprise profits for self-employed women by 30 percent.

Measures of nutritional status and health status have also been shown to have positive impacts on wages and productivity, and these effects are greater for the poor than for the nonpoor. Strauss and Thomas (1997) show that, controlling for a range of factors, taller men in the United States earn more—a 1 percent increase in height is associated with a 1 percent increase in wages. The relationship is much more powerful for Brazilian males: a 1 percent increase in height is associated with a 7 percent increase in wages. In their survey of the literature Strauss and Thomas (1998) conclude that improvements in health do result in increases in productivity and wages and that (more important for our analysis) the health of the poorest and least educated is likely to improve the most.

Without the basic building blocks of health and education, the poor are unable to take advantage of the income-earning opportunities that come with growth, and society suffers the loss of their potential contributions.[16] The provision of basic social services, besides being important in its own right, therefore constitutes an important element in the growth of a society. As one would expect, national comparisons do indeed indicate a broad correlation between income levels and life expectancy, literacy, infant mortality, and so on. But growth in income by itself does not necessarily translate into improvements in health status or educational attainment, nor does improved health or better education necessarily lead to increases in income.

For example, there are some striking outliers from the general correlation between income and other measures of well-being. The UNDP's *Human Development Report 1994* showed that Sri Lanka, Nicaragua, Pakistan, and Guinea all had per capita incomes in the US$400–$500 range but life expectancies of, respectively, 71, 65, 58, and 44 years and infant mortality rates of, respectively, 24, 53, 99, and 135 per 1,000 live births. Outliers often provide valuable insights, but there are at least two interpretations in this case.

First, the resources generated by growth may not be used in a way that promotes improvements in other indicators. Growth provides an opportunity, but that opportunity has to be seized. Anand and Ravallion (1993) provide support for this view. Using a sample of 22 countries, they show that the observed relationship between improvements in life expectancy and increases in mean income disappears once measures for income and poverty and for per capita public spending on health are introduced. This suggests that growth in mean income translates into improvements in life expectancy only if growth reduces poverty (increased incomes for the poor are critical to significant improvements in life expectancy) and if adequate provision is made for public health care. It is how the fruits of economic growth are used that is critical. In this perspective, Sri Lanka has used its income effectively, whereas Guinea has not.

But there is a second interpretation. The structure of incentives and the complementary investments needed to ensure that society—especially the poor—will reap the maximum benefit, including increased incomes, from investment in education and health may not be in place (Squire 1993). There is evidence to support this view, especially for education. Cross-country regressions suggest that the effect of growth in educational capital on growth in GDP per worker is "consistently small and negative" (Pritchett 1996). Pritchett squares the circle between the apparently positive effect of education at the individual level and its apparently insignificant effect at the aggregate level by distinguishing between rent-seeking and productive activities (Murphy, Shleifer, and Vishny 1991). If the returns to education go, at least in part, into rent-seeking, individuals receiving education will enjoy increases in income, but national income will not necessarily rise. According to this view, countries such as Sri Lanka have enjoyed the immediate benefits of better health and more education but have not realized the increases in income that could accompany them.

The arguments that growth does not necessarily translate into social progress and, alternatively, that improvements in health and education do not necessarily lead to higher incomes can, of course, be turned around. When countries have used the benefits of growth to finance basic health care and access to education for all, and when they have put in place incentive structures and complementary investments to ensure that better health and education lead to higher incomes, the poor have benefited doubly: they are healthier and better educated, and their consumption has increased. *World Development Report 1990* argued that the two efforts were mutually reinforcing and that one without the other was not sufficient. Progress on both fronts was the foundation of its two-part strategy.

Most East Asian countries, before the crisis of the late 1990s, were illustrations of what can be achieved by such a strategy. Poverty fell dramatically in East Asia between 1975, when roughly 6 out of 10 East Asians lived in absolute poverty, and 1995, when only about 2 did. At the same time, and in part propelling these achievements, governments invested in human capital through public expenditures on education and health. Between 1975 and 1995, in a sample group of six East Asian countries, life expectancy increased by more than 9 years, average years of education rose by 60 percent, and infant mortality fell from 73 per 1,000 births to 35.[17] Although these achievements may have been eroded to some extent during the crisis of the late 1990s, their lasting effect still represents a degree of progress not seen elsewhere.

Several recent empirical studies at the household level, using panel data, provide further support for a strong interaction between human development and income growth. For example, a study of 891 households in Peru during the period 1994 to 1997 found that the higher the education of the household head in 1994, the larger the growth in expenditure per capita in the subsequent period (Chong and Hentschel 1999). Panel data for 2,678 Vietnamese households covering the period 1993 to 1998 pointed to the same conclusion. On average, expenditure per capita for households whose head had no education declined, but it increased for households whose head had a primary education or more, and the increase for those with upper secondary education was three times that for those with primary education (Glewwe, Gragnolati, and Zaman 2000).

Incorporating other dimensions of poverty—longevity and literacy—into our definition expands considerably the range of policy instruments available for alleviating poverty. Even if incomes do not increase, policies that improve the health of individuals and increase their capacity to absorb and exchange information improve the quality of their lives. But—and this is the lasting lesson from precrisis East Asia—where policies and programs to improve health and expand education are combined with government action designed to promote investment and broadly based growth, the benefits to the poor are that much greater. Additional country-level research designed to illuminate the appropriate balance between policies for countries at different levels of development would yield valuable lessons. How to transfer such lessons to the countries of Sub-Saharan Africa and South Asia, home to 70 percent of the world's poor, remains an important challenge in the fight to reduce poverty.

Even as this challenge goes unanswered, new challenges are coming to the fore. The risks, to poor and nonpoor alike, of large fluctuations in capital flows are now abundantly visible in East Asia. And, as we explore in the next section, risk manifests itself in a multitude of forms where the poor are concerned.

Vulnerability and Voice

Conventional measures of poverty draw heavily on the statistical information contained in household surveys, combined with a more or less arbitrary cutoff separating the poor from the nonpoor. An alternative empirical approach to measuring poverty involves asking people what, to them, constitutes poverty. Initial investigations along these lines were designed to elicit information about an expenditure-based or an income-based poverty line. For example, respondents might be asked what income they considered the minimum needed to make ends meet (see, for example, Goedhart and others 1977; Hagenaars 1986). More recent work—using, for example, participatory poverty assessments—is much more open-ended, interactive, and qualitative and allows people to describe what constitutes poverty in whatever dimensions they choose.

Participatory surveys are designed to learn how individuals from various social groups assess their own poverty and existing poverty reduction strategies, how various survival strategies operate, which government poverty reduction strategies people prefer, and which they are prepared to support. The findings are meant to refocus, elaborate, or validate conclusions drawn from conventional poverty assessments (Salmen 1995). At the same time, participatory poverty assessments pay special attention to process, with the aim of engaging a range of stakeholders, generating involvement, maximizing local ownership, and building commitment to change. Each assessment is different, reflecting the country context, the time available, and the information needs of policymakers (Narayan and Nyamwaya 1996). Thus, the specific questions each one addresses will vary widely.

The World Bank began systematically requiring a poverty assessment of each country as a result of the findings of *World Development Report 1990*. Poverty assessments use a variety of sources to diagnose the structural causes of poverty. Taking their cue from researchers such as N. S. Jodha, Robert Chambers, and Lawrence Salmen who had been asking the poor for their own assessments of their economic status, the poverty assessments began in 1993 to include participatory surveys. The participatory poverty assessments draw their methodology from other analytical instruments used in the World Bank: beneficiary assessments, designed to obtain client feedback, and participatory rural appraisals, which involve stakeholders in helping to form a rapid understanding of a particular location. As of July 1998, 43 policy-oriented participatory surveys had been undertaken at the World Bank, with at least 10 more now under way. Of the 43 completed participatory assessments, 28 were in Africa, 6 in Latin America, 5 in Eastern Europe, and 4 in Asia.

Two aspects of poverty (expressed in different ways) that emerge from participatory assessments and that are not captured in conventional surveys seem especially important. The first, a concern about risk and volatility of income, is often expressed as a feeling of vulnerability. Descriptions by poor people of how market fluctuations, seasons, and crises affect their well-being impart an understanding of poverty as a state not just of having little but also of being vulnerable to losing the little one has. The second dimension is lack of political power. Some see this lack of voice and political rights, often described as a sense of powerlessness, as the most fundamental characteristic of poverty.

Vulnerability "has two sides: the external side of exposure to shocks, stress, and risk; and the internal side of defenselessness, meaning a lack of means to cope without damaging loss" (Chambers 1995). Outside sources of risk range from irregular rainfall and epidemics to crime and violence, the structural vulnerability of homes, and civil conflict. During the civil war in Tajikistan, economic activity in the affected areas ground to a halt, and even after the conflict, women without grown males to protect them felt particularly vulnerable. The poor perceived peace and security as the highest priority, even over better food and shelter. With the restoration of peace, people in Tajikistan felt that the economic and political situation would improve and so would physical security (World Bank 1998b).

Faced with a great deal of risk, the poor try to minimize their vulnerability to disaster by diversifying their income. For example, in Kenya the poor engage in activities such as small-scale subsistence farming, peddling and hawking, manual labor, illicit brewing, welding and cobbling, and operation of small-scale businesses. But as we shall see, these kinds of coping mechanism are inadequate.

The poor suffer from risk because they lack the means to protect themselves adequately against it; this is what makes them vulnerable. If a contingency occurs, the poor have few assets to dispose of to address the problem, and the depletion of those assets must plunge them further into long-term poverty. And they often cannot borrow to meet their needs. In Kenya only 4 percent of the poor have access to credit through banks and another 3 percent through cooperatives, mainly because property requirements exclude them. Similarly, poverty assessments show that the poor in Zambia, Djibouti, and Tajikistan associate poverty with insecurity, uncertainty, and vulnerability (World Bank, 1994, 1997, 1998b).

The Zambia participatory poverty assessment points out that definitions of poverty and vulnerability at the local level often highlight characteristics that refer to people who are on or beyond the margins of the local community; even though an entire village community may be below a standard national "poverty line" measure, most people will still conceive of themselves as coping. Frequently, having a secure livelihood is perceived as more important than maximizing income. Thus, people's understanding about their livelihoods has more to do with vulnerability than with poverty (World Bank 1994: 34). For example, the Zambia report presented evidence that growing a wide range of food and cash crops diminishes vulnerability to both environmental and market-based shocks and reduces the seasonal dimension of vulnerability. Respondents' perception of a combination of age, childlessness, and social isolation of widows and divorcées as characteristic of the rural poor illustrates how vulnerability is seen as lacking the wherewithal to cope.

In Cameroon the poor in all regions distinguish themselves from the nonpoor on five main criteria: hunger in their households; fewer meals a day and nutritionally inadequate diets; a higher percentage of their meager and irregular income being spent on food; nonexistent or low sources of cash income; and a feeling of powerlessness and inability to make themselves heard (World Bank 1995). This last factor can be seen in concrete terms in the inability of most poor people in Cameroon to obtain an identity card; without one, they are legally nonexistent, unable to vote, and barred from work and travel and from economic activities such as having a bank account or obtaining a loan. One retired man in the capital, Yaoundé, said, "The more time passes, the more poor we become; on top of that, we have no security any more, everywhere we are insulted, pushed aside; and we here are poor, even the government ignores us" (Mfoulou and others 1994: 139). A widow stated, "Everywhere, health, food, and school is for the bigwigs who took all the money" (140). Thus, although income or income-related dimensions of poverty do feature prominently, the participatory approach exposes the poor's concern with isolation and powerlessness.

Economically marginalized groups tend to be socially marginalized as well, so that they are disadvantaged with respect to both resources and power (Salmen 1995).[18] In Cameroon, Gabon, Kenya, and Zambia the poor reported that they felt powerless and unable to make their voices heard. In Gabon and Zambia the government carried out projects without consulting the communities that were meant to benefit from them, and in Kenya the poor complained that district officials tended not to go to villages or passed through quickly without talking to the poor about their problems. Interviews with those officials revealed that they were unaware of the basic characteristics of the lives of the poor; for example, they did not know that health clinics regularly charged fees to the poor (Narayan and Nyamwaya 1996).

Where interaction between those in power and the poor does exist, it can be very lopsided. A 1995 participatory poverty assessment in Mexico found that custom dictates a patron-client relationship (*clientilismo*) between politicians and the people, under which political leaders provide services or favors in exchange for votes. This trading is the only way that the poor acquire land, housing, and urban infrastructure such as water and electricity. The system of strong vertical channels has led many to perceive a lack of opportunity to act individually or as a collective group in their own interests and has undermined their willingness to take any initiatives.

The evidence cited above gives a flavor of the complexity and diversity in people's outlook about poverty. Their views on the causes of poverty and its cures can influence public efforts in ways that may be overlooked by conventional surveys. Their insights indicate actions with high benefits for poor people at relatively low financial cost. For example, access to health care emerged as a high priority for the poor in rural and urban communities in Zambia, yet the poor consistently complained that staff in hospitals and clinics were rude and arrogant to them (World Bank 1994). In response to the findings of the participatory poverty assessment, the World Bank's Social Fund supported some of the priorities identified by communities. Under a health project, drought-stricken areas are exempt from paying health fees, and the Ministry of Health has increased the resources allocated to rural areas in an effort to empower health workers and decrease their frustrations (Robb 1998). The same participatory survey revealed a problem rural households had regarding school fees, uniforms, and books and materials. These expenditures typically occur in the preharvest season, when incomes are low and available cash has to go toward emergency stocks of food to cover the period up to the harvest. This finding pointed to the need to distribute school expenses over the year or shift them to another time, and the Ministry of Education is now considering these changes (Robb 1998).

Thus, participatory surveys can enrich our understanding of the poor and lead to public actions that are perceived by the poor to be of benefit to them. That said, these extensions of the definition of poverty—especially the addition of vulnerability and powerlessness—probably do not significantly change our view of who is poor, something that is difficult to establish in a precise way. As is the case with indicators of human development, we do not have household-level measures of vulnerability or powerlessness and so cannot distinguish the poor (on these dimensions) from the nonpoor. Moreover, measures of exposure to risk could be very high for individuals with very large incomes. This is clearly not what people have in mind when they refer to vulnerability.

Empirical evidence on the overlap between vulnerability and powerlessness as measures of poverty and a consumption-based measure are scarce. The one frequently cited study, Jodha (1995), has been questioned by Moore, Choudhary, and Singh (1998). In Jodha's study, most households that had experienced a decline in income by at least 5 percent between 1963–66 and 1982–84 in two villages in Rajasthan reported that they were nevertheless better off according to several other criteria such as less resort to "emergency" income-earning strategies. Moore, Choudhary, and Singh point out that the provision of many public services had improved over this period—piped drinking water had been provided, for example—and also question the evidence on the decline in private income. They comment, "There is no convincing evidence that the poor place a very high value on independence, respect, or personal autonomy if that is to be traded off against food when they are hungry" (Moore, Choudhary, and Singh 1998: 17).

Since vulnerability and powerlessness emerge clearly from participatory surveys, one way of testing whether conventional measures of poverty coincide with measures based on vulnerability or powerlessness is to ask whether conventional surveys and participatory surveys identify the same people as poor. In Kenya, for example, the findings of the 1995 participatory survey using "wealth ranking" can be compared with those of a 1992 National Welfare Monitoring Survey based on an established poverty line (Narayan and Nyamwaya 1996). Where cluster sampling was carried out carefully (and where drought did not seriously affect the district in the intervening years), the estimates of poverty from the participatory survey ended up being virtually identical to estimates from the national survey. In Bornet district the two estimates were 64 percent (participatory) and 65 percent (national); in Busia both were 68 percent, and in Nyamira both were 54 percent.

As more points of comparison become available, the conclusion suggested by the Kenyan example will be confirmed or else modified. One interesting comparison comes from fieldwork in Lugazi, Uganda (Davis and Whittington 1998). The authors administered a questionnaire to 384 households and conducted a series of participatory community meetings throughout Lugazi, with attendance ranging from 50 to 225 people. The purpose of both exercises was to ascertain willingness to pay for improved water and sanitation service. The results are broadly similar. For example, the household survey indicated that one third of households would connect to a piped water supply at the specified price, while the community meetings suggested that one quarter might do so. The authors argue that these differences are not significant from a policy perspective. They also note, however, that the two approaches resulted in samples with significantly different socioeconomic characteristics; despite "best practice" techniques, different samples of individuals were consulted. These results suggest the need for additional research to identify the relative strengths and weaknesses of different approaches and to determine how best to make use of conventional surveys and participatory approaches.

Coping with Risk

Health and education for the poor, as we have seen, are important components of a poverty-reducing strategy in their own right and are essential building blocks to help the poor increase their incomes. There are other factors that provide a platform for reducing poverty; in particular, actions that reduce risk or provide insurance against risk expand the range of opportunities available to the poor and enable them to take better advantage of strategies to reduce poverty, whether these strategies bear on health, education, or income-earning possibilities.

Increasingly, we are realizing that even such victories as the poor can achieve in improving their lot, no matter how virtuously linked to increasingly better outcomes, are ultimately fragile. Risks associated with being poor may wipe out hard-won gains overnight. In many cases risk prevents the poor from undertaking activities that could have high returns. The problem of risk has at least two dimensions: it keeps the poor in low-risk, low-return activities, and it endangers what they already have. The usual remedies for risk—borrowing and insurance— are rarely available to the poor, and their absence lies at the heart of many of the disadvantages they must face.

A well-known study of moneylenders in Chambar, Pakistan, in the early 1980s (Aleem 1993) illustrates the problem in the credit market. Moneylenders invest considerable time and effort in ascertaining the creditworthiness of would-be borrowers. Lacking collateral, the poor require more scrutiny than others. Even if an applicant successfully overcomes this hurdle (the rejection rate in the study was around 50 percent), the moneylender usually begins with a small loan to test the waters. The combination of high administrative costs and small loans leads inevitably to high interest rates. The average rate charged by moneylenders in Chambar was 79 percent a year (Aleem 1993). At these rates, the poor are effectively excluded. Similarly, insurers lack a reliable means of assessing effort on the part of those seeking insurance, especially in agricultural contexts, and thus cannot identify the real cause of, say, a crop failure (Hazell, Pomareda, and Valdés 1986).

Lack of credit and insurance bear heavily on the poor. For example, a study of rural households in southwestern China for the period 1985–90 found that the loss of one year's income as a result of crop failure led, on average, to a 10 percent decline in consumption in the following year for the richest third of households. This is significant, but manageable. In contrast, for the poorest tenth of households the average decline was a devastating 40 percent in the year following a crop failure (Jalan and Ravallion 1999). Similarly, in the south Indian villages intensively surveyed over 10 years by ICRISAT, the average coefficient of variation of household income was 40 percent; for farm profits it was over 125 percent (reported in Morduch 1995).

Poor households react to income volatility in two ways. They may adopt production plans or employment strategies to reduce their exposure to the risk of adverse income shocks, even if this entails lower average income. In addition to such efforts to smooth income, they may try to smooth consumption by creating buffer stocks, withdrawing children from school, and developing informal insurance and credit arrangements. These efforts are both costly and inadequate. They are costly because the poor face a bitter tradeoff: they can accept risk that could lead to disastrous fluctuations in consumption, or they can minimize risk in ways that perpetuate poverty. Their efforts are inadequate because, especially at the village, region, or national level, risks remain against which the poor by themselves are unable to insure. We illustrate these points briefly.

With respect to costs, Morduch (1990) uses the ICRISAT data to show that households which are more vulnerable to income shocks devote a smaller share of their land (9 percent) to risky, high-yielding varieties, compared with about 36 percent for households with better access to coping mechanisms. Jacoby and Skoufias (1997) show that when hit by a drop in income, poor households withdraw their children from school; a 10 percent decline in agricultural income across agricultural seasons leads to a fall in school attendance of about five days in a sample of six Indian villages. Thus, the coping mechanisms available to the poor, although providing some protection in the short run, limit their long-run prospects of escaping poverty.

As for inadequacy, informal mechanisms of insurance are unlikely to be able to cope with systemic risk. In four Muslim villages near Zaria in northern Nigeria a 1988–89 survey revealed the importance of informal credit transactions: over one half of the households had both borrowed and lent during the survey period, and only one tenth of households had neither borrowed nor lent. Loans between villages are much less prevalent than loans within villages, yet more than half the variation (58 percent) in agricultural output in the region was caused by aggregate shocks that affected entire villages. No matter how good the within-village insurance mechanisms, villagers were unable to protect themselves from one of the biggest sources of risk (Udry 1990, 1994).

To counteract the effects of crises on the poor, governments must provide safety nets to cushion the blows and preserve poor people's opportunities to improve their situation. Their ability to do so is benefiting from two recent innovations that alleviate the information problems that so plague credit and insurance markets. These innovations are group lending (group screening and monitoring) and self-revelation of information.

Group Lending. The costs of collecting information and enforcing repayment can be significantly reduced through group lending. Since groups of poor people may know quite a bit about each other and have many opportunities to interact and enforce their social expectations of each other's behavior, such groups may apply for joint loans and monitor each other to ensure repayment. Thus, the information burden to the lender is significantly reduced, and the poor pay less for lenders' uncertainty about them. This idea, pioneered by Grameen Bank in Bangladesh, has now spread in various forms to many countries. About 10 million households worldwide are served by microfinance programs. Repayment rates are high; Grameen, for example, boasts a repayment rate above 95 percent. Interest rates are lower than those in the informal market, and more than 30 programs operate without any subsidy at all (Morduch 1999).

As one might expect, not all programs are equally successful in all dimensions. The programs that have been most successful in reaching the poor are far from financially sustainable. Grameen Bank, for example, has reached over 2 million borrowers, 94 percent of whom are women, by charging relatively low rates of interest—20 percent a year. To operate without any subsidies, however, Grameen would have to increase interest rates to 33 percent a year (Morduch 1999). Group-lending schemes have succeeded where others had failed in providing credit to the poor, but as Morduch (1998b) notes, a large number still face the problem of high operating costs. Morduch proposes two options. The first is to focus on simple programs to reach the poor, such as the simplified administrative procedures and "minimalist credit" approach practiced by Bangladesh's Association for Social Advancement.[19] Alternatively, or simultaneously, governments and donors could undertake to subsidize the administrative costs of programs with significant poverty-focused outreach. The relevant issue here is whether subsidies used for this purpose are a better way of helping the poor than subsidies used for other purposes. Determining that will require careful evaluation of the impact of alternative actions.

The evidence on the outcomes of group lending is mixed. Some find evidence of substantial benefit. Pitt and Khandker (1998b), for example, estimate that household consumption increases by 18 taka for every 100 taka lent to a woman and by 11 taka for every 100 taka lent to a man. They also find evidence that access to credit improves the borrowing household's ability to smooth consumption across seasons (Pitt and Khandker 1998a). There is also evidence, however, that significant increases in consumption are primarily realized by moderately poor households that borrow beyond a threshold loan size (Zaman 1998).[20] Using the same data as Pitt and Khandker and correcting for a possible error in their selectivity correction, Morduch (1998a) finds no increase in consumption but does find evidence of consumption smoothing.

Even if the benefits of group lending are limited to consumption smoothing, this may lead to long-run gains that are not being captured in the surveys currently available. As noted above, the ability to smooth consumption is important not only for its immediate benefit but also because it may help households pursue longer-run strategies to escape poverty that might otherwise be considered too risky. The issue of linkage also arises in other ways. There is evidence that participation in microcredit programs leads to an improvement in nutritional indicators and in children's schooling (Khandker 1998) and that access to credit has an empowering effect on female borrowers, giving them greater control over various aspects of their lives (Hashemi, Schuler, and Riley 1996).[21]

Savings offer another means of smoothing consumption. Although many of the microfinance schemes have not focused on savings mobilization, some successful schemes with such a focus are emerging. In 1986 Bank Rakyat Indonesia (BRI) introduced a saving program, SIMPEDES, that offers modest interest rates but allows withdrawals at any time. It also runs a lottery, with the chances of winning linked to the size of deposits. By 1988 over 4 million poor households were participating, and by the end of 1996, 16 million were (Morduch 1999). As a result, BRI has access to a relatively cheap source of funds amounting to US$3 billion in 1996, and households can accumulate assets, as well as smooth consumption.

Self-Revelation. A second important innovation, self-revelation of information, has been used effectively in public works schemes. For example, in Chile a large public works program undertaken in the wake of a major crisis in the 1980s succeeded in part because it set wages low enough to ensure that the neediest were the main participants (Glewwe and others 2000). In a World Bank project in Argentina in 1997 that offered low-wage work on community projects in poor areas, more than half the participants were from the poorest 10 percent of the population (World Bank 1999: 126). These and many other examples provide a convincing argument that the basic approach has merit. The issues now are how to keep administrative costs down and how to draw the balance between asset creation and insurance. Programs that offer guaranteed employment provide the most insurance but may not create the most productive assets.

Because public insurance schemes may displace private efforts, it is important to understand people's preferences for allocating time. For example, Datt and Ravallion (1994) investigated the opportunity costs to participants in rural public works projects in two Indian villages. In one village the public works participants are mostly unemployed, so their opportunity costs are low and their net benefits from the program are high. In the other village public works employment mostly replaces wage labor and own-farm work, leading to a substantially higher opportunity cost and lower net benefits. Cox and Jimenez (1992) and

Cox, Eser, and Jimenez (1998) examined whether the motive for private transfers in Peru is altruism or exchange; this is important because such motivation can influence the effects of public income transfers. They found that social security benefits "crowd out" private transfers: receiving social security reduces the probability of receiving a private transfer by about 6 percent. The response is stronger in the Philippines, where Cox and Jimenez (1995) found that private transfers would be 37 percent higher in the absence of retirement income.

Although these factors should be borne in mind when designing public action, there are two reasons to persevere with public schemes. First, as we see from these examples, the offset is not one for one. Second, informal mechanisms are unlikely to be able to insure against villagewide or regionwide risks.

The East Asian crisis underscored the importance of safety nets in a dramatic and unfortunate way. Countries such as Indonesia had neither the financial resources nor the administrative mechanisms to deal with the fallout from the crisis. Actions being taken now will strengthen safety nets and social security throughout the region. But there is a lesson for macroeconomic policy, as well. The degree of risk in macroeconomic policy has to be managed in light of the ability to protect citizens in the event of a crisis and the extent to which international action limits the likelihood of a crisis (Stiglitz 1998a, 1998b). Unless there is an adequate domestic safety net and international restraints on investors, the risks in liberalizing financial markets and capital accounts are great.

Many of the participatory poverty surveys reviewed earlier pointed to a concern with risk. Other evidence documents the costs of various actions that the poor take to offset risk or to deal with its consequences. There is also a growing but as yet incomplete body of evidence regarding public action to alleviate the risk dimension of poverty. Although not all the evidence points in the same direction, and further evaluations are clearly needed, experience suggests that a combination of public works programs, group-lending schemes (subsidized, where necessary), and simple deposit schemes offer the poor at least some support in dealing with risk.

From Isolation to Participation

Recent theoretical contributions show how the median voter in a high-inequality, democratic society can bring about more redistributive policies through the vote, albeit at the cost of slower growth (Persson and Tabellini 1994). What is wrong with this picture as applied to actual events in developing countries over the past 25 years? Apart from the inconclusive empirical evidence, the theory assumes that most countries are democracies, in which votes determine policy, and that the policy, once determined, can be effectively implemented. Neither assumption captures the reality of developing countries over the last quarter of the 20th century.

To start with, even as late as 1990 fewer than half the countries in the world were democracies. Inequality in many high-inequality countries is largely a consequence of the disproportionate share of income received by the richest decile. In the high-inequality countries of Latin America the richest decile captures 40 percent of national income. Whether through the political process or outside it, this concentration of economic power must give a small percentage of the population a tremendous capacity to influence the formulation of policy, and if not its formulation, then its implementation. For example, Anand and Kanbur (1991) note that as the targeting of the Sri Lankan rice ration was improved, it was allowed to be eroded by inflation with little or no protest. Those with the power to protest were not benefiting from the ration, and the erosion in its value actually freed resources for other uses that might be to the benefit of the more powerful groups.

Democracy is, however, spreading; the number of countries with electoral democracies increased from 76 in 1990 to 117 in 1995. This development and the increasing commitment to respect civil and political rights (140 countries have so far ratified the International Covenant on Civil and Political Rights) are opening the way to a larger say for the poor in policymaking.

"Ownership" has been shown to be a key factor in the success or failure of structural adjustment loans. A study of 81 adjustment operations supported by the World Bank between 1980 and 1992 developed a measure of borrower ownership that included the locus of the initiative for the program, the level of intellectual commitment of key policymakers, the expression of political will by top leadership, and (of most interest for this discussion) efforts to build consensus. The last element assessed the extent to which the government had undertaken a broad public campaign to elicit support for the program. In the 16 cases in which local ownership was considered very high, 15 of the operations were judged successful; in the 17 cases with very low local ownership, only 3 operations were judged successful (Branson and Jayarajah 1995). Although these and similar results point to the importance of ownership, they do not tell us the extent to which the poor were consulted.

The impact of the poor's voice is more apparent at the project level. Top-down solutions have often failed. Over the past decade development practitioners have become increasingly aware that the poor have better knowledge of their situation and their needs and can contribute to the design of policies and projects intended to better their lot. Once the poor have a say in design, they are more committed to implementation. In direct contrast to the isolation the poor often endure, successful implementation calls for their inclusion and active participation in a wide range of circumstances.

Development practitioners have come to a consensus that participation by the intended beneficiaries improves project performance. There are many examples of the value of participation. In Indonesia the government and an aid organization, CARE, shifted their focus to community demand as the key selection criterion for water supply and sanitation projects, with control in the hands of communities. Over the period 1979–90 the combined cash contributions of CARE and the Indonesian government dropped from approximately 80 percent of project costs to about 30 percent. Communities had provided all cash contributions for physical construction for more than three fourths of the projects, and most had successfully operated and maintained their systems. Many communities had also helped neighboring groups develop their own systems (Narayan 1994).

Econometric evidence leads to the same conclusion as these case studies. In a careful study of 121 rural water supply projects in 49 countries, Isham, Narayan, and Pritchett (1994) found that 7 out of every 10 projects succeeded when the intended beneficiaries took an active part in project design but that only 1 in 10 succeeded when they did not. Government support for a participatory approach greatly increased the likelihood of participation. Case studies of some of these projects confirmed the importance of participation. For example, Phase I of the Aguthi Rural Water Supply Project in Kenya did not involve community members. The project ran into construction delays, cost overruns, and disagreement over payment methods. To get the project back on track, local leaders and project staff organized stakeholder conferences. With community involvement, Phase II of the project was completed on time and within budget (Narayan 1994).

The interactions between voice and other development outcomes and between risk and other development outcomes are perhaps less well understood and less well researched than the links between growth and inequality and between growth and human development that were discussed earlier. Nevertheless, the evidence available to date suggests that these are areas that warrant further attention with respect to information failures (see, for example, Kaufmann, Kraay, and Zoido-Lobatón 1999; Rodrik 1999). They have the potential to increase greatly the effectiveness of project and program implementation by giving the poor more say in matters that concern them. By reducing exposure to risk, they can provide the poor with the security to explore high-return activities that may have been outside their reach in the past but that may be their best hope for escaping poverty.

Outstanding Issues

How would Benjamin Seebohm Rowntree assess the evolution of thought over the past quarter-century from the perspective of his investigation of poverty in York in the early 1900s? We think he would have three reactions. First, he might be surprised that the basic approach to measuring poverty which he used almost 100 years ago is still very much a feature of how we measure poverty today. Second, he would agree that life expectancy, literacy, and morbidity are key aspects of well-being and that the poor in the city of York suffered in all these dimensions. Indeed, Rowntree devoted a chapter to the relation of poverty to health. He observed that "the death-rate is the best instrument for measuring the variations in the physical well-being of the people," and found that "the mortality amongst the very poor is more than twice as high as amongst the best paid section of the working classes." High infant and child mortality, as well as illness and physical underdevelopment, afflicted the poor of York in Rowntree's time.

His third reaction, to the notion of giving the poor voice and providing them with safety nets, would be nuanced. Although his object was "to state facts rather than to suggest remedies," he remarked that "the suffering may be all but voiceless" and that even if all persons in poverty over 65 received old age pensions, it would only reduce poverty by about 1 percent. He criticized the inadequacy of the workhouses and relief administration and noted that the very poor often cannot afford to insure against illness, but he made only vague and passing mention of the prospect that the poor could organize politically or that the state might change its power relations to the individual. In all, Rowntree exhibits a surprising modernity, stressing the importance of education (especially for women), acclaiming the benefits of capacity-building public service, and describing the interconnecting, cyclical nature of poverty, where outcomes also become causes.

Looking back from our vantage point of today, how should we assess the evolution of thinking? Although different methods of defining and measuring poverty inevitably identify different groups as poor, the evidence suggests that the differences may not be that great. The methods' real contribution is not to measurement but to strategy: the way in which poverty is defined drives the strategy for dealing with it. One obvious effect of the broadening of the definition is that a larger range of policy instruments becomes relevant to the task of reducing poverty. A less obvious effect arises from the interactions among different aspects of poverty, which call for a careful integration of policies.

When the focus was confined to income, the key interaction was between growth in the mean and changes in equality. As the definition of poverty expanded to include health status, literacy, and so on, the key interaction became that between efforts to increase income and efforts to improve these other dimensions of well-being. And when the definition was further extended to embrace risk, vulnerability, and voice, then safety nets, access to credit, and participation emerged as critical to the poor's ability to take advantage of risky, poverty-reducing opportunities and to shape economic policy and programs to their benefit.

Looking forward, what are the key outstanding areas in need of additional research? We close with two suggestions. First, additional research is required to increase our understanding of the interactions identified in this review. We began by asserting that the appropriate package of policies would have a greater impact than the sum of their parts because of these interactions. Although we have presented evidence to support this claim, more information about the best combinations of policy for countries with different problems and different capacities would be of great value. In our view, this calls for careful, in-depth country case studies to explore how different policy packages have or have not benefited the poor.[22] Second, we have seen how information failures and knowledge gaps may have undermined the access of the poor to credit and insurance and limited their role in the design and implementation of policies and projects. Again, we gave instances in which these problems seemed to have been overcome through the development of new institutional arrangements. A full assessment of these innovations is, however, lacking. We therefore suggest that another priority is the careful evaluation of institutional innovations to find out what works and why.[23]

Notes

1. The latest report on poverty, World Bank (2000), was published after this chapter was written.

2. For useful surveys, see Callan and Nolan (1991); Lipton and Ravallion (1995).

3. To permit cross-country comparison, *World Development Report 1990* used a range of income, from US$275 to US$370 per person a year in 1985 PPP prices. The range spanned the poverty lines estimated for a number of countries: Bangladesh, the Arab Republic of Egypt, India, Indonesia, Kenya, Morocco, and Tanzania.

4. Dominance conditions are a more formal solution to the problem of uncertainty about the poverty line (Atkinson 1987).

5. The choice of an "equivalence scale" that sets a proportion for children's needs versus those of adults can change commonly held views about poverty. For example, if economies of size are sufficiently strong, the negative relationship between size of household and expenditure per person can be reversed (Lanjouw and Ravallion 1995).

6. Cited in Haddad, Hoddinott, and Alderman (1997).

7. Most of Kuznets's figures were from the United States, the United Kingdom, and Germany, with some references to India, Prussia, Ceylon (now Sri Lanka), and Puerto Rico (Kuznets 1955).

8. Paukert (1973); Chenery and Syrquin (1975); Ahluwalia (1976); Ahluwalia, Carter, and Chenery (1979).

9. Anand and Kanbur (1993); Bruno, Ravallion, and Squire (1998); Deininger and Squire (1998).

10. In his review of income distribution and development, Kanbur (1998) describes this conclusion as the "emerging consensus."

11. The poverty gap is defined as the amount of transfer (perfectly targeted) required to bring every one up to the poverty line, expressed as a proportion of the poverty line times the total population.

12. Authors' calculation using the Deininger-Squire database.

13. See Easterly and others (1993) on growth and Li, Squire, and Zou (1998) on inequality.

14. Authors' calculations using the Deininger-Squire database.

15. See, for example, McGillivray and White (1993) and Ravallion (1997) on the subject of the similar Human Development Index.

16. For example, Ravallion and Datt (1999) show that nonfarm economic growth in India's states was less effective in reducing poverty in states with poor basic education.

17. The data are population-weighted averages for Indonesia, the Republic of Korea, Malaysia, the Philippines, Thailand, and Taiwan (China).

18. Salmen goes on to say that in-depth listening to the poor would reveal whether getting out of poverty is more a problem of lack of representation or lack of material resources—an issue of key importance in poverty reduction.

19. The term "minimalist" credit, whereby only loans are provided, contrasts with the "integrated credit" approach practiced by BRAC in Bangladesh, in which some loans are supplemented with a package of extension services, training, and marketing support.

20. Zaman (1998) estimates this threshold as 10,000 taka in cumulative loans.

21. Hashemi, Schuler, and Riley (1996) develop an empowerment index made up of indicators such as female mobility, ownership and control over resources, and decisionmaking over household purchases. They show that borrowing from Grameen and BRAC has a significant impact on empowerment when a range of other factors is controlled for.

22. Taiwan (China) provides good examples, from the early work of Fei, Ranis, and Kuo (1979) to the more recent work of Chu (1995). Preliminary papers emerging from a research project on income distribution managed by François Bourguignon and Nora Lustig also illustrate the type of detailed analysis that can be undertaken at the country level. See Ferreira and Paes de Barros (1999) for Brazil and Bouillon, Legovini, and Lustig (1998).

23. Good examples to date include work on microfinance (Morduch 1998b, for example) and on public employment schemes (Datt and Ravallion 1994).

References

Ahluwalia, Montek S. 1976. "Inequality, Poverty, and Development." *Journal of Development Economics* 3 (September): 307–42.

Ahluwalia, Montek S., Nicholas G. Carter, and Hollis B. Chenery. 1979. "Growth and Poverty in Developing Countries." *Journal of Development Economics* 6: 299–341.

Alderman, Harold, Pierre André Chiapponi, Lawrence Haddad, John Hoddinott, and Ravi Kanbur. 1995. "Unitary versus Collective Models of the Household: Is It Time to Shift the Burden of Proof?" *World Bank Research Observer* 10 (1, February): 1–19.

Alderman, Harold, Jere R. Behrman, Victor Lavy, and Rekha Menon. 1997. "Child Nutrition, Child Health, and School Enrollment: A Longitudinal Analysis." Policy Research Working Paper 1700. Policy Research Department, World Bank, Washington, D.C.

Aleem, Irfan. 1993. "Imperfect Information, Screening, and the Costs of Informal Lending: A Study of a Rural Credit Market in Pakistan." In Karla Hoff, Avishay Braverman, and Joseph E. Stiglitz, eds., *The Economics of Rural Organization: Theory, Practice, and Policy*, 131–53. New York: Oxford University Press.

Anand, Sudhir, and Christopher J. Harris. 1994. "Choosing a Welfare Indicator." *American Economic Review* 84 (May): 226–31.

Anand, Sudhir, and S. M. R. Kanbur. 1991. "Public Policy and Basic Needs Provision in Sri Lanka." In Jean Drèze and Amartya Sen, eds., *The Political Economy of Hunger*. Vol. 3: *Endemic Hunger*. Oxford, U.K.: Clarendon Press.

———. 1993. "Inequality and Development: A Critique." *Journal of Development Economics* 41 (June): 19–43.

Anand, Sudhir, and Martin Ravallion. 1993. "Human Development in Poor Countries: On the Role of Private Incomes and Public Services." *Journal of Economic Perspectives* 7 (1, winter): 133–50.

Appleton, Simon, and Lina Song. 1999. "Income and Human Development at the Household Level: Evidence from Six Countries." Center for the Study of African Economies, Oxford, U.K. Processed.

Atkinson, A. B. 1987. "On the Measurement of Poverty." *Econometrica* 55: 749–64.

Barro, Robert J., and Xavier Sala-i-Martin. 1995. *Economic Growth*. New York: McGraw-Hill.

Birdsall, Nancy, and Juan Luis Londoño. 1997. "Asset Inequality Matters: An Assessment of the World Bank's Approach to Poverty Reduction." *American Economic Review* 87 (2): 32–37.

Bonilla-Chacin, M., and J. Hammer. 1999. "Life and Death among the Poorest." Paper presented at the Economist's Forum, World Bank, April.

Bouillon, César, Arianna Legovini, and Nora Lustig. 1998. "Rising Inequality in Mexico: Returns to Household Characteristics." World Bank and Inter-American Development Bank, Washington, D.C. Available at <www.iadb.org>, Publications.

Bourguignon, François, and Christian Morrison. 1990. "Income Distribution, Development, and Foreign Trade: A Cross-Sectional Analysis." *European Economic Review* 34 (6): 1113–32.

Branson, William H., and Carl Jayarajah. 1995. "Evaluating the Impacts of Policy Adjustment." *International Monetary Fund Seminar Series* 1 (January). Washington, D.C.

Bruno, Michael, Martin Ravallion, and Lyn Squire. 1998. "Equity and Growth in Developing Countries: Old and New Perspectives on the Policy Issue." In Vito Tanzi and Ke-young Chu, eds., *Income Distribution and High-Quality Growth*. Cambridge, Mass.: MIT Press.

Callan, Tim, and Brian Nolan. 1991. "Concepts of Poverty and the Poverty Line." *Journal of Economic Surveys* 5 (3): [243]–61.

Chambers, Robert. 1995. "Poverty and Livelihoods: Whose Reality Counts?" *Environment and Urbanization* 7 (April): 173–204.

Chen, Shaohua, and Martin Ravallion. 1997. "What Can New Survey Data Tell Us about Recent Changes in Distribution and Poverty?" *World Bank Economic Review* 11 (2): 357–82.

Chen, Shaohua, Gaurav Datt, and Martin Ravallion. 1994. "Is Poverty Increasing in the Developing World?" *Review of Income and Wealth* 40 (December): 359–76.

Chenery, Hollis B., and Moises Syrquin. 1975. *Patterns of Development, 1950–1970*. New York: Oxford University Press.

Chong, A., and J. Hentschel. 1999. "Bundling of Basic Services, Welfare, and Structural Reform in Perú." Development Research Group and Poverty Reduction and Economic Management Network, World Bank, Washington, D.C. Processed.

Chu, Y. 1995. "Taiwan's Inequality in the Postwar Era." Sun Yat Sen Institute, Taiwan, China. Processed.

Clarke, George R. G. 1996. "More Evidence on Income Distribution and Growth." *Journal of Development Economics* 47 (August): 403–27.

Cox, Donald, and Emmanuel Jimenez. 1992. "Social Security and Private Transfers in Developing Countries: The Case of Peru." *World Bank Economic Review* 6 (1, January): 155–69.

———. 1995. "Private Transfers and the Effectiveness of Public Income Redistribution in the Philippines." In Dominique van de Walle and Kimberly Nead, eds., *Public Spending and the Poor: Theory and Evidence*. Baltimore, Md.: Johns Hopkins University Press.

Cox, Donald, Zekeriya Eser, and Emmanuel Jimenez. 1998. "Motives for Private Transfers over the Life Cycle: An Analytical Framework and Evidence for Peru." *Journal of Development Economics* 55: 57–80.

Datt, Gaurav, and Martin Ravallion. 1994. "Transfer Benefits from Public-Works Employment: Evidence for Rural India." *Economic Journal* 104 (November): 1346–69.

Davis, Jennifer, and Dale Whittington. 1998. "'Participatory' Research for Development Projects: A Comparison of the Community Meeting and Household Survey Techniques." *Economic Development and Cultural Change* 47 (October): 73–94.

Deininger, Klaus, and Lyn Squire. 1998. "New Ways of Looking at Old Issues: Inequality and Growth." *Journal of Development Economics* 57 (December): 259–87.

Easterly, William, Michael Kremer, Lant Pritchett, and Lawrence H. Summers. 1993. "Good Policy or Good Luck? Country Growth Performance and Temporary Shocks." *Journal of Monetary Economics* 32 (December): 459–83.

Fei, John C. H., Gustav Ranis, and Shirley W. Y. Kuo. 1979. *Growth with Equity: The Taiwan Case.* New York: Oxford University Press.

Ferreira, Francisco H. G., and Ricardo Paes de Barros. 1999. "The Slippery Slope: Explaining the Increase in Poverty in Urban Brazil, 1976–1996." Policy Research Working Paper 2210. Poverty Reduction and Economic Management Network, World Bank, Washington, D.C.

Fisher, Gordon M. 1996. "Relative or Absolute—New Light on the Behavior of Poverty Lines over Time." *Newsletter of the Government Statistics Section and the Social Statistics Section of the American Statistical Association* (summer): 10–12. Available at <http://aspe.os.dhhs.gov/poverty/papers/relabs.htm>.

Forbes, Kristin. 1998. "A Reassessment of the Relationship between Inequality and Growth." Massachusetts Institute of Technology, Cambridge, Mass. Processed.

Fortmann, Louise, and Dianne Rocheleau. 1989. "Why Agroforestry Needs Women: Four Myths and a Case Study." In *Women's Role in Forest Resource Management: A Reader.* Bangkok: Food and Agriculture Organization of the United Nations, Regional Wood Energy Development Program in Asia.

Glewwe, Paul. 1997. *How Does Schooling of Mothers Improve Child Health? Evidence from Morocco.* Living Standards Measurement Study Working Paper 128. Washington, D.C.: World Bank.

Glewwe, Paul, and Jacques van der Gaag. 1990. "Identifying the Poor in Developing Countries: Do Different Definitions Matter?" *World Development* 18: 803–14.

Glewwe, Paul, Michele Gragnolati, and Hassan Zaman. 2000. "Who Gained From Vietnam's Boom in the 1990s?" Policy Research Working Paper 2275. World Bank, Washington, D.C.

Glick, Peter, and David E. Sahn. 1997. "Gender and Education Impacts on Employment and Earnings in West Africa: Evidence from Guinea." *Economic Development and Cultural Change* 45 (July): 793–823.

Goedhart, T., V. Halberstadt, A. Kapteyn, and B. van Praag. 1977. "The Poverty Line: Concept and Measurement." *Journal of Human Resources* 12: 503–20.

Haddad, Lawrence, and Ravi Kanbur. 1990. "How Serious Is the Neglect of Intrahousehold Inequality?" Policy Research Working Paper 296. Office of the Research Administrator, World Bank, Washington, D.C.

Haddad, Lawrence, John Hoddinott, and Harold Alderman, eds. 1997. *Intrahousehold Resource Allocation in Developing Countries: Models, Methods, and Policy.* Baltimore, Md.: Johns Hopkins University Press.

Hagenaars, Aldi J. M. 1986. *The Perception of Poverty*. Amsterdam: North-Holland.

Hashemi, Syed M., Sidney Ruth Schuler, and Ann P. Riley. 1996. "Rural Credit Programs and Women's Empowerment in Bangladesh." *World Development* 24 (April): 635–53.

Hazell, Peter, Carlos Pomareda, and Alberto Valdés, eds. 1986. *Crop Insurance for Agricultural Development: Issues and Experience*. Baltimore, Md.: Johns Hopkins University Press.

IADB (Inter-American Development Bank). 1998. *Facing Up to Inequality in Latin America*. Washington, D.C.

Isham, Jonathan, Deepa Narayan, and Lant Pritchett. 1994. "Does Participation Improve Project Performance? Establishing Causality with Subjective Data." Policy Research Working Paper 1357. Office of the Vice President, Development Economics, World Bank, Washington, D.C.

Jacoby, Hanan G., and Emmanuel Skoufias. 1997. "Risk, Financial Markets, and Human Capital in a Developing Country." *Review of Economic Studies* 64 (3): 311–35.

Jalan, Jyotsna, and Martin Ravallion. 1998. "Transient Poverty in Postreform Rural China." *Journal of Comparative Economics* 26 (June): 338–57.

———. 1999. "Are the Poor Less Well Insured? Evidence on Vulnerability to Income Risk in Rural China." *Journal of Development Economics* 58 (February): 61–81.

Jodha, N. S. 1995. "Common Property Resources and the Dynamics of Rural Poverty in India's Dry Regions." *Unasylva* 46 (180): 23–29.

Kakwani, Nanak C. 1980. *Income Inequality and Poverty: Methods of Estimation and Policy Applications*. New York: Oxford University Press.

Kanbur, Ravi. 1998. "Income Distribution and Development." Working Paper 98-13. Department of Agricultural, Resource, and Managerial Economics, Cornell University, Ithaca, N.Y.

Kaufmann, Daniel, Aart Kraay, and Pablo Zoido-Lobatón. 1999. "Governance Matters." Policy Research Working Paper 2196. Development Research Group, Macroeconomics and Growth, and World Bank Institute, World Bank, Washington, D.C.

Khandker, Shahidur S. 1998. *Fighting Poverty with Microcredit: Experience in Bangladesh*. New York: Oxford University Press.

Kuznets, Simon. 1955. "Economic Growth and Income Inequality." *American Economic Review* 45 (1, March): 1–28.

Lanjouw, Peter, and Martin Ravallion. 1995. "Poverty and Household Size." *Economic Journal* 105 (November): 1415–34.

Lewis, W. Arthur. 1954. "Economic Development with Unlimited Supplies of Labor." *Manchester School of Economic and Social Studies* 22 (May): 139–91.

Li, Hongyi, and Heng-fu Zou. 1998. "Income Inequality Is Not Harmful for Growth: Theory and Evidence." *Review of Development Economics* 2 (3): 318–34.

Li, Hongyi, Lyn Squire, and Heng-fu Zou. 1998. "Explaining International and Intertemporal Variations in Income Inequality." *Economic Journal* 108 (January): 1–18.

Lipton, Michael, and Martin Ravallion. 1995. "Poverty and Policy." In Jere Behrman and T. N. Srinivasan, eds., *Handbook of Development Economics*, vol. 3. Amsterdam: Elsevier.

Lundberg, Mattias, and Lyn Squire. 1999. "Growth and Inequality: Extracting the Lessons for Policymakers." Policy Research Department, World Bank, Washington, D.C. Available at <http://www.worldbank.org/html/prdmg/grthweb/semiold.htm>.

Manser, Marilyn, and Murray Brown. 1980. "Marriage and Household Decisionmaking: A Bargaining Analysis." *International Economic Review* 21 (1): 31–44.

Marshall, Alfred. 1925. *The Principles of Economics*. 8th ed. London: Macmillan.

Martella, A. 1996. "Djibouti Participatory Poverty Assessment." Background document for the Djibouti Poverty Assessment. World Bank, Washington, D.C.

McElroy, Marjorie, and Mary Jean Horney. 1981. "Nash-Bargained Household Decisions: Toward a Generalization of the Theory of Demand." *International Economic Review* 22 (2): 333–50.

McGillivray, Mark, and Howard White. 1993. "Measuring Development? The UNDP's Human Development Index." *Journal of International Development* 5 (March–April): 183–92.

Mfoulou, J., V. Nga Ndongo, J. Aboa Ngono, A. S. Zoa, and C. Bala. 1994. "Evaluation participative de la pauvreté au Cameroun." Report of study conducted in Yaoundé for the World Bank, July.

Moore, Mick, Madhulika Choudhary, and Neelam Singh. 1998. "How Can We Know What They Want? Understanding Local Perceptions of Poverty and Ill-Being in Asia." IDS Working Paper 80. Institute of Development Studies, University of Sussex, Brighton, U.K.

Morduch, Jonathan J. 1990. "Risk, Production, and Saving: Theory and Evidence from Indian Households." Working Paper. Department of Economics, Harvard University, Cambridge, Mass.

——. 1995. "Income Smoothing and Consumption Smoothing." *Journal of Economic Perspectives* 9 (3, summer): 103–14.

——. 1998a. "Does Microfinance Really Help the Poor? New Evidence from Flagship Programs in Bangladesh." Hoover Institution, Stanford University, Stanford, Calif. Processed.

——. 1998b. "The Grameen Bank: A Financial Reckoning." Hoover Institution, Stanford University, Stanford, Calif. Processed.

——. 1999. "The Microfinance Promise." *Journal of Economic Literature* 37 (4, December): 1569–1614.

Mpol, F., M. Mendouka, A. Bikoï, and L. A. Ndongo. 1994. "Evaluation participative de la pauvreté au Cameroun." Report of study conducted in the East Province for the World Bank, June.

Murphy, Kevin M., Andrei Shleifer, and Robert W. Vishny. 1991. "The Allocation of Talent: Implications for Growth." *Quarterly Journal of Economics* 106 (2): 503–30.

Narayan, Deepa. 1994. *The Contribution of People's Participation: Evidence from 121 Rural Water Supply Projects*. Environmentally Sustainable Development Occasional Paper Series 1. Washington, D.C.: World Bank.

Narayan, Deepa, and David Nyamwaya. 1996. "Learning from the Poor: A Participatory Poverty Assessment in Kenya." Environment Department Paper 34. World Bank, Washington, D.C.

Paukert, Felix. 1973. "Income Distribution at Different Levels of Development: A Survey of Evidence." *International Labour Review* 108 (2–3): 97–125.

Persson, Torsten, and Guido Tabellini. 1994. "Is Inequality Harmful for Growth?" *American Economic Review* 84 (3): 600–21.

Pitt, Mark M., and S. Khandker. 1998a. "Credit Programs for the Poor and Seasonality in Rural Bangladesh." Draft, January 9. Brown University, Providence, R.I., and World Bank, Washington, D.C.

———. 1998b. "The Impact of Group-Based Credit Programs on Poor Households in Bangladesh: Does the Gender of Participants Matter?" *Journal of Political Economy* 106 (October): 958–96.

Poppele, Jessica, Sudarno Sumarto, and Lant Pritchett. 1999. "Social Impacts of the Indonesian Crisis: New Data and Policy Implications." Social Monitoring and Early Response Unit, Jakarta.

Pritchett, Lant. 1996. "Where Has All the Education Gone?" Policy Research Working Paper 1581. Policy Research Department, World Bank, Washington, D.C.

Ravallion, Martin. 1997. "Good and Bad Growth: The Human Development Reports." *World Development* 25 (5, May): 631–38.

———. 1998. "Does Aggregation Hide the Harmful Effects of Inequality on Growth?" *Economics Letters* 61: 73–77.

Ravallion, Martin, and Gaurav Datt. 1999. "When Is Growth Pro-Poor? Evidence from the Diverse Experiences of India's States." Policy Research Working Paper 2263. Poverty and Human Resources, Development Research Group, and Poverty Reduction and Economic Management, South Asia Regional Office, World Bank, Washington, D.C.

Ravallion, Martin, and Dominique van de Walle. 1991. "Urban-Rural Cost of Living Differentials in a Developing Economy." *Journal of Urban Economics* 29: 113–27.

Robb, Caroline M. 1998. *Can the Poor Influence Policy? Participatory Poverty Assessments in the Developing World*. Directions in Development series. Washington, D.C.: World Bank.

Rodrik, Dani. 1999. *The New Global Economy and Developing Countries: Making Openness Work*. Policy Essay 24. Washington, D.C.: Overseas Development Council.

Rowntree, Benjamin Seebohm. 1910. *Poverty: A Study of Town Life*. London: Macmillan.

Salmen, Lawrence F. 1995. "Participatory Poverty Assessment: Incorporating Poor People's Perspectives into Poverty Assessment Work." Environment Department Paper 24, Social Assessment series. World Bank, Washington, D.C.

Sen, Amartya. 1981. *Poverty and Famines: An Essay on Entitlement and Deprivation.* Oxford, U.K.: Clarendon Press.

———. 1984. *Resources, Values, and Development.* Oxford, U.K.: Basil Blackwell.

———. 1999. *Development as Freedom.* New York: Knopf.

Singh, Inderjit, Lyn Squire, and John A. Strauss, eds. 1986. *Agricultural Household Models: Extensions, Applications and Policy.* Baltimore, Md.: Johns Hopkins University Press.

Squire, Lyn. 1993. "Fighting Poverty." American Economic Review, *Papers and Proceedings* 83 (2): 377–82.

Stiglitz, Joseph E. 1998a. "Must Financial Crises Be This Frequent and This Painful?" McKay Lecture, Pittsburgh, Pa., September 23.

———. 1998b. "Responding to Economic Crises: Policy Alternatives for Equitable Recovery and Development." Remarks at the North-South Institute Seminar, "Recovery from Crisis," Ottawa, September 29.

Strauss, John, and Duncan Thomas. 1997. "Health and Wages: Evidence on Men and Women in Urban Brazil." *Journal of Econometrics* 77 (1): 159–85.

———. 1998. "Health, Nutrition, and Economic Development." *Journal of Economic Literature* 36: 766–817.

Thomas, Duncan. 1990. "Intra-Household Resource Allocation: An Inferential Approach." *Journal of Human Resources* 25 (4, fall): 635–64.

Thomas, Duncan, John Strauss, and Maria Helena Henriques. 1991. "How Does Mother's Education Affect Child Height?" *Journal of Human Resources* 26 (2, spring): 183–211.

Udry, Christopher. 1990. "Rural Credit in Northern Nigeria: Credit as Insurance in a Rural Economy." *World Bank Economic Review* 4: 251–69.

———. 1994. "Risk and Insurance in a Rural Credit Market: An Empirical Investigation in Northern Nigeria." *Review of Economic Studies* 61: 495–526.

UNDP (United Nations Development Programme). 1994. *Human Development Report.* New York: Oxford University Press.

van de Walle, Dominique. 1994. "The Distribution of Subsidies through Public Health Services in Indonesia, 1978–87." *World Bank Economic Review* 8 (2, May): 279–309.

van de Walle, Dominique, and Kimberly Nead, eds. 1995. *Public Spending and the Poor: Theory and Evidence.* Baltimore, Md.: Johns Hopkins University Press.

World Bank. 1980. *World Development Report 1980.* New York: Oxford University Press.

———. 1990. *World Development Report 1990: Poverty.* New York: Oxford University Press.

———. 1991. *Assistance Strategies to Reduce Poverty.* Policy Paper. Washington, D.C.

————. 1994. "Zambia Poverty Assessment." Vol. 5: "Participatory Poverty Assessment." November 30. Washington, D.C.

————. 1995. "Cameroon: Diversity, Growth, and Poverty Reduction." Economic Report. Africa Region, Washington, D.C.

————. 1996. *Poverty Reduction and the World Bank: Progress and Challenges in the 1990s*. Washington, D.C.

————. 1997. "Djibouti—Crossroads of the Horn of Africa: Poverty Assessment." Sector Report. Africa Region, Washington, D.C.

————. 1998a. *East Asia: The Road to Recovery*. Washington, D.C.: World Bank.

————. 1998b. "Note on Poverty in the Republic of Tajikistan." Prepared for the Consultative Group Meeting, May 20. Washington, D.C.

————. 1999. *World Development Report 1998/99: Knowledge for Development*. New York: Oxford University Press.

————. 2000. *World Development Report 2000/01: Attacking Poverty*. New York: Oxford University Press.

Zaman, Hassan. 1998. "Who Benefits and to What Extent? An Evaluation of BRAC's Micro-Credit Program." D.Phil. thesis, University of Sussex, Brighton, U.K.

Development Issues: Settled and Open

Shahid Yusuf and Joseph E. Stiglitz

A DEVELOPMENT ISSUE MAY BE defined as a matter regarding the course of development that demands resolution. Our intention in this paper is to present major development issues that will test researchers and policymakers in the decades ahead. As we enter the new century, whether we can sustain the achievements of the past 50 years and whittle away at the worsening problem of poverty (Figure 1) will depend on how these issues are tackled, on two levels—intellectual and practical. Each issue requires careful conceptualization and analysis. Only after such conceptualization and analysis can policies appropriate for a particular context be devised and implemented.

Past Issues

For seven development issues, the years of intensive debate are behind us, although academic skirmishing continues and the econometric chiseling of coefficients remains a furious preoccupation for many. The solutions to these issues, while complex, have graduated to the realm of "normal science," becoming a part of the common wisdom of development economics. This common wisdom serves as a foundation for policy in poor and industrial countries alike.[1]

What Are the Sources of Growth?

Although a precise answer to this question has eluded the most diligent researchers, nearly 40 years of increasingly refined analysis has established the primary importance of capital accumulation and factor productivity that arise from research, learning, technological change, and improvements in the quality of labor. The contribution of human capi-

227

Figure 1. Population Living on Less than $1 PPP a Day
in Developing Regions, Numbers and Population Shares,
1987 and 1993

Millions of people

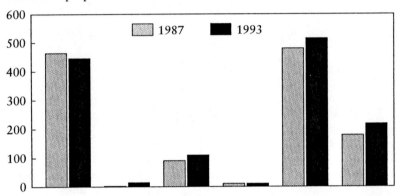

Share of population (percent)

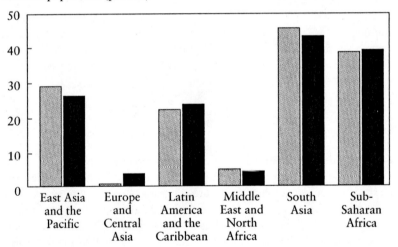

Note: PPP, purchasing power parity. Income is at 1985 prices, adjusted for PPP.
Source: World Bank (1998).

tal, viewed by many as one of the principal drivers of growth in East
Asia, remains contested, and even the role of capital is periodically
challenged.[2] But such skepticism cannot dislodge the body of evidence,
backed by intuition, that links economic growth with investment and

gains in productivity.[3] Thus, promoting investment in equipment and infrastructure and encouraging the accumulation of usable knowledge through a variety of channels are among the central tenets of development. Because investment must, to a large extent, be financed from domestic resources, raising the level of saving is integral to a progrowth strategy.

Does Macrostability Matter, and How Can It Be Sustained?

Concerns about stability arose from the inflationary turbulence of the 1970s and 1980s. The initial findings were equivocal: in countries such as Brazil and the Republic of Korea inflation did not appear to hamper growth, but experience from countries with moderate to high inflation revealed detrimental consequences for investment, equity, allocative efficiency, trade, and foreign direct investment (FDI). By the early 1990s, there was broad consensus that low and stable rates of inflation were desirable goals for developing countries, even though moderate rates of inflation—up to 40 percent a year—were not necessarily injurious to growth (Fischer 1993; Bruno and Easterly 1995; Barro 1997). Research has also shown that macrostability requires flexible labor markets and a prudent and coordinated mix of fiscal, monetary, and exchange rate policies—a mix now enshrined among the fundamentals of macroeconomic policy.

Should Developing Countries Liberalize Trade?

Following World War I and the Great Depression, countries blamed openness for their problems and retreated behind trade barriers (Skidelsky 1996). This policy course carried over into the post–World War II era, when the generation responsible for initiating development saw protection and import-substituting industrialization as the surest road to prosperity (Bruton 1998). Initially, import-substituting industrialization yielded good results, but by the 1980s it was becoming apparent that outward orientation, as practiced by the East Asian economies (under conditions of macrostability and organizational capability), was a more successful strategy on several counts (Rodrik 1998). Apart from the allocative and dynamic gains from freer trade, more open economies showed greater resilience in the face of shocks, attracted larger flows of FDI, enhanced their growth rates through the link between exports and domestic investment, and realized technological progress through export competition, as well as increased access to more technologically sophisticated imports (Lawrence and Weinstein 2000).

By the late 1980s, the debt crisis that afflicted many developing countries in the early 1980s—along with the example of East Asian countries that used exports to overcome the crisis and sustain rapid

Figure 2. Trade, Tariffs, and Nontariff Barriers, East Asia, 1980–94

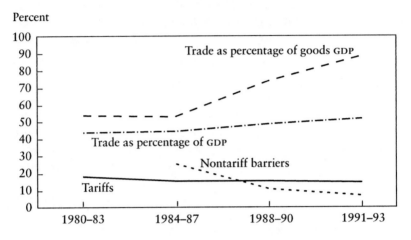

Percent

Note: The figures for tariff and nontariff barriers are weighted averages for all product categories.
Source: Rodrik (1998); World Bank (1998).

growth—caused the pendulum to swing firmly in favor of trade liberalization. Most developing countries became committed to lowering trade barriers by acceding to the rules of the General Agreement on Tariffs and Trade (GATT) and its successor, the World Trade Organization (WTO), and by furthering the cause of international trade disciplines. (Figure 2 illustrates the effect of lower trade barriers on the volume of trade in East Asia.) This trend is reflected in the growth of trade volume. Some countries, however, lagged behind and saw their trade stagnate. The completion of the Uruguay Round of multilateral trade negotiations and the creation of the WTO in 1994 imparted additional momentum to trade liberalization and the elaboration of rules embracing services, intellectual property rights, and FDI. A framework of rules is being put in place, although a multilateral agreement governing FDI is still years away. Barring a reversal stemming from tensions generated by the crisis of the late 1990s, trade liberalization, under the auspices of enforceable multilateral rules, will remain a central tenet of policy for developing countries and the principal avenue for their integration into the global economy.

How Crucial Are Property Rights?

The answer that is now accepted, virtually without dispute, is that secure and enforceable property rights are the lifeblood of an efficient free-market economy. By improving investor confidence, secure property rights boost the flow of capital into productive activities and encourage income growth (Figure 3).[4] Secure property rights also increase FDI and, through it, the volume of both trade and technology transfer.

In the majority of developing countries, many property rights are informally defined and weakly enforced. It is widely accepted that this state of affairs constrains investment. In addition, the recent experience of transition economies has led to general agreement that formally defined rights enjoying the sanction of law are much more useful for economic growth than are informal rights buttressed by custom and enforced through community or extralegal mechanisms.[5]

For transition economies and for most developing countries, maximizing the potential benefits of the market requires that rights be defined and clear enforcement mechanisms be established to protect these rights. In a number of cases this involves fresh delineation of the state's role with respect to the private sector, a substantial augmentation of the state's regulatory and legal capability, and an assertion of the state's

Figure 3. Property Rights Index and Per Capita Income,
Selected Countries, 1990

GNP per capita, PPP (constant 1987 international dollars)

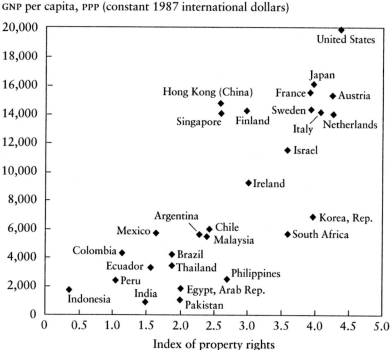

Sources: Ginarte and Park (1997); World Bank (1999).

determination to implement legal and administrative rulings fully and impartially. These measures have their costs; as Holmes and Sunstein (1999: 15) point out, "To the obvious truth that rights depend on government must be added a logical corollary, one rich with implications: rights cost money. Rights cannot be protected or enforced without public funding and support. . . . The right to freedom of contract has public costs no less than the right to health care, the right to freedom of speech no less than the right to decent housing. All rights make claims upon the public Treasury."

History suggests that the struggle to define property rights and place them on a firm legal footing will be a long one (North and Weingast 1989). But in an integrating world environment where markets are the axes of economic activity, the necessity of doing so is now unquestioned.

Is Reducing Poverty a Function of Growth and Asset Accumulation or of Poverty Nets?

The last quarter of this century is distinctive in its acceptance of the reduction of poverty in developing countries as one of humankind's principal goals (World Bank 1990). With over 1.2 billion people living on less than a dollar a day, poverty ranks at the very top of the development agenda.

As we have addressed this challenge, our knowledge about poverty has matured substantially, especially over the past decade. First, there is a far more detailed and nuanced understanding of the nature of poverty. New tools have been developed to measure poverty; poverty traps are better appreciated; the linkages between poverty and other socioeconomic tendencies are in sharper focus; and the dynamics of poverty are undergirded with more perceptive analysis.

Second, the eventual cure for poverty is not pegged exclusively to long-term policy initiatives to maximize growth and improve market functioning. It is now clear that trickle-down, which can take many years to reach the lower income levels, must be supplemented by policies of inclusion that lessen sharp disparities in incomes and assets, enhance human capital accumulation and employment opportunities, and help provide safety nets for the more vulnerable elements of a society.[6]

As experience accumulates, the mix and quality of policy initiatives will undoubtedly change. But the debate is now about exactly how governments and communities can tackle poverty in specific contexts, given the available resources, social capital, and administrative capability.

Can Developing Countries Defer or Downplay Environmental Problems?

After almost two decades of observation, analysis, heated political debate, and assessment of mounting environmental degradation, it has become clear that there is no longer a tradeoff between growth and measures for ensuring environmental sustainability. All developing countries now face the costs of environmental neglect, which in some instances are quite severe. (Environmental degradation may reduce China's gross domestic product by as much as 7 percent.) The salience of concerns regarding ozone depletion, global warming, and biodiversity has also brought out the urgent need for collective action to contain trends that could have potentially disastrous consequences for the world.

Recent research has dissipated much of the fog surrounding earlier discussions. It is clear that developing countries must consciously promote sustainable development with due attention to environmental exigencies. It is also apparent that many countries can immediately embark on win-win policies that lessen environmental costs without diminishing growth prospects. For example, Poland and China have been able to keep carbon dioxide emissions down while achieving economic growth. In addition, possibilities for broader measures are under constant discussion at the international and national levels. Here, the issue is not settled. The awareness that we are eating into our fund of environmental assets has sharpened appreciably through the spread of information and the activities of nongovernmental organizations (NGOs) and international agencies. Furthermore, the knowledge needed to manage the environment sustainably and to reduce damaging emissions is constantly increasing. Still, our understanding of how to arrive at viable international agreements remains sparse. This is a live issue to which we return below.

The readiness of developing countries to pursue environmentally friendly policies is a function of costs, political will, a clearer sense of what needs to be done and how, and the capacity to implement particular actions. Tradeoffs between environmental protection and economic growth are no longer an issue. Only in the short run can depletion of environmental resources lead to growth.

How Closely Should the State Manage and Regulate Development?

Of the major issues of the past half-century, the role of the state has been among the most contentious. At one extreme, the verdict of experience is unequivocal: centrally planned socialism has been convincingly discredited and is no longer viewed as a viable option. Variants of the market system now provide armatures for development throughout the world.

It is also clear, however, that the state has important roles to play. The issue is not whether the state should direct macroeconomic policy, provide public goods, be responsible for safety nets, support privatization, regulate natural monopolies, or manage competition: it should do all these things.[7] A central policy concern is how to equip the state with the administrative capacity to perform these functions efficiently.

What is controversial is whether the state should, in certain circumstances, go beyond these well-posted limits and take a more active part in directing economic activity. Possible policy approaches include direct ownership or close management of industry, direct sponsorship of pilot production facilities, credit allocation, provision of export subsidies, and other strategies for governing the market. Most experience suggests that when a state-owned or state-favored industry is granted preferred or monopoly status—and managed in a way that offers few institutional incentives for high levels of service or productivity growth— direct government support of that industry will prove wasteful or even counterproductive. East Asia offers the primary counterexample; within the geopolitical milieu of East Asia from the 1960s to the 1980s, the state's aggressive role apparently stimulated outward-oriented growth (Crone 1988; Stiglitz 1996; Stiglitz and Uy 1996). The extraordinary growth record of East Asia over recent decades has not been erased by the 1997–99 economic crisis. Over time, however, state intervention in those economies may have subtly shifted from collaborative capitalism to a crony capitalism in which close relationships between government and business focus more on rent-seeking than on raising productivity and enabling aggressive competition in the world economy.

To realize development goals, large and small, it is crucial in East Asia and elsewhere to have a competent, relatively honest, and well-motivated state bureaucracy that can work closely with private and nongovernmental entities.[8] How to create and maintain such a bureaucracy is an issue that is important today and will continue to be important in the early 21st century.

Present Trends

The understanding of development that we command today has been hard-won. It reflects enlightened theorizing, painstaking analysis, an unsparing interrogation of practical experience, and the perspective of a half-century. Many doubts remain regarding the issues sketched above, and these doubts will continue to spark controversy, but we can see our way ahead and can proceed to devising better technical solutions. Even as some of the problems that were critically important in recent decades have been resolved, however, a second generation of equally demanding issues has arisen.

The issues that will engage development thinking have their roots in several ongoing trends with potentially vast consequences. Each of these trends deserves attention.

Globalization

Globalization means the closer integration of the world economy resulting from increasing flows of trade, ideas, and capital and the emergence of multicountry production networks spawned by the investment activities of transnational corporations. Multinationals account for a large share of world production, and perhaps one third of all trade is within firms. But globalism extends beyond economic interdependence to embrace the transformation of time and space as a result of the communications revolution and the spread of information technology. People are now more directly affected by distant events. By the same token, microlevel actions can have macrolevel consequences. A change in the use of fuels or in the energy intensity of production in one part of the world can have significant effects on a host of countries.

The dramatic growth of trade is a major aspect of globalization.[9] Over the past 10 years, trade in goods and services has grown at more than twice the rate of global gross domestic product (GDP), and developing countries' share of trade has risen from 23 to 29 percent.[10] Increasing numbers of firms from developing countries, like their industrial-country counterparts, engage in transnational production and adopt a global perspective in structuring their operations (Prahalad and Liebenthal 1998; United Nations 1998a).

In driving the unparalleled global spread of ideas and innovations, these trade and investment flows have been underpinned by a series of eight rounds of multilateral negotiations to reduce trade barriers, starting with the Geneva Round in 1947. The Uruguay Round, signed in 1994, was the latest and most ambitious. Its lowering of trade barriers is expected to yield economic gains of some US$192 billion, including US$75 billion for developing countries. Its institutional invention, the WTO, allows nations to lock in unilateral trade liberalization—a vital action for development. Of equal importance will be institutional steps to stimulate trade in services, which is likely to be the fastest-growing component in the future.

The acute problems of 1997–99 spotlight the financial interdependencies of countries and are subjecting these interdependencies to intense scrutiny. Although still concentrated in a dozen or so developing nations, international capital flows are rapidly becoming a major force in development, raising the stakes for financial market development, regulation, and liberalization. Financial flows increased dramatically in the 1990s, and although they slipped in 1998, there are good reasons to believe that they will resume their upward trend. Technological developments in computing and telecommunications have drastically lowered transaction costs, and these costs will continue to fall.[11] Alongside these developments, financial innovation has contained risks and offered a rich menu of investment possibilities—another trend that will not be arrested, because the potential rewards are so attractive.[12] More significantly, the supply of financial resources will expand over the next two decades, fed by pension and mutual funds in Western societies.

The rising supply of funds will be matched, if not exceeded, by rising demand, especially from poor countries. Eighty-five percent of the world's population is in countries that are still developing. Half of that population lives in cities. To modernize, industrialize, and urbanize, developing countries will require huge amounts of capital. Most of this capital will come from domestic savings, but well-run developing countries offering solid returns will be able to supplement their domestic savings with resources from all over the globe (Vamvakidis and Wacziarg 1998). Developing countries are also becoming the fastest-growing markets for the products of multinational corporations (United Nations 1998a), and an increasing volume of foreign direct investment will find its way to them, providing jobs for their workers.[13]

The financial markets of the leading industrial nations have melded into a global financial system, permitting ever-larger amounts of capital to be allocated in their economies and to developing and transition economies. Gross FDI by these nations has increased more than 30-fold since 1970.[14] But this growth pales in comparison with worldwide portfolio investment flows, which have shot up to nearly 200 times their 1970 total, exceeding US$1 trillion in 1997.

Mutual funds, hedge funds, pension funds, insurance companies, and other investment and asset managers now compete for national savings. Although this is true primarily in industrial nations, the consequences for developing countries could be significant because institutional investors are diversifying their portfolios internationally, enlarging the pool of potentially available financial capital. In 1995 they managed US$20 trillion, of which an average of 20 percent was invested abroad. This represents a 10-fold increase in the funds held by these institutions and a 40-fold increase in their investment abroad since 1980 (see Figure 4).

Localization

Globalization has led to widened horizons, greater interdependence, and increased awareness of happenings beyond the confines of the community and the nation. It might also be spurring a parallel tendency toward localization—a crystallizing of local or ethnic identities that is, in part, a reaction to globalism.[15] Localization represents a demand for greater political, fiscal, and administrative autonomy in a post–Cold War geopolitical environment in which the pull of centrifugal forces on states has grown stronger. The assertion of identity and the demand for autonomy are tied to the upsurge of participatory politics that has given

Figure 4. Domestic and Foreign Investment by Institutionally Managed Funds, 1980 and 1995

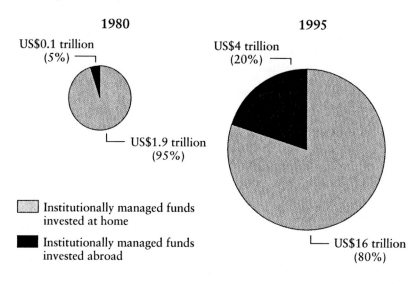

Source: IMF (1998b).

many people a voice and provided foci for organization. Localization trends also reflect the emergence of economic regions comprising linked industrial clusters that have exploited powerful agglomeration economies to enter a virtuous circle of development.[16]

Localization was already on the horizon in the late 1980s. Since then, it has moved toward the foreground. Localization is not exclusively a result of a change in the international political climate; in many countries it stems from acute dissatisfaction with the central government's ability to maintain law and order and to fulfill its promises to raise income, increase the number of jobs, and provide public services. Ethnic divisions, widening regional income disparities, and deepening inequalities between skilled and unskilled workers have at times fanned the discontent, while the rise of national political activity has opened avenues for articulating demands for local autonomy.

The proliferation of new states over the past decade provides strong evidence of centrifugal forces (Alesina and Spolaore 1997; Boniface 1998). In some countries, such as China, Germany, and Italy, prospering provinces are increasingly reluctant to finance transfers to poorer parts of the country. Meanwhile urbanization, by concentrating people in cities, has both facilitated organization and the expression of voice and imparted a municipal focus to decentralization. The discretionary authority of the state has been narrowed, reducing its leverage in bargaining with subnational players. In some instances, desire for local autonomy coincides with the central government's own interest in shedding expenditure responsibilities that exceed its fiscal capability.

These forces drive localization to differing degrees in each developing country. Of 75 developing and transition economies with populations of more than 5 million, 63 are devolving more authority to local governments (Davoodi and Zou 1998). Figure 5 illustrates the same pattern for a sample of 22 developing countries, where the share of local and state governments in total government consumption and investment expenditure is rising.

Environmental Degradation

Environmental pressures, long an international concern, have acquired new urgency. Both the content and the quality of environmental discourse have been completely transformed in the past 20 years. The sheer weight of authoritative scientific evidence now commands the attention of governments and the public. Moreover, with globalization

Figure 5. Share of Subnational Government in Total Government Consumption and Investment

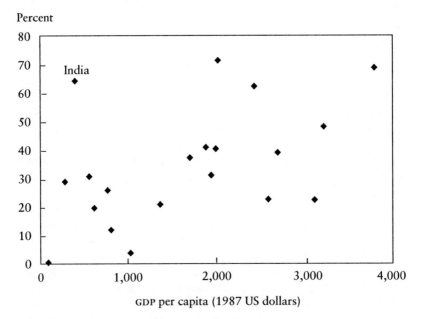

Sources: IMF (1998a); World Bank (1998).

has come new recognition of shared responsibility for the environment. Numerous organizations with a deep interest in this issue, including international, governmental, and nongovernmental organizations, have appeared on the international scene. These bodies have made full use of both the associational arena offered by the United Nations system and the enhanced reach attainable through the new communications technologies to press for stronger institutions to regulate the global commons (Meyer and others 1998).

Global warming, the loss of biodiversity, and other problems related to the global commons are slowly being recognized as problems that the community of nations must take on collectively and that, if left unattended, will worsen as the planet becomes more crowded and development increases resource utilization. This constitutes a major shift in development perspective, even though the implications of environmental change continue to be hotly contested.[17]

Ten years ago, it was possible to brush aside environmental challenges and to emphasize the primacy of growth, stability, and poverty reduction. The world of the 21st century will allow us no such luxury. We can no longer even afford to wait until we have the full scientific picture; action on a broad front is urgently needed to achieve environmental sustainability. Even if the consequences of global warming prove less severe than is now believed, taking immediate steps to arrest the process is cost-effective and appropriate in view of current risk perceptions and the considerable inertia in environmental systems, which could greatly increase mitigation expenses at a later stage.

Demographic Change

The past two decades have witnessed both a gradual tapering in the global fertility rate and a widening gap in population growth rates between countries—a gap that results in populations with widely varying age structures.[18] In most industrial countries and in a substantial number of developing countries, populations are increasing very slowly; in these countries, which include China and several East European economies, the share of older age groups will expand substantially in the next three decades. In other developing countries the situation is quite different; populations are still growing at a rapid clip, and close to half the population is under age 18.

Global population growth slowed from 2.1 percent in the 1960s to 1.5 percent in the late 1990s. The global fertility rate is about 2.7 and is approaching the replacement rate of 2.1. Nevertheless, largely because of the family size preferences of the 2 billion people under age 20 living in developing countries today, world population will rise from 6 billion in 1999 to more than 8 billion in 2025 (Table 1). The sharpest population increases—in Africa, the Middle East, and South Asia—will place

Table 1. World Population by Region, 1995, and Estimates for 2025 and 2050

Region	1995	2025	2050
World	5.69	8.04	9.37
Industrial regions	1.17	1.22	1.16
Developing regions	4.52	6.82	8.20
Africa	0.72	1.45	2.05
Asia	3.47	4.83	5.49
Europe	0.73	0.70	0.64
Latin America	0.48	0.69	0.81
North America	0.30	0.37	0.38

Source: United Nations (1998c).

tremendous stresses on limited natural resources and fragile environments.[19] Moreover, the share of developing-country populations living in cities will rise from one half to well over three quarters. It is worth remembering that in 1900 the earth contained about 1.7 billion people, the vast majority of whom lived in rural areas (Gelbard, Haub, and Kent 1999).

The current population trends have serious economic and political implications. A stagnant and aging population could influence economic growth rates, domestic saving, and the need for social safety nets. Large cohorts of young people will enormously increase the demand for jobs. In countries where growth rates generate insufficient demand for labor, there is high pressure to emigrate and great potential for political turbulence. Combined with the assertion of local identities, an expanding population enlarges the risk of political tension and conflict that is exacerbated by the notable ethnic divisions in many developing countries. Moreover, the increased potential for international migration raises the likelihood of ethnic rivalry in countries that receive streams of migrants.

There is a brighter side to the demographic profile in countries such as Bangladesh that have a youthful population but declining fertility. Here, the falling dependency ratio provides conditions for higher saving and growth, similar to the conditions East Asian economies have experienced. Whether countries can take advantage of this opportunity depends greatly on the domestic and external policy environment.

Food and Water Security

In some regions, population pressure, in conjunction with environmental degradation and global warming, could reduce food security, sharpen frictions over riparian issues, and substantially increase the severity of climate-related shocks. Currently, close to a third of the world's population lives under moderate to severe water stress; this is particularly problematic in the Middle East and North Africa, where 13 countries faced absolute water scarcity in 1990. By 2025, 48 countries, with a total population of 2.8 billion—about one third of the world's projected population—will suffer from water scarcity, and another 9 including China and Pakistan, will be exposed to water stress.[20] The situation could be especially acute in countries such as Egypt, which already uses 97 percent of its available water and faces a growing population. In India it is estimated that by 2025 demand will equal 92 percent of the water supply.[21] Urbanization and industrial development will greatly increase demand for water; industry currently accounts for 50 percent of water use in Europe but for only 5 percent in Africa (Feder and LeMoigne 1994).

In the past, food insecurity has arisen as a source of concern only to dissipate in the face of abundant food supplies. However, uncertainty about future climatic conditions and the diminishing availability of usable water in some densely populated regions introduces additional imponderables. The decline in food supplies could be sharpest at lower latitudes.[22] The increase in grain yields has slowed since 1990, and plant breeders may be approaching the limits of genetic yield potential (see Table 2). Future increases in developing countries' grain output will depend not only on dissemination of better husbandry practices but also on soil, water, and climate conditions (Brown 1997; *Science*, August 22, 1997).

Urbanization

Localizing tendencies, together with a concentration of people in cities, will make urban areas the focus of most economic and political activities. As the 21st century begins, about half of the world's population lives in cities. For higher-income countries in Latin America, Eastern

Table 2. Annual Change in World Grain Yields by Decade, 1950–95

(percent)

Years	Total grain	Rice	Wheat	Corn	Other grains
1950–60	2.0	1.4	1.7	2.6	—
1960–70	2.5	2.1	2.9	2.4	2.3
1970–80	1.9	1.7	2.1	2.7	0.4
1980–90	2.2	2.4	2.9	1.3	1.7
1990–95	0.7	1.0	0.1	1.7	−0.8

— Not available.
Source: Brown (1997).

Europe, and the Middle East, urbanization has already passed its peak, although the social and institutional transformation to an urban society is still occurring in all middle-income countries.

As many Latin American cities enlarge their roles on the national and international stages, Latin American countries are rewriting constitutional rules to regulate and define political and fiscal decentralization. In Eastern Europe and Central Asia governments are struggling to rationalize the structure of cities that have inherited large infrastructures with nonmarket configurations of economic activity and relatively inchoate property rights. In Asia and Africa urbanization is low but is increasing rapidly (see Figure 6), with social and institutional transformation still in its early stages.

Although a current and reliable count of the urban poor in developing countries is not yet available, scattered evidence suggests that several hundred million people are in this category, and the total is rising steadily.[23] As land and job opportunities in the countryside become scarce, more of the rural poor in Brazil, China, India, and many African countries are heading for urban areas. A small fraction finds formal employment. The rest, at least initially, eke out a living in the informal sector or by producing foodstuffs that can be marketed in the city (Losada and others 1998). For many, urban life is precarious and

Figure 6. Urbanization by Region, 1996

Annual growth rate of urban population (percent)

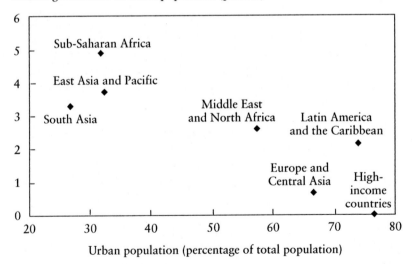

Urban population (percentage of total population)

Source: United Nations (1998c).

involves low and uncertain earnings, a dependence on street foods of uneven quality and safety, lack of shelter, exposure to pollution from a variety of sources, and the threat of violence.

The institutions, social capital, and politics that served a stable, dispersed rural population do not transfer intact to cities. To successfully meet the challenges of industrialization and of population movements into dense urban areas, new institutions and legal structures are required. Much social capital is lost and must be replaced, reconstituted, and augmented.[24] Rural social and market relations, which provide insurance against risks through either patron-client relations or single-stranded market-based interaction, need to be replaced by urban safety nets, formal and informal.[25] Where municipal services are insufficient, communities need to provide services such as waste disposal and to institute their own rules to limit pollution. New and demanding technical, regulatory, and management tasks fall to local governments.

Institutional transitions in cities are influenced by the fact that growing cities have relatively diverse, young, and often disproportionately male populations that are a source of energy and entrepreneurship—although, if jobs are scarce, they can also be a cause of unrest and crime (Bloom and Williamson 1998). Cities are where the middle class emerges and expands. They are focal points for the introduction of modern consumer goods and services and exposure to Western cultures and institutions—a phenomenon accelerated by globalization (Crystal 1997). Each city develops a social order, with demands for local voice and national-level representation, to assess and meet its own unique governance needs.

In several countries, development has led to the emergence of urban industrial networks embracing several municipalities. These interlaced industrial regions account for a sizable share of GDP, exports, and tax revenue (Wu 1997; Scott 1998). Such regions, already a feature of high-income countries such as Germany, Italy, and the United States, have now appeared in Brazil, China, and India. These regions view themselves as local pegs in a globalizing world. Many now see that their interests may not be identical with national interests and look for a more autonomous role in the global trading system. By creating an environment of openness framed by international rules, globalization has made some degree of regional autonomy more feasible.

Issues for the 21st Century

From current global trends arise a range of issues that can be grouped under two headings:

- Multilevel governance and regulation issues
- Issues related to managing resources—human, capital, and natural.

Governance and Regulation

In a world where global and local concerns compete with and occasionally overshadow national concerns, issues of governance are coming to dominate many aspects of the long-running debate about the role of government. The vast increase in international transactions and linkages requires myriad rules, standards, conventions, and protocols. Without these, coordination failures may occur and volatility could increase, enlarging the risk premiums on trade and capital flows and raising transaction costs. To reap the benefits of globalization, it is necessary to have international institutions that put in place commonly agreed on and widely observed rules. With continuing integration, the need for rules to mediate transactions becomes even greater. This means that governments must be willing to accept bounds on their sovereignty and act in concert, creating institutions that confine the permissible within an agreed framework that is either buttressed by enforcement mechanisms (such as the WTO) or informally observed (as in the Basle Banking Accord).[26] Bit by bit, the steady accretion of international institutions, transnational corporations, and NGOs is making global governance a reality in many spheres, constraining the writ of national governments.

The transition from centralized and hierarchical government structures to multicentric and participatory forms of governance is emerging even more insistently within countries because of localizing tendencies. The end of the Cold War extinguished the rivalry between the superpowers that was an important source of geopolitical tension. It also removed one of the supports for centralized governments—a support that was capable of mobilizing the full resources of the country for purposes of security (Deng and Lyons 1998). In the post–Cold War era, fewer countries face external foes, and in a globalizing world, prosperity is unrelated to the acquisition of territory. Hence, the original reason for the creation of states—to define and protect borders by military means—carries far less weight. Likewise, territorial aggrandizement is a goal very few countries would consider pursuing.

There is another reason why the state's capacity to make war or defend against external threat appears less compelling. This is related to the spread of democracy and the apparent reluctance of democracies to pursue their policy objectives by warlike means (Weart 1998). The dismantling of the Berlin Wall did not extinguish humankind's aggressiveness. Armed conflict and violence are unlikely to diminish (Keegan 1998). But wars between states may erupt less frequently.

However, the wars between states that do erupt could become immensely more destructive as countries acquire nuclear and biological weapon technologies. Table 3 shows the costliness of even short-term conventional conflicts over the past 20 years.[27] In this milieu, the pull

Table 3. Costs of 20th-Century Wars
(billions of 1995 U.S. dollars)

Conflict	Cost
World War I	2,850
World War II	4,000
Korean War	340
Suez War	13
Vietnam War	720
Arab-Israeli Six-Day War	3
Yom Kippur War	21
Afghanistan War	116
Iran-Iraq War	150
Falklands War	5
Gulf War	102

Sources: International Institute for Strategic Studies; *Financial Times* April 9, 1999.

of local identity, the quest for greater autonomy, and the demand for rights by groups as well as by individuals will lead a shift away from centralization toward forms of governance that cannot be quelled by pointing to external threats. Thus, the elaboration of international governance will be matched by institutions of local governance that correspond to the morphology of localization. Authority will devolve downward from the center to varying degrees, depending on the circumstances.

There is another side to national governance: the regulation of market entities by the state in the interest of efficiency, equity, and competition. The role of markets is increasing in all developing and transition economies. This trend is propelled by structural reforms, the deliberate pursuit of openness, a conscious turn away from socialism, and the unfolding of privatization programs. The public sector is shrinking, and the task of public agencies is no longer production but, instead, improvement of market function through monitoring and regulation. The state operates as an enabling hand in a predominantly market economy, in many sectors retreating from production to the provision of certain public goods. The enabling role is multisectoral but is more delineated than in the past. Like other governance activities, it has to do with creating, monitoring, and enforcing rules. The state eschews attempts at control in favor of more evenly balanced interaction between itself and other sectors.

A balanced relationship between the public and private spheres is also being dictated by the growing competition between countries for foreign investment and by the market power exercised by many interests. The rewards of FDI—in the form of increased exports, employment, and total factor productivity—are highly attractive for countries that are short of capital, technology, and market access. Hence, investors have plenty of choices. They can demand market-friendly conditions—a style of governance and incentives comparable to those of the more developed countries. The terms of the relationship between the state and industry are also changed by the fact that many of the larger investors are giant multinationals with significant power in the global marketplace. Governments in developing countries can no longer exert bureaucratic control; they can, however, exercise regulatory oversight subject to rules.

If states are to retain their integrity and achieve viable governance regimes, a major concern will be the establishment of constitutional provisions and legal mechanisms that ensure basic rights and scope for participatory politics. There are at least two dimensions to political activity. One is national and relates to the selection of individuals who will direct the central government. A second dimension, which is gaining significance as the perception of local identities grows, is the local or municipal politics that often have a direct bearing on people's daily lives.

For most developing countries, participatory politics is a relatively new experience, one based on institutions in Western countries with different traditions, mores, and social relations. These transplants and the associated framework of legally enforceable rights and patterns of behavior have been slow to take root. A number of countries that have recently embraced participatory politics are nominally democratic, but very few deliver on the promise of democracy at the national or local levels. Corruption, red tape, ineffectual policymaking, and inefficient public organization are the bane of voters newly introduced to democracy (see Figure 7). Even in countries where participatory politics has found roots in indigenous culture, the political system has yet to reach a stage in which it permits ease of entry to individuals with strong leadership qualities and the capacity to present appealing and forward-looking programs to voters.

Participatory politics in developing countries, while it may represent a significant advance over the authoritarianism of yesteryear, has in general failed to provide the newly enfranchised with good government, substantially improved economic outcomes, and real choices. In a world subject to the forces of globalization and localization, a failure of governance poses a grave risk to the stability of developing countries and is arguably the most serious impediment to future growth.

There are no simple solutions to the problem of ineffectual governance. The problem must be addressed by tackling at least five different issues: participatory politics, organizational capability, decentralization, inequality, and urban governance.

Participatory Politics. A formal basis for good governance can be secured by devising constitutional ground rules for national politics and

Figure 7. Local Entrepreneurs' Perceptions of State Corruption

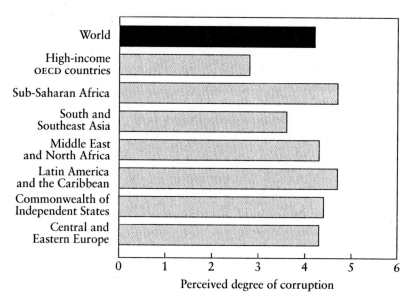

Note: Local entrepreneurs were asked to rank corruption on a scale from 1 (no problem) to 6 (extreme problem).
Source: Brunetti, Kisunko, and Weder (1997).

institutions that define the rights of the electorate, as well as the responsibilities of elected representatives. A necessary first step is to set in place credible rules that are fair and enforceable and that result in fruitful competition between a small number of well-organized political parties. But formulating such rules is difficult, and very few developing countries have built a legal infrastructure that has endured. There are plenty of good ideas in the air, and there is considerable experience against which to test them. Nevertheless, creating a few clear guidelines has proved elusive. Finding an institutional framework for viable, context-friendly, participatory policies that can be supported by organizations and resources is surely one of the priorities for development thinking.

Organizational Capability. Getting the politics right will not yield meaningful results until developing countries can find ways to strengthen public organizations. The failure of organizations has been a consistent brake on progress. Furthermore, the importance of organizational efficiency will only increase with the swelling flow of information and the growing duties of state agencies that shoulder complex regulatory responsibilities such as the successful oversight of privatization.[28]

Research on public bureaucracies has identified three main weaknesses (Grindle 1997; Evans 1998):

- There is a *chronic shortage of skills.* Public agencies struggle to attract adequate numbers of talented people and have a poor track record for cultivating skills in-house and retaining trained individuals. Islands of expensively created bureaucratic excellence have vanished in all but a handful of countries.
- *Management incentives and organization structure* are generally inadequate and highly resistant to reform, even with the best technical assistance.
- The *institutional environment* within which public bodies operate is often not conducive to efficiency and accountability. By and large, constitutionally mandated oversight is rarely effective, legal safeguards insufficiently enforce agency responsibility, and monitoring by the press or NGOs has little effect. More recently, international pressure has been shown to improve organizational performance on occasion—but only in special circumstances, and rarely in a way that leaves a lasting impression.

Building organizational capability is vital for good governance and development. It has attracted a vast amount of attention and billions of dollars in international assistance. It remains a live issue, however, and weakness of organizational capability will continue to undermine efforts in other areas.

Decentralization. The centrifugal forces released by localizing tendencies could easily become seriously disruptive for many countries. Experience during the past decade points toward not only an upsurge of economic tensions between regions but also the possibility of armed conflict. In fact, civil strife and internal wars—possibly leading to secession—are bigger threats than conflict between nations. This has become painfully apparent in southeastern Europe and parts of Sub-Saharan Africa. Civil wars are not only more destructive than international wars; they also undermine the state and cause a loss of GDP during and after the conflict.[29] Clearly, processes of decentralization and rules governing relationships between the center and subnational entities must be crafted consultatively and with a close eye to the local context. This calls for sound and tested general rules, along with detailed local knowledge.

Although decentralization has been high on the development agenda for some time, processes of decentralization have occurred in decidedly uneven ways. General fiscal rules for effective decentralization provide guidance, but there is much less clarity about how to sequence decentralization or about political rules for sharing power and wealth between the center and subnational entities. Nor is there much clarity about building organizational capacities so that provinces and municipalities can make the best use of the discretionary authority devolved to them. There is no dearth of proposals, but proposals have failed to resolve the issue. The push to decentralize only increases the urgency of resolving important decentralization issues.

Inequality. The ambivalence toward participatory politics in developing countries, the worldwide trend toward localization, and increasing levels of violence all draw some of their impetus from high and growing levels of inequality. Between the mid-1960s and the mid-1990s, the poorest 20 percent of the world population saw its share of income fall from 2.3 to 1.4 percent. Meanwhile the share of the wealthiest quintile increased from 70 to 85 percent (UNDP 1996).

Although poverty has declined in many countries—a significant achievement—the rise in inequality is profoundly disturbing. This rise is leading to a growing gap between affluent middle and upper classes and a relatively disadvantaged majority that is falling further and further behind, even though per capita incomes may be increasing.

The disadvantaged often feel politically marginalized and lacking in voice. This breeds apathy, an unwillingness to participate, and, ultimately, anger. Democratic politics is hollowed out, and institutions have little chance of securing legitimacy. As a result, political change and the desirable transition from centralized government to a more participatory governance can stall.

Widening regional inequalities can give rise to tensions that are capable of tearing countries apart. Cross-regional inequality is one of the main drivers of localization. Up to a point, such inequality can be papered over by political compacts and rules for fiscal transfers. But making these work requires mature and resilient political institutions, along with a durable sense of national identity. Where such institutions and such a sense of identity are absent—as in the majority of developing countries—the strains quickly begin to show, and only a very strong center can even temporarily ward off the efforts of richer provinces to prevent resource transfers to poorer ones.

Research shows that regions within countries are slowly converging. Unfortunately, the rate of convergence is modest even in the fastest-growing economies. In many instances the maturing of political institutions—which could provide the glue to hold countries together—may not be able to compensate for this lag.

People outside cities may be insulated from the violent consequences of political apathy and regional economic divergence, but urban dwellers—a growing majority—cannot avoid the violence that may come in the wake of widening social cleavages. This violence is a persistent and

worsening economic hemorrhage in developing countries.[30] It damages
the quality of life of all citizens, especially the poor. Often, the government appears helpless to control its spread, and public security forces
are suspected of abetting the perpetrators of organized resistance. As a
result, the state loses credibility, and it becomes even more difficult to
create desirable governance institutions.

Containing or reversing inequality is likely to be integral to achieving good governance and could influence longer-term growth prospects.[31] Research has succeeded in measuring the march of inequality,
identifying its multifarious causes, and showing how small reductions
in inequality can have large effects on poverty. However, attempts to
redistribute income or assets have achieved only limited success. Land
reforms favoring the poor face strong opposition from entrenched elites.
There is resistance to the use of progressive direct taxes to finance targeted poverty alleviation programs. And the sorry policy implementation record of many governments in developing countries makes it
difficult to win tax compliance (Alesina and Spolaore 1997).

This leaves as remedies education and training programs and measures to provide land rights to slum dwellers and squatters in urban
areas. Education and training have failed to stem worsening inequality, even in East Asian countries with a good human development
record. The urban land rights policies face administrative bottlenecks
and political opposition, and their implications for inequality are
poorly understood.

Recent trends point toward an inexorable increase in inequality as
globalism widens the income gap between the skilled and the unskilled.
Localization threatens to erode the already limited effectiveness of national programs for redistributing income. Thus far, growth—at least
in the United States and East Asia—has not been constrained by divergences in income. But unless careful analysis is used to identify more
clearly the processes that cause inequality and to serve as a basis for
inclusive policies, growing inequality will compromise the longer-term
performance of developing countries.

Urban Governance. The linkage between urban development and welfare is tightened by localization, as well as by the concentration of people
in urban areas. There is a role here for the central government, but the
larger responsibility will rest on the quality of urban governance.

The central government can provide the infrastructure to support
urbanization while adopting spatially neutral policies that give equal
opportunity to all regions, rather than encouraging a focus on a few
metropolitan areas. Central governments can also provide a regulatory
framework and institute fiscal transfers to supplement resources mobilized by municipalities themselves. But the center is rarely in a position
to induce cities to enhance their economic performance or to improve

their livability. Cities must pull themselves up by their own bootstraps, and here governance is critical.

The transfer of people from rural areas to cities in the past 50 years has improved life chances, lessened morbidity, and raised life expectancy. The squalor, violence, congestion, and continued high incidence of infectious diseases in urban areas, however, indicate that the majority of people in developing countries do not derive anywhere near the full benefits of the structural changes sweeping these countries.[32] Localization and greater political participation may have drawbacks but may also yield advantages if cities are positioned to seize them. Greater autonomy will compel cities to diversify their financing instead of depending solely on the state or on provincial sources. But cities will also be able to pursue a wider range of initiatives and compete aggressively for business. Success will depend on their capacity to govern, to manage efficiently, and to mobilize adequate resources.

The problem for most cities is how to capitalize on greater political freedom to build durable partnerships between the public sector and private entities such as the business sector, NGOs, and the ever more numerous slum dwellers. Such partnerships harness a broad spectrum of urban stakeholders to provide an avenue for gaining commitment to objectives, tapping a wide range of innovative development possibilities, and pursuing a multifaceted but coordinated effort.

Viable partnerships rest on trust and a clear sense of rules, as well as obligations, for all of the participants. In an urban context, achieving such partnerships depends, according to Putnam (1993), on the efficacy of the horizontal relationships that are subsumed under social capital. It also is a function of the perceived efficiency and fairness of the institutions governing political activity. If there is little public sector accountability, if the poor have no voice, if elections do not offer meaningful choice, if public and private entities are unable to work together to achieve common goals, and if legal or administrative remedies are available only to a select few, participatory governance is unlikely.

This failure of governance is the rule in the urban centers mushrooming throughout the developing world. Twenty years ago, when most people lived in rural areas and there was hope that administrative reforms, combined with technological change, would yield answers, the situation in the cities was only serious. Now, amid the debris of failed attempts to create dynamic and livable cities, the world confronts an incipient crisis. Its acute nature is apparent from the near absence of success stories. The tiny band of cities that have attained cult status among social scientists—Curitiba, Brazil; Hong Kong, China; Singapore—has not grown for a decade. None of the existing and future megacities in Asia or Latin America qualifies as a model, and few provide clues about how to improve governance and implement good policies. There is no dearth of theory and empirical analysis, but we do not have reci-

pes that can make cities work, ensure effective partnerships among diverse public and private entities in the absence of an organizational
structure specifying rules of interaction, or quell the increasing squalor
and violence bred by paucity of jobs, lack of voice, and fading hope.

Management of Human and Natural Resources

Two demographic issues will take on a new urgency over the coming
decades: cross-border migration and the global adequacy of savings in
a world divided between countries with large cohorts of older people
who are dissaving and those with vast cohorts of young people who
will find higher-paying jobs in the formal sector only if there are high
levels of investment. Priority issues in management of natural resources
will be the global commons and food and water security.

Cross-Border Migration. People—along with goods, services, and investment—are crossing borders in record numbers. Each year, between
2 million and 3 million people emigrate. In 1998 some 130 million
people lived in countries other than those in which they were born—a
number that has been rising at about 1.9 percent annually (see Figure
8). In absolute terms, the number of migrants is modest—2.3 percent
of world population—but they are concentrated in just a few regions:
North America, Western Europe, Oceania, and the Middle East. In North
America and Western Europe, the growth of the migrant population

Figure 8. Immigration into the Largest Host Countries, 1960–94

Thousands of migrants

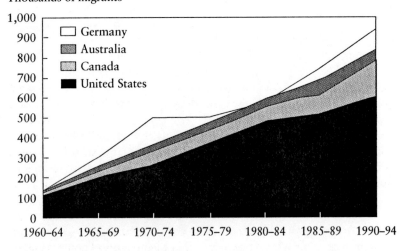

Source: Zlotnik (1998).

during 1965–90 was 2.5 percent a year, a share that far outstripped overall population growth. One in every 13 people living in these four regions is foreign born (Zlotnik 1998). Although the cost-benefit calculus of migration is largely positive for receiving countries and for many of the originating countries, migration has caused ethnic and labor market tensions in urban areas to worsen. The belief, strongly articulated by politically vocal groups, that immigrants displace local workers in low-skilled jobs, make large claims on social services, and are responsible for increasing rates of crime is creating a climate of opinion that supports the raising of barriers to immigration (Tonry 1997). Several industrial countries, including the United States, France, and Germany, have been tightening immigration controls, recapitulating similar moves in the early part of the 20th century. It is unclear whether this tendency will persist in the face of declining populations, but sensitivities toward immigration are increasingly apparent. Even as industrial countries move to limit the flow of migrants, the potential for migration from some developing regions is on the rise.

Shortages of agricultural land and of urban employment will be two important concerns for the poorest countries, with spillover effects for other countries. In Africa, South Asia, and parts of the Middle East, intense competition for jobs could sharpen incentives to emigrate. Conflict and natural disasters have already led to a dramatic increase in refugees, from 2.5 million in 1975 to 25 million in the late 1990s (Kane 1995; Korn 1999).[33] These cross-border spillovers, when they involve large populations, can be a source of conflict, misery, and disease. They can also be difficult to reverse (*Wall Street Journal*, April 22, 1999). The widespread availability of small arms compounds the severity of conflict, while life in refugee camps magnifies the possibility of disease outbreaks.[34]

There is very little possibility that countries, especially developing countries, will be able to seal off their borders, nor does it appear likely that the circulation of weaponry will diminish. Hence, population movements, sometimes accompanied by localized conflagrations (such as the one that erupted in the Great Lakes region of Africa during 1998–99), could become a recurring nightmare for the poorest countries—and could abruptly reverse years of slow progress.

Darkening demographic prospects and the likelihood that cross-border flows of people could impose severe strains on recipient countries have not elicited fresh ideas or institutional proposals. The only comfort that economics can offer is that greater trade and financial integration, along with the possibility of some increase in emigration to member countries of the Organisation for Economic Co-operation and Development (OECD), could enable the low-income countries to cope with population pressures during the demographic transition. By accelerating growth and increasing employment opportunities in low-income countries, foreign investment and trade could reduce incentives to emigrate (Borjas 1998). The shrinking and aging of the populations of Europe and Japan might also boost demand for migrant workers, as happened in Western Europe between the mid-1950s and the mid-1970s. This would call for a framework of immigration policies and institutions akin to those needed for the movement of capital (Sassen 1997). It would also presage the spread of multiethnic communities in industrial countries, which could involve major social adjustments.

At this stage, there is no evidence of any readiness to put in place international institutions to manage cross-border flows of people. Little thought has been invested in this issue, nor has there been any effort to mobilize international opinion to support major new global governance initiatives for managing migration. And substantial research on multiethnic communities has yet to establish the social conditions and political mechanisms that would ensure stability with economic dynamism.

Aging and Capital Supplies. The aging of populations in developed countries and in some industrializing East Asian countries could significantly constrain the international supply of capital 20 or 30 years from now. Three factors will be critical. One is the effect of aging populations and rising dependency ratios on household saving behavior in industrial and developing countries. A second is the trend in the retirement age. A third is the extent and funding of social security systems.

The bleakest scenario projects a substantial drop in household savings in industrial and East Asian economies as the number of people over age 65 increases. It points to a rising tendency for people to retire in their 50s, as is already common in Europe. It also indicates that unreformed, pay-as-you-go social security schemes will be bankrupted or at least will come under great pressure.

The median age of the population in northeast Asia will rise from 28 to 36 between 1995 and 2015—a transformation that took twice as long in industrial countries, from 1955 to 1995 (Eberstadt 1998). Just 12.5 percent of the U.S. population and 11.8 percent of the Japanese population was over 65 in 1990; these proportions will rise to 18.7 and 26.7 percent by 2025. Between 1990 and 2025, rapid aging will raise the share of the 65-plus cohort from 6 to 13.3 percent in China and from 5 to 15 percent in the Republic of Korea.

With countries beginning to gray, labor force participation rates for males in the 60–64 cohort dropped precipitously during 1960–95, from 80 to 55 percent in the United States, from 80 to 20 percent in Italy, and from 70 to 15 percent in France. One might expect as a result a severe global capital shortage that raises interest rates and depresses growth, trade, and commodity prices.

A second, and much brighter, scenario, suggests that a savings crunch can be avoided. Household surveys show that aging may not lead to the steep decline in saving revealed by cross-country studies. Rising rates of female participation in the work force will partially offset the effect of declining male rates. And policies and institutions might narrow (if not close) the savings gap in some industrial countries and prevent shortages in industrializing economies.

Research on Japan and East Asia supports the view that saving could decline as populations age but that diminishing rates of investment would more than offset lower saving (Horioka 1990; Higgins and Williamson 1997; Kosai, Saito, and Yoshiro 1998). As dependency ratios in South Asia fall during the next two decades, saving could climb, and countries in the region could gradually become capital exporters like the East Asian and Southeast Asian economies. In fact, some recent research on the United Kingdom and the United States suggests that saving rates may increase as baby boomers approach retirement in the next two decades (Attanasio and Banks 1998).

Even if the more favorable scenario comes to pass, industrial and developing countries with aging populations need to make haste in two areas. Industrial countries whose pay-as-you-earn social security schemes will run out of money over the next two to three decades should increase social security funding, shave benefits, and contain—if not reverse—the fall in the retirement age. There will be a great deal of resistance to raising payments or cutting benefits, but this pain must be faced. The total bill for pensions and medical care for the aged over the next 30 years is estimated at US$64 trillion (Peterson 1999).

Sociologists such as Anthony Giddens believe that the decline in the retirement age will be reversed (Giddens 1998a). If this happens—and there are plenty of contrarian views that stress the attractiveness of retirement and the declining price of recreation—a savings shortfall in industrial countries might pose less of a problem (Costa 1998).

For industrial countries, the issue here is not so much governance as it is how to reshape institutions to provide a minimum fiscally supportable public safety net while bolstering savings so as to enlarge private mechanisms to support people in retirement (Deaton 1998). For developing countries, it is how to build a combination of publicly and privately financed safety nets in the first place and how to keep older people on the job.

Managing the Global Commons. Warnings of impending global food shortages and environmental catastrophes have frequently been voiced. So far, these have not materialized, and perhaps technological ingenuity will enable humankind to sustain development indefinitely. But the magnitude of demographic change that will be telescoped into the next two decades and the certainty that the world will become warmer, lose biodiversity, and push against the limits of the resource envelope are worrisome. Scores of environmental treaties and protocols have been signed over the past few decades, but only one, the Montreal Protocol to protect the ozone layer, can be counted as a true success. There were several reasons for the success of the protocol: the problem and the urgency of remedying it were indisputable; only a handful of countries (with the United States clearly in the lead) produced ozone-destroying chlorofluorocarbons (CFCs) and needed to come to an agreement on phasing them out; substitutes for CFCs were available and new ones were on the horizon; and the industrial nations were willing to make a multilateral fund available to developing countries to help them limit their CFC use.

It is more difficult to devise international institutions that will address other environmental concerns, which do not meet these conditions. Regarding global climate change, for example, the scientific consensus has yet to jell; there is a large variance in estimates of costs and benefits; only the countries for which the dangers from warming loom large—such as Bangladesh, with its densely populated, low-lying deltaic region—are willing to participate; and mechanisms for sharing the costs between countries in an equitable and politically acceptable manner are still in an embryonic stage.

Managing the global commons is a vital and live issue for the future, and one that must be addressed at many levels. For example, countries must deal with the political economy of cost sharing. Enforceable global rules and markets for trading carbon emissions will need to be defined. Policies will need to be evolved to develop new technologies and the means of ensuring their widespread adoption. And attention must be given to bargaining strategies that will enable countries with disparate concerns to reach workable compromises.

Food and Water Security. The issue of food security is related not only to environmental concerns but also to the growth of populations. Changes in the global climate and higher levels of carbon dioxide could adversely influence crop production and yields, especially in the tropics. This would exacerbate the longer-term problem of soil erosion from intensive cropping, poor husbandry practices, and deforestation. Furthermore, the increasing claims on limited supplies of fresh water and the deteriorating quality of water bodies could lead to conflicts between regions and between riparian countries.[35]

Scientific advances in crop genetics are sure to yield varieties that can withstand greater heat, water stress, and salt content without compromising high yields. Scientists, however, have become notably circumspect in their claims about future gains. For poorer countries in the tropics, the achievement of sustainable rates of agricultural output growth, an old issue, is acquiring renewed importance (*Science*, March 5, 1999).

Even if yields can be steadily improved, crops and livestock will still require water. As growth continues, city industries compete against the demands of agriculture, and as pollution degrades water quality, the distribution of available water supplies may have a decisive bearing on regional development prospects.[36] The rules of sharing will also determine whether neighbors remain on peaceful terms, especially where countries rely heavily on external supplies (see Table 4). As Hinrichsen, Robey, and Upadhyay (1998) note, a world short of water could be inherently unstable.

The literature on dividing water resources is rich and insightful. A few parts of the world, including the western United States, have effective regionwide institutions. There are also microlevel institutions—in Chile, China, western India, and other places—that efficiently allocate water, especially groundwater, using market-based or informal mechanisms. But solutions to emerging macrolevel problems are not in sight. Even the adaptation of successful microinstitutions for use in different regions has proved difficult.

It is appropriate that we close this review of issues with food and water security, an issue that was present at the dawn of development

Table 4. Countries Heavily Dependent on Imported Surface Water

Country	Percentage of total flow originating outside own borders	Country	Percentage of total flow originating outside own borders
Egypt, Arab Republic of	97	Iraq	66
Hungary	95	Albania	53
Mauritania	95	Uruguay	52
Botswana	94	Germany	51
Bulgaria	91	Portugal	48
Netherlands	89	Bangladesh	42
Gambia, The	86	Thailand	39
Cambodia	82	Austria	38
Romania	82	Jordan	36
Luxembourg	80	Pakistan	36
Syrian Arab Republic	79	Venezuela, Republica Bolivariana de	35
Congo, Republic of	77	Senegal	34
Sudan	77	Belgium	33
Paraguay	70	Israel[a]	21
Niger	68		

a. A significant proportion of Israel's water supply comes from disputed land.
Source: Wallensteen and Swain (1997).

studies and the importance of which remains undiminished after nearly five decades. The health of agriculture will continue to be a key determinant of welfare, growth, and political stability in the 21st century. In an era of worsening environmental conditions and tightening resource constraints, food security will be a major objective, and one that countries will have to struggle harder to secure. This struggle may extend to water rights. If it does, the chances of conflict in certain parts of the world are significant. Such conflicts could be enormously destructive, given the increasing numbers of countries in possession of sophisticated chemical, biological, and thermonuclear weapons. How to ensure food security and access to water will be an issue that commands the closest attention.

A Search for Answers

The nature and complexity of the development issues that now confront us show how far thinking and practice have evolved. The recent record of moderate growth, increasing stability, and improving standards of human development all suggest that we have made substantial progress in finding workable solutions to tough development problems. But other statistics warn us that the race to develop is far from over. Although a decreasing percentage of people is poor, the number of poor people continues to grow. Few industrializing countries are narrowing the income gap that separates them from industrial economies. Convergence of both incomes and levels of human development could be accelerated by responding to the issues sketched above.

This paper seeks to highlight issues, not to propose solutions. But in the end, fresh thinking on governance, institutions, regulatory policies, and measures for managing resources will lead to the highest payoff. In a world in which global and local concerns have begun to dominate, population growth is beginning to test environmental sustainability, political expectations have been sharpened by literacy, information is becoming more readily available, and rates of urbanization are high and increasing, economic development will depend on our ability to resolve a broad range of complex issues.

These issues are multidisciplinary. They lie at the intersection of economic, political, social, and environmental concerns. Economists must make common cause with other social scientists if the search for answers is to yield fruit.

Notes

This paper draws on research done for *World Development Report 1999/2000*. The authors would like to thank Anjum Altaf, Simon Evenett, and Charles

Kenny for their penetrating comments and Stratos Safioleas, Mohammad Arzaghi, and Noémi Giszpenc for research assistance.

1. An assessment of the policy consensus achieved through the 1980s is provided in World Bank (1991).

2. Pritchett (1997) showed that increased educational attainment did not have a positive effect on output growth. Barro (1997) showed that the positive relationship between the investment ratio and growth found in cross-country regressions reflects a reverse link between growth prospects and investment.

3. This is supported by research on industrial, developing, and East Asian countries surveyed by Fagerberg (1994); Oulton (1997); Crafts (1998).

4. A positive relationship between property rights and growth has been reported by Barro (1997) and Keefer and Knack (1997). Olson (1996) maintained that developing countries have not exploited their full growth potential because of weak institutions for protecting contracts and rights.

5. Different kinds of legal systems, however, confer differing degrees of protection. La Porta and others (1998) show that the degree of investor protection and legal enforcement is greater in common law countries than in countries with a system based on civil law. Enforcement also tends to improve as income rises.

6. See Ahmad and Yang (1991); Newman, Jorgensen and Pradhan (1991); Pissarides (1991); Squire (1991). Dasgupta (1998) draws attention to the association between poverty and undernourishment, high fertility, and environmental degradation.

7. Brada (1996) discusses the constraints on rapid privatization in the transition economies, the options available, and the viability of partial schemes in which the government retains a role. White and Bhatia (1998) examine the checkered but broadly positive record of privatization in Africa.

8. Both the "market friendly" and the industrial policy models demand high bureaucratic capability (see Evans 1998).

9. One striking measure of globalization is the doubling of global output that is exported, from one tenth in 1950 to one fifth in 1990. This trend is mirrored by the increase in GATT/WTO membership, from 23 countries when the first treaty was signed in 1947 to 134 in 1999. Another 30 countries have applied to join (see Anderson 1998).

10. Flexible supply-chain management of products for large retailers and other buyers by regionally diversified export trading companies (such as Hong Kong's Li and Fung) is also changing the nature of design, sourcing, and assembly of products (see Magretta 1998).

11. The cost of a three-minute transatlantic telephone call dropped from US$31.58 in 1970 to less than US$1 in 1998. Meanwhile computer use is exploding, more and more people have Internet access, and access speeds have risen from 14.4 kilobytes per second to 10 megabytes per second.

12. See Feldstein (1999). These and other technological developments are the possible harbingers of a "new economy" (see Greenspan 1998).

13. See OECD (1998). So far, however, much of the foreign direct investment in developing countries goes to fewer than a score of East Asian and Latin American economies (Fry 1995: 257).

14. Foreign direct investment (FDI) consists of investment in physical capital and other production-related assets. It is distinguished, conceptually at least, from foreign portfolio investment (FPI), which refers to purchases of foreign liquid financial assets. In reality, the distinction is somewhat fuzzy, as financial transactions may involve elements of both. However, the higher liquidity of FPI underlies the presumption that it is more footloose than FDI.

15. Giddens (1998b: 31) notes that globalization "pushes down—it creates new demands and also new possibilities for regenerating local identities."

16. Cooke and Morgan (1998); Porter (1998); Scott (1998). Silicon Valley and the Emilia Romagna region of northeastern Italy are the most famous examples, but they are being joined by many others in India and China.

17. For example, current forecasts indicate that in 2100 carbon dioxide concentrations will reach 600 parts per million (ppm)—two to three times the level in 1750. Average temperatures could rise by some 2° Celsius from now. This projection continues to be disputed, however, because the variability of climate over the eons, driven by little-understood natural mechanisms, is well documented. Still in the realm of scientific conjecture are the severity of weather fluctuations in a warming world, the global distribution of the effects of warming on agriculture and living conditions, and the extent of adaptation to warming. Although higher carbon dioxide concentration might enhance plant growth and will certainly increase the efficiency of water use, changes in tissue chemistry will render plants less palatable, and heat and water stress on vegetation will offset some of the gains from increased carbon dioxide (see Goudie 1997; *Science*, July 25, 1997: 496).

18. This is now evident in most regions and is mirrored by the rising rates of contraceptive use (Gelbard, Haub, and Kent 1999).

19. Population projections using a probabilistic approach indicate that the populations of Sub-Saharan Africa, North Africa, and the Middle East will triple by 2050 and quadruple by 2100, according to Lutz, Sanderson, and Scherbou (1997). In some Sub-Saharan African countries the AIDS epidemic will slow population growth by shortening life expectancy by nearly 17 years between 2010 and 2015, but even countries such as Botswana, where a quarter of the adult population is HIV positive, can expect their populations to double by 2050 (see United Nations 1998b; *AIDS Analysis Africa* 1998).

20. It is sobering to note that the world's supply of fresh water is no greater now than it was 2,000 years ago, when the population was 3 percent of today's size. In this century alone, water withdrawals have increased sixfold (Hinrichsen, Robey, and Upadhyay 1998).

21. See World Bank (1998). A condition of water stress is reached when annual per capita water availability is between 1,000 and 1,700 cubic meters. When the annual supply drops below 1,000 cubic meters, a country faces water scarcity. Below 500 cubic meters, there is absolute water scarcity (see Wallensteen and Swain 1997). On the increasing severity of water constraints in the Middle East, see Rogers and Lyndon (1994).

22. A recent report indicates that a 3 percent warming of the climate over the next 100 years would lead to a 90 million ton shortfall in food supplies by

2050, increasing the number of people at risk of hunger to 30 million. About 18 percent of Africa's population could be affected if this projection holds (*Financial Times,* November 3, 1998).

23. Haddad, Ruel, and Garrett (1999a, 1999b) refer to an estimated number of 300 million urban poor in the late 1980s.

24. Elster (1989) strikes a similar note when he discusses how social norms might be weakened in modern society because of mobility, the ephemeral nature of interactions, and the pace of change. Although the public provision of a safety net for the poor to replace informal kin- or patron-based insurance schemes has been widely discussed, creating viable schemes is and will remain a considerable challenge. Experience with targeted transfers has revealed high political and administrative costs and substantial leakages even when there is self-targeting of the poor using inferior goods such as coarse grains. Local community efforts, which might become more important for some countries in the future, will also have to overcome such hurdles as the inadequacy of administrative and revenue-raising capacity, capture of local safety net programs by local elites, and the need for state- or national-level coordination of programs subject to significant externalities (see Bardhan 1996).

25. See Scott (1976). Popkin (1979) rightly maintained that the moral economy based on patron-client relations can often be constraining and that the commercialization of the rural economy improves the overall prospects of the peasantry, including the capacity to survive shocks.

26. The Basle Banking accord was established in 1988. In the aftermath of the East Asian financial crisis of the late 1990s, the Basle committee is proposing a widening of the rules to include not only revamped risk-based capital adequacy rules but also enhanced disclosure and supervisory practices that give greater discretion to regulatory agencies.

27. Morrison and Tsipis (1998) estimate that during 1914–90 wars resulted in about 110 million excess deaths. They recommend a global community security regime that would allow countries to drastically reduce arms spending, provide a vehicle for effective armed response to crises, and free resources for economic progress, thereby reducing sources of tension.

28. Nellis (1999) suggests that mass privatization in some of the transition economies has generally failed to induce enterprise restructuring or improve performance because institutions were not in place and public or private organizations for monitoring and regulating the newly privatized entities were weak.

29. Collier (1999) estimates that during civil wars GDP per capita declines at an annual rate of 2.2 percent relative to the counterfactual. If a war lasts only one year, the loss of growth in the next five years of peace is 2.1 percent per year.

30. Studying Latin American countries, Bourguignon (1998) estimates that over 7 percent of their GDP is lost because of violence. The cost of crime and violence to South Africa is believed to equal 6 percent of GDP (*Business Times,* February 14, 1999).

31. See Kanbur (1998). Campos and Root (1996) view egalitarianism as one of the keys to East Asia's success.

32. The concentration of people in urban areas improves the chances of reducing the incidence of water- and insect-borne diseases, but it can worsen the spread of droplet-borne infections such as tuberculosis and influenza and of sexually transmitted diseases such as AIDS (see Ridley 1997). The spread of AIDS is one of the greatest threats to development in Africa (*Lancet*, February 20, 1999).

33. The Gulf War displaced 5.5 million people, and the conflict in Afghanistan is responsible for the 2 million refugees living in Iranian border camps and for an additional 1 million in Pakistan (*Economist*, "Exporting Misery," April 17, 1999).

34. Klare (1999) estimates that the total number of small arms in circulation worldwide ranges from 500 million to 1 billion, of which 200 million–250 million are privately owned by individuals in the United States. Close to 70 million AK-47 automatic rifles and 8 million M-16 automatic rifles have been produced since 1947.

35. The main threats are from chemical effluents, untreated sewage, and agricultural runoff (see Pielou 1998).

36. Urbanization could result in a large increase in per capita use of water for domestic purposes, which is currently only 8 percent of total consumption. In the United States, average annual household use rose from 10 cubic meters in 1900 to 200 cubic meters in the 1990s. About 36.5 cubic meters a year are needed to maintain good health (see Feder and LeMoigne 1994; Hinrichsen, Robey, and Upadhyay 1998).

References

Ahmad, Ehtisham, and Yan Wang. 1991. "Inequality and Poverty in China: Institutional Change and Public Policy, 1978 to 1998." *World Bank Economic Review* 5 (2, May): 231–57.

Alesina, Alberto, and Enrico Spolaore. 1997. "On the Number and Size of Nations." *Quarterly Journal of Economics* 112 (4, November): 1027–56.

Anderson, Kym. 1998. "Globalization, WTO and Development Strategies of Poorer Countries." Background paper for *World Development Report 1999/2000: Entering the 21st Century.* World Development Report Office, World Bank, Washington, D.C.

Attanasio, Orazio, and James Banks. 1998. "Trends in Household Saving Don't Justify Tax Incentives to Boost Saving." *Economic Policy* 27 (October): 547–84.

Bardhan, Pranab. 1996. "Research on Poverty and Development Twenty Years after *Redistribution and Growth*." In Michael Bruno and Boris Pleskovic, eds., *Annual World Bank Conference on Development Economics 1995.* Washington, D.C.: World Bank.

Barro, Robert. 1997. *Determinants of Economic Growth*. Cambridge, Mass.: MIT Press.

Bloom, David E., and Jeffrey G. Williamson. 1998. *Demographic Transitions and Economic Miracles in Emerging Asia.* Technical Paper 40, Consulting Assistance on Economic Reform Project. Cambridge, Mass.: Harvard Institute for International Development and U.S. Agency for International Development.

Boniface, Pascal. 1998. "The Proliferation of States." *Washington Quarterly* 21 (3, summer): 111–27.

Borjas, George J. 1998. "Economic Research on the Determinants of Immigration: Lessons for the European Union." Working paper prepared for the World Bank. Kennedy School of Government, Harvard University, Cambridge, Mass.

Bourguignon, François. 1998. "Crime as a Social Cost of Poverty and Inequality: A Review Focusing on Developing Countries." Background paper for *World Development Report 1999/2000: Entering the 21st Century.* World Development Report Office, World Bank, Washington, D.C.

Brada, Josef C. 1996. "Privatization Is Transition—or Is It?" *Journal of Economic Perspectives* 10 (2, spring): 67–86.

Bratton, Michael, and Nicholas van de Walle. 1997. *Democratic Experiences in Africa: Regime Transitions in Comparative Perspective.* Cambridge, U.K.: Cambridge University Press.

Brown, Lester R. 1997. "Can We Raise Grain Yields Fast Enough?" *World Watch* 10 (4, July–August): 8–17.

Brunetti, Aymo, Gregory Kisunko, and Beatrice Weder. 1997. "Institutional Obstacles to Doing Business: Region-by-Region Results from a Worldwide Survey of the Private Sector." Policy Research Working Paper 1759. World Development Report Office, World Bank, Washington, D.C.

Bruno, Michael, and William Easterly. 1995. "Inflation Crisis and Long-Run Growth." NBER Working Paper 5209. National Bureau of Economic Research, Cambridge, Mass.

Bruton, Henry J. 1998. "A Reconsideration of Import Substitution." *Journal of Economic Literature* 36 (2, June): 903–36.

Campos, Jose Egardo, and Hilton Root. 1996. *The Key to the East Asian Miracle: Making Shared Growth Credible.* Washington, D.C.: Brookings Institution.

Collier, Paul. 1999. "On The Economic Consequences of Civil War." *Oxford Economic Papers* 51(1, January): 168–83.

Cooke, Philip, and Kevin Morgan. 1998. *The Associational Economy.* Oxford, U.K.: Oxford University Press.

Costa, Dora L. 1998. *The Evolution of Retirement.* Chicago, Ill.: University of Chicago Press.

Crafts, Nicholas F. R. 1998. "Forging Ahead and Falling Behind: The Rise and Relative Decline of the First Industrial Nation." *Journal of Economic Perspectives* 12 (2): 193–210.

Crone, Donald K. 1988. "Social Elites and Government Capacity in Southeast Asia." *World Politics* 40 (2): 252–68.

Crystal, David. 1997. *English as a Global Language*. Cambridge, U.K.: Cambridge University Press.

Dasgupta, Partha. 1998. "The Economics of Poverty in Poor Countries." *Scandinavian Journal of Economics* 100 (1): 41–68.

Davoodi, Hamid, and Heng-fu Zou. 1998. "Fiscal Decentralization and Economic Growth: A Cross-Country Study." *Journal of Urban Economics* 43 (2, March): 244–57.

Deaton, Angus. 1998. "Global and Regional Effects of Aging and of Demographic Change." Background paper for *World Development Report 1999/ 2000: Entering the 21st Century.* World Development Report Office, World Bank, Washington, D.C.

Deng, Francis M., and Terrence Lyons, eds. 1998. *African Reckoning: A Quest for Good Governance*. Washington, D.C.: Brookings Institution.

Eberstadt, Nicholas. 1998. "Asia Tomorrow, Gray and Male." *National Interest* 53 (fall): 56–65.

Elster, Jon. 1989. *The Cement of Society: A Study of Social Order.* Cambridge, U.K.: Cambridge University Press.

Evans, Peter. 1998. "Transferable Lessons? Re-examining the Institutional Prerequisites of East Asian Economic Policies." *Journal of Development Studies* 34 (6, August): 66–86.

Fagerberg, Jan. 1994. "Technology and International Differences in Growth Rates." *Journal of Economic Literature* 32 (3, December): 1147–75.

Feder, Gershon, and Guy LeMoigne. 1994. "Managing Water in a Sustainable Manner." *Finance and Development* 31 (2, June): 24–27.

Feldstein, Martin. 1999. "International Capital Flows: Introduction." In Martin Feldstein, ed., *International Capital Flows*. Chicago, Ill.: University of Chicago Press.

Fischer, Stanley. 1993. "The Role of Macroeconomic Factors in Growth." *Journal of Monetary Economics* 32 (3, December): 485–512.

Fry, Maxwell J. 1995. *Money, Interest and Banking in Economic Development*. Baltimore, Md.: Johns Hopkins University Press.

Gelbard, Alene, Carl Haub, and Mary Kent. 1999. "World Population beyond Six Billion." *Population Bulletin* 54 (1, March): 1–44.

Giddens, Anthony. 1998a. *Conversations by Anthony Giddens*. Cambridge, U.K.: Polity Press.

———. 1998b. *The Third Way—The Renewal of Social Democracy*. Cambridge, U.K.: Polity Press.

Ginarte, Juan C., and Walter G. Park. 1997. "Determinants of Patent Rights: A Cross-National Study." *Research Policy* 26 (3, October): 283–301.

Goudie, Andrew. 1997. *The Future of Climate*. Predictions Series, vol. 5. London: Phoenix.

Greenspan, Alan. 1998. "Is There a New Economy?" *California Management Review* 41 (1, fall): 74–85.

Grindle, Merilee S., ed. 1997. *Getting Good Government: Capacity Building in the Public Sectors of Developing Countries*. Cambridge, Mass.: Harvard Institute for International Development, Harvard University Press.

Haddad, Lawrence, Marie T. Ruel, and James L. Garrett. 1999a. "Are Urban Poverty and Undernutrition Growing? Some Newly Assembled Evidence." *World Development* 27 (11): 1891–1904.

———. 1999b. "Some Urban Facts of Life: Implications for Research and Policy." *World Development* 27 (11): 1917–38.

Higgins, Matthew, and Jeffrey G. Williamson. 1997. "Age Structure Dynamics in Asia and Dependence on Foreign Capital." *Population and Development Review* 23 (2): 261–93.

Hinrichsen, Don, Bryant Robey, and Ushma D. Upadhyay. 1998. "Solutions for a Water-Short World." Population Information Program, Johns Hopkins School of Public Health. *Population Reports* 26 (1, September). Available at <http://www.jhuccp.org/pr/m14edsum.stm>.

Holmes, Stephen, and Cass R. Sunstein. 1999. *The Cost of Rights: Why Liberty Depends on Taxes.* New York: W. W. Norton.

Horioka, C. Y. 1990. "Why Is Japan's Household Saving So High? A Literature Survey." *Journal of Japanese and International Economics* 4 (1): 49–92.

IMF (International Monetary Fund). 1998a. *Government Finance Statistics Yearbook.* Washington, D.C.

———. 1998b. *International Capital Markets: Developments, Prospects, and Key Policy Issues.* Washington, D.C.

———. 1998c. *Balance of Payments Statistics Yearbook.* Washington, D.C.

Kanbur, Ravi. 1998. "Income Distribution and Development." Working Paper 98-13. Department of Agricultural, Resource, and Managerial Economics, Cornell University, Ithaca, N.Y.

Kane, Hal. 1995. "What's Driving Migration?" *World Watch* 8 (1, January–February): 23–33.

Keefer, Philip, and Stephen Knack. 1997. "Why Don't Poor Countries Catch Up? A Cross-National Test of an Institutional Explanation." *Economic Inquiry* 35 (3, July): 590–602.

Keegan, John. 1998. *War and Our World.* London: Hutchinson.

Klare, Michael. 1999. "The Kalashnikov Age." *Bulletin of the Atomic Scientists* 55 (1): 18–22.

Korn, David A. 1999. *Exodus within Borders.* Washington, D.C.: Brookings Institution.

Kosai, Yutaka, Jun Saito, and Nashiro Yashiro. 1998. "Declining Population and Sustained Economic Growth: Can They Coexist?" *American Economic Review* 88 (2): 412–16.

La Porta, Rafael, Florencio Lopez-de-Silanes, Andrei Shleifer, and Robert W. Vishny. 1998. "Law and Finance." *Journal of Political Economy* 106 (6, December): 1113–55.

Lawrence, Robert, and David Weinstein. 2000. "The Role of Trade in East Asian Productivity Growth: The Case of Japan." In Joseph Stiglitz, ed., *Rethinking the East Asian Miracle.* Washington, D.C.: World Bank.

Losada, H., H. Martínez, J. Vieyra, R. Pealing, R. Zavala, and J. Cortés. 1998. "Urban Agriculture in the Metropolitan Zone of Mexico City: Changes over Time in Urban, Suburban and Peri-Urban Areas." *Environment and Urbanization* 10 (2): 37–54.

Lutz, Wolfgang, Warren Sanderson, and Sergei Scherbou. 1997. "Doubling of World Population Unlikely." *Nature* 387 (6635, June): 803–05.

Magretta, Joan. 1998. "Fast, Global, and Entrepreneurial: Supply Chain Management, Hong Kong Style. An Interview with Victor Fung." *Harvard Business Review* 76 (5, September–October): 102–14.

Meyer, John W., David John Frank, Ann Hironaka, Evan Schofer, and Nancy Brandon Tuma. 1998. "The Structuring of a World Environmental Regime, 1870–1990." *International Organization* 51 (4, autumn): 623–51.

Morrison, Philip, and Kosta Tsipis. 1998. *Reason Enough to Hope: America and the World of the Twenty-First Century.* Cambridge, Mass.: MIT Press.

Nellis, John. 1999. "Time to Rethink Privatization in Transition Economies?" *Transition* 10 (1): 4–6.

Newman, John, Steen Jorgensen, and Menno Pradhan. 1991. "How Did Workers Benefit from Bolivia's Emergency Social Fund?" *World Bank Economic Review* 5 (2): 367–93.

North, Douglass C. 1997. "Prologue." In John N. Drobak and J. V. C. Nye, eds., *The Frontiers of the New Institutional Economics.* San Diego, Calif.: Academic Press.

North, Douglass C., and Barry Weingast. 1989. "Constitutions and Commitment: The Evolution of Institutions Governing Public Choice in Seventeenth Century England." *Journal of Economic History* 49 (4, December): 803–32.

OECD (Organisation for Economic Co-operation and Development). 1998. *Foreign Direct Investment and Economic Development.* Paris.

Olson, Mancur, Jr. 1996. "Big Bills Left on the Sidewalk: Why Some Nations Are Rich, and Others Poor." *Journal of Economic Perspectives* 10 (2): 3–24.

Oulton, Nicholas. 1997. "Total Factor Productivity and Growth and the Role of Externalities." *National Institute Economic Review* 162 (October): 99–111.

Peterson, Peter G. 1999. *Gray Dawn: How the Coming Age Wave Will Transform America—and the World.* New York: Times Books.

Pielou, E. C. 1998. *Fresh Water.* Chicago, Ill.: University of Chicago Press.

Pissarides, Christopher A. 1991. "Macroeconomic Adjustment and Poverty in Selected Industrial Countries." *World Bank Economic Review* 5 (2): 207–29.

Popkin, Samuel L. 1979. *The Rational Peasant.* Berkeley, Calif.: University of California Press.

Porter, Michael E. 1998. "The Adam Smith Address: Location, Clusters and the 'New' Microeconomics of Competition." *Business Economics* 33 (1. January): 7–13.

Prahalad, C. K., and Kenneth Liebenthal. 1998. "The End of Corporate Imperialism." *Harvard Business Review* 76 (4, July–August): 68–79.

Pritchett, Lant. 1997. "Where Has All the Education Gone?" Policy Research Working Paper 1581. Policy Research Department, World Bank, Washington, D.C.

Putnam, Robert D. 1993. *Making Democracy Work: Civic Traditions in Modern Italy.* Princeton, N.J.: Princeton University Press.

Ridley, Matt. 1997. *The Future of Disease*. Predictions Series, vol. 3. London: Phoenix.

Rodrik, Dani. 1998. *New Global Economy in Developing Countries: Making Openness Work*. Baltimore, Md.: Johns Hopkins University Press.

Rogers, Peter, and Peter Lyndon. 1994. *Water in the Arab World: Population and Prognosis*. Cambridge, Mass.: Harvard University Press.

Sachs, Jeffrey, and Andrew Warner. 1997. "Fundamental Sources of Long-Run Growth." *American Economic Review* 87 (2): 184–88.

Sassen, Saskia. 1997. "Immigration Policy in a Global Economy." *SAIS Review* 17 (2, spring–summer): 1–19.

Scott, Allen J. 1998. *Regions and the World Economy*. Oxford, U.K.: Oxford University Press.

Scott, James C. 1976. *The Moral Economy of the Peasant*. New Haven, Conn.: Yale University Press.

Skidelsky, Robert. 1996. *The Road from Serfdom: The Economic and Political Consequences of the End of Communism*. New York: Penguin Press.

Squire, Lyn. 1991. "Introduction: Poverty and Adjustment in the 1980s." *World Bank Economic Review* 5 (2): 177–85.

Stiglitz, Joseph E. 1996. "Some Lessons from the East Asian Miracle." *World Bank Research Observer* 11 (2, August): 151–77.

Stiglitz, Joseph E., and Marilou Uy. 1996. "Financial Markets, Public Policy, and the East Asian Miracle." *World Bank Research Observer* 11 (2, August): 249–76.

Tonry, Michael, ed. 1997. *Ethnicity, Crime and Immigration: Comparative and Cross-National Perspectives*. Chicago, Ill.: University of Chicago Press.

UNDP (United Nations Development Programme). 1996. *Human Development Report 1996*. New York: Oxford University Press.

United Nations. 1998a. *World Investment Report*. New York.

———. 1998b. "World Population Nearing 6 Billion." Population Division Note. New York.

———. 1998c. *World Population Prospects: The 1996 Revision*. Population Division. New York.

Vamvakidis, Athanasios, and Romain Wacziarg. 1998. "Developing Countries and the Feldstein-Horioka Puzzle." International Monetary Fund Working Paper WP/98/2. Washington, D.C.

Wallensteen, Peter, and Ashok Swain. 1997. *Comprehensive Assessment of the Freshwater Resources of the World*. Stockholm: World Meteorological Association and Stockholm Environment Institute.

Watson, Robert T., and others. 1998. *Protecting Our Planet, Securing Our Future: Linkages among Global Environmental Issues and Human Needs*. Washington, D.C.: United Nations Environment Programme, U.S. National Aeronautics and Space Administration, and World Bank.

Weart, Spencer R. 1998. *Never at War: Why Democracies Will Not Fight One Another*. New Haven, Conn.: Yale University Press.

Weingast, Barry R. 1997. "The Political Foundations of Limited Government: Parliament and Sovereign Debt in 17th and 18th Century England." In

John N. Drobak and J. V. C. Nye, eds., *The Frontiers of the New Institutional Economics*. San Diego, Calif.: Academic Press.

White, Oliver Campbell, and Anita Bhatia. 1998. *Privatization in Africa*. Directions in Development series. Washington, D.C.: World Bank.

World Bank. 1990. *World Development Report 1990: Poverty*. New York: Oxford University Press.

———. 1991. *World Development Report 1991: The Challenge of Development*. New York: Oxford University Press.

———. 1998. *World Development Indicators 1998*. Washington, D.C.

———. 1999. *World Development Indicators 1999*. Washington, D.C.

Wu, Chung-tong. 1997. "Globalization of the Chinese Countryside: International Capital and the Transformation of the Pearl River Delta." In Peter J. Rimmer, ed., *Pacific Rim Development: Integration and Globalisation in the Asia-Pacific Economy*. Canberra: Allen and Unwin.

Zlotnik, Hania. 1998. "International Migration 1965–96: An Overview." *Population and Development Review* 24 (3, September): 429–68.

Distributive Conflicts, Collective Action, and Institutional Economics

Pranab Bardhan

IN RECENT YEARS, as the pervasive influence of Walrasian models in economics has waned, it has become generally recognized that "institutions matter" and that the associated incentive structures substantially influence economic performance. Two recent strands of institutional economics have been influential in the development literature. One is associated with the theory of imperfect information: the underlying rationale of institutional arrangements and contracts (formal or informal) is explained in terms of strategic behavior under asymmetric information among the different parties involved. This theory has been fruitfully used in modeling many key agrarian and other institutions in poor countries, which are seen as substitutes for missing credit, insurance, and futures markets in an environment of pervasive risks, information asymmetry, and moral hazard. The literature on this interpretation started with sharecropping and went on to interlocking transactions in labor, credit, marketing, and land lease and to labor tying, credit rationing, joint liability in group lending schemes, and so on. Examples and overviews of the models can be found in Bardhan (1989a); Nabli and Nugent (1989); and Hoff, Braverman, and Stiglitz (1993).

The other school, associated primarily with North (1981, 1990) and Greif (1992, 1997), concentrates on comparative historical analysis of development processes, mainly in Western Europe and North America. North pointed to the inevitable tradeoff in the historical growth process between economies of scale and specialization, on the one hand, and transaction costs, on the other. In a small, closed, peasant community where transactions are face to face, transaction costs are low but production costs are high because specialization and division of labor are severely limited by the extent of the market defined by the personalized exchange process of the small community. In a large-scale, complex economy, as the network of interdependence widens, the impersonal exchange process gives considerable scope for all kinds of opportunistic behavior, and transaction costs can be high. Greif examined the self-enforcing institutions of collective punishment for malfeasance in long-distance trade in the late medieval period and, in a comparative study of Maghribi and Genoese traders, explored the institutional foundations of commercial development.

In Western societies, over time, complex institutional (legal and corporate) structures have been devised to constrain the participants, to reduce the uncertainty of social interaction, and, in general, to prevent excessive transaction costs and thus allow the productivity gains from a larger scale and improved technology to be realized. These institutions include elaborately defined and effectively enforced property rights, formal contracts and guarantees, trademarks, limited liability, bankruptcy laws, large corporate organizations with governance structures to limit agency problems, and what Williamson (1985) has called ex post opportunism. In developing countries some of these institutional structures are nonexistent, weak, or poorly devised and implemented. The state in these countries is either too weak to act as a guarantor of rights and institutions or much too predatory in its own demands, posing a threat to them.

Both strands of institutional economics have provided major insights into the microfoundations of institutional arrangements in developing countries and in our understanding of underdevelopment as an institutional failure. Both underline the multiplicity of equilibria, given the strategic interactions that result in the institutions as equilibrium outcomes and allowing for the historical initial conditions and cultural beliefs (which coordinate agents' expectations) that influence the selection of a particular equilibrium. At the same time, it is clear that the literature has barely scratched the surface of an as yet largely unexplored story in poor countries. Particularly lacking are theoretically informed, inductive, historical analyses of institutional change (or atrophy) in these countries of the kind that Greif has so incisively carried out for late medieval Europe. In this chapter, I only speculate on a few broad analytical themes that have not been given enough attention in the theoretical institutional economics literature, in particular, (a) the persistence of dysfunctional institutions in poor countries, (b) institutional impediments as outcomes of distributive conflicts, (c) the collective action problems these conflicts exacerbate, and (d) the critical need for coordination and, accordingly, for a more complex and nuanced role for the state, which many (though not all) states fail to fulfill.

The Evolution of Institutions in Developing Countries

The institutions a society develops (or fails to develop) for long-distance trade, credit, and other intertemporal and interspatial markets where the transactions are not self-enforcing provide an important indicator of that society's capacity for development. In this context the analyses of North (1990), Milgrom, North, and Weingast (1990), Greif (1992), and Greif, Milgrom, and Weingast (1994) have brought to our attention the importance of such institutions. Examples include the merchant guilds in Italian city-states and the Hansa, a league of German cities; the law merchant system as illustrated by the private judges who recorded institutionalized public memory at the Champagne fairs (an important nexus of trade between northern and southern Europe); and the community responsibility system in Mediterranean and European trade which arose during the commercial revolution that took place between the 11th and 14th centuries. These institutions facilitated economic growth by reducing opportunism in transactions among people largely unknown to one another and by providing a multilateral reputation mechanism supported by frameworks of credible commitment, enforcement, and coordination.

Greif has suggested that in the informal enforcement of mercantile contracts, contracts that depend on bilateral reputation mechanisms (that is, in which the cheater is punished only by the party that is cheated) are usually more costly than multilateral reputation mechanisms, in which punishment is inflicted by the whole community to which the cheated party belongs, or a community responsibility system, in which a whole community is jointly liable if one of its members cheats. In the case of bilateral reputation mechanisms, simple efficiency-wage considerations suggest that to keep a long-distance trading agent honest, the merchant (the principal) has to pay the agent a wage higher than the agent's reservation income. In more "collectivist" forms of enforcement this wage need not be as high, since the penalty for cheating is higher or peer monitoring makes cheating more difficult. But in a world with information asymmetry, slow communication, and plausibly different interpretations of facts in a dispute, an uncoordinated multilateral reputation mechanism may not always work and may need to be supplemented by a more formal organization for coordinating the expectations and responses of different members of the collectivity and for enforcement. In medieval Europe the merchant guild was such an organization. In governing relations between merchants, their various towns, and the foreign towns with which they traded, the guilds were able to coordinate merchants' responses to abuses against any merchant and to force merchants to participate in trade embargoes. This credible threat of collective action by the guilds enabled medieval rulers to commit to respecting the property rights of alien merchants and thus facilitated exchange and market integration.

Many developing countries have a long history of indigenous mercantile institutions of trust and commitment based on multilateral reputation mechanisms and informal codes of conduct and enforcement. Examples of institutions of long-distance trade and credit abound among mercantile families and groups in precolonial and colonial India, Chinese traders in Southeast Asia, Arab "trading diasporas" in West Africa, and so on. In precolonial India, for example, Bayly (1983) cites many cases of caste-based (and sometimes even multicaste) mercantile associations and *panchayats* (local tribunals or arbitration panels) that acted much like the merchant guilds and the law merchant system, respectively, of medieval Europe, within a vigorous and far-flung mercantile economy. Credit instruments such as *hundis* (bills of exchange) governed trade across thousands of miles even though their negotiability was not recognized in formal courts of law. Firms kept lists of creditable merchants whose credit notes—*sahajog hundis*—could expect a rapid discount in the bazaar. Bayly primarily discusses such community institutions in the area of the "burgher cities" of Allahabad and Benares in precolonial northern India., Rudner (1994) studied the southern Indian, caste-based, mercantile organization of the Nattukottai Chettiars in the colonial period, whose elaborate system of *hundis* transacted over long distances (with the caste elite firms, or *adathis*, acting as clearinghouses), collective decisions on standardization of interest rates, and caste *panchayats* with customary sanctions provided the basis for indigenous banking networks that spread over large parts of southern India and British-ruled southeastern Asia.

The institutional economics literature suggests that traditional institutions of exchange in developing countries often did not evolve into more complex (impersonal, open, legal-rational) rules or institutions of enforcement as they did in early modern Europe, and it emphasizes the need for such an evolution. The dramatic success story of rapid industrial progress in Southeast Asia in recent decades, often under the leadership of Chinese business families, suggests that more "collectivist" organizations can be reshaped in particular social-historical contexts to facilitate industrial progress and that clan-based or other particularistic networks can sometimes provide an alternative to contract law and impersonal ownership. In a study of 72 Chinese entrepreneurs in Hong Kong, Indonesia, Singapore, and Taiwan (China), Redding (1990) shows how, using specific social networks of direct relationships or clan or regional connections, these entrepreneurs built a system dependent on patrimonial control by key individuals, bonds of personal obligation, relational contracting, and interlocking directorships.[1]

As Ouchi (1980) had noted some years back, when ambiguity of performance evaluation is high and goal incongruence is low, the clan-based organization may have advantages over market relations or bureaucratic organizations. In clan-based organizations, goal congruence (and thus low opportunism) is achieved through various processes of socialization; performance is evaluated through a subtle reading of signals that are observable by other clan members but not verifiable by a third-party authority. As might be expected, there are some constraints on arrangements in these Chinese business families: reliance on centralized decisionmaking and control, internal finance, a small pool of managerial talent, a relatively small scale of operations, and, in large organizations, a tendency to subdivide into more or less separate units, each with its own products and markets. A major problem of "collectivist" systems of enforcement is that the boundaries of the collectivity within which rewards and punishment are awarded may not be the most efficient ones and may inhibit potentially profitable transactions with people outside the collectivity.

In general, even when the indigenous institutions of a mercantile economy thrived, the process, familiar from Western history, of the development of sequentially more complex organizations suited to industrial investment and innovations did not take place in developing countries. Contrary to usual practice, I shall refrain from putting all the blame on colonial or neocolonial policies, not because I think they are unimportant but because here I want to keep away from the familiar litany of nationalist historiography. I will confine myself to a discussion of indigenous institutional impediments to development and will link it with my critical assessment of the institutional economics literature.

A major institutional deficiency that blocked the evolution of the mercantile economy into an industrial economy in many poor countries has to do with financial markets.[2] Even when caste-based or clan-based mercantile firms thrived in their network of multilateral reputation and enforcement mechanisms, these mechanisms were often not adequate for supporting the much larger risks of longer-horizon industrial investment. The mercantile firms, by and large, had limited capacity (in finance or in specialized skills) to pool risks and mobilize the capital of the society at large in high-risk, high-return industrial ventures. The usual imperfections of credit and equity markets emphasized in the literature on imperfect information are severe in the early stages of industrial development. Investment in learning by doing is not easily collateralizable and is therefore particularly subject to the high costs of information imperfections. The technological and pecuniary externalities in investment between firms (and industries), which are difficult to pin down empirically but are emphasized analytically in early as well as more recent development literature, give rise to "strategic complementarities" and positive feedback effects, resulting in multiple equilibria.[3] This is particularly important when information externalities and the need for a network of proximate suppliers of components, services, and infrastructural facilities with economies of scale render investment decisions highly interdependent and make it particularly difficult to raise capital from the market for the whole complex of activities.[4] Historically, in some countries (for example, in postwar East Asia) the state has played an important role in resolving this kind of "coordination failure" by facilitating and complementing private sector coordination.

In this context one may note Gerschenkron's (1962) emphasis on the role of state-supported development banks for the late industrializers of Europe in the 19th century. Government-supported development banks have played a crucial role in long-term industrial finance and in the acquisition and dissemination of financial expertise in new industrial sectors in periods of large-scale reconstruction and acute scarcity of capital and skills. Examples include the Credit Mobilier in 19th-century France, Credit National in France and Société National de Credit à l'Industrie in Belgium after World War I, and, after World War II, Germany's Kreditanstalt für Wiederaufbau, the Japan Development Bank, and the Korea Development Bank. But experience with such banks in other developing countries (as in India or Mexico in recent decades) has been mixed at best. Armendáriz de Aghion (1999) points out that in contrast to the banks in France, Germany, and Japan, development banks in developing countries have often been controlled by the government in an exclusive and heavy-handed way. There has been little or no scope for cofinancing (or coownership) arrangements with private financial intermediaries (which would help with diversification of risk and dissemination of expertise) or opportunities to specialize in a small number of sectors, which would promote acquisition of specialized expertise. This is even apart from the usual moral hazard problem that arises in subsidizing the sometimes necessary losses of pioneering development banks and the ever-present danger that loan operations will become involved in the distribution of political patronage.

Thus, in the crucial leap between the mercantile economy and the industrial economy, the ability of the state to act as a catalyst and a coordinator in the financial market can sometimes be important. In much of the literature on the new institutional economics, the importance of the state is recognized but in the narrow context of how to use state power to enforce contracts and property rights and how to establish the state's credibility that it will not make confiscatory demands on the private owners of those rights. This dilemma is implicit in the standard recommendation in this literature for a "strong but limited" government. It is, however, possible to argue that in the successful cases of East Asian development (including that of Japan), the state has played a much more active role: intervening in the capital market in subtle but decisive ways; using regulated credit allocation (sometimes threatening withdrawal of credit in not so subtle ways) to promote and channel industrial investment; underwriting risks and guaranteeing loans; establishing public development banks and other financial institutions; encouraging the development of the nascent parts of financial markets; and nudging existing firms to upgrade their technology and to move into sectors that are important in an overall vision of strategic developmental goals. In this process, as Aoki, Murdock, and Okuno-Fujiwara (1995) have emphasized, the state has enhanced the market instead of supplanting it; that is, it has induced private coordination by providing various kinds of cooperation-contingent rents. In the early stages of industrialization, when private financial and other related institutions were underdeveloped and coordination was not self-enforcing, the East Asian state created opportunities for rents conditional on performance or outcome (through mobilization of savings, commercialization of inventions, export "contests," and so on) and facilitated institutional development by influencing the strategic incentives facing private agents through an alteration of the relative returns to cooperation in comparison with the adversarial equilibrium.

One should not, of course, underestimate the administrative difficulties of such aggregate coordination, and the issues of micromanagement of capital may be much too intricate for the institutional capacity and information-processing abilities of many a state in Africa, Latin America, or South Asia.[5] One should also be wary, as the more recent East Asian experience of financial crisis warns us, about the moral hazard problems of too cozy a relationship between public banks and private business and the political pressures for bailout that a state-supported financial system inevitably faces. Nevertheless, I think that institutional economics will be richer if we admit the possibility of a more nuanced theory of the state, beyond the oversimplifications of either the Marxist theorist's class-driven state or the public choice theorist's rentier or predatory state.

Dysfunctional Institutions

One of the as yet inadequately resolved issues in institutional economics in the context of underdevelopment is why dysfunctional institutions often persist for a long time. Unlike the followers of the property rights school, who often displayed a naive presumption of the survival of the "fittest" institution, the two strands of institutional economics identified above are quite clear in not ascribing optimality properties to the institutions as (Nash) equilibrium outcomes. North (1990), Bardhan (1989b), and others have pointed to the self-reinforcing mechanisms for the persistence of socially suboptimal institutions when path-dependent processes are at work. Borrowing an idea from the literature on the history of technological change, one can see that there are increasing returns to adoption of a particular institutional form: the more it is adopted, the more it is attractive or convenient for others to conform on account of infrastructural and network externalities, learning and coordination effects, and adaptive expectations. A path chosen by some initial adopters to suit their interests may "lock in" the whole system for a long time to come, denying later, perhaps potentially more appropriate, institutions a footing.

North, more than others, has emphasized how in this path-dependent process the interaction between the "mental models" the members of a society possess and the incentive structure provided by the institutions works to shape incremental change.[6] The path-dependent process is further complicated by the frequent cases of unintended consequences. More than a century ago, Menger ([1883] 1963) made a distinction between "pragmatic" and "organic" institutions. Pragmatic institutions are the direct outcome of conscious contractual design, as in the institutional models in the theory of imperfect information or transaction costs. Organic institutions, as in Menger's theory of the origin of money, are comparatively undesigned and evolve gradually as the unintended and unforeseeable result of the pursuit of individual interests. Elster (1989) has referred to intermediate cases in which an institution may have originally come into existence unintentionally but is then consciously preserved by agents, once they become aware of the function the institution performs for them.

In the new institutional economics literature, the main stumbling block to realizing potential gains from trade is political. Looking over the past few hundred years of history, North, Weingast, and others have focused on a particular political mechanism of credible commitment that made much of the difference between the success stories of Western Europe and North America and the stagnation in large parts of the rest of the world over this period.[7] The mechanism in the West essentially involved self-binding by the rulers, who credibly committed themselves to be nonpredatory and thus secured private property rights, allowing private enterprise and capital markets to flourish. (For example, in England in 1688 the king gave up royal prerogatives, increasing the powers of Parliament.)

Although I do not deny that such self-binding mechanisms can play a very important role in history, I think it is possible to argue that they are neither necessary nor sufficient for economic development. They are not sufficient because there are other (technological, demographic, ecological, and cultural) constraints on the development process, not all of which will be relaxed by the rulers' disabling themselves. They are not necessary, as a few non-Western success stories (such as Japan since the Meiji Restoration, the Republic of Korea and Taiwan, China, since 1960, and coastal China since 1980) suggest; in most of these cases, although rulers often adopted prudent policies (and sometimes even acquired reputations to this effect), they were far from disabling their discretion. Major economic transactions in the successful East Asian cases have often been relation based rather than rule based. Although charges of cronyism have been bandied about in the diagnosis of the recent Asian financial crisis, the long-term success stories, even with relation-based systems, cannot be denied.

The political stumbling blocks to beneficial institutional change in many poor countries may have more to do with distributive conflicts and asymmetries in bargaining power. The "old" institutional economists (including Marxists) used to point out how a given institutional arrangement that serves the interests of some powerful group or class acts as a long-lasting barrier to economic progress (or a "fetter" on it, to quote a favorite word of Marx's). As has been suggested by Bardhan (1989b) and Knight (1992), the new institutional economists sometimes understate the tenacity of vested interests, the immensity of the collective action problem that has to be solved to bring about institutional change, and the differential capacity of different social groups for mobilization and coordination.[8]

The collective action problem can be serious even when the change would be Pareto superior for all groups. Two kinds of collective action problems are involved: the well-known free-rider problem of sharing the costs involved in bringing about change, and a bargaining problem in which disputes about sharing the potential benefits from the change may lead to a breakdown of the necessary coordination.[9] An institution that nobody individually likes may persist because it is upheld by a mutually sustaining network of social sanctions in which each individual conforms out of fear that infractions will lead to loss of reputation.[10] Potential members of a breakaway coalition in such situations may have grounds to fear that it is doomed to failure, and failure to challenge the system can become a self-fulfilling prophecy.

The problem may be more acute when, as is more often the case, there are winners and losers from a productivity-enhancing institutional change. The costs of collective action to bring about such a change may be too high. This is particularly so, as we know from Olson (1965), when the losses of the potential losers are concentrated and transparent, whereas the benefits to potential gainers are diffuse or are uncertain for a given individual, even though not for the group, as suggested by Fernandez and Rodrik (1991).[11] There is also the inherent difficulty, emphasized by Dixit and Londregan (1995), that the potential gainers cannot credibly commit to compensate the losers ex post.[12] Ideally, the state could issue long-term bonds to buy off the losers and could repay itself by taxing the gainers. But in many developing countries the government's ability to tax and its credibility in keeping inflation under control are seriously limited, and the bond market is thin. Potential losers may also fear that by giving up an existing institution, they may lose their position for lobbying with a future government in case the promises are not kept. (That is, "exit" from a current institutional arrangement could damage their "voice" in the new regime in the future.) The losers therefore resist a change that is potentially Pareto improving, in the sense that the gainers could compensate the losers.

The obstruction by vested interests can be formalized as a simple Nash bargaining model. The institutional innovation may shift the bargaining frontier outward (creating the potential for gains by all parties), but in the process the disagreement payoff of the weaker party may also rise—often because of the better options for both "exit" and "voice" that institutional changes may bring in their wake—and the erstwhile stronger party may end up losing in the new bargaining equilibrium. (How likely this is will, of course, depend on the nature of the shift in the bargaining frontier and the extent of the change in the disagreement payoffs.)[13] As Robinson (1995) emphasized in his theory of predatory states, it may not be rational for a dictator to carry out institutional changes that safeguard property rights, law enforcement, and other economically beneficial structures, even though they may fatten the cow that the dictator has the power to milk, if in the process his preexisting rent-extraction machinery could be damaged or weakened. The dictator may not want to risk upsetting the current arrangement for the uncertain prospect of a share in a larger pie.

The classic example of the persistence of inefficient institutions as the lopsided outcome of distributive struggles relates to the historical evolution of land rights in developing countries. In most of these countries the empirical evidence suggests that economies of scale in farm production are insignificant (except in some plantation crops) and that the small family farm is often the most efficient unit of production. Yet the violent and tortuous history of land reform in many countries suggests that there are numerous roadblocks, put up by long-standing vested interests, in the path of a more efficient reallocation of land rights. Why do the large landlords not voluntarily lease out or sell their land to small family farmers and grab much of the surplus arising from this efficient reallocation? There clearly has been some leasing out of land, but monitoring problems, insecurity of tenure, and the landlord's fear that the tenant will acquire occupancy rights to the land have limited the efficiency gains and the extent of tenancy. The land sales market has been particularly thin, and in many poor countries the sales go the opposite way, from distressed small farmers to landlords and moneylenders. Low household savings and severely imperfect credit markets mean that the potentially more efficient small farmer is often incapable of affording the going market price of land. Binswanger, Deininger, and Feder (1995) explain that land, as preferred collateral that carries all kinds of tax advantages and speculative opportunities for the wealthy, is often priced higher than the capitalized value of the agricultural income stream for even the more productive small farmer, rendering mortgaged sales uncommon (since mortgaged land cannot be used as collateral to raise working capital for the buyer). Under these circumstances, and if public finances (and the state of the bond market) are such that landlords cannot be fully compensated, land redistribution will not be voluntary.

Landlords also resist land reforms because the leveling effects reduce their social and political power and their ability to control and dominate even nonland transactions. Large landholdings may give their owner special social status or political power in a lumpy way.[14] (That is, the status or political effect from owning 100 hectares is greater than the combined status or political effect accruing to 50 new buyers owning 2 hectares each.) Thus, the social or political rent of landownership for the large landowner will not be compensated by the offer price of the numerous small buyers. Under the circumstances, the landowner will not sell, and inefficient (in a productivity, not Pareto, sense) land concentration persists.

Of course, even if there are increasing returns to landownership in terms of political rent, land concentration is not always the unique or stable political equilibrium. Much depends on the nature of political competition and the context-specific and path-dependent formation of political coalitions. Nugent and Robinson (1998) provide an interesting example from comparative institutional-historical analysis. They compare the divergent institutional and growth trajectories of two pairs of Latin American countries—Costa Rica and Colombia, and El Salvador and Guatemala—that share the same Spanish colonial background and produce the same principal crop, coffee, by the same methods. Institutional economics would be richer for more such comparative historical studies rather than additional cross-country regressions.

An important aspect of political rent that is overlooked in the usual calculations of the surplus generated by a given institutional change is that all sides are really interested in *relative*, rather than absolute, gain or loss. In a power game, as in a winner-take-all contest or tournament, it is not enough, if an institutional change is to be acceptable, that it increases the surplus for all parties concerned. One side may gain absolutely but lose relative to the other side and thus may resist change. If both sides have to continue to spend resources to seek (or preserve) power or improve their future bargaining position, and if the marginal return from spending such resources for one party is an increasing function of such spending by the other party (that is, if power-seeking efforts by the two parties are "strategic complements"), it is easy to see why the relative gain from an institutional change may determine its acceptability.[15]

Distributive Conflicts

If distributive conflicts constitute an important factor behind the persistence of dysfunctional institutions, they also make collective action difficult at the level of the central state agency (for example, in its coordination of macroeconomic policy) and at the level of local governments and community organizations (for example, in the provision and management of local public goods). At the macro level, collective action is necessary in formulating cohesive developmental goals with clear priorities and avoiding prisoners' dilemma–type deadlocks in the pursuit of commonly agreed on goals. Where wealth distribution is relatively egalitarian, as in large parts of East Asia (particularly when it is a result of land reform and widespread expansion of education and basic health services), it has been somewhat easier to enlist the support of most social groups—and isolate the extreme political wings of the labor movement—for short-run sacrifices in times of macroeconomic crises and for coordination of stabilization and growth-promoting policies.[16] There is some cross-country evidence that inequality and other forms of polarization make it more difficult to build a consensus on policy changes in response to crises and that they result in instability of policy outcomes and insecurity of property and contractual rights.[17]

The contrast between East Asia and South Asia is instructive in this respect. When society is extremely heterogeneous and conflict-ridden, as in India, and no individual group is powerful enough to hijack the state by itself, the democratic process tends to install an elaborate system of checks and balances in the public sphere and meticulous rules of equity in sharing the spoils, at least among the divided elite groups. (For an analysis of the continuing fiscal crisis and developmental gridlock in India as an intricate collective action problem in an implicit framework of noncooperative Nash equilibria, see Bardhan 1984, 1998.) The internal organization of such a state may exhibit what sociologists call "institutionalized suspicion" and a carefully structured system of multiple veto powers. (In India the institutionalized suspicion was no doubt enhanced by the legacy of colonial rulers, who were suspicious of the natives, and the earlier legacy of the Moghul emperors, who were suspicious of the potentially unruly *subadar*s and *mansabdar*s, the local potentates.) The tightly integrated working relationship of government with private business that characterizes much of East Asia is difficult to contemplate in this context. Not merely is the cultural distance between the "gentleman (or lady) administrator" and the private capitalist rather large in India (although it is declining in recent years), but, much more important, in the Indian context of a plurality of contending heterogeneous groups, a close liaison and harmonization of the interests of the state with private business would raise an outcry of foul play and strong political resentment among the other interest groups (particularly among organized labor and farmers). Indian politicians are much less able to ignore this reaction than the typical East Asian politician. It is difficult for the ruling groups in India to have what Olson (1982) called an "encompassing interest," that is, a structure that can internalize the distortions caused by its own policies. In general, at the level of the macro political economy, inefficient and uncoordinated state interventionism (which is usually the villain in the schematic scenario of public choice theory) is often a symptom of deeper conflicts in society.

Even more acute than at the macro level is the institutional failure at the local community level in many poor countries, and this is often ignored in the broad state-versus-market debates. The day-to-day livelihood of vast masses of the poor in the world, particularly in rural areas, crucially depends on the provision of local public goods (roads, extension services, power, irrigation, education, and public health and sanitation) and the management of the local commons (forests, fisheries, grazing lands, and so on). Yet well-functioning institutions of local self-government are often nonexistent, and development programs are usually administered by a distant, uncoordinated, and occasionally corrupt central bureaucracy that is unaccountable and insensitive to the needs of the local people.

On grounds of leaving decisionmaking in the hands of those who have information that outsiders lack and increasing the flexibility of public programs with respect to local conditions, the case for decentralization or devolution of authority to local governments is very strong. However, in addition to the usual administrative problems of coordination across jurisdictions and the lack of local revenue-raising and technical capacity, most schemes of decentralized governance are hindered by a major shortcoming related to distributive conflicts.[18] In areas of high social and economic inequality, the problem of "capture" of local governing agencies by the local elite can be severe, and the poor and the weaker sections of the population may be left grievously exposed to their mercies and malfeasance.[19] The central government can also be "captured," but for many reasons, the problem may be more serious at the local level. For example, because of the fixed costs of organizing resistance groups or lobbies, the poor may sometimes be more unorganized at the local level than at the national level, where they can pool their organizing capacities. Similarly, collusion among elite groups may be easier at the local level than at the national level, and policymaking at the national level may represent a greater compromise among the policy platforms of different parties. When local government is captured by the powerful and the wealthy, instances in which subordinate groups appeal to supralocal authorities for protection and relief are not uncommon. In such cases intervention by the long arm of the state in remote corners of a poor country has been by invitation, not always by arbitrary imposition (as is usually implied in the public choice or the new institutional economics literature).

The same problem clearly afflicts local (nongovernmental) community organizations with respect to management of the local commons. Extreme social fragmentation in India, for example, makes cooperation in community institution building much more difficult than in socially homogeneous Korea or Japan. There is also some scattered evidence that community-level institutions work better in enforcing common agreements and cooperative norms when the underlying property regime is not too skewed and the benefits generated are more equitably shared. Putnam's (1993) study of regional variations in Italy also suggests that "horizontal" social networks (those involving people of similar status and power) are more effective in generating trust and norms of reciprocity than "vertical" ones. One beneficial by-product of land reform that is underemphasized in the usual economic analysis is that such reform, by changing the local political structure in the village, gives more "voice" to the poor and induces them to get involved in local self-governing institutions and in the management of the local commons.

Economists belonging to the property rights school would, of course, point out the basic inefficiency of resource use in the commons. They favor the establishment of well-defined private property rights over the common resources, to generate incentives for greater internalization of externalities and for careful husbanding of resources by the private owners. But even if we ignore the serious distributional consequences of privatization of common-property resources, particularly in the form of disenfranchisement of the poor—from the enclosure movement in English history to the current appropriations of forests and grazing lands in developing countries by timber merchants and cattle ranchers, it has been the same sad story—it is possible to argue that privatization can create important problems even from the point of view of efficiency. As Seabright (1993) has pointed out, when contracts are necessarily incomplete, attempts to enforce private property rights may weaken the mechanisms of cooperation that previously existed among the users—who may have shared implicit noncontractual rights in the common-property resource—in two important ways.

First, privatization typically shifts bargaining power sufficiently in favor of those who acquire the property rights so that the parties may no longer share enough interdependence—or what Singleton and Taylor (1992) call "mutual vulnerability"—to make cooperation credible. In fact, when privatization is perceived as unfair by the dispossessed previous users, it can lead some of these users to irresponsible and destructive practices, and ultimately everyone, including the owner of the newly created property right, may be worse off. Second, a central characteristic of most private property rights is their tradability, and tradability may undermine the reliability of a long-term relationship among beneficiaries of a resource. Relationship-specific investments in the maintenance and preservation of a resource may be discouraged.[20] A self-governing local community may thus actually have efficiency advantages over both the bureaucratic and the private market mechanisms: it has the local information advantage over the bureaucratic mechanism, and it has the above-mentioned advantages in cases of incomplete contracts over the private market mechanism. A local community organization, particularly if it has a stable membership and well-developed structures for transmission of private information and norms among the members, and if it has the power of social sanctions to enforce agreements, has the potential to provide a more efficient coordination device. There are several documented examples of successful local community-level cooperation in management of common-property resources (see Ostrom 1990 for examples from different parts of the world). There are, of course, more numerous cases of failure of such cooperation in poor countries.

Going back to the issue of distributive conflicts and possible failures in the management of the local commons, in the economics literature the complex relationship between inequality of endowments and successful collective action is still an underresearched area. On the one hand, there is the well-known suggestion of Olson (1965) that in a heterogeneous group a dominant member enjoying a large part of the benefits of a collective good is likely to see to its provision even if he has to pay all the costs himself, with the small players free-riding on the contribution of the large player. On the other hand, there are cases in which the net benefits of coordination for each individual may be structured in such a way that in situations of marked inequality some individuals (particularly those with better exit options) may not participate, and the resulting outcome may be more inefficient than in the case with greater equality. Furthermore, the transaction and enforcement costs for some cooperative arrangements may increase with inequality.[21]

In general, contrary to the presumption of much of mainstream economics, there need not always be a tradeoff between equality and efficiency, as is now recognized in the literature on imperfect information and transaction costs. The terms and conditions of contracts in various transactions that directly affect the efficiency of resource allocation crucially depend on who owns what and who is empowered to make which decisions. Institutional structures and opportunities for cooperative problem solving are often forgone by societies that are sharply divided along economic lines. Barriers faced by the poor in the capital markets (through a lack of collateralizable assets that borrowers need to have to improve the credibility of their commitment) and in the land market (where the landed oligarchy hogs the endowments of land and water) sharply reduce a society's potential for productive investment, innovation, and human resource development. Under the circumstances, if the state, even if motivated by the desire to improve its political support base, carries out redistributive reform, some of the reform may go toward increasing productivity, enhancing the credibility of commitments on the part of the asset-poor, and creating socially more efficient property rights. Even the accountability mechanisms for checking state abuse of power at the local level work better when the poor have more of a stake in the asset base of the local economy. By dismissing all state-mandated redistribution as mere unproductive rent creation, some of the new institutional economists foreclose a whole range of possibilities. The state, however, in trying to correct inequities, has to be careful about incentive compatibility issues and its own political and administrative limitations. In general the state, the market, and the local community are all highly imperfect coordinating mechanisms. Each can do some things better than others, while each fails miserably in some matters.

We started with the historical role of the "collectivist" mechanisms of Eastern mercantile economies (as opposed to the more formal Western institutions) and the critical coordination role the state can sometimes play in the leap from the mercantile to the industrial economy. The difficult question is to identify the factors that may predispose a state to have an encompassing interest in the economic performance of the country and the conditions under which the state frequently fails. Much of the new institutional economics literature focuses on various, undoubtedly important, government failures, in particular, the failure to provide mechanisms of credible commitment to ensuring property rights. In this chapter we directed attention to other kinds of institutional failure that may be equally important. The institutional arrangements of a society are often the outcome of strategic distributive conflicts among different social groups, and inequality in the distribution of power and resources can sometimes block the rearrangement of these institutions in ways that would have been conducive to overall development. We have drawn particular attention to the inevitable collective action problems in this rearrangement, both at the macro level of the state—where these problems are at the root of the difficulty of breaking out of the policy deadlock, of which inefficient interventionism is only a symptom—and at the local level, where they make provision and management of crucial local public goods highly inefficient.

Notes

1. As Redding (1990) points out, "Many transactions which in other countries would require contracts, lawyers, guarantees, investigators, wide opinion-seeking, and delays are among the overseas Chinese dealt with reliably and

quickly by telephone, by a handshake, over a cup of tea. Some of the most massive property deals in Hong Kong are concluded with a small note locked in the top drawer of a chief executive's desk, after a two-man meeting." (Page 213). (One hears similar stories about the Hasidic diamond traders of New York and about firms in industrial districts in northern Italy.)

2. Another equally important institutional deficiency in this context relates to the agrarian institutions that can provide a sustainable rural base for industrialization programs (see "Dysfunctional Institutions," below).

3. The analysis of externalities has a long history in the postwar development literature, from Rosenstein-Rodan (1943) to Murphy, Shleifer, and Vishny (1989). For more recent theoretical contributions to this literature, see the special issue on "Increasing Returns, Monopolistic Competition, and Economic Development," *Journal of Development Economics*, April 1996.

4. Motivated by some historical examples from 19th-century continental Europe, Da Rin and Hellmann (1996) show, in a model with complementarities of investments of different firms, that private banks can act as catalysts for industrialization provided that they are sufficiently large to mobilize a critical mass of firms and that they possess adequate market power to make profits from costly coordination. These necessary conditions were not met, for example, in the case of unsuccessful industrial banks in Spain and Russia in the 19th century. In a model of a decentralized banking system, Dewatripont and Maskin (1995) show that banks tend to underinvest in long-term projects that involve large sunk costs requiring cofinancing by several banks. This is because such cofinancing leads to a free-rider problem in monitoring by each bank.

5. As the example of Japan in recent years shows, when technologies become more complex and the exploration of new technological opportunities becomes highly uncertain, the state loses some of its efficacy in guiding private sector coordination. (See Aoki, Murdock, and Okuno-Fujiwara 1995.)

6. A related example may be cited from the comparative study in Guinnane (1994) of credit cooperatives in German and Irish history. The Raiffeisen agricultural credit cooperatives that were successful in 19th-century rural Germany provided a model for the introduction of similar organizations in Ireland in 1894. They did not succeed in Ireland, however, partly because the social and cultural norm of mutual monitoring and collective punishment among members of a cooperative, which worked in rural Germany, did not in the Irish countryside.

7. See North and Weingast (1989). For some empirical criticisms of the argument with respect to English history, see Carruthers (1990) and Clark (1995).

8. North (1990) is an exception in this tradition. He points to the contrasting and path-dependent processes of change in bargaining power of the ruler versus the ruled in different countries, particularly in the context of the fiscal crisis of the state. In earlier historical literature on the transition from feudalism in Europe, Brenner (1976) departed from the usual analysis of transition in terms of demography or market conditions. He provided a detailed analysis of the contrasting experiences with transition in different parts of Europe (be-

tween western and eastern Europe and between the English and the French cases) in terms of changes in the bargaining power of different social groups or in the outcomes of social conflicts. Brenner showed that much depends, for example, on the cohesiveness of landlords and peasants as contending groups and on their ability to resist encroachments on each other's rights and to form coalitions with other groups in society

9. Although most economists identify the collective action problem with the free-rider problem, political philosophers such as Elster (1989) and behavioral economists working with ultimatum games, such as Rabin (1998), have emphasized the bargaining problem that arises from unequal benefits.

10. For a well-known static analysis of such a case, see Akerlof (1984). For a more complex model in terms of stochastic dynamic games explaining the evolution of local customs or conventions, see Young (1998).

11. As Machiavelli reminds us in *The Prince*, (1513), ch. 6, "the reformer has enemies in all those who profit by the old order, and only lukewarm defenders in all those who would profit by the new."

12. Of course, some societies may be able to develop, as situations recur, appropriate norms of compensation to losers, but preservation of such a norm may itself require collective action.

13. This is the case even if we abstract from the usual case of deadlocks arising in bargaining with incomplete information, with possible misrepresentation of the "type" of the bargaining players.

14. In an interesting paper, Baland and Robinson (1998) formalized increasing returns in political benefits from landownership in terms of a model of voting with Shapley value that determines the political rents each landlord gets as a function of the number of workers whose votes he controls. (Since a single peasant's influence is very small in relation to that of the landowner, in a wide set of circumstances the single vote he has is never pivotal electorally.) As Baland and Robinson note, the analysis would be similar for the collective action problem of numerous small peasants in deriving political benefits.

15. For a model of power-seeking on these lines that explains why two parties may not agree to transactions that are obviously mutually advantageous, even when there are simple enforceable contracts and side transfers of fungible resources to implement them, see Rajan and Zingales (1999).

16. The benefits of relatively equal distribution are, of course, not unique to East Asia. In fact a major institutional lesson that Adelman and Morris (1989) draw from their historical research on the development experience of 23 countries in the 19th century is similar: "Favorable impacts of government policies on the *structure* of economic growth can be expected only where political institutions limit elite control of assets, land institutions spread a surplus over subsistence widely, and domestic education and skills are well diffused."

Campos and Root (1996) observe, "In contrast with Latin America and Africa, East Asian regimes established their legitimacy by promising shared growth so that demands of narrowly conceived groups for regulations that would have long-term deleterious consequences for growth were resisted. In particular, broad-based social support allowed their governments to avoid having to make concessions to radical demands of organized labor."

17. See Keefer and Knack (1995). Rodrik (1999) cites cross-country evidence for his hypothesis that the economic costs of external shocks are magnified by the distributional conflicts that are triggered and that this diminishes the productivity with which a society's resources are utilized. This is also related to the literature on inequality and delayed stabilization in Latin America. See, for example, Alesina and Drazen (1991).

18. See Bardhan and Mookherjee (1998) for a theoretical framework for appraising the various tradeoffs involved in delegating authority to a central bureaucracy (as opposed to an elected local government) for delivery of public services from the point of view of the targeting and cost-effectiveness of public spending programs in developing countries.

19. This idea should be familiar in the United States, where movements in favor of state rights that would diminish the power of the federal government have been interpreted, with some historical justification, as regressive, working against poor minorities.

20. Seabright (1993) is, however, careful to stress that the circumstances under which this problem occurs are somewhat special. Long-term implicit contracts are not weakened by the mere fact of tradability of property rights in assets; it is tradability plus a sufficient likelihood of the presence of potential new owners with different out-of-equilibrium payoffs that is the key factor.

21. For a theoretical exploration of these cases, see Baland and Platteau (1997, 1998); Dayton-Johnson and Bardhan (1997).

References

Adelman, Irma, and Cynthia Taft Morris. 1989. "Nineteenth-Century Development Experience and Lessons for Today." *World Development* 17 (9): 1417–32.

Akerlof, G. A. 1984. *An Economic Theorist's Book of Tales.* New York: Cambridge University Press.

Alesina, Alberto, and Allan Drazen. 1991. "Why Are Stabilizations Delayed?" *American Economic Review* 81 (5, December): 1170–88.

Aoki, Masahiko, K. Murdock, and Masahiro Okuno-Fujiwara. 1995. "Beyond the East Asian Miracle: Introducing the Market Enhancing View." Stanford University, Stanford, Calif. Processed.

Armendáriz de Aghion, Beatriz. 1999. "Development Banking." *Journal of Development Economics* 58 (1): 83–100.

Baland, Jean-Marie, and Jean-Philippe Platteau. 1997. "Wealth Inequality and Efficiency in the Commons. Part I: The Unregulated Case." *Oxford Economic Papers* 49 (4): 451–82.

———.1998. "Wealth Inequality and Efficiency in the Commons. Part II: The Regulated Case." *Oxford Economic Papers* 50 (1): 1–22.

Baland, Jean-Marie, and James A. Robinson. 1998. "Land and Power." Centre de Recherches en Economie de Développement, Facultés Universitaires Notre-Dame de la Paix, Namur, France.

Bardhan, Pranab. 1984. *The Political Economy of Development in India.* Oxford, U.K.: Basil Blackwell.

———, ed. 1989a. *The Economic Theory of Agrarian Institutions.* Oxford, U.K.: Clarendon Press.

———. 1989b. "The New Institutional Economics and Development Theory: A Brief Critical Assessment." *World Development* 17 (9, September): 1389–95.

———. 1998. *The Political Economy of Development in India.* Expanded ed. New Delhi: Oxford University Press.

Bardhan, Pranab, and Dilip Mookherjee. 1998. "Expenditure Decentralization and the Delivery of Public Services in Developing Countries." CIDER Working Paper. Center for International and Development Economics Research, University of California at Berkeley.

Bayly, C. A. 1983. *Rulers, Townsmen and Bazaar: North Indian Society in the Age of British Expansion 1770–1870.* Cambridge, U.K.: Cambridge University Press.

Binswanger, Hans P., K. Deininger, and Gershon Feder. 1995. "Power, Distortions, Revolt and Reform in Agricultural Land Relations." In Jere R. Behrman and T. N. Srinivasan, eds., *Handbook of Development Economics,* 2659–2772. Amsterdam: Elsevier.

Brenner, Robert. 1976. "Agrarian Class Structure and Economic Development in Pre-industrial Europe." *Past and Present* 70 (1): 30–70.

Campos, José Edgardo, and Hilton L. Root. 1996. *The Key to the Asian Miracle: Making Shared Growth Credible.* Washington, D.C.: Brookings Institution.

Carruthers, B. E. 1990. "Politics, Popery, and Property: A Comment on North and Weingast." *Journal of Economic History* 50 (3): 693–98.

Clark, Gregory. 1995. "The Political Foundations of Modern Economic Growth: England, 1540–1800." *Journal of Interdisciplinary History* 26: 563–88.

Da Rin, Marco, and Thomas Hellmann. 1996. "Banks as Catalysts for Industrialization." Stanford University, Stanford, Calif. Processed.

Dayton-Johnson, Jeff, and Pranab Bardhan. 1997. "Inequality and Conservation on the Local Commons: A Theoretical Exercise." CIDER Working Paper. Center for International and Development Economics Research, University of California at Berkeley.

Dewatripont, M., and E. Maskin. 1995. "Credit and Efficiency in Centralized and Decentralized Economies." *Review of Economic Studies* 62 (4): 541–55.

Dixit, Avinash K., and John Londregan. 1995. "Redistributive Politics and Economic Efficiency." *American Political Science Review* 89 (4): 856–66.

Elster, Jon. 1989. *The Cement of Society: A Study of Social Order.* Cambridge, U.K.: Cambridge University Press.

Fernandez, Raquel, and Dani Rodrik. 1991. "Resistance to Reform: Status Quo Bias in the Presence of Individual-Specific Uncertainty." *American Economic Review* 81 (5, December): 1146–55.

Gerschenkron, Alexander. 1962. *Economic Backwardness in Historical Perspective*. Cambridge, Mass.: Belknap Press of Harvard University Press.

Greif, Avner. 1992. "Institutions and International Trade: Lessons from the Commercial Revolution." *American Economic Review* 82 (2): 128–33.

_____. 1997. "Microtheory and Recent Developments in the Study of Economic Institutions through Economic History." In D. M. Kreps and K. F. Wallis, eds., *Advances in Economic Theory*, vol. 2, 79–113. New York: Cambridge University Press.

Greif, Avner, Paul Milgrom, and Barry Weingast. 1994. "Coordination, Commitment, and Enforcement: The Case of the Merchant Guild." *Journal of Political Economy* 102 (3): 745–76.

Guinnane, T. W. 1994. "A Failed Institutional Transplant: Raiffeisen's Credit Cooperatives in Ireland, 1894–1914." *Explorations in Economic History* 31 (1): 38–61.

Hayami, Yujiro, and Vernon W. Ruttan. 1985. *Agricultural Development: An International Perspective*. Baltimore, Md.: Johns Hopkins University Press.

Hoff, Karla, Avishay Braverman, and Joseph E. Stiglitz, eds. 1993. *The Economics of Rural Organizations: Theory, Practice, and Policy*. New York: Oxford University Press.

Keefer, Philip, and Stephen Knack. 1995. "Polarization, Property Rights and the Links between Inequality and Growth." American University, Washington, D.C. Processed.

Knight, Jack. 1992. *Institutions and Social Conflict*. Cambridge, U.K.: Cambridge University Press.

Menger, Carl. 1963. *Problems of Economics and Sociology*. Translated by Francis J. Nock. Urbana, Ill.: University of Illinois Press. First published 1883.

Milgrom, Paul R., Douglass North, and Barry Weingast. 1990. "The Role of Institutions in the Revival of Trade: The Law Merchant, Private Judges, and the Champagne Fair." *Economics and Politics* 2: 1–23.

Murphy, Kevin M., Andrei Shleifer, and Robert W. Vishny. 1989. "Industrialization and the Big Push." *Journal of Political Economy* 97 (5, October): 1003–26.

Nabli, Mustapha K., and Jeffrey B. Nugent, eds. 1989. *The New Institutional Economics and Development*. Amsterdam: Elsevier.

North, Douglass C. 1981. *Structure and Change in Economic History*. New York: Norton.

_____. 1990 *Institutions, Institutional Change and Economic Performance*. Cambridge, U.K.: Cambridge University Press.

North, Douglass, and Barry Weingast. 1989. "Constitutions and Commitment: Evolution of Institutions Governing Public Choice in Seventeenth Century England." *Journal of Economic History* 49 (4, December): 803–32.

Nugent, Jeffrey B., and James A. Robinson. 1998. "Are Endowments Fate? On the Political Economy of Comparative Institutional Development." Department of Economics, University of Southern California, Los Angeles, Calif.

Olson, Mancur. 1965. *The Logic of Collective Action: Public Goods and the Theory of Groups.* Cambridge, Mass.: Harvard University Press.

——. 1982. *The Rise and Decline of Nations: Economic Growth, Stagflation, and Social Rigidities.* New Haven, Conn.: Yale University Press.

Ostrom, Elinor. 1990. *Governing the Commons: The Evolution of Institutions for Collective Action.* New York: Cambridge University Press.

Ouchi, W. G. 1980. "Markets, Bureaucracies, and Clans." *Administrative Science Quarterly* 25: 129–41.

Putnam, Robert D. 1993. *Making Democracy Work: Civic Traditions in Modern Italy.* Princeton, N.J.: Princeton University Press.

Rabin, Matthew. "Psychology and Economics." *Journal of Economic Literature* 36 (1998).

Rajan, R. R., and Luigi Zingales. 1999. "The Tyranny of the Inefficient: An Enquiry into the Adverse Consequences of Power Struggles." Working Paper. Graduate School of Business, University of Chicago. Chicago, Ill.

Redding, S. G. 1990. *The Spirit of Chinese Capitalism.* New York: Walter de Gruyter.

Robin, Matthew. "Psychology and Economics." *Journal of Economic Literature* 36 (1998).

Robinson, James A. 1995. "Theories of 'Bad Policy.'" Department of Economics, University of Southern California, Los Angeles, Calif. Processed.

Rodrik, Dani. 1999. "Where Did All the Growth Go? External Shocks, Social Conflicts, and Growth Collapses." *Journal of Economic Growth* 4 (December): 385–412.

Rosenstein-Rodan, Paul N. 1943. "Problems of Industrialization of Eastern and South-Eastern Europe." *Economic Journal* 53: 202–11.

Rudner, David West. 1994. *Caste and Capitalism in Colonial India: The Nattukottai Chettiars.* Berkeley: University of California Press.

Seabright, Paul. 1993. "Managing Local Commons: Theoretical Issues in Incentive Design." *Journal of Economic Perspectives* 7 (fall): 13–34.

Singleton, Susan, and Michael Taylor. 1992. "Common Property, Collective Action and Community." *Journal of Theoretical Politics* 4 (3): 309–24.

Williamson, Oliver E. 1985. *The Economic Institutions of Capitalism: Firms, Markets, Relational Contracting.* New York: Free Press.

Young, H. P. 1998. *Individual Strategy and Social Structure: An Evolutionary Theory of Institutions.* Princeton, N.J.: Princeton University Press.

Comment

Irma Adelman

THIS IS AN EXTRAORDINARILY DIFFICULT chapter to discuss because it is so subtle, supported by far-ranging examples spanning several centuries and continents, and because its major points are valid. Under the circumstances, a discussant has two basic choices: one can give one's own paper, or one can make a few disjointed remarks that underscore some of the points made or suggest some questions related to the subject that deserve tackling. In my discussion, I will adopt the second approach.

First, this is a pessimistic paper with respect to possibilities of institutional change. It suggests that, because of distributional conflicts, the hurdles a proposed institutional modification will have to surmount are high. Therefore, the benefits from institutional change have to be very large and unequivocally clear before a proposed reform has a chance—and even then, the reform may not be implemented if it upsets the *relative* distribution of power. The point is unfortunately correct and applies to a large number of countries. After all, over two thirds of all developing countries are plagued by high degrees of ethnic or religious inhomogeneity, and a quarter have extreme degrees of concentration of income and wealth. I am reminded of the standard approach of the first-generation development economists when faced with a policy proposal they wanted to sink: "Yes, but will it work in India?" (Incidentally, the analogous comment with respect to urban policy was, "Yes, but will it work in New York City?")

However, one can also make the converse point: egalitarian societies, not plagued by distributional conflicts, are ready to change institutions that have become dysfunctional. True, cohesive societies that are not plagued by distributional conflicts are rare and may well be limited mostly to East Asia. But they nevertheless exist and—one hesitates in saying this—can be forged by a mixture of policies: opening access to asset-accumulation opportunities in a way that is skewed towards the poor and the ethnically discriminated against; implementing development strategies that raise the value of the assets of the poor and ethnically disadvantaged (their unskilled labor); and making assets that complement the assets of the poor (credit or irrigation) more readily available to them. In this context, I have been struck by the great ease with which the Republic of Korea has been able to implement even radical institutional change.

Korea is a very homogeneous society (Song Byng Nak 1997: ch. 4); it has no ethnic minorities and is largely Confucian in tradition. Confucianism advocates communitarian values that assign great utility to benefits to the community as a whole and consider benefits to the individual secondary. Furthermore, Korea started its accelerated development from a very egalitarian distribution of assets. Before the Korean War there were two redistributive land reforms; then the partition, the war, and the aftermath of the war leveled the distribution of real wealth; inflation leveled the distribution of financial wealth; the benefits from rent-seeking were confiscated in the first month of the Park regime; and educational opportunities were distributed in an egalitarian manner, stressing first the expansion of primary education and then, when that was universal, the expansion of secondary education, and limiting enrollments in tertiary education. The result was an egalitarian society, not plagued by distributional conflicts, that could easily be mobilized to do what it took to lift itself from a state of abject poverty. Of course, the Toynbee effect emanating from competition with the Democratic Republic of Korea contributed significantly to the extraordinarily high level of social capability characteristic of Korea in the 1960s.

It is not an exaggeration to say that in Korea each new major policy initiative was preceded by the creation of a new institution or the reform of an old one. A case in point comes from my own experience as adviser in 1964–65 for the design of Korea's Second Five Year Plan, which launched the economy on its export-led growth trajectory (Adelman 1969). When I was first brought to Korea to advise on the plan and looked at the institutional arrangements for its implementation, I found that the Economic Planning Board, which was to be in charge of implementation, had no direct access to the executive. It was subordinated to the Ministry of Finance, which was preoccupied with the formulation of annual budgets and short-term macroeconomic policies, and it could not interact directly with other economic ministries or with the vice president. I wrote a report stating that unless this situation was remedied, planning would be a futile exercise, as short-term considerations would always win the day over long-term objectives. I then went back home, expecting that this would be the end of it. To my great surprise, a month later I received a cable stating, "We have done what you recommended; now come help us with the design of the plan."

Korea has retained its high level of social capability to the present. This has been evident in its adjustment to the 1997–98 financial crisis (Adelman and Song Byung Nak forthcoming). When the crisis first broke, women lined up at banks to turn in their gold jewelry without compensation to help with the acquisition of much-needed foreign exchange. Households also voluntarily curtailed their purchases of imports, even before the precipitous devaluation made imported goods excessively expensive. And in structuring its corporate adjustment, those who could bear the costs best took the initial hit: the salaries of managers and professionals were cut first, and an effort was made to shelter rank-and-file workers by preserving employment in the chaebols. Although unemployment developed later, it was primarily due to bankruptcies of less strongly capitalized small and medium-size firms. Unions were persuaded to call off a national strike, and when, months later, major strikes did materialize, the protests concerned the dismemberment of the chaebols, as well as the new flexibility in employment contracts imposed by adjustment under International Monetary Fund (IMF) conditions. Chaebol owners were persuaded to go along with measures to streamline the conglomerates by divesting themselves of their noncore businesses and by putting their personal wealth, which had been protected by limited liability laws, into the chaebols they owned, thus shoring up the firms' solvency and reducing the excessively large debt-equity ratios. The adjustment, while rapid and relatively drastic, has not generated much social turmoil and political protest, in contrast to the situation in the distributionally more unequal Indonesia, where the middle class and the poor have borne the brunt of adjustment to the financial crisis.

The contrast between crisis management in Korea (and Singapore), on the one hand, and in Indonesia and the Philippines, on the other, reinforces both Bardhan's proposition and its converse. It indicates the importance of social consensus for the relatively painful adjustments needed to cope with the crisis. This also ties in well with Rodrik's (1997, 1998) thesis that in societies in which inequalities are relatively small and the institutions which can manage and contain distributional conflicts arising out of globalization are strong (as they are in Confucian societies), the economic shocks arising from globalization can be contained. These societies can move relatively quickly and with relatively little social friction to implement the necessary corporate restructuring.[1] Conversely, in societies where inequalities are large and institutions for conflict management are weak or absent, the economic and social costs of external shocks will be magnified and perpetuated over time by distributional conflicts.

My second general observation is that Bardhan overstates somewhat the difficulties of converting merchant capital into industrial capital, or indeed the need to do so in the earliest stages of industrialization. After all, in the 19th century the Rothschilds financed European wars, and the financial requirements of wars are no smaller than those of industrialization, nor were the Rothschilds experts in the technology of war. In this context, I am reminded of the following joke: Mama Rothschild is at a social gathering at which the imminence of war between England and France is the major subject of discussion. She says, "Don't worry. My son won't finance it."

Another illustration of the possibilities for converting merchant capital into industrial capital is offered by the story of how the richest man in Taiwan (China), Mr. Wong, became so rich. In 1949 the head of the Taiwanese planning commission wanted to establish a plastics industry. He called the chairman of the Bank of Taiwan and asked, "Who is your largest depositor?" The banker replied, "The merchant Mr. Wong." The chairman of the planning commission then called Mr. Wong in and told him, "I want you to establish a plastics industry." Mr. Wong tried to argue that he had no experience in industry and knew nothing of plastics. To which the chairman replied, "You can hire experts in both." Reluctantly, Mr. Wong complied. For the first two years he had to build warehouses to hold his ever-mounting inventories of plastics and was going broke. Then came the Korean War, and the rest was history.

Converting merchant capital into industrial capital is not the only way to finance industrialization. We have learned from Gerschenkron that governments can substitute for missing or insufficient finance and can import missing technical know-how. The histories of Germany, Italy, Japan, and Russia abound with examples from their early stages of industrialization. In addition, W. Arthur Lewis has stressed the importance of agricultural capital flowing into industry. In financing its early industrialization, Taiwan converted agricultural capital into industrial capital by compensating large landowners for their confiscated and redistributed lands with industrial bonds, redeemable in industrial assets that had yet to be created (Kuo, Ranis, and Fei 1981).

How, then, can institutions be discarded when they become dysfunctional or introduced when they are appropriate? Bardhan's focus is on evolutionary change that is inhibited by distributional conflict. But, as the histories of the latecomers to the Industrial Revolution and of East Asian industrialization demonstrate, institutional change can also come from above, aided by leadership commitment to development and spurred by state power, external pressures, and internal and external challenges that encourage the laying aside of distributional conflicts. Of course, these institutions can initially be hijacked by the power elite and used to further their own, rather than social, interests. For example, a Yugoslav sociologist who studied worker council meetings in worker-managed enterprises found that only managers and professionals spoke up and that the rank and file ended up voting to support their recommendations.

Modern institutions can function in a manner analogous to that of the old institutions they are intended to replace. For instance, the first microcredit banks had a very poor repayment record. Borrowers at first interpreted the loans as being like traditional loans from landlords, on which repayment was not expected: peasants were born in debt and died in debt. But if the new institutions are monitored closely enough and are redesigned appropriately when flaws become apparent, and if sufficiently heavy penalties for hijacking are imposed, the modern institutions will eventually lead to the intended "modern behavior." This will not happen overnight, but with sufficient inventiveness, dedication, and perseverance, functional, modern institutions appropriate to the economy's stage of technological and social development will evolve.

So, we can end the discussion of possibilities for institutional change on a note of guarded optimism.

Note

1. In this context, it is interesting that the strikes in the Republic of Korea in the 1990s have been by workers protesting against the dismemberment of the chaebols rather than by unions urging their breakup.

References

Adelman, Irma, ed. 1969. *Practical Approaches to Development Planning: Korea's Second Five Year Plan.* Baltimore, Md.: Johns Hopkins University Press.

Adelman, Irma, and Song Byung Nak. Forthcoming. "The Korean Financial Crisis of 1997–98 and Its Implications for the Global Financial System." In Ro Naastepad and Servas T. H. Storm, eds., *Festschrift for George Waardenburg.* Delhi: Oxford University Press.

Kuo, Shirley W. Y., Gustav Ranis, and John C. H. Fei. 1981. *The Taiwan Success Story.* Boulder, Colo.: Westview Press.

Rodrik, Dani. 1997. "The 'Paradoxes' of the Successful State." *European Economic Review* 41: 411–42.

————. 1998. " Globalisation, Social Conflict and Economic Growth." *World Economy* 21: 143–58.

Song Byung Nak. 1997. *The Rise of the Korean Economy.* New York: Oxford University Press.

Comment

Paul Collier

BARDHAN HAS EXPLORED SOME of the ways in which institutions can persist even if they are, in economic terms, inefficient. One case is that in which institutions have "unintended consequences"; another is when they are the arena for distributive conflict. I am going to focus on one institution, kin groups, and show how they can have powerful unintended effects and become the arena for contests.

In traditional societies the kin group can reasonably be interpreted as an efficient institution (Posner 1980). Especially in environments of high natural risk and limited opportunities for accumulating assets, such as prevailed in much of Africa, people need institutions that provide insurance and intergenerational transfers. Insurance is, however, subject to severe problems of adverse selection and moral hazard, making it one of the most difficult services for a market to provide. The kin group overcomes these problems. The criterion for membership being birth, the problem of self-selection is avoided, while the high observability that comes from frequent social interaction reduces the problem of moral hazard. Thus, in traditional societies kin groups provide an efficient web of reciprocal obligations. They are what is often termed "social capital." Now, consider what happens when kin group members participate in the modern economy.

In African manufacturing, black-owned firms compete with firms owned by ethnic minorities—typically, Asians in East Africa, Lebanese in West Africa, and whites in southern Africa. A study of manufacturing firms in Kenya (Biggs, Raturi, and Srivastava 1996) found an important difference between Asian-owned firms and black-owned firms. Asian kin groups and African kin groups are probably about the same size, but most members of a typical African kin group work in peasant agriculture, whereas the typical Asian kin group is highly specialized in manufacturing and related trading. As a result, an Asian owner of a manufacturing firm can use his kin group to get much more information about manufacturers than could a black owner. Biggs, Raturi, and Srivastava found that as a consequence, Asian and black firms used completely different strategies for evaluating the creditworthiness of potential new customers. The typical Asian firm used its social network, whereas the typical African firm had to resort to the presumably more costly and less accurate method of going to look at the outside of the prospective client's premises. Not surprisingly, these effects have repercussions. If new business is risky to take on, a firm will stay with a narrow range of clients and will be less diversified and less able to grow. A related finding by Biggs, Raturi, and Srivastava is that small Asian firms have much better access to credit than small black firms.

Barr (1996) analyzed the diversity of informational sources used by networks of Ghanaian manufacturers and found that the more diverse was the social network, the higher was firm productivity. Foreign, usually ethnic minority, firms had much more diverse networks than did black-owned firms. They also had higher productivity, but this was fully explained by the greater diversity of their networks.

An implication of these studies is that although kin groups indeed perform useful functions in the modern economy, the differing compositions of the kin groups of ethnic minorities and ethnic majorities may give the former a substantial advantage. Their kin groups are both more specialized as to sector and more diversified internationally.

In the public sector we find precisely the opposite story: kin groups are a menace, and ethnic majorities are at an advantage. The preexisting webs of obligation that constitute kin groups find new arenas for action within the modern sector labor market. Once a member of a kin group is in a management position, with power to recruit and to promote, other members of the group can exert pressure for favors.

Kin groups were obviously not originally designed with such an eventuality in mind, but the general-purpose obligations they create make them readily adaptable to the opportunities and risks of urban life. Managers cannot choose to withdraw from kin groups. The underlying enforcement mechanisms—essentially, beliefs about the efficacy of kin group punishment—have been inculcated over centuries precisely to prevent members of kin group insurance schemes from withdrawing when they discover that they are atypically successful. For example, in a celebrated Kenyan court case, a successful Luo man left a will specifying that he was to be buried by his wife in Nairobi rather than by his kin group in his home district. The kin challenged the right of the wife to conduct such a burial. The Kenyan high court overturned the will, siding with the kin group. This decision was important because the kin group's ultimate sanction against recalcitrant members is to bury them near their ancestors, who can be expected to exact retribution. The Kenyan high court was upholding the social obligations inherent in kin group membership.

Thus, kin group obligations are alive and well in the modern economy. Managers are subject to pressures from kin and from other members of the same ethnic group for preference. This imposes an additional constraint on the operation of the organization. If its managers meet these obligations, the organization will perform less efficiently because less qualified people will be appointed and promoted over more qualified people. The owner of the organization thus faces a principal-agent problem with the managers. Whether the owner can design an incentive system for the managers that successfully negates the pressures for kin group patronage depends on how easy it is to monitor performance and on the strength of the pressures. Managers in all parts of the modern economy can be presumed to face similar pressures, but sectors differ radically in the ease with which performance can be monitored.

Probably the most basic distinction in sectoral performance is that between the market and nonmarket sectors. One reason that governments engage in activities in the nonmarket sector is that output is harder to measure and harder to sell. Hence, managers in the public nonmarket sector are likely to be less subject to incentives that offset kin group patronage pressures than their counterparts in the market sector.

Using detailed geographic data on employee characteristics across the Ghanaian labor market, I was able to test this proposition (Collier and Garg 1999). There are many tribes in Ghana, and each is disproportionately clustered in a particular region. If managers favor their own kin groups or their own tribes in promotion decisions, workers who are members of the locally dominant tribe should have an advantage. They are much more likely to be working under a manager from the same kin group than are workers who are immigrants to the locality, and so they are more likely to be favored in promotion. We found that, controlling for a wide range of worker characteristics, including measured cognitive skills, workers in the Ghanaian public sector received a wage premium of 25 percent if they were from the locally dominant tribe. In the private sector there was no such premium. The public sector problem was compounded by the lack of remuneration for cognitive skills, again in contrast to the private sector.

Thus, the labor market evidence supports the analytical prediction (and the casual evidence from interviews with managers) that ethnic loyalties introduce new constraints into organizational performance. The problems posed by such loyalties are not generally insuperable. Like other incentive problems, they can be overcome if the "owner" has sufficient information about the performance of the firm. However, at least in Ghana, it appears that the public sector, where measurement is more difficult, has not succeeded in neutralizing the effects of ethnic allegiance.

Finally, I combine these two stories of kin groups as economic institutions. We have seen that in the private sector, kin groups are useful, but ethnic minorities have an advantage. In the public sector, kin groups are harmful, but ethnic majorities have an advantage. An obvious consequence would be that ethnic minorities would tend to select careers in private entrepreneurship, whereas ethnic majorities would select careers in the public sector. The potential implications for public policy are unattractive. The ethnic majority would tend to be suspicious of the private sector while favoring the expansion of the public sector. In effect, we have a Bardhan-style case of an ethnic distributive clash, deeply rooted in the functioning of kin groups, with the potential to scale up into a bias in economic policy.

References

Barr, A. M. 1996. "Entrepreneurial Networks and Economic Growth." Doctoral dissertation. Oxford University, Oxford, U.K.

Biggs, Tyler, Mayank Raturi, and Pradeep Srivastava. 1996. "Enforcement of Contracts in an African Credit Market: Working Capital and Finance in Kenyan Manufacturing." RPED Discussion Paper 71. World Bank, Regional Program on Enterprise Development in Africa, Washington D.C.

Collier, Paul, and Ashish Garg. 1999. "On Kin Groups and Wages in the Ghanaian Labour Market." *Oxford Bulletin of Economics and Statistics* 61 (2, May): 133–57.

Posner, R. A. 1980. "A Theory of Primitive Society with Special Reference to Law." *Journal of Law and Economics* 23: 1–53.

Historical Perspectives
on Development

Nicholas Crafts

THIS CHAPTER DISCUSSES SOME ASPECTS of the changing relationship between the study of economic history and development economics. Forty years ago the subjects seemed to be quite closely linked: senior figures straddled both areas, the development history of industrial countries was frequently studied with a view to deriving lessons for development policy, and economic historians made broad generalizations as to what these lessons were. In the 1990s things appear different. There is much less overlap between the fields of development and history, historians have largely retreated from the brash claims of the early postwar generation, and developing countries have their own well-documented recent history from which to draw lessons. This state of affairs is clearly reflected in a recent edition of Meier (1995), in which the historical perspective on development is still derived largely from Gerschenkron and Rostow.

This suggests the following questions:

1. Did anything of lasting value come out of the generalizations of the early postwar pioneers?

2. Have more recent practitioners of economic history any big messages for development economics?

3. Has development economics much to gain from resuming a closer relationship with economic history?

I return to these questions near the end of the chapter. In the following sections, I outline some of the outstanding claims about history and development put forward from the 1950s through the early 1960s, as well as the "new economic history" of the later 1960s and 1970s, and draw on the experience of the Industrial Revolution in Great Britain to review some reasons why the older work fell into disrepute. I next examine more recent studies on the historical process of growth and go on to argue that insights from economic history and appropriate historical comparisons have much to offer analysts of both the miracle and the crisis in East Asia. I describe the trend in cliometrics toward focusing more on living standards and less on production and suggest that this is an area for fruitful interaction between development economists and economic historians. Finally, I venture some brief answers to the three questions posed above.

The Legacy of Two Old Generations of Economic Historians

The early postwar generation of senior economic historians produced some high-profile generalizations about the historical experience of economic development that seemed to have wide policy implications and that impinged heavily on the consciousness of most economists. Shortly thereafter, the early cliometricians took center stage, and a neoclassical economic history that was rather suspicious of those earlier assertions came to the fore. Given that cliometrics was firmly grounded in orthodox mainstream economics, it was less likely to produce startling claims that would make development economists sit up and take notice, although it was still noteworthy for continuing, at least on occasion, to treat institutions and technological change as endogenous. This section offers a retrospective on what we have learned from the contributions of these two generations.

The Demographic Transition

Although there were predecessors, the classic statement of the theory of the demographic transition is in Notestein (1953), whose formulation was a dominant paradigm in both development economics and economic history until about the early 1970s. The approach was that of a stage theory of development: societies pass from a phase of low population growth in which both birth and death rates are high, through a phase of rapid population growth in which modernization causes decreases in mortality, and then, after a lag, to a mature phase in which both birth and death rates are low and population growth is once again modest. This vision, based on impressions of historical European experience—and widely interpreted as implying that "development is the best contraceptive"—contained both good news and bad news. Although eventually economic development would solve the population problem because modernization changes the economics of childbearing, in the short term it would inevitably exacerbate demographic pressure.

Progress in medical science and public health programs made mortality much less dependent on economic growth and much lower than past experience might have suggested (Preston 1975). The challenge implied by this finding was to the details of projections based on European economic history rather than to the basic premise of transition theory. Much more fundamental problems and different policy implications emerged from the historical study of fertility, especially in light of the results of the European Fertility Project (Coale and Watkins 1986) and the careful formulations of the microtheory of household contraceptive choice (Easterlin 1978).

Among the results of this research were the findings that changes in the costs of contraception or changes in tastes, as well as the more obvious income and female wage variables, might influence desired family size; that fertility decline in Europe occurred almost simultaneously in countries at very different stages of economic development; that predecline fertility was variable and well below the biological maximum; and that the cultural setting influenced the spread of birth control. A clear implication was that family planning programs had much greater potential to influence fertility, even at low levels of development, than the proponents of transition theory would have imagined (Knodel and van de Walle 1979).

Clearly, the prediction that demographic transition would accompany economic development is not invalidated by this or more recent historical experience, but what has disappeared is any pretence that the precise point at which fertility will fall is predictable (Kirk 1996). Thus, Bongaarts and Watkins (1996) find that in today's developing countries fertility seems generally unresponsive when the Human Development Index (HDI) is below 0.4 but that when the HDI rises past 0.6, nearly all countries are in transition. This seems also to have been the case in the European fertility transition, using the HDI estimates in Crafts (1997). (In 19th-century Europe, France is a huge outlier, with substantial family limitation setting in by the 1820s, when the HDI must have been well below 0.3.)

Many historians are happy to emphasize the importance of culture in fertility outcomes. Even they recognize, however, that the present state of knowledge is distinctly unsatisfactory in that it is quite unclear about what the decisive aspects of culture are or to what extent they might operate by influencing the diffusion of birth control (contraceptive costs) or by way of changing ideas on the acceptability of small or childless families—that is, through changes in tastes (Alter 1992). It should also be remembered that more narrowly economic factors related to the costs of children, such as women's employment opportunities and schooling, seem to have had an effect on fertility during the decline (Crafts 1984a; Anderson 1998).

Much more historical research remains to be done to reach an adequate understanding of the European fertility decline. It is clear that the view embodied in the original theory of the demographic transition was far too simplistic and was seriously misleading for policymakers. More sophisticated description has come out of the European Fertility Project, but at present there is no convincing general analysis on which development economists can draw.

Growth Accounting

Growth accounting was an idea that came to fruition in the early 1950s. It was, essentially, a tool of historical description emanating from the historical national income research program at the National Bureau of Economic Research (NBER) under the leadership of Kuznets. The early messages coming from it were all based on a long-run view of American economic growth. The big and startling claim that arose was that over eight decades a very high proportion—perhaps 90 percent—of per capita output growth came from the residual (Abramovitz 1956). Similar findings were reported by Solow (1957), who linked the result to growth theory, and by Kendrick (1961), who supplied the original magnum opus on American productivity trends. An international program of research was developed under the leadership of Abramovitz and Kuznets to produce similar long-run studies of other industrial countries, including France, Japan, and the United Kingdom. Maddison (1987) provides an overview of these and other studies.

The technique of growth accounting, subsequently much refined and reinterpreted, has proved to be of lasting value. In the 1990s it experienced a notable resurgence in the context of the debate on the sources of rapid growth in East Asia (Young 1995, 1998; Collins and Bosworth 1996; Hsieh 1997), and it has been reconnected with modern growth theory (Barro 1998). As more research has been done, the original assertion of the overwhelming importance of the residual has not proved to be either generalizable or even particularly robust. In part, this is a result of better measurement of factor inputs and, especially, the explicit acknowledgement of the role of human capital.

It also appears that the measured contribution varies substantially from country to country and from period to period, even when estimates are constructed using similar weights and procedures, as reported in Table 1. The variation seems to reflect several factors that have become better known since the pioneering work of the 1950s. These include the different contributions of scale economies and improvements in the efficiency of resource allocation that may lead growth in total factor productivity (TFP) to exaggerate technological change. Conversely, conventional TFP growth may understate the contribution of technological change where there is endogenous innovation or where there is a capital-deepening and labor-saving bias combined with inelastic factor substitution. The factor-saving bias of technological change has differed greatly in various epochs (Abramovitz 1993).

Table 1. Growth Accounting: Comparisons of Sources
of Growth, Selected Countries and Periods

(average annual percentage change; numbers in parentheses are percentages
of total)

Country and period	Capital		Labor		Total factor productivity		Output
United Kingdom							
1780–1831	0.6	(35)	0.8	(47)	0.3	(18)	1.7
1831–73	0.9	(38)	0.7	(29)	0.8	(33)	2.4
1873–1913	0.8	(42)	0.6	(32)	0.5	(26)	1.9
United States							
1800–55	1.4	(35)	2.4	(60)	0.2	(5)	4.0
1855–90	2.0	(50)	1.6	(40)	0.4	(10)	4.0
1890–1905	1.6	(42)	1.3	(34)	0.9	(24)	3.8
1913–50							
France	0.6	(55)	–0.2	(–19)	0.7	(64)	1.1
Germany	0.6	(46)	0.4	(31)	0.3	(23)	1.3
Japan	1.2	(55)	0.3	(13)	0.7	(32)	2.2
United Kingdom	0.8	(62)	0.1	(7)	0.4	(31)	1.3
United States	0.9	(32)	0.6	(21)	1.3	(47)	2.8
1950–73							
France	1.6	(32)	0.3	(6)	3.1	(62)	5.0
Germany, Fed. Rep.	2.2	(37)	0.5	(8)	3.3	(55)	6.0
Japan	3.1	(34)	2.5	(27)	3.6	(39)	9.2
United Kingdom	1.6	(53)	0.2	(7)	1.2	(40)	3.0
United States	1.0	(26)	1.3	(33)	1.6	(41)	3.9
1973–92							
France	1.3	(57)	0.4	(17)	0.6	(26)	2.3
Germany, Fed. Rep.	0.9	(39)	–0.1	(–4)	1.5	(65)	2.3
Japan	2.0	(53)	0.8	(21)	1.0	(26)	3.8
United Kingdom	0.9	(56)	0.0	(0)	0.7	(44)	1.6
United States	0.9	(38)	1.3	(54)	0.2	(8)	2.4
1978–95							
China	3.1	(41)	2.7	(36)	1.7	(23)	7.5
1960–94							
Hong Kong (China)	2.8	(38)	2.1	(29)	2.4	(33)	7.3
Indonesia	2.9	(52)	1.9	(34)	0.8	(14)	5.6
Korea, Rep. of	4.3	(52)	2.5	(30)	1.5	(18)	8.3
Malaysia	3.4	(50)	2.5	(37)	0.9	(13)	6.8
Philippines	2.1	(55)	2.1	(55)	–0.4	(–10)	3.8
Singapore	4.4	(54)	2.2	(27)	1.5	(19)	8.1
Taiwan (China)	4.1	(48)	2.4	(28)	2.0	(24)	8.5
Thailand	3.7	(49)	2.0	(27)	1.8	(24)	7.5

(Table continues on the following page.)

Table 1 (continued)

Country and period	Capital	Labor	Total factor productivity	Output
1960–94				
South Asia	1.8 (43)	1.6 (38)	0.8 (19)	4.2
Latin America	1.8 (43)	2.2 (52)	0.2 (5)	4.2
Africa	1.7 (59)	1.8 (62)	−0.6 (−21)	2.9
Middle East	2.5 (56)	2.3 (51)	−0.3 (−7)	4.5

Sources: United Kingdom, 1780–1913: Matthews, Feinstein, and Odling-Smee (1982); Crafts (1995). (Estimates for years prior to 1856 refer to Great Britain.) United States, 1800–1905: Abramovitz (1993). "Group of 7" members: 1913–50, Maddison (1991); 1950–92, Maddison (1996). East Asia: derived from Collins and Bosworth (1996) except for Hong Kong, based on Young (1995), and China, based on Maddison (1998), both with factor shares adjusted to match Collins and Bosworth's assumptions. South Asia, Latin America, Africa, and Middle East: Collins and Bosworth (1996).

Technological change has greater effects on overall TFP growth when it assumes "yeast-like" rather than "mushroom-like" attributes, as is the case with general-purpose technologies with lots of spillovers. American TFP growth seems to have been yeasty in the 1920s but mushroomy in the 1960s (Harberger 1998; David and Wright 1999). We have also learned that economies vary substantially in their TFP growth capabilities for reasons that even mainstream economists now admit are not readily compatible with traditional neoclassical economics (Prescott 1998). Finally, the pace of underlying technological progress has been higher, on average, in the 20th than in the 19th century.

While the simple generalization with which we started has been lost, the wealth of knowledge gained in growth accounting research has resulted in the availability of a useful diagnostic tool for evaluating growth outcomes—albeit one that is quite demanding of data. In particular, when standardized factor weights are imposed across groups of countries, growth accounting has considerable value for benchmarking performance, as recent work on East Asia underlines (see "The East Asian Miracle and Crisis," p. 319).

The Kuznets Curve

Simon Kuznets was one of the most important founding fathers of the study of modern economic growth. He was more circumspect than others of his generation but produced a claim that continues to spark empirical investigation to this day. This was his suggestion, based on early empirical work, that during the process of economic development income distribution might follow an inverted-U shape, becoming first more and then less unequal (Kuznets 1955).

This claim is still fiercely contested by development economists, whose results seem highly sensitive to statistical methodology and the data set employed. Two of the most recent studies using large cross-country and longitudinal data sets reached diametrically opposing views on the validity of the Kuznets curve in recent development experience (Jha 1996; Deininger and Squire 1998). Long-run analysis by economic historians produces mixed results. Early modern Western Europe may have experienced a Kuznets curve upswing based on the urbanization mechanism that Kuznets himself invoked (van Zanden 1995). For two centuries, until the mid-1970s, American experience probably bears out Kuznets's conjecture, but British experience after 1688 does not clearly show the upswing. In both countries inequality has risen sharply in the past 25 years (Lindert 1997). In the globalization period before 1914, mass migration seems to have created rising inequality in receiving regions such as the United States but the opposite in sending regions, including Italy and Sweden (Williamson 1997). At best, it seems that the evidence for Kuznets's generalization is mixed.

Although the historical studies undertaken in response to Kuznets's conjecture have not supported the supposition, we have learned where research should be directed, and we can discard the misleading but apparently strong inference of an inevitable tradeoff between development and equality. Instead, a number of potentially powerful forces appear to be acting on pretax income inequality. Some of these forces are amenable to policy, and many of them have varied in their impact in different epochs. They include demographic change, human capital formation, biases in technological change, and Engel effects. This suggests that seeking to estimate Kuznets curves as a means of projecting future income distributions or as a guide to policy formation is a misplaced, mechanistic exercise.

Rostow's "Stages" and Gerschenkron's "Backwardness"

The highest-profile contribution of the early years was Rostow's stage theory of economic growth and, in particular, his notion of "the take-off into self-sustained growth," first set out in an article (Rostow 1956) and then in a short book (Rostow 1960). The idea was of a linear progression to an advanced economy through five stages, of which takeoff was the third, following "traditional society" and "preconditions for takeoff." The paradigm case was Great Britain, and other countries were portrayed as following in that country's footsteps. Takeoff required a doubling of the productive investment rate, the development of one or more leading sectors with substantial backward and forward linkage effects, and an appropriate institutional framework that could deliver an industrial revolution in two to three decades. The antecedent preconditions stage was one of investment in social overhead capital, the development of an institutional and legal infrastructure that facilitated investment and innovation, and a dynamic agriculture that released factors of production and fed a growing nonagricultural labor force.

The publication of Rostow's work generated a torrent of comment in the short term and added impetus to longer-term empirical research that examined the quantitative support for his hypotheses. The main lines of opposition soon became clear and are well captured in a conference volume that appeared shortly after the book was issued (Rostow 1963). On the theoretical level, these include objections to the failure to explain how economies move from one stage to the next or to set out necessary and sufficient conditions for being in a stage; suggestions that takeoff could (and did) occur in the absence of at least some of the preconditions; and arguments that the experiences of a pioneer industrializer and a follower country were bound to be different. Perhaps even more damning were empirical investigations that failed to identify a takeoff in the economic history of countries such as France (Marczewski 1963) or found that Great Britain appeared to be an outlier and that investment rose by far less during European industrialization than Rostow supposed (Crafts 1984b) or questioned the role of railways as a leading sector in American economic growth (Fogel 1964).

In part, the abandonment of Rostow was a consequence of the enormous influence of the alternative approach advanced by Gerschenkron (1962), who was in the forefront of those who doubted the idea of preconditions for takeoff. He put forward the proposition of substitutes for prerequisites: institutional innovation could circumvent the establishment of market-based relationships; the state could substitute for the private capital market; monopoly profits could generate the savings to finance investment; the banking system could supply entrepreneurship; and external trade could replace domestic agriculture in sustaining domestic industry.

The power of Gerschenkron's vision lay in his suggestion that the patterns of substitution for alleged prerequisites could be understood as responses to economic backwardness at the start of industrialization. For example, retained profits and private investors would dominate in well-advanced countries, bank finance and entrepreneurship would be important in conditions of moderate backwardness, and in extreme backwardness the state would be the key to industrial investment (Sylla 1991). There were also clear similarities to the "big push" view of industrialization in developing economies popular in the 1940s and to recent research on the developmental state in East Asian industrialization (Amsden 1989; Wade 1990).

A crude summary version of Gerschenkron's ideas provided the basis for some statistical tests of the "backwardness hypothesis," focusing in particular on his suggestion that backwardness offered greater opportunities for rapid growth once a successful institutional response had been created; growth would tend to be based on industry rather than on agriculture, and on investment and the output of producers' goods rather than on consumer goods. Statistical investigation of these hypotheses turned up mixed results rather than clear-cut support (Trebilcock 1981; Crafts 1984b). In particular, the notion that backwardness was associated with a great decisive spurt in growth of industrial output seems to be rejected by the available data when subjected to time-series analysis (Crafts, Leybourne, and Mills 1990).

Probably the most researched aspect of Gerschenkron's account of backwardness in European industrialization is the role of banking. Here too, serious doubts were raised, notably in the context of the claims made about the impact of universal banking early in industrialization in the pivotal case of Germany (Fohlin 1998). Although the picture of investment banking that emerges is more subtle and nuanced than Gerschenkron suggested, his claims appear to have some validity. It seems clear that in analyzing the effects of finance on development, attention needs to be paid to the entire range of institutional arrangements and their legal underpinnings (Sylla 1991). This resonates with recent work on the role of financial institutions in economic development.

The literature of European economic history rapidly dropped the Rostovian schema and regrouped around the idea that there were different paths of development to the modern world. Although the spirit of Gerschenkron's approach may still be useful in thinking about economic development (Sylla and Toniolo 1991), the general conclusion has been that there is no typology for the study of industrialization in 19th-century Europe (O'Brien 1986). The empirical rejection of the stylized facts in these grand theories has relied heavily on the results of empirical investigations, originally spearheaded by Kuznets, in the historical national income accounting tradition. This still flourishes and, as compiled and evaluated by Maddison (1982, 1995), has made a major contribution to empirical growth economics.

Although unsatisfactory as descriptive generalizations, the work of Rostow and, especially, Gerschenkron contains insights that may appeal more to mainstream economists today than in the 1960s and 1970s. Thus, particularly in the context of new economic geography, Rostovian linkage effects are back in vogue in models that feature imperfect competition, pecuniary externalities, and increasing returns to scale in analyzing, for example, patterns of industrialization (Puga 1998). Similarly, the ideas of the potential importance of coordination problems in development and of state intervention to escape a bad equilibrium have been formalized in models with increasing returns and nontradability of some inputs (Ciccone and Matsuyama 1996; Rodrik 1996a), thus rehabilitating to some extent the notion of the big push favored by Gerschenkron.

The literature of asymmetric information and transaction costs can be used to capture and to sharpen Gerschenkron's insights on the boundaries of the firm, the role of the state, and the type of finance likely to be appropriate under conditions of backwardness. Thus, a powerful state can play an important role in promoting and directing investment when capital markets are immature, but it needs a commitment technology to guard against rent-seeking behavior (Lee 1992). Bank finance has strong advantages in monitoring firms in the early stages of industrialization, but the supply of bank credit depends crucially on the quality of the legal system (Levine 1998). External finance will not be forthcoming when outside investors have few rights and contract enforcement is weak (La Porta and others 1997). The development of business groups is a way of reducing holdup problems (Khanna 1999).

Both the transaction costs argument and the incomplete contracts argument indicate more hierarchy and less reliance on markets when legal systems are weak, markets are thin, and asset specificity is intensified. It seems clear, however, that as development progresses, a shift toward more orthodox market-based arrangements and financial liberalization will be attractive—in particular, for improving productivity performance and allocative efficiency. The need to make such a transition and the difficulties to which it may give rise have, unfortunately, not been much discussed.

The possibility that Gerschenkron can be construed in terms of modern microeconomics does not mean that his underlying view of the role of the state in the development process is acceptable. On the contrary, it appears to lay far too much emphasis on the role of capital and far too little on the importance of productivity improvements, and it appears to be too sanguine about the dangers of government failure as opposed to market failure. Nevertheless, a clear message that derives from Gerschenkron and does still appear to be valid is that economies which develop from backwardness will probably go through the early stages of development with institutional configurations that look quite different from those of, say, the United States and that optimal arrangements will alter as development progresses.

New Economic History

The onset of the cliometric revolution in economic history is conventionally marked by the first of the annual Cliometrics Association meetings at Purdue, in 1960. The early work of the cliometric school was dominated not so much by econometric wizardry as by the application of mainstream neoclassical economics, notably price theory, to expose weaknesses in the logic of the stories told by traditional historians. Over several decades this has matured into a solid corpus of detailed studies, gradually encompassing more sophisticated econometrics and the microeconomics of agency problems, transaction costs, and so on, that is available as a storehouse of knowledge to be drawn on by the economics profession.

This type of work tends to produce far less than its predecessor in the way of startling generalizations to grab the development economist's attention. In part, this is because much new economic history entails the application of standard techniques of applied economics, so that there is less novelty in the findings. In addition, much of the effort devoted to quantification of the past has actually involved discovering that the old generalizations are at best half-truths. And, as McCloskey put it in his survey of early work in the field, "the conclusions have often been variations on the theme 'The Market, God Bless It, Works'" (McCloskey 1978: 21). A prominent example of this approach was the success of new economic history in debunking the notion of entrepreneurial failure in the late-Victorian British economy by demonstrating that controversial choices of technique were justified on profit-maximizing criteria at British relative factor costs (McCloskey and Sandberg 1971) and that returns on foreign investment amply justified the use of a large fraction of British savings abroad rather than at home (Edelstein 1976).

For economic growth, the big message that emerged was that the effect on overall growth of even the most profound technological breakthroughs is modest, especially at first. This finding emerged strongly from the pioneering studies of Fogel (1964) and Fishlow (1965) on the impact of railroads on American economic growth, in a period when social savings as a proportion of gross domestic product (GDP) were estimated to be the equivalent of only a couple of years' growth. Water transport was a good substitute for rail transport in many cases, and railroads were never that large in relation to the total capital stock of the U.S. economy. This lesson about the impact of inventions on the economy seems robust and has been revived recently in the context of late 20th century computer technology in a study reminiscent of the Fogel-Fishlow era (Sichel 1997).

It should be recognized that the new economic history of those early years was heavily dependent on the assumptions embodied in the neoclassical economics of the day. Some of this orthodoxy has subsequently been challenged, and—as analytical techniques have improved, in particular to bring the concepts of imperfect competition and increasing returns into the mainstream—old certainties have been superseded. Thus, the new industrial economics, the new international economics, the new economic geography, and the new growth economics all potentially call for some rethinking of early cliometric results.

For example, Fogel's estimate of the social saving from railroads is essentially a conventional cost-benefit analysis of a (large) transport project on the basis of a fixed trip matrix designed to obtain an upper-bound measure that regards the transport benefits as an acceptable estimate of overall economic benefits and disregards linkage effects. Given perfect competition and constant returns to scale, together with an exogenous growth model, this would be correct. Work in the new economic geography, however, undermines these assumptions. It has progressed to the point at which computer general equilibrium (CGE) modeling can embody different setups, including imperfect competition, agglomeration effects, and changes in the number of producers in the transport-using sector. Using a calibrated model, Venables and Gasiorek (1998) find that for freight traffic, the ratio of benefits to those captured by orthodox cost-benefit analysis may be in the range 1.4 to 1.65. Similarly, Baldwin (1989), in a review of the European single market, notes that incorporating endogenous growth into the analysis may add significant growth-rate effects to the static cost-benefit result. None of this, however, would allow the reinstatement of the myth of the indispensability of the railroads.

More generally, the key weakness of new economic history, despite brave attempts and in common with its predecessors, has been the inadequacy of its analytical tools for addressing the central themes of long-run economic history: endogenous institutional and technological change. An ability to develop powerful lessons in these areas might be just what development economists would most like from economic history, since these issues lie at the heart of long-run economic divergence.

Cliometricians—for example, Rosenberg (1982) and Mokyr (1990)—have made distinguished contributions to the history of technology, and, in general, analysis of technological change is one of the highlights of research in economic history. Moreover, this work has shown a subtle appreciation of the economics of technology diffusion and transfer (David 1991; Nelson and Wright 1992) and of the impact of factor endowments on choice of technique (James and Skinner 1985) and learning processes (David 1975; Allen 1983) that has been highly influential in the economics of technology.

Nevertheless, the unease of cliometrics when faced with questions about the determinants of technological change was readily exposed by the Habbakuk debate on the role of factor endowments in American and British 19th-century technology, as the overview in David (1975) so clearly reveals. Moreover, while recognition of the consequences of factor-saving bias in technological change is a strong theme in cliometric history, explanation of these time-varying biases remains in its infancy. Cliometricians have been successful in debunking crude Kondratieff-cycle formulations of fluctuations in the pace of technological change (Solomou 1987) but unsuccessful in accounting for the timing of the Industrial Revolution.

The early phase of cliometric history was also notable for pioneering attempts to endogenize institutional change along Coasian lines and as a response to changing relative prices. The boldest essay was that of North and Thomas (1973). The senior author has subsequently become one of that book's most perceptive critics. North now stresses that institutional change is a more complicated process than early cliometrics acknowledged because we cannot rely on the implementation properties of efficient markets and we must pay heed to informal constraints and the likelihood of path-dependent outcomes.

The First Industrial Revolution

In the 1950s, economic history written with development economists in mind often took the Industrial Revolution in Great Britain as a reference point. Subsequently, and especially in the past 20 years, quantitative reassessment of this experience has undermined many of the early claims. The main development has been much lower estimates, for the years 1780–1830, of economic growth and TFP growth (Crafts and Harley 1992) and of investment rates (Feinstein 1988a); see Table 2.

One implication of this work is that Rostow's notion of the takeoff seems to be completely discredited. GDP growth exhibited a steady acceleration over perhaps half a century and peaked at less than 3 percent a year, and there is no sign of the rapid doubling of the investment rate postulated by Rostow. The notion of leading sectors has also fared badly in light of the strong emphasis in the recent literature on the small initial size of cotton textiles in relation to GDP or even industrial output. Weighting of index numbers to reflect this point properly has been fundamental to reduced estimates of growth in industrial output.

Table 2 also reports the rapid deagriculturalization of the British labor force; by 1870 the proportion employed in agriculture had fallen to levels not reached in continental Europe until after World War II. This can only be explained in an open-economy context. CGE modeling suggests that it probably reflects a combination of technological prowess in leading industrial exports and the pressure of population growth on a domestic agriculture sector with an inelastic supply of land (Harley and Crafts 1998). In any event, it makes the British development trajectory an unusual one that was not followed elsewhere, and it is another reason to discard Rostow's linear model.

The Kuznets curve also seems a doubtful characterization of the British industrialization experience, and any changes in overall income inequality were probably small. The data are weak, however, and some modest rise and decline in inequality may have occurred. Williamson (1985) asserted that sectorally unbalanced technological progress and associated shifts in the supply of and demand for skilled and unskilled labor during the 19th century generated a Kuznets curve in an economy in which human capital formation was slow to respond to the new environment, but that claim has not survived Feinstein's (1988b) critique.

Table 2. Aspects of the First Industrial Revolution,
Selected Years, 1780–1913

Indicator	1780	1820	1870	1913
Gross domestic product (GDP)				
per capita ($1990 PPP)	1,787	2,099	3,263	5,032
GDP growth rate (percent)	1.0	1.9	2.4	1.4
Total factor productivity (TFP)				
growth rate (percent)	0.05	0.40	0.75	0.45
Share of agricultural employment				
(percent)	45	35	22.7	11.8
Investment as percentage of GDP	6.0	8.3	8.7	8.7
Research and development expenditure				
as percentage of GDP				0.02
Adult literacy (percent)	50	54	76	96
Primary school enrollment (percent)		36	76	100
Secondary school enrollment (percent)			1.7	5.6
Crude birth rate (per 1,000 population)	34.9	40.2	35.2	24.1
Life expectancy at birth (years)	34.7	39.2	41.3	53.4
Average direct tax rate (percent)	2.4	3.9	1.4	1.7
Gini coefficient for income	48.7	51.9	47.1	48.2

Note: Estimates refer to Great Britain through 1820 and the United Kingdom thereafter. Growth and investment rates are period averages.

Sources: Crafts (1998), where fuller details are given; for Gini coefficient, which is for nearest available year, Williamson (1985) as corrected by Feinstein (1988a).

Research on the English experience has been a key element in undermining the traditional view of the demographic transition. Remarkable progress has been made in using inverse projection techniques, taking samples of baptisms and burials in Anglican parish registers, to develop estimates of English population and vital rates back to 1541 (originally in Wrigley and Schofield 1981 and revised slightly in Wrigley and others 1997). These estimates have radically revised English population history and have generated a new conventional wisdom, although they are still the subject of considerable critical comment in the historical demography world (Razzell 1998). The account of English demographic history emerging from the estimates stresses that preindustrial fertility was regulated by nuptiality and was quite variable in a weakly homeostatic Malthusian system characterized by preventive checks.

During the Industrial Revolution fertility rose sharply as marriage behavior changed, and this accounted for most of the additional population growth through about 1821. The general spread of family limitation did not begin until the 1870s, when Britain was already a highly developed economy—a delay that contrasts with the case of France and is still not really understood. The rate of natural increase peaked at about 1.5 percent a year, a modest figure compared with those in developing countries in recent years, and this partly accounts for Britain's ability to develop without major increases in the rate of investment. The enhanced growth potential of the economy as technological progress accelerated enabled the economy to cope with population pressure that would have undermined living standards and evoked preventive checks in earlier centuries.

Even so, British industrialization does not appear to be a case in which growth is dominated by the residual—which may seem paradoxical, given the common interpretation of this episode as a period in which, for the first time, modern technological change came into its own. This is partly explained by the point made earlier that even major technological breakthroughs do not have big initial impacts on GDP as a whole; for example, it has been estimated that the social savings attributable to James Watt's steam engine were around 0.2 percent of GDP in 1800 (von Tunzelmann 1978: 157). It is also partly explained by the unevenness of technological change, which had little impact in many service sectors, and by the fact that achievement of full exploitation of new technologies depended on learning by doing and by using and thus took time. At a deeper level, it has been suggested that from an endogenous innovation perspective, this was still an economy which, by later standards, had many limitations, including weak science and technology, small markets, and many attractive rent-seeking opportunities for the talented (Crafts 1995).

Indeed, a World Bank economist, given a basic description of the late 18th century British economy without knowing to which country it applied, might well conclude that here was a case of very poor development prospects. Table 2 shows weak investment in formal schooling and in physical capital, despite very low direct taxes. The economy was engaged in an expensive war and was becoming increasingly protectionist, with a ballooning national debt. The outstanding plus points were in fact probably nonquantifiable and related to the constitutional underpinnings of property rights (North and Weingast 1989) and to a comparative advantage in microinventions based on expertise and on institutions that fostered relatively rapid technological diffusion and learning (Mokyr 1993).

Ongoing research has created a picture of the British Industrial Revolution that differs substantially from that which gave rise to the development history of the 1950s. If there is a lesson to be derived, it may be that, in many respects, the British experience is not a role model for the developing world today.

Third-Generation Economic History in a World of Growth Regressions

In the past 10 years or so the generalizations about economic growth used by development economists have frequently been taken from growth regressions. To an extent, this enterprise has stemmed from the work of Maddison (1982, 1995) in compiling long-run data on economic growth, but most of the vast growth regressions literature has used the Summers and Heston postwar data set (1988) and the subsequent updates. Both sources offer purchasing power parity (PPP)–adjusted estimates of real output per worker or per person in past years and so have been used to investigate issues of convergence and divergence, as well as the sources of growth.

Whereas growth economists have used growth regressions to attempt to discriminate between competing claims in growth theory, development economists have used them to project future growth (Barro 1997), to evaluate growth performance across countries (World Bank 1993), to bolster generalizations relating to the role of factor accumulation and initial backwardness in growth (Levine and Renelt 1992), and to support claims such as that openness is good for TFP growth (Edwards 1998) or that corruption is bad for growth (Mauro 1995). In this sense, growth regressions can be seen as the natural successors to the work of Kuznets and Rostow in the 1950s. An overview of the whole enterprise and some discussion of the technical econometric problems that are involved can be found in Barro (1997).

The growth regressions literature has quickly passed through two stages. In the early days the emphasis in terms of right-hand-side variables was on measures of accumulation and initial income levels as determinants of growth, with a strong emphasis on human capital. The implication of these models, taken literally, was that the transition economies of Eastern Europe could expect rapid growth because they had high school enrollments and a massive initial productivity gap. Mankiw, Romer, and Weil (1992) argued that the evidence was largely consistent with an augmented-Solow model as a good approximation of growth experience. Barro and Sala-i-Martin (1991) saw the future of Eastern Europe as a kind of neoclassical transition process in which conditional convergence to the steady state would proceed at 2 percent a year. These claims do indeed look odd set against the long-run historical record, which, as has been stressed recently, is one of "divergence, big time" (Pritchett 1997).

The next round of growth regression models pays much more attention to institutional quality as a right-hand-side variable and is characterized by innovative attempts to measure this factor, stimulated by the well-known paper by Knack and Keefer (1995). That paper, quickly followed by many others, used data from country risk guides published for international investors (International Country Risk Guide, ICRG) to assess the quality of property rights, the enforceability of contracts, the quality of bureaucracy, and so on and showed that these measures appeared to have a strong impact on growth performance. The underlying argument points to the importance of the appropriability of returns, freedom from holdup problems for investment, and managerial efforts for cost reduction. The relationship to economic history is in a way quite close, and North (1990) is cited as the explicit motivation for the research. The implications of this line of argument for the growth prospects of some of the former communist countries may be much less optimistic, given the weaknesses of their institutional arrangements (EBRD 1997: ch. 6). The most recent developments in this literature are characterized by pioneering attempts to explain the quality of institutions and policies. Thus, the regressions in Easterly and Levine (1997) and in Rodrik (1999) bring in contextual variables related to social conflict and ethnic division.

By now, this literature can be seen as converging with an important strand in the next generation of work in economic history, one that has sought to bring institutional change back to the forefront of generalization about the historical experience of growth. The two seminal references in this context are Abramovitz (1986) and North (1990). These historians can be seen, by implication, as probing more deeply than did Gerschenkron into the relationship between backwardness and growth (Abramovitz) and into the capability of the state to transform a backward economy (North). Abramovitz and North can both also be seen as elaborating a much broader version of the endogenous-innovation approach to economic growth developed by Grossman and Helpman (1991) and Aghion and Howitt (1998) but as quite far away from the neoclassical views in Mankiw, Romer, and Weil (1992). In these terms, the point to note is the fundamental importance of solving agency and appropriation problems in creating an environment conducive to innovation and productivity improvement.

The famous discussion of catch-up growth in Abramovitz (1986) stressed two points in particular. First, catch-up involves reducing a technological gap, not merely a factor intensity gap, and this requires technological congruence of the followers with the leaders. Second, catch-up requires "social capability." By this is meant the ability effectively to assimilate advanced countries' technology. Abramovitz admitted that this ability was hard to pin down precisely or to quantify. It requires not only adequate levels of human capital but also appropriate institutions, openness, and a political system that does not block reform or impede innovative activity. The combination of technological gap and social capability defines a country's potential for productivity advance by way of catch-up, while factors such as macroeconomic conditions and facilities for the international diffusion of knowledge influence the realization of that potential (Abramovitz 1986: 390).

Catch-up is far from automatic. A golden age of catch-up is rare but occurs when all the factors come together in a favorable conjuncture, as in most of Western Europe after World War II but not after World War I. Policy choices played a significant role after World War II, with many countries achieving "social contracts" between capital and labor that were conducive to high investment and to wage moderation based on the creation of commitment technologies and monitoring devices (Eichengreen 1996). Here, and in the incentives that it gave to trade liberalization, lay the importance of the Marshall Plan, rather than in the amounts of investment or technical assistance involved (Eichengreen and Uzan 1992).

Although in the case of postwar Europe there was a very clear and remarkably strong inverse correlation between initial income level and subsequent growth, there are still outliers, including the United Kingdom, that grew unusually slowly. Here, too, social capability probably played a role, perhaps through the industrial relations system, which politicians were unable or unwilling to reform, with its adverse (holdup) implications for TFP growth (Bean and Crafts 1996). This lack of capability would not be captured by standard growth regressions, underscoring the need to undertake historical case studies to identify key aspects of social capability rather than simply hope to find a proxy variable to use in cross-sections.

North (1990) also emphasized the crucial importance of institutions for growth—a theme that runs through several decades of his work. Well-defined, enforceable property rights that reduce transaction costs (in the form of exposure to opportunistic holdup) and thus support productive investment and innovation lie at the heart of North's view of the growth process. Strong but limited government is required; that is, government is needed to promote the rule of law, but it must be credible in renouncing opportunistic behavior. For autocrats with short time horizons, looting makes more sense than nurturing long-term perspective in the business world.

What is less clear is how these desirable attributes are achieved. North pointed out that not only is there no natural selection process that ensures the replacement of inefficient with efficient institutions but that network externalities, informal constraints, and the vested interests that surround existing arrangements tend to make institutional change a slow, incremental process and give it a path-dependent character. A central message is that creating social capability is very difficult; indeed, the policy advice that seems to follow most naturally from this concept is, "Get a new history!" An inability to explain when it is politically feasible to reform institutional and policy frameworks also characterizes the development economics literature on the political economy of reform, although some progress has been made in understanding status quo bias and wars of attrition (Rodrik 1996b).

North, like Abramovitz, does not try to quantify his ideas on the relationship between institutional quality and economic growth and would probably regard the attempts using ICRG in the growth regressions literature as brave but limited. Indeed, an interesting question is just what this variable captures; for example, is it failure of the legal system to enforce contracts that hobbles the financial system (Levine 1998), or do the effects run through the impact of corruption as a tax on foreign direct investment (Wei 1997)? If the corruption "tax" is perceived as the key problem, a more subtle view suggests that the amount of damage will differ depending, for example, on whether the corruption tax is more similar to lump-sum taxation by a powerful government or to overfishing by roving bandits (Bardhan 1997)— a distinction that echoes well-known themes in new institutional economic history. Here, too, it seems likely that ICRG-type growth regressions need to be supplemented by historical case studies.

In sum, the coming together of the growth regressions industry and some of the major themes in recent overviews of the growth process by economic historians is encouraging and may provide an opportunity for fruitful interaction between development economists and economic historians in exploring aspects of growth that are excluded from the augmented-Solow view of the world.

The East Asian Miracle and Crisis

Until recently, the remarkable growth performance of many East Asian economies was widely praised, and the crises of the late 1990s were not generally foreseen. The crises have triggered a period of reassessment of East Asian development. This experience provides a good opportunity to reflect on the difference that a historical perspective drawing on insights informed by the big ideas in economic history and some of the relevant cliometric research results can make.

The assessment in World Bank (1993) provides a good starting point for looking at the mainstream development economics view of East Asia in the early 1990s. High-performing East Asian economies were seen as benefiting from excellent TFP growth linked to their outward-oriented policies. The unusual success of these economies was attributed to government success in solving coordination problems while adopting policy frameworks that contained rent-seeking and were generally market friendly. Rapid deepening of financial markets was taken to be a great stimulus to investment and growth, while industrial and directed-credit policies were not seen as damaging. The World Bank's evaluation of the growth record was backed up by first-generation growth regressions in which dummy variables suggested that high-performing East Asian economies had outperformed the world sample by about 1.7 percent a year, compared with underperformance of 1.3 and 1.0 percent signaled by the Latin American and African dummies, respectively (World Bank 1993: 54).

Second-generation growth regressions include measures of institutional quality. Particularly if estimates for the 1990s are used, leading

East Asian countries also score well on these variables. Growth projections based on an equation of this type, including a "rule of law" variable with a large coefficient, were presented by Barro (1997: 44). They suggested further high growth in many East Asian countries, with the Republic of Korea right at the top of the world list.

The miracle years were already the subject of some reassessment prior to the crises as economists turned to the standard economic history methodology of growth accounting (Young 1995; Collins and Bosworth 1996). The messages were somewhat different from those coming from growth regressions, since the impact of the Asian demographic transition (Bloom and Williamson 1997) and the initially low capital-output ratios (Fukuda 1999) had not been reflected in regressions that used investment shares and population growth as right-hand-side variables. When put in historical context, the clear message of benchmarking through growth accounting, which appears robust to arguments about the data and factor-saving bias in technological change, is that East Asian TFP growth is far from outstanding, although, obviously, it compares well with that in Africa or Latin America.

From the columns for capital and labor in Table 1, it is clear that East Asian growth has relied much more on the contribution of rapid factor accumulation of both capital and labor than did Europe's fast growth in its golden age. Conversely, East Asian TFP growth has not been as strong as that in the European countries that experienced rapid catch-up growth in the early postwar decades. Indeed, the "Asian tigers" have fallen well short of Japan's achievement in this aspect of growth. Moreover, when one normalizes for the opportunities for catching up presented by the initial productivity gaps and levels of education, the tigers' TFP growth appears in a much less favorable light and seems rather disappointing (Crafts 1999).

At least for the more successful Asian economies, this should not detract from their unusually fruitful efforts to accumulate human capital and to improve and develop imported technology (Dahlman 1994). These achievements suggest that the tigers' disappointing TFP growth had its roots in other weaknesses in the Gerschenkronian developmental state model. A danger noted but understated in World Bank (1993) is that these weaknesses spawn government policies that serve the interests of special-interest groups and actually inhibit economic growth by inducing misallocations of resources—for example, through industrial policy.

Although there is no consensus in the literature on the overall effects of these policies, econometric analysis is increasingly tending to find that selective interventions, on balance, retarded rather than stimulated growth in both Korea and Taiwan (China). An analysis of the growth of industrial productivity across sectors in Korea during 1963–83 found that tax and financial incentives did not enhance productivity growth, while nontariff barriers to trade reduced both capital accumulation and TFP growth (Lee 1995). Similar results apply to Taiwan in the 1980s (Smith 1995).

The faltering Japanese productivity growth in the past 20 years underlines the point that catch-up growth is not automatic, as the neoclassical model would have us believe; it depends on social capability and can be eroded by poor policy choices. Japan's experience also underlines the need for transition after the first phase of a Gerschenkronian escape from backwardness. The distinctive Japanese institutional arrangements that emerged from the wartime experience addressed transaction cost problems effectively, mobilized support for the drive to modernization, and delivered the golden age, but they are now increasingly seen as in need of serious reform (Ito 1996). Yet reform is proving politically extremely difficult to implement. Readers of Abramovitz and North would not be greatly surprised by this outcome.

In part, poor Japanese TFP performance reflects excessive and wasteful investment and thus weaknesses in the financial system and in corporate governance (Ide 1996). Policy errors, however, have also played a part. As elsewhere in East Asia, industrial policies appear to have diverted resources away from high-growth sectors and toward declining industries and did not have a positive effect on TFP growth during 1960–90 (Beason and Weinstein 1996). The Japanese economy has also been subjected to excessive regulation, which has been costly to productivity, and it has continued to have high hidden unemployment in nontradables. The scope for TFP gains from deregulation in Japan appears to be about six times as large as in the United States (Blondal and Pilat 1997). Slow growth in the 1990s was exacerbated by a flawed financial liberalization in the 1980s, leading to a banking crisis, with severe implications for the financing of investment (Bayoumi 1999).

Understandably, the developmental states in East Asia have been aware of the need for reform if they are to catch up fully to the leading Organisation for Economic Co-operation and Development (OECD) economies in due course. Since the mid-1980s a major thrust of this reform effort has embraced financial liberalization, which, as theory does suggest, would be appropriate, in principle. The financial sector policies of a developmental state had tended to place little weight on proper auditing, accounting, credit rating, capital adequacy, and disclosure requirements or on experienced and independent regulators (Park 1994). Financial liberalization meant that prudential regulation and supervision assumed much greater importance. Failure to adapt quickly could lead to severe problems of moral hazard, which have indeed emerged (World Bank 1998). Thus, the current crisis in countries such as Korea can also be seen as illustrative of the difficulties of transition in a Gerschenkronian-style development. In addition, a student of North might want to add the insight that a transition to more orthodox financial arrangements might be expected to be fraught with difficulty, given the political clout of the interest groups associated with the original system.

An obvious lesson from economic history is that the record shows many examples in which financial crises and ensuing severe downturns have occurred in basically sound and strong economies that had high growth potential but were exposed to macroeconomic shocks when the banking system was inadequately regulated. The classic example is surely the United States in the 19th and early 20th centuries, most notoriously in the Great Depression of the 1930s (Mishkin 1991; Grossman 1993). In each case, resolution of the crisis permitted the resumption of strong growth.

In sum, a well-informed economic historian would surely have wanted to qualify the World Bank (1993) report on the sources of the "East Asian miracle" and would have emphasized that the capacity for effective institutional reform on a continuing basis is central to sustaining strong catch-up growth as a country develops. The historian would not think that financial crisis per se necessarily indicated weak long-term growth potential or presented an insuperable obstacle to the resumption of rapid growth, given an effective policy response to the problems exposed in the financial system.

Living Standards

Both development economists and economic historians have become increasingly concerned with developing measures of living standards that are more comprehensive than real wages or real GDP per capita. This is partly because attention has increasingly turned to the lives that people lead rather than the incomes that they enjoy and partly because in most circumstances a substantial element of well-being is not derived by way of personal command over resources but depends on provision by the state. This tends to be true of health and education in many countries and is universally the case for civil and political rights (Dasgupta and Weale 1992).

Studies of industrialization, in particular, have alerted economic historians to the possibility that there may be circumstances in which material prosperity increases while other aspects of living standards, such as life expectancy, deteriorate (Engerman 1997). It has long been recognized that industrialization in 19th-century conditions, at least for most workers, implied a tradeoff between higher wages and a worse environment (Williamson 1990). Research in historical demography has emphasized that over the past century or so, changes in life expectancy have been largely independent of changes in real incomes (Preston 1975). Although, traditionally, economic historians have concentrated largely on seeking to quantify real wages, this effort is increasingly seen as only part of what is required.

Since the late 1970s one of the most substantial research efforts in cliometrics has been devoted to investigation of human physical stature. This has involved laborious compilation of data, especially from military records, and the development of appropriate statistical methods to deal with the truncated distributions that these records often report (Wachter and Trussell 1982). The potential value of height in the context of measuring living standards is that it is known to reflect nutritional status and to be sensitive to factors that are not captured by real wages, such as work effort and the disease environment to which a person is exposed (Steckel 1995). Its role is as a diagnostic rather than as a measure of welfare per se.

Declines in height during the 19th century have been reported for several countries. In both the American and British cases it has been suggested that the height data indicate that economic growth and rising real wages are to some extent misleading indicators of changes in living standards. Having said this, it is not yet clear what exactly the diagnostic is picking up and thus what are the welfare implications. It could be costs of urbanization in terms of exposure of workers to adverse urban disease environments (Floud, Wachter, and Gregory 1990), or increased inequality of income, as regression results obtained in Steckel (1983) might imply, or a reduction in consumption of food in response to a rise in its relative price, as argued by Komlos (1995).

Economic historians have begun to embrace the Human Development Index (HDI). Floud and Harris (1997) assert that "there is a strong case for using . . . the HDI to investigate the level of human welfare in the past" (114). Costa and Steckel (1997) regard the HDI as "a retrospective index of welfare . . . relevant for understanding the past . . . the HDI measures how far an economy has come along the path to modern living standards" (73f). Historical estimates of the HDI or close approximations to it are possible back to the early 19th century in some countries, and estimates have started to appear (see Table 3).

The HDI is described and refined in successive issues of the *Human Development Report* (UNDP various years). Its focus is the escape from poverty, which is seen as depending on public services as well as on private incomes. The HDI is a composite of three basic components: longevity, knowledge, and income. Human development is seen as a process of expanding people's choices. Income is assumed to affect choices primarily at low levels of material well-being, and above a threshold level it is considered to make a sharply diminishing contribution, eventually tailing off to nothing. Longevity, measured by life expectancy at birth (e_0), and knowledge, measured by a weighted average of literacy (*LIT*) and school enrollment (*ENROL*), are regarded as central to the enhancement of capabilities but as not closely correlated with or strictly dependent on private income. The components are combined in a single index by measuring the distance traveled between the minimum and maximum values of the components ever observed and averaging these scores into one index. The precise formula is given in Table 3.

The HDI has obvious weaknesses as a measure of economic welfare that may not yet be fully appreciated by economic historians. It runs into difficulties with weighting. It is possible in this case to calculate the implicit set of weights that it embodies, but when that is done, their

Table 3. Human Development Index (HDI), 1870 and 1973

Period and country	GDP per capita ($1990 int.)	Life expectancy (years)	Literacy (percent)	Enroll- ment (percent)	HDI
1870					
France	1,858	42.0	69	40.7	0.400
Germany	1,913	36.2	80	41.6	0.397
Italy	1,467	28.0	32	16.3	0.187
United Kingdom	3,263	41.3	76	35.4	0.496
United States	2,457	44.0	75	43.8	0.466
1973					
France	12,940	72.4	97	66.7	0.881
Germany	13,152	70.6	99	66.6	0.876
Italy	10,409	72.1	94	58.4	0.862
United Kingdom	11,992	72.0	99	66.7	0.883
United States	16,607	71.3	99	83.1	0.900
China	1,186	63.2	27	64.2	0.407
India	853	50.3	34	28.1	0.289
Sri Lanka	1,733	65.0	77	49.0	0.547

Note: The HDI is defined as follows:

Life expectancy $(L) = (e_0 - 25)/(85 - 25)$

Schooling $(S) = 0.67LIT + 0.33ENROL$

Income $(I) = (Y_{adj} - 200)/(5,385 - 200)$

Each of these components has a value between 0 and 1, as does $HDI = (L + S + I)/3$. Adjusted income is measured by the following formula, which heavily discounts income above the threshold level, $y^* = 5,120$ ($1,990 int):

$Y_{adj} = y^* + 2[(y - y^*)^{1/2}]$ for $y^* < y < 2y^*$

$Y_{adj} = y^* + 2[(y - y^*)^{1/2}] + 3[(y - 2y^*)^{1/3}]$ for $2y^* < y < 3y^*$

and so on. $5,385 is an approximate maximum for this formula.

Source: Crafts (1997), Tables 1, 4, and 5.

justification is obscure, they vary dramatically at different income levels, and they are sensitive to the choice of extreme values. The very low weight given to income above an arbitrary threshold level is particularly difficult for many commentators to accept (Gormely 1995). Moreover, if the basic rationale of the index stems from a concern with capabilities and with the impact of social arrangements, the coverage of the HDI might well be regarded as too narrow.

Despite these reservations about the HDI, it may be valuable in historical research. Certainly, comparing today's developing countries with their European predecessors on the basis of the HDI gives a quite different impression from that obtained using historical national accounts, as is reflected in the estimates for India and Italy in Table 3. Since it is generally agreed that most improvements in mortality experience have resulted from "exogenous" factors such as advances in science and public health programs, it is likely that the growth of living standards since 1870 as measured by real national income per capita is substantially underestimated. To confirm this, however, we would need a way to value the exogenous change in life expectancy in terms of income, and the HDI methodology does not provide a way of carrying this out.

Usher (1980: ch. 7) provides a detailed rationale and methodology for making imputations to growth rates for environmental changes, that is, for variables that contribute to welfare but are not counted directly or indirectly as part of income and for which the average amount enjoyed changes over time. He takes pollution, crime, life expectancy, and leisure to be potentially important examples. All are clearly relevant to a long-run view of living standards and probably should eventually be addressed by economic historians, but only the last two have been quantified thus far, and then only very crudely. The main point is simply that imputations along these lines tend to be rather large, suggesting that conventional GDP growth rates may substantially understate the rate of improvement of average living standards in the past century (Crafts 1997).

The results shown in Table 3 contain an important message for development economists as well. It is clear that any index of living standards that gives a substantial weight to life expectancy will make the developing countries of the recent past look much better in welfare comparisons with the leading countries of 1870 than does a judgment based simply on real GDP per capita. This might prompt one of two basic reactions: either to say that this shows how important it is not to judge progress in development by GDP alone, or to say that it underlines how important it is to pay more serious attention to the index-number problems of measuring changes in living standards.

In fact, both reactions are probably valid. If so, they map out an important area in which future collaboration between economic historians and development economists should be fruitful, especially since historical research has revealed cases of bias in both directions in using growth of real GDP per capita to measure growth of average living standards.

Conclusions

In the light of this extended review of the literature, what might be the answers to the questions posed in the introduction?

The early postwar pioneers in economic history still have something to offer development economists. In general, however, what they offer is useful insights rather than generalizations that remain defensible. Notions such as takeoff, demographic transition theory, and the Kuznets curve have been largely discredited. But Gerschenkron's work on development from conditions of economic backwardness still deserves to be read and might usefully be revisited from the perspective of modern microeconomics.

Three big messages stand out in recent work in economic history. First, the attempts to force patterns of economic growth and development into the framework of the augmented-Solow neoclassical growth model are seriously misconceived. Second, institutions matter for economic growth, but countries can be expected to diverge significantly and persistently in their institutional arrangements. Third, it is important to distinguish between growth in real wages or GDP per capita and growth of living standards. In different stages of growth or in different epochs, the relationship between them has varied greatly.

These messages all suggest that economic historians and development economists have more to gain from continued and closer interaction than might have seemed to be the case 25 years ago in the heyday of revisionist new economic history. The example of the analysis of recent East Asian economic development has been used in the paper to illustrate that a bit more history and a bit less interpretation based on growth regressions might be helpful.

Note

The author is grateful to Douglass North and participants at the Dubrovnik conference for many helpful comments. He also received useful suggestions from Timothy Guinnane. Any errors are the responsibility of the author.

References

Abramovitz, Moses. 1956. "Resource and Output Trends in the United States since 1870." *American Economic Review* 46 (2, May): 5–23.

———. 1986. "Catching Up, Forging Ahead, and Falling Behind." *Journal of Economic History* 46 (2, June): 385–406.

———. 1993. "The Search for the Sources of Growth: Areas of Ignorance, Old and New." *Journal of Economic History* 53 (2, June): 217–43.

Aghion, Philippe, and Peter Howitt. 1998. *Endogenous Growth Theory.* Cambridge, Mass.: MIT Press.

Allen, Robert C. 1983. "Collective Invention." *Journal of Economic Behavior and Organization* 4 (1, March): 1–24.

Alter, George. 1992. "Theories of Fertility Decline: A Nonspecialist's Guide to the Current Debate." In John R. Gillis, Louise A. Tilly, and David Levine, eds., *The European Experience of Declining Fertility, 1850–1970,* 13–27. Oxford, U.K.: Basil Blackwell.

Amsden, Alice H. 1989. *Asia's Next Giant.* New York: Oxford University Press.

Anderson, Michael. 1998. "Highly Restricted Fertility: Very Small Families in the British Fertility Decline." *Population Studies* 52 (2, July): 177–99.

Baldwin, Richard E. 1989. "The Growth Effects of 1992." *Economic Policy* 0 (9, October): 247–81.

Bardhan, Pranab. 1997. "Corruption and Development: A Review of Issues." *Journal of Economic Literature* 35 (September): 1320–46.

Barro, Robert J. 1997. *Determinants of Economic Growth.* Cambridge, Mass.: MIT Press.

———. 1998. "Notes on Growth Accounting." NBER Working Paper 6654. National Bureau of Economic Research, Cambridge, Mass.

Barro, Robert J., and Xavier Sala-i-Martin. 1991. "Convergence across States and Regions." *Brookings Papers on Economic Activity* 0 (1): 107–58.

Bayoumi, Tamim. 1999. "The Morning After: Explaining the Slowdown in Japanese Growth in the 1990s." IMF Working Paper WP/99/13. Washington, D.C.: International Monetary Fund.

Bean, Charles, and Nicholas F. R. Crafts. 1996. "British Economic Growth since 1945: Relative Economic Decline . . . and Renaissance?" In Nicholas F. R. Crafts and Gianni Toniolo, eds., *Economic Growth in Europe since 1945,* 131–72. Cambridge, U.K.: Cambridge University Press.

Beason, Richard, and David E. Weinstein. 1996. "Growth, Economies of Scale, and Targeting in Japan, 1955–1990." *Review of Economics and Statistics* 78 (2, May): 286–95.

Blondal, Sveinbjorn, and Dirk Pilat. 1997. "The Economic Benefits of Regulatory Reform." *OECD Economic Studies* 28 (1): 7–48.

Bloom, David E., and Jeffrey G. Williamson. 1997. "Demographic Transitions and Economic Miracles in Emerging Asia." NBER Working Paper 6268. National Bureau of Economic Research, Cambridge, Mass.

Bongaarts, John, and Susan Cotts Watkins. 1996. "Social Interactions and Contemporary Fertility Transitions." *Population and Development Review* 22 (4, December): 639–82.

Ciccone, Antonio, and Kiminori Matsuyama. 1996. "Start-Up Costs and Pecuniary Externalities as Barriers to Economic Development." *Journal of Development Economics* 49 (April): 33–59.

Coale, Ansley J., and Susan Cotts Watkins, eds. 1986. *The Decline of Fertility in Europe.* Princeton, N.J.: Princeton University Press.

Collins, Susan, and Barry Bosworth. 1996. "Economic Growth in East Asia: Accumulation versus Assimilation." *Brookings Papers on Economic Activity* 2: 135–91.

Costa, Dora L., and Richard H. Steckel. 1997. "Long Term Trends in Health, Welfare, and Economic Growth in the United States." In Richard H. Steckel and Roderick Floud, eds., *Health and Welfare during Industrialization,* 47–89. Chicago, Ill.: University of Chicago Press.

Crafts, Nicholas F. R. 1984a. "A Cross-Sectional Study of Legitimate Fertility in England and Wales." *Research in Economic History* 9: 89–107.

———. 1984b. "Patterns of Development in Nineteenth Century Europe." *Oxford Economic Papers* 36: 438–58.

———. 1995. "Exogenous or Endogenous Growth? The Industrial Revolution Reconsidered." *Journal of Economic History* 55 (4, December): 745–72.

———. 1997. "The Human Development Index and Changes in Standards of Living: Some Historical Comparisons." *European Review of Economic History* 1 (3, December): 299–322.

———. 1998. "Forging Ahead and Falling Behind: The Rise and Relative Decline of the First Industrial Nation." *Journal of Economic Perspectives* 12 (2): 193–210.

———. 1999. "East Asian Growth before and after the Crisis." *IMF Staff Papers* 46 (June): 139–66. Washington, D.C.: International Monetary Fund.

Crafts, Nicholas F. R., and C. K. Harley. 1992. "Output Growth and the British Industrial Revolution: A Restatement of the Crafts-Harley View." *Economic History Review* 45: 703–30.

Crafts, Nicholas F. R., S. J. Leybourne, and T. C. Mills. 1990. "Measurement of Trend Growth in European Industrial Output before 1914: Methodological Issues and New Estimates." *Explorations in Economic History* 27: 442–67.

Dahlman, Carl J. 1994. "Technology Strategy in East Asian Developing Countries." *Journal of Asian Economics* 5 (winter): 541–72.

Dasgupta, Partha, and Martin Weale. 1992. "On Measuring the Quality of Life." *World Development* 20 (1, January): 119–31.

David, Paul A. 1975. *Technical Choice, Innovation and Economic Growth.* Cambridge. U.K.: Cambridge University Press.

———. 1991. "Computer and Dynamo: The Modern Productivity Paradox in a Not-Too-Distant Mirror." In Organisation for Economic Co-operation and Development, *Technology and Productivity,* 315–48. Paris.

David, Paul A., and Gavin Wright. 1999. "Early Twentieth Century Productivity Growth Dynamics." Paper presented to the Economic History Society Conference, Oxford, U.K., March 26–28.

Deininger, Klaus, and Lyn Squire. 1998. "New Ways of Looking at Old Issues: Inequality and Growth." *Journal of Development Economics* 57: 259–87.

Easterlin, Richard A. 1978. "The Economics and Sociology of Fertility: A Synthesis." In C. Tilly, ed., *Historical Studies of Changing Fertility,* 57–113. Princeton, N.J.: Princeton University Press.

Easterly, William, and Ross Levine. 1997. "Africa's Growth Tragedy: Policies and Ethnic Divisions." *Quarterly Journal of Economics* 112 (4, November): 1203–50.

EBRD (European Bank for Reconstruction and Development). 1997. *Transition Report.* London.

Edelstein, Michael. 1976. "Realized Rates of Return on UK Home and Overseas Portfolio Investment in the Age of High Imperialism." *Explorations in Economic History* 13: 283–329.

Edwards, Sebastian. 1998. "Openness, Productivity and Growth: What Do We Really Know?" *Economic Journal* 108 (447, March): 383–98.

Eichengreen, Barry. 1996. "Institutions and Economic Growth: Europe after World War II." In Nicholas F. R. Crafts and Gianni Toniolo, eds., *Economic Growth in Europe since 1945,* 38–72. Cambridge, U.K.: Cambridge University Press.

Eichengreen, Barry, and Marc Uzan. 1992. "The Marshall Plan: Economic Effects and Implications for Eastern Europe and the Former USSR." *Economic Policy* 0 (14, April): 13–76.

Engerman, Stanley L. 1997. "The Standard of Living Debate in International Perspective: Measures and Indicators." In Richard H. Steckel and Roderick Floud, eds., *Health and Welfare during Industrialization,*17–45. Chicago, Ill.: University of Chicago Press.

Feinstein, Charles H. 1988a. "National Statistics, 1760–1920." In C. H. Feinstein and S. Pollard, eds., *Studies in Capital Formation in the United Kingdom, 1750–1920,* 257–471. Oxford, U.K.: Clarendon Press.

———. 1988b. "The Rise and Fall of the Williamson Curve." *Journal of Economic History* 48 (3, September): 699–729.

Fishlow, Albert. 1965. *American Railroads and the Transformation of the Ante-Bellum Economy.* Cambridge, Mass.: Harvard University Press.

Floud, Roderick, and Bernard Harris. 1997. "Health, Height and Welfare: Britain, 1700–1980." In Richard H. Steckel and Roderick Floud, eds., *Health and Welfare during Industrialization,* 91–126. Chicago, Ill.: University of Chicago Press.

Floud, Roderick, Kenneth Wachter, and Annabel Gregory. 1990. *Health, Height and History.* Cambridge, U.K.: Cambridge University Press.

Fogel, R. W. 1964. *Railroads and American Economic Growth: Essays in Econometric History.* Baltimore, Md.: Johns Hopkins University Press.

Fohlin, C. 1998. *Financial System Structure and Industrialization: Reassessing the German Experience before World War I.* California Institute of Technology Social Science Working Paper 1028. Pasadena, Calif.

Fukuda, S. 1999. "Sources of Economic Growth in East Asian Economies: Why Did Capital Stock Grow So Rapidly?" In Organisation for Economic

Co-operation and Development, *Structural Aspects of the East Asian Crisis*, 29–56. Paris.

Gerschenkron, Alexander. 1962. *Economic Backwardness in Historical Perspective*. Cambridge, Mass.: Belknap Press of Harvard University Press.

Gormely, Patrick J. 1995. "The Human Development Index in 1994: Impact of Income on Country Rank." *Journal of Economic and Social Measurement* 21 (4): 253–67.

Grossman, Gene M., and Elhanan Helpman. 1991. *Innovation and Growth in the Global Economy*. Cambridge, Mass.: MIT Press.

Grossman, Richard S. 1993. "The Macroeconomic Consequences of Bank Failures under the National Banking System." *Explorations in Economic History* 30 (3, July): 294–320.

Harberger, Arnold C. 1998. "A Vision of the Growth Process." *American Economic Review* 88 (March): 1–32.

Harley, C. K., and Nicholas F. R. Crafts. 1998. *Productivity Growth during the First Industrial Revolution: Inferences from the Pattern of British External Trade*. London School of Economics Department of Economic History Working Paper 42. London.

Hsieh, Chang-tai. 1997. "What Explains the Industrial Revolution in East Asia?" University of California at Berkeley. Processed.

Ide, Masasuke. 1996. "The Financial System and Corporate Competitiveness." In Paul Sheard, ed., *Japanese Firms, Finance and Markets*, 191–221. New York: Addison-Wesley.

Ito, Takatoshi. 1996. "Japan and the Asian Economies: A 'Miracle' in Transition." *Brookings Papers on Economic Activity* 0 (2): 205–60.

James, John A., and Jonathan S. Skinner. 1985. "The Resolution of the Labor Scarcity Paradox." *Journal of Economic History* 45 (3, September): 513–40.

Jha, S. K. 1996. "The Kuznets Curve: A Reassessment." *World Development* 24: 773–80.

Kendrick, J. W. 1961. *Productivity Trends in the United States*. Princeton, N.J.: Princeton University Press.

Khanna, Tarun. 1999. "Policy Shocks, Market Intermediaries and Corporate Strategy: The Evolution of Business Groups in Chile and India." In Centre for Co-operation with Non-members, *Structural Aspects of the East Asian Crisis*, 91–124. Paris: Organisation for Economic Co-operation and Development.

Kirk, D. 1996. "Demographic Transition Theory." *Population Studies* 50: 361–87.

Knack, Stephen, and Philip Keefer. 1995. "Institutions and Economic Performance: Cross-Country Tests Using Alternative Institutional Measures." *Economics and Politics* 7 (3, November): 207–27.

Knodel, John E., and Etienne van de Walle. 1979. "Lessons from the Past: Policy Implications of Historical Fertility Studies." *Population and Development Review* 5: 217–45.

Komlos, John. 1995. *The Biological Standard of Living on Three Continents.* Oxford, U.K.: Westview Press.

Kuznets, Simon. 1955. "Economic Growth and Income Inequality." *American Economic Review* 45 (1, March): 1–28.

La Porta, Rafael, Florencio Lopez-de-Silanes, Andrei Shleifer, and Robert W. Vishny. 1997. "Legal Determinants of External Finance." *Journal of Finance* 52 (July): 1131–50.

Lee, Chung H. 1992. "The Government, Financial System, and Large Private Enterprises in the Economic Development of South Korea." *World Development* 20 (February): 187–97.

Lee, Jong-Wha. 1995. "Government Interventions and Productivity Growth in Korean Manufacturing Industries." NBER Working Paper 5060. National Bureau of Economic Research, Cambridge, Mass.

Levine, Ross. 1998. "The Legal Environment, Banks and Long-Run Economic Growth." *Journal of Money, Credit and Banking* 30 (August): 596–620.

Levine, Ross, and David Renelt. 1992. "A Sensitivity Analysis of Cross-Country Growth Regressions." *American Economic Review* 82 (4, September): 942–63.

Lindert, P. H. 1997. *Three Centuries of Inequality in Britain and America.* UC Davis Working Paper 97–09. University of California at Davis.

Maddison, Angus. 1982. *Phases of Capitalist Development.* Oxford, U.K.: Oxford University Press.

———. 1987. "Growth and Slowdown in Advanced Capitalist Economies: Techniques of Quantitative Assessment." *Journal of Economic Literature* 25 (2, June): 649–98.

———. 1991. *Dynamic Forces in Capitalist Development.* Oxford, U.K.: Oxford University Press.

———. 1995. *Monitoring the World Economy, 1820–1992.* Paris: Organisation for Economic Co-operation and Development.

———. 1996. "Macroeconomic Accounts for European Countries." In B. van Ark and N. F. R. Crafts, eds., *Quantitative Aspects of Postwar European Economic Growth,* 27–83. Cambridge, U.K.: Cambridge University Press.

———. 1998. *Chinese Economic Performance in the Long Run.* Paris: Organisation for Economic Co-operation and Development.

Mankiw, N. Gregory, David Romer, and David Weil. 1992. "A Contribution to the Empirics of Economic Growth." *Quarterly Journal of Economics* 107 (2, May): 407–37.

Marczewski, Jean. 1963. "The Take-Off Hypothesis and French Experience." In W. W. Rostow, ed., *The Economics of Take-Off into Sustained Growth,* 119–38. London: Macmillan.

Matthews, R. C. O., C. H. Feinstein, and J. C. Odling-Smee. 1982. *British Economic Growth, 1856–1973.* Stanford, Calif.: Stanford University Press.

Mauro, Paolo. 1995. "Corruption and Growth." *Quarterly Journal of Economics* 110 (3, August): 681–712.

McCloskey, Donald N. 1978. "The Achievements of the Cliometric School." *Journal of Economic History* 38 (1, March): 13–28.

McCloskey, Donald N., and L. Sandberg. 1971. "From Damnation to Redemption: Judgements on the Late Victorian Entrepreneur." *Explorations in Economic History* 9: 89–108.

Meier, Gerald M., ed. 1995. *Leading Issues in Economic Development.* Oxford, U.K.: Oxford University Press.

Mishkin, Frederic. 1991. "Asymmetric Information and Financial Crises: A Historical Perspective." In R. Glenn Hubbard, ed., *Financial Markets and Financial Crises*, 69–108. Chicago, Ill.: University of Chicago Press.

Mokyr, Joel. 1990. *The Lever of Riches.* New York: Oxford University Press.

———. 1993. "Editor's Introduction: The New Economic History and the Industrial Revolution." In Joel Mokyr, ed., *The British Industrial Revolution: An Economic Perspective*, 1–131. Oxford, U.K.: Westview Press.

Nelson, Richard R., and Gavin Wright. 1992. "The Rise and Fall of American Technological Leadership: The Post-War Era in Historical Perspective." *Journal of Economic Literature* 30 (4, December): 1931–64.

North, Douglass C. 1990. *Institutions, Institutional Change and Economic Performance.* Cambridge, U.K.: Cambridge University Press.

North, Douglass C., and Robert Paul Thomas. 1973. *The Rise of the Western World.* Cambridge, U.K.: Cambridge University Press.

North, Douglass C., and Barry Weingast. 1989. "Constitutions and Commitment: The Evolution of Institutions Governing Public Choice in Seventeenth Century England." *Journal of Economic History* 49 (4, December): 803–32.

Notestein, F. W. 1953. "Economic Problems of Population Change." In *Proceedings of the Eighth International Conference of Agricultural Economists*, 13–31. London: Oxford University Press.

O'Brien, P. K. 1986. "Do We Have a Typology for the Study of European Industrialization in the XIXth Century?" *Journal of European Economic History* 15: 291–333.

Park, Yung Chul. 1994. "Concepts and Issues." In Hugh T. Patrick and Yung Chul Park, eds., *The Financial Development of Japan, Korea and Taiwan: Growth, Repression and Liberalization*, 3–26. New York: Oxford University Press.

Prescott, E. C. 1998. "Needed: A Theory of Total Factor Productivity." *International Economic Review* 39: 525–51.

Preston, Samuel H. 1975. "The Changing Relation between Mortality and Level of Economic Development." *Population Studies* 29 (2, July): 231–48.

Pritchett, Lant. 1997. "Divergence, Big Time." *Journal of Economic Perspectives* 11 (3, summer): 3–17.

Puga, Diego. 1998. "Urbanization Patterns: European versus Less Developed Countries." *Journal of Regional Science* 38: 231–52.

Razzell, Peter. 1998. "The Conundrum of Eighteenth-Century English Population Growth." *Social History of Medicine* 11: 469–500.

Rodrik, Dani. 1996a. "Coordination Failures and Government Policy: A Model with Applications to East Asia and Eastern Europe." *Journal of International Economics* 40 (1–2, February): 1–22.

———. 1996b. "Understanding Economic Policy Reform." *Journal of Economic Literature* 34 (1, March): 9–41.

———. 1999. "Where Did All the Growth Go? External Shocks, Social Conflict and Growth Collapse." *Journal of Economic Growth* 4 (December): 385–412.

Rosenberg, Nathan. 1982. *Inside the Black Box.* Cambridge, U.K.: Cambridge University Press.

Rostow, W. W. 1956. "The Take-Off into Self-Sustained Growth." *Economic Journal* 66 (261, March) 25–48.

———. 1960. *The Stages of Economic Growth: A Non-Communist Manifesto.* Cambridge, U.K.: Cambridge University Press.

Rostow, W. W., ed. 1963. *The Economics of Take-Off into Sustained Growth.* London: Macmillan.

Sichel, D. E. 1997. *The Computer Revolution: An Economic Perspective.* Washington, D.C.: Brookings Institution.

Smith, Heather. 1995. "Industry Policy in East Asia." *Asian-Pacific Economic Literature* 9 (May): 17–39.

Solomou, Solomos. 1987. *Phases of Economic Growth, 1850–1973.* Cambridge, U.K.: Cambridge University Press.

Solow, Robert M. 1957. "Technical Change and the Aggregate Production Function." *Review of Economics and Statistics* 39: 312–20.

Steckel, Richard H. 1983. "Height and Per Capita Income." *Historical Methods* 16: 1–7.

———. 1995. "Stature and the Standard of Living." *Journal of Economic Literature* 33 (4, December): 1903–40.

Summers, Robert, and Alan Heston. 1988. "New Set of International Comparisons of Real Product and Price Levels Estimates for 130 Countries, 1950–1985." *Review of Income and Wealth* 34 (1, March): 1–25.

Sylla, Richard. 1991. "The Role of Banks." In Richard Sylla and Gianni Toniolo, eds., *Patterns of European Industrialization: The Nineteenth Century,* 45–63. London: Routledge.

Sylla, Richard, and Gianni Toniolo. 1991. "Introduction." In Richard Sylla and Gianni Toniolo, eds., *Patterns of European Industrialization: The Nineteenth Century,* 1–26. London: Routledge.

Trebilcock, Clive. 1981. *The Industrialization of the Continental Powers, 1780–1914.* London: Longman.

UNDP (United Nations Development Programme). Various years. *Human Development Report.* New York: Oxford University Press.

Usher, Dan. 1980. *The Measurement of Economic Growth.* Oxford, U.K.: Basil Blackwell.

van Zanden, J. L. 1995. "Tracing the Beginning of the Kuznets Curve: Western Europe during the Early Modern Period." *Economic History Review* 48: 643–64.

Venables, A. J., and M. Gasiorek. 1998. "The Welfare Implications of Transport Improvements in the Presence of Market Failure." U.K. Department of Environment, Transport, and the Regions. London. Processed.

von Tunzelmann, G. N. 1978. *Steam Power and British Industrialization to 1860.* Oxford, U.K.: Oxford University Press.

Wachter, Kenneth W., and James Trussell. 1982. "Estimating Historical Heights." *Journal of the American Statistical Association* 77 (378, June): 277–93.

Wade, Robert. 1990. *Governing the Market: Economic Theory and the Role of Government in East Asian Industrialization.* Princeton, N.J.: Princeton University Press.

Wei, Shang-Jin. 1997. "How Taxing Is Corruption on International Investors?" NBER Working Paper 6030. National Bureau of Economic Research, Cambridge, Mass.

Williamson, Jeffrey G. 1985. *Did British Capitalism Breed Inequality?* London: Allen and Unwin.

———. 1990. *Coping with City Growth during the Industrial Revolution.* Cambridge, U.K.: Cambridge University Press.

———. 1997. "Globalization and Inequality, Past and Present." *World Bank Research Observer* 12 (August): 117–35.

World Bank. 1993. *The East Asian Miracle: Economic Growth and Public Policy.* New York: Oxford University Press.

———. 1998. *East Asia: The Road to Recovery.* Washington, D.C.: World Bank.

Wrigley, E. A., and R. S. Schofield. 1981. *The Population History of England 1541–1871.* London: Arnold.

Wrigley, E. A., R. S. Davies, J. E. Oeppen, and R. S. Schofield. 1997. *English Population History from Family Reconstitution 1580–1837.* Cambridge, U.K.: Cambridge University Press.

Young, Alwyn. 1995. "The Tyranny of Numbers: Confronting the Statistical Realities of the East Asian Growth Experience." *Quarterly Journal of Economics* 110 (August): 641–80.

———. 1998. "Alternative Estimates of Productivity Growth in the NICs." NBER Working Paper 6657. National Bureau of Economic Research, Cambridge, Mass.

Comment

Avner Greif

IN HIS ILLUMINATING CONTRIBUTION, Professor Crafts has argued that the relationships between economic history and development economics have gone through two phases and are entering their third. The first phase was characterized by attempts to use economic history to produce generalizations about the process of development. Although these generalizations have failed the test of time, they provided important insights about development. The second phase was characterized by an extensive reliance on neoclassical economics. It left no noticeable mark on development economics, since it was aimed at demonstrating that markets functioned well in past economies. The third and current phase is characterized by three important realizations. First, "attempts to force patterns of economic growth and development into the framework of the augmented-Solow neoclassical growth model are seriously misconceived." Second, "institutions matter for economic growth." Third, "it is important to distinguish between growth in real wages or [gross domestic product] per capita and growth of living standards" (p. 326). Crafts concludes that focusing on living standards is "an important area in which future collaboration between economic historians and development economics should be fruitful" (p. 325).

The merit of these observations notwithstanding, this comment provides a complementary perspective on the relationships between economic history and development economics and stresses another future common area of research. Throughout the period discussed by Crafts, both fields have traveled and are traveling along the same route in trying better to understand processes of growth and stagnation. Until recently, they searched for what may be called "The Economic Theory of Development" (with capital letters). Both fields have now come to grips with the realization that economic development is a complex historical process in which economic, political, social, and cultural factors interrelate to influence the well-being of the individuals involved. The study of the past and present processes of economic development thus necessitates a transition from broad generalizations based on macrolevel econometric analyses that reveal (important) correlations but not the underlying lines of causation. Studying processes of growth and stagnation requires microlevel theoretical and empirical analysis that takes into account the particularities of the society under consideration and exposes the institutions that determine economic, political, and social outcomes. In examining development from such a microlevel institutional perspective, collaboration between economic development and economic history has been and will be fruitful. The economic history of industrial and developing countries alike provides a valuable data set. Such institutional analysis is inherently historical, since it requires studying a society's historical heritage as expressed in that society's institutions and their economic, political, social, and cultural aspects. (For a discussion of the related methodology, see Greif forthcoming.)

During the two first phases discussed by Crafts, scholars in economic history and economic development focused on the theory of economic development. It had been postulated that economic development follows basically the same path in all countries. The early phase was devoted to the search for broad generalizations. In the latter phase neoclassical economics was thought to provide the foundation for an encompassing theory. Over time, however, theoretical and empirical advances led to qualitative reorientation in both economic history and development economics, and similar factors contributed to the decline of the neoclassical economics framework in both fields. Advances in contract theory, information economics, endogenous growth theory, and game theory revealed the limitations of the neoclassical framework. In particular, these theoretical advances have shown that Pareto-ranked equilibria can prevail in common situations and that factors not captured in the neoclassical framework are important for growth. On the empirical side, case studies and econometric analyses based on data from current and past economies revealed the limited ability of the neoclassical growth model to direct development policy.

Instead of a concentration on measuring growth and the factors correlated with it, the emerging research agenda calls for a deeper probe into lines of causation. This reorientation requires us to enrich our understanding of the processes of development on the basis of microlevel, context-specific institutional analysis. To understand development and the implications of various policies in a particular time and place, we have to identify and analyze the incentive structure that influences the actions of the relevant economic or political decisionmakers. Thus, this research agenda calls for going beyond the argument that institutions matter but that they are products of history and that therefore the best—indeed, the only—policy advice we can give is to "get a new history." It postulates that to foster development we have to understand how history manifests itself in the details of the current institutional structures and hence how we can foster its growth-enabling or mitigate its growth-inhibiting properties.

Such a research agenda has already begun to take shape in economic history and economic development. Let me stress that this research agenda does not challenge the benefit of using modern economic theory and econometrics to provide useful analytical and statistical tools. Indeed, it is the sophistication of current tools that enables this research to flourish. Furthermore, the research builds on insights gained from past and present scholars who used case studies or econometric analysis to reveal factors that influence well-being. The importance of, for example, markets, government actions, population growth, corruption, financial systems, and education is not being challenged. What this new research agenda emphasizes is that to understand how these factors influence well-being in a particular society and to devise an appropriate policy, we first have to understand the details of that society's institutions.

This emerging research agenda has been applied to a wide variety of issues, ranging from the internal organization of firms and business communities to the inner workings of the government. Let me illustrate by briefly elaborating on two concepts that have been central to economic history and economic development: markets and states. Markets and their boundaries have always been considered both the ideal governance for organizing exchange and the yardstick for evaluating the development of an economy. In the first phase discussed by Crafts, scholars in both fields elaborated on conditions for the emergence of markets. In the later phase scholars held strong beliefs that markets are an optimal means of providing incentives, coordination, and information; accordingly, they have labored to demonstrate that markets prevailed in the past and have measured their extent in past and present economies.

The emerging research agenda aims at going beyond the view of the market as a primitive unit of analysis. It emphasizes that to understand the nature of markets in a particular time and place, we have to examine their institutional foundations. Markets do not function in a vacuum and do not carry their own weight; they require contract enforcement, coordination, and information, and the details of their operation, their extent, and their consequences for efficiency and distribution depend on their underpinning institutions. Thus, it is ultimately these institutions that determine which exchanges will take place, who can exchange, and what the terms of the exchange will be. Alongside the factors that neoclassical economics emphasizes as important for determining outcomes in markets, contract enforcement and other institutions shape the nature of the supply and demand curves. Such institutions can be, and have been shown to be, interrelated with various economic, social, and political aspects of a society. Social structures, trade associations,

exchange norms, legal rules, and political structures can and do constitute an integral part of these institutions. For an understanding of how
development policy can foster efficiency and well-being by extending
the reach of markets in a particular society, it is first necessary to un-
cover the nature of the institutions that foster or hinder the operation
of existing and missing markets (Greif and Kandal 1995; Greif 1998a).

Implicit in the above statement is a claim that markets do not always
rely on formal institutions, such as property rights and legal contract
enforcement, that are provided by the state. Both theory and empirical
research indicate that the limited ability of formal institutions reflects
such factors as asymmetric information and incompleteness of contracts.
But the emerging research agenda emphasizes that this limited ability
also reflects that the operation of the state itself—and hence its ability
to support exchange, protect property rights, and provide public goods—
is dependent on its own institutional foundations. In contrast, the first
generation of scholars described by Crafts considered the state itself to
be a social actor that could be taken as exogenous when considering
growth. The state has been considered a social planner, even a benevolent social planner, that acts to foster economic development. The second generation of scholars also held a distinct view of the state,
considering it to be a poor mechanism for resource allocation and inferior to markets.

The new research agenda considers the state to be an endogenous
economic and political agent, a positive analysis of which requires an
understanding of its institutional foundations and their specific characteristics in a particular society. One cannot regard the state as a unitary
actor, a benevolent social planner, or a resource allocation mechanism
inferior to the market in the society under study. The nature of the state
itself reflects the broader society within which it is embedded, and its
operation depends on the incentive structure that various individuals
constituting its apparatus face (see, for example, Aoki, Kim, and Okuno-
Fujiwara 1997; Weingast 1997; Greif 1998b). Similarly, one cannot
assume that the legal system is a guardian of civil society. For an understanding of the economic implications of a legal system, it is necessary
not just to study its legal codes but also to study the institutions that
motivate and direct the decisions of judges and those who are supposed
to enforce their judgments (Rosenthal 1992).

I could continue to provide examples, drawing from works on such
diverse issues as technology transfer (Abramovitz and David 1996) and
the endogeneity of resources (Wright 1990). Two conclusions, however, are common to all these works. First, to understand the operation
of an economy, and hence the appropriate development policy, we need
to study its microlevel institutions and particular conditions. Second,
such an analysis is inherently historical. Institutions embody, reflect,
and shape a society's economic, political, social, and cultural aspects,

and these aspects have an inertia of their own; they are societal features that transcend the conditions that led to their emergence. Hence, development policy appropriate for a particular society has to take the society's institutions and their endurance into account. A prime challenge facing economic development in the third millennium is to be able to advance our knowledge regarding institutions, their nature, and the ability to manipulate them. Economic development and economic history are again cotravelers in the search for this knowledge.

References

Abramovitz, Moses, and Paul A. David. 1996. "The Mosaic of Economic Growth." In Ralph Landau, Timothy Taylor, and Gavin Wright, eds., *Convergence and Deferred Catch-up: Productivity. Leadership and the Waning of American Exceptionalism*, 21–62. Stanford, Calif.: Stanford University Press.

Aoki, Masahiko, Hyung-Ki Kim, and Masahiro Okuno-Fujiwara, eds. 1997. *The Role of Government in East Asian Economic Development*. Oxford, U.K.: Clarendon Press.

Greif, Avner. 1998a. "Contracting, Enforcement, and Efficiency: Economics beyond the Law." In Boris Pleskovic and Joseph E. Stiglitz, eds., *Annual World Bank Conference on Development Economics 1997*. Washington, D.C.: World Bank.

———. 1998b. "Self-Enforcing Political Systems and Economic Growth: Late Medieval Genoa." In Bob Bates, Avner Greif, Margaret Levi, Jean-Laurent Rosenthal, and Barry Weingast, eds., *Analytic Narrative*. Princeton, N.J.: Princeton University Press.

———. Forthcoming. *The Institutional Foundations of States and Markets. Historical and Comparative Institutional Analysis of Genoa and the Maghribi Traders*. Cambridge, Mass.: Cambridge University Press.

Greif, Avner, and Eugene Kandal. 1995. "Contract Enforcement Institutions: Historical Perspective and Current Status in Russia." In Edward P. Lazear, ed., *Economic Transition in Eastern Europe and Russia: Realities of Reform*, 291–321. Stanford, Calif.: Hoover Institution Press.

Rosenthal, Jean-Laurent. 1992. *The Fruits of Revolution*. Cambridge, U.K.: Cambridge University Press.

Weingast, Barry R. 1997. "The Political Foundations of Democracy and the Rule of Law." *American Political Science Review* 91 (2, June): 245–63.

Wright, Gavin. 1990. "The Origins of American Industrial Success, 1879–1940." *American Economic Review* 80 (4, September): 651–68.

Comment

David Landes

THE READER WILL BE IMPRESSED by Crafts's familiarity with and coverage of the literature, especially that by economists and by what I shall call historical economists rather than economic historians. Why do I make this distinction? Because Crafts is not much interested in the writing of historians who deal with development, and we must use some terminological precision to assess his survey. I am struck by the fact that I have no place in his bibliography. (I know he reads me, if only to disagree.) Nor, for that matter, do such economists as Paul Krugman and Amartya Sen have a place. There's no accounting for taste.

I would make one general point about language, at the risk of disqualifying myself. We have a problem here: economists and their imitators have adopted a jargon often incomprehensible to lay readers. Even efforts to vivify the prose by means of simile and metaphor (as in the contrast between yeast and mushrooms) are insider talk. Style is frequently heavy. I found myself on occasion in a slough of verbal despond. Such language, it occurs to me, reflects intellectual isolation and indifference to outsiders.

Let me take up some topics in their order in the Crafts chapter.

Demographic Transition. Crafts is much impressed by the importance of this subject and the quality of the specialists working in the area. His review makes clear, however, that there is no unambiguous, unidirectional link between growth of numbers and growth of output. In rich countries population increase can help; in poor countries it can be a handicap. I am particularly sensitive to and grateful for his comments because of criticisms of my neglect of demography in my own book, *Wealth and Poverty*. It is not a simple issue. Crafts returns to it later, but it is clear that economists and demographers have yet to settle these matters and indeed may never do so. Each case may have to be seen and judged in context.

Growth Accounting. Here, the literature makes much of the size and character of the so-called residual. Crafts notes that with "more research," original assertions of the importance of the residual have "not proved to be either generalizable or even particularly robust." I think it is crucial to recognize the character of this further "research." It has produced not so much new knowledge as redefinition, incorporating once-residual factors into traditional factors. One goes, for example, from the simple summing of labor-hours to weighting these hours by, say, quality, educational level, or equipment, thus pumping up the old components and reducing the new. But nothing about the importance of technology as a residual factor of production has changed.

This, may I say, strikes me as an abiding weakness of much quantitative economics: the effort to change the results by altering definitions. For example, Alwyn Young and Paul Krugman have argued that East Asian gains in output over the past 15 or 20 years have come from increases in manpower and capital, not from improvements in technology, and that there is thus little residual. But the data show that East Asian workers of today are better educated than those of yesterday, while management, entrepreneurship, and the composition of capital have improved with increased participation from abroad.

A similar example is the recent effort to argue that information technology is less important to productivity growth than had been estimated because the estimates include older industries—chemicals, steel, and automobiles—whereas they should properly be confined to those branches strictly concerned with informatics. But that is surely nonsense, since a good economic historian will look for and find the contributions of new knowledge wherever they alight.

Kuznets Curve. Crafts notes that scholars are still working on Kuznets's suggestion that income distribution over the course of economic development follows an inverted-U track, first more unequal, then less. The results are mixed, and Crafts states that "seeking to estimate Kuznets curves as a means of projecting future income distributions or as a guide to policy formation is a misplaced, mechanistic exercise." Too true. The problem here, as elsewhere, is the tendency of historical economists to think they have done their job when they establish statistical correlations. What they should be trying to understand is *why.* Why does income inequality increase or decrease? Crafts says the influences include demographic change and human quality.

Rostow and Gerschenkron. Crafts clearly feels that the Rostow thesis of stages of growth was an influential, if erroneous, contribution to economic history. Most of us old-timers found Rostow's metaphor of a takeoff misleading—too quick, too pat—and we found his fifth stage (development for all) romantically optimistic. We also felt, as does Crafts, that Rostow never gave a general explanation for the move from one stage to another. How could he? Every country has its own sequence, similar to and yet different from that of other places. That's history. Crafts also stresses that damning empirical results showed no takeoff in the story of such countries as France. But J. H. Clapham had already made this point 30 years before the Rostow thesis came under collective scrutiny at a conference in Constance, Germany, where Rostow faced his accusers and eventually edited the resulting volume of papers and comments. (I sometimes have the feeling that historical economists read only the latest work, at great cost to their understanding—an eerie, ahistorical view.)

At a later point in the chapter, Crafts implies that the work of Robert Fogel and Albert Fishlow on U.S. railroads refutes Rostow's emphasis on railroadization and other "technological breakthroughs" as major factors in growth. I am not so sure of that. For one thing, studies of the role and effect of railways in other nations show significant variation. For another, Fogel's own calculations give rise to serious problems. His estimates of the cost of water transport rest on the optimistic promises of U.S. Army engineers, who had their own reasons for encouraging rivers and harbors projects. And Fogel pointed out that all of this would not hold for the western third of the country, where topography made the railroad a significantly cheaper and superior mode of transport. The train, moreover, was faster than barge or boat, and that made all the difference in transport of people as against goods, as the British found out in the early railway age. Crafts finds the argument that specific inventions had only a limited impact on the economy seemingly "robust" and cites similar results in studies of today's computer technology. I would differ because, as noted above, these calculations do not grasp the full effects; in particular, they ignore or avoid linkages. Fogel did find examples of scholars who had written of the indispensability of the railroad, and Crafts gratefully recalls his dismissal of this thesis. But indispensability was always nothing more than loose rhetoric, and Fogel had no trouble discrediting a myth.

Crafts seems to believe that Gerschenkron's work on development was published in 1962 and pushed Rostow aside. In fact, it was published a decade earlier and addressed a different set of problems, in particular, patterns of catch-up by late developers. Still, it is fair to say that economists did prefer Gerschenkron and saw him more as a professional colleague. This preference was primarily academic-political. Note that Gerschenkron's model of spurts and late development generated as many contradictions as any other large generalization, including Rostow's. (See Crafts's comments on Rodrik and others who, he says, seem to have rehabilitated the spurt thesis.) Much of this new work strikes me as proving the obvious—for example, that poor legal systems and inadequate contractual enforcement deter investment and credit. No kidding! Meanwhile Gerschenkron did raise important issues and did come up with one indisputable, if obvious, finding: that there are many ways to skin a cat. But that, too, was an old story. Indeed, it was the whole point of Clapham's comparison of France and Germany.

The So-Called New Economic History. For me, this was the least satisfactory aspect of the chapter, and that worries me. Crafts dates the "cliometric revolution" from the first of the meetings at Purdue in 1960. In fact, we have an anticipatory literature, including early essays by Walt Rostow. But 1960 was the beginning of the club, of a conscious intellectual identity. Crafts notes with much satisfaction what he sees as the achievements of the new school, in particular, the examination of traditional interpretations in the light of classical and neoclassical economic theory. Among the signal successes, Crafts points to the debunking of the old myth of entrepreneurial failure in Victorian Britain. Crafts feels that D. N. McCloskey and Lars Sandberg have shown that business decisions accorded with rational standards of profit and loss; if people chose not to invest, it was because more profitable uses were available.

I must say, if this is success, where lies failure? The notion that profit-maximization resides exclusively in short-term calculations of givens is the sort of thing that only nonbusiness people will believe. It takes a bemused historical economist to think that a dollar is a dollar, whether used to produce organic chemicals and computers, on the one hand, or movies and saxophonists, on the other. Or to assume that comparative advantage stands still. Or to believe that British entrepreneurs were models of rationality, or that Britain's loss of industrial leadership in Europe was ineluctable. The irony is that one hears or reads these things from British scholars, too. They should know better, especially if they have traveled.

Crafts also likes what the "new economic history" has done to increase our knowledge of technology. True. One thinks of Nate Rosenberg and Paul David. But what about the huge literature that preceded them: Usher, Ashton, and, yes, me? And the literature that followed: Crafts should look again at the work of his old colleague Maxine Berg. And what of the Industrial Revolution? Crafts feels and regrets that even the cliometricians have not been able to account for the timing of this major change in the pace and composition of technology. If that were true, it would be a sad reflection on the capabilities of cliometrics. Usher had no problem with this, as far back as 1920. But then he used simple numbers, such as changes in the price of cotton yarn.

Truly, it's not the numbers that matter; it's what one does with them. The notion of leading sectors, we are told, has "fared badly," with a "strong emphasis in the recent literature on the small initial size of cotton textiles in relation to [gross domestic product] or even industrial output." But isn't that the point? Cotton starts tiny and becomes huge. It reshapes the entire textile industry by showing what machines can do. That's what most of us would call a leading sector.

All in all, Crafts's tale of the cliometric results more or less wipes out the story of British achievement. "Indeed, a World Bank economist, given a basic description of the late 18th century British economy without knowing to which country it applied, might well conclude that here was a case of very poor development prospects"!!! Shouldn't alarm bells be going off? The only "plus points" he finds are property rights and a comparative advantage in microinventions. To be sure, and why not add entrepreneurship and note that under Mokyr's definition of micro, cotton textile machines fall in the micro category?

In sum, Crafts feels, the more recent research on the Industrial Revolution differs substantially from the picture given by development history in the 1950s. No doubt. But he could have had a much more plausible version by going back to the work of the preceding generation—or to observations of contemporaries, in Great Britain and abroad, in the early 19th century.

For me, the big ray of hope is that economists, much more than historical economists, are beginning to reckon with the cultural aspects of change and development. Many still avoid the term "cultural." But when Moses Abramovitz writes of "social capability," which in Crafts's words means "the ability effectively to assimilate advanced countries' technology," that's what he is talking about. "Hard to pin down precisely or to quantify," no doubt, but that does not excuse scholars from taking these things into account and trying to understand them. For Crafts, it would seem, such notions do not deserve attention until issued by members of the guild or club. That, I think, is a sad commentary on one corner of the economics profession. Fortunately, it's just a corner.

I would end on a positive note. Crafts notes the limitations of regressions and calls for "historical case studies to identify key aspects of social capability." Hear, hear!

In Quest of the Political: The Political Economy of Development Policymaking

Merilee S. Grindle

POLITICAL ECONOMY IS ALIVE and well among those who seek to explain policy decisionmaking in developing and transition countries. That this is the case can be credited to the assiduity of the "real world" in outpacing our ability to explain politics. During two decades of extraordinary policy and institutional change, real-world experiences consistently raised intriguing and difficult-to-answer questions about the intersection of policies and politics: Why would governments select and maintain policies that are demonstrably inefficient for economic development? Why do some governments choose to alter development policies and strategies in significant ways while others adhere to policies that are economically, socially, and politically destructive? Why are some reforming countries able to sustain new policies while others are forced to abandon them? How do institutions shape opportunities for reform?

Efforts to provide responses to these puzzles spawned a small industry of case studies and cross-national analyses of the determinants of policy and institutional change in developing and transition countries. As a result of such work, produced by political scientists, economists, and sociologists, we know a great deal more about the political economy of development policy, and particularly about when and why it is likely to change, than we did 20 years ago. We have extensive evidence about how powerful economic interests develop around policies and the ways in which they resist reductions in the benefits they receive from these policies.[1] We have gained significant insight into how to calculate the distributional consequences of policy change.[2] We have seen considerable evidence that economic crises—particularly crises associated with inflation, hyperinflation, and foreign exchange shortages—are powerful stimuli for reform initiatives.[3] We have also learned, however, that

crisis is neither a necessary nor a sufficient condition for spurring successful reform initiatives.[4] In other work, researchers have shown that
opportunities to introduce new policies tend to cluster in "honeymoon
periods" directly after elections.[5] Moreover, we have good reason to
believe that the actions of policy entrepreneurs and the character of
technocratic teams are critical to the success of reform initiatives.[6] In
addition, we have gained greater appreciation for the role of ideas and
leadership in the process of change.[7] And we have begun to generate
insights into why new institutions are created and what their consequences are for the management of policy.[8]

Luckily for the employment prospects of political economists, despite considerable advances in our understanding of policy and institutional change, the real world continues to provide interesting puzzles
about development policymaking. And, usefully for scholarly debate,
there is considerable difference of opinion about the most appropriate
way to go about studying these puzzles. In this chapter I consider some
of the central debates in the application of political economy to development policymaking. At the outset, I am particularly interested in the
insights that distinct traditions of political economy—some drawn from
economics, others based in sociological theory—generate about why
and when change is likely to occur in policies and institutions. Subsequently, I consider whether such traditions provide effective guidance
about the politics of decisionmaking and the process of policy reform
and whether they generate helpful insights for reformers interested in
encouraging such processes. Throughout the chapter, then, I am concerned with the connection between theory, empirical observation, and
the practice of policy decisionmaking. Just as other authors in this volume strive to demonstrate the origins and legacies of debates in the
field of economic development, I seek to show how two divergent traditions in political economy provide strikingly different interpretations
of development policy choice and change.

I suggest that current approaches to political economy present a
stark tradeoff between parsimony and elegance, on the one hand, and
insight into conflict and process, on the other. I also find that both
traditions of political economy borrow assumptions about political
interactions from contexts that may not be fully relevant to developing and transition countries. In addition, when theory is compared
with the extensive empirical literature that now exists about experiences with policy and institutional change, it fails to provide convincing explanations for some of the most important characteristics of
real-world politics: leadership, ideas, and success. Furthermore, much
theoretical and empirical work in political economy has fallen far
behind in exploring the policy agendas that now confront developing
and transition countries. I draw modest conclusions from this survey
of how political economists approach the issue of policy choice and

change, the ways in which theories model reality, and the research agenda for the future: political economists of whatever persuasion should consult the empirical world more frequently, question assumptions more assiduously, stretch theory beyond overgeneralization or overspecificity, and keep an eye open for the policy agendas of today and tomorrow, as well as those of yesterday.

I have opted to define political economy broadly. In this understanding, political economy refers to efforts to investigate the intersection of economics and politics in policy choice and in policy and institutional change, whether these efforts reflect the "new political economy" rooted in economics or a distinct tradition of analysis based in sociology (see Meier 1991). For some in each tradition, political economy means understanding how economic interests shape political behavior. For others, the central question is how political behavior shapes economic policy. At the end of the chapter I suggest an even broader arena for political economy in a series of policy issues that go beyond traditional concern with economic interests and economic policies to focus on the reform of the state and the emergence of demands related to social policy. My purpose in doing so is to highlight some of the relatively unexplored territory in the real world that should stimulate the interest and challenge the ingenuity of political economists.

Policy Choice and Change: Contending Paradigms

Currently, two broad traditions in political economy provide alternative ways of understanding choices about policy and the factors that influence the adoption, implementation, and consolidation of policy reform initiatives.[9] These approaches not only differ fundamentally as to the structure and meaning of competition over policy decisions; they also provide distinct ways of understanding institutions and the relationship between institutions and actions. In the following pages I describe traditions that draw on economics and sociology to attempt to understand the responses to four real-world puzzles: Why and when are politicians interested in supporting policy change? How do political institutions affect the choices made by politicians? How are new institutions created or transformed? What are the consequences of new rules of the game for economic and political interaction?

Economists are most familiar—perhaps exclusively familiar—with a neoclassical political-economy tradition that stretches back to Adam Smith and that has been made relevant to development in the work of Robert Bates, Dani Rodrik, Alberto Alesina, Barbara Geddes, Anne Krueger, and many others. Indeed, for most of those whose work is represented in this volume, political economy means the application of the tools of economic analysis to political phenomena, often referred to as the "new political economy." In this tradition, microeconomic assumptions about the centrality of self-interest are applied to political actors. As a consequence, political behavior can be modeled along with economic behavior. Despite the claim that "economists have always been better at telling policymakers what to do than at explaining why policymakers do what they do," the new political economy has provided economists and political scientists with important ways of exploring transactions within political markets (Rodrik 1993: 356).

But there is another tradition of political economy, one that is often overlooked or dismissed by economists. This tradition traces its roots to sociological theory and to work by Karl Marx, Max Weber, Talcott Parsons, and others. Currently, it is identified with the work of Theda Skocpol, Peter Evans, Peter Hall, and many who work in the area of comparative politics. They draw on sociology rather than on economics and focus on concepts of conflict, group consciousness, institutions, and power. In this tradition, causality is almost always complex and multifaceted, and explorations of hypotheses generally involve considerable immersion in historical cases. A variety of theoretical orientations fit comfortably within this tradition, but they are drawn together by deep appreciation of the role of structures of power in political decisionmaking.

The divide between political economists who draw on economic theory and those who draw on sociological theory to explain policy is deep and often contentious. Those who look to economics for insight into policy seek to develop a general theory of politics that is deductive, powerful, and rigorous.[10] They are in search of explanations that hold across an extensive range of empirical cases. In contrast, those who draw on sociology insist that political behavior is always deeply rooted in context and specificity and that to be useful, theory must be able to evoke, explore, and explain this complexity and specificity.[11] They further assert that political institutions are central to explaining why the study of policy is primarily a study of how similar issues in collective life work out differently in distinct contexts. These two approaches offer strikingly different responses to questions about policy choice and change. They also pose a stark contrast as to whether generality or specificity is the best way to understand political dynamics, as indicated by their diverse responses to the four questions set out at the beginning of this section and to which we now return.

Why and when are politicians interested in supporting policy change?
In the real world, politicians must initiate, support, or accept new policies if change is to occur. During the 1980s and 1990s politicians' support became critically important to officials of international financial institutions and other policy advocates who were deeply committed to encouraging major policy reforms. Many times, however, they found

that politicians rejected reform proposals, even when these were clearly superior to a broken or deeply inefficient status quo. Other politicians embraced policy change and assumed active leadership of efforts to introduce and sustain major innovations in national development strategies. Ongoing involvement with a series of reform initiatives provided sufficient evidence that the desire to enhance social welfare, the suasion of technical analysis, or surrender to the pressure of international agencies could not explain the diversity of responses to the economic stagnation and crisis afflicting countries around the world (see Haggard and Kaufman 1992a).

Other chapters in this volume indicate that the task for development economists has generally been to generate and assess optimal policies and strategies for development. In contrast, political economists have been more concerned to explain why and when changes would be adopted. Some political economists have turned to economics to understand the motivations of politicians in resisting or embracing policy change. Much of the ensuing effort has drawn on rational-choice theory. The rational-choice approach asserts that political actors, like *homo economicus,* act to maximize utility, which is generally assumed to reflect their self-interest. Voters, politicians, lobbyists, bureaucrats, and party officials are understood to be rational in that they have preferences and seek to achieve them through action. Preferences are taken as given and, in research, must be asserted ex ante, usually as a statement of reasonable first-order objectives. Thus, in seeking to explain the behavior of politicians, rational-choice theorists generally assert that politicians naturally prefer more power to less, survival in office to defeat, reelection to loss, and influence to irrelevance. Voters naturally prefer politicians who provide benefits that improve their individual welfare to those who do not. Bureaucrats naturally prefer higher budgets to lower ones, more discretion to less, more opportunities to promote their own welfare to fewer, and career promotion to demotion. These individuals are distinct from economic actors only in that they are conceptualized to be interacting in a political market in which competition is for power to provide or receive benefits from public policy, public investments, and resources controlled by the government.

If politicians prefer power, survival in office, influence, and electoral support to not having these things, then in democratic systems politicians must be particularly sensitive to the interests of voters or particular constituencies that help them achieve their objectives. The interests of voters are important in rational-choice political economy because they constrain the choices available to politicians and compel them to make decisions that are characteristically geared toward electoral gains. Moreover, because of periodic elections, politicians must discount the future heavily. Thus, it is rational for politicians to sacrifice policy choices that will pay off in the longer term to those that produce short-term advantages, such as staying in office. In some cases, so powerful is the need of politicians to trade policy benefits for votes that policymaking can be captured by particular interests that extort preferential treatment in return for votes or contributions to electoral campaigns (see Krueger 1974; Bates 1981). In such cases the politicians and the particular interests are both engaged in rent-seeking.

Individuals are the unit of analysis in a rational-choice approach to the explanation of political behavior. But empirically, much political activity involves the behavior of groups, and Mancur Olson (1965) and others have therefore examined how and when self-interested individuals will act collectively to achieve their policy goals. Individuals will do so when they can be assured that the energy exerted in acting as a group will pay off efficiently in terms of individual benefits received. For reasons having to do with the potential for free riders to benefit from group action without expending the energy necessary to cooperate, groups tend to coalesce around very specific interests that, if achieved, will not provide benefits to those outside the group. Politically, this translates into the tendency for exchanges between politicians and a multitude of interest groups, each of which is pursuing a narrowly focused and usually immediate benefit. The task for the politician becomes that of parceling out public policy or public resources to a large number of competing groups, each of which has some capacity to punish the provider. The larger purposes of government, such as "the public interest," are difficult to achieve, given the exchange relationships between politicians and interests.

Rational-choice theory offers at least two hypotheses about why and when politicians would support policy change. In one case, politicians could make a rational strategic calculation that promoting policy reform would bring them increased support at the ballot box; they could also choose to resist championing change because of their rational expectation that doing so would diminish their chances of staying in office. An alternative hypothesis is somewhat different in that it posits pressure from particular interests that is intense enough to give politicians no option but to support (or resist) change; if they do not respond to the pressures, they will lose their jobs.[12] In the first case, support of policy reform is a strategic option; in the second case, it is the result of lack of options, given the preferences of politicians.

Comparative institutionalism, a broader and less theoretically rigorous tradition in social science, provides a distinct way of approaching the question of policy choice and change.[13] Drawing on sociology for analytical tools and on history for empirical insights, researchers who follow this tradition view political actors as embedded within contexts that shape their behavior in profound ways. These contexts are far more than the strategic decisionmaking arenas described in rational-choice theory. They are complex environments that have roots in the past and that not only constrain and channel action but also actually shape the perspectives, preferences, and values of the political actors. Comparative institutionalists understand political actors to be groups, classes, interests, or other collectivities. Although these are the primary units of analysis, it is important that the behavior of such political actors be analyzed and understood as an outcome of the complex and historically evolved context within which they find themselves. Thus, central to the tradition is the notion that events such as policy change are resultants of collectivities interacting within a specific context. Frequently, scholars in this tradition assess the extent to which the state itself, or state institutions such as bureaucracies, set the context in which conflict is played out.

In addition, comparative institutionalists place conflict at the center of political analysis in ways that differ significantly from an economic perspective.[14] In rational-choice theory conflict exists when two or more individuals simultaneously seek to act on their preferences and when these cannot be achieved through joint action. Comparative institutionalists, by contrast, view conflicts as ongoing interactions through which groups compete for predominance in particular economic, social, and policy arenas and in which prior conflicts shape the nature of current conflicts and determine the issues that are contested. Conflict over policy is the normal stuff of politics, then, and outcomes are shaped by the relative power of distinct groups—a condition that is itself determined by the outcomes of prior conflicts and the particular way in which states and regimes allocate power.

As a result of these premises, analysts who draw on the sociological tradition tend to produce research that is rich in depth and complexity rather than in breadth and parsimony. Although the origins of comparative institutionalism are in the "grand theory" tradition of Marx and Weber, today's practitioners tend to be less interested in a general theory of politics than in understanding the conditions under which political actors will behave in particular ways; they tend to generate middle-range theory and to be intensely engaged in understanding the historical record around particular conflicts. Far more than is true of those who explain policy from a rational-choice perspective, they are concerned about institutions, including the state. And although they focus on the factors that shape the actions of collectivities rather than on the logic of individual choice, they have also sought to understand "statecraft."[15] In pursuit of this goal, comparative institutionalists have studied the ways in which individual political actors or political entrepreneurs maneuver within institutional contexts to build coalitions, engineer consensus, negotiate, and bargain to generate new policies, new legislation, and new institutions.[16] They find that some individuals are motivated to bring about change, while others resist it. The motivations of these politicians can draw on ideas, collective identities, group interests, and values, as well as on self-interest. Within this tradition, some politicians are more skilled in the use of political resources than others, and some have greater or lesser access to these resources.

In contrast to the hypotheses put forward by the new political economy that draws on economics, comparative institutionalists offer much more contingent statements about why and when politicians will initiate or support policy change.[17] The position taken depends on the nature of existing and past conflicts over policy, the ways in which institutions privilege or discriminate against particular individuals or groups, and the commitments and skills of the politicians who are contending over policy. Choices are not discrete but are influenced by positions on other policy matters, choices made in the past, and larger strategic issues that are important to the longer-term concerns that divide and unite groups in political conflict. For political economists who draw on this tradition, much of the story of policy choice and change can only be understood if institutions are properly taken into consideration and if the state is taken seriously as a structure that profoundly affects the allocation of power in a society.

How do political institutions affect the choices made by politicians?
No one who has tried to untangle the web of day-by-day politics in any country can ignore the ways in which policy decisionmakers are constrained by the formal and informal rules of the political game. Decisions are affected by such institutions as party and electoral systems, formal allocations of power within government, legal systems, and informal norms about how political debates are carried out. Who is entitled to make decisions is an outcome of institutions that constrain and privilege various actors. The processes mandated for approving and implementing policies can determine the policies' success or failure. Who has access to policy debates and how opposition is manifested are determined by formal and informal institutional arrangements that vary from country to country. What electoral rules are in force shape the ways in which political actors calculate the costs and benefits of various courses of action. In these and other ways, institutions affect the resources available to political actors and the dynamics of policy choice. Because institutions are complex and multifaceted, however, analysts do not agree on how they influence the activities of politicians or the options available to them. Indeed, the rational-choice and comparative institutionalist approaches vary considerably as to how they assess the role of institutions in policy choice.

Although the rational-choice approach is rooted in assumptions about the preferences of generic individuals, it is not blind to the context in which political behavior occurs. Context, in terms of the particular constraints imposed by political institutions or incentive systems, shapes the opportunities available to political actors in pursuing their preferences.[18] In this way, politicians become strategic actors who accumulate information about the options available to them and select the actions that are most likely to allow them to maximize power, votes, influence, or political survival within the political context that surrounds them. From the perspective of research, given assumptions about the preferences of political actors, knowledge of the context in which they operate provides information necessary to explain and predict the policy choices they make. In seeking to produce generalizable statements about the political behavior of individuals, rational-choice theory deals with institutions as a strategic arena for individual choice.

Comparative institutionalists place institutions much more at the center of explanations of policy. They insist that to understand political actors as generic individuals pursuing generic preferences is to miss the role of institutions and of history in determining the preferences, orientations, values, and strategies of collective actors. The nature and meaning of conflict is similarly influenced by institutions, which channel and influence how conflict is played out. Thus, institutions are much more than contexts that inform rational strategic action. For comparative institutionalists, political actions are embedded in historically evolved institutions that are, in turn, the site of ongoing struggles to define public policy and distribution of economic and political power. In this way, institutions are determining factors in policy decisionmaking. This perspective allows comparative institutionalists to explain how similar policy problems—the provision of health care in modern industrial countries, for example—have found distinct solutions in different contexts (see Immergut 1992; King 1992). The outcomes are the results of the distinct institutional environments that have shaped the goals and behaviors of groups and interests and have determined how they contest for influence over policy.

Comparative institutionalists generally argue that political actions are influenced by institutions, which in turn are shaped by the actions of political agents. In fact, however, they tend to focus much more on how actions are shaped by institutions than on the transformative effect of action on institutions. This reflects quite realistically the dynamics of everyday politics in most advanced industrial countries, where much of the work in this tradition has been carried out. In such countries, political actions take place in relatively stable institutional settings. Moreover, these institutions and the political actions they spawn are understood to be embedded in the political system (Evans 1995). Embeddedness means that new institutions are evolutionary descendants of older institutions, altered to accommodate new power relationships or the consequences of conflicts over policy. Thus, an important question for political economy generally is the issue of institutional creation or evolution.

How are new institutions created or transformed?

Throughout much of the 1980s, many of those concerned about the prospects for development of poor countries insisted on the importance of "getting the policies right." As it turned out, however, only some of the countries that adopted the "right" policies were able to generate sustained economic growth. Gradually, policy advisers and policymakers came to the conclusion that the ability of new policies to generate improved welfare depended on the kinds of institutions that were in place for managing economic and political transactions. This perspective was spurred by analyses of the "East Asian miracle" that pointed to the role of government institutions in paving the way for sustained development (see Wade 1990; World Bank 1993). In a very different way, this view received added impetus from the early experiences of postcommunist countries that adopted a wide range of market-oriented policies in the absence of formal and informal institutions for managing market transactions (Coase 1992). Democratization—a struggle occurring in large numbers of countries around the world—called attention to equally important rules of the game for political interactions.[19]

Thus, creating or transforming institutions of governance acquired increased importance as policy reformers undertook initiatives to put in place autonomous central banks, independent tax authorities, securities and exchange commissions, professional civil services, authoritative legal systems, party and electoral systems, and other new institutions. Analysts of these experiences sought understanding about how such changes could occur. They found that political economists had more than one response for their questions.

Many of those working within the rational-choice approach were particularly intrigued by the creation of new institutions that constrained the power of politicians, such as independent central banks and autonomous tax agencies. Given the assumptions of the theory, how could this behavior be explained? One answer invoked standard assumptions about the preferences of politicians: if politicians are acting both rationally and strategically, they might create new institutions that would constrain their power over the longer term in order to achieve some immediate political advantage, such as winning an election, or they might be responding to overwhelming pressure from electoral constituents. This is consistent with the rational-choice hypotheses about why and when politicians might support policy change.

More interesting responses focused on the relationship between new institutions and the preferences of reformist politicians. If politicians have supported policy reform, they may create new institutions to signal commitment to it or to lock in their choices so that future incumbents cannot alter them.[20] In the first case, that of signaling commitment, the message is meant to convince domestic and international economic agents that the policy choices made will remain stable, unaffected by the immediate electoral needs of (implicitly, other) politicians. In the second case, the target is future politicians who might seek to undo a set of reforms and thus undermine the preferences of current incumbents. The logic of these choices is interesting: politicians choose to constrain their power in the future, rather than maximize their power in the present, in order to reduce uncertainty about future choices, particularly those that might be made by other politicians. Thus, the creation of institutions that lock in policy preferences can actually be understood as a way of maximizing individual preferences over the longer term.

Despite these forays into explaining institutional creation, rational-choice political economists have been widely criticized for their failure to generate a broader understanding of how institutional contexts emerge, persist, and change. Led by Douglass North and others, a "new institutionalist" perspective has sought to address this shortcoming.[21] An important strand of the new institutionalism takes as a founding insight the idea that all exchanges involve transaction costs.[22] In economics, transaction costs, such as acquiring information or enforcing rules, decrease the efficiency of exchange relationships. A critical insight in North's approach is that institutions are not simply a result of efforts to lower the transaction costs of market exchanges but are also a function of political and social interests and differences in the allocation of power in a society. Thus, institutions "are not necessarily or even usually created to be socially efficient; rather they, or at least the formal rules, are created to serve the interests of those with the bargaining power to devise the rules. In a zero-transaction-cost world, bargaining strength does not affect the efficiency of outcomes, but in a world of positive transaction costs it does" (North 1990: 16). Institutional change is promoted when actors with power perceive that their interests can be better achieved through alternative sets of rules.

Extrapolating from this explanation, transaction costs also exist in political life and are present in political exchanges such as those that occur between politicians and voters or between politicians and interest groups. Politicians often do not have full information on the activities and interests of important constituencies or the time or ability to acquire such information. They may also face conflicting demands from different interest constituencies. Voters and particular constituencies may not have full information on the behavior of the public officials they want to respond to their concerns, nor do they necessarily know how many votes are needed or how much campaign money is efficient for getting what they want from the politicians. Legislators do not necessarily have information on the preferences of other legislators. The difficulty of acquiring such information increases the risks of making choices for politicians, voters, campaign contributors, and others. To lower these transaction costs, implicit or explicit rules of the game emerge that allow politicians and voters to act on the basis of incomplete information without undue risk or without having to invest heavily in collecting information.

In this way, institutions such as electoral systems, political parties, and rules or procedures in legislatures emerge over time to lower the transaction costs of doing politics. At the same time, these rules structure the interactions of citizens, politicians, and would-be politicians by providing incentives and sanctions for behaving in certain ways and by distributing bargaining power differentially. The behavior of political actors becomes predictable over time as it conforms to these incentives, sanctions, and power relationships. Moreover, these rules and procedures structure the way other transaction-cost problems are treated. When such problems emerge and, over time, generate pressures for change or for the introduction of greater stability in how they are dealt with, legislation is introduced, debated, and voted on according to the rules that have evolved for dealing with legislation, debates, and votes. As change occurs in the nature of transaction costs, the institutions themselves can evolve in ways that lower these costs, although such a response is not always timely or efficient.

Over time, institutions accommodate to important changes in the nature of transactions, such as those stemming from technological innovation, the availability of information, and the influence of other institutions (which are also evolving). Over time, also, history demonstrates certain path dependencies that result from the way power relationships lock in distributional biases. Thus, the histories of different countries or different regions of the world are likely to differ as each pursues a path that evolves from institutional adjustment and adaptation, producing an economic theory that explains why "history matters." What North refers to as "discontinuous change" occurs much less frequently and is generally a result of revolution or conquest. "Although formal rules may change overnight as the result of political or judicial decisions, informal constraints embodied in customs, traditions, and cultural constraints not only connect the past with the present and future, but provide us with a key to explaining the path of historical change" (North 1990: 6).

The new institutionalism of North and others is particularly concerned with explaining institutional evolution and adaptation. An "institutional design" approach provides an interesting alternative for explaining institutional creation. This approach is explicitly theoretical and nonempirical in that it posits characteristic problems faced within organizations or institutions, typically of a principal-agent nature, and seeks to develop rules and organizational principles that allow for the efficient solution of these problems.[23] Principal-agent problems are found everywhere in political life—in the relationships between the voter and the representative, the politician and the bureaucrat, the bureaucratic superior and the subordinate, and the policymaker and the implementer. The essential problem is that the principal (in these cases, the voter, the politician, the bureaucratic superior, or the policymaker) does not have sufficient information or control over the actions of the agent (the representative, the bureaucrat, the subordinate, or the implementer) to ensure that his or her commands are actually being carried out. This creates a problem of moral hazard for the principals in that they cannot be certain about the motivations or actions of those entrusted with carrying out their promises or wishes.

The task for institutional design, then, is to find ways to structure this difficult relationship so as to minimize the principal-agent problem. Characteristically, work in this field focuses attention on the incentive structures that surround the actions of agents. That is, it is concerned with ensuring that agents have incentives that encourage them to be attentive to the wishes of the principals and efficient in responding to them. In solving principal-agent problems, the institutional designer asks how rules, procedures, and incentive structures can be created to ensure that agents *commit* to the goals of the principal. Often, the issue is posed in terms of the principal's desire to ensure future commitment to particular policy or institutional preferences.

Approaching the issue of institutional creation through an institutional design perspective is intriguing because it suggests that history and process are not important and that path dependence is not a constraint. With this perspective, explaining the creation of new institutions at particular moments means demonstrating how political actors self-consciously design new rules of the game through a technical process of analysis, much as an engineer would analyze a particular problem relating to say, weight-bearing capacity and then design a structure that solves the particular problem. Indeed, the "reengineering" approach to organizational change is based on similar assumptions. The reorganization of New Zealand's public sector in the 1990s was significantly influenced by such a design experience (Horn 1995). This approach suggests that new institutions are created because a group of institutional designers sits around a metaphorical table, identifies a set of ongoing principal-agent problems to be solved, self-consciously designs new ways to resolve them, and then puts them into effect. In a recent study of "democratizing reforms" in three countries, I found such institutional designers playing critical roles in each case (Grindle 2000).

Comparative institutionalists would balk at such an apolitical explanation of institutional change. They would wonder what drove the institutional designers to the table in the first place and what authorization they had to solve the problems they identified. They would argue that such a rational problem-solving explanation cannot explain away conflict over goals and the allocation of power. They would assert instead that conflicts and differences in the power of collectivities can result in new rules being negotiated or imposed on society. New rules thus emerge out of past conflicts and past structures of power. Comparative institutionalism suggests that new institutions come into being as a result of historically embedded conflicts over the distribution of power and benefits in a society and can be understood as negotiated or imposed resultants of contestation among interests (Skocpol 1979; Knight 1992). They might deal with transaction costs or principal-agent problems, but only as contingent outcomes of conflicts over power.

What are the consequences of new rules of the game for politics?
When new institutions are created and take on reality, they introduce new rules and new incentives for decisionmaking. When put into practice, they can alter long-existing power relationships, resolve long-standing problems, introduce new sources of conflict, or alter the motivations of political actors in important ways. Thus, the story of institutional creation is incomplete unless it also addresses the consequences of new rules of the game for political actors and policy decisionmaking. Again, distinct political-economy approaches provide very different responses to this puzzle.

A rational-choice explanation of the consequences of introducing new institutions would anticipate that a new set of constraints on the options available to politicians would lead to new strategies for achieving first-order preferences. Politicians would have to adjust to new constraints in their efforts to maximize power, survive in office, or win elections. Thus, given institutional change, political actors will select policies that are rational in terms of their predictable preferences for more power rather than less, more electoral advantage rather than less, more career stability rather than less, and so forth. Rational-choice theorists would accordingly anticipate a new equilibrium in policy decisionmaking, reintroducing stable expectations about rational behavior.

If, as in the new institutionalism, rules of the game are created in response to transaction-cost problems in politics, it can be predicted that new institutions will lower the costs of engaging in politics. The task for empirical research would be to focus on the extent to which this is true. Even where institutional disjuncture occurs, it could be predicted that path dependence would reassert itself as an explanation for the subsequent evolution of institutions. Presumably, new institutions eventually experience the accumulation of transaction-cost problems, followed by the further evolution of the institution or its rupture through the creation of a new institution. The institutional design literature offers a similarly interesting hypothesis: if new institutions are created with an eye toward resolving principal-agent problems, we should anticipate that they will create more accountability in the sense of ensuring a closer link between what principals want and what agents do.

A comparative institutionalist assessing the consequences of the creation of new institutions would explore a more dynamic hypothesis about change. In distinction to the equilibrium situation predicted in economic models, a sociological approach would anticipate that institutional change would create new sources of conflict, new claims for resources, new spaces for contestation, or efforts by various collectivities to undo the impact of the new institutions on their claims to power and influence. It would also encourage research on new political actors—whether these are collectivities, their leaders, or those who benefited or lost from the redistribution of power and access to benefits—and new ways of organizing for political contests. Political actors would reorganize, recombine, or reassert themselves to take advantage of new resources or reclaim lost ones, and they would reconnect in conflict, coalition building, and bargaining over the distributional consequences of change, probably with reconfigured access to political, economic, and leadership resources.

The two distinct theoretical traditions discussed here exhibit important contrasts in how they explore and explain policy decisionmaking and policy and institutional change. They differ significantly in purposes of theory building, levels of analysis, assumptions about the nature of politics, and methods of inquiry. In recent years adherents of each tradition have been outspokenly harsh about the other side. Those who favor the elegance and parsimony of economic models of political behavior as developed in the new political economy accuse comparative institutionalists of avoiding rigorous theory and scientific methodology and of producing primarily descriptive studies (Miller 1997). Those who work from within the sociological tradition retort that economic models produce political banalities and historically inaccurate analyses that ignore empirical evidence (Evans 1995: ch. 2). Acrimony, as well as very distinct basic assumptions, makes talking across this divide in political economy increasingly difficult. Indeed, it is rare to find scholars working in either tradition acknowledging the work of the other.

The purpose of this section has not been to choose sides in this debate but, rather, to review how distinct visions of political economy deal with central questions of policy decisionmaking. Having done so, it is time to consider whether the theoretical lenses of the economic and sociological traditions are helpful in providing insights into what we know about policymaking and about policy and institutional change in developing and transition countries. This comes somewhat closer to choosing sides. As the following discussion suggests, however, when we hold theory up to the mirror of empirical studies and ask how usefully theory models reality, both schools of political economy turn out to be deficient in important ways.

When Theory Meets Practice

To be relevant in the real world, political-economy theory ought to be useful in at least one of two ways. (1) It ought to be able to model reality by reflecting the basic dynamics of political interactions in the design and implementation of development policy and in the creation or transformation of institutions. If it can do this, it can inform the strategic actions of those actively engaged in promoting policy and institutional change. (2) In addition, or alternatively, theory ought to be able to predict the behavior of political agents in designing, adopting, and implementing policy change or to predict the political consequences of alternative policy and institutional choices. This is another way of informing the strategic choices that policy reformers make.

Of course, theory does not necessarily have to be relevant to the real world. Its objective can be to give added insight into generic questions about cause-and-effect relationships, to supply frameworks for thinking about issues in ways that add to our understanding of them, to provide elegant statements of logical deduction, or to predict outcomes given certain assumptions. At the level of theory, if the logic of the argument is rigorous and parsimonious, if the modeling is elegant, or if the ideas advanced are novel and interesting, it may not matter whether the underlying assumptions of political-economy approaches are inadequate or wrong. This is a position that has at times been associated with the new political economy in economics.

At the same time, and as evidenced by numerous chapters in this volume, development economics has long sought to bridge the gap between theory and the real world in an effort to understand which policies and strategies can best lead to improvements in welfare in developing, and now transition, countries. Just as insistently, it has sought to apply the insights of theory to advice about what policies developing and transition countries ought to adopt. The investigation of how such advice is filtered through political and decisionmaking contexts to inform strategic action is merely an extension of this long-existing concern to link theory to practice. Political-economy analysis should be able to feed back into helpful ideas about what might be done to improve practice. If it identifies inappropriate dynamics about why reform is initiated, who the principal actors are, and what conditions characterize the institutions within which decisions are made, the advice is likely to be unrealistic or misleading. In consequence, it is appropriate to ask how well different political-economy approaches model characteristic features of politics in developing and transition countries and how well they account for characteristic features of policy reform efforts in those countries.

Imagining Reality

The political-economy traditions of interest here emerged primarily through scholarship in and on advanced industrial countries. The new political economy in economics has been most frequently propounded in the United States. European scholars have been much more drawn to sociological theory for understanding politics, although that tradition is strong in the United States also. Inadvertently, perhaps, their origins show through in the underlying assumptions about the normal behavior of political actors and the characteristics of political institutions.

Both traditions tend to view politics as society-centric, in the sense that initiative for action, including policy change, emerges from parties, interest groups, public opinion, and other mechanisms in civil society. This assumption may not necessarily hold for characteristic aspects of politics in developing and transition countries, where politics has much more often reflected the actions of elites within government rather than the pressures of civil society on the government or on political officials.[24] In this more state-centric dynamic of policy choice and change, interest groups are often more reactors to proposals for change than initiators of it. The state-centric tradition acknowledges that political elites have some scope for autonomous action, although the extent of their room for maneuver will vary over time and by country and issue area. As democratization progresses in many countries, this tradition is undergoing change, yet in many countries policy decisionmaking is still carried out in relatively closed contexts and often as a result of the political entrepreneurship of elected and appointed government officials. In addition, politics is often conducted in unstable institutional settings—a significant difference from the institutional environments of industrial countries.

Assumptions that conform to the basic conditions of politics in the United States underlie much of the work that derives from economics. Typically, for example, such approaches assume that voters are sovereign and that votes are meaningful in the sense that they unambiguously decide outcomes. Political parties are generally considered to be nonprogrammatic and decentralized, to be electoral organizations that mobilize voters around periodic elections, and to be few in number. It is assumed that politicians can be reelected and that they face frequent electoral contests. In addition, it is assumed that interest groups are concerned with single issues, that government is highly porous to interest-group pressure, that politicians and political leaders react to pressure rather than initiate policy agendas, and that the power of political executives is highly circumscribed by the power of other institutions, such as legislatures and courts. Perhaps most important, politics is considered to be played out in stable institutional environments in which past behavior provides a template for predicting current and future behavior.

Assumptions about normal politics in comparative institutionalism are more diverse, but certainly much of the orientation of the approach best fits European contexts. In this perspective, the most important identities of those who engage in political conflict are class based or derive from the structural conditions of the economic and political systems. Parties provide important ideological and programmatic foundations for their membership and thus are often movement or membership organizations rather than electoral parties. They accordingly embrace and define their adherents more fully than is true of the main electoral parties in the United States. It is normally assumed that politicians represent group interests and are accountable to those interests for programmatic commitments. History and structure matter deeply in that the legacies of past conflict and relationships emerge in current conflict. As a consequence, continuities are more likely than disjunctures in politics and positions on policy issues. Institutions are stable and evolve over time. Conflict is the normal stuff of day-to-day politics, and negotiation over issues is endemic.

Both images omit important features of politics in developing countries. There, voters are not necessarily sovereign but are often nodes in long chains of clientelistic relationships controlled by political bosses. Votes often ratify decisions already made, compete with other ways of deciding outcomes—such as the use of force—or are in other ways peripheral to deciding outcomes. Parties tend to be highly centralized, and often they are ephemeral. Some systems have only one party; others have numerous parties that compete for positions of influence in government. Victory in elections often opens extraordinary opportunities for patronage and spoils, and changes in government can be extensively reflected in the public service, the public purse, and conflict over the rules of the game. Politicians may be barred from reelection to the same position. Interest groups can be powerful but organizationally inchoate and thus difficult to identify empirically. The government is often highly centralized and closed to formal lobbying while at the same time very porous to informal relationships of influence or public displays of power, such as strikes, protest marches, and even violence. High-level politicians often initiate policy and have extensive formal and informal power. In this regard, politics is frequently more state-centric in terms of the source of initiative for change. Policy is often approved with no intention of putting it into practice, playing havoc with the interpretation of official pronouncements. Negotiation as a form of conflict resolution is frequently joined by confrontation, coercion, and winner-take-all faits accomplis. In many cases institutions are unstable and are changed frequently. Even the basic rules of the game for how politics is to be carried on can change radically and frequently, as when regimes are overthrown or when new constitutions are introduced.

What happens, then, when theoretical lenses are focused on instances of policy decisionmaking and policy and institutional change in these unstable institutional contexts? The inherent power of the rational-choice model, based on the simplicity of its assumptions and its deductive logic, can easily lead to research that is logically compelling but empirically false—and thus unhelpful. For example, it can encourage students of political economy to focus on the behavior of individuals, groups, and institutions as if they mattered, when in fact they may be peripheral to the dynamics of real-world policy and institutional choice and change. In many parts of the world, for example, legislatures are minor actors in much policy decisionmaking. Yet political economists of this tradition have at times chosen to study legislatures as though they were powerful influences in this process, in part because legislative voting data can be readily used to test hypotheses but also, more fundamentally, because of inappropriate assumptions about the importance of legislatures in the policy process (see, for example, Geddes 1994).

Similarly, practitioners of the new political economy frequently fail to make a distinction between groups as organized interests and as unorganized collectivities of individuals who happen to share a similar economic interest. The use of the term "interest groups" is often taken to signal sectoral interests ("industrialists," "trade unions," or "agricultural producers") that are then treated as if they were organized entities capable of actively representing interests in policy discussions, such as a national association of manufacturers, a teachers' union, or a rice growers' association. In predicting action without considering the implications of organization—or lack of it—for the representation of interests, an economics approach to politics fails to specify actors and power relationships accurately.

Moreover, the approach emphasizes the society-centric origin of pressure for policy change. It thus tends to reason forward from interests (given particular interests, groups will press for particular kinds of policies) or backward from outcomes (if certain interests benefit from policy, they must have been central to influencing policy choices).[25] In either case process is treated as a black box, and the questions of who takes the initiative to promote policy and institutional change, and of what interests are represented and how, are assumed rather than investigated empirically. Reasoning backward or forward from interests to outcomes can easily lead to misspecification of actors in empirical cases. The only way to avoid such errors is to inquire into process—to open up the black box of political decisionmaking. This is particularly important if the purpose of political research is to improve decisionmaking about policy.

Despite its origins, comparative institutionalism has generally shown itself to be more adaptive than the economics approach to the realities of developing- and transition-country policymaking. This tradition is in fact more inductive and empirical in its practice and, given its sensitivity to the importance of context, more geared to unfolding the particularities of cases. It is also an approach that, because of its interest in investigating conflict and how it plays out, is able to focus analytical attention on process. As a fairly open-ended framework of analysis, it invites investigation of a broad range of issues and questions, constrained only by the tendency to see groups, conflict, and contextual peculiarities behind every bush. It does not suffer from the problems of aggregation that beset economic approaches that are based on methodological individualism. Moreover, because it does not claim to be predictive, it is better able to deal with the unintended consequences of policy and institutional choice. It is an approach that can deal with overarching structures such as states and regimes, as well as with groups and the actions of individuals. As we have seen, however, the approach tends to inhibit generalization. Outcomes are highly contingent, and while the approach is rich in the ability to reconstruct, describe, and analyze what has happened, it eschews the capacity to predict what will or might happen. Moreover, it tends to emphasize pressures for change that are located in social groups and movements rather than allow for the possibility of change being initiated and championed from within the government.

Underexplaining Reality

Case studies of the political economy of policy decisionmaking regularly point to important determinants of outcomes that are not fully considered in either political-economy tradition. At least three factors appear to be underexplained. First, leadership consistently plays an important role in reform situations but continues to be largely exogenous to theory. Second, ideas—particularly ideas about the appropriate content of development policies—emerge as important factors in case study research and have been shown to have significant connections to power relationships. Theory has little to say about ideas, however. Third, the real world is full of examples of the successful introduction of reformed policies and improved institutions. Theory, however, overdetermines resistance, stasis, and failure.

Leadership. Leadership matters in reform initiatives—for the timing of reform initiatives, the content of reform proposals, and the process of generating support and managing opposition to change. Studies of policy reform initiatives indicate that for successful change to occur, reform leaders must emerge, commit themselves to the content of a reform, empower and protect technocrats who provide substantive input into reform planning, mobilize reformist coalitions, provide a vision of a more hopeful future to help citizens tolerate the disequilibrium of change, and deal effectively with those whose opposition threatens to derail reform (Nelson 1990; J. Williamson 1994b; Wallis 1998). In fact, the empirical literature is almost unanimous: reform leadership is essential to successful policy and institutional change.

In political-economy theory, however, leadership is not well explained. Both the economic and the sociological traditions are uncomfortable with the notion of agency in history. The considerable evidence that individuals can make a difference to the destinies of countries fits poorly with the desire to identify generic rationales for human behavior or to analyze how institutional structures and rules constrain behavior. Moreover, because the issue of leadership is difficult to pin down, academics have tended simply to observe it and then to underexplain its implications for both theory and analysis.

Political-economy approaches that draw on economics for insight into human behavior anticipate reform leadership only when such action can be clearly linked to political self-interest. For example, sponsorship of policy change can be expected when it will result in electoral advantage or when politicians are forced to accede to the wishes of powerful interests whose support is necessary if the politicians are to remain in office. The empirical record of many policy changes put in place in the 1980s and 1990s fits uncomfortably with this logic, however. In the cases of policies for stabilization and structural adjustment, proposals for policy change generally meet with widespread opposition unless politicians are attempting to control very high levels of inflation. This opposition is normal because, as pointed out by political economists from the economics tradition, potential losers from altered policy tend to be well organized and conscious of the losses they face, while winners tend to be dispersed and generally unaware of the benefits of reform (Nelson 1990; Frieden 1991; Schamis 1999). Given the strong likelihood of opposition to change, economics-based approaches predict lack of political leadership for change and must resort to altruism or exogenous factors to explain it (see Srinivasan 1985).

Since many politicians in developing countries are constitutionally barred from reelection, these political economists have proposed another motive—keeping a political party in office. But this hypothesis is also suspect in light of the considerable evidence that reform leaders often act against the wishes of their political parties and support reforms that impose costs on their traditional support bases.[26] Reformist leaders consistently act in the absence of a preexisting coalition of support and often in the face of overwhelming opposition from powerful groups in the population (see Grindle 1996, especially ch. 4). In fact, one of their critical roles is to identify and mobilize a reform coalition in the absence of any powerful constituency for it. Empirical studies also demonstrate consistently that politicians who are forced unwillingly into reform by powerful international actors renege on their agreements (Kahler 1992). In many cases, then, leaders appear to act autonomously from the stated preferences of powerful groups and even against their own immediate political self-interest.[27] Those who draw on the logic of economics and political self-interest are generally stymied in explaining such behavior.

The new institutionalism is largely silent on the issue of agency. The model, for example, does not specify actors. Institutions evolve naturally over time to deal with transaction costs, but in the real world particular actors take particular decisions that cause change to happen. Thus, it would be interesting to consider how transaction costs are identified, to whom they accrue, how affected interests behave, who takes the initiative for change, and so forth.[28] A more difficult problem is that of predicting whether transaction costs are in fact lowered in something as complex as a political market. In a recent study I found that new political institutions raised transaction costs for some actors, lowered them for others, and made no difference to yet others. It was similarly difficult to determine whether politics in general was proceeding more efficiently in the wake of change (Grindle 2000).

For comparative institutionalists, the issue of why politicians behave as they do is an empirical question and need not be asserted ex ante, as in rational-choice approaches. Furthermore, comparative institutionalism has traditionally recognized the importance of statecraft in its research agenda. This approach therefore does somewhat better in providing insight into the leadership roles of reform politicians. Leaders are generally not accorded much autonomy, however. Given the basis of the approach in assumptions about the role of collectivities and conflict, leadership is usually treated as a function of group interests and resources for engaging in conflict over policy and institutional preferences. Thus, leaders are those who represent and advance group interests in conflicts. At the same time, leaders can be counted as resources that groups have—or do not have—in their quest for policy results. For example, some groups or interests have leaders skilled in negotiation and some do not, some have leaders in powerful official positions and others do not, and so forth. The notion that leaders act more autonomously in the sense that they initiate proposals and mobilize group support around particular policy issues is elusive in this theory, although it appears to be a normal case in practice.

The issue of reform leadership, then, emerges strongly in empirical literature but is underdetermined in theory. Nevertheless, generating greater understanding of reform leadership will be a difficult challenge for any theory. Indeed, on the basis of a wide range of case studies on policy reform, it is tempting to conclude that leadership is idiosyncratic—which would mean that it could only be studied case by case. It might be useful, however, to devote time to exploring how leaders emerge, on what basis they claim to exert leadership, what particular political tasks they must perform, and what strategies they select to promote reform in particular contexts. An interesting insight of the case study literature is that leaders often invoke ideas as reasons for championing reform and as ways of mobilizing support for it. Thus, leadership and ideas may have to be explored jointly.

Ideas and Power. Ideas matter in reform initiatives. They appear to play an important role in how problems are interpreted and how options for dealing with those problems are selected and assessed (Hall 1989; Grindle 1996: ch. 5; Wallis 1998). In the past two decades, for example, neoclassical economics has had a significant effect on the development of policy in a wide range of countries. In a typical case, reformers are convinced that their country is in economic stagnation or crisis as a result of development policies that accorded a leading role to the state in economic development. They believe that the country must liberalize markets and international trade and diminish the size and role of the state to allow more scope for markets to function well. They champion reform because they have come to believe in the superiority of markets to states in the process of development. These reformers have often had important educational experiences that convinced them of the rightness of neoclassical economics, or they are part of transnational networks of practitioners who speak a common language of ideas.[29] Not infrequently, leaders of reform initiatives act on the basis of ideas that directly contradict ideas they espoused in the past.[30]

Understanding the role of ideas in policy reform initiatives is also important because of the link between ideas and power. Those who have found ideas to be important ingredients of the reform situations they study are often implicitly or explicitly arguing that expertise affects the distribution of power in the reform process. For example, one of the more interesting insights to emerge from early case studies of economic policy reform was the central role that technocratic teams played in crafting reform initiatives (Nelson and others 1989; J. Williamson 1994a). Disciplinary training, particularly in economics, underlay the way in which such teams understood national economic problems and the language they used to communicate about these problems among themselves, with influential policymakers, and with international actors. Although the power of the technocrats was derived from their relationship to political leaders, they frequently filled seats at the policy table that had previously been occupied by representatives of interest groups, economic elites, party officials, or heads of line ministries (Grindle 1996: ch. 5). In a very direct way, then, ideas reshaped power relationships in many policy decisionmaking situations. Similarly, ideas became explicitly political resources as policy entrepreneurs used them to bring people together around reformist agendas, to put together broad new reform coalitions, and to define issues in conflict situations.

Implicitly, many international actors promote policy change as if ideas mattered. International financial institutions, for example, put money into research and training for their own staff and also for others who are or might be engaged in policy discussions. They promote policy dialogue and consensus-building on the basis of discussions of ideas about, for example, how economies work most efficiently. They engage with technocrats in the countries they deal with and help generate national development strategies that owe much to current understanding of how market economies are developed and sustained. Thus, ideas may be an important means through which international actors become players in domestic policy debates.

In political-economy theory, however, ideas generally get short shrift, overshadowed by a focus on the economic interests of political actors. In economic approaches, with the exception of institutional design, ideas are not treated seriously. The normal case is one in which politicians and others make decisions on the basis of self-interested logic that leaves no room for the influence of ideas. In the comparative institutionalist literature, ideas are acknowledged to have a role in group consciousness and in both inter- and intragroup conflict. Ideas thus help groups understand their own situation or define their identity and interests in distinction to those of others. They can, for example, be the fault lines along which conflict occurs. In some cases (for example, in Marxian analysis) ideas are treated primarily as consciously adopted window dressing for the promotion of economic interests. Most commonly, ideas are understood as political resources—a form of capital that is used to promote particular positions or to influence the outcome of decisions. In neither the economic nor the sociological approach is there much attention to how political actors take on commitments to ideas, how ideas can be distinguished from interests, or how ideas about ways of solving particular problems become the dominant language of policy discussion.

As with the concept of leadership, there is good reason for theoretical caution when dealing with the issue of ideas. Ideas are difficult to track and measure and to separate from interests. The influence of ideas must be inferred from the statements and policy preferences of actors. It is almost always a conundrum to know to what extent individuals or groups are acting out of conviction or out of some more self-interested motivation. Only when actors assert and act on ideas that are in direct conflict with their immediate and longer-term self-interest can a good case be made for the independent influence of ideas. In practice, the impact of ideas in policy reform situations is frequently asserted, but rarely is it possible to provide fully convincing proof that ideas explain policy choices. Nevertheless, given the frequency with which ideas emerge in experiences of reform, it is a concept that deserves more attention in political-economy theory.

Success. In surveying the policy history of countries around the world in the past 20 years, the extent of change is remarkable. Although countries have moved at different speeds and with varying degrees of completeness, most have adopted market-oriented economic development strategies and have moved far in the direction of trade liberalization, privatization, and government retrenchment and reorientation. The rapid pace of economic globalization has certainly pushed many governments in this direction, but historical memories should remind us how far so many countries have come in the past 20 years. Whatever the forces at work, each country has had to devise new policies, find political support for them, put them in practice—often through the creation of new institutions—and work to sustain them over time. They have generally done so in the face of considerable opposition. This represents an extensive record of success in initiating and implementing reform.

Meanwhile, political-economy theory continues to predict failure in efforts to promote policy and institutional change. The larger the change, the more theory would anticipate resistance and reaction rather than successful adaptation.[31] In many ways, current political-economy approaches begin and end in agreement with Machiavelli's pronouncement, written in 1513:

> It must be considered that there is nothing more difficult to carry out, nor more doubtful of success, nor more dangerous to handle, than to initiate a new order of things. For the reformer has enemies in all those who profit by the old order, and only lukewarm defenders in all those who would profit from the new order, this lukewarmness arising partly from the fear of their adversaries, who have the laws in their favor; and partly from the incredulity of mankind, who do not truly believe in anything new until they have had the experience of it.

Notwithstanding growing evidence of the adoption of significant policy changes, theory continues to approach the politics of reform by anticipating factors that are likely to inhibit it (see Rodrik 1993). The reasons for this focus are both empirical and theoretical. Empirically, it is true that in most cases reform does threaten important or broad interests and imposes costs that have real meaning in the calculations of politicians. Success often occurs despite Machiavelli's warning. More to the point of theory, however, failure in policy reform initiatives may be overdetermined because both economic and sociological approaches to political economy begin with a concept of individuals or groups acting within contexts that limit action and initiative. Constraints come in the guise of negatively affected interests, the machinations of other politicians, or the political institutions that limit the power of reformers. As indicated, all these factors are important, and usually they are empirically identifiable. The problem is not whether constraints exist; it is rather that an initial concern for identifying constraints tends to bias researchers to focus on why reform will not fly. Thus, most begin with a conservative bias in considering the likely outcomes of reform efforts.

For example, a general theory of politics—the objective of the new political economy rooted in economics—is a theory about politics understood generally, concerned with explaining what is likely to happen most frequently or most of the time. It is most appropriate in stable institutional contexts in which the objective is to explain the behavior of the generic politician, voter, bureaucrat, or interest-group member. Such an approach may fail to anticipate the kinds of choices that can make a real difference in political life. Although it takes individuals as the unit of analysis, the approach can be criticized for not taking individuals seriously enough, in the sense that individuals can be agents of history, not simply captives of the "games" that are in play.

Moreover, in the economics-based political-economy literature, politics is treated as a negative input into policy decisionmaking. In this approach, the politics of self-interest distort policy choice so that general purposes and social welfare objectives become lost as all actors pursue narrow individual and group interests. Theory predicts that the resultant policies are likely to be ones that are socially and economically irrational, even though they serve the interests of identifiable individuals and groups. Again, the bias is toward anticipating socially unproductive policies. Economic models of political behavior present a uniformly cynical view of the purpose of political action and a very narrow assessment of the motivations of political actors.

It is, however, possible to view politics through more neutral lenses and to understand policymakers as "strategic managers within complex policy contexts who have a set of complex preferences and who are seeking politically, bureaucratically, and economically viable outcomes" (Grindle 1991: 67). Viewed in this way, the outcome of a process of decisionmaking could be good, bad, or indifferent with regard to change in policies or institutions. A more process-oriented approach to understanding policy decisionmaking illuminates more fully the fact that contexts offer both constraints and opportunities for change and that good analysis demonstrates not only how constraints will be felt but also how opportunities can be identified and acted on. Moreover, if the notion of assumed preferences is held in abeyance, it becomes possible to understand the motivations of actors as complex, mixed, and subject to empirical observation and analysis.

A process-oriented approach also draws more attention to the fact that the power of particular individuals or groups can fluctuate considerably over time, altering the dynamics of politics in important ways.

Again, particularly in economic approaches, interests are treated as fixed in terms of their positions of power and in the preferences they have. But it is useful to remember that part of the reason many macroeconomic reform packages were introduced without greater resistance was that in many countries the power of unions and import-substituting interests had declined considerably under the impact of the global recession and the domestic economic crises of the early 1980s. Static concepts of power cannot explain why what appears to be a constraint one day becomes an opportunity the next. Theory needs to attempt to capture more fully the dynamic interactions that surround policy decisionmaking and the dynamics of change over time in the power and interests of political actors.

Conclusion: Agendas for Political Economy and Policy Reform

In the past decade or more, real-world initiatives for change have been ahead—often far ahead—of what political economists have chosen to study. In fact, much work on the political economy of development policymaking remains focused on the factors that affect decisionmaking about stabilization and structural adjustment—the so-called first-generation reforms. Yet a quick visit to many countries in the world today is sufficient to note that the development policy agenda is long on other issues. In many countries the policies promoted to engender a sound, market-oriented economy are accepted as necessary, and the political economy surrounding their adoption and sustainability has become less crisis ridden. Of course, the Asian financial crisis reintroduced issues related to macroeconomic management in the context of volatility in international capital markets, and these remain on the table as critically important concerns for policy discussion and debate. In addition, a considerable body of work on the international institutions and policy regimes that increasingly influence the domestic politics of developing and transition countries is illuminating important political-economy issues. Among these are the conditions under which such institutions influence decisionmaking, the ways in which international and domestic actors form alliances to affect domestic policies, the range of options available to countries for managing globalization in institutions and policy regimes, and explanations for the choices they make. At the same time, other issues have crowded onto the table, and they have received much less attention from political economists than they warrant.

An important area that deserves greater attention is institutional change. Although there is an evolving literature on the political economy of institutional creation and change in terms of those that are important for economic management—central banks, tax agencies, and ministries of finance—much work remains to be done in terms of the reform of the state in general, in such areas as decentralization, civil service reform, and capacity building. Political economists need to consider where the initiative for institutional change comes from, how new institutional models are generated, in what ways the dynamics of institutional creation may differ from those of institutional evolution, and how political and economic actors adapt to such changes.

One of the most important policy issues at present is improvement in the quality and reach of social policies and their impact on poverty alleviation. Political economists should be challenged to explore how and why the politics of education, health, social security, and labor reform differ from the experiences of first-generation reforms that focused primarily on macroeconomic stability and liberalization. They also need to consider how new structures and incentive systems affect bureaucratic behavior in social service delivery organizations, the distributional consequences of alternative social policies and delivery systems, and the effect of alternative models on poverty alleviation.[32]

Equally important issues surround a wealth of real-world experiments with political reform around the world. The recent empowerment of local governments, efforts to incorporate participation by civil society in policy decisionmaking (through, for example, participatory budgeting), the creation of ombudsmen's offices and national consumer protection agencies, the reform of judicial systems, the emergence of new political parties, and the introduction of mechanisms to increase accountability and transparency in public affairs are among the innovations that hold the potential to alter political dynamics in important ways. Political economists ought to be studying these phenomena more assiduously and seeking to stretch theoretical models to provide useful insights into what political interactions bring them into being and what consequences they have for the way politics get done.

If much theory seems stuck on understanding the political roots and implications of stabilization and structural adjustment while the tasks for development in the real world have expanded far beyond this focus, the agenda for political economists is a challenging one in the future. Despite the political turmoil they involve, the kinds of changes made through first-generation reforms are relatively simple in terms of political interactions. In the typical case political leaders initiate proposals for change, empower technocratic teams to design reform programs, negotiate at high levels with international financial agencies, and centralize power in the executive branch to facilitate decisionmaking, which is often carried out in secret within a relatively small group of officials. Many macroeconomic reforms do not require extensive implementation. So-called "stroke of the pen" reforms—deregulation is a good example—call on governments to desist from doing things, thus avoiding issues of institutional capacity and the management of implementation. Decisions are difficult to make because of the political costs they impose, but once made, they are relatively easy to carry out. (Sustaining them, however, can be difficult.)

This is a highly stylized portrait of what has occurred in adopting and implementing first-generation reforms, and it does not hold for more complex tasks such as privatization and regulation. Still, the experience with such policy changes stands in considerable contrast to efforts to build credible and capable new institutions; promote important reforms in health and education services, social security, and labor policy; and create more decentralized and participatory forms of governance.[33] These activities involve many more moving parts in terms of how they are planned and put in practice. They also require extensive consultation, negotiation, and consensus building if they are to be successfully adopted. They call for decentralized forms of decisionmaking and need continual and time-consuming monitoring and capacity building if they are to be implemented. In contrast to the general consensus that exists about macroeconomic policy, many of the newer reforms do not have well-recognized templates that explain the central problem and the appropriate solution to it.[34] Policymakers are thus dealing in much more complex political environments and often walking blind as to what needs to be done to resolve issues of public importance.

The politics involved in these second-generation reforms are more complicated than those of the earlier economic policy changes and appear to be contingent on histories of conflict and the structural characteristics of the relationship between the state and the society in particular countries. Yet these complex policy and institutional changes may be as important for encouraging development as the macroeconomic reforms already adopted. They are important subjects for theory building and analysis, even though they may require the development of new theoretical models and more contingent explanations of change. Given the number of policymakers and advisers who are struggling with these issues currently, the quest to understand their political dynamics can be directly useful in the real world, if not to provide answers, at least to suggest strategies for improving the chances of a wide variety of welfare-enhancing changes.

Notes

1. See Krueger (1974, 1992); Bates (1981); Alesina and Drazen (1991); Bates and Krueger (1993). On industrial countries, see Olson (1982).

2. See Nelson (1990); Fernandez and Rodrik (1991); Frieden (1991); Haggard and Kaufman (1992b); Tommasi and Velasco (1996); Schamis (1999).

3. See Nelson (1990); Drazen and Grilli (1993); Krueger (1993: ch. 7); Widner (1994); J. Williamson (1994b); Grindle (1996).

4. Crisis hypotheses encounter difficulty in specifying threshold conditions that define a crisis and in accounting for why some governments act expeditiously in the face of a crisis or to avert crisis while other governments allow situations to go from bad to worse to worse yet. See Nelson (1990); Rodrik (1994); Grindle (1996).

5. See, for example, Haggard and Webb (1994).

6. See Nelson and others (1989); J. Williamson (1994a); Grindle (1996: ch. 5); Domínguez (1997).

7. See Hall (1989); Puryear (1994); Stone, Denham, and Garnett (1998).

8. See North and Weingast (1989); Root (1989); Persson and Tabellini (1994); Weingast (1995); Grindle (2000).

9. Useful overviews of a range of approaches to political economy can be found in Caporaso and Levine (1992) and Banks and Hanushek (1995).

10. For reviews of the literature that draws on economics, see Caporaso and Levine (1992); Rodrik (1993); Geddes (1995); Miller (1997).

11. For discussions of the literature that draws on sociology, see Granovetter (1985); Migdal (1988); Steinmo, Thelen, and Longstreth (1992); Evans (1995: ch. 2).

12. This is an important dynamic underlying the explanation of economic and political decay in Africa, according to the foundational work in this area by Robert Bates (1981).

13. The term "comparative institutionalism" is taken from discussions at a World Politics symposium (1995). In Steinmo, Thelen, and Longstreth (1992) this approach is referred to as "historical institutionalism." Among those who are often cited as leaders in this tradition are Theda Skocpol, Peter Katzenstein, Peter Evans, and Peter Hall. See also work by Charles Tilly (1985) and Alain Touraine (1985).

14. See, especially, Thelen and Steinmo (1992), as well as the case studies in Steinmo, Thelen, and Longstreth (1992), for discussions of the importance of institutions, conflict, and history in comparative analysis. See also contributions to the symposium in World Politics (1995).

15. Max Weber, a principal icon of comparative institutionalism, considers the work of statecraft in "Politics as a Vocation" ([1919] 1946). See also Ascher (1984) and Domínguez (1997).

16. See the case studies presented in Steinmo, Thelen, and Longstreth (1992) and Skowronek (1993).

17. Typically, scholars in this tradition explore the context within which political actions take place as a dense set of rules and relationships that actually shape motivations and inform action.

18. According to Barbara Geddes (1995: 82), "[t]he most compelling use of this approach results from the creative synthesis of the rational actor assumptions with, one, a plausible attribution of goals and, two, a careful interpretation of the effects of institutions and other factors on the feasible strategies available to actors for achieving these goals."

19. See Przeworski (1991); Nelson (1994); Haggard and Kaufman (1995); Lipjhart and Waisman (1996).

20. See North and Weingast (1989); Rodrik (1989); Levy and Spiller (1994); Persson and Tabellini (1994).

21. See, especially, North (1990). See also Alston, Eggertsson, and North (1996); O. Williamson (1994, 1998).

22. Foundational work in this tradition is generally traced to Ronald Coase's 1937 work "The Nature of the Firm." For analysis of a new institutionalist approach that focuses on imperfect information, see Bardhan (1989).

23. "The principal-agent model is an analytical expression of the agency relationship in which one party, the principal, considers entering into a contractual agreement with another, the agent, in the expectation that the agent will subsequently choose actions that produce outcomes desired by the principal" (Moe 1984: 756). The problems of delegation and commitment are thus central concerns in a principal-agent framework. See, especially, Horn (1995).

24. On the distinction between state-centric and society-centric explanations of politics, see Grindle and Thomas (1991).

25. This is characteristic of Marxian analysis also, as it is with many scholars who treat policy decisionmaking as a "black box."

26. President Carlos Menem in Argentina is the most frequently cited example of this kind of situation, but Carlos Salinas in Mexico and Carlos Andrés Pérez in Venezuela are also good examples.

27. Thus, leaders of economic reform are referred to as heroes in some discussions. See Harberger (1993).

28. Empirical work is beginning to respond to these questions. See the case studies in Alston, Eggertsson, and North (1996).

29. See Domínguez (1997). Considerable work on "epistemic communities" in international and domestic arenas has also illuminated the impact of ideas on policy choice. See, for example, Drake and Nicolaïdis (1992).

30. Again, Menem in Argentina and Pérez in Venezuela are good examples.

31. Kurt Weyland has used "prospect theory" to advance an argument as to why decisionmakers may take large risks when confronted with the potential for high losses. See Weyland (1996).

32. For an example of the kind of work that needs to be done in this area, see Corrales (1998). In addition, useful work is currently under way in areas related to regulatory, pension, and labor market reform.

33. First- and second-generation reforms are described in Naím (1995) and Graham and Naím (1998).

34. This point is made by Nelson (1997).

References

Alesina, Alberto, and Allan Drazen. 1991. "Why Are Stabilizations Delayed?" *American Economic Review* 81 (5, December): 1170–88.

Alston, Lee J., Trainn Eggertsson, and Douglass C. North, eds. 1996. *Empirical Studies in Institutional Change.* Cambridge, U.K.: Cambridge University Press.

Ascher, William. 1984. *Scheming for the Poor: The Politics of Redistribution in Latin America.* Cambridge, Mass.: Harvard University Press.

Banks, Jeffrey S., and Eric A. Hanushek, eds. 1995. *Modern Political Economy: Old Topics, New Directions.* Cambridge, U.K.: Cambridge University Press.

Bardhan, Pranab. 1989. "The New Institutional Economics and Development Theory: A Brief Critical Assessment." *World Development* 17 (9, September): 1389–95.

Bates, Robert. 1981. *Markets and States in Tropical Africa.* Berkeley, Calif.: University of California Press.

Bates, Robert, and Anne O. Krueger, eds. 1993. *Political and Economic Interactions in Economic Policy Reform: Evidence from Eight Countries.* Oxford, U.K.: Basil Blackwell.

Caporaso, James A., and David P. Levine. 1992. *Theories of Political Economy.* Cambridge, U.K.: Cambridge University Press.

Coase, Ronald H. 1937. "The Nature of the Firm." *Economica* 4: 386–405.

———. 1992. "The Institutional Structure of Production." *American Economic Review* 82 (September): 713–19.

Corrales, Javier. 1998. "The Politics of Education Reform Implementation." Amherst College, Amherst, Mass. December. Processed

Domínguez, Jorge. 1997. *Technopols: Freeing Politics and Markets in the 1980s.* University Park, Pa.: Pennsylvania State University Press.

Drake, William, and Kalypso Nicolaïdis. 1992. "Ideas, Interests and Institutionalization: 'Trade in Services' and the Uruguay Round." *International Organization* 46 (1, winter): 37–100.

Drazen, Allan, and Vittorio Grilli. 1993. "The Benefit of Crises for Economic Reforms." *American Economic Review* 83 (3, June): 598–607.

Evans, Peter. 1995. *Embedded Autonomy: States and Industrial Transformation.* Princeton, N.J.: Princeton University Press.

Fernandez, Raquel, and Dani Rodrik. 1991. "Resistance to Reform: Status Quo Bias in the Presence of Individual-Specific Uncertainty." *American Economic Review* 81 (5, December): 1146–55.

Frieden, Jeffry. 1991. *Debt, Development, and Democracy.* Princeton, N.J.: Princeton University Press.

Geddes, Barbara. 1994. *Politician's Dilemma: Building State Capacity in Latin America.* Berkeley, Calif.: University of California Press.

———. 1995. "The Uses and Limitations of Rational Choice." In Peter Smith, ed., *Latin America in Comparative Perspective: New Approaches to Methods and Analysis.* Boulder, Colo.: Westview Press.

Graham, Carol, and Moisés Naím. 1998. "The Political Economy of Institutional Reform in Latin America." In Nancy Birdsall, Carol Graham, and Richard H. Sabot, eds., *Beyond Trade-offs: Market Reform and Equitable Growth in Latin America.* Washington, D.C.: Inter-American Development Bank and Brookings Institution Press.

Granovetter, Mark. 1985. "Economic Action and Social Structure: The Problem of Embeddedness." *American Journal of Sociology* 91 (3, November): 481–510.

Grindle, Merilee S. 1991. "The New Political Economy: Positive Economics and Negative Politics." In Gerald M. Meier, ed., *Politics and Policy Making in Developing Countries: Perspectives on the New Political Economy.* San Francisco, Calif.: ICS Press.

———. 1996. *Challenging the State: Crisis and Innovation in Africa and Latin America.* Cambridge, U.K.: Cambridge University Press.

———. 2000. *Audacious Reforms: Institutional Invention and Democracy in Latin America.* Baltimore, Md.: Johns Hopkins University Press.

Grindle, Merilee S., and John W. Thomas. 1991. *Public Choices and Policy Change: The Political Economy of Reform in Developing Countries.* Baltimore, Md.: Johns Hopkins University Press.

Haggard, Stephan, and Robert R. Kaufman. 1992a. "Introduction: Institutions and Economic Adjustment." In Stephan Haggard and Robert R. Kaufman, eds. *The Politics of Economic Adjustment.* Princeton, N.J.: Princeton University Press.

———, eds. 1992b. *The Politics of Economic Adjustment.* Princeton, N.J.: Princeton University Press.

———. 1995. *The Political Economy of Democratic Transitions.* Princeton, N.J.: Princeton University Press.

Haggard, Stephan, and Steven Webb, eds. 1994. *Voting for Reform: Democracy, Political Liberalization, and Economic Adjustment.* New York: Oxford University Press.

Hall, Peter. 1989. *The Political Power of Economic Ideas: Keynesianism across Nations.* Princeton, N.J.: Princeton University Press.

Harberger, Arnold. 1993. "Secrets of Success: A Handful of Heroes." *American Economic Review* 83 (2, May): 343–50.

Horn, Murray. 1995. *The Political Economy of Public Administration: Institutional Choice in the Public Sector.* Cambridge, U.K.: Cambridge University Press.

Immergut, Ellen. 1992. "The Rules of the Game: The Logic of Health Policy-Making in France, Switzerland, and Sweden." In Sven Steinmo, Kathleen Thelen, and Frank Longstreth, eds., *Structuring Politics: Historical Institutionalism in Comparative Analysis.* Cambridge, U.K.: Cambridge University Press.

Kahler, Miles. 1992. "External Influence, Conditionality, and the Politics of Adjustment." In Stephan Haggard and Robert R. Kaufman, eds., *The Politics of Economic Adjustment.* Princeton, N.J.: Princeton University Press.

King, Desmond S. 1992. "The Establishment of Work-Welfare Programs in the United States and Britain: Politics, Ideas, and Institutions." In Sven Steinmo, Kathleen Thelen, and Frank Longstreth, eds., *Structuring Politics: Historical Institutionalism in Comparative Analysis.* Cambridge, U.K.: Cambridge University Press.

Knight, Jack. 1992. *Institutions and Social Conflict.* Cambridge, U.K.: Cambridge University Press.

Krueger, Anne O. 1974. "The Political Economy of the Rent-Seeking Society." *American Economic Review* 64 (3, June): 291–303.

————. 1992. *Economic Policy Reform in Developing Countries*. Oxford, U.K.: Basil Blackwell.

————. 1993. *Political Economy of Policy Reform in Developing Countries*. Cambridge, Mass.: MIT Press.

Levy, Brian, and Pablo Spiller. 1994. "The Institutional Foundations of Regulatory Commitment: A Comparative Analysis of Telecommunications Regulation." *Journal of Law, Economics, and Organization* 10 (2, October): 201–46.

Lipjhart, Arend, and Carlos Waisman, eds. 1996. *Institutional Design in New Democracies*. Boulder, Colo.: Westview Press.

Meier, Gerald M., ed. 1991. *Politics and Policy Making in Developing Countries: Perspectives on the New Political Economy*. San Francisco, Calif.: ICS Press.

Migdal, Joel. 1988. *Strong Societies and Weak States: State-Society Relations and State Capabilities in the Third World*. Princeton, N.J.: Princeton University Press.

Miller, Gary J. 1997. "The Impact of Economics on Contemporary Political Science." *Journal of Economic Literature* 35 (3, September): 1173–1204.

Moe, Terry M. 1984. "The New Economics of Organization." *American Journal of Political Science* 28 (4, November): 739–77.

Naím, Moisés. 1995. *Latin America's Journey to the Market: From Macroeconomic Shock to Institutional Therapy*. Occasional Paper 62. International Center for Economic Growth. San Francisco, Calif.: ICS Press.

Nelson, Joan M., ed. 1990. *Economic Crisis and Policy Choice: The Politics of Adjustment in the Third World*. Princeton, N.J.: Princeton University Press.

————. 1994. *A Precarious Balance: Democracy and Economic Reform in Eastern Europe*. San Francisco, Calif.: ICS Press.

————. 1997. "Reforming Social Sector Governance: A Political Perspective." Paper prepared for a conference on "Governance, Poverty Eradication, and Social Policy," Harvard University, November 12–14.

Nelson, Joan M., John Waterbury, and contributors. 1989. *Fragile Coalitions: The Politics of Economic Adjustment*. New Brunswick, N.J.: Transaction Books.

North, Douglass C. 1990. *Institutions, Institutional Change and Economic Performance*. Cambridge, U.K.: Cambridge University Press.

North, Douglass C., and Barry R. Weingast. 1989. "Constitutions and Commitment: The Evolution of Institutions Governing Public Choice in Seventeenth Century England." *Journal of Economic History* 49 (4, December): 803–32.

Olson, Mancur. 1965. *The Logic of Collective Action: Public Goods and the Theory of Groups*. Cambridge, Mass.: Harvard University Press.

————. 1982. *The Rise and Decline of Nations: Economic Growth Stagflation, and Social Rigidities*. New Haven, Conn.: Yale University Press.

Persson, Torsten, and Guido Tabellini, eds. 1994. *Monetary and Fiscal Policy*. Cambridge, Mass.: MIT Press.

Przeworski, Adam. 1991. *Democracy and the Market: Political and Economic Reforms in Eastern Europe and Latin America*. Cambridge, U.K.: Cambridge University Press.

Puryear, Jeffrey M. 1994. *Thinking Politics: Intellectuals and Democracy in Chile*. Baltimore, Md.: Johns Hopkins University Press.

Rodrik, Dani. 1989. "Promises, Promises: Credible Policy Reform via Signaling." *Economic Journal* 99 (September): 756–72.

———. 1993. "The Positive Economics of Policy Reform." *American Economic Review* 83 (2, May): 356–61.

———. 1994. "The Rush to Free Trade: Why So Late? Why Now? Will It Last?" In Stephan Haggard and Steven Webb, eds., *Voting for Reform: Democracy, Political Liberalization, and Economic Adjustment*. New York: Oxford University Press.

Root, Hilton L. 1989. "Tying the King's Hands: Credible Commitments and Royal Fiscal Policy during the Old Regime." *Rationality and Society* 1 (2, October).

Schamis, Hector E. 1999. "Distributional Coalitions and the Politics of Economic Reform in Latin America." *World Politics* 51 (2, January): 236–68.

Skocpol, Theda. 1979. *States and Social Revolutions: A Comparative Analysis of France, Russia, and China*. Cambridge. U.K.: Cambridge University Press.

Skowronek, Stephen. 1993. *The Politics Presidents Make: Leadership from John Adams to George Bush*. Cambridge, Mass.: Belknap Press of Harvard University Press.

Srinivasan, T. N. 1985. "Neoclassical Political Economy, the State and Economic Development." *Asian Development Review* 3 (2): 38–58.

Steinmo, Sven, Kathleen Thelen, and Frank Longstreth, eds. 1992. *Structuring Politics: Historical Institutionalism in Comparative Analysis*. Cambridge, U.K.: Cambridge University Press.

Stone, Diane, Andrew Denham, and Mark Garnett, eds. 1998. *Think Tanks across Nations: A Comparative Approach*. Manchester, U.K.: Manchester University Press.

Thelen, Kathleen, and Sven Steinmo. 1992. "Historical Institutionalism in Comparative Politics." In Sven Steinmo, Kathleen Thelen, and Frank Longstreth, eds., *Structuring Politics: Historical Institutionalism in Comparative Analysis*. Cambridge, U.K.: Cambridge University Press.

Tilly, Charles. 1985. "Models and Realities of Popular Collective Action." *Social Research* 52 (4): 717.

Tommasi, Mariano, and Andres Velasco. 1996. "Where Are We in the Political Economy of Reform?" *Journal of Policy Reform* 1 (2): 187–238.

Touraine, Alain. 1985. "An Introduction to the Study of Social Movements." *Social Research* 52 (4): 749–87.

Wade, Robert. 1990. *Governing the Market: Economic Theory and the Role of Government in East Asian Industrialization*. Princeton, N.J.: Princeton University Press.

Wallis, Joe. 1998. "Understanding the Role of Leadership in Economic Policy Reform." *World Development* 27 (1, January): 39–53.

Weber, Max. 1946. "Politics as a Vocation." In H. H. Gerth and C. Wright Mills, eds., *From Max Weber: Essays in Sociology.* New York: Oxford University Press. First published 1919.

Weingast, Barry R. 1995. "The Political Foundations of Limited Government: Parliament and Sovereign Debt in 17th and 18th Century England." Paper prepared for a conference on "The Frontiers of Institutional Economics," Washington University, St. Louis, Mo., March 17–19.

Weyland, Kurt. 1996. "Risk Taking in Latin American Economic Restructuring: Lessons from Prospect Theory." *International Studies Quarterly* 40 (2): 185–208.

Widner, Jennifer A., ed. 1994. *Economic Change and Political Liberalization in Sub-Saharan Africa.* Baltimore, Md.: Johns Hopkins University Press.

Williamson, John. 1994a. "In Search of a Manual for Technopols." In John Williamson, ed., *The Political Economy of Policy Reform.* Washington, D.C.: Institute for International Economics.

————, ed. 1994b. *The Political Economy of Policy Reform.* Washington, D.C.: Institute for International Economics.

Williamson, Oliver E. 1994. "The Institutions and Governance of Economic Development and Reform." In Michael Bruno and Boris Pleskovic, eds., *Proceedings of the World Bank Annual Conference on Development Economics 1993,* 171–97. Washington, D.C.: World Bank.

————. 1998. "The Institutions of Governance." *American Economic Review* 88 (2, May): 75–79.

World Bank. 1993. *The East Asian Miracle: Economic Growth and Public Policy.* New York: Oxford University Press.

World Politics. 1995. "The Role of Theory in Comparative Politics: A Symposium." *World Politics* 48 (1): 1–49.

Comment

Gustav Ranis

MERILEE GRINDLE NEED NOT worry about the employment prospects for political economists. There is much work to be done. However, she hit a sensitive nerve when she observed that her invitation as the only noneconomist at Dubrovnik seemed intended to illustrate the new-found interdisciplinary openness of the profession.

In fact, the situation, while changing, is still not radically different from what it was before we discovered institutions and politics. Instead of working with political scientists in a symmetric, relatively balanced fashion, economists who venture into the borderline areas seem to be intent on imperialist expansion into the field of political science. As a consequence, the choice Grindle describes, between the parsimony and elegance of economic models, on the one hand, and rich, sociology-based insights into conflict situations and power relations, on the other, is being carried into political science itself, with an increasing number of young professionals rallying to the "economistic" banner. The result has been increasingly marked battle lines within the political science profession, between those coopted by economists' methodology and those adhering to the broader, more flexible, sociology-oriented way of examining the political dimensions of development policy. Meanwhile, there is much less tension on display in economics. Neoclassical orthodoxy remains strong and generally in control. Those assembled at Dubrovnik did not by any means represent a cross-section of the profession but rather, in the main, a cross-section of deviants.

Grindle provides an interesting test of how these two traditions answer four critical questions: why politicians do or do not support policy change; how political institutions affect the choices made by politicians; how institutions are created or transformed; and what the consequences of new rules of the game are for politics. For example, the economistic answer to the first is to supply rational-choice theory, plus a healthy dosage of myopia, to ensure reelection. The sociological answer calls on a historically evolved, much more complex, context to answer the same query. The second question is again addressed alternatively by invoking rational-choice theory, now including institutions as part of the choice set, or by insisting that institutions are themselves shaped by political agents and subject to path dependency. The third question is answered, in one tradition, by expanding the scope of transaction costs to include the political kind, while the other appeals to power struggles and the effort to protect rents. And so on. In short, the economists and their economistic allies on the other side force additional exogenous variables, such as institutions, onto their canvas and call it a day; the sociologically oriented political scientists try to endogenize institutions in terms of political and possibly underlying cultural and ethnic forces.

I have no problem in favoring the process of change-oriented, historically evolved, and collectively determined alternatives over the extended version of the individualistic rational-choice model. But what concerns me is whether the "middle-range theories" Merilee Grindle rightly calls for have indeed begun to emerge from the second school. There is clearly a need for a differentiation from the work of anthropologists, who are also entering this arena of late with their often very interesting and instructive "narratives" that do not pretend to seek generalization. What is clearly called for is not necessarily formal modeling to seek the approbation of economists but the generation of frameworks in which a basket of theories, tailored to individual, time-bound country situations and useful for policymakers, can find a place.

What is also called for, on the other side of the fence, is a bit less triumphalism and a little more humility. Economists have certainly little to crow about, whether we are focusing on recent events in East Asia or in the transition countries of the former Soviet Union. We have to stop thinking of politics as an exogenous interference—ranging from an annoyance to the wholesale thwarting of the reform package—and of the median voter as the average expression of sovereign individual preferences, rather than as possibly dominated by vested interests.

There are a few dimensions that were missing and that Grindle might have usefully considered. One is the state, which presumably plays a critical third-party role along with politicians and voters. It is hard to see how, in the end, issues of policy formation can be addressed without considering the kind of a state and how it relates to political parties and to voters and productive agents. In that connection, both vertical decentralization, conventionally understood, and horizontal decentralization—that is, the relative influence of legislatures, the judiciary, and civil society, including indigenous nongovernmental organizations—are bound to be highly relevant for the issues raised here. Another dimension is the need to extend the agency issue to the international arena—to concern ourselves not only with the nexus of internal goal-setting, monitoring, and rewards but also with the relations among such institutions as the international financial institutions, multinational corporations, international commercial banks, and such intermediate developing-country institutions as central banks, private intermediaries, and development banks.

Finally, it is hard to see how bureaucracy can be left out of the picture if the implementation as well as the formation of policy is to be part of the analysis. The political economy of development policymaking, is, after all, the title of Grindle's chapter, and all of us have seen the critical role of the bureaucracy—once again, preferably treated endogenously—in making, or, more frequently, breaking the best-laid plans of voters and politicians.

Comment

Timothy Besley

MERILEE GRINDLE PROVIDES an interesting and wide-ranging discussion of the political economy of policy reform. Political economy has been alive and well in development studies for a long time. For much of the past 30 years, however, it has been much less well represented in mainstream policy analysis, in spite of important interventions by leading figures in the economics profession such as Jagdish Bhagwati and Anne Krueger. An often-suggested dichotomy is between models of the policy process that assume benevolent governments which care about efficiency and equity and a political-economy approach that stresses the possible failures of the state in living up to this ideal. Looking at the experience of many of the world's poorest countries, the benevolent view of government seems untenable as a positive model. This reality may suggest that an approach to policy analysis informed by a political-economy approach must have the edge over traditional economic approaches.

There is some merit in this indictment of the technocratic approach to policymaking, but the indictment is often misconstrued. In this comment I try to suggest a somewhat different perspective on the role of the study of politics and economics in an understanding of policy reform. This approach preserves a role for normative policy analysis of a technocratic kind but argues that institutional arrangements for delivering policy, as much as the policies themselves, should be the object of study. This is in tune with the general theme in contemporary development debates on the importance of finding appropriate institutional remedies for problems, not just recommending policy solutions in the absence of the vehicles needed to deliver the policies.

There are two key roles for a *political*-economy analysis of policy. The first is positive: to understand the policy process better. Many of the main issues for developing countries lie in understanding the forces that shape key policy reforms, and Grindle expertly surveys a number of different approaches. A crucial difference between approaches concerns the extent to which they admit *general* lessons from reform experiences. This is where theory is important: if we have models of what drives policy reforms, built from underlying precepts about human motivation, we can use them to understand a broader context. Detailed case studies of particular reform experiences are hard to generalize unless they aim explicitly at testing underlying theories. Broader-brush approaches that begin with a more fully specified set of theoretical presumptions rarely do justice to the nuances of particular reform experiences. Neither approach should be granted a monopoly.

My own inclination is to downplay (in comparison with Grindle's account) the contrast between rational-choice and more institutional approaches. The contrast creates an artificial fault line that is far more important to academic turf wars than to real-world policy discussions. It is probably fair to say that certain modes of analysis rely too much on stylized facts and a priori reasoning than would be ideal. But this has nothing intrinsically to do with rational-choice explanation.

The really important agenda is to bring creative theory and analysis of data together. This is a tried and tested formula for success in most branches of the social sciences, but it presents difficult questions as to where to start; that is, what is to be treated as given for the purposes of the analysis. For analytical purposes it is often convenient to take some combination of political institutions, culture, and constitutional rules as given. However, there are many contexts where this is not sustainable. I doubt that the right approach can be determined in the abstract; it will depend on the scope and aims of particular studies.

Ultimately, the issue is really about the role that our understanding of political processes will play in developing a portable framework for understanding policy reforms *in other contexts*. Underlying this effort is a rejection of the view that given cultural features determine everything of relevance. Thus, there is an important agenda for determining which institutional and constitutional changes might lead to particular effects.

The second (and arguably more important) role of political-economy analyses is to facilitate policy advice. The technocratic approach to policy advice sees planning as the key to a better world. A good example is the cost-benefit tradition, the aim of which is to identify interventions that meet certain social objectives. That approach constitutes the best practice for identifying desirable directions for policy reform. The World Bank has for many years championed it as a cornerstone of its lending policy for a whole range of projects.

There are two reasons why actual policy reform might diverge from the ideal. The first concerns distributional judgments. The cost-benefit analyst must assign weights to gainers or losers to reach an aggregate judgment. If the policy process uses different weights, there may be divergences in both directions: policies will be chosen that fail the cost-benefit test in question, and apparently desirable projects will not be adopted. It is not difficult, using a political-economy analysis, to understand why these divergences from a cost-benefit test are so common. A key role of a democratic political process is to decide whose social preferences will prevail. That in many countries policies are weighted in favor of elites and diverge from some cost-benefit test which weights the poor more heavily may be regrettable, but it is hardly a surprise.

Policy reform can also diverge by choosing a policy that is not picked by a cost-benefit test *for any distributional weights*. These are the real political failures. A classic example is the use of tariff protection, which economic theory has long shown is Pareto dominated by some combination of a production subsidy and a tax on consumers. Yet we see tariff protection the world over. A growing body of work in political economy views these inefficiencies as rooted in the way in which political institutions operate—in particular, in the turnovers of power that typify democratic processes in which politicians choose policies to manipulate future elections. This may end up serving nobody's interest!

What, then, is the role of a policy analyst? There is a danger that we will simply take a *que será será* view of policy. If the political system is an autonomous entity that makes its own decisions regardless of what is recommended, the notion of recommending policy becomes anodyne. Economists have long been attached to consumer sovereignty. This outlook argues for democratic sovereignty to boot.

I am not persuaded by this argument. There is scope for a role for analysis in improving the world. The traditional technocratic view of the policy process worked in a market context in which it was accepted that markets might fail to produce a socially acceptable distribution of income and that the system was susceptible to market failure. The natural extension of this view to the policy process recognizes that political institutions which allocate resources may similarly bring about maldistribution and inefficiency.

The form of policy advice, however, is rather different and depends very much on what one views as the primitives and the policy levers. Many of the interesting policy levers are now institutional and constitutional rules, and, moreover, it is often through changes in these rules that policy reforms become credible. Many of the leading questions on the development agenda reflect such concerns. Is it better for societies to have more transparent policymaking, a strong press, limits on campaign spending, and so on? Are rules that mandate representation of low-caste groups or women likely to lead to policies that favor these traditionally disadvantaged groups? Is centralization, decentralization, or privatization more likely to benefit the poor? Should judges be elected or appointed? This kind of welfare political economy presents a challenging and important agenda for the future and is at the heart of attempts to improve the quality of government in developing countries.

Doing good political economy is a tall order. It requires a close understanding of both the political and the economic dimensions of policy. Moreover, the agenda has to be both theoretical and empirical—neither alone will suffice. A balance will also have to be struck between case studies and broader comparisons, reflecting the tradeoff between the values of specificity and portability. One of the largest divides between political scientists and economists concerns the relative weights that they attach to case studies and to wider comparisons in formulating policy.

An area in which I wish to emphasize my agreement with Grindle is her notion that we need to have a better grasp of the importance of leadership and the power of ideas in shaping policy. This ties in with the view that the role of civil society is important. It is striking how strengthening social institutions at the grassroots level can lead to the emergence of community leaders. Dissemination of ideas also requires a better understanding of the role of the media in shaping policy processes and a sharper appreciation of the importance of transparency in the political process. This has not been studied enough, especially in a developing-country context. The social benefits of increased literacy and open discussion of ideas could be far higher than their private benefits once spillovers into the political process are taken into account. This may be an area in which technological change in the form of portable communications (for example, cellular phones) can yield an important payoff by widening citizens' access to information about their own society, as well as others. Moreover, political control of information flows is much more difficult in such circumstances.

A key role of a political-economy analysis is to emphasize that the context of decisions and the nature of decisionmaking institutions are critical to the quality of government. There is, of course, a larger question of how we can bring about actual changes in institutions and in constitutional rules. Just as with low-quality economic policies, there are likely to be strong vested interests in maintaining low-quality institutions. Here, analysis is key—creating the possibility of demonstrating that certain practices benefit particular groups at the expense of others. The role of high-quality, evidence-based policy analysis of institutional changes should not be underestimated. Moreover, there is a strong case for the validity of normative analysis along the lines that I have argued. The study of political economy does not preclude using analytical tools to *persuade* policymakers that there are ways to improve the world. It is important to dispel the myth, in part created by some sections of the public choice school of political economy, that modeling and understanding government leads to a case for dismantling the state. High-quality governments, like high-quality firms, are likely to expand the domain in which they operate. The key issue is to identify the activities in which government can be effective and then to design institutional solutions to guarantee this effectiveness over the long run. It is the latter part that underlines the importance of *political economy*.

Modern Economic Theory and Development

Karla Hoff
Joseph E. Stiglitz

THE PAST 50 YEARS have seen marked changes in our understanding of development. We know that development is possible, but not inevitable. We have had a wealth of experiments. There are clearly no sure-fire formulas for success; if there were, there would be more successes. Some strategies seem to work for a while and then stall; some strategies seem to work in some countries and not in others.[1] Economic theory has evolved to account for the successes and failures. This chapter attempts to describe these changes in economic theory—both in the kinds of models used and in the factors that are identified as playing key roles. It focuses on two pivotal questions: What forces can explain the divergence in incomes across countries? What implications can we draw for the nature of the interventions most likely to promote development?

A basic theme of this chapter is that industrial countries differ from developing countries by much more than their level of capital—or even their human capital. More capital may be helpful, but, remarkably, even a transfer of funds may not have a large effect on economic growth (see World Bank 1999a). Eliminating government-imposed distortions is also obviously desirable but seems neither necessary nor sufficient for sustained growth.[2] A view shared by all the perspectives on development that we explore in this chapter is that industrial and developing countries are on different production functions and are organized in different ways. Development is no longer seen primarily as a process of capital accumulation but rather as a process of organizational change.

We discuss work done in three broad, interrelated research programs—the economics of information, the theory of coordination problems, and institutional economics. These research programs depart from the strong assumptions of neoclassical theory. In that theory, every equilibrium is a Pareto optimum, and, in general, the equilibrium is unique.[3] In contrast, in the research programs considered here, individuals need not make the right tradeoffs. And whereas in the past we thought the implication was that the economy would be slightly distorted, we now understand that the interaction of these slightly distorted behaviors may produce very large distortions. The consequence is that there may be multiple equilibria and that each may be inefficient. Given some initial equilibrium, even though each individual may know that there is another equilibrium at which all would be better off, individuals are unable to coordinate the complementary changes in their actions necessary to attain that outcome. This chapter provides examples in which rent-seeking, inefficient institutions, and underinvestment in research and development and training can each be explained as a *coordination failure*.[4]

The research programs discussed here entail a major shift in focus and in conclusions from neoclassical models. Such models hypothesize that one can explain output, growth, and the differences between industrial and developing countries by focusing on "fundamentals"—resources, technology, and preferences. If preferences are the same across countries, then differences across countries in capital resources are explained only by the fact that some countries started to accumulate before others. That is, underdevelopment is a result of a late start, and, in the long run, all countries will converge in per capita incomes. Appendix A analyzes the neoclassical growth model (Solow 1956) and argues that low capital cannot explain underdevelopment.

Neoclassical theory contends that the particular set of institutions in an economy does not matter. This position rests on three points: (a) outcomes are determined by fundamental forces (reflecting resources, preferences, and technology), (b) these forces lead to Pareto-efficient outcomes, and (c) institutions do not even influence the choice of the equilibrium. For example, whether a society has an institution in which the bride's family pays a dowry, or the groom's family pays a bride price, or neither one, neoclassical theory would contend that—with given fundamentals—the distribution of incomes will be the same as it would have been without those institutions (Becker 1973). The standard modeling technique in neoclassical economics is to solve for the outcomes that would emerge from an impersonal setting with a market for all goods, all periods, and all risks, where people make trades "with the market." History does not matter. Not even the distribution of wealth matters if one is interested solely in efficiency. These are strong hypotheses. And in leaving out institutions, history, and distributional considerations, neoclassical economics leaves out the heart of development economics. Modern economic theory argues that the fundamentals are not the only deep determinants of economic outcomes.

Neoclassical theorists could not, of course, turn a blind eye to the fact that the kind of convergence predicted by theory was not occurring, and thus they had to look to some "outside" intervention. *Government failures provided an easy out.* When neoclassical economists go beyond the fundamentals of resources, technology, and preferences, they focus almost exclusively on government—it is government impediments to markets that prevent the economy from working smoothly. But many versions of such theories are inherently unsatisfactory. In some versions the government failures are assumed to be exogenous, leaving unexplained why they should be larger in some societies than in others. In other versions political-economy models are used to explain the government failures—in which case they typically do not explain how or when certain recommended interventions would overcome the political forces that initially led to the distortions. Surely, a pious speech from an outside adviser would seem unlikely to displace fundamental political forces! More broadly, as we note below, the "government-induced distortion" theory of underdevelopment does not do well in explaining key aspects of the development process.

Today we recognize that government failures can be critically important. But we also recognize that they need to be, and often can be, explained; with appropriate institutional design, they can even be limited. We recognize, as well, that even without government failures, market failures are pervasive, especially in developing countries.[5] The purpose of this chapter, however, is to go beyond the standard discussion of market failures and development in order to identify a broad set of basic influences on outcomes. We focus on four: institutions, the distribution of wealth, history, and "ecology"—by which we mean the behaviors of other agents in the economy that have spillover effects.

Institutions. Neoclassical theory pierced the veil of institutions, seeing through (so it argued) to the deeper determinants of economic outcomes—the economic fundamentals. Today we recognize that information and enforcement problems impose limits on economic possibilities that are just as real as the limits of technology. Nonmarket institutions arise in response to those limits and influence outcomes. But improvements in those institutions—"good mutations"—may not survive on their own if they require complementary changes in other social institutions. "If the institutional matrix rewards piracy, then piratical organizations will come into existence . . ." (North 1994: 361). There is no teleology—no evolutionary force that ensures that outcomes will be efficient. If a Nash equilibrium in institutions exists, it may not be efficient. We will provide many illustrations.

Going inside the black boxes of institutions. A major thrust of modern development economics is to shift the boundary between what we black-box (for example, treat as an institutional rigidity) and what we explain with our models. Early theoretical work that focused on institutional issues and the scope for policy in development attempted to identify specific institutional characteristics of developing countries and incorporated them as exogenous features of models. This was the "structuralist" approach to development; an overview is Chenery (1975). Later work tried to evaluate policies within the context of articulated economic models that explained the problems which the policies were designed to solve.

The shift in this boundary has had strong implications for our views about policy. The chapter provides five examples.

• *Complementarities in industrialization.* Earlier models of the "big push" (Rosenstein-Rodan 1943) simply assumed complementarities in demand so that expectations of low investment could be self-fulfilling. The implication was that the government should intervene in the industrialization process. Later models developed frameworks in which complementarities were derived as an equilibrium outcome. In some cases, the complementarities were shown not to produce inefficiencies (Murphy, Shleifer, and Vishny 1989: sect. 3) or to vanish once an economy was opened to international trade. But in other cases, complementarities did produce inefficiencies, and there were no easy policy measures to resolve them. For example, there may be no simple way around search costs.

• *Rural credit.* Earlier models simply assumed that rural credit markets did not work well. Later models derived credit market imperfections from information and enforcement costs. An implication of these models was that standard interventions through credit subsidies might be ineffective but that institutional interventions could improve credit markets.

• *Labor markets.* Earlier models of urban unemployment treated the urban wage as fixed and therefore argued that it did not reflect the opportunity cost of labor. Later models explained why in equilibrium the urban wage might exceed the rural wage but nonetheless reflect the opportunity costs of expanding urban employment.

• *Saving rates.* Earlier models assumed that a higher fraction of profits than of wages or rural incomes was saved and that therefore rural incomes should be disproportionately taxed. Later experience demonstrated that rural saving rates could be very high, and theory shed light on institutional influences on saving.

• *Political constraints.* Political processes are endogenous. Earlier models tended to ignore political processes and to assume that outside intervention could effectively change policies. We distinguish "deep" interventions, which affect underlying economic and political forces and therefore change policies, from "shallow" ones, which do not and which may actually make things worse.

Inseparability among distribution, institutions, and efficiency. Neo-classical economics argued that neither institutions nor wealth distribution mattered for efficiency; productive resources always gravitated through market exchange into the hands of the person who valued them the most. An even stronger statement of that idea is the Coase theorem. When an economy departed from the complete-markets assumption of the neoclassical model, Coase (1960) argued, private bargaining would provide an antidote so that the economy would still be efficient. To be sure, Coase recognized that his theorem would not hold in the presence of transaction costs (McCloskey 1998). If a situation *does* have trans-action costs or information problems, then it *does* matter how wealth and property rights are distributed. Transaction costs are important, particularly in developing countries. Modern economic theory empha-sizes that transaction costs depend on institutions, that institutions are endogenous, and that the distribution of wealth affects economic effi-ciency both directly and through its effect on institutions.[6]

It is easy to see how the distribution of wealth affects efficiency in principal-agent relationships. In these relationships the principal (say, a lender) controls a resource that he entrusts to another individual, his agent (say, the borrower), and there is imperfect information concern-ing either what action the agent has undertaken or what he should undertake. In many situations the actions of an individual are not eas-ily observable. For instance, a bank entrusts resources to a borrower but cannot perfectly monitor his investments and initiative; an agricul-tural landlord entrusts land to a tenant but cannot easily monitor his effort and care. The task of the principal is to design an incentive scheme to try to align the agent's incentives with his own. The principal-agent literature focuses on the design of contracts to motivate the agent to act in the principal's interest. Contract provisions that can achieve this are collateral, bonds, and provisions that shift the risk of poor output onto the agent. The greater the agent's ability to post collateral, put up a bond, pay rent in advance, or absorb risk, the greater the agent's incen-tives to take the appropriate actions.[7] In these ways, an agent's wealth will affect his incentives and productivity. Wealth in the form of collat-eral plays a *catalytic role* rather than a role as *input* that gets used up in the process of producing output (Hoff 1996).

The first key point is that the extent to which wealth does play this role depends on its distribution. Clearly, if the distribution of wealth is so unequal that some individuals have more than enough wealth to put their skills to best use while others have so little wealth that they can-not even obtain credit to undertake a productive project, the catalytic role of wealth will be limited. A second key point is that because the wealth distribution affects the market decisions of individuals, it af-fects *macrovariables* such as prices and wages, and so the welfare of any single agent depends, in general, on the entire distribution of wealth.[8]

Perhaps the clearest illustration of the effect of wealth distribution on contracts is sharecropping, which is ubiquitous in developing countries. Sharecropping arises as a result of inequality in the distribution of wealth (landholdings) and the absence of better ways to share risks, or the limited ability of the tenant to absorb losses. It creates a principal-agent problem between landlord and tenant that imposes potentially huge costs on the economy—the distortions associated with a 50 percent share are similar to those associated with a 50 percent marginal tax rate. (A case study is Banerjee, Gertler, and Ghatak 1998.) Overall agency costs in labor and capital markets can be reduced by interlinking those contracts, but such interlinkage may reduce the effective degree of competition in the economy (Braverman and Stiglitz 1982, 1989; Ray and Sengupta 1989).

A third key point is that because wealth distribution affects contracts, incentives, and outcomes in one period, it affects the distribution of wealth in the next. An individual with no or few assets may be relatively unproductive (that is, relative to his output in entrepreneurial occupations or under high-powered incentive contracts that he could enter if he had more wealth). And if there are many individuals with no or few assets, wage rates will be low. With low wages, individuals with initially low wealth will make low bequests to the next generation. Thus, an initial highly unequal distribution of wealth may *reproduce* itself from one period to the next. Banerjee and Newman (1993) show that the effects of an initial highly unequal wealth distribution can last forever and can permanently limit growth. Mookherjee and Ray (2000) present an even stronger result, for they allow agents to save over their infinite lifetimes to maximize their lifetime utility. Why, they ask, do not poor agents save aggressively in order to increase their productivity in the future? In answer, they demonstrate that these agents *will* do so if the market is competitive, but "if agents have no bargaining power [and lenders can only write one-period contracts], then the returns to saving of poor agents are appropriated entirely by lenders, resulting in poverty traps" (Mookherjee and Ray 2000: 1).

History. There are other ways besides the distribution of wealth that history affects economic outcomes. History influences a society's technology, skill base, and institutions. It is not necessarily true that the impact of past events erodes over time. Those events may set the preconditions that drive the economy to a particular steady state.[9]

The case in which a transitory event has persistent effects is known as *hysteresis.* For example, the loss of life from the Black Death and the resulting shortage of labor induced labor-saving innovations in Europe, with profound implications for the historical evolution of the continent.[10]

History also affects outcomes by affecting beliefs. An obvious case is that in which expectations are (at least partly) adaptive: individuals expect people to behave in the future as they have in the past. But even with fully rational expectations, history can cast a long shadow. For example, an outbreak of corruption, or the revelation that some firms in an industry passed off shoddy goods as high-quality goods, can tarnish the reputation of the whole industry. That, our intuition tells us, can reduce the incentive of every member of the group to behave honestly in the future. Tirole (1996) explores this idea formally. He assumes that the reputation of a member of the group (for example, an employee in an organization or a firm in an industry) depends on his own past behavior and also, because his track record is observed with noise, on the group's past behavior. The revelation that any member of the group was dishonest in the past will *increase* the time it takes for any given agent to establish a reputation for honesty. This will *lower* the individual's incentives to be honest and may create a *vicious circle of corruption*, where "the new members of an organization may suffer from the original sin of their elders long after the latter are gone. (p. 1)" This is an example of *path dependency*, where the level of a variable in the future depends on its level in the past.

History also matters because it affects exposure to cultural models, which shapes preferences. Changes in the ways that members of one generation earn their living may influence the next generation through changes in childrearing, schooling, informal learning rules such as conformism, role models, and social norms. The market itself is a social institution that shapes preferences; it may foster characteristics of openness, competitiveness, and self-interestedness. (Interesting discussions are in Acemoglu 1995: sect. 4, and Bowles 1998.) Preferences, technology, and institutions are all endogenous, and transitory events can have persistent effects on them.

Multiple equilibria. One of the major insights of general equilibrium theory is that what happens in one market has ramifications for others. In the standard neoclassical models the interactions are mediated by prices, and normally there is a unique equilibrium. If, on the contrary, a continuum of equilibria were associated with any set of fundamentals, then general equilibrium theory would not be very helpful: one could not explain much of the variation across economies by focusing on fundamentals. In fact, Solow's neoclassical growth model went further than asserting that there was a unique equilibrium at a moment in time. In his model, equilibrium in the long run did not depend on history, institutions, or the distribution of wealth.[11] The celebrated prediction of his model was the *convergence* of per capita incomes across economies. But once one broadens the analysis in the way we have suggested, it is easy to construct models that have multiple equilibria, as we will show below.

"Ecological economics." More generally, modern development economics rejects the very notion of "equilibrium" that underlies tradi-

tional neoclassical analysis. In that analysis, the dynamics of the economy are mechanical: knowledge of the fundamentals and the initial conditions enables one to predict with precision the course of the "evolution" of the economy.[12] Even if there are stochastic events, if one knows the stochastic processes affecting the relevant variables, one can predict the probability distribution of outcomes at each date. By contrast, modern development economics tends to be influenced more by biological than physical models. Whereas the latter emphasize the forces pulling toward equilibrium—and with similar forces working in all economies, all should be pulled toward the same equilibrium—the former focus more on evolutionary processes, complex systems, and chance events that may cause systems to diverge.

Near the end of *The Origin of Species*, Charles Darwin wrote, reflecting on the Galapagos Islands:

> [The plants and animals of the Galapagos differ radically among islands that have] the same geological nature, the same height, climate, etc. . . . This long appeared to me a great difficulty, but it arises in chief part from the deeply seated error of considering the physical conditions of a country as the most important for its inhabitants; whereas it cannot, I think, be disputed that the nature of the other inhabitants, with which each has to compete, is at least as important, and generally a far more important element of success. (Darwin [1859] 1993: 540)

The economy is like an ecosystem, and Darwin was implicitly recognizing that ecosystems have multiple equilibria. Far more important in determining the evolution of the system than the fundamentals (the weather and geography) are the endogenous variables, the ecological environment. Luck—accidents of history—may play a role in determining that environment, and thus in the selection of the equilibrium.

If this is the case, development may be both easier and harder than was previously thought. Under the older theory, "all" one had to do to ensure development was to transfer enough capital and remove government-imposed distortions. Under the new theories, "all" one has to do is to induce a movement out of the old equilibrium, sufficiently far and in the right direction that the economy will be "attracted" to a new, superior equilibrium. Although this may require fewer resources, it may take more skill. Some perturbations could lead the economy to an even worse equilibrium—as, some would argue, may have been the case in certain economies in transition. In this broader perspective, the "deep" fundamentals of neoclassical theory—preferences and technology—are themselves endogenous, affected by the social and economic environment.

Although neoclassical economics has failed to provide us with a theoretical framework for thinking about the problems of development, it has played a critical role in the evolution of development theory. By arguing that institutions do not matter, it has forced us to think about why they do. By arguing that wealth distribution does not matter, it has forced us to think about why it does. And by arguing that the main interactions in an economy are mediated by prices, it has forced us to think about the myriad of other important interactions in our ecosystem.

I. Obstacles to Development:
Beyond Capital Endowments and
Government-Induced Price Distortions

How can we explain why the gap in incomes between industrial and developing countries has not narrowed over the past 50 years? A view shared by all the nonneoclassical perspectives on development is that the two groups of countries are on different production functions and are organized in different ways. The deeper question concerns the sources of these differences. This part explores in greater detail three complementary hypotheses: institutions, "ecology," and knowledge.

Institutions, Organization, and Social Capital

A central insight of recent theoretical work is that although the institutions that arise in response to incomplete markets and contracts may have as their intention an improvement in economic outcomes, there is no assurance that improvement will actually result. Institutions may be part of an equilibrium and yet be dysfunctional. For example, Arnott and Stiglitz (1991) examine the effects of a social institution that arises because of incomplete insurance provided by markets faced with moral hazard problems. They show that informal social insurance may crowd out market insurance and decrease social welfare. With endogenous institutions, developing countries may be caught in a vicious circle in which low levels of market development result in high levels of information imperfections and these information imperfections themselves give rise to institutions—for example, informal, personalized networks of relationships—that impede the development of markets. (Other examples are Kranton 1996; Banerjee and Newman 1998.)

A precondition for effective markets, especially those associated with intertemporal trades, is the existence of institutions that make rights to private property secure, enforce contracts, and provide for disclosure of information. This requires government. To be sure, Mafia-style enforcement mechanisms are used in many places, but such enforcement mechanisms have their own drawbacks (Gambetta 1993). To name just one, the same extralegal mechanisms used to enforce contracts are typically used to deter entry. It is not just a too overbear-ing state that impedes markets; frequently, a too weak state is the prob-lem (World Bank 1997).

In some cases, private parties can enforce property rights through their individual efforts, but there is no presumption that such enforce-ment will have any optimality properties. De Meza and Gould (1992) demonstrate this result in a setting where the state defines property rights over a natural resource such as land or minerals but enforcement depends on the individual owner's decision to expend a fixed cost for enforcement—for example, to fence in or patrol his land. If the owner does not incur the enforcement cost, then, by assumption, other indi-viduals will have free use of his property. The benefit to an owner from enforcing his property right is that he can hire labor to work with his natural resource and can collect the resource rents. In deciding whether to enforce his property right, an owner compares his potential rents with the fixed cost of enforcement. These rents will be larger, the lower the reservation wage of workers. In equilibrium, the reservation wage of workers itself depends on how many other owners are enforcing their property rights: as the fraction of property owners who enforce their rights *increases*, the outside opportunities of workers fall and so does the reservation wage. With lower wages, potential resource rents *rise*. Two stable equilibria may therefore exist—one in which all own-ers enforce their property rights and obtain high rents, and one in which none do and the rent that a single owner could obtain from enforce-ment is low.[13] (See Figure 1.)

As Coase (1937) emphasized, when enforcement of private property rights is costly, a market may or may not be the best allocation system. But as Coase did not recognize, whatever the best allocation system is, a decentralized economy with private enforcement costs may not reach it. Recent historical accounts go beyond this observation and show that systems of contract enforcement exhibit path dependence.[14]

Social capital (including norms, information networks, reputation mechanisms, and social sanctions) can sometimes serve as a substitute for formal enforcement mechanisms. Implicit contracts, enforced by repeated engagements, may be as important in ensuring "good behav-ior" as explicit contracts. There is a concern that early in the process of development, norms and information networks become weakened and thus social sanctions become less effective. As traditional communities break down with widespread migration out of villages and with high rates of change (for example, labor mobility), enforcement of implicit contracts becomes difficult. The problem is exacerbated if interest rates are high. Breakdowns in informal enforcement mechanisms normally occur prior to the reestablishment of new bonds and the development of effective formal mechanisms: social capital is destroyed before it is recreated.

Figure 1. Multiple Equilibria (with Corner Solutions) in the Level of Enforcement of Property Rights

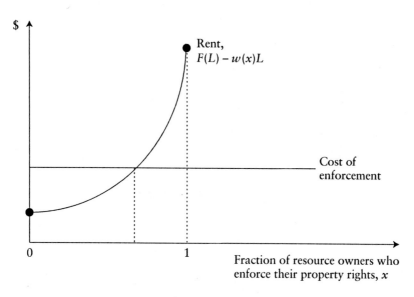

We view society as an *organization*, in which exchange and production are mediated not just by markets but by an array of formal and informal arrangements. Early stages of development are often characterized by retrogression and decay rather than by an increase in social and informational capital; these losses are compensated for (partially or wholly) by increases in physical and human capital. The consequence of the losses is that increases in productivity are smaller than might otherwise have been expected. For instance, the widening of markets reduces the role of community enforcement and may increase the need for uniform standards and for screening institutions, but these may emerge only slowly over time. (An informal account is Klitgaard 1991.) Until they emerge, technical change can actually exacerbate information problems to such an extent that some, all, or even more than all of the gains from the technical change are dissipated (Hoff 1998).[15]

The pacing and sequencing of government-imposed reforms may attenuate or exacerbate these disorganizational forces. Ancillary effects of reform can largely offset or more than offset efficiency gains from otherwise desirable reforms. For instance, a potentially huge, unintended effect of rapid reforms in banking standards or exchange rate adjustments is to destroy the franchise values of banks and reduce other asset values. This weakens banks (which are then more likely to engage in looting or excessive risk-taking) and thus increases the likelihood of bank failure. If banks fail, the resulting credit contractions cause firm bankruptcies, leading to further destruction of organizational and informational capital.

Many developing countries face the dual challenge of a loss of social capital as development proceeds and a lack of formal and informal institutions to constrain government to act within a rule of law. Democracy is a check on government. The ability of government to act as an agent of development may depend on the strength of democratic forces and on the extent to which voters are divided along class or ethnic lines. Many developing countries are polarized by class or ethnicity, which impedes the ability of the state to act as a "developmental state" in decisions about public goods (Easterly 1999) or redistribution (Tornell and Lane 1999). Others face problems with increasing levels of violence. In Africa civil disturbances have proved to be an important impediment to development (Easterly and Levine 1997).

Viewing development from an ecological/evolutionary perspective introduces new elements into the dynamic process. It is a matter of tracing out not just the dynamics of capital accumulation (on which traditional neoclassical economics focused) or even the transmission of knowledge (on which Schumpeterian theory focused) but also the evolution of social, economic, and political institutions. We need to know how, for instance, particular interventions affect the costs of forming certain institutions, which in turn affect the kinds of reform that can be enacted subsequently. We shall return to these themes in Part II.

Some Examples of Coordination Problems

Only limited progress has been made in modeling the dynamic process of institutional change described in the preceding paragraph, but there has been considerable progress in the formulation of models in which coordination failures can occur.[16] Here, we present an overview of that work. The work captures the idea that a myriad of activities that are central to the development process, such as innovation, honesty in trade, investment, labor training, and saving, can create externalities. The externalities may be mediated by (a) changes in beliefs and information, (b) effects on the technology of the individual agent, (c) changes in the set of markets that exists, (d) changes in the size of the market, and (e) changes in search costs. These externalities affect the rewards to activities and can lead to the existence of multiple equilibria, each with a different reward structure. Thus, this work describes settings in which a given set of fundamentals—analogous to the geology, climate, and natural resources of the Galapagos Islands described by Darwin—can support as an equilibrium any one of a wide set of behaviors.

We postpone until Appendix B a formal treatment of the mathematical structure of these models, and until Part II a brief discussion of dynamics. To anticipate the latter discussion, we note here that it is possible to embed the static equilibria we will describe in an intertemporal model, as Adserà and Ray (1998) do, and to show that even when agents have perfect foresight, there may not exist an equilibrium path along which an economy is able to break out of a "bad" equilibrium. The trap holds.

We present below models of *market* economies with a large number of participants, so that each ignores the effect of his actions on others, and, in fact, that effect is infinitesimal. (We thus focus on the Nash equilibria.) The models are structurally similar to *games* with strategic complementarities, but there are some important conceptual distinctions. In the game-theoretic models, the very notion of strategic interactions suggests that each player is aware that his actions may affect the actions of others, whereas in the market equilibrium models on which we focus, such strategic interactions are ruled out by assumption. We would argue that for analyzing problems of markets, the market models are far more relevant than the game-theoretic models (although the latter may be important in understanding the interaction between an isolated tenant and his landlord).

1. R&D Spillovers. One way to conceptualize the kind of R&D that most producers undertake is that it is a transformation of a set of known facts and accepted principles into a potentially profitable new application. In this view, the expected return to an investment in R&D rises as the stock of ideas that are in the public domain increases. If some part of the outcome of private research seeps into the "public pool," the more private research that is conducted, the larger is the pool of ideas on which each producer draws. With a richer stock of ideas, the incentive of each producer to undertake R&D rises (Romer 1986).

To analyze this situation, consider a simple model in which the profit (utility) of any producer (all producers are assumed identical) depends on prices, his own level of R&D (his action a^i, which can be any value between 0 and 1), and the level of R&D of all others (their action a). Since we will be concerned here only with symmetric equilibria, we consider only the case in which all other producers choose the same action. Thus, we write the profit function as $U^i[a^i; a, p(a)]$, where p is the price vector (which itself depends on the vector of actions of the agents). Assume for each agent decreasing marginal returns to an increase in the level of its action. Each agent chooses its action to maximize its profit, given the actions of others. (Each agent is small enough that there are no strategic interactions, and it ignores its effect on p.) The reaction function

$$(1) \qquad u^i_1[a^i; a, p(a)] = 0$$

characterizes the action that the representative agent i will take for all possible values of a selected by the remaining actors. The function u^i_1 is

Figure 2. Dual Stable Equilibria in a Model
with Symmetric Actors

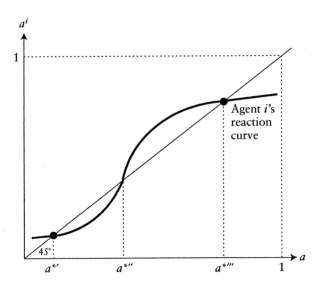

the partial derivative of u^i with respect to the first argument a^i. Equation (1) states that, given a, the agent cannot obtain a higher payoff through a marginal change in the level of his action. Figure 2 depicts the case in which a higher action a by all other agents will lead the remaining agent i to follow suit: formally, a higher action by other agents increases the marginal return to higher action by each. We say that the actions of different agents are *complements*.

The interior, symmetric equilibria are values of a^* that solve the equation:

$$(2) \qquad\qquad u^i_1 [a^*; a^*, p(a^*)] = 0.$$

Multiple equilibria may occur if the complementarities across agents are sufficiently large. Figure 2 illustrates a stable low-level equilibrium at $a^{*\prime}$ and a stable high-level equilibrium at $a^{*\prime\prime}$. When others do little R&D, it does not pay any firm to do much R&D. A shock that changes the level of R&D by each firm to a level even slightly above $a^{*\prime\prime}$ may generate a response that shifts the equilibrium to $a^{*\prime\prime\prime}$ (see Romer 1986 and Krugman 1991 for a discussion of dynamics).

The model captures the simple idea of positive spillovers across agents. In contrast, in neoclassical theory the only endogenous variables that affect an agent are prices. Prices always point the way to efficient allocations because markets are *complete*. (That is, there would need to be a mechanism by which one firm would be compensated by other firms for the spillover effects of its R&D.)

2. Spillovers from Bureaucrats, Rent-Seekers, and Collectivist Enforcers. The literature on coordination problems concerns not only the *level* of activities (such as R&D or investment) but also the *kinds* of behaviors and institutions that characterize an economy. Do individuals behave bureaucratically, or do they seek out innovations? Do they rent-seek, or produce? In order to enforce contracts, do they rely on sanctions applied by informal groups, by the individual, or by the state? An individual's behavior creates externalities. The externalities can determine the *ranking* of alternative courses of behavior. This can lead, as in the preceding example, to the existence of multiple equilibria, each with a different reward structure. We consider these three cases below.[17]

"Bureaucratic" versus "innovative" behavior. Sah and Stiglitz (1989a) formulate a model of societal equilibrium in which individuals can choose to behave "bureaucratically" or "innovatively." Bureaucrats make life more difficult for innovators, and conversely.

Let x be the fraction of the population that chooses to be innovative. Let $U(I; x, p)$ be the utility associated with the innovative strategy, and let $U(B; x, p)$ be the utility associated with the bureaucratic strategy. Each individual chooses the activity that yields him the greater utility, taking x and the price vector p as given. If most people choose to behave bureaucratically, the rewards to innovation will be low, and it may pay only a few people to behave innovatively. But if most people behave innovatively, the rewards to innovation may be high, rendering that also an equilibrium. An interior equilibrium (where x is between 0 and 1) is a fraction x^* that solves the equation

$$U[I; x^*, p(x^*)] = U[B; x^*, p(x^*)]$$

and there may be multiple such equilibria. "Corner" equilibria where all agents make the same choice may also exist—one entailing bureaucratic behavior if

$$U[I; 0, p(0)] < U[B; 0, p(0)]$$

and another entailing innovative behavior if

$$U[I; 1, p(1)] > U[B; 1, p(1)].$$

A slight variant of this model can be used to explore evolutionary dynamics. Assume that, rather than the individual's *choosing* to be either innovative or bureaucratic, differential reproductive rates are a function of utility levels, so that

$$d \ln x/dt = k[U(I; x, p) - U(B; x, p)]$$

for some positive constant k. Then the set of equilibria will be the same as before, and the equilibrium on which the economy converges depends on its history. Historical events—for example, the opening of a country to international competition that differentially hurts "bureaucratic" firms—may move the economy from one equilibrium to another, thereby affecting the long-run rate of technological progress.

Rent-seekers versus producers. Another variant of the preceding model focuses on rent-seeking (Murphy, Shleifer, and Vishny 1993; Acemoglu 1995). This variant sheds light on why some countries fail to grow at all when public and private rent-seeking makes property rights insecure. One reason is that "rent-seeking, particularly rent-seeking by government officials, is likely to hurt innovative activities more than everyday production" (Murphy, Shleifer, and Vishny 1993: 409). "Public rent-seeking attacks innovation, since innovators need government-supplied goods, such as permits, licenses, import quotas, and so on . . ." (412).

Murphy, Shleifer, and Vishny consider a farm economy in which individuals choose to undertake one of three activities. An individual can be an "innovator," which in some economies might mean merely producing a cash crop for the market; the key point is that his output is vulnerable to rent-seeking. Or he can produce a subsistence crop, in which case his output is not vulnerable to rent-seeking. Or he can be a rent-seeker and expropriate part of the output of the innovators. An equilibrium is an allocation of the population among the three activities. The authors make the plausible assumption that over some range, as more resources move into rent-seeking, returns to innovation fall faster than returns to rent-seeking do. As a consequence, the returns to rent-seeking relative to innovation increase, and this can give rise to multiple equilibria. In one equilibrium, the fraction of innovators is low and returns to innovation are low because the fraction of rent-seekers is high. But there is another equilibrium at which the reverse is true.

"Collectivist" versus "individualist" enforcement. Most development economists are now agreed that among the most important sets of institutions in an economy are those that provide for the enforcement of contracts. Greif (1994) examines the cultural factors that might explain why two premodern societies (the Maghribi in North Africa and the Genoese) evolved along different trajectories of societal organization. To illustrate the main ideas, he presents a model in which there are two kinds of actors: merchants and agents. Agents carry out overseas trade on behalf of the merchants. A merchant makes one decision: he chooses either collectivist or individualist enforcement of his contracts with agents. Collectivist enforcement entails punishing (by refusing to hire) an agent who is known to have cheated any merchant in the collective group. Individualist enforcement entails a merchant's punishing

only agents who have cheated him. Greif shows that if the merchant believes that collectivist enforcement is likely to occur, in general it will not be in his interest to hire an agent who is known to have cheated other merchants. That makes such expectations self-fulfilling. The intuition for this result is straightforward: an agent who already has damaged his reputation has little to lose by cheating again, and so he will be more easily tempted to cheat his current employer than would an agent with an unblemished reputation. That makes the agent who has already damaged his reputation by cheating less desirable to hire. If, however, the merchant believes that individualist enforcement will occur, the motive for collectivist enforcement is absent. Thus, two equilibria, one entailing collectivist enforcement and one entailing individualist enforcement, can exist. The equilibrium that is "selected" will depend on beliefs (culture).

In the short run, reliance on individualist enforcement will be more costly, since it forgoes the stronger, group-level punishment mechanism. But in the long run, individualist enforcement will strengthen the forces that contribute to the emergence of formal, state-level mechanisms to enforce contracts and adjudicate conflicts. By facilitating the widening of markets, such institutions tend to promote long-run growth. Greif (1994) interprets the history of the West in just such terms.

3. Spillovers and Inequality. An important feature of economies is the way that differences in individual attributes give rise to differences in outcomes. Does the market reproduce, attenuate, or magnify them? Is the "mapping" unique? We present two examples where it is not; there can be multiple, Pareto-ranked equilibria.

Informational externalities. The actions that people take often reveal information not only about themselves but also about others who did *not* take those actions. This will be true whenever some hidden quality of an individual is correlated with the net benefit of taking that action. Intuition might suggest that rational individuals would always make the efficient choices over screening. But because their choice creates "informational externalities," this need not be the case, as illustrated in one of the earliest models of coordination problems (Stiglitz 1975).

The model is based on the idea that a key role of education is not only to produce human capital but also to screen individuals by innate ability. Education credentials sort people into distinct groups in the labor market. Stiglitz (1975) presents a model in which education has *no* effect on innate abilities but can serve as a screen. The model addresses two simple questions: Is the equilibrium unique? Is it Pareto optimal?

Individuals are assumed to have private information about their ability. The higher their ability, the lower their nonpecuniary cost (e.g., the cost of effort) of obtaining an education credential. Employers cannot directly ascertain an individual's ability, but they can observe whether or not he has a credential. They can also observe the *average* ability of those who are, and who are not, credentialed.

In choosing whether to obtain a credential, an individual compares the gain—the difference between the wage of a credentialed and an uncredentialed worker—with the cost of obtaining the credential. The cost is given by $C = C(z)$, which depends on ability z. Consider the simplest case, where an individual is either high ability, H, or low ability, L. It is easy to see that two equilibria exist, one entailing screening for the high-ability type and one entailing no screening, if

$$C(L) > w(H) - w(L) > C(H)$$

and

$$w(H) - \mu < C(H)$$

where μ represents the average productivity level in the population. The above inequalities imply that in the no-screening equilibrium, the high-ability as well as the low-ability individuals obtain *higher* incomes. Yet if all other high-ability agents obtain a credential, each high-ability agent is better off doing likewise, and so the case of screening is also an equilibrium.

This model illustrates the idea of *complementarities in the process of market creation*. To see this, let action a, where a is binary, be "to screen" or "not to screen." Individuals' choices determine whether there is one labor market or two (one for each ability level). If the above inequalities are satisfied, then two equilibria exist, and the one with just one labor market is better for everybody.[18]

The structure of ownership: A parable of capitalism. The next example considers the choice of contracts made by individuals of differing wealth. Hoff and Sen (2000) consider an economy in which capital markets are imperfect and, as a result, the cost of obtaining an equity stake in one's business or home is higher for low-wealth individuals. But an equity stake is valuable because it creates high-powered incentives for effort. The standard treatment of this problem assumes no spillovers across agents. But the evidence suggests that spillovers are important. Ideas spill over across firms in Silicon Valley; a breakthrough into an export market by one entrepreneur increases opportunities to export by others in the economy; an improvement by one homeowner unavoidably increases the value of the parcels owned by others in the neighborhood.[19] Thus, one impact of a larger number of entrepreneurs (or homeowners) is that the return to entrepreneurship in an industrial belt (or to homeownership in a neighborhood) may increase. As in the preceding example, there may be multiple, Pareto-ranked equilibria in the choices made by an individual of a given type. And once we allow for an additional level of complexity—free migration across industrial belts (or residential neighborhoods)—the consequences of coordination failures can be magnified.

To be more specific, consider an environment in which the cumulative distribution function of endowment wealth is $F(W)$. (For the moment, we treat the set of agents in the interaction environment as fixed.) Suppose that each firm is managed by either a salaried wage earner or an individual with a substantial equity stake in the firm (an "entrepreneur"). The capital market is imperfect: the interest rate for individual borrowers is higher than that for lenders. This means that an individual with low wealth will choose to become an entrepreneur only if his expected return is high enough to offset the transaction costs of borrowing. Each individual chooses the activity that yields him the greater utility, taking as given the fraction x of firms in the economy managed by entrepreneurs. Let $V(e, x, W)$ be the utility associated with high effort e and any given wealth level W, and let $V(n, x, W)$ be the utility associated with the same parameters and with low effort, n. Then if an interior equilibrium exists, it is characterized by a critical level of endowment wealth, W^*, at which the individual is just indifferent between entrepreneurship and wage-earning; that is,

$$V[e, x, W^*] = V[n, x, W^*].$$

An increase in x raises the left-hand side more than the right-hand side if there are complementarities among entrepreneurs. A fall in wealth lowers the left-hand side more than the right-hand side, since, in addition to the loss of consumption, there is an increase in the transaction costs of borrowing. Therefore associated with a higher x is a lower W^*: we can write the cutoff wealth level as

$$W^* = W^*(x).$$

Given the distribution of wealth in the economy, $F(.)$, associated with any value of wealth W is a proportion of the population, x, whose income exceeds W. We can write this proportion as

$$x = 1 - F(W) \equiv x(W).$$

The simultaneous solution of these two equations characterizes the equilibria of the model. These two downwardly sloping curves can have multiple crossings. As illustrated in Figure 3, there may exist a low-level equilibrium in which a minority fraction $x^{*\prime}$ of individuals buys enough equity to become entrepreneurs (who put in high effort); the resulting local positive externalities are low; and this outcome supports the majority decision to stay with a wage contract and produce low output. Only individuals with wealth at or above the critical level $W^{*\prime}$ become entrepreneurs. By contrast, when a larger fraction ($x^{*\prime\prime}$ or $x^{*\prime\prime\prime}$) of individuals become entrepreneurs by buying equity in the firms they manage, they generate the higher level of local spillovers that makes

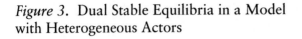

Figure 3. Dual Stable Equilibria in a Model
with Heterogeneous Actors

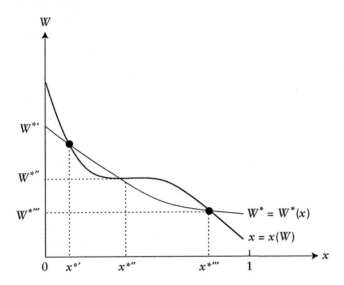

that better state of affairs an equilibrium. The critical wealth level falls, respectively, to $W^{*''}$ or $W^{*'''}$.

A further level of complexity and realism can be introduced into this model by recognizing that many of the spillovers that are critical for growth are *local*, not *global* (for example, they are restricted to a Silicon Valley or a single residential community, and agents are spread across various industrial belts or residential communities). Intuition might suggest that free migration across areas would resolve the problem of coordination failures. This would indeed tend to happen if individuals could costlessly form new groups and move into new business or residential areas. Suppose, however, that suitable land is in fixed supply. Then land prices will equilibrate to make even those areas with coordination failures desirable to some set of individuals. In this case migration can exacerbate the consequences of a coordination failure. Hoff and Sen (2000) show that when complementarities among entrepreneurs (or homeowners) are sufficiently strong, rich and poor agents will stratify by "contract type" and income—the rich in areas with a high level of "stakeholders" and positive externalities, and the poor in areas with low levels of both. In this way one can explain "pockets of underdevelopment" within an industrial country without assuming any innate differences in abilities or preferences among agents.[20]

4. *"Big Push" Theory: Linkages.* Rosenstein-Rodan's (1943) "big push" theory is a celebrated early statement of coordination problems in development. Rosenstein-Rodan suggested a variety of mechanisms through which a coordination failure can occur. Consider his example of "missing linkages." He argued that it did not pay a firm to make, for instance, steel if there were no firms that used steel, but no firm would be created that used steel if steel was not available. Such problems do not arise in the neoclassical model because there is a complete set of markets for commodities that are or could be produced, and the "virtual" prices of steel would induce entry of both steel-producing and steel-using firms. But even in the absence of a complete set of markets, this particular example lacks cogency because a single firm would normally be able to produce both steel and products that use steel. Only if it could be argued that there were large diseconomies of scope would the coordination failure problem seem to be significant.

A crucial feature on which the relevance of the big push models rests is diffuse externalities, where the interaction effects occur through systemwide variables such as aggregate demand, industrial demand for inputs, or search costs. Murphy, Shleifer, and Vishny (1989) formalized the big push theory by focusing on a variety of such diffuse spillover effects. The best-known of their models focuses on demand spillovers: expansion of the high-productivity manufacturing sector leads to higher incomes, which leads to higher demand for the products of that sector.

But although diffuse externalities are necessary for a convincing big push theory, they are not sufficient. For example, in a global economy a steel-using firm could purchase steel from abroad, and a steel-producing firm could sell steel abroad. International trade resolves the coordination problem, as Tinbergen (1967) recognized early on. A small developing country should, at least in the long run, be able to find an essentially boundless demand for its products. The experience of the export-oriented strategies of the East Asian economies suggests that limitations in demand have not played a critical role in limiting those economies' growth.

But there are other formalizations of Rosenstein-Rodan's theory in which international trade does not resolve the coordination failure. Modern technologies often require a variety of *local* inputs and support services. One version of big push theory focuses on the nontradability of a range of differentiated, intermediate inputs used in the "advanced sector" of the economy that are produced under increasing returns to scale and imperfect competition (Helpman and Krugman 1985; Rodríguez-Clare 1996; Rodrik 1996). An expansion of the "advanced sector" increases the demand for these nontraded inputs, which lowers their average costs and increases the available variety. With greater variety of intermediate inputs, production is more efficient. (The intermediate sector is modeled as one of differentiated products, as in

Dixit and Stiglitz 1977.) It can thus be the case that when all other firms enter the "advanced sector," it pays the remaining firm to do so, but when all other firms remain in the traditional, low-technology sector, it pays the remaining firm to do so, too. A low-level equilibrium can thus be sustained even when the economy is fully open to international trade.

There are several ways of thinking about the nontradable inputs. One is that they represent physical input goods. Another is that they represent different categories of specialized skilled labor, such as computer technicians and software designers. As Rodrik (1996: 2) argues, "A worker's decision to invest in a specialized skill depends both on the demand for the particular skill and the existence of complementary skills in the economy." But this example raises the question, why cannot a single firm train the labor force it needs and thereby internalize the externalities? The next section presents a two-period model that shows why even perfect contracting *within* a firm may fail to provide a complete solution to the interdependence among the decisions made by workers and firms.

5. "Big Push" Theory: Search Costs. This version of the big push theory focuses on the problem of search in the labor market. The productivity of training depends on the ability of trained labor to find employers who have innovated; this ability, in turn, depends on the proportion of firms in the economy that have innovated. To capture this idea, we sketch a simple version of the model of Acemoglu (1997). There are two types of actors: firms, which may adopt new technology or not, and workers, who may become trained to use the new technology or not. The numbers of firms and workers are large and equal, and each firm employs just one worker. There are two time periods. In the first period each firm is matched with one worker; they jointly make decisions about training and innovation, and there is complete contracting between them—that is, there are no information problems or transaction costs. At the end of the first period there is some risk of separation. If separation occurs, a firm has to find a new worker, and a worker has to find a new firm. In the second period, output is produced.

If the worker is trained and his firm is one that has adopted new technology, the value of joint output is increased by α. Skills and technology are assumed to be strongly complementary, so that if either training or innovation does not occur, there is no payoff to skills or to new technology. Let C represent the combined cost of the two investments (training and innovation), and let r represent the interest rate. To make the model interesting, assume that training and innovation are potentially valuable: that is, $\alpha > C(1 + r)$.

A potential coordination failure arises in this economy because there is a risk of separation between the firm and the worker at the end of period 1. Assume that with probability s, the worker and firm will receive an adverse, match-specific shock that causes them to separate. In that event, a firm has to find a new employee, and a worker has to find a new employer. The time line is illustrated below:

Period 1		*Period 2*
Decisions about investment in innovation and training are made by the firm and the worker.	Separation between the firm and the worker occurs with probability s.	Output is produced.

Training imparts to the worker skills that he can use with any firm that has adopted the new technology. Therefore, if there were no search costs in the labor market, separation between a firm and an employee would not create a loss: if separation occurred, the worker would simply move on to another firm that had adopted the new technology, and all the surplus from training and investment would be captured by the firms and workers that made the investments. But suppose that search is costly. Then matching will be imperfect. There is no guarantee that the firm with the investment in the new technology will be matched with the worker who has the training.

Let ϕ represent the probability of a good match. For simplicity, we assume that the matching process is random (but any assumption short of costless, perfect matching would serve, too). Then ϕ is the proportion of firms with the new technology (which is equal to the proportion of the workers who are trained). From the perspective of the firm and its worker making their investment decisions in period 1, the combined returns from training and innovation are equal to $-(1 + r)C + (1 - s)\alpha + s\phi\alpha$. This says that with probability $1 - s$, the pair does not separate and so they capture the return α on their investment. With probability s, the pair separates, and thus the expected combined return on their investment is only $\phi\alpha$.

By substituting $\phi = 1$, we can see that an equilibrium at which all firms innovate and all workers are trained exists: the private returns to training and investment are positive. By substituting $\phi = 0$, we can see that an equilibrium without training and innovation may also exist. The combined expected gains to the firm and the worker from innovation and training when no one else adopts the new technology are only $(1 - s)\alpha - (1 + r)C$, which will be negative if s is sufficiently close to one. In this example, therefore, *a possible equilibrium is no innovation and no training in the economy.* Another consequence of costly search, which we do not develop here but which Acemoglu (1997) develops, is that there is imperfect competition in the labor market. This depresses the worker's return to training and further erodes his incentives to train.

The reason for the multiplicity of equilibria is that a firm's likelihood of finding the right worker depends on the *thickness* of the market (the number of trained workers). Similarly, the worker's likelihood of finding the right employer depends on the *thickness* of the market provided by firms that have adopted the new technology.[21] Of course, without a risk of separation ($s = 0$), there would be no inefficiencies, since there would be no interactions with future employees or employers. The inefficiency arises because of an externality between the worker and his *future* employer, and between the firm and its *future* employee, that cannot be internalized because the identity of the actor with whom one may be matched is unknown.

To recapitulate, the example shows how search costs in the labor market can make the decisions of firms and workers highly interdependent in ways that are not captured by prices. Some economies may not invest in new technology and training as a result of a coordination failure arising from search costs.

Gaps in Knowledge

The preceding set of hypotheses about obstacles to development focuses on coordination problems ("ecology"). Another, distinct set of hypotheses argues that it is gaps in knowledge—between industrial and developing countries, and between more advanced firms within developing countries and less advanced ones—that account for lack of development.

There are two separate issues. One is barriers to the flow of knowledge: the disease environment of an economy can be a barrier if technology transfer requires the flow of people. Accounts of Africa's interactions with the rest of the world over the past 500 years suggest that malaria has been a major barrier to Africa's normal integration into the world economy (Gallup and Sachs 1999). Nonnatives lack the resistance to the disease that Africans have acquired, and available medicines are imperfect.[22] Bloom and Sachs (1998) estimate that the economic effect of the single deadliest strain of malaria is to reduce growth of gross domestic product (GDP) by more than 1 percent per year.

Another issue is underinvestment in knowledge. Knowledge has public good properties, and even when it is not a pure public good, there can be important externalities (see, for example, Arrow 1962a; Gilbert, Dasgupta, and Stiglitz 1982; Stiglitz 1999). Arrow (1962b) hypothesized in his famous model of learning-by-doing that in an emerging industry, each firm's profitability depends on the accumulated experience in the industry. Such spillovers would mean that market forces will not elicit optimal investment.

Spillovers occur as well in the process of acquiring *localized* information that is relevant to production. Uncertainty about the suitability of local conditions for production means that individual producers, as they experiment with new technology, can play a role in reducing, in future periods, the information barriers to adoption of new technology (Hoff 1997). Economists have begun to try to measure such information spillovers (Besley and Case 1994; Foster and Rosenzweig 1995; Conley and Udry 1999). For instance, Conley and Udry survey Ghanaian villages in which an established system of maize and cassava production is being transformed into intensive production of pineapple for export to Europe. Their objective is to determine exactly what farmers know about others' agricultural activities and how they know it. They find that adoption decisions, as well as the profitability of a farmer's pineapple operation, depend on local characteristics of the farmer's information network. This helps to explain why in some survey areas— but not in others with similar soils, climate, and so on—little pineapple is grown, despite its seemingly high potential profitability. The characteristics of information networks seem to explain why there is technological divergence *even across villages.*

II. Perspectives on Policy

The changes in economic theories of development outlined in previous sections imply marked changes in policy perspectives. Some of the implied changes are obvious: if differences between industrial and developing countries depend on differences in knowledge as much as on differences in capital, policies to narrow the knowledge gap take on a first-order importance. As a consequence, improvements in secondary and tertiary education systems, not just increased access to primary education, become important (World Bank 1999b). If geography matters, policies need to focus on addressing the limitations imposed by geography—for example, on malaria eradication and on migration policies. In this part, we want to go beyond specific policy recommendations to theoretical issues regarding the nature of interventions and reform strategies.

Two Extreme Views: "Rational Development" and Public Choice Theory

Implicit in much of the policy discussion in the past have been two extreme views of policy interventions. One is based on the premise of "rational development": all that is required is to provide individuals in the economy with information about the consequences of different policies, and Coasian rationality will ensure that the parties will make use of that information to arrive at an efficient solution. To be sure, there may be market failures, but social institutions arise spontaneously to address them. Thus, only lack of information could lead to "inefficient outcomes." (In some variants of this view, government appears as a benevolent dictator outside the economy, with the ability to act freely on it. Thus, all that a policy analyst needs to do is to find out which policies maximize social welfare and transmit that information to the government, and it will be acted on.)

Few today hold to that view. If the adviser shows that there is an optimal set of tariffs and encourages the government to put in place a highly differentiated tariff structure, the advice might be followed. The tariff structure, however, will depend not on the subtle deadweight-loss arguments of the policy adviser but, rather, on the corrupting influence of special-interest groups trying to seize the opportunities afforded by a differentiated tariff structure to increase protection for their industries. To be sure, they may even follow the "rules of the game," hiring economic analysts to show that an industry satisfies the conditions stipulated for higher tariff protection. But of course, both they and the government know that these are simply arguments needed to satisfy public demands for probity.

The second polar view is the extreme *public choice* view: as social scientists, we can just watch and interpret the playing out of the development drama—we cannot change policies. In this view, political forces produce an equilibrium set of policies. There are no degrees of freedom for normative intervention—a situation that has been called the *determinacy paradox* (Bhagwati, Brecher, and Srinivasan 1984).

We—and we dare say most development economists—reject both of these extreme views of the role of outsiders' advice. Conditional on the information available, equilibria are often not Pareto efficient. Institutions that arise in response to a market failure may not only fail to cure it but may actually make matters worse, as we saw in the previous sections. Outsiders can, however, have an effect on outcomes—and in ways other than simply changing the information sets of participants. But our understanding of the processes by which interventions do affect outcomes is seriously incomplete, and many of the failures of the past can be traced to naïveté in intervention strategies.

For instance, there is mounting evidence that the practice of conditioning foreign aid to a country on its adoption of policy reforms does not work, at least in the sense of leading to sustained changes in policies that increase growth and reduce inequality and poverty. One cannot "buy" good policies (World Bank 1999a). There are good reasons for this: it is widely recognized today that successful policies need to have the country's "ownership"—not only the support *of* the government, but also a broad consensus *within* the population—to be effectively implemented. Policies imposed from the outside will be circumvented, may induce resentment, and will not withstand the vicissitudes of the political process (see Bruno 1996; Stiglitz 1998c).

Theories of the Ineffectiveness of Government Intervention

The issue raised by the public choice school is whether an adviser can influence policy. A second, distinct issue is whether, in a market economy, government intervention can promote good outcomes. There is a long tradition in economics that the only proper role for the government is to define and enforce property rights and to provide public goods. Beyond that, government interventions are likely to be—in the extreme versions, inevitably will be—ineffective, unnecessary, or counterproductive.[23]

The fact that most of the "success" cases of economic growth have involved heavy doses of government intervention provides a strong counterweight to these general allegations. For instance, in the United States the government has, since 1863, played a role in financial market regulation. Evidence that since World War II downturns have been shallower and shorter and expansions longer is consistent with the hypothesis that better macroeconomic management does work. Even in industrial policies, the United States has a credible history—from the founding of the telecommunications industry, with the first telegraph line between Baltimore and Washington in 1842, to its most recent contribution to that industry, the creation of the Internet; from the support of research and dissemination in the dominant sector of the 19th century, agriculture, to support of research in the dominant high-technology industries of today. Still, it is worth disposing quickly of the major theoretical arguments underlying the ineffectiveness of intervention.

Government is unnecessary: anything the government can do, the private sector can do better. The fact is that government is endowed with powers which the private sector does not have, and these powers are essential in addressing the public good and externality problems that are rife throughout the economy. Coasians are simply wrong in arguing that private parties by themselves, with given, well-defined property rights, always resolve these issues.[24]

Anything government does will be undone by the private sector. Although there are specific models for which this assertion is true (see, for instance, Lucas 1973; Lucas and Prescott 1974), it is generally not true—for example, when government changes relative prices through taxation. Still, there is an important moral to these models: the actual consequences of government policies can be markedly different from the intended ones.

Government is always captured by special-interest groups (Stigler 1971). To be sure, there are incentives for producer special-interest groups to try to capture, for instance, the regulatory process. But there are countervailing incentives for other groups. Stigler does not explain why in some states it is consumer groups that capture, say, electricity regulation, while in others it appears to be producer groups. In this, too, there is an important moral: political processes are critical, but the outcome of political processes is more complicated than simple theories of capture would suggest.

A variety of interventions can affect outcomes. Below we consider several broad kinds of interventions: (a) interventions to solve coordination problems, (b) information as an intervention, (c) interventions to change the dynamics of the political process, and (d) interventions to change the distribution of wealth.

Interventions to Solve a Coordination Problem

Some of the multiple-equilibria models discussed above suggest interventions that can move an economy to a more favorable equilibrium. But just as the equilibrium set of behaviors in a decentralized economy may not be Pareto efficient, one cannot jump to the conclusion that Pareto improvements are likely to emerge from the political process. (At the end of this part we provide examples of cases in which they do not.)

Moreover, to make the analysis of intervention precise requires a dynamic framework. For example, only in a dynamic framework can one ask whether an initial coordination failure will in fact transmit itself over time. Why would not forward-looking agents, with sufficiently low discount rates, adopt a *path* (which might include the option of changing their behavior several times) that would permit as an equilibrium a self-fulfilling move away from a bad equilibrium to a good one? Is there really any scope for policy? Adserà and Ray (1998) address these questions in a setting in which each agent makes a discrete choice between two activities (which could be interpreted as entry into a high-tech versus a low-tech sector). They obtain a striking result: *if* the positive externalities from moving to the more favorable set of activities appear with a time lag (that can be made arbitrarily short), *then the final outcome depends entirely on initial conditions unless there is some gain to being the first to switch*. To put it another way, unless there is some gain to being among the first to switch, each agent will rationally wait for others to switch first, and so no one will switch at all! Initial conditions will thus determine the entire equilibrium outcome.

Adserà and Ray's model shows that in a variety of circumstances there is a *potential* role for policy to enable an economy to break free of history. A temporary subsidy can "force" an equilibrium, and yet once the equilibrium is attained, the subsidy is no longer necessary to support it. We consider several such interventions below.

1. Affirmative Action and Anticorruption Programs. A change in a legal statute may be able to force an equilibrium if the path to the new equilibrium entails a revision of beliefs and the revised beliefs sustain the new equilibrium. Stiglitz (1974b) shows how affirmative action programs can eliminate equilibria in which productivity is unequal between groups (e.g., races or ethnic groups) whose innate abilities are identical but whose histories are different. Productivity between groups may be unequal if, for example, individuals' preferences for education depend on their parents' education and if the resulting differences in education lead to differential expectations by employers regarding the payoffs to training workers. Decisions by employers may then lock different groups into different positions in the income distribution. An affirmative action program changes the behavior of employers, the new behavior creates a new "history" and reveals information about the discriminated-against group, and the revised information can lead to an equilibrium in which prospective employers no longer want to discriminate. Similarly, Tirole's (1996) model of group reputation, discussed above, demonstrates the role that an anticorruption program of sufficient duration and severity can play in switching an economy from an equilibrium with high corruption—sustained by expectations of high corruption—to one with low corruption, sustained by expectations of low corruption.

2. Enactment of Social Norms into Law. Following Cooter (2000), suppose that a person who punishes someone for violating a social norm risks confrontation or revenge but that this risk falls as the proportion of people willing to punish increases. Suppose also that enactment into statutory law of the social norm (say, to use generally accepted accounting standards, or to send children to school) lowers the individual's private cost of enforcement because it creates the possibility that violators of the norm will face civil punishment. In doing so, it may cause the individual to believe that other individuals will enforce the norm, and the expectation can be self-fulfilling. Enactment of the law can thus "pull in" private activity rather than "crowding it out" (as occurs in traditional analysis of government provision of public goods). By extension, a state governed by laws that mirror social norms (a "rule of law state") tends to be one that is hard to corrupt, whereas a state in which law is imposed and enforced from above (the "rule of state law") tends to be costly, ineffective, and easily corrupted (Cooter 1997). A related view of statutory law is developed by Basu (2000), who argues that the *only* way government-enacted law can influence an economy is to switch it from one equilibrium to another: if an outcome (including a set of norms consistent with that outcome) is not a candidate equilibrium absent the law, it is still not an equilibrium under any conceivable legal regime.

3. Temporary Wage Floors. There are situations in which an economy is characterized by multiple equilibria, some preferred by a policymaker over others, but in which the equilibria cannot be Pareto ranked. In those cases there may be interventions that switch an economy to the better equilibrium by forcing a change in the distribution of income. The classic example of multiple equilibria in the neoclassical model arises when the labor supply curve is backward-bending. Then there may exist one market equilibrium with low wages, high labor supply, and high profits and another with high wages, low labor supply, and low profits. The low-wage equilibrium is more favorable to capitalists, the other to workers. In such a setting, minimum wage legislation could serve to "rule out" the low-wage equilibrium. Once the high-wage equilibrium was attained, the minimum wage law would not be a binding constraint. That is, no effort would need to be expended to enforce the wage because, starting from the high-wage equilibrium, there is no supply of workers at the lower wage.[25]

Information as an Intervention

Although by itself information often is not sufficient to ensure that more efficient equilibria predominate, it can be an effective intervention in many cases, for it does change the behavior of participants (see, for example, Dixit 1996). Rules concerning the disclosure of information and standards of accounting change behavior, if only by drawing attention to certain relevant "facts." Disclosure of information can also make possible informal enforcement of community standards. In the area of pollution control, for instance, there is evidence that informal enforcement has had significant effects (see Pargal and Wheeler's 1996 study of pollution levels across Indonesian districts).

It is precisely because information does affect the behavior of voters that governments often work so hard to keep it secret (Stiglitz 1998b). Although there is no general theorem ensuring that private parties will engage in the socially desirable level of disclosure, there are strong reasons to believe that incumbents in the political process will work hard to suppress relevant information.[26]

Indeed, information about the importance of information has even affected the amount of information that is disclosed and the form in which it is disclosed. While it is true that different disclosure rules may induce behavior to try to circumvent the requirements, typically these are imperfect, particularly if the disclosure requirements are well designed.

Interventions That Affect the Dynamics of the Political Process

Public choice theory has provided considerable insights into the nature of political processes, including the problems associated with the formation of interest groups (Olson 1965; Becker 1983). For instance, free-rider problems play an important role in determining which interest groups form, just as they play an important role in the provision of public goods more generally. Public actions affect the costs and benefits associated with interest-group formation. Since the costs of interest-group formation are, to some extent at least, fixed costs, interventions that affect the dynamics of the political process—thereby affecting subsequent outcomes—can be thought of as *deep* interventions. They entail irreversibilities.

An example of the dynamics of the political process may help illustrate what we have in mind. Assume that the government is contemplating privatizing a monopoly. There are several potential buyers. Each has an interest in ensuring that the regulations that prevail after privatization allow him to continue to enjoy the monopoly profits and perhaps even leverage the monopoly power further. But each, thinking that he has a small probability of winning, is unwilling to spend much to ensure this "collective" good (or bad, depending on one's perspective). Moreover, each may face large costs of identifying who the other potential buyers are. Even if a potential buyer succeeds in identifying the others, if they are numerous there will still be a free-rider problem, each claiming publicly that he himself will obtain high profits through increased efficiency rather than by exploiting monopoly power.[27] But *once the privatization has occurred*, there is a single party who is the "winner." There no longer is a collective-action problem, and the winner has the incentive and resources to fight legislation imposing regulation or competition. Thus, before the privatization, it may be possible to pass rules to promote competition (since there is no organized resistance in the private sector) and there may be (admittedly weak) public interest groups pushing for it.[28] The sequencing of reforms—that is, whether regulatory policies precede or follow privatization—matters. In one sequence, the result may be a competitive or regulated industry, where the benefits of privatization in terms of lower consumer prices are realized. In the other sequence, one may end up with an unregulated monopoly, which, to be sure, may be more efficient than it was as a public sector producer but which may be more efficient not only in producing goods but also in exploiting consumers.

Deep interventions need to be distinguished from the *shallow* interventions that typically make up a part of "reform" packages in negotiations between borrower countries and international financial organizations. Consider measures to lower tariffs. Interventions that impose such tariff reforms as part of conditionality or as part of a World Trade Organization (WTO) agreement do not necessarily change the underlying political forces. If they do not, a process that Finger (1998) calls *political fungibility* occurs: the political forces that generated the initial trade barriers simply look for other, WTO-legal, interventions. These may have the same protective effect but may be more distortionary.

The increased use of nontariff barriers, including antidumping measures, in developing countries is consistent with this theory.

It is precisely because history matters that interventions can be effective in the long run. A perturbation to the system at one date can have permanent effects. (By contrast, in neoclassical and related theories, it is fundamentals—including those associated with the political process—that determine long-run outcomes.) A particular set of circumstances in which history can matter is when there are multiple equilibria and an historical shock "selects" the equilibrium. A large enough disturbance can move an economy in a direction that converges to a different steady-state equilibrium.

Interventions to Change the Distribution of Wealth

Among the most important sets of interventions are those that change the distribution of wealth. Such interventions can lead to a new steady-state distribution of wealth, W^*, defined by

$$W^* = A(W^*)W^*$$

where A is the transition matrix and W is the vector of wealth levels. We write $A = A(W)$ to emphasize that the transition matrix depends on the distribution of wealth, the vector W. As was discussed in Part I, the wealth distribution affects economic performance through many channels. It affects the severity of agency problems (for example, access to financial markets), vulnerability to risk, and the institutions that arise to cope with agency problems and risk (such as sharecropping). These factors affect outcomes directly and also indirectly through the effect on prices, wages, interest rates, and the distribution of wealth in *succeeding* generations.

The wealth distribution also affects *political* support for institutions that, by facilitating or impeding individuals' participation in commercial activity, influence growth. Ongoing research explores the empirical relationship between the distribution of wealth and institutional development in New World economies beginning in the 1700s (see Engerman and Sokoloff 1997; Engerman, Haber, and Sokoloff 1999). These authors find that societies which began with greater inequality tended to place greater restrictions on access to primary schooling, access to land, the franchise, the right to vote in secret, the right to create a company, and the right to patent an invention and to protect that right in the courts. In Latin America these restrictions tended to perpetuate inequality and limit growth.

A Word of Caution: Deep versus Shallow Interventions

When interventions to promote economic reform are not "deep" in the sense defined above, not only may their effects be undone through a process of political fungibility, but they may actually be harmful, at least in some dimensions. Consider again the issue of privatization. One of the principal arguments against governments' running enterprises is that public officials skim off the rents. It is also argued that privatization eliminates the scope for this kind of political abuse.[29] In many cases, unfortunately, this has not proved to be the case. One should have been suspicious when allegedly corrupt political leaders embraced the doctrine of privatization. Perhaps it was not so much that they were converted by the sermons of the visiting priests of the new orthodoxy to give up their corrupt ways; rather, they may have seen in their preaching an opportunity to exploit the public even more. They realized that by corrupting the privatization process, they could appropriate not only some of today's rents but also a fraction of the present discounted value of rents of the future. Why leave those rents around for future politicians to grab? Should it thus come as a surprise that so many cases of privatization have been plagued by corruption? In many cases we have learned that clothing the "grabbing hand of government" in the "velvet glove of privatization" does little to impede its ability to grab.

In many cases, too, we have learned that the privatization process may even have limited efficacy in stemming the flow of *ongoing* rent-seeking by government. For instance, if local authorities have regulatory oversight (environmental, building permits, and so on), local government approval is needed for continued operation of a business. It matters not what pretext the government uses to "hold up" the company; eliminating one pretext still leaves a plethora of others. Privatization thus does not effectively tie the hands of government. Only a deep intervention that changes the nature of government behavior will succeed in addressing these concerns.[30]

Looking into Black Boxes

The issues raised above reflect one of the central themes of this chapter: modern development economics has been looking into, trying to explain, the black boxes of the past. How do we explain institutions? What are the sources of failures of markets and of governments (an issue that we develop further in the next section)?

In the past, development theory and policy often took certain variables as *exogenous* institutional rigidities or political constraints. Modern theory has shifted the boundary between what we black-box (treat as an institutional rigidity) and what we explain within our models. This shifting boundary has strong implications for our views about policy. Here we present two further examples—on credit markets and on unemployment—each of which has been the subject of an enormous literature.

Rural Credit Markets. Early views in development economics were that village moneylenders charged usurious interest rates and that nothing could be done about it. Policy interventions had to deal with such constraints. Because the source of the market failure was not well analyzed, it was hard to tell the true nature of the institutional constraint, and this left policy in a precarious position. Assume that one really believed that high rural interest rates merely reflected the monopoly power of the moneylender. Then one might view as the solution the creation of a system of government-subsidized rural lending institutions, on the assumption that this would "provide a positive institutional alternative to the moneylender himself, something which will compete with him, remove him from the forefront, and put him in his place" (Reserve Bank of India 1954, cited in Bell 1990: 297). But once one recognizes that there are information and enforcement problems in lending to the poor which formal lenders are not well positioned to solve, it is not surprising that subsidized lending in the rural sector reached primarily large farmers who could pledge land as collateral, while small farmers continued to rely on the informal financial sector.

Pushing the analysis one step further—to the structure of competition in the informal credit sector and the determinants of the moneylender's transaction costs—Hoff and Stiglitz (1998) showed that a subsidy to rural banks need not even "trickle down" to the poor. The subsidy will normally increase the number of moneylenders (and moneylenders in many settings also act as traders, taking a part of the farmers' crop as payment for their debt). When borrowers in the informal sector have a larger number of potential outlets for their crops and more potential sources of credit, it may be harder for each moneylender to enforce repayment. With higher enforcement costs, the interest rates that moneylenders charge may even rise in response to a subsidy to rural banks! Recognition of the information and enforcement problems in rural financial markets has redirected policy in recent years toward the creation of microfinance programs and the improvement of savings institutions that are accessible to the poor (Morduch 1999).

Urban Unemployment and the Urban-Rural Wage Gap. To take a second example, assume that one believed that urban unemployment existed because the urban wage was fixed in nominal terms. Then one might impose a tax on food to raise revenues, which could be used to finance a wage subsidy, expanding employment. But surely, one might think, whatever the economic or political forces determining the wage level, workers are not so irrational as to fail to see through such a lowering of the real wage; it is real wages that all participants in the market care about. Thus, pushing the analysis beyond the simple assumption of a nominal fixed wage, one quickly comes to the presumption that it is some measure of real wages that should be assumed rigid. The early models, however, simply assumed that the nominal level of urban wages was fixed and that the size of the urban labor force (the sum of the urban employed plus unemployed) was also fixed. Thus, hiring one more laborer meant moving a worker from zero productivity (unemployment) to productive work and so was clearly desirable.

Later, Harris and Todaro (1970) showed that hiring one more laborer at a wage in excess of the rural wage would induce migration; the opportunity cost of hiring a seemingly unemployed worker is not zero but is equal to the reduced rural output resulting from the induced migration. Stiglitz (1974c) formulated a simple model in which urban wages were set endogenously (the efficiency-wage model) and migration equalized the expected income of migrants and the rural wage. In the central case examined, the opportunity cost of hiring an additional worker in the urban sector was actually equal to the urban wage. The shadow wage *was* the market wage, even though the unemployment rate could be quite high! Thus, explaining seeming rigidities in terms of more fundamental factors of information and incentives reversed the policy implications of earlier models, which had treated many aspects of the labor market as fixed constraints.

Rational Expectations and Political Barriers to Economic Development

In democratic societies interventions are enacted through political processes. Economists have naively tended to assume that such processes would surely enable any Pareto improvement to occur; there should be unanimity in favor of such reforms. Distortions might arise as one group tried to force a movement that improved its welfare at the expense of others, but presumably such distortions would then be undone as the political process once again moved toward the "utility possibilities curve." This does not seem to be the case: even changes that seem to be Pareto improvements are often resisted (Stiglitz 1998b). The theory of deep interventions helps explain this. With rational expectations, participants in the political process anticipate the consequences of any action—and those consequences are not necessarily limited to the immediate effects: participants see through the political dynamics. They will resist a Pareto improvement in the short run that will subsequently lead to a movement along the utility possibilities curve in a way that will disadvantage them in the long run. For example, an incumbent will be deterred from undertaking a Pareto-improving investment (one that provides to every individual direct net benefits) if it changes the identity of future policymakers in a way that is disadvantageous to his supporters (Besley and Coate 1998). Participants in the political process compare where they are with where the political process is likely to lead. The limited ability of governments (or political actors) to make commitments, and, in particular, to commit not to make subsequent adverse changes, makes change—even seeming Pareto improvements—more difficult.[31]

The fact that individuals are risk averse and cannot possibly know the full ramifications of any change today makes reform even more difficult. A reform may yield *riskless aggregate* benefits greater than costs but entail *individual-specific uncertainty* about who the winners are. If compensation is not provided to the losers, the gains have to be large enough to compensate for the downside risk of losses. Majority voting may lead citizens to oppose such a reform in order to maintain the benefits generated by the status quo (Fernandez and Rodrik 1991; Krusell and Rios-Rull 1996).

Jain and Mukand (1999) develop a model in which the government is assumed to have the ability to identify ex post the losers from reform and to compensate them, but there is a political constraint on credible commitment: policymakers can be punished for breaking a commitment to compensate the losers only by being voted out of office. In this environment, a reform that *hurts* a majority of 51 percent (while *benefiting* a minority of 49 percent) can be implemented, whereas one in which the fractions of winners and losers are reversed cannot be. In the former case the government can credibly commit to compensate the losers, but in the latter case it cannot, for violation of the contract will not spark a successful revenge movement at the ballot box against the government.

The problem of credible commitment, and the resulting missed opportunities for economic development, arise in a different form in dictatorships. Consider three situations. In the first situation there is a dictator, many poor farmers, and one guerrilla fighter who would like to topple the dictator. By building a road, the dictator has the potential to increase both the farmers' wealth and his own. With just one guerrilla, it is plausible that the dictator could obtain a commitment from the farmers to bar the guerrilla from using the road to attack the dictator. Then he would build the road. Now change the situation by supposing that every farmer can become a guerrilla fighter. The difficulty of contracting to constrain the actions of all the farmers may then be insuperable, and the dictator may not build the road. Finally, consider the actual case of President Mobutu Sese Seko, the longtime dictator of Zaire. When President Juvenal Habyarimana of Rwanda asked for armed support to help fight an insurgency, Mobutu responded:

> I told you not to build any roads . . . building roads never did any good . . . I've been in power in Zaire for thirty years and I never built one road. Now they are driving down them to get you. (*Jeune Afrique* 1991; cited in Robinson 1999: 2)

Mobutu's perspective contrasts with Olson's (1993) view that a dictator who has an "encompassing interest" in his nation will choose, in his self-interest, to provide property rights and other public goods. That view would be correct if there were no difficulties of commitment to ensure that the empowered population would not try to unseat the dictator. There is convincing evidence, however, that many dictators see an underdeveloped society as key to maintaining control of the country (Robinson 1999: sect. 4, and citations therein). "For predatory states, 'low-level equilibrium traps' are not something to be *escaped*; they are something to be *cherished*" (Evans 1995; cited in Robinson 1999: 3; emphasis added). More generally, a fundamental obstacle to economic development in all states, not only dictatorships, can be posed by groups whose political power is threatened by progress (Besley and Coate 1998; Acemoglu and Robinson 1999).

Some Observations on Recent Reform Experiences

Recent experiences of liberalization in East Asia and of transition to market economies in Eastern Europe have imposed huge costs on many groups in those societies. The manner in which reforms have been carried out in the past has perhaps reinforced a rational skepticism, a risk aversion to change. For instance, reformers hailed financial market liberalization in East Asia as holding out the promise of faster growth. Workers saw little evidence of substantial increases in growth but soon saw disastrous consequences in the form of unemployment and wage cuts.

There is a plethora of economic models, with differing predictions concerning the outcome of various policies. If economists cannot resolve some of these differences (and in many cases we do not have the evidence needed to decisively test between competing models, while in other cases it would seem that ideological presuppositions have prevailed over a close look at empirical evidence or coherent theorizing), how is an untrained worker to judge other than by "reduced-form observations" concerning consequences?

The record of reforms is indeed one that should leave risk-averse workers and farmers wary. They have seen not just the capital market liberalizations, which have had such devastating effects in the past two years, but also financial market liberalizations in Africa that have led to higher, not lower, interest rates (Aleem and Kasekende 1999) and movements to market economies in the former Soviet Union that have led to plummeting standards of living, not higher incomes. What is being judged is not only the reforms but also the reformers; their reputations and the accuracy of their predictions have been on the line, and in many cases they have been found wanting. Just as there is a need for greater differentiation in markets so that investors can distinguish between good and bad firms, well managed and poorly managed countries, so too does there need to be greater differentiation in evaluating reforms, reform processes, and reformers. The good news is that around the world, there seems to be evidence of such increased differentiation.

Increased institutional capacity in developing countries has enabled these countries to differentiate better the recipes of the ideologues from prescriptions based on more solid evidence and theory.

Given risk aversion and the ambiguous track record of reform, the extent to which reforms are being embraced around the world is thus perhaps more of a surprise than that there have not been more reforms. Vested interests have lost out. How can we explain these changes? The answer lies in part in the complexity of democratic processes and the strength of the democratic movement. The process of democratization has a historical force that vested interests cannot fully control. To be sure, they will attempt to contain it; moneyed interests will—and do—affect the outcome of elections, and vested interests will try to keep from public scrutiny a variety of activities that favor their groups.[32] Even in democratic societies, not everyone has a seat at the table—or at least not all seats are the same size.

But economic and political processes are sufficiently complex that no one can fully predict or control their evolution or the evolution of reforms emanating through them. Consider, for instance, the recent debates over transparency. The focus on transparency in financial reporting as a key factor behind the East Asian crisis served strong political interests. It shifted blame from lenders in industrial countries to the borrowers in developing countries. It shifted blame from the industrial countries that had pushed rapid capital account and financial liberalization—without a corresponding stress on the importance of strong institutions and regulatory oversight—to the governments of developing countries, which had failed to enforce information disclosure. And it provided assurance to those in industrial countries—where presumably there was greater transparency—that they were not likely to be afflicted with similar problems.

The evidence concerning the role that lack of transparency played in the crisis was scant.[33] But once the specter of transparency was raised, it took on a life of its own. Following the publicly engineered (but privately financed) bailout of the U.S. firm Long-Term Capital Management, there were calls that increased transparency should extend to the highly leveraged institutions (hedge funds). It may not have been in the interests of some groups to see disclosure and other forms of regulation imposed on these institutions, but virtually every industrial country other than the United Kingdom joined in these demands, and eventually a study by the U.S. Treasury endorsed recommendations for increased disclosure. Had the financial community seen where calls for increased transparency would eventually lead, they might have taken a different tack earlier. But in the complex evolution of society, participants can see only a short distance ahead. If strategic interactions are like a game of chess, then the players can see, at most, only a few moves ahead in the chess game.

Concluding Remarks

In many ways, development theory has come full circle. Thirty or 40 years ago, linkages among the parts of the society as well as the parts of the economy were stressed. The need for balance, not only among the sectors of the economy but also among the elements of society, was emphasized. Development was viewed as more than the elimination of distortions and the accumulation of capital. Indeed, it was recognized that there were other elements of a society that limited its absorptive capacity—its ability to use transfers of capital well.[34] It was recognized that a plantation economy or a dual economy was not a developed economy, although it might see increases in GDP.

But in the ensuing decades, much has changed. Our understanding of market economies has increased enormously, and with that understanding has come an appreciation of the difficulties entailed in making market economies work. The assumptions of perfect competition, perfect information, perfect contract enforcement, and complete markets and contracts are far from trivial, although the latter three sets of assumptions were not even mentioned in the classic statement of the competitive model (Arrow and Debreu 1954). We were always told that the neoclassical model was "just a benchmark"—a tool for thinking through complicated problems—but now there is increasing recognition that its implications are likely to be misleading in realistic settings where there are diffuse externalities. We have shown that formal theory now extends to many areas of imperfect information and incomplete contracting. This work has established that in many different settings, nonmarket interactions can give rise to complementarities, which may be associated with multiple equilibria. It is not just preferences and technologies that determine outcomes and behavior. The most important determinant of actions is one's environment, including the particular institutions in that environment. More important, these institutions cannot be derived from the "fundamentals" of the neoclassical model. And it is not just institutions, prices, and choices that are endogenous; even preferences and technologies are. Given history, beliefs, and chance, certain behaviors and traits are rewarded and others are not. Rewarded behaviors and traits will tend to increase relative to others, and that may further increase the rewards to those behaviors and traits. Initial differences in circumstances or beliefs may thereby not only persist but be magnified over time.

So too have views about the goals of development evolved. While lip service is always paid to environmental amenities, today the environment has a far more central place in our perceptions of sustainable development. Fifty years ago we often saw rapid development and democratic participation as entailing a tradeoff (Huntington 1968). Today we are more likely to see them as complements, to stress the need for voice and participation as a means of ensuring that reforms are politically sustainable, and to recognize as a fundamental right individuals' having a say over the decisions that affect their lives and livelihoods (Sen 1999). Fifty years ago increases in inequality were seen not only as a natural accompaniment of development (Kuznets 1955) but as actually facilitating development (Lewis 1954). Today we recognize that not only are such increases in inequality not necessary but that they may actually be detrimental to growth—by increasing agency costs in credit and land rental markets, by tending to lead to political regimes that restrict access to education and to markets, and by exacerbating social conflicts.

Although evolving societal preferences and values may have changed the relative weights associated with various developmental objectives, modern theory has cast new light on strategies for achieving those objectives. While our understanding of market economies has been enormously enhanced—markets no longer sit on the pedestal to which they were at one time assigned—our appreciation of the importance of noneconomic forces (in particular, political forces) in the reform process has also increased. But our understanding of these processes is far from complete. We are at least at the stage at which we know that we do not know. That is, perhaps, a good way to begin the new century.

Appendix A. Why Low Capital Does Not Explain Underdevelopment

If the fundamental cause of lack of development is simply a shortage of capital, then (given diminishing returns to capital) why do not incomes in all economies tend to converge over time? This appendix takes up the neoclassical perspective on development, in which the cause of underdevelopment is simply a shortage of capital or skilled labor. We will argue that this view is inconsistent with the evidence on private capital flows. Instead, a shortage of capital must be a symptom, not a cause, of underdevelopment.[35]

Implications of the Neoclassical Production Function

If all countries had the same production function,

$$(A\text{-}1) \qquad\qquad Y = F(K, L)$$

with output being a function of capital and labor and with diminishing returns to each factor (when the other is held fixed), countries with a capital scarcity would have higher rates of return. Capital would flow from capital-rich to capital-poor countries, and in short order, as the returns to capital were equalized, so too would be GDP per capita.[36] Gross national product (GNP) would not be so quickly equalized, as some of the capital in the poor countries would be owned by those in the rich countries. But eventually, even incomes per capita would be equalized, so long as saving rates were the same. If saving rates differed, differences in incomes could be totally explained by those differences in saving rates (Stiglitz 1969).

Not only does trade not seem to equalize factor prices, but capital flows from industrial to developing countries are, to say the least, far weaker than the theory would suggest. Only since 1990 have private capital flows to developing countries been significant (see Figure A-1), and the flows have been highly concentrated, with much larger flows going to middle-income countries than to low-income countries. This is true whether the flows are measured in absolute amounts, as shown in the upper panel of the figure, or as a fraction of GDP, shown in the lower panel.

If capital accumulation were at the center of development, and *if* international capital flows were limited (because of "institutional" or "informational" impediments), *then* features of the economy that increased domestic savings rates would ensure growth. The dual-economy models provided one response to W. Arthur Lewis's famous statement of the development problem:

> The central problem in the theory of economic development is to understand the process by which a community which was previously saving and investing 4 or 5 per cent of its national income or less, converts itself into an economy where voluntary saving is running at about 12 to 15 per cent of national income or more. This is the central problem because the central fact of economic development is rapid capital accumulation (including knowledge and skills with capital). (Lewis, 1954: 155)

Two hypotheses were key to the dual-economy models (Lewis 1954; Fei and Ranis 1969):

• Capitalists saved a higher fraction of their income than workers or peasants, so that policies which increased inequality—giving higher profits to the high-saving capitalists—would promote growth.
• There was surplus labor in the rural sector.

If the first hypothesis were true, tax policies to ensure the continued ready supply of labor from the rural sector would promote development. Such policies would keep urban wages low and thus contribute to the pool of profits out of which savings were accumulated. The second hypothesis—that there was a close to infinite elasticity of labor under the "right" policies—reinforced the emphasis on capital: it was a shortage of capital, not of labor, that prevented industrial growth.

Figure A-1. Net Private Capital Flows to Low- and
Middle-Income Developing Countries, 1972–98

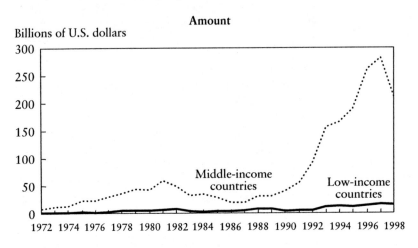

Amount

Billions of U.S. dollars

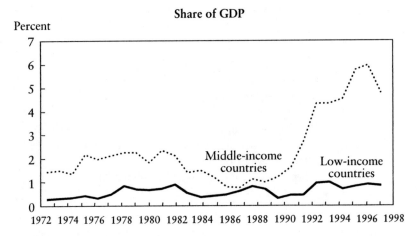

Share of GDP

Percent

Note: The classification of economies is based on per capita income. For 1998, the
per capita cutoff levels are as follows: low income, US$760 or less; middle income,
US$761 to US$9,360.
Source: Statistical Information and Management Analysis (SIMA), World Bank.

Experience has not been kind to these theories. One problem is that
the "right" policies were not implementable. For instance, in many countries the government can tax only tradable goods—through marketing
boards or at the port. But once a tax on tradables is imposed, farmers
tend to shift out of such goods. A second problem is that if farmers

Figure A-2. Average Savings Rates and Inequality,
East Asia and the Rest of the World, 1960–95

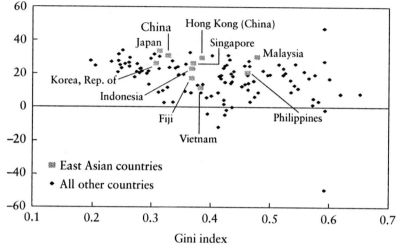

Average gross domestic savings as percentage of GDP

Source: Statistical Information and Management Analysis (SIMA), World Bank.

come to believe that any agricultural surplus will be taxed away, they lose all incentive to respond to new productive opportunities. For example, as reported in Krueger (1993), in the early 1980s it was not uncommon for prices received by farmers in developing countries to be less than 20 percent of the border price of agricultural commodities. The consequence of the tax wedge and of governmental inefficiency in marketing was that in Ghana the real producer price of cocoa in 1984 was about 10 percent of its price some 30 years earlier. "Small wonder that Ghanaian exports of cocoa fell as farmers had first virtually ceased replanting, and then stopped picking the crop" (Krueger 1993: 98).

The East Asian experience also helped undercut these theories. East Asia showed that countries could generate a very high rate of voluntary savings without high levels of inequality. Figure A-2 shows that over the period 1960–95 the East Asian economies had much higher than average saving rates and average or below-average inequality. For example, Japan and the Republic of Korea had saving rates of 33.6 and 26.2 percent, respectively (compared with an average for all countries of 17.6 percent), and both had Gini coefficients of approximately 0.31 (compared with an average for all countries of 0.40).

High savings and low inequality translate into high growth and low inequality. Figure A-3 plots growth and inequality, measured in two

Figure A-3. Average Growth Rates and Inequality,
East Asia and the Rest of the World, 1960–95

Growth rate (percent)

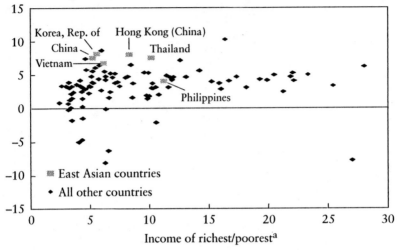

Income of richest/poorest[a]

Growth rate (percent)

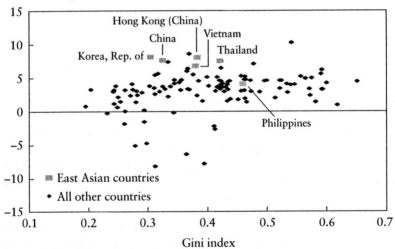

Gini index

a. Ratio of income of richest 20 percent of population to income of poorest 20
percent.
Source: SIMA.

different ways. In the upper panel the inequality measure is the income
share of the top quintile as a proportion of the income share of the
bottom quintile. In the lower panel the inequality measure is the Gini
index. Using these measures, the higher than average growth for the

East Asian countries is associated with average or below-average inequality.

The East Asian experience raised a new question: how could one explain the high rate of saving? Empirical research showed that in East Asia saving rates increased with growth rates. One hypothesis was that saving *functions* in East Asia were similar to those elsewhere but that along this function, saving rates increased with growth rates. It is easy to construct theoretical models for which that might plausibly be the case.[37]

The interesting feature of such a saving function is that it can explain multiple transition paths through which an economy would approach the long-run equilibrium growth rate of the neoclassical model. In this view, East Asia was the first region where countries had jumped to the high-growth path to long-run equilibrium (and in that sense, its development differed from that of earlier industrializers, none of which nad had such high saving rates). If the saving rate depends on the rate of growth of income per capita, g, and if the rate of growth of population is n, then from a Cobb-Douglas version of the aggregate production function in equation (A-1),

(A-2) $$Y = AK^\alpha L^{1-\alpha}$$

we have

$$\frac{\Delta Y}{Y} = \frac{\Delta A}{A} + \alpha \frac{\Delta K}{K} + [1 - \alpha]n$$

and so (since $g = \Delta Y/Y - n$),

(A-3) $$g = \Delta A/A + \alpha[s\beta(k) - n]$$

where $\beta(k)$ is the output-capital ratio, a decreasing function of capital per worker, k.

In the neoclassical growth model (Solow 1956), there is a fixed fraction s of income saved and a steady-state growth rate fixed uniquely by the exogenous rate of technical change, $\Delta A/A$. Starting from a point *out of* steady state—e.g., a low capital-labor ratio, so that $s\beta(k) > n$—the model predicts a unique transition path to the steady state. But if the saving rate increases with the growth rate, there may be multiple values of the equilibrium growth rate at a moment in time, as illustrated in Figure A-4, and thus multiple transition paths that asymptotically converge to the same growth rate and the same income level, as illustrated in Figure A-5—the high-growth, high-saving-rate path that characterized East Asia, and the low-growth, low-saving-rate path that characterized most of the rest of the world.

Notice that the body of this chapter focused on multiple equilibria and argued that there may be *no* forces for convergence, even in the long run. Here we make a quite different point. Even if one conceded

Figure A-4. Multiple Short-Run Equilibria in the Levels of Savings and Growth

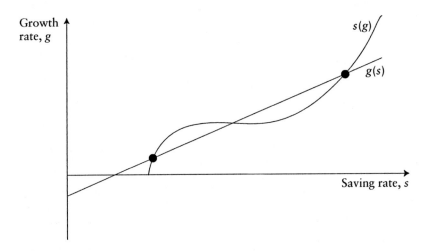

that the neoclassicals were right about the very long run, there could be multiple rates at which an economy approached the long-run equilibrium. There is an ecological environment and a set of expectations that foster high savings and high growth and another such combination that does not.[38]

But it seems that while the high growth rate can explain some, or even much, of East Asia's high saving rates, other factors were at play. Stiglitz and Uy (1996) argue that the high saving rates were attributable at least in part to public policies that promoted institutions designed to mobilize savings, especially in the rural sector. Modern theory, which emphasizes information and enforcement costs, has played an important role in enhancing our understanding, and changing our perceptions, of the kinds of policy likely to promote saving. Savings, especially savings available for industrialization, will be larger if the transaction costs of saving through financial institutions are smaller, if risk is reduced, and if return is increased. The East Asian experience has provided insights into the magnitudes of these effects. While large negative real returns, associated with financial repression (Shaw 1973), have had adverse effects on savings, the interest elasticity of savings has been relatively low: as long as returns were positive, individuals cared more about risk. Government postal savings accounts, for instance, with low transaction costs, low risk, and low return, succeeded in mobilizing enormous savings in Japan.

In summary, low capital seems an unsatisfactory basis for explaining low rates of development, for two reasons. First, if low capital is

Figure A-5. Multiple Transition Paths to the Steady State

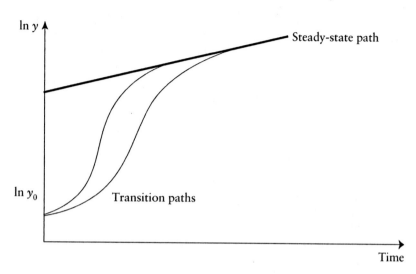

itself the barrier to growth, returns to capital should be sufficiently high to attract large capital inflows. The problem would thus be self-correcting in a market environment. Second, the experience of the East Asian economies shows that under at least some set of institutions, it is possible for an economy to generate enormously high rates of savings and domestic investment. This leads us to ask whether there is a way, *by relaxing certain of the neoclassical assumptions about the production function,* to account for the fact that even as government-imposed barriers to the flow of capital have been brought down, capital has not flowed to many of the countries most starved of capital. We consider, in turn, two possible explanations: (a) the role of skilled labor in enhancing the marginal product of capital in capital-rich countries, and (b) aggregate economies of scale. We present a theoretical model consistent with (a) but argue that (b) does not provide a persuasive explanation of low capital flows to poor countries.

Increasing Returns to Skilled Labor. The production function model suggests that it is a shortage of complementary factors—not labor in general but, rather, skilled and educated labor—that may explain limited capital flows to capital-poor countries. But the phenomenon of brain drain raises questions about this explanation. Why, for instance, would skilled labor migrate from India to the United States if there was a shortage of skilled labor in India and if that shortage explained India's lack of development?

There are simple models that go beyond the neoclassical model with constant returns to scale and that can in fact explain the seeming anomaly. If the production function exhibits *increasing returns to scale in skilled workers,* it will pay for all the skilled workers to cluster together. Consider, for instance, two islands, each with the same endowment of capital and unskilled labor (assumed to be unable to migrate between islands) and an endowment of skilled labor, which can migrate freely from one island to the other. Assume that the production function is

(A-4) $y = K^{\alpha}L^{\beta}(S + 1)^{\gamma}$ with $\alpha + \beta < 1$ and $\gamma > 1$.

Then all the skilled labor will migrate to one island. The marginal productivity of both capital and skilled labor will be higher on that island, which we will call the "developed island." This is true even though the developed and less developed islands have the same production functions.

Kremer's (1993) O-ring theory of production is a striking example of a production function with the key features of equation (A-4), namely, that there are increasing returns to skilled labor. The O-ring theory takes its name from the space shuttle *Challenger,* which exploded because one of its thousands of components, an O-ring, failed. The explosion dramatized the complementarity among inputs to a production process. No matter how good the other parts may be, if one part malfunctions, the other parts may create little, if any, value.

To capture that idea, Kremer proposes an unusual production function. He supposes that there are n tasks in a production process. For simplicity, let $n = 2$. Each worker has a skill q, where q is between 0 and 1. Let q_1 denote the skill of the person performing the first task, and let q_2 denote the skill of the person performing the second task. A firm's production function is $y = Aq_1q_2$. One way to interpret the model is that q is the probability that a job is done correctly. Under this interpretation, the value of a firm's output if both jobs are done correctly is A, and the probability of that joint event is q_1q_2.

Competitive equilibrium is characterized by a wage function, denoted by $w(q)$, and an allocation of workers to firms. Given the wage function, each firm will choose q_1 and q_2 to maximize its expected income, $Aq_1q_2 - w(q_1) - w(q_2)$. The first implication of the model is the "skill-clustering theorem": competitive forces will lead to the clustering of a high-skill worker with other high-skill workers, and similarly for low-skill workers.

To see this is straightforward. Consider any distinct values a and b. Since $(a - b)^2 = a^2 + b^2 - 2ab > 0$, it must be true that $a^2 + b^2 > 2ab$. If we let the values a and b represent the skill levels of the individuals who perform the first and second tasks, it follows that expected output is higher when the skill levels of the workers in the two tasks are matched

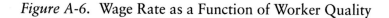

Figure A-6. Wage Rate as a Function of Worker Quality

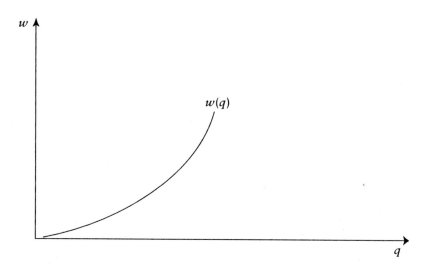

than when they are not. Intuitively, it does not pay to "waste" a worker with a high probability of success by pairing him or her with a co-worker who has a low probability of success. This means that whatever the wage and skill levels are, competitive forces will lead workers of a given skill level to be grouped together in any production unit. If this model captures forces present in the economy as a whole, there will be increasing returns to skill, as illustrated in Figure A-6, and incentives for human capital to flow to the richest countries—the brain drain.

Scale Economies. Besides the phenomenon of skill clustering, there is a second way one might retain the hypothesis that industrial and developing countries have the same production function but that industrial economies have a higher marginal product of capital: scale economies. Ironically, in postulating scale economies, one has to abandon the standard competitive model, unless one argues that all the returns to scale are external to the firm (Marshall 1897).[39] With returns to scale at the national level, a larger country will be more productive than a smaller one and so will tend to attract higher capital investments. Although such scale economies underlie several of the theories of development that have received extensive attention in the past 15 years, we find these theories implausible because they miss the fundamental units across which scale economies might operate.[40] This is especially the case when the scale economies arise from an externality. Then it is simply assumed that the externality is conferred on others in the country but does not

extend beyond the boundaries of the country. With increased globalization (with firms, for instance, operating across national boundaries),
this hypothesis seems dubious. Hong Kong and Singapore have high
per capita incomes, although their aggregate income remains low simply because they are small. If economies of scale operate at the level of
the whole economy, China should be relatively rich, and Hong Kong
and Singapore should be poor. But with the growth of international
trade, it is less persuasive that the natural unit is the country or economy.
If the economies of scale operate at the level of cities (from agglomeration economies), then it is possible that poor countries will have growth
poles in rich cities. To the extent that economies of scale operate at the
level of an industry, poor countries could again enjoy the benefits of
scale simply by concentrating in particular industries.[41]

Distortions: Harberger Triangles and Krueger Rectangles

As we noted in the introduction, neoclassical theorists typically hypothesize that government-induced distortions—stemming from taxes,
tariffs, and quotas, for example—are critical to explaining divergent
economic performances across economies. Government controls over
economic activity not only misallocate resources among productive
activities, inducing Harberger (1964) triangles, but also invite competition for government protection that leads to the dissipation of resources
in rent-seeking activities such as lobbying. In a limiting case—constant
returns to scale in rent-seeking—the rent-seeking activities will dissipate the total value of the rents, producing Krueger (1974) rectangles
of deadweight loss.

Government-induced distortions can be so large as to destroy an
economy's potential to develop, but the evidence suggests that more
than the elimination of price distortions is at stake in creating the preconditions for development. The experience in the aftermath of liberalization in Brazil—where these distortions were reduced enormously, if
not eliminated—was that growth remained limited (even more limited
than during earlier periods such as Brazil's import-substitution phase).
Similarly, the contrast between the transformation to a market economy
of the countries in Eastern Europe and the former Soviet Union, on the
one hand, and China, on the other, suggests that something important
was missing in the usual prescriptions of liberalization and privatization.
Even as the distortions were reduced, output fell—in marked contrast
to the predictions of the standard neoclassical theory (Blanchard and
Kremer 1997; Stiglitz 2000).

In a sense, there was a close similarity between those who saw the
problem of underdevelopment as one of *government-induced failures*
and those, such as the dual-economy theorists, who saw it as one of
easily remedied market failures. Both thought that straightforward in-

terventions to address the problem of resource misallocation—moving to the production possibilities frontier from inside the frontier—provided the key to successful economic transformation. Economic distortions are costly, particularly to poor countries that can ill afford them. Reducing them can undoubtedly transform a very poor developing country into a poor developing country. But reducing distortions—whether by planning or by eliminating government-induced market distortions—seemingly provides neither necessary nor sufficient conditions for sustained growth.[42]

Appendix B. Coordination Problems: A Mathematical Treatment

In Part I we presented a series of models of coordination problems. This appendix highlights their common mathematical structure.

Each model has three elements: a set of *actors;* the set of feasible actions for each actor, i.e. *strategy sets;* and the *payoff functions.* The payoff functions depend in general on one's own actions, the actions of others, and prices (which depend on the actions of all individuals).

In some specializations of the model, the impact of other individuals' actions is entirely through prices; that is, the only externalities are pecuniary ones. Then the payoff functions can be written as a function of only one's own actions and prices. All that matters is the "atmosphere," which can be represented solely by the price system. Examples include the screening model (Stiglitz 1975), the property rights enforcement model (de Meza and Gould 1992), and the "big push" model of Murphy, Shleifer, and Vishny (1989: sect. IV).[43]

Table B-1 provides a taxonomy that distinguishes three ways of modeling actors: as identical (column I), with individual differences in payoff functions (column II), or with individual differences in strategy sets (column III). The table distinguishes two ways of modeling strategy sets: continuous (top row) or discrete (bottom row). The models described in Part I can be placed into the six categories defined by this matrix (I-C, I-D, and so on). Although we did not describe such cases here, there are also hybrids of these six types. For example, in one version of Acemoglu (1997) the workers' choice variable (training) is continuous, but the firms' choice variable (innovation) is discrete.

Class I-C. Identical Actors and Continuous Actions

The first class of models hypothesizes identical actors with the preferences (profits) of agent i being $u^i(a^i; a, p)$, where a^i is the actor's own action, a is everyone else's action, and p is a vector of prices—itself a function of the entire vector of actions. Each action is a continuous

Table B-1. **A Taxonomy of Models of Coordination Problems**

| | Actors | | |
Actions	I. Actors are identical	II. Actors differ in their payoff functions	III. Actors differ in their strategy sets
C. Continuous-choice variable	R&D (Romer 1986) Savings (Appendix A in this chapter)		Training and innovation (Acemoglu 1997)
D. Discrete-choice variable	Innovative behavior (Sah and Stiglitz 1989a) Contract enforcement (Greif 1994) Rent-seeking (Murphy, Shleifer, and Vishny 1993; Acemoglu 1995)	Education as screening (Stiglitz 1975) Innovative behavior (Sah and Stiglitz 1989a) Structure of ownership (Hoff and Sen 2000)	"Big push" models (Helpman and Krugman 1985; Murphy, Shleifer, and Vishny 1989; Rodriguez-Clare 1996; Rodrik 1996) Training and innovation (Acemoglu 1997)

variable. An increase in everyone else's action raises u^i (that is, $u^i_2 > 0$). We summarize everyone else's action by the variable a because we limit our discussion to the case of *symmetric* equilibria.

Assuming decreasing marginal returns to an increase in one's own action (that is, $u^i_{11} < 0$), the representative agent's behavior is described by the reaction function:

$$(B-1) \qquad u^i_1[a^i; a, p(a)] = 0.$$

That is, if all others choose some action a, the ith agent's incentive would be to choose a^i to satisfy (B-1). At that point he would be at an optimum, given his environment. As noted in Part I, the interior symmetric equilibria are the values of a^* that solve

$$(B-2) \qquad u^i_1[a^*; a^*, p(a^*)] = 0$$

for at a^*, all actors are optimizing.

Complementarities are captured in this model by the condition that $u^i_{12} > 0$, and if complementarities are sufficiently large, there will be multiple equilibrium values of a^* (see Figure 2). All individuals are better off in the equilibrium at which all choose a higher action, since for any given a^i, an increase in others' action increases utility ($u^i_2 > 0$).

That an individual then finds it optimal to increase a^i increases his welfare further.

Class I-D. Identical Actors and Discrete Activities

The next class of models assumes identical actors who have *discrete* actions. The simplest case is where there are just two possible actions or activities (a binary choice). Then the payoff to any activity depends on the fraction x of agents that undertake, say, the first activity. The utility function of the ith agent can be written as $U^i = U^i[a^i; x, p(x)]$, where $a = 1$ if the individual undertakes the first activity and $a = 2$ if he undertakes the second activity. The value p is a function of x: $p = p(x)$. The individual chooses his activity, a^i, to maximize $U^i[a^i; x, p(x)]$, taking x as given. With a continuum of agents, an equilibrium in which $x \in (0, 1)$ is described by the values of the fraction x that solve

$$(B\text{-}3) \qquad U^i[1; x^*, p(x^*)] = U^i[2; x^*, p(x^*)].$$

This states that when a fraction x^* of the population undertakes the first activity, every agent is indifferent between the two activities. Complementarities exist in this model if the relative return to the first activity is increasing in x: that is, if the partial derivative of the payoff function with respect to x, denoted U^i_x, satisfies

$$(B\text{-}4) \qquad U^i_x[1, x, p(x)] - U^i_x[2, x, p(x)] > 0.$$

When complementarities are sufficiently strong, the *ranking* of activities 1 and 2 for each agent can change with x, and thus there can be multiple values of x^* that solve (B-3).

With complementarities, corner solutions are also possible. A corner solution where all individuals choose activity 1 exists if

$$(B\text{-}5) \qquad U^i[1; 1, p(1)] > U^i[2; 1, p(1)]$$

and another corner solution exists where all choose activity 2 if

$$(B\text{-}6) \qquad U^i[2; 0, p(0)] > U^i[1; 0, p(0)].$$

(B-5) states that when all other individuals choose the first activity, it is individually optimal to choose the first activity. (B-6) states that when all other individuals choose the second activity, it is individually optimal to choose the second activity.

This binary choice model can be generalized to an arbitrarily large number of discrete activities. In Murphy, Shleifer, and Vishny (1993), there are three activities: cash-crop production, a subsistence activity, and rent-seeking (predation). The returns to the subsistence activity, denoted by γ, are exogenous, while the returns to cash-crop production and rent-seeking are decreasing in the ratio n of rent-seekers relative to cash-crop producers. An interior equilibrium is described by a value n^* that solves

$$(B\text{-}7) \qquad U^i[1; n^*, p(n^*)] = U^i[2; n^*, p(n^*)] = \gamma.$$

Suppose that over some range of n, returns are decreasing more steeply for cash-crop production than for rent-seeking. This implies that over some range of n, the *relative* returns to rent-seeking are increasing in n. In this case, multiple Pareto-rankable equilibria may exist. Some are characterized by a low fraction of rent-seekers where all individuals' payoffs exceed γ (thus there are no subsistence producers). Other equilibria are characterized by a high fraction of rent-seekers where all actors' payoffs are driven down to the subsistence return γ.

Class II-D. Individual Differences in Payoff Functions and Discrete Activities

In the preceding class of models, some individuals chose one action and others chose another. All individuals were identical, and so the theory provides no explanation of why this happened—and, in fact, it makes no difference. All that is required is that individuals be indifferent as to what they do. But, in general, there *are* important individual differences. Whenever such differences exist, they may explain why some individuals choose one action rather than another. The next category of models entails individual differences in payoff functions.

The structure of these models is such that there is some characteristic of the individual, reflected in, say, his utility function or wealth and denoted for simplicity by c, and there is a probability distribution of individuals according to c, say $F(c)$. Suppose as before that individuals have a binary choice of activities. Each individual chooses his activity, a^i, to maximize his payoff, say $V^i(a^i; x, c)$, taking x as given. [For simplicity, we suppress the dependence of payoffs on $p(x)$.] The utility functions have the structure that we can order individuals by c such that there exists a critical value c^* that satisfies:

$$(B\text{-}8) \qquad V[1, F(c^*), c] \gtreqless V[2, F(c^*), c] \quad \text{as } c \gtreqless c^*$$

This states that individuals whose attribute is above c^* prefer activity 1, individuals whose attribute is equal to c^* are indifferent, and individuals whose attribute is below c^* prefer activity 2.

Complementarities are defined, as in equation (B-4), by the condition that the relative return to activity 1 is increasing in the fraction x of individuals undertaking activity 1: $V_x^i(1, x, c) - V_x^i(2, x, c) > 0$. When complementarities are sufficiently strong, there can exist multiple solutions for c^*.

Class III. Individual Differences in Strategy Sets

Coordination failures can also emerge from the interaction of different kinds of actors. Consider a situation with two groups of actors that differ in their strategy sets—for example, firms that can innovate or not, and workers who can train or not. For simplicity, we will represent each group by a single actor, but in fact each group can consist of a large number of actors. In that case, we solve for the symmetric equilibrium of each class of actors using the techniques of Class I-C.

Suppose there are two groups of actors, and suppose the action of the first is a continuous variable denoted by a and the action of the second is a continuous variable denoted by b. Then the first group maximizes a payoff function $v^1[a; b, p(a, b)]$ with respect to a, given b and p, and the second maximizes $v^2[a; b, p(a, b)]$ with respect to b, given a and p.

An interior equilibrium is a solution to the reaction functions

(B-9) $$v_a^1[a^*, b^*, p(a^*, b^*)] = 0$$

and

(B-10) $$v_b^2[a^*, b^*, p(a^*, b^*)] = 0.$$

There may exist multiple values of (a^*, b^*) that solve these equations if there are complementarities between the two groups of actors, which is captured by the condition that $v_{ab}^i > 0$.

Notes

The authors thank Abhijit Banerjee, Arnold Harberger, Gustav Ranis, and Debraj Ray for helpful comments. The first draft of this chapter was prepared while Hoff was a visiting faculty member at Princeton University and Stiglitz was vice president (Development Economics) and chief economist, World Bank. Financial support for Hoff from the John D. and Catherine T. MacArthur Foundation is gratefully acknowledged.

1. For instance, Brazil's import substitution policy yielded growth rates averaging 10 percent per year for nine years (1968–76), but evidently it was not sustainable, or at least was not sustained. Brazil's "liberalization" strategies of the 1980s finally began to yield fruit in the 1990s, although growth was more modest than in the earlier period and the growth spurt was shorter lived; it, too, seems to have stalled in the global financial crisis of 1998. It is too soon to know whether, and for how long, growth will be restored.

2. The low-income country with the most sustained economic growth has been China, which has not privatized, still has a somewhat restricted trade regime, and has only gradually eliminated price distortions.

3. We use the term *neoclassical theory* as shorthand for models that postulate maximizing agents who interact through a *complete* set of perfectly competitive markets. This narrow definition of neoclassical theory is for convenience only. Much of the early work in institutional economics was neoclassical in spirit because it argued that institutions filled in for missing markets in such a way as to lead to efficiency, once the costs of writing and enforcing contracts were taken into account. Douglass North's early work (which one might call "North I") exemplifies that position. That work argued that superior institutions would ultimately eliminate inferior ones so that efficiency would be achieved (see North and Thomas 1970, 1973). North's later work, which one might call North II because its conclusions differ sharply from those of his earlier work, disparages the prospects for understanding economic history as a more or less inevitable movement toward more efficient institutions: "Throughout most of history, the experience of the agents and the ideologies of the actors do not combine to lead to efficient outcomes" (North 1990: 96; see also North 1994). A review is in Hoff (1992).

4. Table B-1 lists our central examples.

5. See, for example, Stiglitz (1989). Floro and Yotopoulos (1991) and Hoff, Braverman, and Stiglitz (1993) provide many case studies demonstrating the importance of market failures in rural credit markets of developing countries.

6. The link between distribution and efficiency is demonstrated in a framework of *bargaining* in William Samuelson (1985). One of the first general equilibrium models to relate inequality to aggregate functioning was Dasgupta and Ray (1986). Models of economies with *principal-agent* relationships that demonstrate the link between distribution and efficiency include Bowles (1985), Braverman and Stiglitz (1989), Banerjee and Newman (1993), Hoff (1994), Hoff and Lyon (1995), Legros and Newman (1996), Aghion and Bolton (1997), Mookherjee (1997a, 1997b), and Hoff and Sen (2000). This link is also studied in models of *collective action* by Bardhan and Ghatak (1999) and in a *political economy* model by Robinson (1999). We briefly discuss in Part II evidence from Engerman and Sokoloff (1997) and Engerman, Haber, and Sokoloff (1999) of the political channels by which initial inequality of wealth affects institutions and growth.

7. Similarly, a firm's incentives will depend on its net worth (Greenwald, Stiglitz, and Weiss 1984; Bernanke and Gertler 1990; Greenwald and Stiglitz 1993).

8. It is easy to lose sight of this, perhaps because the "first generation" of principal-agent models (Ross 1973; Stiglitz 1974a) were *partial* equilibrium models. We are indebted to Ray's comment in this volume for underlining this point. What might be called the "second generation" of principal-agent models differs from the first in that it analyzes moral hazard under *general* equilibrium, where agency problems may affect wage rates (Banerjee and Newman 1993; Legros and Newman 1996), interest rates (Aghion and Bolton 1997; Piketty 1997), and the path of asset prices (Hoff and Sen 2000).

9. There is a vast literature on this topic. A very selective list of interesting results includes Azariadis and Drazen (1990), Krugman (1991), Ljungqvist (1993), Acemoglu (1995), and Mookherjee and Ray (1998). A simple diagrammatic treatment of the effect of an initial wealth distribution on the steady state is Banerjee (2000).

10. For example, once high wages induce a labor-saving innovation, it is not the case that a subsequent fall in the wage "undoes" the innovation. For a broader discussion, see Landes (1998).

11. Indeed, Stiglitz (1969) showed in a variant of the Solow model that the distribution of income did not even depend on initial conditions.

12. We place "equilibrium" and "evolution" within quotation marks because neoclassical analysis ignores institutions and yet, as we have argued, institutions do affect resource allocations. Moreover, institutions evolve in response to changes in endowments, technology, and policy, and these interactions can be among the most important influences on development.

13. Formally, suppose each resource owner who enforces his property rights hires L workers and that the value of their output is $F(L)$. His rents are thus $F(L) - w(x)L$, where w is the wage function, which decreases with the fraction x of resource owners who enforce their property rights.

14. See, for example, Bardhan (2000) and Greif (1997). Greif notes, "Since the relative efficiency of a particular system of [contract enforcement] depends on the economic environment as well as [social, cultural, and political factors], there is no reason to expect a particular system in a particular society to be economically efficient" (257).

15. To see this, note that until screening institutions are created, heterogeneous but observationally identical goods trade at the same price. The price depends on average quality, which is like a common-property resource in that (a) it yields an income flow to producers, (b) the income flow depends on the actions of all producers, who can lower or raise it according to whether they are low- or high-quality producers, and (c) no producer has private property rights to it. If a technical change induces new entry of marginal, low-quality producers, they can lower average quality by so much that no producer gains from the technical change. The intuition is the same as that of the tragedy of the commons.

16. Here we focus on applications of the theory of coordination problems to development. Cooper (1999) treats applications to macroeconomics.

17. In Part I we discussed a fourth example arising from complementarities in the process of property rights enforcement (de Meza and Gould's 1992 model). In this model, complementarities in the enforcement actions of property owners lead to multiple equilibria, some with higher aggregate social surplus than others. But the equilibrium outcomes are not Pareto-rankable (in this model, the workers always prefer less enforcement), and so a *coordination failure* cannot arise.

18. The idea that the set of markets might be inefficient is demonstrated also in Hart (1975). A recent treatment is Makowski and Ostroy (1995). Regarding the problem of why one cannot have complete markets, even in the absence of

the kinds of asymmetric information problems emphasized in Stiglitz (1975), Matsuyama (1997: 145) notes, "Even if one succeeded in making the list of everything, it would be impossible to open markets for all: even with very small costs of setting up markets, all the resources in the economy would be absorbed so that nothing would be left over to be used in performing these activities."

19. For example, when any set of firms in a country establish themselves as successful exporters, foreign buyers are more likely to establish local offices, which in turn raises the return to each entrepreneur's efforts to expand its exports. This issue is highlighted in Morawetz's (1981) case study of Colombia's garment industry.

20. Durlauf (1999) surveys recent work on group effects with endogenous stratification. The contribution of this literature is to study interdependencies in behavior or outcomes across agents in which the grouping of individuals within a given interaction environment (e.g., a neighborhood, school, or firm) is *endogenous,* not fixed.

21. For seminal work on thick market complementarities (in a Keynesian context) see Diamond (1982).

22. Malaria kills primarily children. Natives of Africa who survive to adulthood have some resistance to the disease, which nonnatives lack.

23. A general statement is found in Hayek (1978); an application to the conduct of monetary policy is in Lucas (1973, 1976); and an application to developing countries is in Krueger (1993).

24. For example, Farrell (1987) shows that a clumsy compromise made by a bureaucrat with imperfect information can be a better starting point for bargaining between two parties than either party's most-preferred outcome. Hoff and Lyon (1995) show that when there is adverse selection in the credit market and lenders cannot enforce exclusivity in credit contracts, the government can create a Pareto improvement by a tax-transfer policy that transforms part of an individual's risky future income into a (virtually) riskless transfer payment that can serve as collateral. The increase in collateral mitigates incentive problems and thereby reduces borrowing costs, which makes everyone better off.

25. Other examples of temporary policy that can force a shift from one to another equilibrium are bankruptcy law and a ban on child labor. Miller and Stiglitz (1999) present a model in which a bankruptcy law that establishes stronger debtor rights eliminates the "bad" equilibrium in which there are large numbers of bankruptcies as a result of the large transfers associated with large creditor-friendly bankruptcies. Basu and Van (1998) show how child labor laws can eliminate a "bad" equilibrium with child labor. In the good equilibrium that results, no one actually wants to have his children work.

26. The example in Part I of credentialing illustrates a case of multiple Pareto-ranked equilibria in the disclosure of information; see also Grossman (1989).

27. Palfrey and Rosenthal (1984) present a model in which the *larger* the number of potential beneficiaries of a discrete public good, the *less* likely the public good is to be supplied.

28. In the next section we discuss the case, which is especially relevant in transition economies, of organized resistance *within the government* to privatization.

29. In the transition economies, it has been argued that privatization of natural monopolies and highly concentrated industries should proceed even when the government is too divided between pro- and antireform forces to create a regulatory regime prior to privatization (Boycko, Shleifer, and Vishny 1996). But this argument would seem to violate the following straightforward criterion of consistency: if one argues that government cannot implement a policy α (e.g., industry regulation) because of a trait β (a divided government), then one cannot also argue that government should do a policy P (privatization) unless one can show that P is consistent with trait β. If the reformers have enough power to impose privatization, the argument that they cannot impose regulation is consistent—in the above sense—only if privatization is less costly to the ministries than regulation would be; that is, *because the ministries privatize to themselves* (Hoff and Stiglitz 2000).

30. Such issues arise, of course, in industrial as well as developing countries. Successful reforms require some form of commitment (some fixed costs of undoing the reforms). For instance, when the United States abolished its distortionary farm subsidies—giving farmers a lump-sum payment as compensation—many economists lauded the reform. Others were more skeptical. The strength of the farm lobby was undiminished. Why, having received the lump-sum subsidy, would farmers not subsequently try to restore their distortionary subsidies? There was no real commitment on this point—and how could there be? To be sure, they would wait for a "bad year," with plummeting prices, to press for relief, for a reinstatement of subsidies. And that is precisely what seems to be happening.

31. Besley and Coate (1998: 151–52) provide a definition of *political failure* that is parallel to that of *market failure*. One begins in each case by defining the set of technologically feasible utility allocations. For the case of political failure, this reflects the available policy instruments—for example, taxes, transfers, and investments. Political institutions are then modeled. By analogy with a *market* failure, a *political* failure arises when equilibrium policy choices result in an outcome in which it is technologically feasible (given available tax and transfer instruments, information, and so on) to implement a Pareto-improving policy, but that policy is not an equilibrium choice.

32. For instance, financial interests will make cogent arguments for an independent central bank and, using that cover, push not only for a central bank that is independent but for one whose governance is not representative of the parties affected by macroeconomic policies.

33. For an empirical and theoretical analysis casting doubt on the centrality of transparency as a cause of the crisis, see Furman and Stiglitz (1999).

34. See Rostow (1952, 1960); Adelman and Morris (1965); Abramovitz (1986); Stiglitz (1995a); Temple and Johnson (1998).

35. As North and Thomas argue in *The Rise of the Western World* (1973: 2), "innovation, economies of scale, education, capital accumulation . . . are

not causes of growth; they *are* growth." Easterly and Levine (2000) document four stylized facts of economic growth that they argue are not well explained by the factor accumulation models.

36. See Stiglitz (1988). In fact, among countries with not too disparate capital-labor ratios, factor prices would be equalized simply by trade (Samuelson 1948).

37. Capital market constraints make consumption levels backward-looking: consumption today (c_t) will depend on the time profile of income in the past. For simplicity, suppose $c_t = f(y_{t-1})$ where y_{t-1} is last period's income and $f' > 0$. When the growth rate is high, y_{t-1}/y_t is low. Hence, c_t/y_t is low, which implies that the saving rate is high. In this way, constraints on borrowing against future income can make saving rates an increasing function of growth.

38. Stiglitz (1973) showed in a variety of models that expectations can play a key role in determining savings and the long-run accumulation path of the economy. He noted that expectations may even cause an economy to oscillate between different techniques and saving rates, neither converging to a balanced growth path nor diverging from it; the economy "simply 'wobbles along'" (141). These results do not depend on incorrect expectations but may hold where expectations of prices in the immediate future are fulfilled.

39. Note that the model presented in the previous section exhibited aggregate increasing returns to scale. If capital and labor were both mobile, they would all end up on the same island. If only capital was mobile, it would move disproportionately to the island with the clustering of skilled labor. Incomes per capita would persistently differ across the two islands.

40. For a discussion of the role of multinationals in diffusing new technologies, see World Bank (1999b). For a discussion of the implications of alternative hypotheses for market equilibrium, see Dasgupta and Stiglitz (1988).

41. Earlier we showed that there can exist multiple equilibria arising from economies of scale associated with nontraded goods (see pp. 409–10). Similarly, the hypothesis in Lucas (1988) that early developers can "choose" industries with steep learning curves fails to explain their sustained higher incomes and growth rates. First, it assumes that the learning cannot be transmitted across national boundaries. Second, it fails to note that if some industries have steeper learning curves, faster rates of productivity growth will typically be reflected in faster rates of decline in relative prices; see Skeath (1993).

42. For an elaboration on this point, see Rodrik (1995); Stiglitz (1998a).

43. A general framework with many other examples of pecuniary externalities in a setting of moral hazard and adverse selection is in Greenwald and Stiglitz (1986). For a framework emphasizing pecuniary externalities arising from innovation, see Makowski and Ostroy (1995).

References

Abramovitz, Moses. 1986. "Catching Up, Forging Ahead, and Falling Behind." *Journal of Economic History* 46 (2, June): 385–406.

Acemoglu, Daron. 1995. "Reward Structures and the Allocation of Talent." *European Economic Review* 39: 17–33.

———. 1997. "Training and Innovation in an Imperfect Labour Market." *Review of Economic Studies* 64 (220, July): 445–64.

Acemoglu, Daron, and James A. Robinson. 2000. "Political Losers as a Barrier to Economic Development." *American Economic Review* 90 (2, May): 126–30.

Adelman, Irma, and Cynthia Taft Morris. 1965. "A Factor Analysis of the Interrelationship between Social and Political Variables and Per Capita Gross National Product." *Quarterly Journal of Economics* 79 (4, November): 555–78.

Adserà, Alicia, and Debraj Ray. 1998. "History and Coordination Failure." *Journal of Economic Growth* 3 (3, September): 267–76.

Aghion, Philippe, and Patrick Bolton. 1997. "A Theory of Trickle-Down Growth and Development." *Review of Economic Studies* 64 (2, April): 151–73.

Aleem, Irfan, and Louis Kasekende. 1999. "Reforming Finance in a Low-Income Country: Uganda." Finance Team, Development Research Group, World Bank, Washington, D.C. Processed. Information available at <www.worldbank.org/research/projects/finliber.htm>.

Amelina, Maria, 2000. "Why Is the Russian Peasant Still a Kolkhoznik?" *Post-Soviet Geography and Economics.* Forthcoming.

Arnott, Richard, and Joseph E. Stiglitz. 1991. "Moral Hazard and Nonmarket Institutions: Dysfunctional Crowding Out or Peer Monitoring?" *American Economic Review* 81 (1, March): 179–90.

Arrow, Kenneth. 1962a. "The Economic Implications of Learning by Doing." *Review of Economic Studies* 29 (3): 155–73.

———. 1962b. "Economic Welfare and the Allocation of Resources for Invention." In *The Rate and Direction of Inventive Activity: Economic and Social Factors,* 609–25. Princeton, N.J.: Princeton University Press.

Arrow, Kenneth, and Gerard Debreu. 1954. "Existence of an Equilibrium for a Competitive Economy." *Econometrica* 22 (3, July): 265–90.

Atkinson, Anthony B., and Joseph E. Stiglitz. 1969. "A New View of Technological Change." *Economic Journal* 79 (September): 573–78.

Azariadis, Costas, and Allan Drazen. 1990. "Threshold Externalities in Economic Development." *Quarterly Journal of Economics* 105 (2): 501–26.

Banerjee, Abhijit V. 2000. "The Two Poverties." Massachusetts Institute of Technology, Cambridge, Mass.

Banerjee, Abhijit V., and Andrew F. Newman. 1993. "Occupational Choice and the Process of Development." *Journal of Political Economy* 101 (2, April): 274–98.

———. 1998. "Information, the Dual Economy, and Development." *Review of Economic Studies* 65 (October): 631–53.

Banerjee, Abhijit V., Paul Gertler, and Maitreesh Ghatak. 1998. "Empowerment and Efficiency: The Economics of Tenancy Reform." Massachusetts Institute of Technology, Cambridge, Mass. Processed.

Bardhan, Pranab. 2000. "The Nature of Institutional Impediments to Economic Development." In Mancur Olson and Satu Kähkönen, eds., *A Not-So-Dismal Science,* 245–68. Oxford, U.K.: Oxford University Press.

Bardhan, Pranab, and Maitreesh Ghatak. 1999. "Inequality, Market Imperfections, and Collective Action Problems." CIDER Working Paper C99-108. Center for International and Development Economics Research, University of California, Berkeley.

Basu, Kaushik. 2000. *The Social and Political Foundations of Economics: A Prelude to Political Economy.* Oxford, U.K.: Oxford University Press.

Basu, Kaushik, and Pham Hoang Van. 1998. "The Economics of Child Labor." *American Economic Review* 88 (3, June): 412–27.

Becker, Gary. 1973. "A Theory of Marriage: Part I." *Journal of Political Economy* 81(4, July–August): 813–46.

———. 1983. "A Theory of Competition among Pressure Groups for Political Influence." *Quarterly Journal of Economics* 98 (3, August): 371–400.

Bell, Clive. 1990. "Interactions between Institutional and Informal Credit Agencies in Rural India." *World Bank Economic Review* 4 (3): 297–328. Reprinted in Karla Hoff, Avishay Braverman and Joseph E. Stiglitz, eds., *The Economics of Rural Organization: Theory, Practice, and Policy,* 186–213 (New York: Oxford University Press).

Bernanke, Ben, and Mark Gertler. 1990. "Financial Fragility and Economic Performance." *Quarterly Journal of Economics* 105 (1, February): 87–114.

Besley, Timothy, and Anne Case. 1994. "Diffusion as a Learning Process: Evidence from HYV Cotton." Research Program in Development Studies Discussion Paper 174. Woodrow Wilson School of Public and International Affairs, Princeton University, Princeton, N.J.

Besley, Timothy, and Stephen Coate. 1998. "Sources of Inefficiency in a Representative Democracy: A Dynamic Analysis." *American Economic Review* 88 (1): 139–54.

Bhagwati, Jagdish, Richard Brecher, and T. N. Srinivisan. 1984. "DUP Activities and Economic Theory." In David Colander, ed., *Neoclassical Political Economy: The Analysis of Rent-Seeking and DUP Activities,* 17–32. Cambridge, Mass.: Ballinger.

Blanchard, Olivier, and Michael Kremer. 1997. "Disorganization." *Quarterly Journal of Economics* 112 (4, November): 1091–126.

Bloom, David E., and Jeffrey D. Sachs. 1998. "Geography, Demography, and Economic Growth in Africa." *Brookings Papers on Economic Activity* 0 (2, September): 207–73.

Bowles, Samuel. 1985. "The Production Process in a Competitive Economy: Walrasian, Neo-Hobbesian, and Marxian Models." *American Economic Review* 75: 16–36.

———. 1998. "Endogenous Preferences: The Cultural Consequences of Markets and Other Economic Institutions." *Journal of Economic Literature* 36 (1, March): 75–111.

Boycko, Maxim, Andrei Shleifer, and Robert W. Vishny. 1996. "Second-Best Economic Policy for a Divided Government." *European Economic Review* 40 (3–5, April): 767–74.

Braverman, Avishay, and Joseph E. Stiglitz. 1982. "Sharecropping and the Interlinking of Agrarian Markets." *American Economic Review* 72 (4, September): 695–715.

———. 1986. "Cost Sharing Arrangement under Sharecropping: Moral Hazard, Incentive Flexibility and Risk." *Journal of Agricultural Economics* 68 (3, August): 642–52.

———. 1989. "Credit Rationing, Tenancy, Productivity and the Dynamics of Inequality." In Pranab Bardhan, ed., *The Economic Theory of Agrarian Institutions*, 185–202. Oxford, U.K.: Clarendon Press.

Bruno, Michael. 1996. *Deep Crises and Reform: What Have We Learned?* Directions in Development series. Washington, D.C.: World Bank.

Chenery, Hollis B. 1975. "The Structuralist Approach to Development Policy." *American Economic Review* 65 (2, May): 310–16.

Coase, Ronald H. 1937. "The Nature of the Firm." *Economica* 4: 386–405.

———. 1960. "The Problem of Social Cost." *Journal of Law and Economics* 3: 1–44.

Conley, Timothy, and Christopher Udry. 1999. "Learning and Innovation: The Adoption of Pineapple in Ghana." Working Paper, Agrarian Studies Colloquium Series. Yale University, New Haven, Conn.

Cooper, Russell W. 1999. *Coordination Games: Complementarities and Macroeconomics.* Cambridge, U.K.: Cambridge University Press.

Cooter, Robert D. 1997. "The Rule of State Law and the Rule-of-Law State: Economic Analysis of the Legal Foundations of Development." In Michael Bruno and Boris Pleskovic, eds., *Annual World Bank Conference on Development Economics 1996*, 191–238. Washington, D.C.: World Bank.

———. 2000. "Law from Order: Economic Development and the Jurisprudence of Social Norms." In Mancur Olson and Satu Kähkönen, eds., *A Not-So-Dismal Science*, 228–44. Oxford, U.K.: Oxford University Press.

Darwin, Charles. 1993. *The Origin of Species by Means of Natural Selection.* Modern Library edition. New York: Random House. First published 1859.

Dasgupta, Partha, and Debraj Ray. 1986. "Inequality as a Determinant of Malnutrition and Unemployment." *Economic Journal* 96 (384, December): 1011–34.

Dasgupta, Partha, and Joseph E. Stiglitz. 1988. "Learning-by-Doing, Market Structure and Industrial and Trade Policies." *Oxford Economic Papers* 40 (2): 246–68.

de Meza, David, and J. R. Gould. 1992. "The Social Efficiency of Private Decisions to Enforce Property Rights." *Journal of Political Economy* 100 (3, June): 561–80.

Diamond, Peter. 1982. "Aggregate Demand Management in Search Equilibrium." *Journal of Political Economy* 90: 881–94.

Dixit, Avinash K. 1996. *The Making of Economic Policy: A Transaction Cost Politics Perspective.* Cambridge, Mass.: MIT Press.

Dixit, Avinash K., and Joseph E. Stiglitz. 1977. "Monopolistic Competition and Optimum Product Diversity." *American Economic Review* 67 (3, June): 297–308.

Durlauf, Steven. 1996. "Neighborhood Feedbacks, Endogenous Stratification, and Income Inequality." In William A. Barnett, Giancarlo Gandolfo, and Claude Hillinger, eds., *Dynamic Disequilibrium Modeling: Theory and Applications. Proceedings of the Ninth International Symposium in Economic Theory and Econometrics*, 505–34. Cambridge, U.K.: Cambridge University Press.

———. 1999. "The Memberships Theory of Inequality: Ideas and Implications." In Elise S. Brezis and Peter Temin, eds., *Elites, Minorities, and Economic Growth*, 161–77. Amsterdam: Elsevier Science.

Dyck, Alexander. 1999. "Privatization and Corporate Governance: Principles, Evidence and Future Challenges." Harvard Business School, Cambridge, Mass. Processed.

Easterly, William. 1999. "The Middle Class Consensus and Economic Development." Policy Research Working Paper 2346. Macroeconomics and Growth, Development Research Group, World Bank, Washington, D.C.

Easterly, William, and Ross Levine. 1997. "Africa's Growth Tragedy: Policies and Ethnic Divisions." *Quarterly Journal of Economics* 112 (4, November): 1203–50.

———. 2000. "It's Not Factor Accumulation: Stylized Facts and Growth Models." Policy Research Group, World Bank, Washington, D.C. Available at <www.worldbank.org/research/growth/wpdate.htm>.

Engerman, Stanley L., and Kenneth L. Sokoloff. 1997. "Factor Endowments, Institutions, and Differential Paths of Growth among New World Economies: A View from Economic Historians of the United States." In Stephen Haber, ed., *How Latin America Fell Behind: Essays on the Economic Histories of Brazil and Mexico, 1800–1914*, 260–304. Stanford, Calif.: Stanford University Press.

Engerman, Stanley L., Stephen Haber, and Kenneth L. Sokoloff. 1999. "Inequality, Institutions, and Differential Paths of Growth among New World Economies." Department of Economics, University of California, Los Angeles. Processed.

Evans, Peter. 1995. *Embedded Autonomy: States and Industrial Transformation*. Princeton, N.J.: Princeton University Press.

Farrell, Joseph. 1987. "Information and the Coase Theorem." *Journal of Economic Perspectives* 1 (2, fall): 113–29.

Fei, John C., and Gustav Ranis. 1969. "Economic Development in Historical Perspective." *American Economic Review* 59 (2, May): 386–400.

Fernandez, Raquel, and Dani Rodrik. 1991. "Resistance to Reform: Status Quo Bias in the Presence of Individual-Specific Uncertainty." *American Economic Review* 81 (5, December): 1146–55.

Finger, J. Michael. 1998. "GATT Experience with Safeguards: Making Economic and Political Sense of the Possibilities That the GATT Allows to Restrict

Imports." Policy Research Working Paper 2000. Trade, Development Research Group, World Bank, Washington, D.C.

Floro, Sagrario, and Pan Yotopoulos. 1991. *Informal Credit Markets and the New Institutional Economics: The Case of Philippine Agriculture*. Boulder, Colo.: Westview Press.

Foster, Andrew, and Mark Rosenzweig. 1995. "Learning by Doing and Learning from Others: Human Capital and Technical Change in Agriculture." *Journal of Political Economy* 103 (6, December): 1176–1209.

Furman, Jason, and Joseph E. Stiglitz. 1999. "Economic Crises: Evidence and Insights from East Asia." *Brookings Papers on Economic Activity* (2): 1–114.

Gallup, John Luke, and Jeffrey Sachs, with Andrew Mellinger. 1999. "Geography and Economic Growth." In Boris Pleskovic and Joseph E. Stiglitz, eds., *Annual World Bank Conference on Development Economics 1998*, 127–78. Washington, D.C.: World Bank.

Gambetta, Diego. 1993. *The Sicilian Mafia: The Business of Private Protection*. Cambridge, Mass.: Harvard University Press.

Gilbert, Richard, Partha Dasgupta, and Joseph E. Stiglitz. 1982. "Invention and Innovation under Alternative Market Structures: The Case of Natural Resources." *Review of Economic Studies* 49: 567–82.

Greenwald, Bruce, and Joseph E. Stiglitz. 1986. "Externalities in Economies with Imperfect Information and Incomplete Markets." *Quarterly Journal of Economics* 101 (May): 229–64.

———. 1993. "Financial Market Imperfections and Business Cycles." *Quarterly Journal of Economics* 108 (1, February): 77–114.

Greenwald, Bruce, Joseph E. Stiglitz, and Andrew Weiss. 1984. "Informational Imperfections in the Capital Markets and Macroeconomic Fluctuations." *American Economic Review* 74 (2, May): 194–99.

Greif, Avner. 1994. "Cultural Beliefs and the Organization of Society: A Historical and Theoretical Reflection on Collectivist and Individualist Societies." *Journal of Political Economy* 102 (5, October): 912–50.

———. 1997. "Contracting, Enforcement, and Efficiency: Economics beyond the Law." In Michael Bruno and Boris Pleskovic, eds., *Annual World Bank Conference on Development Economics 1996*. Washington, D.C.: World Bank.

Grossman, Sanford J. 1989. "The Informational Role of Warranties and Private Disclosure about Product Quality." In Sanford J. Grossman, ed., *The Informational Role of Prices*, 166–89. Wicksell Lectures. Cambridge, Mass.: MIT Press.

Harberger, Arnold C. 1964. "Taxation, Resource Allocation, and Welfare." In John Due, ed., *The Role of Direct and Indirect Taxes in the Federal Revenue System*. Princeton, N.J.: Princeton University Press.

Harris, John R., and Michael P. Todaro. 1970. "Migration, Unemployment and Development: A Two-Sector Analysis." *American Economic Review* 60 (1, March): 126–42.

Hart, Oliver. 1975. "On the Optimality of Equilibrium When the Market Structure Is Incomplete." *Journal of Economic Theory* 11 (3, December): 418–43.

Hayek, Friedrich A. 1978. "Competition as a Discovery Procedure." In *New Studies in Philosophy, Politics, Economics and the History of Ideas.* Chicago, Ill.: University of Chicago Press.

Hellman, Thomas, Kevin Murdock, and Joseph E. Stiglitz. 1996. "Deposit Mobilization through Financial Restraint." In Niels Hermes and Robert Lensink, eds., *Financial Development and Economic Growth,* 219–46. New York: Routledge.

Helpman, Elhanan, and Paul Krugman. 1985. *Market Structure and Foreign Trade: Increasing Returns, Imperfect Competition, and the International Economy.* Cambridge, Mass.: MIT Press.

Hoff, Karla. 1992. Review of Douglass C. North, *Institutions, Institutional Change and Economic Performance. Kyklos* 45 (4): 582–85.

———. 1994. "The Second Theorem of the Second Best." *Journal of Public Economics* 54: 223–42.

———. 1996. "Market Failures and the Distribution of Wealth: A Perspective from the Economics of Information." *Politics and Society* 24 (4): 411–32.

———. 1997. "A Bayesian Model of the Infant Industry Argument." *Journal of International Economics* 43 (3–4): 400–36.

———. 1998. "Adverse Selection and Institutional Adaptation." Working Paper Series 98-02 (February): 1–40. Department of Economics, University of Maryland, College Park, Md.

———. 2000. "The Logic of Political Constraints and Reform, with Applications to Strategies for Privatization." World Bank, Washington, D.C. Processed.

Hoff, Karla, and Andrew Lyon. 1995. "Non-Leaky Buckets: Optimal Redistributive Taxation and Agency Costs." *Journal of Public Economics* 58 (3. November): 365–90.

Hoff, Karla, and Arijit Sen. 2000. "Homeownership, Community Interactions, and Segregation." World Bank, Washington, D.C. Processed.

Hoff, Karla, and Joseph E. Stiglitz. 1998. "Moneylenders and Bankers: Price-Increasing Subsidies in a Monopolistically Competitive Market." *Journal of Development Economics* 55 (2, April): 485–518.

Hoff, Karla, Avishay Braverman, and Joseph E. Stiglitz, eds. 1993. *The Economics of Rural Organization: Theory, Practice, and Policy.* New York: Oxford University Press.

Huntington, Samuel. 1968. *Political Order in Changing Societies.* New Haven, Conn.: Yale University Press.

Jain, Sanjay, and Sharun Mukand. 1999. "Redistributive Promises and the Adoption of Economic Reform." George Washington University, Washington, D.C., and Tufts University, Medford, Mass. Processed.

Klitgaard, Robert. 1991. *Adjusting to Reality: Beyond "State versus Market" in Economic Development.* San Francisco, Calif.: ICS Press.

Kranton, Rachel E. 1996. "Reciprocal Exchange: A Self-Sustaining System." *American Economic Review* 86 (4, September): 830–51.

Kremer, Michael. 1993. "The O-Ring Theory of Economic Development." *Quarterly Journal of Economics* 108 (3, August): 551–75.

Krueger, Anne O. 1974. "The Political Economy of the Rent-Seeking Society." *American Economic Review* 64 (3, June): 291–303.

———. 1993. *Political Economy of Policy Reform in Developing Countries.* Cambridge, Mass.: MIT Press.

Krugman, Paul. 1991. "History versus Expectations." *Quarterly Journal of Economics* 106 (May): 651–67.

Krusell, Per, and Jose-Victor Rios-Rull. 1996. "Vested Interests in a Positive Theory of Stagnation and Growth." *Review of Economic Studies* 63 (2, April): 301–29.

Kuznets, Simon. 1955. "Economic Growth and Income Inequality." *American Economic Review* 45 (1, March): 1–28.

Landes, David S. 1998. *The Wealth and Poverty of Nations: Why Some Are So Rich and Some So Poor.* New York: W. W. Norton.

Legros, Patrick, and Andrew F. Newman. 1996. "Wealth Effects, Distribution, and the Theory of Organization." *Journal of Economic Theory* 70 (2, August): 312–41.

Lewis, W. Arthur. 1954. "Economic Development with Unlimited Supplies of Labour." *Manchester School of Economic and Social Studies* 22 (May): 139–91.

Ljungqvist, Lars. 1993. "Economic Underdevelopment: The Case of a Missing Market for Human Capital." *Journal of Development Economics* 40: 219–39.

Lucas, Robert E. 1973. "Some International Evidence on Output-Inflation Tradeoffs." *American Economic Review* 63 (3): 326–34.

———. 1976. "Econometric Policy Evaluation: A Critique." *Journal of Monetary Economics* 1 (2, supplement): 19–46.

———. 1988. "On the Mechanics of Economic Development." *Journal of Monetary Economics* 22 (July): 3–42.

Lucas, Robert E., and E. C. Prescott. 1974. "Equilibrium Search and Unemployment." *Journal of Economic Theory* 7 (2): 188–209.

Makowski, Louis, and Joseph Ostroy. 1995. "Appropriation and Efficiency: A Revision of the First Theorem of Welfare Economics." *American Economic Review* 85 (4): 808–27.

Marshall, Alfred. 1897. "The Old Generation of Economists and the New." *Quarterly Journal of Economics* 11 (2, January): 115–35.

Matsuyama, Kiminori. 1997. "Economic Development as Coordination Problems." In Masahiko Aoki, Hyung-Ki Kim, and Masahiro Okuno-Fujiwara, eds., *The Role of Government in East Asian Economic Development: Comparative Institutional Analysis.* Oxford, U.K.: Clarendon Press.

McCloskey, Deirdre. 1998. "The So-Called Coase Theorem." *Eastern Economic Journal* 24 (3, summer): 367–71.

Miller, Marcus, and Joseph E. Stiglitz. 1999. "Bankruptcy Protection against Macroeconomic Shocks: The Case for a Super Chapter 11." Presented at a conference on "Capital Flows, Financial Crisis, and Policies," World Bank, April 15–16, Washington, D.C. Available at <http://www.warwick.ac.uk/fac/soc/Economics/miller/>.

Mookherjee, Dilip. 1997a. "Informational Rents and Property Rights in Land." In John H. Roemer, ed., *Property Relations, Incentives, and Welfare: Proceedings of a Conference Held in Barcelona, Spain, by the International Economic Association.* New York: St. Martin's Press.

———. 1997b. "Wealth Effects, Incentives, and Productivity." *Review of Development Economics* 1 (1, February): 116–33.

Mookherjee, Dilip, and Debraj Ray. 1998. "Persistent Inequality and Endogenous Investment Thresholds." Boston University, Boston, Mass. Processed.

———. 2000. "Contractual Structure and Wealth Accumulation." Boston University, Boston, Mass. Processed.

Morawetz, David. 1981. *Why the Emperor's New Clothes Are Not Made in Colombia: A Case Study in Latin American and East Asian Manufactured Exports.* New York: Oxford University Press.

Morduch, Jonathan. 1999. "The Microfinance Promise." *Journal of Economic Literature* 37 (4, December): 1569–1614.

Murphy, Kevin M., Andrei Shleifer, and Robert W. Vishny. 1989. "Industrialization and the Big Push." *Journal of Political Economy* 97 (5, October): 1003–26.

———. 1993. "Why Is Rent-Seeking So Costly to Growth?" *American Economic Review* 83 (2, May): 409–14.

North, Douglass C. 1990. *Institutions, Institutional Change and Economic Performance.* Cambridge, U.K.: Cambridge University Press.

———. 1994. "Economic Performance through Time." *American Economic Review* 84 (3, June): 359–68.

North, Douglass C., and Robert Paul Thomas. 1970. "An Economic Theory of the Growth of the Western World." *Economic History Review* 23: 1–17 (second series).

———. 1973. *The Rise of the Western World.* Cambridge, U.K.: Cambridge University Press.

Olson, Mancur. 1965. *The Logic of Collective Action: Public Goods and the Theory of Groups.* Cambridge, Mass.: Harvard University Press.

———. 1993. "Dictatorship, Democracy, and Development." *American Political Science Review* 87 (3, September): 567–76.

Palfrey, Thomas, and Howard Rosenthal. 1984. "Participation and the Provision of Discrete Public Goods: A Strategic Analysis." *Journal of Public Economics* 24 (2, July): 171–93.

Pargal, Sheoli, and David Wheeler. 1996. "Informal Regulation of Industrial Pollution in Developing Countries: Evidence from Indonesia." *Journal of Political Economy* 104 (6): 1314–27.

Piketty, Thomas. 1997. "The Dynamics of the Wealth Distribution and the Interest Rate with Credit Rationing." *Review of Economic Studies* 64 (2, April): 173–89.

Ray, Debraj, and K. Sengupta. 1989. "Interlinkages and the Pattern of Competition." In Pranab Bardhan, ed., *The Economic Theory of Agrarian Institutions*. Oxford, U.K.: Clarendon Press.

Robinson, James A. 1996. "Distribution and Institutional Structure: Some Preliminary Notes." Paper presented at MacArthur Foundation, May 3. University of Southern California, Los Angeles. Processed.

———. 1999. "When Is a State Predatory?" University of California, Berkeley. Processed.

Rodriguez-Clare, Andrés. 1996. "The Division of Labor and Economic Development." *Journal of Development Economics* 49 (April): 3–32.

Rodrik, Dani. 1995. "Trade and Industrial Policy Reform." In Jere Behrman and T. N. Srinivasan, eds., *Handbook of Development Economics*, vol. 3B, 2925–82. Amsterdam: North-Holland.

———. 1996. "Coordination Failures and Government Policy: A Model with Applications to East Asia and Eastern Europe." *Journal of International Economics* 40 (1–2, February): 1–22.

Romer, Paul M. 1986. "Increasing Returns and Long-Run Growth." *Journal of Political Economy* 94 (5, October): 1002–37.

Rosenstein-Rodan, Paul. 1943. "Problems of Industrialization of Eastern and South-Eastern Europe." *Economic Journal* 53: 202–11.

Ross, Stephen. 1973. "The Economic Theory of Agency: The Principal's Problem." *American Economic Review* 63 (2, May): 134–39.

Rostow, Walt Whitman. 1952. *The Process of Economic Growth*. New York: Norton.

———. 1960. *The Stages of Economic Growth: A Non-Communist Manifesto*. Cambridge, U.K.: Cambridge University Press.

Sah, Raaj Kumar, and Joseph E. Stiglitz. 1989a. "Sources of Technological Divergence between Developed and Less Developed Countries." In Guillermo Calvo and others, eds., *Debt, Stabilizations and Development: Essays in Memory of Carlos Diaz-Alejandro*, 423–46. Cambridge, Mass.: Basil Blackwell.

———. 1989b. "Technological Learning, Social Learning and Technological Change." In Sukhamoy Chakravarty, ed., *The Balance between Industry and Agriculture in Economic Development*, 285–98. New York: St. Martin's Press in association with the International Economic Association.

Samuelson, Paul A. 1948. "International Trade and the Equalization of Factor Prices." *Economic Journal* 58 (230, June): 163–84.

Samuelson, William. 1985. "A Comment on the Coase Theorem." In A. E. Roth, ed., *Game-Theoretic Models of Bargaining*. New York: Cambridge University Press.

Sen, Amartya. 1999. *Development as Freedom*. New York: Knopf.

Shaw, Edward. 1973. *Financial Deepening in Economic Development*. New York: Oxford University Press.

Skeath, Susan. 1993. "Strategic Product Choice and Equilibrium Traps for Less Developed Countries." *Journal of International Trade and Economic Development* 2 (1, June): 1–26.

Solow, Robert. 1956. "A Contribution to the Theory of Economic Growth." *Quarterly Journal of Economics* 70 (1, February): 65–94.

Stigler, George. 1971. "The Economic Theory of Regulation." *Bell Journal of Economics* 2 (spring): 3–21.

Stiglitz. Joseph E. 1969. "Distribution of Income and Wealth among Individuals." *Econometrica* 37 (3, July): 382–97.

———. 1973. "Recurrence of Techniques in a Dynamic Economy." In J. Mirrlees, ed., *Models of Economic Growth,* 138–61. New York: Macmillan.

———. 1974a. "Incentives and Risk Sharing in Sharecropping." *Review of Economic Studies* 41 (2, April): 219–55.

———. 1974b. "Theories of Discrimination and Economic Policy." In G. von Furstenberg, Ann R. Horowitz, and Bennett Harrison, eds., *Patterns of Racial Discrimination,* 5–26. Lexington, Mass.: D. C. Heath, Lexington Books.

———. 1974c. "Alternative Theories of Wage Determination and Unemployment in L.D.C.'s: The Labor Turnover Model." *Quarterly Journal of Economics* 88 (2): 194–227.

———. 1975. "The Theory of Screening, Education and the Distribution of Income." *American Economic Review* 65(3): 283–300.

———. 1987. "Learning to Learn, Localized Learning and Technological Progress." In Partha Dasgupta and Paul Stoneman, eds., *Economic Policy and Technological Performance,* 125–53. New York: Cambridge University Press.

———. 1988. "Economic Organization, Information, and Development." In Hollis Chenery and T. N. Srinivasan, eds., *Handbook of Development Economics,* vol. 1, 93–160. Amsterdam: North-Holland.

———. 1989. "Markets, Market Failures, and Development." *American Economic Review* 79 (2, May): 197–203.

———. 1990. "Some Retrospective Views on Growth Theory." In P. Diamond, ed., *Growth/ Productivity/ Unemployment,* 50–68. Cambridge, Mass.: MIT Press.

———. 1992a. "Alternative Tactics and Strategies for Economic Development." In Amitava Krishna Dutt and Kenneth P. Jameson, eds., *New Directions in Development Economics,* 57–80. Aldershot, U.K.: Edward Elgar.

———. 1992b. "Explaining Growth: Competition and Finance." *Rivista di Politica Economica* (Italy) 82 (169, November): 225.

———. 1993. "Comments on 'Towards a Counter-Counterrevolution in Development Theory.'" In Michael Bruno and Boris Pleskovic, eds., *Annual World Bank Conference on Development Economics 1992,* 39–49. Washington, D.C.: World Bank.

———. 1994a. "Economic Growth Revisited." *International and Corporate Change* 3 (1): 65–110.

———. 1994b. "Endogenous Growth and Cycles." In Y. Shionoya and M. Perlman, eds., *Innovation in Technology, Industries, and Institutions,* 121–56. Ann Arbor: University of Michigan Press.

————. 1994c. "The Role of the State in Financial Markets." In Michael Bruno and Boris Pleskovic, eds., *Annual World Bank Conference on Development Economics 1993*. Washington, D.C.: World Bank.

————. 1995a. "Interest Rate Puzzles, Competitive Theory and Capital Constraints." In Jean-Paul Fitoussi, ed., *Economics in a Changing World*, vol. 5, 145–75. New York: St. Martin's Press.

————. 1995b. "Social Absorption Capability and Innovation." In Bon Ho Koo and D. H. Perkins, eds., *Social Capability and Long-Term Economic Growth*. New York: St. Martin's Press.

————. 1996a. "The Role of the Government in the Economy of Less Developed Countries." In *Development Strategy and Management of the Market Economy*. New York: United Nations.

————. 1996b. "Some Lessons from the East Asian Miracle." *World Bank Research Observer* 11 (2, August): 151–77.

————. 1998a. "An Agenda for Development in the Twenty-first Century." In Boris Pleskovic and Joseph E. Stiglitz, eds., *Annual World Bank Conference on Development Economics 1997*. Washington, D.C.: World Bank.

————. 1998b. "The Private Uses of Public Interests: Incentives and Institutions." *Journal of Economic Perspectives* 12 (spring): 3–22.

————. 1998c. "Reflections on the Theory and Practice of Reform." Paper presented to Stanford University, September 17.

————. 1999. "Knowledge as a Global Public Good." In *Global Public Goods*. New York: United Nations Development Programme.

————. 2000. "Whither Reform? Ten Years of the Transition." In Boris Pleskovic and Joseph E. Stiglitz, eds., *Annual World Bank Conference on Development Economics 1999*, Washington, D.C.: World Bank.

Stiglitz. Joseph E., and Marilou Uy. 1996. "Financial Markets, Public Policy, and the East Asian Miracle." *World Bank Research Observer* 11 (2, August): 249–76.

Temple, Jonathan, and Paul A. Johnson. 1998. "Social Capability and Economic Growth." *Quarterly Journal of Economics* 113 (3, August): 965–90.

Tinbergen, Jan. 1967. *Economic Policy: Principles and Design*. Amsterdam: North-Holland.

Tirole, Jean. 1996. "A Theory of Collective Reputations (with Applications to the Persistence of Corruption and to Firm Quality)." *Review of Economic Studies* 63 (1, January): 1–22.

Tornell, Aaron, and Philip R. Lane. 1999. "The Voracity Effect." *American Economic Review* 89 (1, March): 22–46.

World Bank. 1997. *World Development Report 1997: The State in a Changing World*. New York: Oxford University Press.

————. 1999a. *Assessing Aid: What Works, What Doesn't, and Why*. World Bank Policy Research Report. New York: Oxford University Press.

————. 1999b. *World Development Report 1998/99: Knowledge for Development*. New York: Oxford University Press.

Comment

Gustav Ranis

THIS IS AN INTERESTING AND stimulating chapter. It begins with a rather heart-warming broadside against the smugness of the neoclassical paradigm, which tends, among other things, to blame government failure and the resulting distortions for everything that has gone wrong and Pareto-efficient equilibrium for everything that has gone right. Of course, by means of engulfing, like an amoeba, anything uncomfortable that comes along by converting it into risk, governance, or transaction costs, orthodoxy is trying to protect itself, amend the Washington consensus at the margin, focus increasingly on the market-friendliness of government interventions, broaden the objectives of development, and the like. But the emerging "Dubrovnik consensus," as reflected in the chapter by Hoff and Stiglitz, goes beyond that. It points to the real problems: that neoclassical economics is timeless and ahistorical and therefore cannot handle dynamic processes; that unique equilibria usually do not exist; and that markets are incomplete and represent work in progress. As complicated as it makes the world, what neoclassical economics assumes as given—not only distribution, technology, preferences, and policy choices, but also institutions—should be viewed as endogenous. Indeed, behind institutions we find path dependency interacting with ideology and even culture, possibly based on ethnicity. All this can quickly become a mind-blowing exercise, but, as Hoff and Stiglitz point out, logic forces us to enter the jungle.

As we do, we should remember that while Solow's models are neoclassical, do not incorporate distribution, and tend to have unique equilibria, Solow himself should not be associated with the religious wing of the party. Indeed, his sensitivity to the importance of history and of initial conditions has been evident on many occasions. I would add that Kenneth Arrow, often viewed as the high priest of neoclassicism, similarly recognized—appropriately, at the New Delhi meeting of the International Economic Association—that when it comes to development economics, dualism is a reality, and equilibrium can be achieved only in the long run.

But let us not kid ourselves. Orthodoxy still has the profession firmly in its grip. Development economics is viewed by the preponderant majority of economists as just another applied field of economics—and after all, we do have a neat and coherent conceptual machinery at our disposal. Moreover, when Hoff and Stiglitz present their positive analysis in the second part of their paper, we indeed find a "myriad of other important interactions" other than prices that determine outcomes. But while we find many "trees," we don't yet see the outlines of the alternative "forest." Not that we should expect Hoff and Stiglitz to dramatically unveil the outlines of a brand new "theory of development"; instead we expect explanatory frameworks to be developed that are typology specific or even country specific. But the four classes of admittedly very interesting and challenging models presented here seem more like the collected works of Stiglitz and his associates—plus others he admires—than the beginning of any kind of even partially woven tapestry.

This paper is clearly a work in progress—the beginning, not even yet the middle, of wisdom. Perhaps the main criticism I have of the authors' innovative and fascinating tour de force is that it promises too much. In the very introduction we are told that the authors intend to bring theory to bear on the differential performance of the developing countries of Asia, Africa, and Latin America, and they promise to tell us which government interventions are most likely to lead to success. This they do not come close to doing. In fact, aside from an occasional episodic example, there is little indication as to which of the four classes of multiple equilibrium models is likely to be more relevant to which part of the developing world. The models emphasize the importance of institutions in place of investments, of distortions in place of equilibrium, and of knowledge, social capital and, most emphatically, coordination failures and development traps as obstacles, but there is no effort to begin to construct a general theory or shed light on actual development experience. We cannot, of course, expect delivery of something so ambitious. But I am obliged, with Dani Rodrik, to remind the authors that "promises, promises" raise expectations and should therefore probably be toned down.

The policy section of the chapter is rather thin. One suspects that time and space ran out but also that the authors became aware that they had to pull in their horns. Nevertheless, I found the difference between "deep" and "shallow" interventions instructive and the example of the support of the Russian *nomenklatura* for privatization (since they could expect to reap larger rents over longer periods of time) sadly convincing.

These are a few dimensions of intervention choice that I was surprised not to find represented, especially since the, at least partial, endogeneity of policy is very much in the picture. The dichotomy of "chosen" versus "pressing" problems relates rather well to the role of ample natural resources and the availability of foreign capital "for the asking" in taking the pressure off the need for policy reform. This extension of the "Dutch disease" phenomenon into the decisionmaking sphere was, I think, well illustrated in India during the early 1990s, when foreign capital ceased to come in and serious reforms were initiated; in Taiwan (China) in the early 1960s, when a ballooning of economic assistance was associated with the announcement that the aid would come to an end by middecade; and in Indonesia and Mexico, where, over time, we can clearly discern a relationship between better policies and lower oil prices.

Another surprising omission, especially since Hoff and Stiglitz cite it as one of the goals of development, is that of the role of political democracy in the choice of interventions, as well as in their sequencing. The "big bang" associated with the radical application of neoclassical economics could have been usefully contrasted with an institutionally sensitive gradualism, even though we can deduce much from the authors' overall emphasis on induced institutional change.

I have a specific, if minor, comment on one of the examples presented: that relating to the efficiency-wage hypothesis, which permits the determination of an equilibrium industrial real wage. I have always viewed this model, based on Stiglitz's Kenya experience, as an example of a neoclassical effort to force institutional facts into an orthodox, market-determined bottle. If unskilled sweepers in a Nairobi subsidiary of a multinational corporation earn five times the wages of unskilled sweepers in a local firm, turnover differential arguments must be based either on an ex ante quality differential at the hiring stage (that is, a selection bias) or on the conversion by the efficiency wage of the employee of the multinational corporation into a sweeper with much higher productivity—both possible but, in my view, pulled by the hairs. I would rather attribute this phenomenon, in line with the authors' emphasis on institutions and history, to the fact that wage-setting in Kenya was heavily influenced by the effort to Kenyanize expatriate jobs in large-scale industry—including their high wage levels, which then cascaded down to unskilled labor. Institutional wages in the Harris-Todaro sense, applied to unskilled industrial labor (like institutional wages in the Lewis-Fei-Ranis sense, applied to unskilled agricultural labor) would seem more consistent with the main thrust of the paper.

Finally, a well-intentioned—that is, friendly—obiter dictum. I believe it has been heart-warming and of considerable encouragement to professionals, especially outside the United States, to have someone of Stiglitz's recognized intellectual stature—not to speak of his position of influence in the World Bank—question the conventional neoclassical wisdom, at both the macro and micro levels. All of this has indeed come as a breath of fresh air and is a tribute to a new intellectual openness, in contrast to some earlier incumbencies at the Bank. This is all to the good and provides considerable encouragement to those who have believed for some time that the positions of international financial institutions have often been too closed-circle, monolithic, and self-congratulatory. But there are also risks if the critique of neoclassical equilibrium analysis is not relatively soon converted into a coherent set of alternative propositions useful for policy analysis. The experience with Paul Krugman's "new trade theory" heterodoxy of some years ago illustrates the possible downside if that does not happen relatively quickly. Krugman's stress on the impact of economies of scale, imperfect competition, and intermediate goods exchanges on traditional trade theory, which emphasized the free exchange of final goods, was interpreted by many analysts and policymakers in developing countries as an intellectually respectable argument for returning to the import-substitution policies of yesteryear. Krugman was ultimately forced to state in print that he meant the "new trade theory" to apply mainly to North-North trade, not to developing countries—but most of the damage had already been done. A similar danger looms here. Departures from the neoclassical machinery should not be allowed to constitute an invitation for "anything goes."

The challenge, therefore, is clear: to move as quickly as possible toward combining the ideas of North and the analytical virtuosity of Stiglitz into analytical packages with both empirical and policy content. We are agreed that the search should not be for a general theory of development but for one that captures the reality of particular regions or countries and interprets the World Bank's "comprehensive development" approach in this pragmatic fashion.

Comment

Abhijit V. Banerjee

Once upon a time there was an ugly duckling called development economics. It was full of strange assumptions and contrary logic, and all the other economics made fun of it. But as it grew up, it beefed up its theoretical muscles and shed its ugly assumptions, and with its emphasis on institutions and market imperfections, it became the envy of all the rest.

THIS IS THE STORY OF development economics, give or take a bit of fancy, told by Hoff and Stiglitz. It is a heartening story—all the more so because it has the advantage of being largely correct, at least in one interpretation.

I think the story is largely accurate in its description of the views of the current generation of academic development economists *about how the economy functions*. Most would agree with the authors in their view that market failures are so pervasive to as make complete markets of an Arrow-Debreu model substantially irrelevant. Moreover, it is now widely recognized that Coasian bargaining is simply not a realistic way to internalize externalities that involve many participants and, often, more than one market. The second welfare theorem notwithstanding, few now believe that questions of efficiency and growth can be resolved independent of issues about distribution.

But there is much more disagreement in the development community as to what policymakers should make of all this. There are many, especially among practical development economists, who would say with some justice, "Sure, markets do not work in Africa, but then what does?" In other words, where there are market failures, there are also government failures, and it is not at all clear that the cure (in the form of an additional government intervention) may not sometimes be worse than the disease (the market failure).

This is all perfectly true. And therefore, it is argued—and here we see the leap of faith—perhaps governments should stick to their traditional roles of enforcing contracts, carrying out regulation, protecting property rights, disseminating information, maintaining a stable currency, and making sure that there is enough investment in human capital and infrastructure.

Hoff and Stiglitz have a response to this "retro-neoclassical" position. Their view, in brief, is that the category of government failure is too broad to be useful. Governments do not always fail, and even when they do, there are degrees of failure. Therefore, the authors argue, what we as policymakers need is an articulated theory of why and where governments fail. A significant and interesting part of their paper introduces the reader to some of the potential dimensions of such a theory.

What is not in their paper, and perhaps this is logical, is their view of what the appropriate domain for the government might be. In particular, it is not clear whether, after understanding the government better, we would want to go back to the retro-neoclassical view. Hoff and Stiglitz clearly imply that this need not be the case, but they do not say much that is specific about where and why we might want to deviate from the standard agenda. This is what I attempt here: my comment is necessarily based on a very ad hoc view of government, but it has the advantage of being quite specific and therefore perhaps more effective in advertising the distinctive view of the world implicit in their chapter.[1]

Markets and Market Failures

Are there market failures that deserve to be taken seriously? Let me begin with what are in some sense the easiest answers, which relate to what have been the traditional domains of public action. In the case of education, for example, a number of careful recent studies have suggested that the private rates of return on investment in education in developing countries are significantly higher than the comparable cost of capital.[2] The lack of investment, despite the very favorable rates of return, signals either limited access to capital or unwillingness on the part of parents to put up the money. Under either scenario, it is at least arguable that public investment in education can increase output and may even lead to a Pareto improvement.

There is also some evidence—circumstantial, rather than direct—of underinvestment in children's health. There is clear documentation that poor children are smaller than their potential. There is also a significant amount of less clear evidence that smaller people earn less. Finally, there are data indicating that poor families are not using their food expenditures optimally from the point of view of maximizing child health: there is too much emphasis on "quality" as against nutritional value.[3] The combination of these facts seems to suggest that parents do not value their children's nutrition as much as productivity calculations would dictate.

Although the case for government intervention in human capital development is relatively noncontroversial, there is controversy about what is the best way to intervene. The traditional recipe—investment in public schools and hospitals—seems to work reasonably well in some places but not in others. For example, in many areas of India, such as Rajasthan and Uttar Pradesh, both the public school system and the public health system are almost defunct as a result of widespread apathy and corruption, but there are also areas (for example, Himachal Pradesh and Kerala) where things work much better. As of now, there are no signs that the worse areas are moving in the direction of the better ones (see Drèze and Sen 1995; Probe Team 1998).

Overexploitation of environmental resources is another orthodox argument for public intervention. While I am not aware of rigorous empirical analysis proving that there is overexploitation (showing, for example, that the observed rate of deforestation is not what people want), the prima facie evidence and the logic of theory are so compelling that the case for some intervention seems straightforward.[4] At this point the concern seems to be that government interventions do not appear to have been very successful in arresting deforestation in the developing world. Over the period 1990–95 the annual deforestation rate in low-income countries was 0.7 percent, which in the long run is clearly unsustainable. The comparable rate in high-income countries was –0.2 percent; that is, those countries were actually adding forested land (World Bank 1999).

There is disagreement as to why government regulation in this area has been so ineffective. For a long time the dominant view among economists was that governments in developing countries were relying too much on regulation and too little on creating private property rights in environmental resources; forests get cut down, in this view, because no one owns them. Private property rights, however, have the significant disadvantage that they only work when a few individuals control a large enough volume of resources; to take an extreme example, putting fences around single trees is rarely cost-effective. Moreover, for many resources, such as biodiversity, the private value of their conservation may be lower than the social value.[5] All this has led to a growing interest in other ways of dealing with this problem, which I discuss in a later section.

Development economists have also traditionally emphasized the inefficiencies that arise from sheer lack of knowledge. People often do not know what the best practice or the latest technology might be and are surprisingly slow to move to the best-practice technology. Hybrid corn took 20 years to be fully accepted in the United States, and the process of diffusion of Green Revolution technology in India has been even slower (Munshi 1999).

Although the case for trying to speed up this process seems clear, actual experience with government extension programs that advocate new technologies has been mixed. In fact, diffusion of both hybrid corn and high-yielding varieties of wheat and rice was slow even though well-established extension programs existed. The problem is that farmers do not fully trust the extension worker: they feel that the extension worker may not have understood their specific context well enough. As a result, in recent years a growing literature has emphasized the process whereby people learn about new technologies and practices from people like themselves. This is clearly a valuable source of additional knowledge, but it creates problems of its own. Because people learn from other people's experience, each person who tries out a new technology is doing all his neighbors a favor, and in equilibrium, it is likely that too few people will strike out in a new direction. In some cases the result could be that everyone sticks to an inefficient older technology even if a newer and better option is available; essentially, each person makes the wrong choice because everyone else does.[6]

To summarize at this point, the evidence does seem to support the need for intervention in what were traditional domains of the government, but the history of such interventions has been rather disappointing, and as a result the exact role of the government has to be rethought. I next turn to other, less orthodox, arguments for intervention.

Shaban (1987) explored the failure of the land market to provide adequate incentives and estimated the loss of productivity stemming from the fact that the owner of the land is not the one who cultivates it at 16 percent. Banerjee, Gertler, and Ghatak (1998) found that a reform which strengthened tenants' rights in the Indian state of West Bengal led to a 12 percent increase in the overall agricultural output of the state. These estimates imply that the free-market outcome provides inadequate incentives for agricultural production and suggest that both equity and efficiency may be promoted by some form of redistribution.

Consumption-smoothing is another area in which there has been a lot of recent research. The concern is that the poor, because they own so little in assets, may find it difficult to deal with even temporary downturns in their incomes. In extreme cases this could mean living in semistarvation until incomes recover.

The evidence on this is rather mixed. The most dramatic evidence seems to be that from famines, when, as Amartya Sen has argued, people starve to death even though the per capita availability of food may be only marginally lower than in other years. Fortunately, famines are not particularly common, and most people would probably agree that feeding people in a famine is an acceptable role for the government. More-over, famines are, by their very nature, correlated shocks that affect everyone in an area. Insuring against famines requires an arrangement that involves people from different areas or even different countries and that, as a result, cannot exist without a certain amount of formal institutional structure.[7] For this reason the ability of markets to pro-vide insurance against famines is probably a less interesting question than the ability of villagers to coinsure against idiosyncratic shocks.

This is certainly the view in the literature; almost every study of risk-sharing takes the village as its natural unit (Townsend 1995 is an ex-ception) and studies the effect of temporary income shocks on consumption. The evidence that emerges from these studies gives cre-dence to the view that even poor, semiliterate people are able to reduce their exposure to idiosyncratic income risk without any help from the government. It remains true, however, that the data frequently reject the prediction of perfect insurance at the village level. Deaton (1997), in a study of coinsurance in Côte d'Ivoire, finds that a US$1 fall in a person's current income, with no change in average village income, can lead to a decline in current consumption of up to 35 cents.

There is also reason to believe that these studies may severely under-estimate the full efficiency effect of lack of insurance. As Morduch (1993) pointed out, a part of the effect of imperfect insurance is to induce people to make choices that reduce their risk exposure. This in turn can induce other people to distort their choices through the pecuniary ex-ternalities that they generate.[8]

The fact that insurance is not perfect does not, of course, imply that the market outcome can be improved on through government interven-tion, but there is some reason to believe that this may be the case. Both Townsend (1995) and Deaton (1997) find wide variations in the extent of consumption insurance across villages. While this finding could re-flect unobservable differences in risk characteristics or in the taste for bearing risk, it is at least as likely that it reflects institutional differ-ences. After all, most observed insurance arrangements tend to be in-formal and are presumably enforced through some collective monitoring and punishment mechanism. Such mechanisms are obviously vulner-able to free-riding by those who are supposed to enforce them. More-over, since the mechanisms have to be self-enforcing, there is the usual problem of multiple equilibria: effective insurance is possible in only some of the equilibria, and there is no guarantee that the desirable equi-libria are the ones that get chosen.[9]

Expensive and limited access to credit is another important limita-tion of the "free" market. Lack of access to credit prevents people who do not have their own money from making the investments that best match their talents and therefore both slows growth and promotes in-equality. Lack of access to credit is also one reason why there is imperfect insurance: if the credit market were perfect, short-run fluctuations in income would have no effect on consumption.

Aleem (1993) provides direct evidence on imperfections in the credit market. Using data gathered from moneylenders in Pakistan, he argues that the cost of implementing a loan contract (which includes screening costs and collection costs) with borrowers who have little or no collateralizable wealth is between 30 and 45 cents for each dollar lent. This is pure waste from the collective point of view and would be avoided if the government simply gave the dollar to the borrowers. Of course, the government would then have to pay for these gifts by using general tax revenues, and taxation is costly, but there is no reason to believe that zero redistribution maximizes the social surplus. We will come back to this issue in the next section.

A Role for Government?

In the last section, we reviewed a subset of Hoff and Stiglitz's much more comprehensive list of areas in which it is possible to improve on the market outcome. However, the existence of obvious and costly market failures does not by itself imply an expanded role for governments. I have, after all, also suggested that government intervention in the traditional areas needs to be refocused and revamped. In this section I argue that it is important that we do ask more of governments, at least in certain specific areas.

Redistribution

I have already suggested that redistribution might promote efficiency in the markets for credit and land. Insuring people better may also require some ex post redistribution. Redistribution on a large scale is by no means easy. Land reforms, to take the one modern example of attempted redistribution on a substantial scale, have failed more often than they have succeeded (see Banerjee 2000). This is hardly surprising, given that the traditionally powerful landlord class has a stake in undermining the reform and that government officials can be bribed or coerced to go along with them.

There is, however, an important asymmetry between a failed attempt to redistribute and a successful one. After a failed reform, we go back, more or less, to the status quo. A successful reform, by contrast, might start us on what has been called the virtuous cycle of poverty reduction: by making the tenant the owner of the land, it raises his productivity and hence his income. A higher income allows the tenant to save more and to invest more, raising his income even further, and so on.[10] A similar argument can be made in the case of a credit market failure.

Extra wealth leads to higher creditworthiness. This leads to more credit, which leads to higher investments, higher incomes, and, ultimately, higher wealth. Getting richer might enhance people's willingness to take risks, which in turn leads to more wealth and more risky investments. Finally, being richer might make people more self-confident and more patient, encouraging them to set their goals higher.

The general implication is that successful redistributions come with a multiplier that makes their productivity effect much larger than the direct effect of the reform. Moreover, a successful redistribution can take other burdens off the government. If parents have enough money they can (and usually do) invest in their children's health and education, relieving the government of that particular responsibility. If people have rewarding occupations, they are much less likely to cut down trees illegally or to poach rare animals. Finally, in developing countries, communities that are wealthy enough often provide a part of their own infrastructure.[11] The chance of a really successful redistribution can be worth the risk of a few failures.[12]

I also believe that thinking hard about strategies and applying what we understand about incentive theory can make redistribution much more likely to succeed. First, it is useful to broaden the constituency for the redistribution. If, for example, land is being redistributed, the urban middle classes may be a natural ally of the rural poor (especially if they are the ones whose taxes are paying for the reform), and they can help make sure that the program is properly implemented.

Second, there are many ways to redistribute, and the most obvious method may not be the best. To take an example, even if the goal is more equal distribution of land, it does not follow that land itself should be redistributed. Sometimes it may be better to give money to the poor for the purpose of buying land.[13] It may also be possible to achieve the effects of redistributing land by adopting what I have elsewhere called empowerment strategies (see Banerjee, Gertler, and Ghatak 1998). These are strategies that empower the tenant in the sense of strengthening his bargaining position vis-à-vis the landlord. If, for example, he no longer has to rely on the landlord for help in an emergency (because, say, the government has set up an emergency income assistance program), he can afford to be tougher when he bargains with the landlord, and this could increase his share of the output and improve his incentives. Tenancy reforms that strengthen the legal rights of the tenant also fall in the class of empowerment strategies.[14] Similarly, giving a poor family money may not be the best way to help it.

Third, the eligibility requirements for being part of the program should be chosen carefully. Having no requirements may be too costly because everyone would want to join, but having a large number of complicated requirements distorts the incentives of the potential participants and, perhaps more important, makes it easy for corrupt bureaucrats to extract bribes from potential beneficiaries of the program. In the case of land reform, for example, trying to identify the true landless may be too costly. Giving the current tenant the right to buy out the owner might reduce the efficacy of the program but has the advantage of being more difficult to manipulate.[15]

Fourth, the net size of the gift to the beneficiaries should not be too large. Very large gifts attract the attention of greedy bureaucrats who will then try to make sure that they get a piece. Note that the dynamic effects of the transfer do not depend on the net welfare gain (what we have called the gift); they depend on the net increase in the beneficiary's wealth. In other words, an ideal program increases the beneficiary's wealth by a large amount but his welfare, at least in the short run, by a smaller amount. This can be achieved by inflicting nonmonetary costs on the beneficiary. From this point of view, workfare is clearly better than pure transfers.[16]

Finally, it may be easier to subsidize the accumulation of assets by poor people than to actually transfer assets to them. Subsidization can be accomplished by paying poor people higher than market returns on their deposits in banks or other financial institutions or by using public money to improve access to these financial institutions.[17] On the borrowing side, as is discussed below, it may be possible to substantially improve credit access among poor people by developing and promoting microcredit institutions.

Promoting Innovations

The other area in which I see a greater role for the government is as a promoter of innovation. As Hoff and Stiglitz, following Bloom and Sachs (1998), point out, research on a vaccine for malaria is severely underfunded, and a public initiative could make a difference here. Of course, the exact mechanism for encouraging innovation needs to be worked out carefully since, as Kremer (1999) has argued, it is easy to end up wasting a lot of money.[18]

A less obvious example is what has come to be called microcredit. In recent years a number of nongovernmental organizations (NGOs) have had remarkable success in lending to relatively poor people in very poor countries. They have been able to achieve a combination of very high repayment rates and relatively low interest rates—at least compared with what moneylenders charge—without requiring massive subsidies. It is not entirely clear why they have been so successful. Some NGOs (and some scholars) stress the benefits of group lending, arguing that careful screening and monitoring of borrowers by other members reduces agency problems in the credit market. Others have stressed the importance of a long-term relationship—borrowers repay because they want credit in the future. In either case it is likely that the direct effect will generate a further multiplier effect: as borrowers' incentives improve, the interest rate that they are charged will fall, further improving their incentives and leading to another round of falling interest rates, improved incentives, and so on. This kind of amplification may explain why these programs have done so well.[19] Whatever the basis of their success, it is clear that there has been an innovation in the technology of lending. Moreover, given that the innovation was arrived at through a process of trial and error, there is every reason to believe that further innovations are possible.[20]

There have been important innovations in other areas as well. In environmental management there is growing support for vesting the primary property rights for forests and water sources in the local community (see Baland and Platteau 1996). It is argued that the local community has the strongest incentives for protecting the local environment and has enough resources to be able to effectively monitor its use. In recent years a number of governments in India, Nepal, and elsewhere have adopted the joint forest management model, transferring control over state property to elected local bodies.

More generally, I firmly believe that by the creative application of ideas from mechanism design, it ought to be possible to generate better risk-sharing, better schools, and even less corrupt governments.[21] Of course, these are not the kinds of innovation that will be promoted by the lure of profits.[22] Governments can help by subsidizing the innovators but also by creating a political framework within which such innovation is possible. Thus, joint forest management requires the government to create an institutional framework that will eventually exclude the government from any role in managing forests.

The government also has an important role to play in promoting the *adoption* of innovations. In part, this is just a matter of coordinating people. Risk-pooling arrangements, for example, work because a lot of people join the group, thereby reducing the overall level of risk. No one will want to join a group that has very few members. Townsend (1995) suggests that in Thailand having a leader who takes the initiative to coordinate all the people in the village interested in risk-sharing is crucial. In the absence of such a leader, the government could take on this function.

In many cases the problem is less one of coordination than of communication. As I pointed out earlier, people seem to be more influenced by the experience of their peers than by the recommendations of government personnel. Therefore, an effective strategy for the government may be to subsidize people who are willing to try out new technologies; the government would then publicize the results of those trials. The most important change here may be in the attitudes of government agents: instead of telling people what to do, they will have to let them try out the various options and decide for themselves.

Promoting innovations, like everything else that governments do, creates opportunities for corruption. It is possible, for example, that money could be handed out to specific people in the name of encouraging innovation. It is clear, however, that in comparison with the case of redistribution, the stakes will be much smaller, and so, probably, will be the likelihood of corruption. After all, almost no one would benefit from blocking these innovations. It may well be that the mindset of government officials is the more important constraint in this case; historically, government bureaucracies have not been friendly to new ideas, which may reflect the incentives that they are usually given.[23] Changing these incentives, and the attitudes that go with them, will be important for the success of this kind of effort.

Conclusion

Good governance is one of the scarcest resources in developing countries. Anyone who suggests new things for the government to do must therefore have ideas about what could be sacrificed. In most developing countries, governments produce steel and electricity, run hotels and mines, deliver the mail, and more. I would want most of that out of the government's hands, even if it were not important to make space for other things. As it is, tying a privatization program to a subsequent redistribution plan helps make the privatization more palatable and the redistribution more effective.

Notes

The author is grateful to Karla Hoff for detailed discussions.

1. This way of posing the problem ignores the role played by nongovernmental organizations (NGOs), which are increasingly doing things that used to be expected of the government. NGOs are not immune to corruption or bureaucratic ineptitude and at least a part of the discussion here ought to apply to their interventions as well.

2. A careful study by Duflo (2000) argues that the rate of return on public money invested in the construction of new primary school buildings in Indonesia in the 1970s was around 10.5 percent, after allowing for a 20 percent deadweight loss from taxation and making conservative projections about growth after 1997. That is considerably higher than the average real rate on Indonesian government bonds in the same period, which was about 5 percent. This calculation does not control for the opportunity cost of the time spent in school, but primary school students earn very little. Moreover, Duflo's calculation leaves out the gains to those who would have completed primary schooling even before the program. These children presumably benefited from now having schools closer to them. See also Clark and Hsieh (1999) and Spohr (1999) for related evidence from Taiwan (China).

3. For a comprehensive survey of the available evidence, see Strauss and Thomas (1998).

4. It is hard to imagine that Coasian bargaining could solve the problem, at least when the number of potential beneficiaries is large and there is some

asymmetric information about people's tastes. Mailath and Postlewaite (1990) formalize this idea.

5. It is also worth emphasizing that the argument that property rights and free markets guarantee the optimal long-run use of natural resources relies heavily on the assumption that there is a large enough number of far-sighted agents who are able and willing to do arbitrage over a very long period. It is not clear that this is a reasonable assumption in the context of developing countries. Baland and Platteau (1996) provide a more elaborate discussion of the case for and against privatization.

6. Banerjee (1992) and Bikhchandani, Hirshleifer, and Welch (1992) provide theoretical analyses of the effects of learning externalities. Besley and Case (1994), Foster and Rosenzweig (1995), and Munshi (1999) are empirical analyses which find that the timing of decisions to adopt a new agricultural technology is correlated within a village, even after controlling for all obvious observable sources of such a correlation; this result suggests that learning from other people does take place. Moreover, both Foster and Rosenzweig and Munshi show strong evidence for certain other predictions of the social learning model.

7. For example, the enforcement of cross-border insurance contracts is difficult without the backing of international law.

8. See Banerjee and Newman (1998) for a formalization of this argument.

9. For a formalization of an insurance arrangement as repeated game, see Kimball (1988). Greif (1993) argues that history plays an important role in choosing among the set of possible equilibria.

10. This kind of virtuous cycle and its counterpart, the vicious cycle of poverty, are modeled in Banerjee and Newman (1994) and Galor and Zeira (1993). Banerjee and Newman (1993) argue that there may be additional vicious and virtuous cycles if we take account of the fact that the wage rate is endogenous.

11. Many town and village enterprises in China, as well as the textile town of Tirupur in India, are examples of such communities.

12. This is particularly true if there is enough political pressure from the poor that the government has to make some gesture towards them from time to time. If this gesture costs real money and yet does not help the poor to escape from poverty—as is frequently the case—we would need to compare the cost of all the gestures that would have to be made in the future with the current cost of a large-scale reform.

13. A number of recent programs for redistributing land have gone in this direction (this what the World Bank calls market-assisted land reform). For a discussion of the pros and cons of giving money as against redistributing land, see Banerjee (2000).

14. It should be emphasized that each of these empowerment strategies works only under specific conditions.

15. I discuss issues relating to the design of land reforms in Banerjee (2000).

16. This assumes that the labor market is not perfect. There is, however, a lot of evidence that people in rural areas are underemployed in the dry season,

and rural employment schemes that pay people for working on public projects in the dry season already exist in more than one country. Note also that this argument for workfare is different from the more standard argument that emphasizes the screening role of work requirements (see Besley and Coate 1992).

17. There is probably a substantial amount of pent-up demand among poor people for savings instruments that give them moderate rates of return. Aportela (1998) estimates that the Pahnal program in Mexico, which substantially improved poor people's access to moderately rewarding savings instruments (the real rate of return on the most popular program, the Cuentahorro, was at most 2–3 percent), raised their saving rate by around 7 percentage points, starting from a base of about 3 percent.

18. Kremer (1999) also proposes a mechanism that avoids many of these problems.

19. Since the effect of a subsidy is also amplified, even the rather small subsidies that these organizations receive may contribute significantly to their success.

20. In fact, this is how I read the recent papers (Laffont and N'Guessan 1999; Rai and Sjöström 1999) which argue that it is possible to improve on the observed group-lending mechanisms.

21. It should be possible, for example, to improve the quality of the public education system by adopting better systems of incentives for teachers. Giving more power and resources to a committee of parents may be one way of improving incentives. A more radical strategy would be to give the parents school vouchers and allow them the choice of sending their children to private schools. See Banerjee (1997) for a discussion of how the government may be reengineered to reduce corruption.

22. It is in any case not true that the market provides optimal incentives for innovation even in the case of much more marketable commodities; see Aghion and Howitt (1998).

23. For example, the popular stereotype is that bureaucrats are not rewarded for success but are punished for important failures.

References

Aghion, Philippe, and Peter Howitt. 1998. *Endogeneous Growth Theory.* Cambridge, Mass.: MIT Press.

Aleem, Irfan. 1993. "Imperfect Information, Screening and the Costs of Informal Lending: A Study of a Rural Credit Market in Pakistan." In Karla Hoff, Avishay Braverman, and Joseph E. Stiglitz, eds., *The Economics of Rural Organization: Theory, Practice, and Policy,* 131–53. New York: Oxford University Press.

Aportela, Fernando. 1998. "Effects of Financial Access on Savings by Low-Income People." Massachusetts Institute of Technology, Cambridge, Mass. Processed.

Baland, Jean-Marie, and Jean-Philippe Platteau. 1996. *Halting Degradation of Natural Resources.* New York: Oxford University Press.

Banerjee, Abhijit V. 1992. "A Simple Model of Herd Behavior." *Quarterly Journal of Economics* 107 (3): 797–817.

———. 1997. "A Theory of Misgovernance." *Quarterly Journal of Economics* 112 (4): 1289–1332.

———. 2000. "Land Reforms: Prospects and Strategies." In Boris Pleskovic and Joseph E. Stiglitz, eds., *Annual World Bank Conference on Development Economics 1999*. Washington, D.C.: World Bank.

Banerjee, Abhijit V., and Andrew F. Newman. 1993. "Occupational Choice and the Process of Development." *Journal of Political Economy* 101 (2, April): 274–98.

———. 1994. "Poverty, Incentives, and Development." *American Economic Review* 84 (2): 211–15.

———. 1998. "Information, the Dual Economy, and Development." *Review of Economic Studies* 65 (4, October): 631–53.

Banerjee, Abhijit V., Paul Gertler, and Maitreesh Ghatak. 1998. "Empowerment and Efficiency: The Economics of a Tenancy Reform." Massachusetts Institute of Technology, Cambridge, Mass. Processed.

Besley, Timothy, and Anne Case. 1994. "Diffusion as a Learning Process: Evidence from HYV Cotton." Research Program in Development Studies Discussion Paper 174. Woodrow Wilson School of Public and International Affairs, Princeton University, Princeton, N.J.

Besley, Timothy, and Stephen Coate. 1992. "Workfare vs. Welfare: Incentive Arguments for Work Requirements in Poverty Alleviation Programs." *American Economic Review* 82 (March): 249–61.

Bikhchandani, Sushil, David Hirshleifer, and Ivo Welch. 1992. "A Theory of Fads, Fashion, Custom, and Cultural Change as Informational Cascades." *Journal of Political Economy* 100 (5): 992–1026.

Bloom, David E., and Jeffrey D. Sachs. 1998. "Geography, Demography, and Economic Growth in Africa." *Brookings Papers on Economic Activity* 0 (2, September): 207–73.

Clark, D., and C.-T. Hsieh. 1999. "Schooling and Labor Market Impact of the 1968 Nine-Year Education Program in Taiwan." University of California, Berkeley. Processed.

Deaton, Angus. 1997. *The Analysis of Household Surveys: A Microeconometric Approach to Development Policy*. Baltimore, Md.: Johns Hopkins University Press.

Drèze, Jean, and Amartya Sen. 1995. *India: Economic Development and Social Opportunity*. Delhi: Oxford India Press.

Duflo, Esther. 2000. "Schooling and Labor Market Consequences of School Construction in Indonesia: Evidence from an Unusual Policy Experiment." Massachusetts Institute of Technology, Cambridge, Mass. Processed. Available at: http://web.mit.edu/eduflo/www/indpapaer.pdf

Foster, Andrew, and Mark Rosenzweig. 1995. "Learning by Doing and Learning from Others: Human Capital and Technical Change in Agriculture." *Journal of Political Economy* 103 (6, December): 1176–1209.

Galor, Oded, and Joseph Zeira. 1993. "Income Distribution and Macroeconomics." *Review of Economic Studies* 60 (1): 35–52.

Greif, Avner. 1993. "Contract Enforceability and Economic Institutions in Early Trade: The Maghribi Traders' Coalitions." *American Economic Review* 83 (3): 525–48.

Kimball, Miles S. 1988. "Farmers' Cooperatives as Behavior toward Risk." *American Economic Review* 78 (1): 224–32.

Kremer Michael. 2000a. "Creating Markets for New Vaccines: Rationale." Forthcoming in *Innovation Policy and the Economy*. See http://post.economics. harvard.edu/faculty/kremer/papers.html

———. 2000b. "Creating Markets for New Vaccines: Design Issues." *Innovation Policy and the Economy*. Forthcoming. See http://post.economics. harvard.edu/faculty/kremer/papers.html

Laffont, Jean-Jacques, and T. N'Guessan. 1999. "Collusion and Group Lending with Adverse Selection." Draft. Institut d'Economie Industrielle, University of Toulouse, France.

Mailath, George J., and Andrew Postlewaite 1990. "Asymmetric Information Bargaining Problems with Many Agents." *Review of Economic Studies* 57 (3): 351–67.

Morduch, Jonathan. 1993. "Risk, Production and Saving: Theory and Evidence from Indian Households." Working Paper. Department of Economics, Harvard University, Cambridge, Mass.

Munshi, Kaivan. 1999. "Learning from Your Neighbors: Why Do Some Innovations Spread Faster Than Others?" University of Pennsylvania, Philadelphia. Processed.

Ostrom, Elinor, R. Gardner, and J. Walker. 1994. *Rules, Games and Common-Pool Resources*. Ann Arbor: University of Michigan Press.

Probe Team. 1998. *Public Report on Basic Education in India*. Delhi: Oxford University Press.

Rai, Ashok, and Tomas Sjöström. 1999. "Efficient Lending Schemes in Village Economies." Harvard University, Cambridge, Mass. Processed.

Shaban, Radwan Ali. 1987. "Testing between Competing Models of Sharecropping." *Journal of Political Economy* 95 (5, October): 893–920.

Spohr, Christopher. 1999. "Formal Schooling and Workforce Participation in a Rapidly Developing Economy: Evidence from 'Compulsory' Junior High School in Taiwan." Massachusetts Institute of Technology, Cambridge, Mass. Processed.

Strauss, John V., and Duncan Thomas. 1998. "Health, Nutrition, and Economic Development." *Journal of Economic Literature* 36 (2): 766–817.

Townsend, Robert. 1995. "Financial Systems in Northern Thai Villages." *Quarterly Journal of Economics* 110 (4): 1011–46.

World Bank. 1999. *World Development Report 1998–99: Knowledge for Development*. New York: Oxford University Press.

Comment

Debraj Ray

THE CHAPTER BY HOFF AND STIGLITZ reviews new theoretical approaches to the study of economic development. The literature they discuss is of immense significance for our understanding of the development process. It is time that this material became standard reading for students, and their chapter will contribute usefully toward that end.

In these brief comments I summarize the new points of view, mainly to complement the Hoff-Stiglitz chapter but also to point out one or two areas on which more emphasis may be warranted.

Much of the traditional literature in economic development has been based on the neoclassical growth model, which embodies the following assumption and attempts to trace its implications:

> Capital-scarce countries should have a higher rate of return. If they were to save the same fraction of income as their capital-rich counterparts, and if they had the same population growth rates, their per capita income would grow faster. It follows that, all other things being equal, countries should converge in terms of per capita income. If we do see systematic differences, it must be because other things, such as savings and population growth rates, are not equal.

What causes the differences, according to this view? A variety of "exogenous" cultural, historical, and even religious factors are invoked at this stage: corrupt cultures, problematic social attitudes toward high fertility, the absence of a Protestant ethic, a lack of democracy, incompetent government, traditions that promote conspicuous consumption . . . you name it.

This is the situation—in my view, an unsatisfactory one—in which development economics has floundered for several decades. It is important to understand that this is not just a world view; it has a definite influence on policy. A policy would then be a persistent attempt to shore up variables such as saving rates or to bring down variables such as population growth rates. A policy would have to be persistent because without it, the "fundamental" intercountry, intersociety differences would simply take over again.

This view of development as some conditional form of convergence (conditional on the fundamentals being correct) has come under some criticism. Sustained growth, in this view, is the outcome of tweaking some parameters such as the saving rate and making sure that they are kept in place by a judicious mix of policy interventions. At worst, if there are large setup costs, economies of scale, or other "nonconvexities" at the level of the economy, some large-scale resource transfers from industrial to developing countries would be needed, in addition to these policies. But as Hoff and Stiglitz correctly argue, it is hard to see what sort of scale economies come into play at the national level, and in any case "even a transfer of funds may not have a large effect on economic growth."

The literature discussed in this chapter takes a rather different view. Briefly, one might interpret this literature as implicitly arguing—or at least taking as its working presumption—that there are no fundamental differences across societies. That is, the very same fundamental society can display very different, self-reinforcing modes of behavior. Initial historical legacies, by pinning down expectations or some other, more concrete variable such as the distribution of assets, can precipitate one or more of these self-reinforcing outcomes, which remain persistently different across societies.

The lucid exposition in the Hoff-Stiglitz contribution gives me room for a little extra—but, I hope, useful—abstraction. It will be helpful to distinguish between two forms of self-reinforcing equilibria (the terminology is borrowed from Mookherjee and Ray forthcoming).

Inertial Self-Reinforcement

These are the multiple equilibria that Hoff and Stiglitz discuss in detail. They illustrate such equilibria beautifully by using models in which, for instance, several aggregate saving rates, or research and development rates, or degrees of property rights enforcement could persist under the same fundamentals. I wish to emphasize a different aspect of these multiplicities, and my choice of terminology will reflect this.

At any given moment of time, a particular equilibrium is in force and has possibly been in force in that society in the medium- or long-run past. Suppose that this is indeed the bad equilibrium in any one of the examples given by Hoff and Stiglitz. Rosenstein-Rodan (1943) and

Hirschman (1958) have argued that this initial situation—the fact that by force of inertia we are in the bad equilibrium to begin with—is what one might mean by underdevelopment. At the same time, the claim that multiple equilibria are at the bottom of it all does not appear to be central to these writers (although recent rediscoverers of this phenomenon have lingered long over it). The harder question is, how is a particular equilibrium pinned down by the force of historical inertia, and what will it take to unpin it?

Unfortunately, the multiple equilibrium or coordination-game paradigm is not of much use in this regard beyond the demonstration that multiplicities (may) exist. The very same paradigm is at a loss to explain historical inertia: repeat a multiple equilibrium story, and all sorts of dynamic equilibria emerge, including those in which the society jumps between the bad and the good equilibria in all sorts of deftly coordinated ways.

This indeterminacy and disregard for inertia have been of recent concern to macroeconomists as well as development economists, even though the steps taken so far have been quite tentative.[1] Rosenstein-Rodan and Hirschman were certainly concerned with this issue, although they did not make much serious headway on it—witness the debate between "balanced" and "unbalanced" growth, a topic of great interest in the 1950s.

I would like to place this problem on the table as one that demands serious research attention. Let me emphasize that this would not merely be an application of "modern" economic theory to development. In fact, a coherent theory for this sort of "equilibrium transition" simply does not exist at this time (nor does a serious theory of expectations inertia).[2]

It goes without saying that central to such a theory of equilibrium transition would be a particular view of economic policy. In this world there is no such thing as a persistent policy (although this is not to argue that there is never any need for such policies in other, equally appropriate descriptions). Economic policy, in this view, is an equilibrium-tipping device. The most important feature of these policies is that they are intrinsically ephemeral: once the equilibrium has been tipped, the new equilibrium will hold on its own.

Historical Self-Reinforcement

Inertial self-reinforcement describes multiple equilibria and therefore directs our attention to the beliefs or expectations of the economic agents that lock them into any one of the equilibria. This view of underdevelopment may be usefully complemented by a related but distinct approach. This is the observation that historical legacies may actually select for different sets of equilibria (quite apart from the possible multiplicities in each set). In short, history may echo persistently into the future, and not just via the determination of expectations.

Hoff and Stiglitz discuss these equilibria as well, arguing that historical pressure may come from sources as diverse as legal structure, traditions, or group reputations (see also Ray 1998, especially ch. 4). Notice that the question I raised in the previous section becomes less relevant here. The problem of explaining expectational inertia no longer arises because historical self-reinforcement can coexist with a unique equilibrium (under each history). A parallel question, however, emerges, equally if not more important for policy: how do changes in "initial conditions" map into equilibrium (or long-run-equilibrium) changes? To illustrate, I will focus on what is possibly the most important instance of historical self-reinforcement: that caused by initial inequalities in the distribution of assets.

Notice that in the standard neoclassical growth model, differences in initial endowments across countries are predicted to disappear in the long run (at least conditionally). This sort of argumentation creeps into some of the first- and second-generation theories of income distribution dynamics (see, for instance, Champernowne 1953; Loury 1981), which may be viewed as several copies of the neoclassical growth model running in parallel, without any interaction across individuals. The diminishing-returns postulate in the standard growth model forces ahistoricity, and the presence of uncertainty (as in Loury's framework), while weakening the deterministic notion of convergence, does nothing to remove this ahistoricity.

More recently, models of inequality that emphasize interaction across individuals have emerged. In these theories the distribution of assets at any date has an impact on macroeconomic variables, such as equilibrium prices and wages or employment and output, at that date. One important reason why these variables are affected by inequality is that credit markets are typically missing or imperfect, so that wealth constraints affect market decisions. In such scenarios, initial inequalities may be reproduced in each period or even magnified. The connection between "initial" and "final" inequality can be complex, as the following example shows. (The discussion that follows is based on Mookherjee and Ray 2000.)

Suppose that output is produced using two types of labor: skilled and unskilled. At each date there is a generation of individuals, some of whom are skilled and some unskilled. Members of this generation receive a wage commensurate with their skills, which they can divide between their own consumption and investment in their offspring. For simplicity, assume that the needed investment is zero if the child is to be left unskilled but some fixed cost if the child is to be given skills. Each person maximizes some utility function that depends on her own consumption and the utility of her offspring (as in Loury 1981). This story repeats itself period after period.

This would be no different from a "noninteractive" inequality model if wages were constant. But I take wages to depend on the proportion of skilled people in that generation, with either wage rising to very high levels as the proportion of that type becomes vanishingly scarce. (The aggregate production function needs both types of labor.) Now we have a typical "interactive" model.

Suppose that all individuals in a particular generation have equal wealth. Is it possible for all of them to make the same choices regarding child education? The answer is, in general, no. If all of them choose to leave their descendants unskilled, the return to skilled labor will become enormously high, encouraging some fraction of the population to educate their children. (This will be true as long as credit markets are not entirely missing.) Similarly, it is not possible for all parents to educate their children if unskilled labor is also necessary in production. Thus—and precisely because of this interdependence—identical agents are forced to take nonidentical actions. This means, of course, that from the viewpoint of the next generation, some inequality must emerge. Over subsequent generations, inequality can continue to grow.

At the same time, there are other initial distributions that can lead to a progressive reduction of inequality across generations. Finally, there are distributions—in general, a multiplicity of them—that are self-perpetuating.

The multiplicity of equilibria that occur under inertial self-reinforcement is now replaced, under historical self-reinforcement, by a multiplicity of steady states. The implications for policy are different. Interventions in this context must shift their focus from changing equilibria (through the enactment of some temporary law, for instance) to changing some objective entitlement, such as property rights. Moreover, the example above suggests that an interventionist policy must take note of the dynamics that follow such an intervention: some interventions may be useless if inequality can "grow back."

At the same time, to the extent that there are multiple self-reinforcing distributions, some types of property rights interventions will certainly matter. We need progress on economic theories of the evolution of inequality (not just theories of steady states) to settle these concerns. As Hoff and Stiglitz put it, while economic policy under this sort of world view "may require fewer resources, it may take more skill."

Information and Credit

The preceding discussion leads to a final point that is worth mentioning. First, continuing the theme of policy prescriptions, the models of historical self-reinforcement draw attention not only to initial inequalities but also to the imperfections of credit markets. Given the immense political and informational obstacles to asset redistribution, it may not be much of an exaggeration to say that credit market reform is the most important policy issue facing developing countries. As the pace of development picks up and mobility increases, informal credit markets may get worse, not better, at serving their clientele.[3] This is the result of an erosion in informational networks, which will presumably be replaced—but not just yet—by databases that track individual credit histories. I would therefore place the study of credit markets (with limited information flows) on the agenda of essential problems that merit our attention, from both the theoretical and the policy perspectives.

What sorts of questions might one ask regarding credit market policy? There are several, some of which are mentioned by Hoff and Stiglitz.

- Can one design banks that accept collateral in unorthodox form, such as crop output or labor? (One could, if banks were to take a page out of the literature on interlinked contracts.)
- Can limited enforceability of contracts be compensated for, at least partially, by group lending? (It can, if borrowers know more about one another than banks do, as in Ghatak 1999 and van Tassell 1999.)
- Will an expansion of credit to formal banks or large moneylenders ultimately benefit poor borrowers? (It may not, as Floro and Ray 1997, Hoff and Stiglitz 1997, and Bose 1998 have pointed out.)
- How might property ownership, or even use rights, affect access to credit?
- Are enforceability considerations for fixed-capital loans fundamentally different from those for working-capital loans?
- What sustains an informal credit market when information flows are limited?

The need for theoretical research in these areas is great.

To summarize, there are three implications of this emerging point of view for economic development.

Our understanding. Convergence, even in its fancier "conditional" form, is essentially an ahistorical theory. Initial economic differences will ultimately be wiped away, unless impeded by some fundamental variations across societies. Belief in these fundamentals—assuming it is not restricted to innocuous examples such as geography and climate— can deeply shape one's world view. It certainly is a very different world view from the one that emerges from theories of the multiplicity of self-reinforcing outcomes in (otherwise) identical societies. The latter view does not rely on fundamental economic or cultural differences to explain the divergence in income or wealth across countries, and it is profoundly historical. This is the broad approach that many authors now espouse and that Hoff and Stiglitz so ably summarize.

What is exogenous? Many factors taken as fundamental under the standard view are now up for grabs. For instance, a "culture of corruption" can now be viewed as a self-reinforcing equilibrium for a society that can just as well appear noncorrupt in some other equilibrium. The same is true of a variety of phenomena as diverse as fertility, hyperinflation, technology standards, saving rates, and social norms and attitudes. This opening of the black boxes, as Hoff and Stiglitz describe it, is very much in line with the comments in the preceding paragraph. If our world view does not permit us to believe in fundamental differences, then all differences demand an explanation. At least, that is the ambitious agenda set by these theoretical developments.

Policy. From a broad methodological perspective, the policy implications are of two kinds. First, there are policies that are designed to overcome inertial self-reinforcement. Essentially, they promote a move to a new equilibrium without permanent intervention. That does not mean that such policies are costless in terms of the policymaker's skills: as Hoff and Stiglitz and many other authors have noted, they require delicate interventions to overcome a possibly vicious cycle of expectations reinforcement. Moreover, such policies may be costly in terms of resources, especially in the monitoring of the transition to the new equilibrium.

The second kind of policies is designed to overcome historical self-reinforcement. These policies are different: they require interventions that are not merely of the coordination variety. Wealth, or perhaps other assets such as land, may need to be redistributed. The structure of use rights may have to be changed. These policies are based on the theoretical presumption that history matters. (If all history were to be wiped out, either initial distributions would not matter or changes to them could be reversed anyway.)

Notes

1. See, for example, Krugman (1991); Matsuyama (1991); Chamley and Gale (1994); Adserà and Ray (1998); Cooper (1999).

2. To be sure, one can construct a model in which historical conditions simply preclude the good equilibrium as a possible outcome. I will take up instances of such theories below, but it should be pointed out that these are not multiple equilibrium models but theories of multiple steady states.

3. On this point, see Ghosh and Ray (1996); Ray (1998: ch. 14); World Bank (1999).

References

Adserà, Alicia, and Debraj Ray. 1998. "History and Coordination Failure." *Journal of Economic Growth* 3 (3, September): 267–76.

Bose, Pinaki. 1998. "Formal-Informal Sector Interaction in Rural Credit Markets." *Journal of Development Economics* 56 (August): 265–80.

Chamley, Christopher, and Douglas Gale. 1994. "Information Revelation and Strategic Delay in a Model of Investment." *Econometrica* 62 (September): 1065–85.

Champernowne, David. 1953. "A Model of Income Distribution." *Economic Journal* 64: 318–51.

Cooper, Russell. 1999. *Coordination Games: Complementarities and Macroeconomics.* Cambridge, U.K.: Cambridge University Press.

Floro, Maria Sagrario, and Debraj Ray. 1997. "Vertical Links between Formal and Informal Financial Institutions." *Review of Development Economics* 1: 34–56.

Ghatak, Maitreesh. 1999. "Group Lending, Local Information and Peer Selection." *Journal of Development Economics* 60: 27–50.

Ghosh, Parikshit, and Debraj Ray. 1996. "Cooperation in Community Interaction without Information Flows." *Review of Economic Studies* 63 (3, July): 491–519.

Hirschman, Albert O. 1958. *The Strategy of Economic Development.* New Haven, Conn.: Yale University Press.

Hoff, Karla, and Joseph E. Stiglitz. 1997. "Moneylenders and Bankers: Price-Increasing Subsidies in a Monopolistically Competitive Market." *Journal of Development Economics* 52 (April): 429–62. (Reprinted in 1998 with corrections to notation.)

Krugman, Paul. 1991. "History versus Expectations." *Quarterly Journal of Economics* 106 (May): 651–67.

Loury, Glenn C. 1981. "Intergenerational Transfers and the Distribution of Earnings." *Econometrica* 49: 843–67.

Matsuyama, Kiminori. 1991. "Increasing Returns, Industrialization, and Indeterminacy of Equilibrium." *Quarterly Journal of Economics* 106 (May): 617–50.

Mookherjee, Dilap, and Debraj Ray. 2000. "On the Persistence of Inequality." Institute for Economic Development, Boston University, Boston, Mass. Processed.

———. Forthcoming. "Introduction." In Dilap Mookherjee and Debraj Ray, eds., *A Reader in Development Economics.* Oxford, U.K.: Basil Blackwell.

Ray, Debraj. 1998. *Development Economics.* Princeton, N.J.: Princeton University Press.

Rosenstein-Rodan, Paul. 1943. "Problems of Industrialization of Eastern and South-Eastern Europe." *Economic Journal* 53: 202–11.

van Tassell, Eric. 1999. "Group Lending under Asymmetric Information." *Journal of Development Economics* 60 (1): 3–25.

World Bank. 1999. *World Development Report 1998/99: Knowledge for Development.* New York: Oxford University Press.

*Reflections by
Nobel Laureates*

A Research Agenda

Lawrence R. Klein

FROM MY PERSPECTIVE—in building models for developing economies for integration into a total world system and constructing interesting scenarios that seek to enhance performance in the world of emerging economies in a smooth way—I find the following research needs:

1. Introduction of a demographic module that shows population and closely related trends in some detail

2. The ability to generate patterns of income and wealth distribution for judging fairness to the population at large

3. A system of comprehensive sectoral performance, starting from a standard input-output system but moving toward analysis of such issues as technological progress and the changing relationships between primary, secondary, and tertiary activities within economies

4. The integration of developing economies into the evolving world trade and payments system

5. The analysis of financial flows, patterned, where possible, after the interactive detail of the input-output system

6. The expansion of the scope of development indicators, far beyond the elements of the above issues but embracing such things as health, education, communication, environmental protection, and peaceful coexistence.

Each of these six lines of analysis is naturally being investigated in one way or another, but it does not seem to me that they are being appropriately studied in such a way as to bring them all together in a meaningful and manageable system. In particular, they are highly interrelated and may be examined either one at a time or in terms of their mutual feedback effects.

I believe that the information flow, software development, and hardware are all available now in user-friendly mode so that significant progress can be made in the development of a total and consistent system. In small steps, we have been able to extend the UN-LINK model beyond trade flows and ordinary social accounting. A next step would be financial flows, culminating in a complete flow-of-funds system, as nearly worldwide as possible. For individual countries, such as the Philippines and Chile, demographic groupings (age and sex) have been introduced to improve the way the total population module handles birth and mortality. Income distributions by income size, age, and sex have been introduced successfully into the analysis for the Philippines and for Chile. These are stepping stones that show what is potentially possible on a much wider scale.

The various development indexes regularly tabulated in the United Nations Development Programme's *Human Development Reports* provide an excellent information source for further work under the sixth point listed above.

Needed: A Theory of Change

Douglass C. North

THE PROBLEMS IN DEVELOPMENT economics are straightforward. We come to these problems with a heritage from neoclassical theory, which is a static body of theory and, at least in its pure form, looked at frictionless perfect markets. What we try to understand in development is the process of formation, change, and development of both political and economic markets and the way in which that process occurs. In order to do that, we have to evolve a new body of theory, or at least to modify existing theory to integrate it with those parts of neoclassical theory that are of value. This means that, first, we need a clear understanding of the new institutional economics, since it is the evolution of institutions that is a fundamental source of political and economic change and formal institutions are the only instrument we possess to alter the way in which economies perform. Second, we must develop a body of political-economic theory, since it is the polity that specifies and enforces the economic rules of the game and we still do not have a clear understanding of the interplay between politics and economics that would allow us to get a better grasp of this subject. Third, we need to have a better understanding of the social norms and informal constraints that are a fundamental source of either good performance or poor performance in developing countries. This entails gleaning from anthropologists and sociologists what they have come to learn about informal constraints and integrating that knowledge with economic and political theory so that we can arrive at some generalizations that will help us.

The problem is straightforward. We know both the economic conditions and the institutional conditions that make for good economic performance. What we do not know is how to get them. For that, we need a body of theory that explores the process of economic, political, and social change. When we have such a theory, we will make much better progress toward solving problems of development.

Sparks and Grit from the Anvil of Growth

Paul A. Samuelson

NEW GROWTH THEORY IS NOT so new as it thinks itself to be. Not surprisingly, then, old growth theory is less obsolete than it is often painted. Both will be proved by time to be less useful than their adherents hope them to be and have claimed them to be. Both will be found to have in them more lasting and testable usefulness than cynical nihilists have granted them. Their combined wisdoms will add up to less than the sum of their separate wisdoms. What else is new?

Capital Deepening: The Early Elixir for Growth

Both economic history and plausible economic logic nominate, as one material way for a society to progress in opulence, the "accumulation of Kapital." Adam Smith believed that Holland's superiority in productivity over China's could be traced partially to past Dutch successes in stepping up saving (at the expense of available consuming). Long before Robert Solow, or Paul Douglas, or J. B. Clark, or Eugen von Böhm-Bawerk, Smith's readers did not attribute this outcome to Mother Nature's rewarding of thrift as merely a virtue in itself. Smith, the hard-headed Deist, believed past net saving to be good because of his empirical inference that when saving does create increments of the vectoral stocks of *produced* inputs (Kapitals), that would add to society's (gross and net) vectors of sustainable consumptions.

One useful insight need not blot out another: in the comparison between China and Holland, the lessened density of labor per unit of land did figure in Smith's eclectic comparison. Indeed, long before Cournot, Dupuit, Marshall, or Fleeming Jenkin drew (p, q) diagrams of demand, Smith's predecessors would have expected, other things being equal, an increase in the corn crop or in congeries of capital goods or in employable population size each to induce a drop in, respectively, the *p* of corn, the real interest and profit rates, and the frequency spread of wage rates. (Around 1815, Malthus, West, and Ricardo coined such phrases as "the law of diminishing returns." But of course young Malthus, arguing at the breakfast table with his father, the Condorcet optimist, was already using that law in the previous century—as had Benjamin Franklin and other nonilliterates when Smith was still in short pants.)

As an economic theorist kibitzing among growth specialists, I will presently explicate what serious Sraffians can mean when they deny that the valid labor-to-land law of diminishing returns can apply to the *K/L* law of diminishing (interest) returns. Using ink on this topic does not signify my belief in its vital importance; it is just that, in an age when new macroeconomists deplore the lack of kosher microfoundations for the old 1936+ macroeconomics, it is important to know whether conventional textbook *micro*economics itself does lack sound *micro*economic foundations. Later I shall return to this subtlety.

What Seems Important Too: The Residual

A good memory means you recall your past triumphs. It also means you remember your past misses. So I say: Speak, Memory.

I happened to be in Paul Douglas's Chicago classes in the 1932–34 period when he was harvesting his Cobb-Douglas production-function researches. Douglas was a 1913 pupil of J. B. Clark at Columbia graduate school. He wanted to measure anything: $MV = PQ$, S(aving) = I(nvestment), $Q = F(L, K)$, or $Q = F(L, K;$ Land$)$. Using 1899–1923 data on labor supplies and some kind of an index of physical capital, by least squares he estimated real $Q = 1.01$(real labor)$^{0.75} K^{0.25}$.

His *K/L* variable followed closely a rising (nonlinear) trend. In the three-space of $(L, K; Q)$, a fit of $Q = aL + bK$ would have yielded a similarly high R^2. But so ill conditioned were his sample data, an epsilon change in one or a few data points (I found in learning exercises on multiregression analysis à la Munroe calculators) could have changed $(0.75, 0.25)$ to $(0.5, 0.5)$ or worse. Douglas deserved his pre-Nobel Hart Schaffer & Marx prize. But, like Ricardo, he had early critics who were *not* all wrong.

What interests us here was Schumpeter's reaction when I levitated from Chicago's undergraduate school to Harvard's graduate school. "My dear Samuelson, how could any savant leave out for the 1899–1923 years the palpable fact of technological change?" Naturally I tried out a $Q = aL + bK + ct$, or $\log Q = \alpha \log L + \beta \log K + \gamma t$, with or without a constraint of $\alpha + \beta = 1$. Ill-conditioning of that sample precluded interesting results. In view of recent revivals of Smith-Young-

Graham-Ohlin increasing returns to scale, I dimly recollect that I had to agree with a casual remark of George Stigler's that those data could not robustly identify the strength of a t influence relative to a $(\alpha + \beta - 1)$ influence. Samuelson's (1979) posthumous survey of Paul Douglas's production work records why I believe Douglas's misspecified *cross-sectional* studies could not cogently resolve these time-series difficulties.

Once America stayed near to high employment after World War II, I was content in my journalisms to use a Slichter-like $Q = (1.025)^t L^{0.75} K^{0.25}$ as a makeshift. Later, Solow (in the office next door to mine but with a Chinese Wall in between) made theory sense of total factor productivity (Solow 1957). But the historical survey of the residual by Zvi Griliches (1996) gives too little attention to how Solow resolved the ill-conditioning of the $(L, K, t; Q)$ data. Solow augmented it, in effect, by using $[WL/PQ, (PQ - WL)/PQ]$ data: using the heroic marginal-productivity approximations that, $P\,\partial Q/\partial W = W, \partial Q/\partial K = \partial K/\partial K = i$, better conditioning obtained for a $(K, L; Q)$ fit; and, not by accident, the Cobb-Douglas form with $K^{0.75}L^{0.25}$ turned out to be not too bad a fit; and even Slichter's $(1.025)^t$ residual was not too far off the mark as a normalizing coefficient.[1]

I was not displeased that early researches gave a big role to the residual and a lesser role to the "deepening of Kapital." In many editions of my *Economics* primer, I regarded the single most important diagram in the book as the one that attributed to post-Newtonian science the successful Industrial Revolution. (I must now add this: I do not believe that scientific revolution was crucially accelerated by the bribes the system gave to innovators in ex ante and ex post rent rewards for their efforts. Newton, the Bernoullis, Euler, Lagrange, Faraday, Maxwell, and Helmholtz—unlike Watt and Edison—benefited from public and private patronage that reflected past inequality of income rather than profit-and-rent-seeking venture capital. As late as 1910, J. J. Thomson, who discovered the electron, was told, "Every broker in the City makes much more than you do in Cambridge." He replied, "Yes, but think of the work they have to do." My late physicist friend at Harvard, Edward Purcell, invented with Robert Pound the MRI scan. The reward they sought, and what they got, was zero—a tale that will surprise my grandchildren.)

One remembered good idea can breed a remembered bad one. In my brash, youthful way I was contemptuous of Lenin as an economist. One of his idiocies was to write, while in hiding during the interval between the February and October Revolutions in Russia, that all a communist society needed to run a capitalist system it had taken over was the arithmetic Rule of Three. Allegedly, gold would gravitate to the production of toilets in the communist utopia. "Electricity + the Soviets ≡ Communism" did not commend itself to me as a slogan. Bernard Shaw and Joan Robinson shared the first of these dicta. Once in existence, society's stock of capital allegedly needed no incentive or market guidance to keep it intact. Hayek (1945), whose *Road to Serfdom* (1944) and *Prices and Production* (1931) were not high on my list of admired works, persuaded me that Lerner-Lange aping of the price mechanism (but playing for matches and not for blood) would falter on the need for "dynamic information."

However, I knew how good pure mathematics was in Stalin's U.S.S.R. Their physicists, when given backing and academic freedom, could create (sans spies) a hydrogen bomb much like ours. Mao's Keystone-Kops bureaucrats could, by adopting the findings of American medical research, achieve life expectancies better than many Western economies had achieved at 10 times China's productivity levels, as measured by the Penn Tables. In short, I erroneously hypothesized that a function F (unskilled labor, skimpy and poorly allocated capital; scientific knowledge, however acquired) might succeed in achieving respectable progress for approximate Q/L estimates of a society.

Something vague, like Harvey Leibenstein's (1969) X-efficiency, I was reluctant to put into such journalistic background production functions. Thus, when unclassified Central Intelligence Agency (CIA) estimates put per capita affluence in 1988 East Germany at, say, three quarters of West Germany's, I used those estimates in successive post-1970 editions of my textbook. After the unification of Germany 10 years ago, my reading of the evidence required marking that ratio down from 0.75 to, say, 0.33. How to explain this? It was not so much lies in government-published economic data. It is rather that the whole *theory* of economic index numbers (to which I had myself contributed) was founded implicitly on some tolerable relationship between the P data in the $(P_1 \ldots P_n; Q_1 \ldots Q_n)$ statistics and the Lagrange-multiplier shadow prices implicit in those noncapitalist societies. Their actual Ps differed from normative Ps so much as to make those little triangles of deadweight losses in consumer surplus add up to much in the total reckoning. There is no logical need for this; nor is there easy empirical testing for it.

Still, to an open-minded scholar of considerable experience, the best ultimate hypothesis to explain growth spurts and growth slumps seemed to be that only a *limited* mixed economy can, for societies as they really are, deliver on the promises of greater productivity plenty. The miracle in Sweden (which a Friedrich Hayek never remotely understood) was not that it grew so well for a long time but that it did so in a contrived regimen of considerable equality and civil liberties. After 1970, however, the trend for societies like Scandinavia's to begin to fall behind their position near the leaders in the Penn Tables showed that one cannot count on miracles. (Never believe in miracles before they happen. It is hard enough to believe in them *after* they do.)

The archetype model for simple capital deepening is a one-sector, one-capital-good model of Ramsey-Solow type

(1)   gross Q = consumption + new capital goods = $C + G = F(L, K)$,

F concave smooth and 1st degree homogeneous.

When capital depreciates exponentially, at a rate δ independent of age and use,

(2)   net $q = C + $ net $\dot{K} = F(L, K) - \delta K = f(L, K)$, $\delta > 0$.

With smooth and substitutable inputs, distribution simplifies to

(3a)   national income = q = wages + interest

(3b) $= L\,\partial f(L, K)/\partial L + K\,\partial f(L, K)/\partial K$

(3c) $= Lw + Ki$

(3d) $i = \partial\dot{K}/\partial K = \partial f/\partial K$, $w = \partial f/\partial L$.

Necessarily, from strong concavity and constant returns

(3e) $\partial w/\partial K = \partial^2 q/\partial L\partial K > 0$.

Nassau Senior's paradigm describes how giving up C in equation (2) in order to accelerate $\dot{K}$ growth there will cause accumulation of K to raise real wage w.

To Joan Robinson, this one-sector case was a contemptible leets model—"leets" is steel spelled backward—designed by capitalist apologists to bamboozle Sunday-school children. To appraise it objectively, we must introduce vectoral capital goods, at least two of them: (K_1, K_2).

The Leets Fable

To shorten a long story about capital deepening without altering its qualitative content, we can reduce the relevant implications of relations (1) to (3) to the following two-capital-inputs case. Net, one has

$$q_1 = C_1 + \dot{K}_1 = F^1(L_1, K_{11}, K_{21}) - \delta(K_{11} + K_{12}), \qquad \delta > 0$$

(4) $$q_2 = C_2 + \dot{K}_2 = F^2(L_2, K_{12}, K_{22}) - \delta(K_{21} + K_{22})$$

$$L_1 + L_2 = L;\ K_{11} + K_{12} = K_1, \qquad K_{21} + K_{22} = K_2.$$

To avoid index number problems connected with consumer-demand functions, agree to make $C_1(t) \equiv 0$ and set $C_2(t) \equiv C(t)$, which give us an easy exact measure of consumption.

Then with smooth convexity for all (both) the $F^i(\ )$ functions, and specifying constant returns to scale, and given factor endowment totals of (L, K_1, K_2), the optimal output possibility function for society of this putty-capital will be achieved by laissez-faire market competition and can be summarized by the following smooth, properly concave Π function with existent partial derivatives:

(5a)
$$C = \Pi(L, K_1, K_2; \dot{K}_1, \dot{K}_2) \quad \text{for all } t;$$

$$\partial\Pi/\partial K_j > 0, \qquad \partial\Pi/\partial \dot{K}_j < 0$$

$$W/P_C = w = \partial\Pi(L, K_1, K_2; \dot{K}_1, \dot{K}_2)\partial L > 0$$

(5b)   stationary-state $i = i^* \equiv (+\partial\dot{K}_1/\partial K_1)_c \equiv (+\partial\dot{K}_2/\partial K_2)_c \geq 0$

$$= -(\partial\Pi/\partial K_1)/(\partial\Pi/\partial \dot{K}_1) = -(\partial\Pi/\partial K_2)/(\partial\Pi/\partial \dot{K}_2).$$

Query: Suppose a Frank Ramsey God were to ordain a slow fall in society's ρ rate of time preference so that $\rho(t)$ falls slowly and $i(t)$ then falls equivalently with negligible delay, what then will happen to $C(t)/L(t)$ of per capita consumption? (We may keep $L(t)$ constant without harm to this sermon.)

When there are $n = 1$ capital goods, the Senior story (which Robinson deems a fairy tale) validly predicts that $C(t)/L(t)$ will slowly *rise* until at $\rho = 0 = i^*$, the golden-rule state of Schumpeter et al., maximal $(C/L)^*$ will be realized.

Here, however, is the surprise—the only true surprise that I got from Sraffa's classic 1960 book. (Don't look for it there. But it is there, hidden in plain sight—and made dramatic by singular cases of "Sraffian double switching," which also are hidden there in plain sight.)

Surprise: In an ideal intertemporal neoclassical model, per capita consumption is always maximal at the golden-rule state where the interest rate and the balanced-growth rate are equal. When, however, i rises *above* the growth rate, then per capita C must at first, if anything, *fall*. Nevertheless it can well happen that this C/L can later turn back up toward (and even "to") the golden $(C/L)^*$ level. Its oscillation up and down can be multifold, and yet never is there any violation of the technology's convexity and its (properly statable) law of diminishing returns.

What does this Joan-Piero finding *not* mean?

• It does not deny that a society that begins outside the golden-rule technology can never get there without doing some Senior "waiting and abstaining." Only some temporary sacrifice of early $(\ldots C_{t-1}, C_t, C_{t+1}, \ldots)$ can get you to maximal C^* if you are not already there.

• It is still true that $|\partial C_{t+1}/\partial C_t|$ equals under intertemporal competition 1 plus the rea-l *own* rate of interest, and whenever derivatives or finite differences of the $(\partial C_{t+1}/\partial C_t, \partial^2 C_{t+1}/\partial C_t^2)$ type are calculated, successive equal increments of C_t abstention will ultimately yield *diminishing* own-rate interest yields. Figure 1 depicts what can and cannot happen.[2]

Figure 1. Intertemporal Consumption

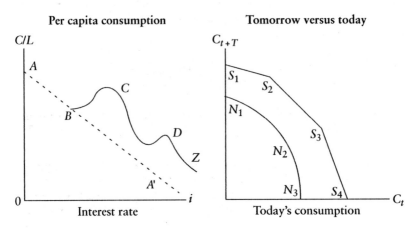

In concluding this discussion of deepening of capital, I leave the realm of deductive logic and try to do justice to empirical economic history and likely growth opportunities for undeveloped economies. The realistic panoply of existent alternative, discrete techniques impresses me as making it likely that successful substitutions of consumption products for realized investment projects can speed up real growth. No poor society has already saved so much, has already accumulated so much capital, as to make properly allocated new investment projects useless in terms of private and social products. This cannot be proved or disproved by the methodology that proves the Pythagorean theorem and disproves the rationality of $\sqrt{2}$. But maybe the same can be said about the potency of penicillin?

Some new growth theorists have proposed that Solow-Clark diminishing returns to capital, $\partial^2 Q/\partial K^2 < 0$, be replaced by the approximation of Q proportional to K and with $\partial Q/\partial K$, a quasi constant. I perceive no particular merit to such a crochet.[3]

Increasing Returns to Scale

Constant returns to scale, sans chance, change, externalities, and information uncertainties, is pretty much a finished book in economic theory. Little wonder, then, that lively scholars ardent to make breakthroughs in science periodically stress deviations from this chaste model. In particular, increasing returns to scale received notice from Smith's division of labor in pin manufacture; as part of the theory of monopoly by A. A. Cournot ([1838] 1929) and J. M. Clark (1923); in connection with international trade by Frank Graham (1923), Bertil Ohlin (1933), R. C. O. Matthews (1950), and Paul Krugman and Elhanan Helpman (1985); and in vague connection with developmental growth in Allyn Young's most famous (1928) article. Always a bridesmaid but never a bride, so to speak. The trouble with increasing scale returns is that after you have said the first things about it, it is deucedly hard to find interesting second and third themes to develop. Most of pretty modern mathematics lacks elegant application to the combinatorial swamp that nonconvexity irreducibly entails.

My conscience was long bothered by our guild's neglect of a subject on the ground that it is so hard to tackle. But I have a confession to make. So global have modern markets become that at century's end my hunch has to be that there obtains in reality *less* unexhausted scale economies than was the case when I first wrote *Economics*. In early editions I felt forced to recognize that the Fortune 500 companies possessed considerable oligopoly rents, which they were compelled to share somewhat with militant trade unions. In today's ruthless mixed capitalism, I doubt that appropriable scale profits have their former long-run importance—which, I suppose, is why antitrust action by the government can these days be optimally reduced. (Not all of this is scale effect; changes in corporate governance can accelerate the virulence of competitive entry.)

External Scale Economies and Market Failure

Because imperfect competition is relatively hard to analyze in an interesting way, we economists are self-indulgent and like to exaggerate the degree to which increasing scale returns can sometimes be connected with *external* economies. This tends to be associated with market failure and non-Pareto optimality of laissez-faire. Despite the patter of Coasian transaction costs, from the beginning of time inventors and innovators have not been led by any invisible hand to optimal intensities of effort and activity. Who invented the wheel, cheese, fermented drink, salting or smoking of perishable meats, and all the great discoveries of the remote past? No precise ideal patent system or ideal temporary regimen of semimonopoly can be formulated out of economic theory itself. Indeed scientific discovery, the importance of which I have already extolled, is probably itself importantly connected with decreasing returns to scale. Ask ourselves: would 10 teams working in parallel back in 1980 to prove Fermat's last theorem have significantly outperformed 5 teams? Not likely.

Darwinian Selection and Pseudo Scale Economies

Furthermore, what may seem like increasing returns to scale may sometimes be a mirage. Here, taken from Fisher-Haldane-Wright theoretical genetics, is the time profile of one species of rabbits growing on a fixed plot of land. When fertile rabbits are few per acre, males may have difficulty in locating mates. Consequently, soon thereafter exponential growth rates may speed up: a genuine short-term operation of increasing returns to scale. Following this can come a regime of constant steady-state growth rate during which rabbits spread over more and more virginal acres.

What follows then can be a third acceleration-of-growth stage that looks like increasing returns to scale. Suppose the rabbit species has more than one subspecies: call them A and B, and let their numbers start out about equal. Suppose that A has both a higher fecundity rate than B and, genetically, a lower mortality rate. Then because of what biologists call "r-selection," the rabbit population under highly non-random mating will grow thus:

$$(6) \qquad N(t) = N_A(t) + N_B(t) = N_A(1)e^{r_A t} + N_B e^{r_B t}, \quad r_A > r_B.$$

This implies that $\dot{N}/N$ will be seen to accelerate from $\frac{1}{2}(r_A + r_B)$ upward toward r_A as A rabbits proliferate faster than B. (This is a crude instance of R. A. Fisher's overtouted 1930 "law of increasing fitness," which he modestly ranks for biology as the second law of thermodynamics ranks for physics.) Later, as land becomes scarce relative to the rabbit population, something like the Verhulst ogive of logistic growth prevails, with

$$(7) \qquad \lim_{t \to \infty} [N_A, N_B] = [K^*, 0].$$

Biologists call this final stage K-capacity-selection. In it, for the (land, rabbits) space, constant returns to scale prevail, and diminishing returns prevail for (N_A, N_B) relative to limited land.

Except for the transitory earliest stage of this Darwinian drama, there is never other than constant returns to scale, even though before the inflection point a weight-shift effect on N_B/N_A might give a spurious appearance of increasing returns to scale. (I have soft-pedaled the Mendelian genetics of the r-selection stage, a simplification that leads to no distortion of qualitative results.)

Learning by Imitation of Others' Doing

The leitmotif of the half-century 1950–2000 is that so many nations have been narrowing the gap separating them from American affluent productivity. This was not so much "learning by doing" as "learning by watching others doing." The process is a million years old; mothers, teachers, and siblings are our mentors and we call it "education." Birds and even worms do it.

Banal? Then ask why after World War I, there did not happen what did happen after World War II. It could have, but it didn't. History is chancy as well as deterministic.

Imitation can be easy. (Why does it not operate in vast regions of Africa and Asia?) Before 1970, I asked myself whether some bicycle riders, after coming close to the American leaders, might possibly break through and leave the United States in their dust. Surprisingly, from the Penn Tables we seem to learn that none has done so. It is harder to innovate—to break the wind—than to ride behind those who do. Don't bet the farm, though, that in the 21st century history will not change.

Increasing Returns and Externalities

Here is a beautiful example of market failure, mandated by external increasing returns to scale, that cannot be circumvented by Coase-like assignments of property rights even though transaction costs are zero.

Labor alone timelessly produces iron and cloth. Iron obeys constant returns to scale. Cloth is produced with a third-degree homogeneous production function:

$$(8) \qquad q_1 = L_1, \, q_2 = L_2^3$$

All workers are alike, and all spend their wage income half-and-half on iron and cloth consumptions. Under laissez-faire push-shove, equilibrium occurs when workers get the same real wage in both occupations and where the P_2/P_1 price ratio equates revenues to unit wage costs. (There can be no monopoly because the scale economies for cloth are purely external.)

On reflection, the reader will realize that free entry will in this case direct half of society's L to L_1 and half to L_2. Outputs are then

$$(9) \qquad (q_1 \, q_2) = [(1)\tfrac{1}{2}L, \, (1)(\tfrac{1}{2}L)^3].$$

Real wage rates equate prices to costs at

$$(W/P_1 \, W/P_2) = (1, \, L_2^3 /L_2) = (1, \, L_2^2)$$

$$(10) \qquad GDP = WL = \sum_1^2 P_j q_j.$$

Exact deflation of nominal gross domestic product (GDP) gives (for this J. S. Mill case of 50-50 demand)

$$(11) \qquad \text{real } y = \sqrt{q_1 q_2} = (\tfrac{1}{16}L^4)^{\tfrac{1}{2}} = \tfrac{1}{4}L^2.$$

However, with Mill's $\sqrt{q_1 q_2}$ as the desideratum, Pareto and Bergson-Edgeworth welfare optimality requires that three fourths of L goes to the increasing returns L_2 and one fourth to L_1. Then,

$$\text{optimized } y^* = \sqrt{q_1^* q_2^*} = [\tfrac{1}{4}L]^{\frac{1}{2}} \, [\tfrac{27}{64}]^{\frac{1}{2}} L^{\frac{3}{2}}$$

(12)
$$= \frac{\sqrt{27}}{16} \, L^2 = 0.325 L^2$$

$$> \tfrac{1}{4}L^2 \quad \text{of laissez-faire.}$$

How serious is this deadweight loss from market failure under external economies from increasing returns to scale? It is quantitatively very serious. We libertarians who opt for laissez-faire will be taking a cut of 23 percent in *real* wages every year from now to eternity![4]

Note that Solow's 1955–57 cap on ultimate real growth does not apply here. Per capita affluences grow like the square of population size. Here it is the Santa Claus world of the late Julian Symons, where the cancer of population explosion breeds eternal growth in net productivity. (In deduction, you reap the harvest you have sown. Solow's cap on ultimate growth rate stems from his cap on L's exponential rate of growth and his first-degree homogeneity axioms sans technical change. Symons fabricated for himself a different script.)

My present scenario has no "common" whose "tyranny" can be circumvented by privatization and auctioned-off hard rents. (Samuelson 1974 and Weitzman and Cohen 1975 have proved that landlords pocket after enclosure more than they add to workers' productivity. See Samuelson 1990 for proof that partial enclosure of the common may be worse than either zero enclosure or total enclosure.)

Finale and Growth Outlook

The value of a theory is limited by the inaccuracy of its implicit predictions. What I have said here can be partially summarized by what it suggests about likely future growth in the next quarter-century.

1. Global growth will most likely accelerate a bit. Most of this will come from "learning by observing others doing," enabling developing regions to narrow their shortfall with respect to the leaders.

2. At the frontier of affluence, growth of total factor productivity ought to remain positive. But as we measure this, the high rates achieved in the third quarter of the 20th century may very well not be realized at the beginning of the new century. Until there is evidence for a recovery from the widespread deceleration of productivity of growth in the 1970–95 period, we would be rash to predict it. Science, particularly genetic medical science, is the likely power source of much that will be important. More dramatic, although not necessarily more important, may be the semiconductor and online revolutions. But people do not live by

doing multiplications rapidly, and the profits of initial public offerings (IPOs) are not a reliable measure of future putative utility.

3. Centrist mixed economies with limited powers of government, it is my hunch, are likely to outperform both laissez-faire polar cases and polar cases of paternalistic do-goodism. Human nature has a quantum of altruism, but that quantum is sufficiently limited to require rationing of altruism for its most important uses. No easy task for populist democracy.

4. Sizable areas of Africa and Asia still show few signs of sharing in the fruits of an advancing global plenty.

Even if the above specified pattern is the most likely one, based on the uncertain evidences now available, more likely than not some other pattern that is not yet rationally predictable will probably prevail in fact. It will be a triumph of some version of today's new growth economics if the pattern that actually does emerge in the future could have been cogently predictable from one or more of the competing new growth paradigms.

Notes

1. Griliches (1996) gave undue credence to the merit of redefining upward a nominated measure of "total input" to calibrate and explicate technological change: rewriting $Q = F[K, L, \ldots; t]$ with $\partial F/\partial t > 0$ as $Q = f[I(L, K, \ldots; t)]$ with $f' > 0$, $\partial I/\partial t > 0$ advances the good cause but little.

2. Precisely the same point can be proved for Böhm-Wicksell neoclassical period-of-production capital models: consider $q_t = f(L_{t-1}, L_{t-2})$, or $q_t = F(L_{t-1}, L_{t-2}, L_{t-3})$, where f and F are concave, differentiable, first-degree homogeneous functions. For f, the Senior sermon does indeed hold. For F, the $[i, q/\Sigma L]$ pattern can rise and fall repeatedly away from $i = 0$!

3. In Samuelson (1991) I addressed the 1930s Kaldor and von Neumann ultimate nonsubstitution theorem. Even without joint production, the tautology does not apply when empirical interest rates are above growth rates for whatever savings reasons. See Kaldor (1937, 1938); Knight (1938).

4. A Pigovian tax on iron balanced out by a subsidy on cloth can achieve the optimum. But that requires the visible and up-to-date hand of coercive government, something that libertarian Coasians had hoped to be able to replace by cleverly assigned "property rights."

References

Clark, J. M. 1923. *Studies in the Economics of Overhead Costs.* Chicago, Ill.: University of Chicago Press.

Coase, R. H. 1991. "The Institutional Structure of Production." Nobel Lecture, Stockholm, December 9. Nobel Foundation.

Cournot, A. A. 1929. *Researches into the Mathematical Principles of the Theory of Wealth.* Translated by N. T. Bacon, New York: Macmillan. First published 1838.

Douglas, Paul. 1934. *The Theory of Wages.* New York: Macmillan.

Fisher, R. A. 1930. *The Genetical Theory of Natural Selection.* Oxford, U.K.: Clarendon Press.

Graham, Frank. 1923. "Some Aspects of Protection Further Considered." *Quarterly Journal of Economics* 36: 220–73.

Griliches, Zvi. 1996. "The Discovery of the Residual: A Historical Note." *Journal of Economic Literature* 34 (3): 1324–30.

Hayek, Friedrich. 1931. *Prices and Production.* London: Routledge.

———. 1944. *The Road to Serfdom.* Chicago, Ill.: University of Chicago Press.

———. 1945. "The Use of Knowledge in Society." *American Economic Review* 35: 519–30. Reprinted in F. A. von Hayek, *Individualism and Economic Order* (London: Routledge & Kegan Paul, 1949).

Kaldor, Nicholas. 1937. "Annual Survey of Economic Theory: The Recent Controversy of the Theory of Capital." *Econometrica* 5: 201–33.

———. 1938. "On the Theory of Capital: A Rejoinder to Professor Knight." *Econometrica* 6: 163–76.

Knight, Frank. 1938. "On the Theory of Capital: In Reply to Mr. Kaldor." *Econometrica* 6: 63–82.

Kravis, I. B., A. Heston, and R. Summers. 1978. *International Comparisons of Real Product and Purchasing Power.* Baltimore, Md.: Johns Hopkins University Press.

Krugman, Paul, and Elhanan Helpman. 1985. *Market Structure and Foreign Trade.* Cambridge, Mass.: MIT Press.

Leibenstein, Harvey. 1969. "Organizational or Frictional Equilibria, X-Efficiency, and the Rate of Innovation." *Quarterly Journal of Economics* 83(4): 600–23.

Matthews, R. C. O. 1950. "Reciprocal Demand and Increasing Returns." *Review of Economic Studies* 17 (2):149–58.

Ohlin, Bertil. 1933. *Interregional and International Trade.* Cambridge, Mass.: Harvard University Press.

Robinson, Joan. 1956. *The Accumulation of Capital.* Homewood, Ill.: Richard D. Irwin.

Samuelson, Paul A. 1948–1998. *Economics.* New York: McGraw-Hill.

———. 1974. "Is the Rent-Collector Worthy of His Full Hire?" *Eastern Economic Journal* 1 (1): 7–10. Reproduced in *The Collected Scientific Papers of Paul A. Samuelson,* vol. 4, ch. 263 (Cambridge, Mass.: MIT Press, 1977).

———. 1979. "Paul Douglas's Measurement of Production Functions and Marginal Productivities." *Journal of Political Economy* 87 (5): 923–39. Reproduced in *The Collected Scientific Papers of Paul A. Samuelson,* vol. 5, ch. 302 (Cambridge, Mass.: MIT Press, 1986).

———. 1990. "When Deregulation Makes Things Worse before They Get Better." In C. Moir and J. Dauson, eds., *Competition and Markets,* ch. 2: 11–20. Basingstoke, U.K.: Macmillan.

————. 1991. "A Sweeping New Non-Substitution Theorem: Kaldor's Discovery of the Von Neumann Input-Output Model." In E. J. Nell and W. Semmler, eds., *Nicholas Kaldor and Mainstream Economics*, ch. 4: 72–87. Basingstoke, U.K.: Macmillan.

Senior, Nassau. 1965. *An Outline of the Science of Political Economy.* New York: Kelley Reprint. First published 1836.

Smith, Adam. 1937. *An Inquiry into the Nature and Causes of the Wealth of Nations.* Edited by Edwin Cannan. New York: Modern Library. First published 1776.

Solow, Robert M. 1957. "Technical Change and the Aggregate Production Function." *Review of Economics and Statistics* 39 (3): 312–20.

Sraffa, Piero. 1960. *Production of Commodities by Means of Commodities: Prelude to a Critique of Economic Theory.* Cambridge, U.K.: Cambridge University Press.

von Neumann, John. 1937. "Über ein ökonomisches Gleichungssystem und eine Verallgemeinerung des Brouwerschen Fixpunktsatzes." In K. Menger, ed., *Ergebnisse eines mathematische Kolloquiums* 8. Translated 1945 as "A Model of General Economic Equilibrium," *Review of Economic Studies* 13 (1): 1–9.

Weitzman, M., and J. S. Cohen. 1975. "A Marxian Model of Enclosures." *Journal of Development Economics* 1 (4): 287–336.

Young, Allyn. 1928. "Increasing Returns and Economic Progress." *Economic Journal* 38: 527–42.

What Is Development About?

Amartya K. Sen

THE RELATIONSHIP BETWEEN freedom and development has been debated for a very long time. Some see freedom as a great ally of progress; others are fearful of individual freedom as a spoiler of development and a source of adversity. The latter group includes different (and often conflicting) schools of thought with very different diagnoses of their favorite poison: democratic rights, civil liberties, freedom of market transactions, or basic social opportunities (such as the emancipation involved in women's schooling). Their common suspicion of freedom leads to the advocacy—and imposition—of unfreedom of one kind or another, in the political, economic, or social sphere.

It is important to counter in a comprehensive and congruous way the diverse manifestations of this skepticism about freedom, which can be found plentifully across the contemporary world. A good starting point for the analysis of development is the basic recognition that freedom is both the primary objective of development and its principal means. The first is an evaluative claim and includes appreciation of the principle that the assessment of development cannot be divorced from the lives that people lead and the real freedoms that they enjoy. Development can scarcely be seen merely in terms of enhancement of inanimate objects of convenience, such as a rise in gross national product (GNP) or in personal incomes, or industrialization, or technological advance, or social modernization. These are, of course, valuable—often crucially important—accomplishments, but their value must depend on their effect on the lives and freedoms of the people involved. For responsible human beings, the focus must ultimately be on whether they have the freedom to do what they have reason to value.

The relation between freedom and development goes, however, well beyond this constitutive connection. Freedom is not only the ultimate end of development; it is also a crucially effective means. This acknowledgment can be based on empirical analysis of the consequences of—and interconnections between—freedoms of distinct kinds and on the evidence that freedoms of different types typically help to sustain each other.[1] What a person has the actual capability to achieve is influenced by economic opportunities, political liberties, social facilities, and the enabling conditions of good health, basic education, and the encouragement and cultivation of initiatives. These opportunities are, to a great extent, mutually complementary and tend to reinforce the reach and use of one another. It is because of these interconnections that free and sustainable human agency emerges as a generally effectual engine of development.

Political Freedom

In analyzing any type of freedom, we have to consider both its evaluative relevance and its consequential role. Take political liberties. It is sometimes asked whether political freedom is "conducive to development." Indeed, a negative answer to this question (including an often-articulated belief that democracy is inimical to economic growth) has fueled authoritarian political tendencies in different parts of the world. In assessing this line of argument, the first thing to note is that this way of posing the question misses the crucial recognition that political liberties and democratic rights are among the *constituent components* of development. Their relevance for development does not have to be indirectly established through their contribution to the growth of GNP. Politically unfree citizens—whether rich or poor—are deprived of a basic constituent of good living.

After acknowledging this central connection, however, we have to subject democracy to consequential analysis, since there are other kinds of freedoms as well. It is worth noting in this context that extensive cross-country comparisons have not provided empirical support for the belief that democracy is inimical to economic growth (see, for example, Przeworski and others 1995; Barro 1996). Indeed, the evidence is overwhelming that growth is assisted by the supportiveness of the economic climate rather than by the ruthlessness of the political system.

We must also pay attention to the evidence that democracy and political and civil rights tend to enhance freedoms of other kinds (such as economic security) through giving voice to the deprived and the vulnerable. The fact that no major famine has ever occurred in a democratic country that has regular polls, opposition parties, and relatively free media—even when the country is very poor and in a seriously adverse food situation—merely illustrates the most elementary aspect of the protective power of political liberty. Although Indian democracy has many imperfections, the political incentives generated by it have been adequate to eliminate major famines right from the time of independence. The Bengal famine of 1943, which I witnessed as a child, was the last such event; the country became independent in 1947. A contrasting case is that of China. Even before the economic reforms of 1979, China did much better than India in many areas, particularly in expanding access to education and basic health care. In 1959–62, however, it experienced the largest famine in recorded history, with a figure of extra mortality that has been variously put between 23 million and 30 million. At present, the countries with continuing famine—Ethiopia, the Democratic Republic of Korea, and Sudan—are also the ones most troubled by authoritarian rule or military control.

The power of democracy in providing protection and security to the vulnerable is, in fact, much more extensive than famine prevention. Those who are relatively worse off in the Republic of Korea and Indonesia may not have given much thought to democracy when the economic fortunes of all seemed to go up and up together. When, however, the economic crises came (and the fortunes of different classes went in disparate directions), political and civil rights and the voice that democracy can give to the poor were desperately missed by those whose economic means and lives were unusually battered. A decline in GNP of 5 or 10 percent is not really a big calamity, seen in an aggregative perspective, if it follows decades-long growth of 5 to 10 percent per year, but if that decline is heaped unequally on the least advantaged sections, they may be in severe jeopardy, requiring social support. Democracy has become a central issue in these countries now (it is making very great progress in the Republic of Korea) and in others, including, most spectacularly, Thailand. We should not really have to wait for an economic crisis to appreciate the protective power of democracy.

Markets and Transactional Freedoms

Let us now consider a different type of example: the role of markets. Again, freedom of exchange and transaction is itself part and parcel of the basic liberties that people have reason to value. This is quite a different point from the more discussed issue of the effectiveness of markets in generating economic prosperity. To be generically against markets is almost as odd as being generically against conversations between people. The freedoms to exchange words, or goods, or gifts do not need defensive justification in terms of their favorable but distant effects; they are part of the way human beings in society live and interact with each other (unless stopped by regulation or fiat).

Related to this issue is the importance of freedom of employment and of working practice—in contrast, say, to slavery or bonded labor. The freedom of market-based employment is a crucial liberty that received favorable attention even from Karl Marx—not invariably a great admirer of capitalism. Indeed, Marx's favorable remarks on capitalism as compared with the unfreedom of precapitalist labor arrangements related exactly to this question, which also produced his characterization of the American Civil War as "the one great event of contemporary history."[2] In the contemporary world, this issue of market-based freedom is quite central to the analysis of bonded labor—common in many developing countries—and the transition to free-market labor arrangements (see, in particular, Ramachandran 1990). This is, interestingly enough, one of the cases in which Marxian analysis has tended to have an affinity with libertarian concentration on freedom as opposed to utility.

To point to this often-neglected consideration is not, of course, to deny the importance of judging the market mechanism comprehensively on the basis of all its roles and effects, including its proven ability to generate economic growth, prosperity, and, under certain circumstances, even economic equity. We must also examine the downsides of unrestrained market operations (especially when there is severe inequality in ownership and endowments) and the general judgments, including criticisms, that people may have of the life-styles and values associated with an exclusively market-centered culture. In seeing development as freedom, the constitutive importance of transactions, as well as the direct and indirect effects of markets, must be considered together. It is important not to lose sight of the interlinkages between freedoms of different kinds.

Social Opportunities

To take yet another type of case, consider the role of the social opportunities that the state and the society may facilitate. Public education, for example, has been an effective means of freeing people from the bondage of illiteracy and ignorance. This freedom is valuable in itself, but it also contributes to economic development (and even to a more shared use of the market mechanism) and to the effective freedoms that result from economic prosperity. That lesson, already implicit in the experience of the West, is spectacularly reinforced by the role of the expansion of human capability in Japan's rapid economic growth. Already at the time of the Meiji restoration in the latter part of the 19th century, Japan had a higher literacy rate than did Europe, even though the latter had a long lead in industrial development. Between 1906 and 1911, education consumed as much as 43 percent of town and village budgets in Japan as a whole. By the early years of the 20th century, very little illiteracy remained, and indeed by 1913 Japan was publishing almost twice as many books as the United States (see Gluck 1985). The great achievements of the East Asian and Southeast Asian economies over the past few decades are also closely related to the interactive impact of their early educational expansion and its far-reaching consequences.

In explaining the relatively modest economic growth of the Indian economy, the overactivity of the state in Indian industrial policy has been blamed, and rightly so: denial of transactional freedoms has made wealth creation much more problematic in India than, say, in the Republic of Korea, Taiwan (China), or postreform China. This handicap is being rectified only very slowly. However, the *under*activity of the Indian state in promoting school education (nearly half the adult population is still illiterate) must bear a large share of the blame. India may have more than five times as many university-trained people as China, but China is much closer to universal literacy among the young. Indeed, China's expansion of basic education goes back to the prereform period, when it was driven by a left-wing political commitment. Interestingly enough (Adam Smith would have seen it as an example of the "unintended consequences of human action"), educational expansion in the Maoist period proved to be of great benefit in the effective spread of marketization in the postreform period. There is no mystery as to why the success of Indian industries that are dependent on higher education and training (India is, for example, the second largest producer of computer software in the world, after the United States) is not at all matched by widespread economic production founded on basic skills and on school education, in which China has truly excelled (see Drèze and Sen 1995).

Fertility and Coercion

A central point to note is that development calls for the simultaneous use of many institutions. As Adam Smith remarked, there are good reasons to take note of the fact that "for a very small expence the publick can facilitate, can encourage, and can even impose upon almost the whole body of the people, the necessity of acquiring those most essential parts of education."[3] Basic education, in particular female education, is associated with many social changes, in particular the reduction of child mortality and a rapid fall in fertility rates. The latter is, in fact, an important test case of the role of freedom, which relates to a confrontation between Condorcet's (profreedom) and Malthus's (antifreedom) arguments of almost exactly 200 years ago.

It was Condorcet, the French mathematician and Enlightenment thinker, who first pointed to the possibility that the size of the population can quite conceivably "surpass their means of subsistence." Malthus's more famous expression of this fear came later, with quotations from Condorcet. But Condorcet had gone on to argue that this eventuality was not likely to occur because there would be freely chosen declines in fertility rates, resulting from more education (including more female education) and "the progress of reason." Malthus totally rejected Condorcet's argument and insisted that nothing short of compulsion would make people reduce fertility rates. There is a tendency in modern Malthusian scholarship to emphasize the changes in some of Malthus's views over the years, but his basic distrust of the power of reasoning and freedom, as opposed to the force of economic compulsion, in leading people to choose smaller families remained largely unmodified. Indeed, in one of his last works, published in 1830 (he died in 1834), Malthus insisted on his conclusion that "there is no reason whatever to suppose that anything beside the difficulty of procuring in adequate plenty the necessaries of life should either indispose this greater number of persons to marry early, or disable them from rearing in health the largest families" (Malthus [1830] 1982: 243).

As it happens, this particular debate is not hard to settle empirically. Not only have fertility rates come down over time, but "the progress of reason" in the development of the new norm of smaller families has played a major part in this evolution. Furthermore, cross-sectional comparisons across countries show that the decline of fertility rates is closely related to the empowerment of young women whose lives are most battered by overfrequent bearing and rearing of children. This lesson also emerges clearly from cross-sectional comparisons across India's hundreds of districts. Not surprisingly, women's education and "gainful" employment, which increases their voice in family decisions, emerge as the two biggest influences in reducing fertility rates.

Although the total fertility rate for India as a whole—despite a drop from 6 children per couple to just over 3—is still substantially higher than the replacement level of 2 per couple, it is interesting and important to note that many districts in India have substantially lower fertility rates than the United States, the United Kingdom, France, or China. The fertility declines in the Indian states of Kerala, Tamil Nadu, and Himachal Pradesh can be closely linked to women's empowerment, related to the rapid enhancement of female education and other influences on the standing and voice of young women.

Another interesting example is Bangladesh, where a very sharp reduction in fertility rates seems to have been associated with the expansion of family planning opportunities, greater involvement of women in economic activities (for example, through microcredit movements), and much public discussion on the need to change the prevailing pattern of gender disparity. All these influences, including the role of family planning facilities in helping young women acquire greater reproductive freedom, contribute to women's empowerment. The expanded social and economic role of women in Bangladesh has been widely noted. The fertility rate has declined from 6.1 to 3.4 in a mere decade and a half (between 1980 and 1996) and is continuing to fall sharply; in early 2000 it was just above 3 children per couple. All this has happened without any coercion, by way of greater social freedom, mainly for young women.

China is often taken as a counterexample, providing positive evidence of the good effects of coercion in family planning (as manifested in the "one-child" policy). There is need for more study on the details of the Chinese experience, but at the aggregate level, fertility decline has been sharp. The question that does arise is whether a somewhat similar decline was not to have been expected, even in the absence of coercion, because of China's achievements in female education and employment. The Indian state of Kerala, where female education has also expanded very rapidly but where there is no compulsory family planning, experienced a similarly sharp decline in the fertility rate. In fact, Kerala's expansion of female education was faster than China's, and so was the decline in its fertility rate, even for 1979, when China introduced the "one-child" policy. China's fertility rate fell from 2.8 to 2.0 between 1979 and 1991; during the same period, Kerala's fell from 3.0 to 1.8. Fertility rates have continued to decline in both places, but Kerala's fertility rate has stayed persistently lower than China's in every period. Also, because in Kerala fertility decline came about through free choice rather than coercion, the infant mortality rate has continued to fall in a way it has not in China: although the infant mortality rate in the two countries was roughly similar in 1979, it is now about twice as high in China as in Kerala and still higher for girls. Both effectiveness and humaneness demand that fertility declines be based on more freedom, not less.

Freedom as an End and as a Means

To conclude, a freedom-centered view of development has several advantages over more conventional outlooks. First, it provides a deeper basis for evaluation of development, allowing us to concentrate on the objective of individual freedom rather than merely on proximate means such as the growth of GNP, industrialization, or technological progress. The enhancement of lives and liberties has intrinsic relevance that distinguishes it from, say, the enlargement of commodity production.

Second, since freedoms of various kinds contribute to enhancing freedoms of other kinds, a freedom-centered view offers instrumental insights. By focusing on the interconnections between freedoms of different types, it takes us well beyond the narrow perspective of seeing each freedom in isolation. We live in a world of many institutions (involving the market, the government, the judiciary, political parties, the media, and so on), and we have to determine how they can supplement and strengthen each other, rather than reduce each other's effectiveness.

Third, this broad perspective allows us to distinguish between (a) *repressive interventions* of the state in stifling liberty, initiative, and enterprise and in crippling the working of individual agency and cooperative action and (b) the *supportive role* of the state in enhancing the effective freedoms of individuals—for example, in providing public education, health care, social safety nets, and good macroeconomic policies and in safeguarding industrial competition and epidemiological and ecological sustainability.

Finally, the freedom-centered view captures the constructive role of free human agency as an engine of change. In terms of the medieval distinction between "the agent" and "the patient," this is a distinctly agent-oriented view of development. It is radically different from seeing people as passive beneficiaries of cunning development programs.

Notes

1. The empirical as well as the conceptual connections are discussed in Sen (1999).

2. Marx (1887), vol. 1, ch. 10, sect. 3: 240; see also Marx (1973).

3. Smith ([1776] 1976), I, ii: 27, and V, I, f: 785.

References

Barro, Robert J. 1996. *Getting It Right: Markets and Choices in a Free Society.* Cambridge, Mass.: MIT Press.

Drèze, Jean, and Amartya Sen. 1995. *India: Economic Development and Social Opportunity.* Delhi: Oxford University Press.

Gluck, Carol. 1985. *Japan's Modern Myths: Ideology in the Late Meiji Period.* Princeton, N.J.: Princeton University Press.

Malthus, T. R. 1982. *A Summary View of the Principle of Population.* Harmondsworth, U.K.: Penguin Books. First published 1830.

Marx, Karl. 1887. *Capital.* London: Sonnenschein.

———. 1973. *Grundrisse.* Harmondsworth, U.K.: Penguin Books.

Przeworski, Adam, and others. 1995. *Sustainable Democracy.* Cambridge, U.K.: Cambridge University Press.

Ramachandran, V. K. 1990. *Wage Labour and Unfreedom in Agriculture: An Indian Case Study.* Oxford, U.K.: Clarendon Press.

Sen, Amartya. 1999. *Development as Freedom.* New York: Knopf.

Smith, Adam. 1996. *An Inquiry into the Nature and Causes of the Wealth of Nations.* R. H. Campbell and A. S. Skinner, eds. Oxford, U.K.: Clarendon Press. First published 1776.

Candidate Issues in
Development Economics

Robert M. Solow

I AM NOT A STUDENT OF DEVELOPMENT. These are the thoughts of an economist from a rich country whose main research interest has been the macroeconomics of the long run and the short run. I may be suggesting research questions that have already been aired in the development literature. With that apology, here are some ideas.

1. How large a research establishment, and of what sort, does a developing economy need? Presumably, its goal should not be to replicate on a small scale what a rich country does, but it must have people and institutions capable of accessing, adapting, and using technical innovations that originate elsewhere. How can this be arranged? What is the role of foreign direct investment in this process?

2. What is the optimal (or at least what is a good) time pattern for developing, exploiting, and conserving renewable and nonrenewable resources in a developing economy? How much of the resource rents should be reinvested, and how should the reinvestment be allocated among resource-intensive and other industries?

3. What is a valid macroeconomic model for a small developing economy? As a small, open economy it has the advantage of finding much of the necessary aggregate demand in world markets. But it is vulnerable to synchronized recession in its main export customers. Is an independent monetary policy of much use to such a country? Can discretionary fiscal policy be used to stabilize the domestic economy without endangering other goals?

4. How can a developing economy avoid some of the failures in urban land-use policy, training and retraining institutions, unemployment insurance, and so on that have beset the rich countries?

Reflections by Pioneers

"Pioneers Revisited"

Sir Hans Singer

IN THE FIRST VOLUME OF *Pioneers in Development*, published in 1984, the Pioneer of Pioneers, Paul Rosenstein-Rodan, concluded his contribution thus: "We know what has to be done—we have to mobilize the will to do it." Since then, we have become even clearer about "what has to be done" as far as the ultimate objective is concerned—the reduction and ultimate abolition of poverty and the reduction of inequality. But this clarity is deceptive in two ways: first, we have come to realize that "poverty" is multifaceted and requires action in many different fields and by many different actors, and second, we do not "know" any general rule for how and in what sequence these different facets of poverty should be tackled in the many different countries, with their different histories, cultures, institutions, resources, climates, ethnic uniformity or diversity, and so on. Growth expressed as the single indicator of gross national product (GNP) per capita tempted many development analysts to look for such general rules, but poverty reduction is too complicated and too country specific. This reality will force development analysts more and more into the hard slog of detailed analysis of different situations. Greater availability of data and greatly increased powers of modeling and examining the data may help, but it would be preposterous to claim that "we know what has to be done" for the myriad of situations that confront us. Rosenstein-Rodan was right in his claim as to our ultimate objective but not as to the ways of getting there for every poor person or household in the world.

The second part of his statement—"we have to mobilize the will to do it"—is equally true and yet oversimplistic. It all depends on who is meant by "we." If his statement implies that "we" as development analysts have done our job in providing knowledge and that now it is up to the politicians to "mobilize the will" to act on it, that is not the view of development analysts today. On the contrary, more and more attention is being given to including in the field of development economics the problems of "architecture" at many different levels—global, regional, national, local, household, and personal. The problems of "governance," including the "governance" of transnational corporations, are increasingly important in development studies. Such subjects as financial regulation, corruption, participation, democracy, gender relations, human rights, prevention of ethnic conflicts, and credit institutions are all designed to "mobilize the will." So are discussions of global governance— the reexamination after 55 years of the United Nations system and the Bretton Woods institutions, as well as newer development agencies such as the World Trade Organization. "How to mobilize the will to do it" has become an integral part of development studies and is likely to become even more important in the new millennium. In the process, the subject is becoming more and more interdisciplinary.

If, however, Paul Rosenstein-Rodan meant to say that "we" as development economists must increasingly help to mobilize the political will to act on such knowledge as we have, while working to increase such knowledge, he showed great wisdom and foresight.

Within this general framework of a shift from paradigm to implementation and governance; from growth to poverty reduction (or rather from growth per se to propoor growth), with its associated emphasis on distribution and the reduction of inequalities; and from general rules to situation specificity, we can now identify with a fair degree of confidence a number of areas that will receive increased attention in the field of development studies.

• *Globalization.* The task here will not be to "promote" or "counteract" globalization but to create genuine (that is, all-inclusive) globalization—to convert it from a "winners and losers" to a "win-win" force. Among the problems on this front are the exclusion of much of Africa and access to the new sources of information, as prominently discussed in the 1999 *Human Development Report.*

• *Urbanization.* Soon, the majority of the population and the majority of the poor will live in towns, often in megacities. This will give added urgency to the problems of local government, civic participation, the urban informal sector, and urban infrastructure and environment.

• *Environmental degradation.* This is a matter of intergenerational equity—of leaving to the next generation the same quality of resources as now exists, or better. This issue will add yet another dimension to the need for increased multidisciplinarity (in addition to a shift toward the politics of implementation) and for studies of urban environments, which will be particularly situation specific. It will also call for the development of new measures of sustainable development.

• *Footloose and volatile financial flows.* This matter deserves a special priority within the previous emphasis on new "architectures" at the global and national levels. In view of the magnitude of these financial flows and the new techniques that favor volatility—both of which were unforeseeable by the "Pioneers"—as well as the recent crises in East Asia and elsewhere, this special priority seems fully justified. Under this heading we may also include the rather different problems of urban and rural microcredit as an instrument for creating new opportunities for poverty reduction.

• *Trade in services, technology, and brainpower.* This increasingly important exchange will involve new measures of trade volumes, terms of trade, openness, balances of trade, and so on. This challenge will be difficult to meet—but it will have to be met.

• *Child poverty* is more than a question of intergenerational equity. With the bulk of the world's children born in poor countries, and the number of children within both poor and rich countries' households an increasing function of poverty, the world's children suffer a much higher incidence of poverty than the world's adults. This will increasingly be seen as incompatible with the overriding objectives of poverty elimination and equality of opportunity to develop the innate capacities of all. How to target action on this objective should be perhaps the most important task for development studies.

No doubt others may want to add to this list of priorities, but even this selective list of six items will call for new Pioneers to take up the extended tasks for development studies in the new century.

International Trade
and the Domestic
Institutional Framework

Hla Myint

IT IS NOW GENERALLY RECOGNIZED that in order to apply economic
theory fruitfully to developing countries, economists must incorporate
institutional factors into the analysis. This chapter illustrates that maxim
in the field of international trade. I argue that economic growth with
export expansion in developing countries cannot be fully explained
purely in terms of formal international trade theory unless we take into
account the changes in the domestic institutional setting. Doing so will
give us a better understanding of the relative roles of the market and
the state in the context of an underdeveloped domestic framework.

To illustrate, let us examine two notable phases of rapid growth and
export expansion in developing countries, one representing the "widening" of the domestic framework and the other the "deepening" of
this framework.

"Widening": Opening Up Traditional Economies

The "vent-for-surplus" phase of export expansion during the colonial
period, when the land-abundant peasant economies were "opened up"
to international trade, is a prime example of the widening process. The
spectacular expansion of labor-intensive manufacturing exports and the
corresponding high rates of economic growth in East Asian economies
such as the Republic of Korea and Taiwan (China) from the 1960s
onward is an equally striking example of the deepening of the domestic
institutional framework, starting initially with heavy population pressure on land. In neither case can the rates of export expansion and
economic growth be entirely explained purely in terms of a more effi-

cient allocation of the given resources according to comparative advantage. We are obliged to search for some "residual" sources of growth.

The vent-for-surplus process of peasant export expansion was brought about by the introduction of an efficient modern administration and by government-sponsored improvements in transport and communications. Given this favorable economic environment, peasant producers responded to market incentives and expanded export production by extending cultivation into the unused hinterland, employing traditional agricultural methods. The chief source of residual growth was the availability of unused land and the underemployed labor in subsistence agriculture. By contrast, in the East Asian economies that experienced heavy population pressure, the chief source of residual growth was the rapid rise in the productivity of resources, in both agriculture and manufacturing, brought about by the deepening of the domestic institutional framework and the intensification of economic relationships between the peasant farmers and small-scale industries dispersed in rural areas.

The widening of the domestic institutional framework under free-market conditions was rapid but uneven. The market system was well developed in the foreign trade sector, where export-import firms reached down to the peasant exporters through a series of middlemen, and the local market's domestic agricultural products also benefited from sharing transport and marketing facilities. But there was still a dualism between the traditional sector—peasant farming, small-scale industries, and other small economic units—and the modern sector, consisting of export-import firms and other large enterprises and the commercial banks.

This dualism was manifested in price differentials between the two sectors, which reflected a relatively underdeveloped market and transport system. It was most pronounced in the domestic capital market. Small borrowers in the traditional sector could only borrow from local moneylenders in the "unorganized" market, at a much higher rate of interest than the prevailing rates charged by the modern banks. The reasons were imperfect information, the high risks of lending to small borrowers, and the slow growth of a professional class of local financial intermediaries with the credit standing needed to borrow from the banks and with sufficiently intimate knowledge of local conditions in the traditional sector to channel the loans into productive uses.

Grand Strategies and the Repression of the Traditional Sector

Before going on to the deepening phase of the domestic institutional framework, it is necessary to digress briefly on the interregnum period of the 1950s, when exports and growth suffered a sharp setback. At that time the newly independent countries, including the peasant export economies, reacted against colonial laissez-faire policies and took wholesale to grand strategies of economic development that were based on planning, direct state controls, and import substitution aimed at promoting domestic industrialization. The switch from free trade to import substitution would by itself have introduced large "distortions" into resource allocation, but on top of that, the domestic institutional framework was damaged by direct controls and the replacement of the market by state agencies. Government controls diverted the lion's share of the limited supplies of foreign exchange and capital funds to large-scale, state-controlled enterprises in the modern sector, on highly favorable terms, thus starving the traditional sector of these much-needed resources. In particular, the domestic capital market was repressed: foreign exchange controls cut banks off from the world capital market, while government policies of keeping official interest rates very low to encourage domestic manufacturing industries reduced domestic savings. Moneylenders and other private intermediaries were denied access to the banks and were subjected to regulations fixing the maximum rate of lending.

In sum, the 1950s strategies of economic development had the effect of repressing the least-developed part of the domestic institutional framework—the "traditional" and "unorganized" sector. As we shall see, it was the regeneration and development of this part of the domestic framework, catering for small farmers and small industrialists in rural areas, that paved the way for the success of Korea and Taiwan in expanding labor-intensive manufactured exports.

"Deepening": Two East Asian Examples

Like other developing economies, Korea and Taiwan went through an initial planning and import-substitution phase during the 1950s and early 1960s. They also followed low-interest-rate policies to encourage domestic manufacturing industries. It was only in the face of high inflation and balance of payments difficulties that they switched to trade liberalization policies and raised their interest rates to very high levels. This not only brought inflation under control and achieved economic stability but also increased domestic savings.

According to the factor-proportions theory of comparative advantage, countries with initial conditions of scarce land and abundant labor could enjoy continuing growth under free trade. Starting from highly labor intensive manufactured exports, they could climb the "ladder of comparative advantage" toward less labor intensive and more capital intensive manufactured exports as the tightening of the labor market and rising wages shifted their comparative advantage in that direction. Yet the rates of export expansion and growth in Korea and Taiwan seem to be too high to be explained purely in terms of the gains from the removal of distortions in resource allocation. This is particularly so considering that these two economies were by no means following text-book free-trade policies. They distorted their resource allocation in fa-vor of exports by offering a variety of export-promotion incentives, and they continued some of their import-substitution policies in the more capital intensive and technologically advanced industries to has-ten the progress of those industries toward industrial maturity. One could, of course, argue that because they pursued these distorting poli-cies in moderation, the gains from trade liberalization outweighed the losses from trade distortions, but that does not seem to offer an ad-equate explanation for their phenomenally high growth rates. We are left to search for the residual factors in the form of the large increases in the productivity of both agricultural and manufacturing resources and to focus attention on the improvements in the institutional framework that made these possible.

Formal international trade theory tends to assume that once trade distortions are removed, a country's potential comparative advantage emerges automatically through the workings of a well-coordinated market system and a fully developed domestic institutional framework. But before a developing country can convert its abundant labor supply into a comparative advantage in labor-intensive manufactured exports, two crucial conditions must be fulfilled. First, agricultural productivity has to be raised, to keep wages down and to release labor to manufac-turing. Second, productivity in manufacturing, relative to the low wages, must be increased, to gain a competitive advantage in the world market for labor-intensive manufactures. Both conditions require great improve-ments in the domestic institutional framework. Here, Korea and Tai-wan were fortunate in inheriting a valuable institutional legacy, in both agriculture and manufacturing, from the Japanese colonial period—the result of Japan's own adaptation to its abundant labor supply when it started its successful economic development.

In agriculture, the two economies were able to build on the rural infrastructure left from the Japanese period to pursue policies of raising agricultural productivity through the introduction of high-yielding seeds and fertilizers and through multiple cropping based on improved irri-gation. Active government policies created organizations and institu-tions that catered for a large number of small farmers dispersed over the countryside—providing them with transport, communications, and electricity; making available improved marketing and credit facilities so that farmers could adopt the new cash-intensive methods of agricul-ture; and improving education and information so that knowledge of the new technology could be transmitted.

In manufacturing, the two economies benefited from the Japanese method of promoting industrialization on a decentralized basis, with government policies that encouraged the growth and efficiency of small-scale, labor-intensive industries dispersed in rural areas. This method avoided the heavy outlay in social overhead capital required for building large-scale factories in urban centers. Instead, the small industries were able to share with the small farmers the rural social infrastructure and the organizational network designed to reach out to a large number of small, dispersed economic units. The small industries also enjoyed the locational advantage of being able to utilize the abundant rural labor supply—cheaply, flexibly, and frequently from within daily commuting distance—allowing use of part-time and seasonal workers. They could also draw on the local supply of agricultural raw materials for processing.

There were other sources of gain. With the widening of local markets brought about by improved transport, many small industries were able to utilize more fully their existing capital equipment and management capacity. The widening of the market let to greater specialization and division of labor (in the Adam Smithian manner) and to improvements in technology adapted to local conditions. Individually, the economies from fuller use of existing capacity and the gains from minor innovation may be small, but in the aggregate they contributed to a large rise in the productivity of the small industries. Export of their products was facilitated by further institutional developments, such as subcontracting, quality control, and the use of large trading firms with specialized knowledge of potential markets abroad.

Finally, we must take account of the contribution of foreign direct investment. Foreign investment entered to take advantage of the initially abundant supply of labor. Investment in the export-processing zones expanded local employment. Later, direct investment from Japan provided an effective method of technology transfer because of congruent factor proportions. As wage costs in Japan rose, Japanese firms found it more profitable to locate their relatively labor-intensive type of manufacturing industry in neighboring economies with low wages. This investment came together with technology, management methods, and work practices that had been successfully tested in Japan and could be readily adopted and duplicated in Korea and Taiwan, with their similar factor endowments. Thus, the two economies' climb up the ladder of comparative advantage was facilitated.

We may now sketch the relative roles of the state and the market suggested by our analysis. The success stories of Korea and Taiwan spearheaded the "neoclassical resurgence." There is no doubt about the importance of familiar neoclassical free-market policies grounded on orthodox fiscal and monetary policies for maintaining macroeconomic stability. I have, however, focused on the less well appreciated aspect of these economies' success: their active government policies for raising the productivity of resources in rural areas in situ by improving social infrastructure and by building up organizations and institutions designed to cater for the needs of small farmers and small industrialists widely dispersed over the countryside. These policies are not only important for Korea and Taiwan; they are also relevant for the application of economic theory to developing countries.

Benefits and Drawbacks of State Intervention

From my perspective, the weakness of the neoclassical theory is that it tends to focus attention on the "negative" policies of removing "distortions" in resource allocation, pushing into the background the "positive" policies for improving the institutional framework of a developing country. Formal international theory implicitly assumes that the domestic institutional framework is already fully developed, as exemplified by a "frictionless" perfect-competition model of the economy. That model, however, is adopted purely for the theoretical convenience of being able to define the distortions as deviations from the optimum allocation of resources. When we explicitly start from an underdeveloped state of the domestic institutional framework, there is clearly a need for positive government policies to enable the market system to work more effectively by reducing transaction and information costs.

"Market-enhancing" policies, in this sense, may be regarded as an extension of free-market policies at a practical level. Thus, even during the colonial laissez-faire period the government accepted as a matter of course that its function included provision of social overhead capital, such as roads to reduce transport costs. In principle, there is little difference between the provision of physical infrastructure to reduce transport costs and the provision of intangible social infrastructure to reduce transaction and information costs.

We may now take a brief retrospective look at the relationship between the elements of the domestic institutional framework—the market system and the administrative and fiscal systems. During the colonial period the widening of this framework was brought about by the introduction of a modern form of administration that efficiently and honestly carried out the basic functions of governance, such as the maintenance of law and order, protection of life and property, and administration of justice. The reaction against colonial laissez-faire policies in favor of development planning in the 1950s resulted in the enormous extension of government functions into the multifarious tasks of controlling the economy. The basic functions of governance were regarded as mere "night watchman's" functions, and scarce fiscal and administrative resources were diverted to the more glamorous task of promoting growth. This overloading of the fiscal and administrative system frequently resulted in inefficiency and corruption in the ordinary administration of the country, which severely undermined the government's ability to pursue its chosen economic goals. I believe that this danger of overloading the government system is ever present, whether the chosen goal is economic growth or other socially desirable goals related to economic development.

The Challenges of Globalization

In the 1980s and 1990s Indonesia, Malaysia, and Thailand began to follow the examples of Korea and Taiwan (and of Hong Kong and Singapore) by achieving rapid growth through export expansion. This strategy was based on a general shift toward the outward-looking policies of economic liberalization that removed restrictions not only on international trade but also on international capital movements. Foreign direct investment again played a vital role in transferring technology and raising the productivity of labor in the second generation of "Asian tiger economies," enabling them to move up the ladder of comparative advantage and export more sophisticated manufactured products. The Pacific Rim region became the fastest-growing area in the world.

Then came the Asian economic crisis of 1997, which started with the devaluation of the Thai baht under speculative pressures and spread to neighboring countries, resulting in further devaluations and sharp falls in the stock markets. The economic growth of the Pacific Rim slowed, and the mystique of the Asian tiger economies was shattered. This revived the older, inward-looking tendencies. Malaysia reacted by imposing controls on its capital market, and its prime minister joined in the chorus of denunciation of the world market economic forces that are now described as globalization.

To what degree can this renewed wave of hostility to world market forces be interpreted as a return to the inward-looking development theories and policies of the 1950s? The Asian economic crisis of 1997 demonstrated clearly that long-term flows of foreign investment could be seriously undermined by volatile movements of short-run speculative funds that bore no relation to economic fundamentals and the productivity of long-run investment. In the Asian context the crisis was brought about by a combination of factors: the removal of controls on capital markets, financial innovations such as securitization and financial derivatives, and the rise of new financial centers in Hong Kong and Singapore. The distinction between long-term portfolio capital and short-term bank funds became blurred, since both could be transferred rapidly between one financial center and another.

The existing international financial institutions are unable to control the truly enormous amounts of speculative funds that swirl around the world's financial centers and to protect the currencies of developing countries against speculators. A speculative run on a currency, once it has started and gathered momentum, would be beyond the capacity of an individual country to resist. The only practical alternative is to avoid attracting speculators in the first place, by imposing strict fiscal and monetary discipline (for example, by not extending unsound bank loans to "political cronies"). Singapore and Taiwan, with their large foreign reserves and high domestic savings ratios, have practiced a preventive approach with success, combining orthodox fiscal and monetary policies with the creation of domestic financial institutions to mobilize domestic savings. A well-known example is Singapore's Provident Fund system, which collects a high rate of compulsory contributions.

Starting from a Keynesian diagnosis of the Asian economic crisis, we seem to have arrived at orthodox policy conclusions! We may also note that although a high ratio of domestic savings to gross domestic product (GDP) is not, as was believed in the 1950s, a key to rapid economic growth, it does provide a valuable shield against short-run economic instability and speculation.

The new wave of hostility toward the world market forces that go under the fashionable label of globalization has encouraged the latent inward-looking tendencies of the developing countries. But on a closer look, there are important differences between the aim and objects of the 1950s type of development economics and the present-day protests against globalization.

The development economists of the 1950s were against the world market system because they believed that it could not bring about rapid economic growth without state intervention and planning and because they believed that the developing countries, typically dependent on one or two main primary exports, would be especially vulnerable to the instability of the world market for primary products. Looking back, it is fair to say that in practice, the policymakers of the 1950s frequently subordinated the goal of reducing vulnerability to the short-run instability of the world market to the overriding goal of promoting long-run economic growth. Thus, state agricultural marketing boards, designed to protect peasant producers from fluctuations in the export market, were soon turned into an instrument for taxing the farmers ruthlessly to subsidize domestic industries. Similarly, demands for international schemes to stabilize the price of primary products soon turned into demands for increasing the flow of long-term international capital to promote growth.

In contrast, present-day writers seem to condemn globalization because it promotes economic growth too rapidly! They would argue that the interaction between economic liberalization policies and rapid technological changes has unleashed disruptive forces on the economic and social life of the countries at a much faster rate than their domestic institutional frameworks can absorb and that it is not sufficient to talk about the need for flexible adjustments without counting the social costs. They believe that failure to keep up with the headlong pace of economic growth and to cope with its dislocating effects leads to social and economic tensions and political instability. This contrasts with the "crash programs" and "big pushes" advocated by development economists in the 1950s.

The critics of globalization are concerned about the disruptive effects of world market forces on all the countries exposed to them, whether industrial or developing. Their argument is most persuasive, however, when applied to a developing country in the long transitional period after traditional social arrangements for relieving economic distress and unemployment have broken down under the impact of market forces but before the emergence of a modern government social welfare system. It is ironic to note that "disguised unemployment," much deprecated by the development economists of the 1950s, should now be reappraised as a valuable element in traditional social welfare arrangements.

What are the policy implications of globalization? We shall have to accept that the process of the breakdown of traditional social welfare arrangements under the impact of market forces is likely to be irreversible, even in the least developed of the developing countries. The only practical alternative is to try to shorten the transition phase by pursuing efficient growth policies in the hope that economic growth will provide the government with an expanding stream of revenues. These revenues, if the government so chooses, can be used to alleviate the worst effects of the social and economic dislocations accompanying economic growth. As for the Asian Pacific Rim countries, despite their severe economic setback since 1997, they are now too well integrated with the world economy to be able to go all the way back to the 1950s style of inward-looking development policies. Thus, Malaysia, after its initial reaction of imposing controls on its capital market, is now reported to have lifted these controls, apparently without ill effects in the form of capital flight. Given the long-run economic prospects of the Pacific Rim countries, their future would still seem to lie in the direction of their previous outward-looking policies, although economic recovery may be slower for the more politically fragile countries such as Indonesia.

There is, of course, no guarantee that the expansion of government revenues from economic growth will lead to better provision of social security and welfare. Apart from the limited administrative capacity of the developing countries (not to speak of bureaucratic inefficiency and corruption), there still remains the ultimate obstacle: lack of political will, or the low priority that their governments attach to social welfare expenditure.

The Economics of a
Stagnant Population

W. W. Rostow

I TAKE IT THAT THE MOST important economic event of the 21st century will be the fall in the world's population that will, in time, embrace the developing world as well as the industrial countries.

• Certain of the precocious developing economies—for example, China, the Republic of Korea, and Taiwan (China)—have already fallen below the replacement fertility rate and will soon experience a decline in population.

• In certain other developing countries (called "transitional" by the World Bank and including Brazil, India, and Indonesia), fertility is above 2.1 but is falling rapidly.

• Elsewhere, the general tendency is for fertility rates to fall, and there is no evidence of a tendency for fertility to remain at the replacement rate of 2.1 rather than to go below. Therefore, we shall be confronted in the 21st century—beginning in the industrial countries—by a massive question of public policy: how to manage our affairs with a stagnant population in prospect.

The essential facts about the world's population as a whole in the first half of the 21st century can be briefly summarized.

A gross fertility rate of 2.1 (children per family) defines the replacement rate. Above that number, a population rises over time; below, it falls. The intervals depend on the previous history of the fertility rate and the size of the backlog of women of fertile age. There is a general tendency for fertility (and population growth) rates to correlate with urbanization, income per capita, and the proportion of the population using modern methods of birth control (see Table 1). These three determinants are obviously autocorrelated to an important degree.

A number of transitional countries, including some with large populations, have rapidly decreasing fertility rates. A few already have fertility rates below 2.1 (Table 2).

Table 1. Total Fertility Rate by Income Group,
1970, 1992, and 2000

Country group	1970	1992	2000 (estimated)
Low income	6.0	3.4	3.1
Lower middle income	4.5	3.1	2.9
Upper middle income	4.8	2.9	2.5
High income	2.4	1.7	1.4
World	—	—	2.9

— Not available.
Source: World Bank (1989): 216, Table 27.

Since the late 18th century, both birth rates and death rates have been falling, but the decrease in death rates outpaced that in birth rates until the Great Depression of the 1930s. After World War II world population rose sharply as a result of the spread of the new antibiotics and the control of malaria. Birth rates have subsequently declined and have converged with death rates irrespective of stage of growth (Table 3).

Although life expectancy in most rich countries has crept up, circulatory diseases and cancer have thus far set a kind of limit to the fall of death rates. Africa south of the Sahara is a regional exception to the pattern, with a fertility rate of 5.6, not far below the maximum.

Against this background, the overall long-run estimates of peak global future population have been systematically falling. The medium-projection figure is now below 10 billion.

The Two Dangers

Since overall world population will increase for some time, there is a real danger of regional crises in food or raw materials. Instability in the

Table 2. Total Fertility Rate, Selected Transitional Countries,
1970, 1992, and 2000

Country	1970	1992	2000 (estimated)
Brazil	4.9	2.8	2.0
India	5.8	3.7	3.4
Indonesia	5.9	2.9	2.7
Mexico	6.3	3.2	3.1
Thailand	5.5	2.2	2.0
Turkey	4.9	3.4	2.6

Sources: For 1970 and 1992, World Bank (1999): Table 26; for 2000, 1998 World Population Data Sheet.

Table 3. Death Rates, Excluding India and China,
1970 and 1992
(per thousand population)

Country group	1970	1992
Low income	19	12
Lower middle income	12	9
Upper middle income	10	7
High income	10	9

Source: World Bank (1989): 216, Table 27.

Middle East may cause difficulties in the energy supply. The possibility of environmental crises with global consequences cannot be eliminated. This set of dangers has been widely studied and debated.

The second danger has not been studied and debated. It arises from the length of time required to regain a 2.1 replacement rate and the noneconomic barriers to such a recovery if the fertility rate is permitted to fall below that level. This has already happened in the rich industrial part of the world—in Europe, Japan, mainland China, Taiwan (China), Hong Kong (China), Singapore, and Korea. It will also be a problem for transitional countries, where the total fertility rate is above 2.1 but is falling. All will face the problem of maintaining full employment and a socially viable society with a stagnant population, if they opt for that objective.

Two Major Economic Problems

The first symptom that population dynamics is finding its way into the political arena is the increased average age of the population in the rich industrial countries and the more precocious developing countries. The proportion of the working force to the dependent population is falling. This is also a major issue in mainland China: by 2030, 33 percent of its people will be over 60, accounting for 21 percent of the population (Rostow 1998: 201–02).

Hamish McRae lists the following measures (in addition to raising the retirement age, which has been much talked about but not yet implemented) that will increase the working force in relation to the dependent population (McRae 1994: 97):

- Female participation in the workforce will climb.
- Part-time work (including work at home) will continue to increase.
- University students will be expected to work part-time while studying, a process already begun.

- Greater efforts will be made to reduce unemployment.
- Retraining for different jobs several times in a career will become more normal.
- Volunteer labor will be used to a greater extent.
- There will be more pressure on children to learn marketable skills.

To this list should be added actions to solve the "underclass" problem: to educate and train for places in the work force the disadvantaged men and women who are now on welfare. This will no longer be a matter of equity or budgets. The training of these men and women for the work force will be a substantial contribution toward buying time.

Immigration has already bought time in certain countries with fertility below 2.1. It is economically simple but politically and socially complex. If there is a decline in the indigenous population, the shortfall can, in theory, be easily made up by bringing in men and women from another country with higher fertility rates, at least until the march of development dries up the pool of potential immigrants. There are two contrary forces that come into play, however: political resistance within the host country to a real or perceived change in the demographic content of the society, and the initially unskilled character of many immigrants, resulting in long-term unemployment and a consequent rise in welfare expenditures. The balancing of these considerations against the additions to the work force could limit the role of immigration in making up the shortfall.

Although these measures will buy time, the ultimate problem confronted by the human race will be to get back to a replacement fertility rate of 2.1 or (where the rate is now above 2.1 but is falling toward that level in the developing world) to achieve a leveling off at that rate if that is the choice made.

Time-buying measures are important because it will take considerable time to get the fertility rate back to the replacement rate. The conclusion of one social scientist–mathematician (Yue 1999: 5–6) is to be taken seriously not merely by Japan, which now has a fertility rate of 1.4, but by all countries that have permitted their fertility rates to drop below 2.1. This evidence, combined with the dynamic theory of population systems, tells us that unless the current trend of a declining birth rate in Japan is reversed, there seems little hope of preventing Japan's total population from declining—a development that will certainly emerge in the early decades of this century. Actions for promoting reproduction in Japan have to be taken as soon as possible because population development is a process with great inertia. The probability of obtaining decisive results from population—and other social and economic—policies is extremely small for a short time period measured in terms of years. In the case of Japan the great inertia of the population system will most likely drag the Japanese population down in the next several decades because birth rates there have been declining during the past 50 years. A policy of doing nothing and waiting for Japan's population to rise violates the natural rules governing the population system.

The U.S. Case

The immigration dilemma of the United States (with fertility at 2.0) is an important component of the population problem as a whole, and it is a heightened version of the problem facing Western Europe, Canada, and Japan. At the moment, the American total fertility rate is sustained by the influx of the Hispanic population (with 2.3 fertility) and the 2.2 fertility of the black population.

Three propositions about immigration into the United States at the close of the 20th century are fairly certain. First, immigration from Latin America and Asia surged in the 1970s and 1980s (see Figure 1).[1] Second, by 2040 this surge, which continues, is likely to produce a substantial decline in the proportion of "whites" in the U.S. population (Bean, Cushing, and Hayes 1997: Table 5). That proportion, it is estimated, will fall by 22 points, from 75.2 percent in 1990 to 52.8 percent in 2050. The third proposition is that people in the Hispanic population, and to a lesser extent in the Asian population, tend to marry persons of different races or ethnic groups, and younger persons are more inclined to marry out of their group than are their elders. Most of these mixed marriages are with "whites." Therefore, with the passage of time, the change in racial composition of the population will be diluted. For example, the proportion of Hispanics in mixed marriages constitutes 34 percent of the total; the proportion of Asians is 22 percent of the total.

A fourth, less certain, proposition is that the number of Hispanics, particularly Mexicans, who will seek to migrate to the United States may well decline by 2050. By World Bank reckoning, in 2010 Mexico will have a total fertility rate of 2.1, and by the middle of the 21st century, if not before, it will probably achieve the hypothetical size of a stationary population (170 million). Mexican income per capita in 2050 will approximate that of New Zealand in 2000. With this easing of the pressure of Mexican population growth and the decrease in relative Mexican poverty, it is not irrational to assume a decline in the pressure to migrate north.

The world stands at a curious point in the evolution of its population. There are countries, notably in Africa, where it is worth going on with great efforts to get fertility rates down. The international bureaucracies in the United Nations and the World Bank are properly focused, as they have been for many years, on this effort. And surely the spread

Figure 1. Average Annual Number of Immigrants Admitted
to the United States, by National Origin, 1821–1993

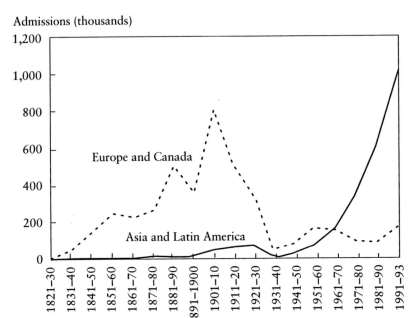

Admissions (thousands)

Source: Bean, Cushing, and Hayes (1997).

of modern methods of birth control has played a role in recent decades
in bringing down fertility levels in the so-called transitional countries
of the developing world. Fertility there is falling fast but still stands,
with certain exceptions, above the replacement rate of 2.1. One would
hope that well before a replacement rate of 2.1 in fertility is reached,
leaders in the transitional countries would argue to their constituents
for a policy that would achieve a stagnant population and a replacement fertility rate at a chosen population level that could be below the
present population level.

    Meanwhile, the fertility level has fallen below 2.1 in most of the
high-income economies. (The oil-rich economies are an exception.) As
emphasized above, however, there is an important time lag between the
achievement of a 2.1 fertility rate and an actual decline in population.
World Bank estimates for the approximate dates when population will
actually fall are presented in Table 4, which also lists the small number
of societies in which an actual decrease in population has already set in.
Those cases are mainly confined to the European nations formerly in
the Soviet Union, plus Hungary and Slovenia.

Table 4. Estimated Trends in Population to 2035

Country	Population trend, 1995–2035	Year in which total population declines	Year in which NRR equals 1.0
Albania	Falls 1995–2000		2005
Austria		2010	
Belarus			2005
Belgium		2010	
Brazil	Rising		2000
China	Rising		2030
Croatia		2000	
Czech Republic	Falls 1990–2000		2030
Denmark		2015	
Estonia	Falling		
Finland		2030	
France		2030	
Germany		2005	
Greece		2015	
Guatemala	Rising		2025
Honduras	Rising		2025
Hungary	Falling		2030
India	Rising		
Ireland	Rising		2030
Italy		2005	
Japan		2015	
Korea, Republic of	Rising		2030
Latvia	Falling		
Lithuania	Falling		
Mexico	Rising		2010
Moldova	Fell 1990–95		1995
Netherlands		2025	
Norway	Rising		
Poland	Rising		
Portugal		2020	
Romania	Falling		
Russia	Falling		2030
Slovak Republic	Rising		2030
Slovenia	Falling		2030
South Africa	Rising		2020
Spain		2010	
Sweden		2035	
Switzerland		2015	
Thailand	Rising		1995
Turkey	Rising		2010
Ukraine	Falling		2030
United Kingdom		2035	
United States	Rising		1995

Note: A net reproduction rate (NRR) of 1.0 is the rough equivalent of a total fertility rate of 2.1. The figures are somewhat suspect and mainly indicate that these countries will begin their population decline before 2035.

Sources: World Bank (1997).

A Hypothesis about Timing

My hypothesis, then, is that we are living in an interval when the relatively rich countries are somewhere between a decline below 2.1 fertility and an actual fall in population and that the turn toward taking the population problem seriously will come when population begins to fall in major countries of the Western world plus Japan—say, around 2005–15. Fairly soon afterward, this turn in the path of the rich countries will probably affect the policies and the social attitudes of the transitional countries. After all, most of them have a chance to stop the decline of the fertility rate at 2.1 if they so choose, and that is an easier task than climbing back to 2.1.

The transition envisaged in this article transcends the technical demographic vocabulary in which the argument has thus far been couched. It runs inevitably into two of the most deeply rooted human impulses.

One has existed at least as long as human beings have lived in organized societies. Keynes once put it well: "We cannot as responsible men do better than base our policy on the evidence we have and adapt it to the five or ten years over which we may suppose ourselves to have some measure of pre-vision . . ." (Keynes 1920: 204). Human beings are extremely conservative and usually base their current decisions "on the evidence we have." The evidence we have is that the global population is still rising. Demography permits us to calculate when a fertility rate below 2.1 will translate into a fall in population itself, given additional information that is generally ascertainable. But in fact, an actual fall in population is only to be observed in the former Soviet bloc, where, perhaps, temporary transitional problems obtain. Most of the world's citizens can go about their business operating on familiar assumptions. They do not study fertility statistics, and the shadows these statistics may cast seem unreal or unlikely or, as psychiatrists say, are denied.

This tendency is reinforced because since the late 18th century the prevailing assumption in the Atlantic world has been that population increase is normal. As the rest of the world moved gradually from the assumption of variations around a static norm to an environment of progress, this assumption has spread, aided by the growing span of the media. Meanwhile, population stagnation got a bum rap.

I suppose the bad repute of stagnation versus progress takes its start from this passage from Adam Smith:

> It is in the progressive state, while the society is advancing to the further acquisition, rather than when it has acquired its full complement of riches, that the condition of the labouring poor, of the great body of the people, seems to be the happiest and the most comfortable. It is hard in the stationary, and miserable in the declining state. The progressive state is in reality the cheerful and the

hearty state to all the different orders of the society. The stationary
is dull; the declining melancholy. (Smith 1776, ch. 8: 69, 81)

The macroeconomics of a stagnant population were briefly set out
in 1937 by J. M. Keynes. By rough calculation, he estimated that for
Britain, "a stationary population with the same improvement in the
standard of life with the same lengthening of the period of production
would have required an increase in the stock of capital of only a little
more than half the increase that actually occurred" (Keynes 1937: 18).
This population-related investment included housing, furnishings, and
automobiles and other consumer durables. This figure was accepted as
the gap that had to be filled in the discussion on the implications of a
static population that was triggered by the rise in unemployment during the Great Depression of the 1930s in the United States.

It should be noted that the scenario considered in this paper was first
outlined by John Stuart Mill. He was, of course, a lifelong advocate of
birth control and of a constant population. But he was also a strong
supporter of public investment in research and development and envisaged a continued rise in productivity and real wages under a regime of
population stagnation.

The Noneconomic Forces

The transition to a constant population would indeed have profound
social, psychological, cultural, and military, as well as economic, significance, but depending on the spirit in which the possibilities and
challenges are pursued, the outcome could be salutary.

One specific consequence would be the required adjustment between
the sexes. The scenario I have set out would require that the fertility
rate in advanced societies be raised to 2.1 and held there. In other societies the decline in fertility should be arrested at 2.1, perhaps after a
further decline in population. The progress of women in the work force—
and, particularly, progress toward professional and executive status—
has been uneven, taking the world as a whole, but it has been virtually
universal in direction. It is most unlikely that women would be willing
to surrender without recompense their hard-won gains and move back
to what they judge to be an inferior social status. And indeed, this scenario demands a true national effort if it is to come to pass. The changes
in attitudes and assumptions that are implied in this analysis will require a concerted effort in each nation and in the world community
that transcends conventional politics.

At this stage one can only conclude that:

• Modern society offers many opportunities to expand investment
in highly productive ways and to maintain full employment under a

regime of stagnant population and rising real wages. The legitimacy of public investment would, however, have to be accepted, and steps would have to be taken to ensure that it would not descend into low-productivity pork-barrel expenditures.

• The success of such a transformation of modern sophisticated societies would not simply consist of a correct series of political-economy measures. A vision would have to be developed that the world of stagnant populations opens many opportunities for creative work. There is no reason to accept passively Adam Smith's reflections before the Industrial Revolution or Keynesian worries about the drying up of investment opportunities in the 1930s.

This transition to a new vision would take place first in the present rich advanced industrial countries that have already fallen below 2.1 fertility. They will soon confront the reality that they will have to buy time with imagination and create a social setting in which their societies raise their fertility to 2.1. In the meanwhile other societies will be coming forward into technological maturity and demanding an enlarged place in the world. It would not be difficult to envisage not a human reconciliation to the attractive world of stagnating populations but a world of ugly struggle between those who came to affluence first and those who came behind them.

But this is an unrealistic dream. After all, the 20th century was largely taken up with the consequences of such dreams by the rulers of Germany (twice), Japan, and Russia. If we count the rather miserable interwar years, as we should, some three quarters of the past century was overshadowed by two world wars and a cold war. The 20th century was hard on those who thought that they could succeed to the hegemony of the colonial powers. The 21st century will prove worse. First, nuclear military power has proved rationally usable only to deter others from using nuclear military power. Second, the link between conventional industrial power and military power has been further diluted by the revolution in the accuracy of delivering conventional weapons exhibited in the Gulf War and especially in the conflict over Kosovo.

The prospects are that those who are coming along behind the present affluent powers could flourish in a world at peace. And they will not be far behind, as China now shows with its considerable industrial prowess but a fertility rate below 2.1. It is not to be ruled out that an enlarging role in a world at peace is the best Chinese option, and the best Russian option, as it now has become for the Germans and Japanese. But that will depend not only on the arms commanded by the Atlantic and European powers but also on their continued vitality and their positive vision of the future.

The vision here differs from the one I set forth in the original *Pioneers* volume and, indeed, from the vision implicit in most of the work on development in the 1950s and 1960s. Then, we were fastened on the task of moving the developing world into sustained growth. We put off to the distant future describing the kind of world that would emerge when the bulk of countries then in the stage of preconditions for take-off or in the early phases of sustained growth achieved sustained growth. I would guess that what underlay our thought was that growth would level off in some distant time either because of diminishing returns to natural resources (including air and water) or because of diminishing marginal utility for income itself. In fact, the prospect we now confront is that the same industrial and technological forces that permitted world population to grow from (say) 760 million to over 6 billion, and that allowed real income per capita to rise by an even larger percentage, have decreed a fall in population that will begin in the advanced industrial world and will quickly spread to most of the developing countries. We will have to make a conscious effort to achieve a fertility rate consistent with a stagnant population if we are to check the forces under way or in prospect. It can be done with sufficient common effort. And if we keep research and development and innovation moving forward, we should be able to enjoy a continued rise in living standards with a constant population. But we will have to earn it, as we have earned sustained growth thus far.

Note

1. The main argument of this passage is derived from Bean, Cushing, and Hayes (1997), which contains an exceedingly useful bibliography. See also the somewhat out of date but classic study by Kotlikoff and Smith (1983). Of continued relevance is the authors' discussion of disincentives to working beyond the age of retirement (and incentives for early retirement) in existing pension schemes in the American private sector (16–18).

References

Bean, Frank D., Robert G. Cushing, and Charles W. Hayes. 1997. "The Changing Demography of U.S. Immigration Flows: Patterns, Projections, and Contexts." In Klaus J. Bade and Myron Weiner, eds., *Migration Past, Migration Future: Germany and the United States,* 120–52. Oxford, U.K.: Berghahn Books.

Keynes, J. M. 1920. *The Economic Consequences of the Peace.* New York: Harcourt, Brace & Howe.

———. 1937. "Some Economic Consequences of a Declining Population." *Eugenics Review* 29(1), 13–17.

Kotlikoff, Laurence J., and Daniel E. Smith. 1983. *Pensions in the American Economy.* Chicago, Ill.: University of Chicago Press for the National Bureau of Economic Research.

McRae, Hamish. 1994. *The World in 2020: Power, Culture and Prosperity: A Vision of the Future.* London: HarperCollins.

Rostow, W. W. 1998. *The Great Population Spike and After.* New York: Oxford University Press.

Smith, Adam. 1776. *An Inquiry into the Nature and Causes of the Wealth of Nations,* ch. 8 ("Of the Wages of Labour").

World Bank. 1989. *World Development Report 1989.* New York: Oxford University Press.

World Bank. 1997. "World Bank Population Projections." *World Development Indicators 1997 on CD-ROM.* Washington, D.C.

World Bank. 1999. *World Development Report 1998/99: Knowledge for Development.* New York: Oxford University Press.

Yue, Piyu. 1999. "A Brief on Dynamics of the Population System and the Future of Japan's Population." Unpublished note. IC^2 Institute, Austin, Tex.

The View from the Trenches:
Development Processes and Policies
as Seen by a Working Professional

Arnold C. Harberger

THIS ESSAY RECORDS A SERIES OF impressions and reflections that arose as I witnessed and participated in the proceedings of the Dubrovnik conference. Obviously, one cannot distill into a few sentences or paragraphs the full richness and variety of the many ideas and interpretations spread before us during those two days of meetings by a cast that consisted of many of the leading figures in the development economics field. So I will not even attempt such a task. Rather, I will concentrate on a certain sense of uneasiness that I was left with as the conference closed. As I put it in a comment during the proceedings, it was as if a very important guest—the working professional—had not been invited to the party.

Now, ask me to characterize this working professional, and I am hard put to produce a simple, straightforward answer.[1] I have to recognize that he or she exists in my mind as an embodiment of a whole set of traits that may never be seen simultaneously in any single individual. I will go on to elaborate on the traits themselves, but just to put readers in the right mood, let me make a short list of people who seem to me to fit pretty well into the suit of clothes I am about to describe: central bankers Alan Greenspan and Mervyn King; U.S. policy experts Michael Boskin and Lawrence Summers; agricultural economists D. Gale Johnson and T. W. Schultz; trade economists Jagdish Bhagwati and Anne O. Krueger; longtime International Monetary Fund (IMF) professionals Manuel Guitian and Vito Tanzi; key Latin American policymakers Pedro Aspe, Hernán Büchi, Domingo Cavallo, and Carlos Massad; and Indian policymakers Raja Chelliah and Manmohan Singh. I could add many more, but these should suffice to give readers something of the flavor of my "working professional."

One thing that these people certainly have in common is that they are anything but naive. They fully appreciate the infinite complexity of the real world and know in their hearts that it is beyond human comprehension. Out of this appreciation arises the imperative of oversimplification. Only through oversimplification do we reach understanding. Hence, to have an idea of theirs attacked because it is alleged to be an oversimplification would hardly bother these people—indeed, they would view such an attack as reflecting more the naïveté of the critic than the vulnerability of the idea. They would, however, take very seriously criticisms that questioned the relevance or usefulness of their oversimplifications.

Respect for Market Forces

Without a doubt, the greatest, most profound, and most useful simplification of economics is the vision of supply and demand interacting in a market. Without this vision, we would be nowhere. Now, are these markets characterized by perfect knowledge, perfect foresight, and perfect competition, with all their nuances? Of course not. And it is naive to think that any important real-world application really rests on such restrictive assumptions. The right way to look at it is to view players as entering the market with the knowledge they have; their supply prices and demand prices are based on this knowledge, and in this context their gains from market transactions are perfectly genuine and real. (Put another way, at the time of any transaction, an omniscient deity could extract the full surplus perceived by both suppliers and demanders, leaving them all feeling just as well off with the transaction as without it.)

It is the same with foresight. Today, supplies and demands (for example, of capital goods and securities) are based on the various agents' perception of what is likely, and their surpluses could in principle be extracted at the moment of any transaction, leaving them just as well off as before. Future events may change this because either (a) the agent's initial vision was faulty (he was not as well off as he thought he was) or (b) new shocks entered to modify a previously correct vision. It is even hard for us poor mortals to tell the difference between (a) and (b), especially when we are dealing with unknown probability distributions in both cases. What we can say for certain is that disturbances of type (b), especially in the form of innovations and real cost reductions of various kinds, are essential ingredients of the growth process.

The same is true of the textbook assumptions of perfect competition. We may need these assumptions to carry out precise analytical proofs, but the big messages that follow from those proofs stay substantially true even when we draw our supply and demand curves with the side of the chalk rather than with its point. It is well to remember that a monopoly markup is, in theory, just like an excise tax (or any other tax) in introducing a wedge between demand price and marginal resource cost. Yet it would be a rare country in which total monopoly and monopsony profits added up to as much as a quarter or a third of total tax revenues. The existence of tax and monopoly distortions does not seriously impede the use of supply and demand in predicting the effects of changes in demand due to income shifts, of changes in supply due to innovations or world price changes, or of changes in market equilibrium as new distortions are introduced or old ones change.

The Limited Scope of Government Action

I don't think any of the people on my list would quarrel with the statement that "equilibria are often not Pareto efficient" (Hoff and Stiglitz, in this volume, p. 414). Indeed, it is likely they would prefer it to be stronger, something like "real world equilibria are never—or hardly ever—efficient in a textbook sense." Why? Because, among other important reasons, government policy is never even close to optimal. Every government in the world inherits from its predecessors a patchwork quilt of policies containing a great many undesirable distortions and often even downright contradictions (one policy undoes the desired effects of another). The task of the government is to improve things. But there is never the option of tearing up the quilt and starting anew. The typical government—certainly the typical democratic government—must proceed by adding its own patches to the quilt. What it is able to do in any given term of office will depend on what political "windows of opportunity" happen to open up during that period. History tells us that major crises open multiple windows of opportunity and that in placid times governments rarely get the chance to institute major reforms; if they do, the reforms are likely to be in selected areas that fate and history conspire to bring under the spotlight of public attention while the particular government holds the reins of power.

What is needed in this setting is solid cost-benefit analysis. This is what will tell policymakers whether adding a particular patch to a given policy quilt will move welfare up or down. The mere mention of this point should remind all of us that in the end, all policy economics represents cost-benefit analysis in some form or other. But we are here distinguishing between the rather ivory-tower, utopian pursuit of the "conditions for an optimum" and the down-to-earth, pragmatic questions of whether a given policy change moves us up or down, or which of two or three plausible alternatives will move us up the most. To answer these latter kinds of question, we must turn to what I call the "economics of the nth best." This really translates into the application of the basic tools of applied welfare economics in a setting with a considerable number of distortions, all but one or two or three of which have to be taken as given as one analyzes today's (or this year's) policy moves.

The analytical machinery exists for doing this type of cost-benefit analysis; indeed, the best "how-to-do-it" courses in economic project evaluation have shown that we can train significant numbers of technicians so that they are able to apply it with a modicum of perceptiveness and subtlety. But what I, and I think a great many "working professionals," would lament is the extent to which hours and days can go by in meetings dealing with policies for promoting economic development without this type of cost-benefit analysis being given a serious place in the discussion, let alone the spot at center stage that we think it deserves.

A Focus on Basic Needs and Opportunities for the Poor Rather Than on Income Distribution Per Se

The limits on what any given government can do are particularly restrictive when it comes to policies focusing on income distribution. I believe that most working professionals sooner or later come to realize that the income distribution is very much an endogenous variable of the overall economy and that most of the factors which determine it are pretty much beyond the range of serious policy influence. It is the market that determines the relative rewards given to the various skills and occupations that make up a nation's labor force. When skills are scarce, the premium on them is high; when menial labor is in short supply, relative to its demand, workers, housemaids, and gardeners end up being "pretty well treated" by the economy.

Education policy is the surest way for a government to set a nation on a path to a more equal distribution. But although the benefits to each individual are unquestionably present at every stage of an educational process, the impact of a changed education policy on the distribution of income comes only slowly, over decades rather than years. Moreover, the internal machinery of the economy can work—as it has over the past 20 years or so—to offset the effects of many decades of educational effort on, say, a country's Gini coefficient.

The true answer here is for societies to get their priorities right, in recognition of the true constraints that face them. Education has been and always will be a principal line of escape for the children of the poor. It is also, very typically in developing countries, a productive economic investment in its own right. The best reasons for opening up educational opportunities for the children of the poor are quite independent of whether the Gini coefficient will go up or down as a result. So let us use the good reasons, not the dubious ones, in motivating and justifying sound education policies.

The same goes for other types of so-called "redistributive" measures. Public finance people are quite aware of how hard it is to produce, in the real world, a tax system that is more than modestly progressive. Most economists are aware that too much zeal in this direction can be counterproductive, entailing enormous efficiency costs for each marginal dollar of revenue. The bottom line from these two observations is that not much redistribution has come, or is likely to come, or even should come, from the tax side of the public finance ledger.

That brings us to the expenditure side. Here, the data reveal somewhat more redistributive potential, but not a great deal more. The trouble seems to be that the benefits obtained by the poor stem from some element of altruism (or sense of fairness) on the part of the nonpoor. We see this in many parts of the world and should not hesitate to applaud. But, typically, our society's altruism is less than 100 percent pure. The nonpoor will vote funds for free public education for the poor provided that most of the nonpoor get it too. The same goes for better access to medical care, for potable water supply and sewerage, etc., etc. In the end, the bottom quintile surely benefits from these and other government-provided or government-assisted services, but they probably do not get much more than their proportionate share of the benefits.

I like to think in terms of what I call a realistic benchmark for the government's impact on the income distribution. This consists of the government's taking from households in proportion to their income and providing services to households in proportion to the number of household members. This benchmark has no moral connotations, but it is helpful to realize that very few countries, and certainly hardly any developing countries, have in fact been able to do as much redistribution as this benchmark implies.

Pursuing these avenues quickly leads one to a recognition that our societies and polities would be better served by focusing on meeting the basic needs of the poor and expanding the opportunities available to them than by constantly sounding the harsh and divisive Klaxon of "redistribution." But is there any hope? My jaded observation is that whenever the income distribution turns toward greater equality, the governing party claims credit for it, and whenever it turns toward greater inequality, the opposition puts the blame on the government. Are we, the economics profession, capable of leading our societies away from this type of fruitless populism? I am not sure, but certainly we will not get far until we instill in ourselves the discipline that comes from recognizing the severe limits that constrain governments' capacity to influence income distribution.

The Importance of "Sources of Growth" Analysis

The idea of breaking down a country's growth rate into a series of components attributable to increased labor input, increased capital input, and a residual incorporating other influences has to be recognized as one of the 20th century's great advances in economic thinking. At the time of its inception, it helped to play down the role of physical capital and play up the role of "technical advance" as elements in the growth process. Very soon thereafter, the role of human capital was given new attention. Still later, the multifaceted nature of the residual term came to the fore. My own predilection is to explicitly label this term "real cost reductions." This label does not change anything, but it helps remind us that this term does not just represent new inventions or economies of scale or externalities and spillovers but, rather, includes all these things plus improved personnel management, better office procedures, modernized inventory control, maybe even successful advertising campaigns, and many other paths to greater profits through greater efficiency.

This "disaggregated" view of the growth process does not fit very well into a framework structured around the concept of the aggregate production function. Rather, its natural point of focus is the firm, where every element of the growth process must ultimately be reflected. This is true at least of the growth of gross domestic product (GDP), which is what has traditionally been measured, since the GDP of a nation (or province) is nothing but the sum total of the GDP contributions of the entities located there. Focusing on the firm and even on breakdowns of growth by two-, three-, and four-digit industries provides a quite different appreciation of the nature of the growth process than one gets by thinking in terms of an aggregate production function. The more disaggregated one's focus, the more Schumpeterian becomes one's vision of the growth process. This is because the great underappreciated *fact* of disaggregated growth analysis is the pervasiveness of real cost increases side by side with real cost reductions. In just about every disaggregated data set that one turns to, there are losers as well as winners—and not just a few losers, but lots of them, often accounting for as much as a third or even half of initial value added.

Some may gravitate toward attributing this fact to mere randomness, but I feel that is like running away from the challenge posed by the phenomenon of widespread declines (side by side with increases) in total factor productivity. I believe, as Schumpeter did, that there is something about it that is not only systematic but also of the essence of the growth process. On top of whatever simple randomness there is, we have the phenomenon of winners beating out losers, all over the economic landscape. The winners are those who find ways of producing the same products for less, or better products for the same money, or totally new products that attract consumer demand. The losers are those who suffer in this process, typically being driven back to production points at which their average costs (the raw material that total factor productivity analysis works with) are higher.

Policies That Promote (or Enable) Real Cost Reductions

Many different studies of the breakdown of growth into its components have come to the conclusion that high-growth situations tend to be characterized (among other things) by high rates of real cost reduction. These real cost reductions occur, in one sense or another, inside business entities. So where does policy come into play? In some cases, such as improving a highway network, it may directly "produce" reductions in real (in this case, transport) costs. In others, such as promoting research and development activities, it may involve operations that can actually "deliver" real cost reductions within the firm. But the overwhelming bulk of relevant policies work in neither of these ways. Instead, they play an "enabling" role, making it easier for firms to encounter new ways of reducing real costs.

First and foremost among growth-enabling policies is the *control of serious inflation.* Much evidence shows that inflation inhibits economic growth. The reasons lie in the many uncertainties that accompany inflation. At least three deserve special mention:

• The blurring of relative prices that invariably accompanies high inflation makes it hard for firms to perceive opportunities for real cost reduction.

• Some of the investable funds that are generated in inflationary economies tend to be diverted to safer havens such as foreign currency or foreign bank and securities accounts.

• The higher the rate of inflation, the greater the fraction of real resources dedicated to finding ways of turning the inflation process to private advantage, even though there is no overall gain to society.

Surmounting inflation, almost by definition, entails pursuing *more sensible fiscal and other macroeconomic policies.* Still, it is worthwhile listing such policies as a separate point. A macroeconomic framework that is economically sound and that is expected to continue to be so in the future opens the door to investments and cost-reducing activities that would otherwise be shunned.

Linked to sound macro policies, but not quite the same thing, is the *reduction of economic distortions,* especially those put in place by the government itself. Taxes, tariffs, quotas, price controls, open and hidden subsidies—these are some of the more important such distortions. Closely related are the distortions imposed by arbitrary regulations, restrictions, licensing procedures, and the like. Some distortions are the inevitable accompaniment of government, but in most real-world cases there is wide scope for reducing their cost to the economy. The idea is to move from an economic system that has lots of "prices that lie" toward one in which there are fewer such prices, and in which the lies they tell are more like fibs and less like gross prevarications. This is important because the greater the degree of distortion in the economy, the more cases there will be of actions that reduce real costs for the economic agents directly involved but actually increase real costs from the standpoint of the economy as a whole. Ill-advised regulations not only work to keep real costs higher than they need to be; they also reduce the rate of growth by slowing the speed at which opportunities for real cost reduction are implemented.

Policies That Promote a More Open Economy

No doubt, policies that promote freer trade in particular and a more open economy in general can be regarded simply as a category under the general heading of policies that reduce economic distortions. But that would tend to underplay the critical role that openness appears to have had in just about every development success story of recent decades. One can argue about the nuances, but not only did both exports and imports grow dramatically in the great growth episodes of Japan, Taiwan (China), the Republic of Korea, Spain, Portugal, Greece, Brazil, Chile and Argentina; they grew even in relation to the very notable growth of GDP.

Openness seems to do much more than just eliminate triangles of excess burden stemming from tariffs, quotas, and similar distortions. It appears that it unleashes, or at least has the potential to unleash, a new dynamism in previously stagnant or sluggish economies. I know it is difficult for many of us economists to accept that economic agents are not always working equally hard to reduce real costs, but the evidence strongly suggests that businesses with a market whose security for the firm is more or less guaranteed (by high protection in one form or other) are more likely to take the comfortable route of sticking with routines that proved successful in the past. Once such businesses are exposed to the rigors of world market competition, they either adapt by reducing real costs or (usually gradually, by a sequence of painful steps) fade out of the picture. Living with market competition for a period of time also tends to change the outlook of business firms, from a more or less static vision of finding a "cash cow" and milking it steadily over a long period to a more dynamic approach of making it part of their regular business routine to constantly look for newer and better products, processes, and methods. In these ways, a turn toward greater openness has an effect not only on a country's GDP (the comparative static effect of trade liberalization) but also on its rate of growth (the dynamic effect).

The "Washington Consensus"

In many discussions, including some at the Dubrovnik conference, the "Washington consensus" has been characterized as a cookie-cutter approach to development policy, derived from a blind application of neoclassical economics to the problems of the developing world. Well, it may be that it is not just beauty that rests in the eye of the beholder. Many economists, including Harberger's working professionals, would see the Washington consensus as a pragmatic distillation derived from some four decades of postwar experience in a host of developing countries.

Who, in particular, can take serious issue with John Williamson's crisp summary of the consensus: "macroeconomic stability, domestic liberalization, and international openness"? As I see it, the Washington consensus, in seeking these ends, has been quite tolerant of moderate fiscal deficits, moderate rates of inflation, moderate ranges of import tariffs, and moderate tax rates generally. The consensus has been antineoclassical in paying little attention to Ramsey rules and other pillars of the modern neoclassical tax literature. Nor has any consensus emerged on the alternatives to Ramsey: uniform, across-the-board ad valorem tariffs and value added taxes at a uniform rate on a broad base. Yet I have not the slightest doubt that, asked to choose between Ramsey tariffs and uniform tariffs, or between a Ramsey-style differentiated value added tax and a broadly based, uniform one, my practicing professionals and Williamson's consensus members would vote overwhelmingly in favor of the uniform-rate alternatives. In doing so they would be expressing not the implications of neoclassical theory but rather what they think of as practical wisdom derived from long experience. In supporting uniform tariffs, they would probably emphasize the guarantee these tariffs provide of equal effective protection to all existing and potential import-competing industries. They would surely also stress how hard it is for *any* single firm or industry to plead for especially favorable treatment for itself when *every* import-substituting activity is equally protected by a general and uniform tariff. This is a political-economy argument for uniformity, not a neoclassical one. Similarly, uniform value added taxation would be seen by these people as a safeguard against pressures for special treatment by all sorts of special interests. At the same time they would see in a uniform rate and broad base a tremendous boon to the equitable and efficient administration of a value added tax. This is because a predictable consequence of differentiated rates is that much evasion will take the form of mislabeling important chunks of value added—that is, putting them in low-rate categories rather than in the high-rate ones where they belong.

These are simply a few examples of how the Washington consensus is something quite different from a faithful reflection of modern neoclassical economics in the medium of economic policy.

Some Examples of "Excess of Zeal"

It should be clear that I am myself a strong supporter of the Washington consensus and feel that many real-world success stories (Argentina, Chile, Hong Kong, Peru, and Taiwan, among others) have emerged from policy packages that fit quite well into its framework. Moreover, I believe that the separate propositions of the consensus have a strong foundation in experience which would stand up well under a rigorous analysis of their costs and benefits.

Yet as an ardent broker for the "cost-benefit approach to economic development," I feel it incumbent on me to recognize cases in which this approach has been cast aside in favor of one or another imagined panacea. The three cases I will treat are privatization, capital and exchange controls, and currency boards and dollarization.

Privatization came to the fore as a policy alternative once economists and others began to see with their own eyes the many trammels under which public sector enterprises typically have to operate. These enterprises are often very severely restricted as to what they can pay their executives; their lower-ranked workers are often paid total compensation (in cash or in benefits) well above the prevailing market wage for comparable work; it is often next to impossible for them to shut down unprofitable lines of activity; modernization is frequently resisted when it would "make too many waves"; and the pursuit of real cost reduction is rarely encouraged. For all these reasons, it would be wise if most of what we have tended to call state-owned enterprises ended up being transferred to the private sector.

But this does not mean transferred "right now, no matter to whom, no matter under what conditions." My position on privatization is very clear. I believe that the government should do the same kind of careful study, the same sort of survey of potential buyers, the same sort of "preparation of the product for sale" as General Electric or General Motors would do if it decided to sell off a division or two. I do not want to be perfectionist here, but one must make serious efforts to avoid the taint of nepotism (à la Somoza, Marcos, Suharto, and so on) or of other corrupt practices such as sales to favored supporters at bargain prices. One must be careful in the case of public utilities that the regulatory framework under which they will operate, once privatized, is based on sound economic principles and is known in advance by all relevant bidders. (One must not make the mistakes that prevailed in the telephone industry in several Latin American countries in which what was sold was in large measure the right to exploit the public via monopoly pricing for a significant period of time.) One must avoid hasty and imprudent contracting, as happened when Mexico authorized the construction of thousands of kilometers of privatized roads. (The contracts were awarded on the basis of the shortest promised payback period. The winners then charged the exorbitant tolls implicit in the abbreviated payback period. At those tolls, traffic was minimal, far below what the government had "guaranteed" when the contracts were let, so the government ended up buying back the roads from their private owners.)

In the eyes of this jaded observer, much of the recent wave of privatization happened for the wrong reason. It was not that most developing-country governments were following the dictates of sound economics; instead, I believe, many of them were simply mesmerized by the thought of getting their hands on "all that money," thus permitting them to "patch over" endemic budget deficits for their own term of office, leaving to successor governments the double problem of finding a real and lasting solution to the deficit problem and coping with the heritage of hasty, poorly prepared privatizations.

Capital and exchange controls have been much in the economic news of late, with the debate often being between purists who are satisfied with nothing less than the complete absence of controls and apologists who defend capital and exchange controls without really explaining what it is they are defending. There seems to be little appeal to evidence from experience on either side of this debate. One point to be made at the outset is that in probably more than half of the "growth miracle" episodes of recent decades, some form of capital or exchange control was in place. Whatever the effect of the controls, it was not so strongly negative as to prevent the "miracles" from happening.

On the other side, the defenders of controls sometimes seem to be defending the idea of controls rather than the instruments involved and the ways in which they might sometimes be fruitfully employed and other times might be quite noxious. Let me try here to sketch how one might proceed. First, let me confess that, on the basis of what I perceive to be the evidence, I am quite close to being a purist on the issue of "compulsory surrender" of export proceeds. This and similar trade-related controls lead rather quickly to black markets in foreign currency and to wholesale evasion based on the underinvoicing of exports together with the overinvoicing of imports. One need but think about it for a few minutes. It is easy for exporters to underinvoice by 10 or 15 percent and for importers to arrange for overinvoicing by a similar magnitude. This permits a hemorrhage of capital from the country, equal to 20 or 30 percent of $[(M + X)/2]$, which could amount to 4 to 6 percent of total production in a country where imports and exports averaged, say, a fifth of GDP. If a country with such controls tried hard to enforce them, it would require a huge diversion of many knowledgeable people from productive activity, turning them into "economic detectives and policemen" when they ought to be out there contributing to the country's productive efforts.

That said, let me add that the developing country I know best (Chile) had some sort of capital controls on the books during both of its major growth episodes of recent decades, 1975–81 and 1985–98. Two mechanisms merit mention. The first was the 1985 decision by Chile's Central Bank to auction off, every few weeks or so, specified amounts of foreign exchange, to be used by private parties to buy up the discounted debt of Chilean private banks in the New York "secondary market." This debt was then repatriated to Chile, with the foreign currency debt being typically replaced by domestic currency instruments. The "profit"—the difference between the discounted New York price and par value—was then split somehow between the Chilean debtor banks and the private impresarios who undertook the "arbitrage" operation. When these operations first began, around 1985, the Central Bank feared that there would be an utter flood of demand for foreign exchange to be used for this purpose, putting in peril the government's objective of trying to keep the real exchange rate (RER) within a specified band. The auctioning of licenses for this purpose (a) prevented the flood of demand, (b) enabled the Central Bank to create its desired amount of demand for foreign exchange at every periodic auction, a capacity that it used artfully over a period of some five years to keep the real exchange rate within the target band, and (c) allowed the Central Bank to make a lot of money from the proceeds of its biweekly auctions.

Whereas the first mechanism, just described, can be classified as a genuine success, the second has clear minuses as well as pluses. Interestingly, this second mechanism was a direct outgrowth of the first. As time passed, the amount of discounted debt available for repatriation kept declining, while the discount at which it sold grew ever smaller. As a consequence, the debt repatriation instrument had practically no leverage left by 1990. Nonetheless, the authorities still wanted to maintain the real exchange rate within a band. They reasoned that if the debt repatriation instrument had functioned well by reducing the external liabilities of private banks while increasing their internal debt, could not one obtain similar results by building up the external assets, in this case of the Central Bank, while increasing the bank's internal debt? Thus, the Central Bank began to create its own desired extra demand for foreign exchange, using funds obtained by the issuance of internal (indexed) debt. Many will recognize in this description the familiar face of "sterilized intervention." It was a pillar of Chilean Central Bank policy from about 1990 until very recently.

This new policy had two drawbacks: first, the reflux back to Chile of some of the foreign exchange the Central Bank was placing abroad, and second, losses incurred because the Central Bank had to pay higher interest rates on the funds it borrowed at home than it received when those same funds (converted to dollars) were placed abroad.

The reflux of funds can be described as follows. First, consider an autonomous capital flow of, say, US$3 billion into Chile. This flow has the effect, not welcomed by the Central Bank, of depressing the real price of the dollar. The Central Bank therefore enters the market with a demand for US$2 billion dollars, to be placed abroad as part of its international reserves. To get the funds for this purchase in a noninflationary way, it issues an equivalent amount of local debt. But this extra supply of Central Bank debt causes market interest rates (both nominal and real) in Chile to rise. Now the world capital market, attracted by the increased rates, sends an "induced" capital flow of, say, an additional US$1 billion to Chile. So, while the Central Bank carried out an operation in the amount of US$2 billion, its effective influence on the net resource transfer into Chile would be only US$1 billion.

This problem had appeared to a degree in the debt repatriation period, but recall that in this case no Central Bank debts (or Central Bank losses) were involved. Moreover, the intensity of the reflux problem grows with the degree of integration of a country into the world capital market. The greater the degree of integration, the larger will be the fraction of each US$1 billion sent abroad that comes back as what I have called a reflux. This fraction may have been as low as 5 or 10 percent when the debt repatriation policy started in 1985, but by the 1990s it was probably in the range of 30 to 50 percent.

To combat this reflux problem, Chile introduced its well-known "tax" on inflows of portfolio funds. This "tax" consisted of a requirement that 30 percent of incoming funds be placed as a non-interest-bearing deposit in the Central Bank for a period of a year. The cost to the investor was the loss of a year's interest in these funds, and the Central Bank made things easy by permitting investors simply to pay 3 percent of the incoming funds up front, as if compensating an intermediary to make the 30 percent deposit for investors. The effect of this was to allow one-year interest rates to be 3 percent higher in Chile than in the world marketplace, without this differential attracting any "reflux" funds. Reflux would now begin only when the interest differential exceeded 3 percent.

The "tax" on inflows of portfolio capital clearly helped reduce the extent of reflux, but it practically guaranteed that Chilean interest rates would be substantially above world market rates, at least so long as portfolio capital was still flowing into Chile. This created a virtual assurance that the Central Bank itself would incur significant losses as it borrowed funds in the domestic market to be placed abroad. Moreover, such losses were generated not on *this year's increment* to domestic debt and international reserves; but on the *whole outstanding stock* of reserves that had been generated in this way. The resulting problem of Central Bank losses became more and more severe as the international reserves of the Central Bank grew from about US$6 billion in 1990 to over US$18 billion in 1997, largely via sterilized intervention operations.

The growth of reserves, and the consequent Central Bank losses, would have been much larger had the Chilean authorities not modified their real exchange rate target band. This action permitted a steady real appreciation of the peso between 1990 and late 1997, when a modest market-induced real devaluation set in, in the wake of the Asian crisis. Subsequently, Chile first lowered and then abandoned its "tax" on capital inflows, and about US$3 billion of the Central Bank's international reserves was sold as Chile responded to the crisis.

I tell this perhaps overlong story to let readers see, from the inside as it were, how serious problems can arise even from a rather mild but quite intelligent set of controls put in place for the "sensible" objectives of using the real exchange rate as a positive signal for producers of tradable goods and perhaps smoothing what might be transitory currency appreciations due to unusual spates of capital inflow. I do not believe that the evidence says that Chile's policy, centered on the use of sterilized intervention to influence the real exchange rate, was a mistake. But certainly one must admit that whatever was gained on the real exchange rate front was bought at a significant price.

Currency boards and dollarization have been the subject of a new wave of enthusiasm in the past few years, with protagonists often claiming almost miraculous powers for these particular nostrums. I believe that both theory and real-world observation feed into a simple distillation of "what we know" about exchange rate regimes. I believe that the correct starting point is the notion of the real exchange rate—the real price, in local currency, of a real unit (measured as its buying power over tradable goods) of foreign currency. Under a flexible exchange rate system, it is possible for a country's domestic price level to remain constant while the nominal exchange rate, E, fluctuates to reflect movements in the equilibrium real exchange rate. Under fixed-rate systems, RER equilibrium is brought about through movements in the domestic price level P_d relative to the world price level of tradables, P^*.

We have had lots of experience with situations calling for an appreciation of the equilibrium real exchange rate—that is, for a fall in $RER = EP^*/P_d$. Typically, when E is fixed, these situations call for the domestic price level, P_d, to rise. This tends to happen with relative ease. Whether caused by a capital inflow or by a boom in the world price of a major export, there is typically a flood of "dollars" on the market, as a consequence of which real spending goes up, pushing up the prices of nontradables. Some people mistakenly think that this type of adjustment should be resisted because it is "inflationary," but in fact it is simply an adjustment by which the real exchange rate is moved to its new equilibrium level.

Unfortunately, the adjustment is not equally easy when a downward movement of the domestic price level is called for. Chile had a fixed exchange rate when the debt crisis of the 1980s struck. Within one year (June 1981 to June 1982), its rate of unemployment rose from less than 10 percent to over 25 percent, and it was years before unemployment was brought back to "normal" levels. Something similar happened in Argentina in the wake of the Mexican crisis of 1994–95. Unemployment rose from around 6 percent to as high as 18 percent before drifting down to 13 percent at the time of the Asian crisis. The crisis gave rise to new pressure on the real exchange rate, causing unemployment to rise again to 15–16 percent.

In both the Chilean and Argentine cases flexible wages and prices surely would have brought about a rapid and smooth path to the new equilibrium real exchange rate. Wages and prices, however, were not flexible enough in a downward direction to permit this happy outcome. Both governments made efforts to stimulate wage flexibility, but to little avail. It is, to me at least, a well-established fact of life that workers accept with relative ease reductions in real wages that come about through the impersonal mechanism of a rising nominal price of the dollar but instinctively resist similar reductions brought about by cuts in nominal wages. This difference is also perfectly understandable. When real wages fall because of a rising price of the dollar, no employees in their right mind would blame their employer. Yet if that employer comes to them and asks them to take a nominal wage cut, they have good reason to view the request with suspicion, as on its face it represents a straight transfer from them to him. Experience has shown us that in these circumstances the use of layoffs rather than wage cuts is preferred by both employers and employees. And it is this fact of life that lies at the root of the asymmetry of RER adjustment under a fixed exchange rate system.

The framers of the Bretton Woods Agreement recognized all this when they provided for a system of fixed rates most of the time, with adjustments to correct situations of "fundamental disequilibrium." I believe that the experience of the Bretton Woods period was a pretty good one. It was massive flows of funds between major financial centers rather than great human misery that brought about that system's demise.

The lesson for developing countries is, I believe, that fixed rates are fine when the equilibrium real exchange rate is stable or falling (appreciating) and may be bearable under moderate rises (depreciations) in the real price of foreign currency. But big depreciations translate into big deflations under a fixed-rate system, and these impose huge costs on the economy and the society. Argentina is in a very special position in this regard, as three "hyperinflations" in a period of less than 20 years have left their mark on the Argentine people. Most of Argentina's best economists, of all political stripes, seem to agree that even a small deviation from parity with the dollar would cause a huge flight from the peso. So here is a case of a country whose people have up to this point, and in a certain sense *willingly,* borne the costs of persistent deflationary pressures, feeling that this is the price they have to pay for stability.

Few developing countries are in Argentina's position, however. For most, the alternative of a somewhat flexible exchange rate system is a perfectly viable option. History holds many examples of flexible rates that are kept constant through central bank policy for years but that retain the legal attribute of flexibility, as well as many other examples of rates whose nominal fix is broken by intermittent devaluations as serious crises emerge. Many other systems—dirty floats, crawling pegs, exchange rate bands (both nominal and real), *tablitas* (setting the nominal rate on a predetermined, typically upward path)—can claim significant periods of successful operation, and all have the capacity to deal with situations that would call for serious deflations in a fixed exchange rate setting.

So why the great enthusiasm for currency boards and dollarization, both of which make devaluation extremely costly—indeed, impossible except by abandoning the system? I believe some of it comes from a misconception that somehow, by imposing a rigid system, one will bring about the type of behavior that is a precondition for such a system to work. Thus, huge and chronic fiscal deficits financed by the banking system are simply incompatible with fixed rates of any kind. A country cannot rationally undertake to have a currency board or to dollarize unless it has surmounted such chronic deficits. But the natural sequence is, first surmount the deficit, then fix the exchange rate in the traditional way, and finally move to a currency board or dollarization.

The same logic applies with respect to international reserves. A country with few (or zero, or negative) international reserves simply cannot contemplate fixing its exchange rate. Significant reserves (in relation to the volume and volatility of the country's trade and capital movements) are required before even the most elementary form of exchange rate fix is possible. For a currency board or for dollarization, the accumulation of reserves must be even greater.

In the end, such exchange rate systems might be good for some countries, but they are certainly no panacea for most developing countries. Both objective facts and policy adjustments can help determine for which countries such mechanisms are suitable. The objective facts concern the likelihood of volatility in the equilibrium real exchange rate in the future. A country whose exports are mainly primary commodities with volatile world prices has a naturally more volatile real exchange rate than economies like Taiwan and Korea whose tradable goods are mainly manufactures with relatively high elasticities of supply (and hence low volatility in their equilibrium relative prices). But, in addition, countries whose political systems have not yet developed strong stabilizing traditions risk RER volatility from this side. The risks of domestic riots and disturbances, of uncertain changes in government, of quick shifts from one governing ideology to another—all these bode ill for any long-term commitment to a peg with the dollar (or other numeraire).

On the side of policy, there is a poorly understood proposition that can be quite critical to the success of, say, a currency board. This concerns the nature of a country's banking system. A country with "its own" banks is much more vulnerable than a country like Panama whose banking system consists mainly of foreign banks. A country's "own" banking system suffers from the link between the asset and liability sides of the banking system's balance sheet. If people significantly reduce their deposits, the banks are constrained to cut private sector credit, which in turn has strong depressive effects on GDP. This sequence has been present in just about every major banking crisis of recent times. It can be avoided if the banking system can somehow maintain its loan portfolio even as deposits decline. This is an easy task for banks that have 70 or 80 percent of their loans and deposits outside the country in question, as is the case in Panama and as was the case in the British colonies (where the four big British banks accounted for most of the banking activity).

I use the city of Peoria, Illinois, as my standard example of a case in which dollarization worked perfectly well and in which a currency board would surely work. Peoria (or any other city within a country with a good capital market) has two attributes that are critical to this success. First, there is no connection between the saving that is done by people and entities resident in Peoria and the investment that occurs there in any given period. Second, there is little connection between the real cash balances held by Peoria residents and entities and the bank loans they receive. These two dislinkages—the unhooking of saving from investment and the unhooking of bank loans from bank deposits—are the real secrets of success of "dollarization" in entities such as cities. Panama and the old British colonies came close to emulating them and enjoyed some success with dollarization and with currency boards, respectively. But how many developing countries can hope to do likewise, and how soon? This, to me, tells us why the zealots of dollarization and of currency boards have gone much too far in urging the general adoption of these systems. Here, as elsewhere in economic policy, there is no substitute for a calm and careful diagnosis of the situation at hand and a subsequent calm and careful weighing of costs and benefits.

Whither Development Economics?

Readers should be able to sense from the preceding sections the directions in which contemporary "working professionals" would like to see our discipline evolve. Here I want to emphasize the vision of a developing country as one small element in the interconnected web we call the world economy. For a small country to contemplate being a closed economy makes no sense at this stage of history. That places at center stage the question of the linkages by which it connects to the world economy.

I want to focus on these linkages, paying special attention to the pervasive roles played by the real exchange rate, by the financial sector, and by real cost reduction. To me, the textbook representations of international trade (two quite symmetrical countries, two products, two factors), although interesting in themselves, shed precious little light on the problems facing a developing country's policymakers in the modern world. Far more relevant is the vision of one country facing a much larger, quite impersonal entity known as the world market. In this market thousands upon thousands of goods and services are traded, for nearly all of which a country must be thought of as a "price taker."

Arrayed against this multitude of world prices, we have the country's own resources, skills, knowledge, tastes, and productive capacity. If the real exchange rate (the real price of the real dollar) is somehow set too low, the people of the country will want to import everything and will be able to export very little. At higher and higher real prices of the dollar, the menu of desired imports gets shorter while the list of profitable exports grows. RER equilibrium is established through the forces of demand for and supply of foreign exchange, including capital flows, debt service, emigrant remittances, and so on, as well as export supply and import demand. This is by far the best way to view the process by which a country's comparative advantage is determined. It reveals, in particular, how that comparative advantage is modified when large inflows of capital or major export price booms cause the equilibrium real exchange rate to fall or when the exigencies of debt repayment or the political and economic uncertainties linked to capital flight cause the equilibrium real exchange rate to rise.

Readers should note how easy is the transition from discussing the real exchange rate as the fundamental equilibrator of a country's international trade and as the basic determiner of its comparative advantage to seeing it as a central variable for the analysis of episodes of debt crisis, capital flight, "Dutch disease," and the collapse of export prices. One should recognize, too, that RER analysis, as we understand it today, was not part of the toolkit of trade and development economists even as little as half a century ago. Understanding of the real exchange

rate began to enter as one branch of international trade economics focused on the "small-country assumption" and as history produced a
series of shocks (oil crises in the 1970s, debt crises in the 1980s, "regional" crises in the 1990s) that carried with them huge movements of
the real exchange rate.

Yet there is much that we have still to learn about RER economics.
We know, for example, relatively little about how the machinery of RER
adjustment works its way through to the allocation of resources in an
economy. We do know that when crises strike, the bulk of the effect of
a sharp rise in the real exchange rate is a severe reduction in imports (to
which declining income and restricted credit also typically contribute).
Effects on the production of tradables and on exports seem not to be
large initially. As time goes by, however, the productive side seems to
take over, with the adjustment process shifting from one dominated by
declining imports to one dominated by rising exports. We need to study
the dynamics of this shift and, in particular, to try to trace empirically
the path by which a higher real exchange rate ends up generating important shifts of resources from the nontradable to the tradable sectors
of the economy.

Another set of questions follows quite directly. Both from theory
and from observation, we can conclude that the dynamics of RER adjustments are quite different under different exchange rate regimes. There
is much greater RER volatility under freely floating rates than under
fixed rates, and substantially greater overshooting of the final equilibrium real exchange rate as the economy adjusts to major shocks. A lot
remains to be learned concerning the whole process of RER adjustment
in the wake of shocks and how the process of adjustment is influenced
by the country's exchange rate regime.

The financial sector was always an important part of the story for
developing economies, but its role has grown as the sector itself has
modernized and developed. To me, the key element that economists
should focus on is the consolidated balance sheet of this sector. If we
draw the boundaries of the sector in the most useful way (so as to
include the central bank, the commercial banks, and other deposit-
receiving institutions such as *financieras*), we have some broad concept
of money as the major liability of the consolidated system and can clas-
sify its assets as consisting of net foreign assets plus credit to the government plus credit to the private (or productive) sector.

This broad picture of a consolidated financial system has been
available to us for a long time in central bank bulletins and in the
International Monetary Fund's *International Financial Statistics*. Unfortunately, we (the economics profession) have not worked hard
enough to exploit the informational riches contained there. The big
picture is as follows.

Economic agents (people and firms) decide how much "broad money" they want to hold. Their tastes and judgments can be captured in the notion of a demand function for, say, M_2. But it is the real amount of money (M_2/P_d), not its nominal amount (M_2 alone), that is the object of their tastes and decisions. Changes in demand, especially large changes, can have dramatic effects on the fortunes of an economy. In every major financial crisis that I can think of, we observe sharp reductions in M_2/P_d. These, for practical purposes, require that one or more of the three major categories of assets be cut. Here we see the convenience of a country's having a large cushion of net foreign assets (international reserves) to act as a shock absorber. In nearly all crises, however, the reserves cushion cannot do anywhere near the full job, and the consequence is a very large reduction in the volume of real credit to the private (or productive) sector.

I cannot emphasize too much that in these crisis situations, the credit contraction is far more worrisome than the monetary contraction itself. To the extent that crises culminate in major recessions or depressions, it is difficult to attribute as the direct cause the reduction in M_2/P_d, for people have to increase their spending in the process of reducing real cash balances. The real culprit lies on the credit side, where a sharp contraction of available funds (in real terms) typically leads to high *real* interest rates (often 20 or 30 percent per year and sometimes much higher). What we undeniably see in such circumstances is widespread loan defaults and business failures.

It is one of the great mysteries of economics how credit contractions can have so strong an effect on real output. Our textbooks would tell us that the marginal product of credit is measured by the interest rate thereon, but this measure greatly understates the fall in output that follows sharp contractions in real credit. One of the great challenges facing us, then, is to study this nexus between the demand for money, the supply of credit, and real output, hoping in the end to dispel much of the mystery that now surrounds it.

The final item on this incomplete agenda for development economics research is *real cost reduction*. Among the items about which we need to learn more are (a) how economic openness functions as a catalyst for real cost reduction, (b) how strong is the influence of particular types of policy measures (controlling inflation, reducing distortions, rationalizing regulations, and so on) on the process of real cost reduction and (c) what are the mechanisms that trigger real cost increases for such a significant fraction of firms (and of disaggregated industries) and whether there are ways in which improved policies can reduce their incidence. Answers to these questions will help us better understand both the nature of the growth process and the ways in which economic policy can improve as policymakers strive to "enable" and to promote economic growth.

Note

1. I know that this is a less than adequate label in that most economists of all stripes see themselves as both "working" and "professional." I earlier used the term "practitioner," which is more restrictive and perhaps more descriptive. But I want the label to cover academics such as Schultz and Krueger, as well as policy people such as Greenspan and Cavallo, and "practitioner" may not be apt for the academics. The characteristic that I think best describes my "working professionals" is their concentration on diagnosing situations and problems and on finding solid and workable solutions for them. They are little concerned either with the current fashions in economic journals or with *Dogmengeschichte* that traces the evolution of concepts over long periods of time.

Contributors and Commentators

Irma Adelman, Professor of Economics, University of California at Berkeley

Philippe Aghion, Professor of Economics, Harvard University

Abhijit V. Banerjee, Professor of Economics, Massachusetts Institute of Technology

Pranab Bardhan, Professor of Economics, University of California at Berkeley

Kaushik Basu, Professor of Economics and C. Marks Professor of International Studies, Cornell University

Timothy Besley, Professor of Economics, London School of Economics

Paul Collier, Director, Development Research Group, World Bank; Professor of Economics, University of Oxford

Nicholas Crafts, Professor of Economic History, London School of Economics

Avner Greif, Professor of Economics, Stanford University

Merilee S. Grindle, Edward S. Mason Professor of International Development, John F. Kennedy School of Government, Harvard University

Arnold C. Harberger, Professor of Economics, University of California at Los Angeles; Swift Distinguished Service Professor, Emeritus, University of Chicago

Karla Hoff, Research Economist, World Bank

Ravi Kanbur, T. H. Lee Professor of World Affairs, Cornell University

Lawrence R. Klein, Benjamin Franklin Professor of Economics, Emeritus, University of Pennsylvania

David Landes, Professor of Economic History, Emeritus, Harvard University

Michael Lipton, Research Professor of Economics, University of Sussex

Gerald M. Meier, Konosuke Matsushita Professor of International Economics and Policy Analysis, Emeritus, Stanford University

Hla Myint, Professor of Economics, Emeritus, London School of Economics

Douglass C. North, Spenser T. Olin Professor in Arts and Sciences, Washington University in St. Louis

Gustav Ranis, Frank Altschul Professor of International Economics and Director, Yale Center for International and Area Studies, Yale University

Debraj Ray, Professor of Economics, New York University

W. W. Rostow, Professor of Economics, Emeritus, University of Texas at Austin

Paul A. Samuelson, Institute Professor of Economics, Emeritus, Massachusetts Institute of Technology

Amartya K. Sen, Lamont University Professor, Emeritus, Harvard University; The Master, Trinity College, Cambridge

Soumitra K. Sharma, Professor of Development Economics, University of Zagreb

Sir Hans Singer, Emeritus Professor and Fellow, Institute of Development Studies, University of Sussex

Robert M. Solow, Institute Professor of Economics, Emeritus, Massachusetts Institute of Technology

Lyn Squire, Director, Global Development Network, World Bank

Joseph E. Stiglitz, Joan Kenney Professor of Economics, Stanford University; formerly Chief Economist and Senior Vice President, World Bank

Paul P. Streeten, Professor of Economics, Emeritus, Boston University

Vinod Thomas, Vice President, World Bank Institute, World Bank Group

David Vines, Fellow in Economics, Balliol College, University of Oxford

Shahid Yusuf, Research Manager, Development Economics Research Group, World Bank

Index